PRODUCTIVITY GROWTH

Wherever possible, the articles in these volumes have been reproduced as originally published using facsimile reproduction, inclusive of footnotes and pagination to facilitate ease of reference.

For a full list of all Edward Elgar published titles visit our website at www.e-elgar.com

Productivity Growth

Industries, Spillovers and Economic Performance

Thijs ten Raa
Associate Professor of Economics
Tilburg University, The Netherlands

and

Edward N. Wolff
Professor of Economics
New York University, USA

Edward Elgar
Cheltenham, UK • Northampton, MA, USA

Published by
Edward Elgar Publishing Limited
The Lypiatts
15 Lansdown Road
Cheltenham
Glos GL50 2JA
UK

Edward Elgar Publishing, Inc.
William Pratt House
9 Dewey Court
Northampton
Massachusetts 01060
USA

A catalogue record for this book is available from the British Library

Library of Congress Control Number: 2012940995

MIX
Paper from responsible sources
FSC www.fsc.org FSC® C018575

ISBN 978 1 78100 344 2

Printed and bound by MPG Books Group, UK

Contents

PART III OUTSOURCING AND PRODUCTIVITY SPILLOVERS

PART IV LABOR AND CAPITAL PRODUCTIVITY

PART V PRODUCTIVITY AND EFFICIENCY ANALYSIS: SYNTHESIS

Acknowledgements

The editors and publishers wish to thank the authors and the following publishers who have kindly given permission for the use of copyright material.

Cambridge University Press for excerpt: Thijs ten Raa (2004), 'A Neoclassical Analysis of Total Factor Productivity Using Input–Output Prices', in Erik Dietzenbacher and Michael L. Lahr (eds), *Wassily Leontief and Input–Output Economics*, Chapter 10, 151–65.

Elsevier via Copyright Clearance Center's Rightslink Service for articles: Thijs ten Raa and Edward N. Wolff (1991), 'Secondary Products and the Measurement of Productivity Growth', *Regional Science and Urban Economics*, **21** (4), December, 581–615; Edward N. Wolff (1994), 'Productivity Measurement Within an Input–Output Framework', *Regional Science and Urban Economics*, **24** (1), February, 75–92; Thijs ten Raa and Edward N. Wolff (2000), 'Engines of Growth in the US Economy', *Structural Change and Economic Dynamics*, **11** (4), December, 473–89; Maury Gittleman, Thijs ten Raa and Edward N. Wolff (2006), 'The Vintage Effect in TFP-Growth: An Analysis of the Age Structure of Capital', *Structural Change and Economic Dynamics*, **17** (3), September, 306–28; Thijs ten Raa and Pierre Mohnen (2008), 'Competition and Performance: The Different Roles of Capital and Labor', *Journal of Economic Behavior and Organization*, **65** (3–4), March, 573–84.

Oxford University Press for excerpt: Edward N. Wolff and David R. Howell (1989), 'Labor Quality and Productivity Growth in the United States: An Input–Output Growth-Accounting Framework', in Ronald E. Miller, Karen R. Polenske and Adam Z. Rose (eds), *Frontiers of Input–Output Analysis*, Chapter 11, 148–62.

President and Fellows of Harvard College for article: Edward N. Wolff (1985), 'Industrial Composition, Interindustry Effects, and the U.S. Productivity Slowdown', *Review of Economics and Statistics*, **67** (2), May, 268–77.

President and Fellows of Harvard College and the Massachusetts Institute of Technology for article: Edward N. Wolff (2003), 'Skills and Changing Comparative Advantage', *Review of Economics and Statistics*, **85** (1), February, 77–93.

Gerald Silverberg and Luc Soete for excerpts: Edward N. Wolff (1994), 'Productivity Growth and Capital Intensity on the Sector and Industry Level: Specialisation among OECD Countries, 1970–1988', in Gerald Silverberg and Luc Soete (eds), *The Economics of Growth and Technical Change: Technologies, Nations, Agents*, Chapter 8, 185–211; Thijs ten Raa (1994), 'Comment on Wolff', in Gerald Silverberg and

Luc Soete (eds), *The Economics of Growth and Technical Change: Technologies, Nations, Agents*, Chapter 8, 212–14.

Springer Science and Business Media B.V. for articles and excerpt: Thijs ten Raa and Edward N. Wolff (2001), 'Outsourcing of Services and the Productivity Recovery in U.S. Manufacturing in the 1980s and 1990s', *Journal of Productivity Analysis*, **16** (2), 149–65; Thijs ten Raa and Pierre Mohnen (2002), 'Neoclassical Growth Accounting and Frontier Analysis: A Synthesis', *Journal of Productivity Analysis*, **18** (2), 111–28; Thijs ten Raa (2005), 'Aggregation of Productivity Indices: The Allocative Efficiency Correction', *Journal of Productivity Analysis*, **24** (2), October, 203–9; Thijs ten Raa (2007), 'Don't Aggregate Efficiency But Disaggregate Inefficiency', in Rolf Färe, Shawna Grosskopf and Daniel Primont (eds), *Aggregation, Efficiency, and Measurement*, 145–51; Thijs ten Raa (2008), 'Debreu's Coefficient of Resource Utilization, the Solow Residual, and TFP: The Connection by Leontief Preferences', *Journal of Productivity Analysis*, **30** (3), 191–9; Thijs ten Raa and Victoria Shestalova (2011), 'The Solow Residual, Domar Aggregation, and Inefficiency: A Synthesis of TFP Measures', *Journal of Productivity Analysis*, **36** (1), 71–7.

Taylor and Francis Ltd (http://www.informaworld.com) for articles: Angel Luis Ruiz and Edward N. Wolff (1996), 'Productivity Growth, Import Leakage and Employment Growth in Puerto Rico, 1967–87', *Economic Systems Research*, **8** (4), 391–413; Edward N. Wolff (1997), 'Spillovers, Linkages and Technical Change', *Economic Systems Research*, **9** (1), 9–23; Edward N. Wolff (2006), 'The Growth of Information Workers in the US Economy, 1950–2000: the Role of Technological Change, Computerization, and Structural Change', *Economic Systems Research*, **18** (3), September, 221–55.

Every effort has been made to trace all the copyright holders but if any have been inadvertently overlooked the publishers will be pleased to make the necessary arrangement at the first opportunity.

Introduction

Thijs ten Raa and Edward N. Wolff

Productivity growth is the main vehicle to increase the standard of living. This book explains the relationships between technological change, efficiency, productivity growth and performance. The emphasis is on the interplay between industries in modern economies. For example, it is shown that the productivity recovery in manufacturing is partly achieved by outsourcing services and that productivity spillovers pinpoint computers as the engine of growth. The book provides a broad yet in-depth input–output analysis of productivity growth by consolidating our papers on the subject.

The book has two distinctive features. First, the chapters range from pure theory – providing a conceptual framework for interrelating alternative productivity and performance measures – to empirical applications at both the national economy level and the sectoral (industry) level. Second, it unifies input–output (I–O) and productivity analyses. We integrate economic theory, I–O measurement and empirical applications. Part I focuses on growth accounting in an I–O framework. Chapter 1, 'Industrial Composition, Interindustry Effects, and the U.S. Productivity Slowdown', investigates the effect of shifts in output composition on the slowdown of productivity growth in the US between 1947–67 and 1967–76. Leontief's I–O framework and the Divisia index of aggregate productivity growth are integrated to separate the effects of changes in sectoral rates of technical progress from the effects of changes in output composition and interindustry flows on the change in overall productivity growth. Of the approximately 2 percentage point decline in overall total factor productivity (TFP) growth, 17–22 percent is ascribed to compositional effects and the remainder to other factors.

This analysis is part of a wide literature that investigates the sources of the productivity slowdown in the US over the 1965–79 period. The main candidates considered in this literature are the following five factors: (1) slowdown in the rate of capital formation; (2) changes in the composition of the labor force; (3) energy price shocks; (4) declines in research and development (R&D) spending (and/or the productivity of R&D); and (5) changes in the composition of output (mainly, the shift to services). This chapter focuses on the fifth of these topics. The general idea is that a shift in resources from a less efficient to a more efficient firm or sector of the economy would by itself cause the overall rate of productivity growth to increase. However, the converse is also true, and the shift of resources out of high-performing industries like manufacturing to low-performing ones like services would cause the overall rate of productivity growth to fall.

We use 87-sector I–O data for the years 1947, 1967 and 1976 to analyse the 'shift effect'. After developing a methodology to separate out the effects of industry-level TFP growth from the change in the composition of final output, and using three different sets of prices (standard Divisia prices, Marxian labor values and Peterson–Harrod prices), between 17 and 22 percent of the overall decline in TFP growth is attributable to the change in the value composition of the final demand vector. Of this effect, about 80 percent is due to changes in the relative prices of sectoral output, with the remainder due to shifts in real final output shares.

Chapter 2, 'Secondary Products and the Measurement of Productivity Growth', shows how our analysis can be extended to modern economic accounts with separate entries for not only the inputs but also the outputs of the industries. In the standard I–O model industries use multiple inputs to produce a single output; I–O coefficients are ratios of the inputs to 'the' output and their reductions measure productivity growth. However, modern enterprises produce multiple outputs and are consequently hard to classify in a single sector, complicating the construction of I–O coefficients and the consequent measurement of productivity growth. The standard procedure, which was also used in Chapter 1, is to construct I–O coefficients as a weighted average of industry input coefficients, which are ratios of inputs to industry output. These are sensitive with respect to prices; the violation of the price invariance axiom by these coefficients creates a bias which is nailed down in Chapter 2, both analytically and empirically. For the period investigated, between 1967 and 1977, the aggregate bias is insignificant, confirming the previous results. At the sectoral level the bias can be quite large (with opposing signs explaining the 'wash out'). Our analysis contributes to the otherwise rather technical theoretical literature on the construction of I–O coefficients, favoring the so-called commodity technology model. In addition, we solve two special methodological problems, namely the treatment of the scrap sector and of the import sector in I–O productivity measurement.

Chapter 3, 'Productivity Measurement Within an Input–Output Framework', takes a wider look at the use of I–O data to measure productivity growth. In particular, the I–O system provides features for the measurement and analysis of TFP growth that are not found in the standard accounting frameworks used for productivity analysis. First, TFP growth can be measured using gross output and incorporating materials as an input. Second, a growth accounting framework can be developed to measure the effect of final output mix changes on aggregate productivity growth. Third, capital can be treated as a produced means of production. Fourth, measures of composite technical change can overcome difficulties engendered by the substitution of externally provided inputs for those previously provided by the firm. Fifth, TFP growth of secondary production can be analytically separated from that of primary output (Chapter 2).

In many respects, the I–O system provides distinct methodological advantages over more standard productivity analysis based on industry gross domestic product (GDP), gross product originating (GPO) or value added. In particular, in the I–O framework, gross output can be used as the measure of industry output, instead of GPO or value added, and intermediate inputs can be specifically incorporated as inputs in the production function. Gross output can be deflated using an industry-level price index. In contrast, GDP in 'constant dollars' requires the use of the so-called 'double deflation' method in which gross output and material (or intermediate) inputs are each deflated by their own price index and the difference is defined as GDP or GPO in constant dollars. There are several difficulties with the latter technique. First, weak separability must be assumed for the production function of each sector for this to be a reliable index. Second, the double deflation method can lead to negative numbers for real GDP if relative price changes are sufficiently great over the period of measurement. Third, since GPO is defined as the difference of two variables, the measurement error in GPO is equal to the sum of the measurement errors in the two components.

Another advantage of the I–O framework in measuring productivity growth is the introduction of productivity measures that reflect changes in total (direct plus indirect) factor requirements of a sector's (final) output. In this approach, based on the Leontief inverse, a sector's composite TFP growth is measured by the rate of decline of its direct plus indirect labor and capital requirements. The rate of composite technical changes has the advantage of avoiding the so-called 'contracting out' problem. Certain activities that were once internal to a firm's operation may be subcontracted out after a certain point of time to firms in other industries. The use of total factor requirements avoids the difficulties associated with this phenomenon.

A still more general approach to TFP analysis is presented in Chapter 4, 'A Neoclassical Analysis of TFP Using Input–Output Prices'. I–O based TFP measures steer close to the national accounts of an economy, but it is not immediate how they connect to the mainstream neoclassical model; this chapter discusses this issue in detail. After reviewing the main results of general equilibrium analysis – the existence of a perfectly competitive equilibrium, its efficiency, and the support of any efficient allocation by perfectly competitive market prices – we specify the fundamentals of an economy consistent with national accounting. The production possibilities are described in terms of the use and make tables, the factor inputs table and the factor endowments, and the preferences are specified using the observed pattern of final consumption. A shortcut makes the transition from the micro data to the macro performance of the economy (the theoretical foundation is left to Chapter 19). The perfectly competitive prices – which are not the observed prices – are derived and the well-known result that factors are priced according to their productivity is used to set up TFP. Disaggregation with respect to industries completes the reconciliation of I–O productivity analysis and the neoclassical model.

Part II of the book treats the subject of international trade and productivity growth. Chapters 5 and 6, 'Productivity Growth and Capital Intensity on the Sector and Industry Level: Specialisation among OECD Countries, 1970–1988' and 'Comment on Wolff' analyse the convergence of aggregate labor productivity among advanced industrial countries, a phenomenon that has been observed by many economists over the years. We consider two possibilities. First, the convergence in aggregate labor productivity may be due to the convergence of labor productivity in individual industries. Second, it may also occur due to the specialization of countries in industries that differ from one another, with modest leads in labor productivity in the country that specializes in them. Of course, both factors may play a role with varying degrees of importance. Data from the Organisation for Economic Co-operation and Development (OECD) International Sectoral Database (ISDB) from 1970 to 1988 are used to address three main questions. First, has convergence in productivity on the aggregate level occurred over this time period? Second, has country specialization also occurred over this time period? In particular, has aggregate convergence continued after 1970 through the uneven development of industries in the individual OECD countries? Third, did countries invest more heavily in industries with rapidly growing TFP?

The aggregate statistics show that convergence of labor productivity, TFP and capital intensity occurred over the period from 1970 to 1988 for the total economy among OECD countries. There was also clear evidence of catch-up, indicated by both rising average productivity and capital intensity of OECD countries relative to the US and a negative correlation between initial levels and rates of growth. On the sectoral level, the variation in labor productivity levels, TFP levels and capital intensity was much higher, on average, than that for the overall economy. Moreover, dispersion on the sectoral level showed only a very modest decline. The same pattern is evident for the dispersion of productivity levels and capital–labor ratios relative to the US across sectors within country. The simple correlation between TFP growth and capital–labor growth was virtually zero across sectors.

For total manufacturing the convergence of productivity levels came to a halt by 1979 or so. There was a slight convergence of labor productivity levels and capital–labor ratios between 1970 and 1979, followed by a slight divergence between 1979 and 1988. On net, there was virtually no change between 1970 and 1988 in the dispersion of labor productivity levels and an actual increase in that of TFP. On the industry level, the variation in labor productivity levels and capital–labor ratios declined slightly, on average, between 1970 and 1979 and increased somewhat between 1979 and 1988. The dispersion of TFP levels remained unchanged between 1970 and 1979 and then increased over the 1979–1988 period. The average dispersion of labor productivity, TFP and capital intensity was higher on the industry level than for total manufacturing. As with the major sectors of the economy, there was virtually no correlation between TFP growth and capital–labor growth on the industry level.

In sum, the simple advantages of backwardness argument (that is, the catch-up effect) as an explanation of aggregate convergence must be modified, at least among the advanced countries of the world. The catch-up effect should show up, if anywhere, on the sectoral (or industry) level. This occurred very weakly among major sectors of the economy in the 1970s and 1980s and among manufacturing industries in the 1970s, but was virtually nonexistent during the 1980s within manufacturing. Instead, specialization in particular industries in terms of investment, with its concomitant technological change, appears to be the main driving force over this period. Thus, while the productivity convergence of the 1970s continued in the 1980s, the main mechanism changed. It was no longer technological catch-up by more backward countries but rather the result of specialization in high-growth sectors (and industries).

The commentary raises some important issues on methodology. TFP growth is measured by the residual between the output growth rate and weighted input growth rates, where the weights are the value shares of the respective inputs. With an appeal to the factor price equalization theorem, these value shares are equated across countries by taking international means. In the estimation of TFP growth, for example, the average ratio of employee compensation to GDP for the twelve countries in the sample over the 1970–1988 period was used to measure factor shares. In the critique, the case of a CES production function is considered. Then, unlike the Cobb–Douglas case, it is possible that in a country (such as Japan) capital becomes so abundant that not only does its relative price decrease but even its value share does. Averaging out with the US, say, will cause an underestimation of the wage share in Japan and overestimation of the capital share. Since in the TFP growth formula, the growth rate of capital dominates that of labor, this will cause an underestimation of TFP growth in Japan. In other words, the high growth rate of capital in Japan may suppress TFP growth but the weight attached to it ought to be smaller than in the US, and this offsetting effect is not taken into account when values shares are averaged across countries. As a result, Japan's TFP performance may have been underestimated.

Chapter 7, 'Productivity Growth, Import Leakage and Employment Growth in Puerto Rico, 1967–87', uses 53-sector Puerto Rican I–O data that cover the period from 1967 and 1987 to investigate both employment growth and productivity growth in Puerto Rico. A standard I–O model is developed with the exception that both the final demand vector and the matrix of total technical coefficients are broken down into a domestic component and an imported component (the Puerto Rican data provide separate matrices for domestic flows and import flows). This allows measurement of the separate contributions on demand from domestic sources and imports. A growth accounting framework is then used to decompose the sources of employment growth into three effects: (i) changes in the vector of total final demand; (ii) the change in technical coefficients; and (iii) the change in import leakages.

Employment growth was found to be led primarily by a rapid increase in final output – 5.1 percent per year – although labor productivity growth was also substantial, at 3.7 percent per year. Import leakages also fell over this period but had little impact on employment growth. Local absorption was more successful than exports in generating new jobs. Employment generated by local absorption grew by 35 percent while that from exports by 29 percent, even though exports increased almost fourfold, while local absorption only doubled. The difference reflects the greater labor intensity of industries that supply local absorption.

There was also a notable shift in the occupational structure toward white-collar employment and away from blue-collar jobs. The main reason for this was the shift in the composition of final output toward industries that relied heavily on white-collar workers. A secondary reason was a bias in technological change, which favored white-collar over blue-collar workers.

Most studies, including ours, measure TFP by the residual between output growth and input growth. Since there are two or more factor inputs and many products, weighted averages must be taken and this raises the question which weights must be used. The observed value shares, or, equivalently, market wage and rental rates are employed for this purpose. For perfectly competitive economies this procedure is correct, as factor inputs are priced according to their marginal productivities. Indeed, the so-called dual or cost-based approach to TFP writes it as the sum of factor productivities, summed over stocks. Market factor rewards, however, are distorted by the exercise of market power and other sources, so accepting them or value shares at face value biases TFP estimates.

Chapter 8, 'Neoclassical Growth Accounting and Frontier Analysis: A Synthesis', takes up the challenge of measuring TFP with endogenous, production-driven value shares instead, replacing observed market valuations by the shadow prices associated with the program that determines the efficient allocation, on the frontier of the production possibility set. The aforementioned main results of general equilibrium analysis associate this efficiency program with perfectly competitive prices, including factor rewards according to productivities. The analysis has some nice implications. First, the wedge between efficient and observed allocations yields a measure for the inefficiency of the economy and permits a decomposition of TFP growth in technical change and efficiency change, in line with the operations research literature. Second, we can contrast the development of imports and exports with their optimal counterparts, the shift in comparative advantage. This resolves an open issue in the literature, namely the role of the terms of trade in productivity. An application shows that the Canadian economy enjoyed strong growth in the 1960s due to technical progress, was stagnant in the 1970s, and regained strength in the 1980s, but offset by adjustment problems, accounted for by inefficiency. The bulk of the structural recovery was due to an improvement in the terms of trade.

Chapter 9, 'Skills and Changing Comparative Advantage', considers the relation between the changing skill base of the US labor force and the country's shifting comparative advantage in the international arena. Standard trade theory predicts that a country will export those products that intensively use those endowments in which it is favored relative to the other countries of the world and import products that are intensive in endowments that are scarce in that country. It was generally believed, for example, that the US exported capital-intensive goods and imported labor-intensive ones, but empirical work showed that US exports tended to be human capital-intensive, and imports capital-intensive (the so-called Leontief paradox). Similarly, does the US tend to export products that embody high-skill labor and import those that embody low-skill labor? How have these trade patterns changed over time? Do they reflect the changing skill composition of the US labor force, which has shifted in favor of cognitive and interactive skills and away from motor skills? With the growth of the information economy (assuming that the US is in the forefront of the world in that dimension as well), is the US comparative advantage shifting in that direction as well? A related issue regards the research and development (R&D) intensity of US trade. During the 1960s and 1970s the major export strength of the US lay in industries whose research was heavily subsidized by the US government (particularly the Department of Defense), including aircraft, armaments, mainframe computers, and medical equipment. Is the US still exporting R&D-intensive products? It is found that the comparative advantage in US international trade was in industries high in cognitive and interactive skills and low in motor skills, and the skill gap between exports and imports widened over time. US exports also had a high content of knowledge workers and a low content of goods workers relative to imports, and the gap grew over time as well. The results also show that imports were more capital- and equipment-intensive than exports but in this case the difference fell over time. Moreover, by 1987 exports were more intensive in office, computing and accounting equipment (OCA) than imports. In contrast, whereas in 1958 the R&D intensity of US exports was much greater than that of imports, by 1996 the R&D intensity of imports was slightly greater than that of exports. We also find that labor productivity rose faster in export than in import industries and the unit labor cost of export industries relative to import industries declined almost steadily over time.

Part III analyses the modern phenomena of outsourcing and productivity spillovers. Chapter 10, 'Outsourcing of Services and the Productivity Recovery in U.S. Manufacturing in the 1980s and 1990s', analyses how much of the recovery in manufacturing can be ascribed to outsourcing of services, which are known to be sluggish productivity growers. The measurement of services productivity is recognized as a problem in the literature. The inputs tend to be measurable, but the outputs not. We overcome this difficulty by making a shortcut from the material services inputs to manufacturing output. Our approach relies indirectly on Marxian analysis, which reduces the value of goods and services to their material contents, ultimately expressed in labor hours. The reduction of the contributions of services to their material contents is not straightforward. We apply Leontief's consolidation alternative to aggregation, simplifying his technique as we go. Imputing service productivity to manufacturing users reduces manufacturing TFP growth from 0.83 to 0.65 percentage points per annum between the periods 1967–1977 and 1977–1987. One-fifth of the recovery can be associated with outsourced services.

Chapter 11, 'Engines of Growth in the US Economy', is on spillovers, another important topic. There is good reason to believe that R&D influences on TFP growth in other sectors are indirect. For R&D to spill over, it must first be successful in the home sector. Indeed, observed spillovers conform better to TFP growth than to R&D in the upstream sectors. Sectoral TFP growth rates are thus interrelated. Solving the intersectoral TFP equation resolves overall TFP growth into sources of growth. The solution essentially eliminates the spillovers and amounts to a novel decomposition of TFP growth. The top ten sectors are designated 'engines of growth'. Engines of growth need not feature high R&D, but once they move in terms of own TFP growth they help to push the entire economy.

Spillovers of technical change are known to drive a wedge between private and social rates of return to R&D. What is less well known is that spillovers render TFP growth in some sectors more critical than in others. In standard growth accounting, the contribution of a sector's TFP growth to overall TFP growth is determined by the value share of the sector in the total economy, without one sector necessarily being more critical than another. However, the story takes a twist when R&D influences TFP growth in other sectors not directly but indirectly – that is, only after it has proven successful in the sector where it has been spent. If this is the case then spillovers interrelate sector TFP growth rates and there are likely to be multiplier effects. The multipliers will depend on the spillover relationships, and these need not be equal to the structure of the material balances in the economy. Hence TFP multiplier effects are not given by the standard multiplier matrix based on the Leontief inverse.

The interdependence of sectoral TFP growth rates is given by a system of equations that account for the spillover effects. We solve the spillover equations for TFP growth rates. The reduced form of the TFP growth rates shows their dependence on sectoral R&D expenditures, and the coefficients measure total returns to R&D, including spillover effects. Observed sectoral TFP growth rates are thereby ascribed to sources of growth.

Using 85-sector US I–O tables for 1958, 1967, 1977 and 1987 to estimate the system of equations, we find that the most important engine of growth was computers and office machinery, followed by electronic components and then plastics and synthetics. This finding throws light on the Solow paradox, '[w]e see computers everywhere, but in the productivity statistics'.

Chapter 12, 'Spillovers, Linkages and Technical Change', further examines the role of technological spillovers between sectors in explaining own sector productivity growth. A standard Divisia measure of industry level TFP growth was applied to 85-sector US I–O tables from the years 1958, 1967, 1977 and 1987. Data were also obtained on R&D expenditures by industry and year. Direct R&D intensity is defined as the ratio of own sector R&D expenditures to the sector's GDP. 'Embodied' R&D of sector j is measured as a weighted average of the R&D intensity of supplying sectors to sector j, where the weights are given by the corresponding interindustry technical coefficients. Embodied R&D is also referred to as 'indirect R&D'. A new contribution of the paper is to introduce an analogous measure for direct productivity spillovers from sector j's supplying industries. This measure is defined as a weighted average of the TFP growth of supplying sectors, where the weights are given, once again, by the corresponding interindustry technical coefficients.

There was strong evidence that industry level TFP growth was significantly and positively relative to the TFP growth of the supplying sectors, with an elasticity of almost 60 percent. R&D intensity, the ratio of R&D expenditures to industry GDP, was also found to be a positive and significant determinant of industry TFP growth, with an estimated return of 10 to 13 percent, and with the return to embodied R&D of 43 percent. Direct productivity spillovers from the technological progress made by supplying industries appear to be more important than spillovers from the R&D performed by suppliers in explaining own industry TFP growth.

Direct productivity spillovers also played a key role in explaining changes in manufacturing TFP growth over time. Changes in the contribution made by direct productivity spillovers to TFP growth accounted for almost half of the slowdown in TFP growth in manufacturing from 1958–1967 to 1967–1977 and for 20 percent of the TFP growth recovery in this sector from 1967–1977 to 1977–1987. Changes in R&D intensity and embodied R&D were relatively unimportant in explaining movements in manufacturing TFP growth over these three periods.

Part IV focuses on both labor and capital productivity. Chapter 13, 'Labor Quality and Productivity Growth in the United States: An Input–Output Growth-Accounting Framework', is concerned primarily with the sources of the productivity slowdown observed in the US during the late 1960s and 1970s, as before, but now the focus is on changes in skill requirements. We argue that the measure of productivity growth should take into account changes in the quality of inputs over time. In the case of labor, change in quality will reflect the evolution of both the skill content of jobs and the mix of jobs. If changes in skill content and job mix result in an upgrading (downgrading) of skill requirements, effective labor input per hour worked will increase (decrease). Most studies that adjust the labor input for labor quality use an index of relative earnings to gauge the relative skill levels of jobs. However, only under extremely strong assumptions will earnings offer a reliable guide to the quality (skill levels) of employed labor. In contrast, we replace earnings with alternative measures of job-skill requirements derived from the Dictionary of Occupational Titles (DOT).

We analyse three sources of overall productivity growth: (i) sectoral technical change; (ii) changes in the composition of final output; and (iii) changes in the skill composition of the labor force, using 47-sector I–O data for the US economy covering the period from 1958 to 1977. The industries were aligned with employment matrices of 47 industries and 267 occupations for decennial Census years 1960, 1970 and 1980. DOT skill scores were provided for each of the 267 occupations. The second part of the paper uses the growth accounting framework to analyse the sources of the US productivity slowdown between the 1958–1967 and 1967–1977 periods. First of all, there is a general upgrading of the skill content of labor inputs from 1958 to 1977. Second, the growth in skill levels accounted for a substantial portion of the growth in unadjusted (that is, not skill-adjusted) TFP growth over the whole period. While unadjusted TFP averaged 1.92 percent per year over this period, cognitive-skill-adjusted TFP growth averaged just 1.34 percent per year. The difference was due to the increase in the average cognitive skill level of the employed labor force over this period. Third, overall productivity growth fell by over one percentage point between the 1958–1967 and the 1967–1977 periods. Of this decline, about one-sixth can be attributed to a slowdown in the rate of increase of the average cognitive skill level of employed workers.

Chapter 14, 'The Growth of Information Workers in the US Economy, 1950–2000: The Role of Technological Change, Computerization, and Structural Change', documents the growth of information workers in the US economy over the postwar period and analyses the sources of their growth. The paper first updates the statistics on the composition of the workforce between information and non-information jobs to 2000. Particular interest is focused on the post-1980 period, which has seen a tremendous growth in the use of computers in production and which some have termed a new 'techno-economic paradigm', based on computer-driven information technology. The occupations were aggregated into four categories: (i) knowledge producers; (ii) data processors; (iii) service workers; and (iv) goods-processing workers.

The information workers (the sum of the first two categories) are found to have increased from 37 percent of the workforce in 1950 to 59 percent in 2000, with the rate of increase for knowledge-producing workers peaking in the 1960s and 1970s and then slowing down somewhat, while that of data workers peaked in the 1960s and then tapered off after that. Yet, all in all, most of the growth in information employment did not take place among high-skilled, high-paid professionals and managers but rather among moderate-skilled, relatively low-paid clerical and sales workers. Another interesting finding is that while in 1950 over half of total employment was found in blue-collar jobs, this proportion slipped to under a quarter by 2000. The results show that the US moved from a society in which people work with their hands to one in which they work with their mind.

The next part of the paper uses an I–O decomposition analysis to break down the changes in the information workers' share of the labor force into three parts: (i) the substitution of information labor for labor of other types within the production process – that is, the change in the proportion of information workers in each industry's labor force; (ii) the change in each industry's share of the economy's total output; and (iii) the change associated with relative variations in labor productivity of the different industries.

The first of these three components indicates the extent to which the composition of the labor force in a typical industry has become more information-intensive (assuming all other things remain the same). The second element relates to different industries' shares of the economy's final output and is pertinent in determining the extent to which the expansion in information-related employment is attributable to an increase in the economy's demand for products with a high information content. The third component plays the part in testing the role of unbalanced growth in the information explosion – that is, the extent to which growth of information workers can be attributed to relatively lower productivity growth in industries using more information.

The growth in information workers is found to have been driven not by a shift in tastes toward information-intensive goods and services (as measured by the composition of final demand) but rather by a roughly equal combination of the substitution of information workers for goods and service workers within the structure of production of industries and the unbalanced growth effect.

The third part of the paper relies on econometric analysis to analyse the sources of growth of information workers on the industry level. The dependent variables are the changes in knowledge and data workers as a percent of total employment in the industry over the period. Independent variables include: (1) TFP growth; (2) expenditure on R&D; (3) investment in new equipment; (4) investment in OCA; and (5) the degree of international competitiveness of an industry. R&D expenditure is found to have a positive coefficient and to be the most significant factor that contributes to the growth in knowledge workers, though it is negatively associated with the growth of data workers. Investment in OCA also exerts a positive effect on knowledge worker employment but it has a strong negative effect on the employment of data workers.

Like Chapter 11, Chapter 15, 'The Vintage Effect in TFP-growth: An Analysis of the Age Structure of Capital', is another instance where we build a neutral general equilibrium model and computers surprise us as key industry. Here, our objective was merely to assess the role of the age of capital in the fluctuation of TFP growth. The idea is that in investment booms capital becomes younger and that this vintage effect spurs TFP growth. In slowdowns the opposite happens. It would be preferable if TFP growth were stable over the business cycle. After all, the point of the so-called 'Solow residual' is that it is a measure of technical change. Technical change should concern the growth of knowledge and knowledge progresses steadily over time rather than cycling up and down. If output growth slides back when the stock of capital becomes obsolete, it is not right to ascribe this to technical regress. In a sense the capital input is reduced and this should enter the growth accounting. Conceptually, the capital growth effect and the technical change effect are disentangled if capital is measured not in physical units, but in efficiency units. We do so by accounting for the vintage structure of different types of capital using not only past investment data, but also data on the average age of capital. If two types of capital have the same investment history, but one stock is younger than the other, its rate of obsolescence must be greater.

In earlier work, Richard Nelson postulated a simple inverse relationship between age and rate of obsolescence and this relationship has been used for a straightforward adjustment of the stock of capital in efficiency units. We show, however, that this formulation is incorrect and that the age data must be commingled with the investment history data to obtain an accurate estimate of the vintage effect. We account explicitly for capital vintages and use maximum likelihood to estimate rates of obsolescence. The greatest rate is found for computer-related equipment. Computer storage devices and computer printers have rates of 0.45, which corresponds with a lifetime slightly over two years. Personal computers have a rate of 0.26, which corresponds with a lifetime of four years. We use these rates of obsolescence to determine the stocks of capital in efficiency units and adjust the Solow residuals accordingly. This, in fact, has a smoothing effect, resolving the puzzle of the pro-cyclicality of measured TFP growth at least to some extent. We back this up by theory. A proposition proves that the sensitivity of measured TFP growth with respect to the rate of obsolescence is proportional to the aging of capital. In times where capital grows older (by a slowdown in investment) measured TFP growth must be corrected upward to take into account the rate of obsolescence and vice versa.

Chapter 16, 'Competition and Performance: The Different Roles of Capital and Labor', combines labor and capital analyses in productivity analysis. A simple insight is that TFP is the sum of labor productivity and capital productivity and that, therefore, TFP growth can be written as a weighted sum of labor productivity growth and capital productivity growth. Real wages and real rental rates can be substituted, provided markets are perfectly competitive so that rewards reflect productivities. In this chapter we address the extremely interesting issue regarding what departures from perfect competition, as occasioned, for example, by the presence of market power, bring about. There is the accounting issue of the appropriate measurement of TFP growth under such conditions and there is the economic issue of whether market power is good or bad.

We use a general equilibrium model of the Canadian economy to solve for perfectly competitive prices, including those of labor and capital. Here we exploit the first welfare theorem, which states that the perfectly competitive equilibrium is efficient. We solve the efficiency program and find that the shadow prices associated with the labor and capital constraints equal to their respective productivities. This methodology is a double-edged sword. On one side it provides TFP growth measures for the Canadian industries that do not (wrongly) assume that market valuations are perfectly competitive. On the other, comparison of these competitive evaluations with the observed ones enables us to estimate mark-ups and, on the basis of I–O analysis, a decomposition of mark-ups into labor and capital components. Finally we relate TFP growth empirically to the mark-ups.

The theoretical literature is divided and the empirical literature is inconclusive. Neoclassical economists argue that competition is good, since it eliminates slack and drives down costs. The neoclassical prediction is a negative relationship between mark-ups and TFP growth. Schumpeterian economists, however, point out that the bulk of R&D is funded by retained profits, predicting a positive relationship between mark-ups and TFP growth. Empirically the relationship is insignificant, as if countervailing forces are at work. Industrial organization models have been developed to generate a nonlinear relationship, but our analysis simply enables us to separate the labor and capital effects. We find that competition in labor markets is good and competition in capital markets is bad for TFP growth. This is consistent with the neoclassical and Schumpeterian arguments. The former pertain to labor markets, such as principal–agent problems, and the latter to capital markets, such as information problems that surround R&D funding.

The final part of our book further distinguishes productivity growth from technical change. Departures from perfect competition not only impact the measurement and development of productivity growth, but also its nature. In a perfectly competitive world TFP growth measures technical change, but inefficient economies can also record TFP growth by becoming more efficient. There are numerous ways to achieve this. Firms may become more efficient. Efficient firms may gain market share. The pattern of specialization may align with comparative advantage. The alternative measures of productivity encountered in the preceding parts of this book, particularly the first, are now consolidated and unified.

A precursor to this unification is Chapter 17, 'Aggregation of Productivity Indices: The Allocative Efficiency Correction'. Here we offer a back-of-the-envelope calculation based on the distance between actual and potential output, $D[x(t), y(t), t] = F[x(t), t] - y(t)$, where x is an input vector, y is output (initially a scalar but later generalized to a vector) and $F(\cdot, t)$ is the production function at time t. Efficiency change is defined as the reduction of this distance, i.e. $EC = -\mathrm{d}D/\mathrm{d}t$ (the ordinary time derivative, with a minus sign). Technical change is defined as the shift of the production function, the partial derivative of F with respect to time t. But this is equal to the partial derivative of the distance function with respect to time t: $TC = \partial D/\partial t$. A firm, industry or economy may perform better by technical change or efficiency change and productivity change is the sum of the two: $PC = \partial D/\partial t - \mathrm{d}D/\mathrm{d}t$. Division of this expression by the level of the output turn is it into a growth rate, namely TFP.

This framework sheds light on the standard expression for TFP (the Solow residual), aggregation issues, and the connection with efficiency versus technical change effects. The back-of-the envelope calculation begins with total differentiation of the distance function. Invoking the chain rule,

$$\mathrm{d}D[x(t), y(t), t]/\mathrm{d}t = \frac{\partial D}{\partial x}\dot{x} + \frac{\partial D}{\partial y}\dot{y} + \frac{\partial D}{\partial t}.$$

Substituting this expression in the formula for PC we obtain

$$PC = -\frac{\partial D}{\partial x}\dot{x} - \frac{\partial D}{\partial y}\dot{y}.$$

By definition of distance function D this reads

$$PC = \dot{y} - \frac{\partial F}{\partial x}\dot{x}.$$

We recognize the Solow residual between output growth and input growth, with perfectly competitive input prices (marginal productivities) as input weights. However, perfect competition is not assumed and there are two sources of productivity growth: technical change and efficiency change.

Productivity measurement is plagued by an aggregation issue. Firm productivities do not sum to industry productivity (and industry productivities do not sum to economy productivity) except when marginal rates of substitution and of transformation are constant in commodity space (linear isoquants and output curves) and these constants are common to all firms. This Blackorby–Russell condition is not fulfilled by Leontief production functions. In terms of our simple framework the condition means that the weights $\partial F/\partial x$ are the same for all units (firms or industries) and aggregation is perfect. If the condition is not fulfilled, units must be assigned idiosyncratic weights and failure to do so generates a bias, which we nail down.

The sequel Chapter 18, 'Don't Aggregate Efficiency But Disaggregate Inefficiency', is a pragmatic solution to the aggregation problem. It proposes to first measure the macro output gap and then to impute it to the micro units and a residual allocative inefficiency term. The term is ignored in the literature and this is another explanation of the aggregation bias.

Chapter 19, 'Debreu's Coefficient of Resource Utilization, the Solow Residual, and TFP: The Connection by Leontief Preferences', offers a solid framework for these ideas and establishes a tight connection with the main concepts in the literature. An economy is described by the following fundamentals: resources, technology and preferences. The efficiency of the economy can be measured by the distance between the resource vector and the frontier of minimal resource vectors that are capable of generating allocations that are at least as good for all consumers, the so-called better set. Debreu has shown that the nearest point of this minimal set is the resource vector obtained by proportional contraction. If this is, say, 90 percent of the actual resource vector, we say the coefficient of resource utilization is 90 percent.

The Achilles' heel of this construct is that consumers' micro data are required to determine the allocations that are acceptable to consumers. Their preferences must be on the table. We show that absent this information a conservative approach is to consider the intersection of all better sets with respect to conceivable preference relationships and that this is equivalent to assuming Leontief preferences. Although these preferences differ between consumers, only aggregate consumption is shown to be needed for the determination of the coefficient of resource allocation. Moreover, we show that TFP growth, defined as the rate of growth of the macro consumption bundle net of the rate of growth of the endowments, is the sum of the Solow residual between output and input in production and the rate of growth of the coefficient of resource allocation, confirming $PC = TC + EC$ on the back of our envelope. The chapter concludes with a decomposition into industry and allocation contributions.

The final Chapter 20, 'The Solow Residual, Domar Aggregation, and Inefficiency: A Synthesis of TFP Measures', consolidates in a unifying framework the four approaches to TFP measurement: (i) growth accounting (Solow residual, Divisia index); (ii) index numbers (Törnqvist index, Fisher index); (iii) Data Envelopment Analysis (Malmqvist index); and (iv) I–O analysis (Domar aggregation of industry Solow residuals). The framework consists of data, a production possibility set and a behavioral assumption. Let us explain each of these three framework components.

Data are inputs and outputs and, possibly, their prices, vectors p and w, respectively. If the prices do not belong to the data, they may be endogenously determined by the inputs, outputs and the other framework components. The production possibility set is assumed to contain the data. (This is not true in a fifth approach to TFP, namely stochastic frontier analysis, where errors may generate observations off the production possibility set.) The behavioral assumption stipulates that prices reflect marginal products on the frontier of the production possibility set. This assumption is consistent with, but weaker than, that of profit maximization or even cost minimization, as productive and allocative inefficiencies are admitted. Yet it is powerful, and in combination with the assumption of constant returns to scale it implies that TFP – defined as the Solow residual between output and input growth rates, each expressed by Divisia indices – must be the sum of the shift of the production possibility frontier and efficiency change.

Next we show that the Törnqvist and Fisher indices approximate the Solow residual if not only prices reflect marginal products, but also slack is absent, rendering efficient change zero. This neoclassical 'if' is a big one. The same no-slack condition yields another result, namely that the Solow residual becomes a Domar weighted average of input coefficient reductions. Here the production possibility set is specified by those input coefficients. The proof is difficult. It uses the fact that the production possibility set can be parametrized by the distance function and that, therefore, the shift of technology is determined by the partial derivative of the distance function with respect to time. The evaluation of the latter requires an analysis of the sensitivity of the value of a linear program with respect to constraint coefficients (which are the input coefficients).

Last but not least, after demonstrating that all mainstream variants of TFP are consistent under the no-slack condition, we show how inefficiencies can be accommodated by adding an efficiency change term. This modification better catches the interest of neoclassical and I–O economists. Although their approaches to TFP differ, they share a tendency to identify TFP growth with technical change. We, however, expect that fluctuations in the efficiency of an economy will attract more attention, including in the policy arena. The groundwork for their analysis is laid.

PART I

GROWTH ACCOUNTING IN AN INPUT–OUTPUT FRAMEWORK

[1]

INDUSTRIAL COMPOSITION, INTERINDUSTRY EFFECTS, AND THE U.S. PRODUCTIVITY SLOWDOWN

Edward N. Wolff*

Abstract—This paper investigates the effect of shifts in output composition on the slowdown of productivity growth in the United States between 1947–67 and 1967–76. I employ a Leontief input-output framework and a Divisia index of aggregate productivity growth to separate the effects of changes in sectoral rates of technical progress from the effects of changes in output composition and interindustry flows on the change in overall productivity growth. Of the approximately 2 percentage point decline in overall total factor productivity growth, 17% to 22% was due to compositional effects and the remainder to other factors.

THE importance of shifts in input or output composition in explaining the recent productivity slowdown in the United States has been a source of some controversy. Estimates of such shift effects vary considerably. For example, Gollop (1982) calculated that resource shifts were actually an offset to the slowdown in productivity growth; Kutscher, Mark, and Norsworthy (1977) estimated that employment shifts had no effect on productivity growth; Thurow (1979) ascribed half of the slowdown between 1965–72 and 1972–77 to employment shifts; and Nordhaus (1972) attributed 77% of the decline from 1948–55 to 1965–71 to employment shifts.

In a related paper, the possible reasons for these disparate results were discussed at length (see Baumol and Wolff, forthcoming). Briefly, these differences stem primarily from the use of different concepts and measures. Actually, three different concepts are used in the literature. The first is a "resource allocation" or "equilibrating shift" effect, which measures the increase in productivity that can result from a more efficient allocation of resources (cf. Denison (1979a, 1979b, and 1984); Norsworthy, Harper, and Kunze (1979); and Gollop (1982)). While interesting in itself, this resource reallocation effect is a somewhat limited notion, measuring the movement toward the efficient frontier instead of the outward movement of the frontier over time. The second concept is the so-called "level" effect, which assesses the effect of resource shifts on overall productivity growth by holding constant the productivity levels of the various sectors of the economy (cf. Nordhaus (1972); Kutscher, Mark, and Norsworthy (1977); and Thurow (1979)). This measure was found to be quite arbitrary, depending on the (arbitrary) choice of base year used in the computation. The third is the so-called "rate effect," which assesses the effect of shifts in resources by holding constant sectoral rates of productivity growth (cf. Nordhaus (1972); Baily (1982), and Gollop (1982)). All three authors found that the rate effect had a negligible influence on the productivity slowdown. This measure is the most theoretically sound of the three, and my measure will fall in this category, though differ in significant ways from previous formulations, and show a greater effect on overall productivity growth from compositional changes.

I shall first develop a general model to measure such shifts or composition effects from a Leontief input-output framework (sections I and II). Results for the U.S. economy over the 1947–76 period will then be reported, with particular emphasis on accounting for the productivity slowdown after 1967 (sections III, IV, and V). Conclusions and a comparison with other results will be discussed in section VI, VII and VIII.

I. The Standard Model

Following the work of Peterson (1979), let us define:

X_t = (column) vector of gross output by sector at time t

Y_t = (column) vector of final demand by sector at time t

a_t = matrix of inter-industry technical coefficients at time t

l_t = (row) vector of labor coefficients at time t, showing employment per unit of output

k_t = (row) vector of capital stock coefficients at time t, showing the capital stock required per unit of output

p_t = (row) vector of prices at time t, showing the price per unit of output of each industry.

Received for publication June 27, 1983. Revision accepted for publication October 19, 1984.

* New York University.

I would like to express my appreciation to Wassily Leontief, William Baumol, M. I. Nadiri, Mark Schankerman, Martin Baily, and Andrew Sharpe for helpful comments and to the Division of Information Science and Technology of the National Science Foundation for financial support.

In addition, let us define the following scalars:

w_t = the annual wage rate (see footnote 2)
r_t = the rate of profit on the capital stock at time t (see footnote 2)
$y_t = p_t Y_t$ = gross national product at current prices at time t
$L_t = l_t X_t$ = total employment at time t
$K_t = k_t X_t$ = total capital stock at time t.

The "standard" measure of the rate of aggregate total factor productivity (TFP) growth will be defined as

$$\rho(pdY - wdL - rdK)/y \tag{1}$$

where the time subscript has been dropped for convenience and d refers to the differential. Alternatively, since

$$dz = z(d\log z)$$

for any variable z, where log is the natural logarithm, then (1) is equivalent to

$$\rho = \frac{p\hat{Y}}{y}d\log Y - \frac{wL}{y}d\log L - \frac{rk}{y}d\log K \tag{2}$$

where a hat (ˆ) over a vector indicates a matrix whose diagonal is equal to the vector and whose other elements are zero. From (2), it should be apparent that ρ is a current value weighted index of productivity growth.[1]

The overall rate of TFP growth can be related to changes in the inter-industry coefficient matrix as follows. From the basic Leontief system,

$$Y = (I - a)X. \tag{3}$$

Therefore,

$$dY = (I - a)dX - (da)X. \tag{4}$$

Moreover, from the definitions of L and K,

$$dL = l\,dX + (dl)X \tag{5}$$
$$dK = k\,dX + (dk)X. \tag{6}$$

Substituting (4), (5), and (6) into (1) yields

$$\rho = [p(I - a)dX - p(da)X - wldX - w(dl)X - rkdX - r(dk)x]/y. \tag{7}$$

[1] Since productivity growth is measured over discrete time periods rather than instantaneously, a modified form of equation (2) is actually used to estimate aggregate productivity growth, where current value shares are replaced by average value shares over the period of estimation. The same approximation is used for the other indices of productivity growth developed in the paper.

Also, from the basic Leontief framework,[2]

$$p = pa + wl + rk \tag{8}$$

or

$$p(I - a) = wl + rk. \tag{9}$$

Hence, from (7) and (9),

$$\rho = -[pda + wdl + rdk]X/y. \tag{10}$$

Let us now define the rate of TPF growth for sector j as

$$\pi_j \equiv -(pda^j + wdl_j + rdk_j)/p_j \tag{11}$$

where π is the corresponding row vector and a^j is the jth column of matrix a. This measure is the continuous analog to a measure of sectoral technical change proposed by Leontief (1953). Then, it follows directly from (10) and (11) that

$$\rho = \pi\hat{p}X/y. \tag{12}$$

Let us now define the total (direct plus indirect) labor and capital requirements per unit of final output as follows:

$$\lambda = lq \tag{13}$$
$$\gamma = kq \tag{14}$$

where $q \equiv (I - a)^{-1}$. Then

$$L = \lambda Y \tag{15}$$
$$K = \gamma Y. \tag{16}$$

[2] Empirically, both wage rates and profit rates differ across sectors. As a result (and for many other reasons such as industry concentration differences), actual market prices deviate from competitive equilibrium prices. Since this analysis assumes competitive equilibrium prices, labor (and capital stock) are assumed to be homogeneous across sectors. A uniform wage rate w is established by dividing total wages by total employment, and a uniform profit rate by dividing total profits by total capital stock. The price vector p is then computed from

$$p = (wl + rk)(I - a)^{-1}.$$

It is straightforward to show that p satisfies the national accounting identity $pY = wL + rk$.

An alternative approach that was also tried is to treat the deviation of the factor compensation in a given sector from the overall factor compensation in the economy as an indicator of the average "quality" of the input in the sector. Thus, if the average wage in a sector is greater than the economy-wide average, then the labor in that sector is assumed to be of higher quality than the average. With this approach, we change our measure of primary inputs to be "quality-adjusted" or "effective" labor and capital stock. The wage rate w is then interpreted as the wage rate of average-quality labor and r the return to average-quality capital stock. The price vector p then becomes the actual sectoral price deflators. The empirical results from this approach differ very little from those reported in tables 1 through 4.

From (8),

$$p = w\lambda + r\gamma. \qquad (17)$$

From (1), (15), and (16),

$$\rho = [pdY - w(d\lambda)Y - w\lambda dY - r(d\gamma)Y - r\gamma dY]/y$$

and, from (17),

$$\rho = -[wd\lambda + rd\gamma]Y/y. \qquad (18)$$

Let us now define the rate of "inverse" sectoral technical change which is the inverse of the rate of decrease in total factor requirements per unit of final output, as follows:

$$\pi_j^* \equiv -(wd\lambda_j + rd\gamma_j)/p_j \qquad (19)$$

where π^* is the corresponding row vector. The measure π_j^* essentially shows the rate of technical progress that would occur in a composite sector j if all the sectors that contributed directly or indirectly to sector j's final output were fully integrated into a new composite sector.

It follows directly from (18) and (19) that

$$\rho = \pi^* \hat{p} Y/y. \qquad (20)$$

As a result,[3]

$$\pi^* = \pi(\hat{p} q \hat{p}^{-1}). \qquad (21)$$

Equation (21) indicates that each π_i^* is a weighted average of the π_j, where the weights are determined by the dollar contribution of each sector j to a dollar of final output of sector i.

It should be emphasized that throughout this analysis the composition of (real) final demand Y is considered exogenously determined. In particular, it is assumed not to be affected by relative price movements and changes in real income, which are themselves consequences of overall and relative productivity movements.

[3] Equation (21) can be derived directly from (11), (13), (14), and (19). A shorter, indirect proof is as follows. From (12) and (20),

$$\pi \hat{p} X/y = \pi^* \hat{p} Y/y.$$

From (3),

$$X = qY.$$

Hence,

$$\pi \hat{p} q Y = \pi^* \hat{p} Y$$

from which (21) follows, since the last equation holds for any Y.

II. The Treatment of Capital as a Produced Means of Production

In the standard model capital is treated as a primary factor of production. One can alternately consider capital a produced means of production, since capital stock, like intermediate inputs, is produced by one or more sectors of the economy. The latter approach has the advantage of incorporating changes in the (primary) resource requirements of producing capital in the measurement of overall technical change.

In order to include capital as an endogenous means of production, a new (endogenous) industry is created, whose row is the capital stock replaced in each sector of the economy and whose column consists of the inputs required to produce the replacement capital stock.[4] Final demand is valued net of replacement investment, and labor is treated as the only primary factor of production. The accounting framework of the standard model is then modified as follows:

g = the row vector showing the amount of capital stock replaced per unit of sectoral output

h = the column vector, showing the inter-industry inputs required to produce one unit of capital stock

$\tilde{a} = \begin{bmatrix} a & h \\ g & 0 \end{bmatrix}$, the augmented inter-industry technical coefficient matrix

$\tilde{Y} = \begin{bmatrix} Y - h(gX) \\ 0 \end{bmatrix}$, the vector of net final output

$\tilde{X} = \begin{bmatrix} X \\ h(gX) \end{bmatrix}$.

Moreover, by construction, $\tilde{k} = \tilde{\gamma} = 0$. The variables $\tilde{\rho}$, $\tilde{p}$, $\tilde{\pi}$, $\tilde{q}$, and $\tilde{\pi}^*$ are then formed in analogous fashion to the standard framework.

Two methods are used here to value the capital stock consumed in each sector : (1) The vector g is set equal to depreciation per unit of output to yield "Marxian labor values." (See Wolff (1979) for more details.) (2) The vector g is set equal to the gross increase in capital stock per unit of output in each sector. This method will be referred to as the "Peterson-Harrod measure," since it was suggested by Peterson (1979), who attributed the idea to Harrod. In both cases, vector h is set equal

[4] It is assumed that no labor or capital stock is directly employed in this fictitious industry.

TABLE 1.—THE UNWEIGHTED AND WEIGHTED AVERAGE OF SECTORAL TFP GROWTH

A. Overall TFP Growth (ρ)

	Periods				
Measure	1947–58	1958–67	1947–67	1967–76	1947–76
1. Standard	.0139	.0188	.0164	−.0024	.0113
2. Marxian labor value	.0213	.0261	.0236	.0025	.0164
3. Peterson-Harrod	.0227	.0256	.0243	.0043	.0180

B. Unweighted Average of Sectoral TFP Growth[a]

	Periods				
Measure	1947–58	1958–67	1947–67	1967–76	1947–76
1. Standard	.0061	.0114	.0082	−.0030	.0068
2. Marxian labor value	.0111	.0170	.0138	.0031	.0099
3. Peterson-Harrod	.0138	.0175	.0152	.0046	.0114

C. Change in Average Sectoral TFP Growth

	Periods			
	1967–76/1958–67		1967–76/1947–67	
Measure	Weighted ($\Delta\rho$)	Unweighted ($\Delta\bar{\pi}$)	Weighted ($\Delta\rho$)	Unweighted ($\Delta\bar{\pi}$)
1. Standard	−.0212	−.0144	−.0188	−.0113
2. Marxian labor value	−.0236	−.0138	−.0211	−.0106
3. Peterson-Harrod	−.0212	−.0128	−.0201	−.0105

[a] This is defined as $\bar{\pi} = \Sigma_j \pi_j / 82$, where 82 is the number of non-dummy industries.

to the coefficients of the gross capital formation vector in final demand.

III. Average Change in Sectoral TFP Growth

Before we consider the effect of sectoral composition on overall TFP growth, it is instructive to compare the weighted and unweighted average change in sectoral technical change. All computations were made from 87-order U.S. input-output tables in constant prices. The years 1947, 1958, 1967, and 1976 were used in this study.[5] Since we are primarily interested in the sources of the productivity slowdown after 1967, we shall focus the empirical results on a comparison of two sets of periods: 1958–67/1967–76 and 1947–67/1967–76.

Panel A of table 1 shows the rate of growth of overall TFP over the indicated periods. The first line shows the value of ρ using the standard definition of TFP growth and "gross national income"—that is, GNP less indirect business taxes—as the definition of total final output y. The second line shows the value of $\tilde{\rho}$ using Marxian labor values and national income (though valued at labor value prices) for total final output $\tilde{y}$. The second line is uniformly greater than the first line, since $\tilde{\rho}$ essentially measures labor productivity growth, which was greater than standard TFP growth. In the third line, the Peterson-Harrod definition of prices is used, and $\tilde{y}$ is equal to gross national income less business capital formation investment valued at the new prices. The third line is slightly greater than the second, except for 1958–67, reflecting mainly a rising ratio of depreciation to gross business investment.[6]

Panel B shows the unweighted average in sectoral rates of TFP growth (π_j in the first line and $\tilde{\pi}_j$ in the second and third lines). In the 1947–58 and 1958–67 periods, the unweighted average rate

[5] See the appendix for a description of the data.

[6] Under normal circumstances (though not all), ρ will be greater than $\tilde{\rho}$. This can be seen indirectly by noting that $\tilde{\rho}$ measures labor productivity growth, whereas ρ measures multi-factor productivity growth. Thus, if the aggregate capital-labor ratio is rising, $\tilde{\rho}$ will generally exceed ρ. See Rymes (1971, 1972), Hulten (1975, 1979), Hulten and Nishimizu (1980), and Rymes (1983) for more technical discussions of this issue and related results.

of TFP growth was uniformly less than the corresponding value of overall TFP growth, and the difference ranged from about 0.7 to 1.0 percentage points. Since, from (12), ρ can itself be construed as a weighted average of sectoral TFP growth rates π_j, with weights proportional to the value of gross output ($p_j X_j$), this result indicates that larger sectors had higher rates of productivity growth than smaller sectors. However, in the 1967–76 period, the unweighted average of sectoral TFP growth rates was about equal to overall TFP growth by each of the three measures, indicating no relation between industry size and productivity growth during this period.

Panel C shows the change in the weighted and unweighted measures of average sectoral TFP growth from the period before 1967 to the period after 1967. Overall TFP growth by each of the three measures fell by over two percentage points between 1958–67 and 1967–76 and by about two percentage points between 1947–67 and 1967–76. In comparison, the change in the unweighted average is typically a full percentage point below the change in the weighted average. This indicates that the largest industries, in terms of the value of gross output ($p_j X_j$), were the ones that experienced the greatest declines in sectoral productivity growth during the 1967–76 period. In this sense, the average rate of sectoral technical progress did not decline as much during the slowdown period as the decline in the overall rate ρ would suggest. Of course, this is only a rough assessment, since the measure of the unweighted average is affected by the classification scheme of input-output sectors. However, insofar as the classification scheme was designed to capture differences in output characteristics rather than differences in the technology of production, the bias in the unweighted measure should be relatively small.

IV. Decomposition of the Overall Rate of TFP Growth

The heart of the analysis is the decomposition of overall TFP growth into a sectoral technical change and composition effect. Such a decomposition can be derived from equations (20) and (21). Let β be the column vector where $\beta_j = p_j Y_j / y$ and $s = \hat{p} q \hat{p}^{-1}$, where s is the Leontief inverse coefficient matrix, showing the dollar value of each input used per dollar of output. Then,

$$\rho = \pi s \beta. \tag{22}$$

If we ignore second-order terms, then the change in the overall growth rate of TFP is given by

$$\Delta\rho \cong \pi s(\Delta\beta) + \pi(\Delta s)\beta + (\Delta\pi)s\beta. \tag{23}$$

This decomposition allows us to separate the change in overall productivity growth into three effects, corresponding to the three terms on the right hand side of (23). (1) The *value share effect* or "composition" effect is the change in ρ that would occur if π and s remained constant but the value composition of final output changed as it did in actuality. Here, it should be noted that β measures value shares, not real shares, and thus $\Delta\beta$ reflects, in part, relative price changes. (2) The *interindustry effect* shows the change in ρ that would occur if π and β remained constant but the interindustry matrix s changed. It should be noted that a positive change in matrix s, which indicates increasing interindustry flows or linkages among sectors in value terms, has a positive effect on overall productivity growth. The change in matrix s also reflects, in part, relative price changes. (3) The *sectoral technical change effect* shows the change in ρ that would occur if s and β remained constant but sectoral rates of TFP growth changed as they had in actuality.[7]

This decomposition might be compared to one based on equation (12):

$$\Delta\rho \cong \pi(\Delta\alpha) + (\Delta\pi)\alpha \tag{23'}$$

where $\alpha_j = p_j X_j / y$. The second term on the right-hand side of (23′) is identical to the last term on the right-hand side of (23), since $\alpha = s\beta$. The first term on the right-hand side of (23′) is thus the sum of the first two terms of (23). In other words, the effect on overall TFP growth from the change in gross output composition is essentially decomposed into two effects in (23): one from the change in final demand composition and the other from the change in the interindustry matrix. The major

[7] This last effect is not independent of the interindustry effect since, from (11), π_j reflects, in part, the change in the interindustry technical coefficient matrix a. That is to say, technically speaking, it is not really appropriate to ask the counterfactual question—what if π changed but s remained constant?—since π already presumes a change in matrix a and hence a change in matrix s. As will be seen below, the interindustry effect and the sectoral technical change effect shall be combined into a single technical change effect, partly for this reason. However, it should be noted that, analytically, equation (23) is still valid.

advantage of (23) over (23′) is that in the former $\Delta\rho$ is related to the shift in final output, which is considered exogenous in a Leontief system, whereas in the latter $\Delta\rho$ is related to the change in gross output, which is considered an endogenous or a derived effect. In addition, since $\alpha = s\beta$, the change in gross output shares may be partly due to changes in the interindustry matrix s, which are themselves a consequence of technical change. Thus, for both reasons, the change in final output shares is, perhaps, methodologically closer to a "pure" composition effect than the change in gross output shares.

The results of the decomposition from (23) are shown in table 2. Since discrete time periods were used, the average value of β in the time period, $\bar{\beta}$, was used in place of β in (22), and the average values of matrix s in the period, $\bar{s}$, in place of s. In addition, both first period and last period weights for $\bar{\beta}$ were used in the decomposition from (23). The change in β over two sets of time periods was considered: 1958–67/1967–76 and 1947–67/1967–76.

The change in final output value shares β accounted for between 5% and 7% of the decline in overall TFP growth between 1958–67 and 1967–76. The value share effect was largely offset by the interindustry effect, which was negative in all cases and reflected the decreased value of interindustry inputs per dollar of final output, which, in turn, was due to diminishing technical coefficients over time. As a result, the sectoral technical change effect almost equalled the total change in ρ. The value share effect was somewhat larger with Marxian labor values or the Peterson-Harrod valuation method than with the standard TFP measure. Moreover, the composition effect was very similar in magnitude with last year weights as with first year weights for β.

The value share effect from the standard framework was slightly greater measured from 1947–67 to 1967–76 than measured from 1958–67 to 1967–76. However, the composition effect measured from the Marxian or Harrod-Peterson framework was considerably greater between 1947–67 and 1967–76, accounting for between 15% and 22% of the overall productivity slowdown. There appear to be two possible reasons that account for the more pronounced composition effect involving the last two measures and the new period. First, there is a 15-year stretch between the midpoint years of the 1947–67 period (1957) and the 1967–76 period (1972). Since the average value of β in each of the two periods, $\bar{\beta}$,

TABLE 2.—DECOMPOSITION OF THE CHANGE IN OVERALL PRODUCTIVITY GROWTH

Periods and Measures	Overall $\Delta\rho$	Percentage Decomposition: Value Share $\pi s(\Delta\beta)/\Delta\rho$	Inter-industry $\pi(\Delta s)\beta/\Delta\rho$	Technical Change $(\Delta\pi)s\beta/\Delta\rho$	Sum of 3 Effects[a]
A. 1958–67/1967–76					
1. Standard					
a. First period weights β	−.0212	5.2%	−4.3%	98.6%	99.4%
b. Last period weights β	−.0212	5.4	−4.3	98.7	99.8
2. Marxian labor value					
a. First period weights β	−.0236	7.3	−3.3	97.4	101.4
b. Last period weights β	−.0236	6.4	−4.4	96.3	98.3
3. Peterson-Harrod					
a. First period weights β	−.0212	6.1	−5.9	100.5	100.7
b. Last period weights β	−.0212	6.7	−6.4	99.4	99.7
B. 1947–67/1967–76					
1. Standard					
a. First period weights β	−.0188	6.0	−4.4	97.0	98.7
b. Last period weights β	−.0188	6.5	−6.3	98.4	98.6
2. Marxian labor value					
a. First period weights β	−.0211	21.7	−7.7	87.3	101.3
b. Last period weights β	−.0211	21.1	−7.2	86.2	100.1
3. Peterson-Harrod					
a. First period weights β	−.0201	14.8	−10.7	97.0	101.1
b. Last period weights β	−.0201	18.8	−8.6	89.5	99.7

[a] The sum of the output, interindustry, and sectoral technical change effects may not equal unity because of the exclusion of second-order terms and rounding errors.

was used in the actual decomposition of (23), there was likely a greater change in $\bar{\beta}$ between 1957 and 1972 than over the corresponding 9 years between the midpoint years of 1958–67 (1963) and 1967–76 periods. The same argument, of course, applies to the standard framework. However, from (21), $\pi^* = \pi s$ and the value share effect can be reformulated as $\pi^*(\Delta\beta)$. The unweighted average value of π^* was about twice as great in the Marxian and Peterson-Harrod measures as in the standard framework, which helped to account for the larger composition effects in the non-standard frameworks.

Second, the interindustry effects were larger in absolute value (actually, more negative) between the 1947–67 and the 1967–76 periods than between the 1958–67 and the 1967–76 periods. Here, again, the apparent reason is that over the longer stretch of time between the midpoint years of the 1947–67 and the 1967–76 periods, the coefficients of the s matrix likely declined more than between the midpoint years of the 1958–67 and the 1967–76 periods. Moreover, the interindustry effects between 1947–67 and 1967–76 were somewhat stronger in the Marxian and Peterson-Harrod framework than in the standard framework. This probably reflects the fact that in the non-standard frameworks, the cost of reproducing capital goods is incorporated within matrix $\tilde{q}$ and, hence, matrix $\tilde{s}$ via vector h. However, it is not the case that the interindustry effect is always greater in the non-standard frameworks than in the standard one.

V. Price and Real Composition Effects

As indicated above, β_j is the value share of the final output of sector j in the total value of final output and thus changes in β_j reflect both changes in relative prices and changes in the share of real final output j in total (real) final output. One can therefore decompose the composition effect into a price and a real share effect.

Let us first deflate relative prices using the GNP deflator:

$$d_{it} = \frac{p_{it}}{p_t Y_t / p_0 Y_t} = \frac{p_{it} \cdot p_0 Y_t}{y_t}$$

where d is a row vector and p_0 is the vector of prices in the base year (1958 was used here). Define the real final output share vector δ by

$$\delta_{it} = p_{i0} Y_{it} / p_0 Y_t = Y_{it} / p_0 Y_t$$

where sectoral base year prices are set equal to unity. Then

$$\beta_{it} = d_{it} \delta_{it}$$

and

$$\Delta\beta \cong (\Delta\hat{d})\delta + \hat{d}(\Delta\delta). \tag{24}$$

This decomposition was carried out in all three frameworks between the 1947–67 and the 1967–76 periods (see table 3). The first two columns of panel A are reproduced from table 2. The change in the value share of final output, as discussed above, accounted for about 6% of the change in overall TFP growth in the standard framework and about 20% in the other two frameworks. Of the 6% in the standard framework, over 7% was attributable to price changes and −1% to the real share effect. Of the 20% in the non-standard frameworks, only 4% was due to the change in the composition of real final demand and the remaining 16% was due to the change in relative prices.

TABLE 3.—DECOMPOSITION OF THE VALUE SHARE EFFECT INTO A PRICE AND REAL SHARE EFFECT BETWEEN 1947–67 AND 1967–76

	$\Delta\rho$	Value Share Effect	Real Share Effect	Price Effect
		$\pi^*(\Delta\beta)/\Delta\rho =$	$\pi^*\hat{d}(\Delta\delta)/\Delta\rho +$	$\pi^*(\hat{d})\delta/\Delta\rho$
1. Standard				
a. First period weights δ	−.0188	6.0%	−1.3%	7.4%
b. Last period weights δ	−.0188	6.5	−1.3	7.8
2. Marxian labor values				
a. First period weights δ	−.0211	21.7	4.8	17.0
b. Last period weights δ	−.0211	21.1	3.6	17.5
3. Peterson-Harrod				
a. First period weights δ	−.0201	14.8	2.1	12.7
b. Last period weights δ	−.0201	18.8	3.4	15.5

TABLE 4.—SUMMARY TABLE: SOURCES OF THE SLOWDOWN IN OVERALL PRODUCTIVITY GROWTH BETWEEN 1947–67 AND 1967–76

	Unweighted Average $\delta\bar{\pi}$[b]	$\Delta\rho$	Percentage Decomposition of $\Delta\rho$[a]: Real Share Effect[c]	Price Effect[d]	Total Technical Change Effect[e]
1. Standard	−.0113	−.0188	−1.3%	7.6%	93.7%
2. Marxian labor value	−.0106	−.0211	4.2	17.3	78.5
3. Peterson-Harrod	−.0105	−.0201	2.8	14.2	83.0

[a] Results are averaged over first year and last year weights, and normalized to sum to 100%.
[b] Defined as $\Sigma_j \Delta\pi_j/82$.
[c] Defined as $\pi^* \hat{d}(\Delta\delta)/\Delta\rho$.
[d] Defined as $\pi^*(\Delta\hat{d})\delta/\Delta\rho$.
[e] Defined as $[\pi(\Delta s)\beta + (\Delta\pi)s\beta]/\Delta\rho = (\Delta\pi^*)\beta/\Delta\rho$.

VI. Summary of Results

A summary of results is presented in table 4 for the slowdown in productivity growth between the 1947–67 period and the 1967–76 period. The results shown are, in addition, averaged between first period and last period weights.

The first column shows the unweighted average decline in the sectoral rate of TFP growth. The unweighted average decline varied between 50% and 60% of the overall (weighted) decline in TFP growth. The difference is attributable to what may be called the *sectoral weighting effect*. The results indicate that larger sectors experienced greater declines in their rate of technical change after 1967 than smaller sectors and this was due to the fact that larger sectors had higher rates of TFP growth than smaller sectors, at least up to 1967. This suggests, in turn, that the "average" decline in the rate of technical change is not as grim as the figure for the overall decline would indicate, where the technology of each sector is given equal weight.

The last three columns present the percentage decomposition of the change in overall TFP growth. The first of these is the real share effect, which shows how much ρ would have changed if real final output shares (δ_j) shifted as they did between 1947–67 and 1967–76 but the relative prices of 1947–67 had remained unchanged. The real share effect was quite small, explaining from −1% to 4% of the overall productivity slowdown. The primary reason for this is that changes in real final output shares between 1947–67 and 1967–76 were uncorrelated with sectoral productivity growth.

The second of these is the price effect, which shows how much ρ would have changed if real final output shares had remained constant but prices changed as they did between 1947–67 and 1967–76. This effect accounted for 7% of the overall change in TFP growth in the standard framework and between 14% and 17% in the non-standard framework. This result indicates that sectors with slower rates of inverse productivity growth (that is, lower values of π^*) increased their *value* share in total final output, over the 1947–76 period.[8]

The third part of the decomposition is the total effect on overall productivity growth from technical change. This consists of two components. The first is the sectoral technical change effect from $\Delta\pi$. The second is the interindustry effect from changes in the inverse value coefficient matrix s. The sum of these two is the effect on overall TFP growth from the change in the inverse sectoral productivity growth rates π^*, since, from (21), $\pi^* = \pi s$. The total technical change effect explained about 94% of the overall productivity slowdown in the standard framework and 80% in the other two. The total composition effect, the sum of the real share and the price effects, explained 6% in the standard framework and about

[8] In a Leontief system, relative prices can change from one of two factors: (i) changes in factor prices and (ii) changes in technical coefficients. This can be shown directly from (17) in the standard framework:

$$dp = [(dw)\lambda + (dr)\gamma] + [w(d\lambda) + r(d\gamma)]$$

where the first term on the right-hand side is the factor price effect and the second term the technical change effect. Then, if real final output shares remain constant over time and factor prices remain unchanged, the relative prices of the slow productivity growth sectors will rise over time, as will their value share in final output. See Baumol, Blackman, and Wolff (forthcoming) for more discussion.

20% in the other two. The composition effect, in turn, reflected the shift in the value of final output to low productivity growth sectors such as business, repair, government, and household services, and this, in turn, was primarily due to the rising relative prices of these sectors.

VII. Comparison with Other Studies

It remains to reconcile our results with those of other researchers who have also measured shift or composition effects. Those who measured the "resource reallocation" effect or the "level effect" were really measuring different phenomena. However, roughly comparable "rate effect" measures were used by Nordhaus (1972), Gollop (1982), and Baily (1982), who all found the effect to be negligible. The primary reason why I measure a stronger composition effect can be seen from equation (22): $\rho = \pi s \beta$. I essentially combine the first two terms on the right-hand side to measure the technical change effect and obtain $\rho = \pi^* \beta$. The others essentially combine the last two terms to measure the composition effect and obtain $\rho = \pi\alpha$. Their decomposition is thus similar to (23′) and their measure of the composition effect essentially incorporates changes in the interindustry matrix, which should more properly be construed as a technical change effect. Since, empirically, the interindustry effect tends to offset the (final output) value share effect, they all obtain lower measures of the composition effect.

There are three other differences in methodology. First, they all treated capital as a primary factor of production. As we saw, estimates of the composition effect were greater in the non-standard frameworks than in the standard framework. Second, they used "gross product originating" (*GPO*) to measure sectoral output and sectoral output shares. *GPO*, also called value added in constant prices, is defined as the difference between gross output in constant prices and the deflated value of intermediate inputs. For sector j at time t,

$$GPO_{jt} = p_{j0} X_{jt} - \sum_i p_{i0} a_{ijt} X_t.$$

Like gross output shares (α), *GPO* shares are determined endogenously from final output shares. In addition, *GPO* as a measure of (real) sectoral *output* is itself contaminated by changes in interindustry coefficients and hence by technical change. Third, the periods they used to measure the composition effect were typically 1958–66 and 1966–75. As was apparent from table 2, the composition effects were greater between 1947–67 and 1967–76 than between 1958–67 and 1967–76. As I argued in section IV, this was primarily due to the fact that output value shares, in general, change more over longer periods of time than over shorter periods, and hence the measured percentage contribution of the composition effect to the change in overall TFP growth will be greater.

VIII. Concluding Remark

One final word might be added. We have considered the composition effect in regard to the change in the *average* annual rate of productivity growth between two *periods* such as 1947–67 and 1967–76. If we looked at the change in overall productivity growth between two individual *years*, such as 1967 and 1976, the measured composition effect would have been much higher. Indeed, with the non-standard measures, it would have explained about half the decline in overall TFP growth between the year 1967 and the year 1976.

APPENDIX

Data Sources and Methods

The 1947, 1958, 1967, and 1972 total flow input-output tables are the standard 87-order Bureau of Economic Analysis versions. (See, for example, "The Input-Output Structure of the U.S. Economy: 1967," *Survey of Current Business*, February 1974, for a discussion of methodology and for a listing of the sectors.) The 1976 table was estimated using the so-called R.A.S. method on the 1972 table, with gross domestic output totals provided in *Time Series Data for Input-Output Industries*, Bureau of Labor Statistics, Bulletin 2018, 1979. Labor coefficients for 1947 and 1958 were obtained from Peter Petri of the Brandeis Economic Research Center (BERC); those for 1967 were obtained in *The Structure of the U.S. Economy in 1980 and 1985*, Bureau of Labor Statistics, Bulletin 1831, 1975; and those for 1976 were from *Time-Series Data for Input-Output Industries*, op. cit. Estimates of the total capital stock owned by each input-output sector are provided in *Capital Stock Estimates for Input-Output Industries: Methods and Data*, Bureau of Labor Statistics, Bulletin 203, 1979. Full capital coefficient matrices for 1947, 1958, and 1975 were obtained from BERC. The 1967 capital coefficient matrix was estimated by interpolating between the 1958 and 1975 matrices. Depreciation rates by sector for 1947 and 1958 were obtained from BERC, and those for other years estimated from *Internal Revenue Service Corporation Tax Returns* for the respective years. Sectoral price indices for years 1947, 1958, and 1967 were provided by BERC and those for 1976 from Bureau of Economic Analysis worksheets. Data on hours worked by sector, though the preferable measure of labor input to employment, were not available by sector and year and therefore could not be incorporated.

Also, sectoral capacity utilization measures, which would have been desirable, were not available for the appropriate years. Additional details on data sources and methods are available from the author.

An important modification that was made to the standard input-output table was to create an "endogenous export column" to balance with the non-competitive import row (sector 80). It was computed by multiplying the export column in final demand by a scalar so that the sum of endogenous exports in current dollars equalled the sum of non-competitive imports. This was done in order to incorporate the change in the sectoral input of non-competitive imports into overall TFP growth. In effect, non-competitive imports are valued by the amount of resources required to produce the exports traded in exchange for them on a dollar-for-dollar basis. This valuation measures, in part, the terms of trade: As the terms of trade move against the United States, the resource value "price" of the non-competitive imports increases with the domestic technology constant, and conversely. Thus, the total factor requirements measure of a product includes the resource content of the exports exchanged for the non-competitive imports used in its production. The endogenous export column was then netted out from the total export column to produce an "exogenous export" column in final demand. It should also be noted that the resource content of competitive imports is essentially valued at their replacement value—that is, at the resource content of their domestic substitute. See Leontief (1941) for more details.

REFERENCES

Baily, Martin Neil, "The Productivity Growth Slowdown by Industry," *Brookings Papers on Economic Activity* (2, 1982), 423–454.

Baumol, William J., Sue Anne Batey Blackman, and Edward N. Wolff, "Unbalanced Growth Revisited: Asymptotic Stagnancy and New Evidence," *American Economic Review* (forthcoming).

Baumol, William J., and Edward N. Wolff, "Input and Output Composition: Measuring the Effect on the Productivity Slowdown," *Journal of Political Economy* 92 (Dec. 1984), 1017–1034.

Denison, Edward F., "Explanations of Declining Productivity Growth," *Survey of Current Business* 59 (8, part II) (Aug. 1979a), 1–24.

——, *Accounting for Slower Economic Growth* (Washington, D.C.: The Brookings Institution, 1979b).

——, "Accounting for Slower Economic Growth: An Update," in John W. Kendrick (ed.), *International Comparisons of Productivity and Causes of the Slowdown* (Cambridge, MA: Ballinger, 1984).

Gollop, Frank M., "Evidence for a Sector-Biased or Sector-Neutral Industrial Strategy: Analysis of the Productivity Slowdown," Boston College mimeo, 1982.

Hulten, Charles R., "Technical Change and the Reproducibility of Capital," *American Economic Review* 65 (Dec. 1975), 956–965.

——, "On the 'Importance' of Productivity Change," *American Economic Review* 69 (March 1979), 126–136.

Hulten, Charles R., and Mieko Nishimizu, "The Importance of Productivity Change in the Economic Growth of Nine Industrialized Countries," in Shlomo Maital and Noah Meltz (eds.), *Lagging Productivity Growth* (Cambridge, Mass.: Ballinger Publishing Co., 1980).

Kutscher, R. E., J. A. Mark, and J. R. Norsworthy, "The Productivity Slowdown and Outlook to 1985," *Monthly Labor Review* 100 (May 1977), 3–8.

Leontief, Wassily, *The Structure of the American Economy, 1919–1939* (New York: Oxford University Press, 1941).

——, *Studies in the Structure of the American Economy* (New York: Oxford University Press, 1953).

Nordhaus, William D., "The Recent Productivity Slowdown," *Brookings Papers on Economic Activity* (3, 1972), 493–536.

Norsworthy, J. R., M. J. Harper, and K. Kunze, "The Slowdown in Productivity Growth: Analysis of Some Contributing Factors," *Brookings Papers on Economic Activity* (2, 1979), 387–421.

Peterson, William, "Total Factor Productivity in the U.K.: A Disaggregated Analysis," in K. D. Patterson and Kerry Schott (eds.), *The Measurement of Capital: Theory and Practice* (London: MacMillan Press, 1979).

Rymes, J. K., *On Concepts of Capital and Technical Change* (Cambridge: Cambridge University Press, 1971).

——, "The Measurement of Capital and Total Factor Productivity in the Context of the Cambridge Theory of Capital," *Review of Income and Wealth*, series 18 (Mar. 1972).

——, "More on the Measurement of Total Factor Productivity," *Review of Income and Wealth*, series 29 (Sept. 1983), 297–316.

Thurow, Lester, "The U.S. Productivity Problem," *Data Resources Review* (Aug. 1979).

Wolff, Edward N., "The Rate of Surplus Value, the Organic Composition, and the General Rate of Profit in the U.S. Economy, 1947–1967," *American Economic Review* 69 (June 1979), 329–341.

[2]

Regional Science and Urban Economics 21 (1991) 581–615. North-Holland

Secondary products and the measurement of productivity growth*

Thijs ten Raa

Tilburg University, 5000 LE Tilburg, The Netherlands

Edward N. Wolff

New York University, New York, NY 10003, USA

Received December 1989, final version received September 1990

The paper considers alternative treatments of secondary products in input–output systems and analyzes their implications for the measurement of productivity growth at both the sectoral and overall level. Two standard models of secondary products are used: (1) the commodity technology model and (2) the industry technology model. It is argued that the first model correctly relates sectoral and overall levels of productivity growth; the second model, though more conventional, aggregates sectoral levels to a biased estimate of overall productivity growth. Estimates of the two measures are provided using U.S. 85-sector input–output data for 1967, 1972, and 1977. The empirical results indicate that the alternative assumptions do not lead to significantly different estimates of commodity-level and industry-level productivity growth over this period for the full economy but do for several sectors. Moreover, changes in secondary production did not contribute significantly to the decline in productivity growth over this period but secondary production was found to have a much lower rate of productivity growth than primary production.

1. Introduction

In almost all recent studies on productivity, industry productivity is defined on the basis of the primary (or major) output of the industry. Productivity growth in the production of secondary (or by-product) output is commingled with that of the primary output. Almost all these studies implicitly assume that productivity growth of secondary products behaves in precisely the same way as that of primary products. Certain technological and market share assumptions are thus embedded in the analysis of productivity growth. As a result, changes in the level, mix, and technology of

*We would like to acknowledge financial support from the Division of Information Science and Technology of the National Science Foundation, the C.V. Starr Center for Applied Economics at New York University, the Netherlands Organization for the Advancement of Research (N.W.O. grant B 45–78) and CentER at Tilburg University. The research of the first author has been made possible by a Senior Fellowship of the Royal Netherlands Academy of Arts and Sciences.

secondary production may potentially bias such estimates of productivity growth.

In this paper, we explicitly consider the role of secondary production in input–output systems for the measurement of productivity growth at both the sectoral and overall level. For this purpose, we formulate two models of secondary production: (i) the commodity technology model and (ii) the industry technology model.[1] Moreover, within each, productivity growth can be measured on either a commodity basis or an industry basis.

We make four contributions on the analytical level. First, we derive the relation between overall productivity growth and individual sectoral productivity growth in each of the models. In particular, we isolate the contribution of secondary output productivity growth to overall productivity growth. Second, special methodological problems are present for both the scrap sector and import sector, and we present solutions for their treatment. Scrap productivity is shown to be given by the rate of recycling, and that of the import sector by the terms of trade. Third, we show analytically how the change in overall productivity growth can be decomposed into several effects, including the change in productivity growth on the sectoral level and shifts in the composition of final output. Fourth, we prove that in the commodity technology model such a decomposition is unbiased, whereas in the industry technology model, a bias is introduced by this type of decomposition.

Empirical results are then presented for the U.S. economy for the period 1967–1977. This period has received particular attention in recent years, because it is one characterized by a sharp productivity slowdown. We make use of the so-called 'make' and 'use' tables provided by the Bureau of Economic Analysis (BEA) on the 85-order level for 1967, 1972, and 1977. These tables show, respectively, the commodities produced by each industry and the commodities consumed in production by each industry. There are three findings of particular interest. First, about 85 percent of the slowdown in overall productivity growth is attributable to reductions in sectoral rates of productivity growth, with changes in the terms of trade faced by the U.S. on the international level accounting for about a quarter of this, and the remaining 15 percent to shifts in the composition of output. This compositional effect is of the same order of magnitude as found in Wolff (1985) for a much longer period (that between 1947–1967 and 1967–1976).[2] Second, though we were able to separate out the secondary product effect, little of the slowdown can be ascribed to changes in secondary product total factor productivity (TFP) growth rates, but the levels of secondary product productivity growth rates are much lower than that of primary products

[1]Also, see ten Raa et al. (1984), Viet (1986), and Kop Jansen and ten Raa (1989) for more discussion of models of secondary production and the properties of such models.

[2]Also see Denison (1979, 1984) and Wolff (1985a) for a discussion of related findings on so-called 'compositional effects'.

throughout the period of analysis. Third, though the bias from using the industry technology model and industry-level measures of productivity growth is low overall, results on the sectoral level indicate that the bias is quite large for several sectors.

Our work seems particularly relevant to multiregional input–output analysis, where the presence of secondary products is more prevalent, and the decomposition of productivity growth into primary and secondary effects admits a natural interpretation. Moreover, the model developed in our paper can be directly adapted to apply to the decomposition of nation-wide productivity movements into regional effects. As a result, our paper appears to have several important implications for the construction of multiregional input–output models.

The remainder of the paper is divided into six parts. The methodological issues are dealt with in the next part, where we present the basic accounting framework and derive the various measures of overall and sectoral productivity growth. In section 3, we present basic results on the growth of secondary production over the period from 1967 to 1977. The treatment of the scrap sector presents special methodological difficulties, since it is exclusively a secondary product, and these are discussed in section 4. Methodological problems also exist for the treatment of imports in a productivity analysis, since they have no domestic inputs in their production, and these are dealt with in section 5. Productivity growth is studied in section 6, where results are shown on sectoral productivity growth over the period and the decomposition of the change in overall productivity growth into sectoral effects, compositional effects, and secondary product effects. Concluding remarks are made in the final section of the paper.

2. The accounting framework and derivation of productivity measures

We follow ten Raa et al. (1984) and Wolff (1985b) in the development of the accounting framework. Define:

U = an input or 'use' commodity-by-industry flow matrix, where u_{ij} shows the total amount of commodity i consumed by industry j;

V = an output or 'make' industry-by-commodity flow matrix, where v_{ij} shows the total output of commodity j produced by industry i;

$\mathbf{1}$ = vector with unit entries;

$X = V^{\mathrm{T}}\mathbf{1}$ = column vector, showing the gross output of each commodity, where a superscript T refers to the transpose of the indicated matrix, and

$X^{\mathrm{I}} = V\mathbf{1}$ is a vector whose elements are the row sums of V, showing the total 'output' of each industry.[3]

[3]We use the expression X^{I} for reasons that will become apparent in subsection 2.3.

For convenience, it is assumed that the number of industries is the same as the number of commodities (that is, each commodity has an industry in which it is primary, and conversely).[4] Moreover, let

L = a row vector, showing total employment by industry;
$\Lambda = L\mathbf{1}$, total employment in the economy;
K = a row vector, showing total capital stock by industry;
$\kappa = K\mathbf{1}$, total capital stock in the economy;
w = the annual wage rate, assumed constant across industries;
r = the rate of profit on the capital stock, assumed constant across industries.[5]

The net output matrix (in terms of commodities) is then given by: $V^{\mathrm{T}} - U$. Note that U, V, L, K, w, and r comprise the data of the system. All other symbols refer to derived constructs.

We can now derive what we shall call the 'standard' row vector of commodity prices, p.[6] Since pV^{T} is the total value of output by industry and pU is the total value of inputs by industry, total value added by industry is given by: $p(V^{\mathrm{T}} - U)$. In competitive equilibrium, value added accrues to labor and capital by industry:

$$p(V^{\mathrm{T}} - U) = wL + rK. \tag{1}$$

Hence,

$$p = (wL + rK)(V^{\mathrm{T}} - U)^{-1}. \tag{2}$$

It should be emphasized that this set of prices is defined by the condition that total value added by industry is equated to factor returns and is determined independently of the model of secondary production. In this case, prices are determined by the actual flow matrix, not the coefficient matrices as in a standard Leontief system, and thus depend on the composition of final or total output.[7] There are other possible choices of price vectors, which we shall comment on below.

[4]This is not exactly true, since scrap output is produced only as a by-product. See below for modifications to the standard models engendered by the treatment of scrap.

[5]It is implicitly assumed that the government sector receives a shadow rate of return r on its capital stock.

[6]It is assumed that each commodity has the same price, irrespective of the technology of production.

[7]In such a system, it is assumed that each sector produces only one output. Then, the price vector p^* is given by:

$$p^* = (wl + rk)(I - A)^{-1},$$

where l is the (row) vector of sectoral labor coefficients, k is the (row) vector of capital coefficients, and A is the standard interindustry technical coefficients. In this system, prices are determined by technology and are invariant with respect to changes in the composition of final or total output.

One other component is needed for the analysis of productivity growth, which is Y, the vector of final demand by commodity. This is simply equal to net output by commodity summed over industries of production or consumption:

$$Y = (V^{\mathrm{T}} - U)\mathbf{1}. \tag{3}$$

The aggregate rate of TFP growth, ρ, is then defined as

$$\rho \equiv (p\,\mathrm{d}Y - w\,\mathrm{d}\Lambda - r\,\mathrm{d}\kappa)y, \tag{4}$$

where $y = pY$ is the ratio of final output.

We can now consider the two models of secondary production.

2.1. Commodity technology model

In this model, it is assumed that each commodity is produced by the same technology, irrespective of the industry of production. In this case, industries are considered independent combinations of outputs j, each with their separate input coefficients (a_{ij}^{c}). As shown in ten Raa et al. (1984), the commodity technology requirements (coefficient) matrix is given by $A^{\mathrm{c}} = UV^{-\mathrm{T}}$, where a superscript of $-\mathrm{T}$ refers to the inverse of the transpose of the indicated matrix (or the transpose of the inverse, since the two operations are communicative). Row vectors of labor and capital stock coefficients can be derived in the same way. Then $l^{\mathrm{c}} = LV^{-\mathrm{T}}$ and $k^{\mathrm{c}} = KV^{-\mathrm{T}}$. Substitution into (1) and multiplication by $V^{-\mathrm{T}}$ yields

$$p(I - A^{\mathrm{c}}) = wl^{\mathrm{c}} + rk^{\mathrm{c}}. \tag{5}$$

Thus, in the commodity technology model, the value added for each commodity unit is directly equal to factor costs. In other words, the national accounting identity between real product and income is fully decentralized on a sectoral basis. As we shall see below, this is not true for the industry technology model.[8] Also, prices depend directly on the technical coefficients and are invariant with respect to changes in final demand composition, as in a standard Leontief system (see footnote 5).

The commodity technology has the added feature that overall TFP growth can be shown to be a weighted sum of sectoral (in this case, commodity-level) rates of TFP growth. A further consequence of the 'decentralization' equation (5) is that[9]

$$\rho = -(p\,\mathrm{d}A^{\mathrm{c}} + w\,\mathrm{d}l^{\mathrm{c}} + r\,\mathrm{d}k^{\mathrm{c}})X/y. \tag{6}$$

[8]Nor is it true for most other models of secondary production. See Kop Jansen and ten Raa (1989) for more details.

[9]See Wolff (1985) for details of the proof.

Since each commodity has a separate technology in this model, the rate of TFP growth for commodity j can be defined as

$$\pi_j^c \equiv -(p\,\mathrm{d}a_{\cdot j}^c + w\,\mathrm{d}l_j^c + r\,\mathrm{d}k_j^c)/p_j, \tag{7}$$

where π^c is the corresponding row vector and $a_{\cdot j}^c$ is the jth column of matrix A^c. It then follows directly that

$$\rho = \pi^c \hat{p} X / y. \tag{8}$$

Thus, the commodity technological model preserves the exact decomposition of overall TFP growth into sectoral components. Moreover, we can also show that overall TFP growth is a function of the sectoral composition of final output. First, by definition of A^c,

$$X = (I - A^c)^{-1}(I - UV^{-T})V^T\mathbf{1} = (I - A^c)^{-1}Y.$$

In other words, the commodity technology model satisfies the material balance equation of Leontief. (This is also true in the industry technology model.) As a result, it follows that (8) can be rewritten as

$$\rho = \pi^c s^c \beta, \tag{9}$$

where $s^c = \hat{p}(I - A^c)^{-1}\hat{p}^{-1}$, the Leontief (value) inverse coefficient matrix, and $\beta = \hat{p}Y/y$, which shows the value composition of final output in terms of commodities.

2.2. Industry technology model

There are two assumptions that are made in this model. First, each industry k has the same input requirements per dollar of output for each commodity that it produces. Second, the market shares for each commodity are fixed among industries. Thus, to produce commodity j, industry k needs $u_{ik}/\sum_1 v_{k1}$ of input i per unit of output j, and its market share $v_{kj}/\sum_1 v_{1j}$ is fixed. Then, as shown in ten Raa et al. (1984), the industry technology requirements per unit of commodity output (coefficient) matrix is given by

$$A^1 = U[\hat{X}^1]^{-1} V \hat{X}^{-1},$$

where a hat (^) denotes a diagonal matrix whose diagonal is equal to the vector. Row vectors of labor and capital stock coefficients can be derived in the same way. Then, $l^1 = L[\hat{X}^1]^{-1} V \hat{X}^{-1}$ and $k^1 = K[\hat{X}^1]^{-1} V \hat{X}^{-1}$. From price equation (2), value added by commodity is

$$p(I-A^{\mathrm{I}})=(wL+rK)(V^{\mathrm{T}}-U)^{-1}(I-U[\hat{X}^{\mathrm{I}}]^{-1}V\hat{X}^{-1}),$$

$$p(I-A^{\mathrm{I}})=(wL+rK)(V^{\mathrm{T}}-U)^{-1}(\hat{X}V^{-1}\hat{X}^{\mathrm{I}}-U)[\hat{X}^{\mathrm{I}}]^{-1}V\hat{X}^{-1}. \tag{10}$$

Factor cost by commodity is

$$wl^{\mathrm{I}}+rk^{\mathrm{I}}=(wL+rK)[\hat{X}^{\mathrm{I}}]^{-1}V\hat{X}^{-1}. \tag{11}$$

Value added by commodity is equal to factor costs by commodity only if the two middle factors in (10) cancel – that is, $V^{\mathrm{T}}=\hat{X}V^{-1}\hat{X}^{\mathrm{I}}$. The presence of secondary production invalidates this condition and hence the equality of value added and factor costs on a commodity basis. The equality does hold for the combination of commodities that make industries and, a fortiori, for the economy as a whole. The distortion at the commodity level is due to the industry technology model notion of industry output, $V\mathbf{1}$. One implication of this, as shown in ten Raa et al. (1984), is that there is no base year price invariance of technology. The invalidation of the commodity value equation between revenues and cost (that is, materials and valued added) is due to the same reasons.

For our present purposes, the most important defect of the industry technology model is that it is no longer possible to decompose overall TFP growth into a weighted average of commodity-level rates of productivity growth. Let us first define the rate of commodity TFP growth in this model as:

$$\pi_j^{\mathrm{I}}\equiv -(p\,\mathrm{d}a_{\cdot j}^{\mathrm{I}}+w\,\mathrm{d}l_j^{\mathrm{I}}+r\,\mathrm{d}k_j^{\mathrm{I}})/p_j. \tag{12}$$

It can be shown directly that the material balance equation holds, namely:

$$Y=(I-A^{\mathrm{I}})X. \tag{13}$$

Hence, from (4) and (13),

$$\rho=[p(I-A^{\mathrm{I}})\,\mathrm{d}X-p(\mathrm{d}A^{\mathrm{I}})X-wl^{\mathrm{I}}\,\mathrm{d}X-w(\mathrm{d}l^{\mathrm{I}})X$$
$$-rk^{\mathrm{I}}\,\mathrm{d}X-r(\mathrm{d}k^{\mathrm{I}})X]/y. \tag{14}$$

Now, however, since factor cost by commodity does not equal value added by commodity [that is, (10) and (11) differ], we cannot derive an equation analogous to (8), at least when secondary production is present. Instead, we obtain from (13):

$$\rho=-(p\,\mathrm{d}A^{\mathrm{I}}+w\,\mathrm{d}l^{\mathrm{I}}+r\,\mathrm{d}k^{\mathrm{I}})X/y+[p(I-A^{\mathrm{I}})-(wl^{\mathrm{I}}+rk^{\mathrm{I}})]\,\mathrm{d}X/y. \tag{15}$$

The commodity technology derivation of (9) and (8) holds here in analogous fashion and, therefore, applies to the first term on the right-hand side of (15). The second term can be considered a residual factor θ. It then follows that

$$\rho = \pi^{\mathrm{I}} s^{\mathrm{I}} \beta + \theta, \tag{16}$$

where $s^{\mathrm{I}} = \hat{p}(I - A^{\mathrm{I}})^{-1}\hat{p}^{-1}$, the Leontief inverse coefficient matrix in the industry technology model, β is the commodity composition of final output, and

$$\theta = [p(I - A^{\mathrm{I}}) - (wl^{\mathrm{I}} + rk^{\mathrm{I}})\,\mathrm{d}X/y. \tag{17}$$

2.3. *Industry-level productivity growth*

The two vectors π^{c} and π^{I} both refer to commodity-level TFP growth – i.e., the productivity growth by individual commodity. The first shows commodity-based productivity growth as calculated using the commodity technology model, while the latter shows commodity-based productivity growth as computed from the industry technology model.

For reasons of comparison, we are also interested in industry-level or industry-based productivity growth, which shows productivity growth by individual industry. The reason is that the traditional and most common method of calculating productivity growth is on an industry basis rather than a commodity basis.[10] Moreover, the use of an industry basis allows us to separate out a specific secondary product effect in decomposing the change in overall TFP growth.

We define industry-level productivity growth as a weighted average of the productivity growth of the individual commodities it produces, where the weights are value shares. To circumvent the independent issue of bias, we shall define industry productivity growth on the basis of the commodity technology model only. By definition, $X = \sum_j v^{\mathrm{T}}_{\cdot j}$, where $v^{\mathrm{T}}_{\cdot j}$ is the jth column of V^{T} – i.e., the jth row of V, showing the industry of production, j. Substituting into (8), we obtain

[10]See, for example Wolff (1985b). It should be noted that the results of this study are based on neither the commodity technology model nor the industry technology model but rather on the so-called BEA transfer method. In this method, the transaction matrix is constructed on an industry by industry basis. A secondary product produced by industry i which is primary to industry j is recorded as a purchase made by industry j from industry i. The actual sales of the secondary product produced in i are then 'transferred' to the sales row of industry j. This method creates artificial transactions and can distort the measurement of productivity growth in both industries i and j. Moreover, they can also affect the measurement of linkages between sectors. The reason for using this method was for consistency with earlier years in the analysis (in particular, 1947, 1958, 1963), for which it was impossible to construct a separate secondary product make matrix.

$$\rho = \sum_j \pi^c \hat{p} v_{\cdot j}^T / y. \tag{18}$$

Note that the coefficients π^c are independent of sector j, by the properties of the commodity technology model. Each term $\pi^c \hat{p} v_j^T$ represents a sectoral contribution to overall TFP growth ρ. Let us define industry-level TFP growth in the commodity technology model for industry j as a weighted average of the TFP growth of the commodities it produces:

$$\psi_j = \pi^c \hat{p} v_{\cdot j}^T / p v_{\cdot j}^T,$$

where the weights are the value shares of the commodity output in the total value of the industry output.

We can now relate industry-level productivity growth rates to overall TFP growth as follows. First, define a matrix of market shares, $M = V\hat{X}^{-1}$. We can now demonstrate that

$$\rho - \pi^c s^c \beta = \psi M s^c \beta. \tag{19}$$

In other words, π^c and ψM act the same way on $s^c\beta$ (though, it should be noted, the two are not generally equal). Since the latter is proportional to the total output vector (in value terms), $\hat{p}X = \hat{p}V^T\mathbf{1}$, it is now necessary to show that $\pi^c \hat{p} V^T \mathbf{1} = \psi M \hat{p} V^T \mathbf{1}$. Now, by the definitions of ψ and M, the right-hand side equals

$$\pi^c \hat{p} V^T [\widehat{pV^T}]^{-1} V \hat{X}^{-1} \hat{p} V^T \mathbf{1} = \pi^c \hat{p} V^T [\widehat{Vp^T}]^{-1} V p^T = \pi^c \hat{p} V^T \mathbf{1}, \tag{20}$$

which is the left-hand side and completes the demonstration.

As an independent line of decomposition, useful in assessing the role of secondary production, we can also define overall productivity growth for primary output as a weighted sum of the commodity-level productivity growth of primary output only. To do this, let matrix P be the diagonal of matrix V (primary products) and matrix S be the off-diagonal elements (secondary products). Then,

$$V = P + S.$$

Productivity growth of primary output is then given by

$$\rho^P = [\pi^c \hat{p} P\mathbf{1} / pP\mathbf{1}] \cdot (pX/y), \tag{21}$$

where the weights are the value shares of primary output in the value of total primary output and the last term is included to reweigh to a corresponding overall productivity growth level. In analogous fashion, secondary product productivity growth is defined as

$$\rho^{s} = \left[\sum_{j} \pi^{c} \hat{p} s_{\cdot j}^{T} / p S^{T} \mathbf{1} \right] \cdot (pX/y), \tag{22}$$

where the weights are the value shares of secondary output in the value of total secondary output. Let $\omega^{p} = pPe/pX$, the value share of primary output in total output, and $\omega^{s} = pS^{T}\mathbf{1}/pX = 1 - \omega^{p}$, the value share of secondary output in total output. Then,

$$\rho = \omega^{p}\rho^{p} + \omega^{s}\rho^{s}. \tag{23}$$

Finally, the change in overall TFP growth can be decomposed into a primary product and secondary product effect, as follows:

$$\Delta\rho = \omega^{p}\Delta\rho^{p} + \omega^{s}\Delta\rho^{s} + \Delta\omega^{s}(\rho^{s} - \rho^{p}), \tag{24}$$

where the first term shows the change in overall TFP growth attributable to the change in productivity growth among primary products, the second term the portion due to the change in productivity growth among secondary output, and the third term the portion due to the change of the share of secondary output in total output.

2.4. A comparison of the three models

From (9) and (16) we now obtain

$$\rho = \pi^{c} s^{c} \beta = \pi^{l} s^{l} \beta + \theta. \tag{25}$$

This now leads directly to another interpretation of θ. Following Wolff (1985b), we first present two alternative growth accounting decompositions of (25). The first of these uses the commodity technology model:

$$\Delta\rho = \pi^{c} s^{c} (\Delta\beta) + \pi^{c} (\Delta s^{c}) \beta + (\Delta\pi^{c}) s^{c} \beta. \tag{26a}$$

In this decomposition, the change in overall TFP growth is decomposed into three effects, corresponding to the three terms on the right-hand side of (26a). The first of these can be called the *final output effect*, the second the *interindustry multiplier effect*, and the third the *sectoral TFP growth effect*.[11] The second decomposition uses the industry technology model:

$$\Delta\rho = \pi^{\mathrm{I}} s^{\mathrm{I}}(\Delta\beta) + \pi^{\mathrm{I}}(\Delta s^{\mathrm{I}})\beta + (\Delta\pi^{\mathrm{I}})s^{\mathrm{I}}\beta + \Delta\theta. \tag{26b}$$

The first three terms on the right-hand side of (26b) are analogous to those in (26a) and may be interpreted in analogous fashion. The last term may be called the *secondary bias effect*, since it shows the bias in the decomposition of overall TFP growth that can be attributed to the presence of secondary products.[12]

Thus, the commodity technology decomposition is unbiased. However, the industry technology decomposition is biased. The bias is from the presence of secondary products and the consequent wedge between the values of net outputs and unit factor costs at the sectoral level when calculated from the industry technology model.

The third model, the industry-level productivity growth, leads to a still different decomposition of overall TFP growth. Thus, in accounting for changes in productivity growth, we essentially get a still further decomposition of the sectoral TFP growth effect into a market share shift effect and an industry-level productivity growth effect. More precisely, by (19),

$$(\Delta\pi^{\mathrm{c}})s^{\mathrm{c}}\beta = \psi(\Delta M)s^{\mathrm{c}}\beta + (\Delta\psi)Ms^{\mathrm{c}}\beta.^{13} \tag{26c}$$

In the empirical analysis of section 6, there are three points of particular

[11]Note that by (2), π^{c}, s^{c} and β are each a function of all basic data, U, V, L, K, w, and r. Although a change in TFP growth can be attributed only to changes in the data, U, V, L, K, w, and r, it can be decomposed formally into the three terms indicated above. It would be interesting to perform a similar decomposition by starting with flows and stocks in constant prices, as is assumed throughout this paper, and attributing TFP growth directly to the real data (U, V, L, K) or the nominal ones (w, r). This can be done analytically by partial differentiations of (8) and then empirical evaluation. However, such an analysis is beyond the scope of the present paper.

[12]This can be seen more formally as follows. From (17),

$$\theta = [(wL+rK)(V^{\mathrm{T}}-U)^{-1}(I-U[\hat{X}^{\mathrm{I}}]^{-1}V\hat{X}^{-1}) - (wL+rK)([\hat{X}^{\mathrm{I}}]^{-1}V\hat{X}^{-1})]\,\mathrm{d}X/(wL+rK)\mathbf{1}$$
$$= (wL+rKL)\{(V^{\mathrm{T}}-U)^{-1}(I-U[\hat{X}^{\mathrm{I}}]^{-1}V\hat{X}^{-1}) - ([\hat{X}^{\mathrm{I}}]^{-1}V\hat{X}^{-1})\}\,\mathrm{d}X/(wL+rK)\mathbf{1}.$$

If there is only one primary production, then $V=\hat{X}$ and the bracketed expression on the right-hand side of the last equation reduces to

$$(\hat{X}-U)^{-1}(I-U\hat{X}^{-1}\hat{X}\hat{X}^{-1}) - \hat{X}^{-1}\hat{X}\hat{X}^{-1} = [(I-U\hat{X}^{-1})\hat{X}](I-U\hat{X}^{-1}) - \hat{X}^{-1}$$
$$= \hat{X}^{-1}(I-U\hat{X}^{-1})^{-1}(I-U\hat{X}^{-1}) - \hat{X}^{-1}$$
$$= \hat{X}^{-1} - \hat{X}^{-1} = 0.$$

Thus, without secondary production, there is no residual term θ. This provides another reason for calling θ a secondary bias effect.

[13]This further decomposition can also be shown to hold in the framework of the industry technology model. In the previous section, we did not address the issue in order to circumvent the independent issue of bias.

interest. The first is the contribution to the change in overall productivity growth from shifts in the composition of final output. In Wolff (1985b), it was found that this accounted for between 17 and 22 percent of the decline in overall TFP between the 1947–1967 and the 1967–1976 periods. However, this computation was implicitly based on the Bureau of Economic Analysis (BEA) transfer model and was therefore biased (see footnote 9). For the mathematics of the transfer model, see Kop Jansen and ten Raa (1989). The bias can be established in precisely the same way as for the industry technology model. Eq. (26a) will allow us to redo this calculation using the unbiased commodity technology model, at least for the 1967–1977 period. The second is the contribution to the decline in TFP accounted for by shifts in the level and composition of secondary output. Since this factor has not received attention in the literature, it will add to our knowledge on the sources of the productivity slowdown in the U.S.

The third is to determine the direction and magnitude of the bias which results from the use of the industry technology model and from the use of the industry-level productivity growth model. Both sorts of biases could be important, particularly since the latter two models are most commonly used. In particular, is the compositional effect greater using a commodity-base model than one using an industry-base model? Is it greater using the commodity-base commodity technology model than the commodity-base industry technology model?

One final comment should be made. We have not said which of the two secondary product models, if either, is the 'true' model of the U.S. economy. Such an analysis is beyond the scope of the present paper.[14] However, the use of both the commodity technology and the industry technology models will provide us with a range of values for both the output composition and the secondary product effects.

3. Secondary output, 1967–1977

As noted in the Introduction, we use the BEA 85-order 1967, 1972, and 1977 'make' and 'use' input–output tables for our analysis.[15] The 1972 and

[14]It is also not possible for the U.S. economy, since we do not have annual input–output tables. However, see ten Raa et al. (1984) for a similar type of analysis for the Canadian economy for which annual input–output tables were available.

[15]These are the only three years for which such data are available. A description of the 1972 tables can be found in Ritz (1979) and Ritz et al. (1979), and documentation of the 1977 tables in U.S. Interindustry Economics Division (1984). The 1967 data were not published as separate make and use tables, but the raw data for them are available on computer tape, which Paula Young of BEA graciously supplied to us. A description of the 1967 total flow tables can be found in U.S. Interindustry Economics Division (1974). Sources and methods for the 1967 and 1972 labor coefficients are described in Wolff (1985b). Employment data for 1977 were obtained from Yuskavage (1985). Capital stock data for all three years were obtained from Gorman et al. (1985).

1977 tables use the same accounting conventions. However, there are four important changes between the 1967 tables and those of 1972 and 1977. First, two dummy sectors, business travel and entertainment and office supplies, are present in the 1967 table but were eliminated in the 1972 and 1977 tables. We follow the later convention and distribute the output of the two dummy sectors to the appropriate using industries. Second, in the 1972 and 1977 tables, the restaurant sector was separated from the trade sector, while in the 1967 table the two are aggregated into a single sector. It was not possible to separate the restaurant sector from the trade sector in the 1967 data. As a result, we have aggregated the two sectors in the 1972 and 1977 data for consistency with the earlier year.[16] Third, in the 1967 table, a portion of the wholesale and retail trade activity and real estate (rental) activity engaged in by the various sectors were recorded as a secondary product of these sectors, whereas in the later years these transactions were recorded as primary to the trade and real estate sectors, respectively. For consistency with the later years, we transferred these secondary outputs to their primary sector.[17] Fourth, in the 1967 table, comparable imports are recorded as if purchased by the industry producing the comparable domestic commodity and then added to that industry's output for distribution to the actual purchasing industries. In the later tables, comparable imports are recorded as directly purchased by the using industry from the comparable domestic industry. We follow the later convention in our work.[18]

The first three tables show some basic results on the change in the importance of secondary products over the three years. Unless otherwise noted, secondary production is defined on the 85-order level. In 1967, 3.9 percent of the total value of output, with the exclusion of scrap output, consisted of secondary products. In 1972, the ratio was somewhat lower, at 3.4 percent, and between 1972 and 1977 the ratio rose to 3.6 percent. In constant 1972 dollar terms, the ratio of secondary to total output fell from 4.0 percent in 1967 to 3.4 percent in 1972 and then rose to 3.9 percent in 1977 (last row of table 2). The importance of secondary output is increased somewhat when the scrap sector is included in the calculation of secondary output. With this definition, the ratio of secondary to total output in current dollars was 4.0 percent in 1967, 3.4 percent in 1972, and 3.7 percent in 1977 (last row of table 3). Though these ratios are rather small, it should be

[16]We refer to the aggregated sector (number 69) as the trade sector.

[17]To balance the flow tables, we adjusted the value added of the trade sector so that its total inputs equalled its new output total and adjusted both the value added of the real estate sector and the real estate input row so that the value of total output and inputs of the real estate sector matched.

[18]Another problem arose with the broadcasting sector, whose output is almost entirely secondary, since it does not sell its broadcasting 'output' to any other sector or to final users. Since its major secondary output is business services (advertizing), we aggregated the broadcasting sector (67) with business services (71) for all three years.

Table 1

Ratio of secondary to total output by industry of production, 10-sectors, current dollars, scrap sector excluded.[a]

	1967	1972	1977	Change 1967–1977
1. Agriculture	0.037	0.043	0.043	0.007
2. Mining	0.060	0.053	0.089	0.029
3. Construction	0.000	0.000	0.000	0.000
4. Non-durable manufacturing	0.063	0.063	0.068	0.004
5. Durable manufacturing	0.066	0.060	0.057	−0.010
6. Transportation, communications, utilities	0.037	0.036	0.033	−0.004
7. Wholesale and retail trade	0.000	0.000	0.000	0.000
8. Finance, insurance, real estate	0.010	0.002	0.002	−0.009
9. Other services	0.007	0.002	0.004	−0.003
10. Government	0.090	0.078	0.095	0.005
11. Total	0.039	0.034	0.036	−0.003

[a]Secondary production based on BEA 85-order classification scheme.

Table 2

Ratio of secondary to total output by industry of production, 10-sectors, constant (1972) dollars, scrap sector excluded.[a]

	1967	1972	1977	Change 1967–1977
1. Agriculture	0.036	0.043	0.046	0.010
2. Mining	0.065	0.053	0.079	0.014
3. Construction	0.000	0.000	0.000	0.000
4. Non-durable manufacturing	0.062	0.063	0.065	0.004
5. Durable manufacturing	0.067	0.060	0.057	−0.010
6. Transportation, communications, utilities	0.035	0.036	0.032	−0.003
7. Wholesale and retail trade	0.000	0.000	0.000	0.000
8. Finance, insurance, real estate	0.011	0.002	0.002	−0.009
9. Other services	0.007	0.002	0.004	−0.003
10. Government	0.106	0.078	0.111	0.005
11. Total	0.040	0.034	0.039	−0.001

[a]Secondary production based on BEA 85-order classification scheme.

stressed that the results on the importance of secondary output is very sensitive to level of aggregation. At more disaggregated levels, secondary output naturally comprises a higher percentage of total output.

There is considerable variation among sectors in the importance of secondary output. Tables 1 and 2 show the ratio of secondary output to total output by major industry of production. In 1972, this ratio varied from a low of zero percent in construction and trade to a high of 7.8 percent in the government sector. The ratio was over 4 percent in agriculture, over 5 percent in mining, and over 6 percent in manufacturing. The importance of secondary output in total production increased most notably in agriculture,

Table 3

Ratio of secondary to total output by commodity type produced, 10-sectors, current dollars.[a]

	1967	1972	1977	Change 1967–1977
1. Agriculture	0.012	0.011	0.014	0.002
2. Mining	0.012	0.010	0.011	−0.002
3. Construction	0.000	0.000	0.000	0.000
4. Non-durable manufacturing	0.041	0.040	0.053	0.013
5. Durable manufacturing	0.064	0.059	0.056	−0.008
6. Transportation, communications, utilities	0.068	0.064	0.068	−0.000
7. Wholesale and retail trade	0.010	0.008	0.008	−0.002
8. Finance, insurance, real estate	0.015	0.001	0.008	−0.006
9. Other services	0.094	0.083	0.066	−0.028
10. Government	0.000	0.000	0.000	0.000
11. Scrap sector	1.000	1.000	1.000	0.000
12. Total (excluding scrap)	0.039	0.034	0.036	−0.003
13. Total (including scrap)	0.040	0.034	0.037	−0.003

[a]Secondary production based on BEA 85-order classification scheme.

mining, and the government sector over the 1967–1977 period, but declined in durable manufacturing and in the finance, insurance, and real estate sector. On the 85-sector level of production, there is even greater variation in the importance of secondary output. Moreover, at this level of disaggregation, secondary output now assumes major importance for some sectors. In 1972, secondary output (excluding scrap) comprised 78 percent of the value of the output of the state and local government enterprise sector (79), 45 percent of the output of the printing and publishing sector (26), 37 percent of the output of chemicals and fertilizer mineral mining (10), 19 percent of the output of the government enterprise sector (78), 15 percent of plastics and synthetic material sector (28), 14 percent of the service industry machinery sector (52) and of the miscellaneous electrical machinery, equipment, and supplies sector (58), 11 percent of general industrial machinery and equipment sector (49), 10 percent of the electric wiring and equipment sector (55), of the electronics components and accessory sector (57), of the professional and scientific instrument sector (62), and of miscellaneous manufacturing (64), and 9 percent of the output of the ordnance sector (13). Moreover, in terms of the number of different commodities produced by a sector, secondary output is also quite important, particularly in manufacturing. In 1972, there were 9 manufacturing sectors which produced 30 or more commodities (excluding scrap), and 20 sectors which produced between 20 and 29 different commodities (excluding scrap).

Table 3 shows the ratio of secondary to total output on the basis of commodity type. In 1972, one percent of agriculture output was produced as another sector's secondary product. This ratio varied from zero percent for construction and government output to 100 percent for scrap output in 1972.

Four percent of non-durable manufactures, 5.9 percent of durables, 6.4 percent of transportation, communication, and utility output, and 8.3 percent of other service output was produced as a secondary output. The most notable changes over the 1967–1977 period were the increase in importance of secondary non-durable output and the decline in secondary other service output.

The last change is particularly noteworthy, since it indicates that many establishments which produced these services in addition to their primary output during the 1960s sloughed off this production during the 1970s. The most dramatic change was in business services (73), in which the proportion of total output accounted for by secondary production fell from 25 to 17 percent. These results suggests that many of these services switched from being produced internally in many establishments to being produced in specialized establishments and being purchased externally through market transactions. It is interesting that Carter (1970) found an increase in the total requirements of service output over the 1947–1967 period in the U.S., but could not decompose this into a real interindustry effect of greater specialization and a specious effect from the reclassification of such service activities from secondary to primary output. Such a distinction is important for pinning down the sources of technical change. The table confirms Carter's intuition that the shift in service output is important. Section 6 of the paper will address the decomposition issue raised but not resolved in Carter's work.

Of the 85-sector level, there were a number of commodities for which the proportion of their total output accounted for by secondary production exceeded 10 percent in 1972. Besides business services (73), these included forestry and fishery products (3), agricultural, forestry and fishery services (4), miscellaneous fabricated textile products (19), chemicals (27), plastics and synthetic materials (28), fabricated metal products (42), engines and turbines (43), metalworking machinery and equipment (47), household appliances (54), electronic components and accessories (57), professional and scientific instruments (62), and electrical, gas, water, and sanitary services (68). Of these, the most dramatic changes were in agricultural services, where the proportion of secondary production declined sharply from 19 to 12 percent, engines and turbines, where it fell from 18 to 123 percent, and miscellaneous textile products, where it declined from 21 to 16 percent. Reversing these trends were chemicals and plastics, in which secondary production grew from 16 to 20 percent and from 12 to 22 percent, respectively.

4. The treatment of the scrap sector

The treatment of the scrap sector, 81, poses a special methodological problem, since it is an important secondary product of many sectors and yet there is no primary output that corresponds to it and hence has no input structure in the use table. Unlike the other sectors, it provides no information. One price equation and one production vector equation are missing. It is impossible to allocate value added between net scrap output and net commodity output. Neither can material inputs be ascribed to scrap output vis-à-vis commodity output. As a result, we must make certain assumptions to fill the gaps.

As regards the price of scrap, the use value seems to be determinate. An engineering approach would be to estimate the equivalent metal ore content of scrap. For this purpose we would need time-series analysis, from which we shy away because of identification problems in the presence of technical change. A better way to determine the economic metal content of scrap is to use an additional bit of information. In this case, we can just as well make a shortcut by using an exogenous price of scrap. This is what we do.

As regards the input structure of scrap, the material components seem to be zero. Nevertheless, scrap is no bonus contributor to productivity. A factor cost is involved, namely capital or, more precisely, replacement investment. In our model, which is not dynamic but rather a sequence of static models, this cost is disguised in rK, the cost of capital. The latter is assumed to be proportional to output, both in the commodity and in the industry technology approaches, which is a reasonable reduced form of a full dynamic model, provided that capital decays exponentially. Intuitively, a high rate of scrap is unproductive, because of the replacement involved. This, however, is taken care of by the value of rK, or its change over time. The use of scrap, as a material input, is unambiguously productive. Under the capital decay assumption, scrap is most appropriately modeled as proportional to capital stock. However, the proportion may vary with the production process.

We can formalize these ideas as follows. The basic data of the system are U, V, L, K, w, r, plus p_{81}, the price of scrap. The vectors $u_{.81}$ and $v_{81.}$ for the scrap sector are zero. It is convenient to partition the use and make tables as follows:

$$U=\begin{pmatrix} U^\circ & 0 \\ u_{81.} & 0 \end{pmatrix} \quad \text{and} \quad V=\begin{pmatrix} V^\circ & v_{.81} \\ 0 & 0 \end{pmatrix}.$$

Here U° and V° are the 80-by-80 use and make tables, respectively, of the economy without the scrap vector; $u_{81.}$ is the 80-row vector of scrap inputs; and $v_{.81}$ is the 80-column vector of scrap outputs. Labor and capital are partitioned similarly:

$$L=(L^\circ \;\; 0) \quad \text{and} \quad K=(K^\circ \;\; 0).$$

This new formulation entails certain modifications of the original model. Eq. (1) still remains valid, though it can now be written as

$$p^{\circ}(V^{\circ T}-U^{\circ})+p_{81}(v_{.81}^{T}-u_{81.})=wL^{\circ}+rK^{\circ}. \tag{1'}$$

Eq. (2) must be rectified as follows:

$$p^{\circ}=[wL^{\circ}+rK^{\circ}+p_{81}(u_{81.}-v_{.81}^{T})](V^{\circ T}-U^{\circ})^{-1}. \tag{2'}$$

In effect, the exogenous value of the net scrap input is implicitly included in factor costs as a depreciation term. Eqs. (3) and (4), which define net output and overall TFP growth, respectively, remain intact. We are now prepared to reconsider the two models of secondary production.

4.1. Commodity technology model

In this new formulation, we now define:

$$A^{\circ c}=U^{\circ}V^{\circ -T},\quad l^{c}=L^{\circ}V^{\circ -T}\quad \text{and}\quad k^{c}=K^{\circ}V^{\circ -T}.$$

Similarly we have scrap input coefficients $a_{81.}^{c}=u_{81.}V^{\circ -T}$. In accordance with the assumptions of the commodity technology model, it is assumed that the proportion of capital stock scrapped per unit of commodity produced is the same for each sector that produces that commodity. To determine the scrap output coefficients, consider sector 1. It has stock $k_1^c v_{1,1}+\cdots+k_{80}^c v_{1,80}$ for its respective outputs. Let b_i^c be the fraction of the capital stock of output i that is scrapped for each commodity i. Then, sector 1 scraps a total of $b_1^c k_1^c v_{1,1}+\cdots+b_{80}^c k_{80}^c v_{1,80}$. This must match the observed output of scrap in sector 1, $v_{1,81}$. Similar equations can be derived for the other sectors, and we obtain $v_{.81}^{T}=b^{c}\hat{k}^{c}V^{\circ T}$. Hence, the scrap output coefficients are specified by

$$b^{c}=v_{.81}^{T}V^{\circ -T}\hat{k}_{c}^{-1}.$$

The price equation for the commodity technology model must now be modified. Substitution into (1′) and multiplication by $V^{\circ -T}$ yields

$$p^{\circ}(I-A^{\circ c})=wl^{c}+rk^{c}+p_{81}(a_{81.}^{c}-b^{c}\hat{k}^{c}). \tag{5'}$$

Multiplication of both sides of eq. (5′) by the Leontief inverse, $(I-A^{\circ c})^{-1}$, yields commodity prices as a function of the technical coefficients, factor prices, and the price of scrap. The material balance equation remains $Y=(I-A^{c})X$, where

$$A^{c} = \begin{pmatrix} A^{oc} & 0 \\ a^{c}_{81.} & 0 \end{pmatrix}.$$

From (5′), it then follows that[19]

$$\rho = -(p\,\mathrm{d}A^{c} + w\,\mathrm{d}l^{c} + r\,\mathrm{d}k^{c})X^{\circ}/y - p_{81}b^{c}\hat{k}^{c}\,\mathrm{d}X^{\circ} + p_{81}\,\mathrm{d}x_{81}.$$

Recall that scrap output coefficients were derived from $v^{T}_{.81} = b^{c}\hat{k}^{c}V^{\circ T}$. By adding components and using the fact that sector 81 has zero output, we obtain $x_{81} = b^{c}\hat{k}^{c}X^{\circ}$.

Hence,

$$\mathrm{d}x_{81} = b^{c}\hat{k}^{c}\,\mathrm{d}X^{\circ} + (\mathrm{d}k^{c})\hat{b}^{c}X^{\circ} + (\mathrm{d}b^{c})\hat{k}^{c}X^{\circ}.$$

Substitution of this for $\mathrm{d}x_{81}$ into the previous equation now yields

$$\rho = -[p\,\mathrm{d}A^{c} + w\,\mathrm{d}l^{c} + \mathrm{d}k^{c}(r - p_{81}\hat{b}^{c}) - p_{81}(\mathrm{d}b^{c})\hat{k}^{c}]X^{\circ}/y. \tag{7′}$$

In this equation, the rate of return on capital is now net of (scrap) depreciation, and the productivity gains from the recycling of scrap as an input in production has now been captured.[20]

4.2. *Industry technology model*

In accord with the assumptions of this model, we assume here that the rate of scrapping depends only on the sector of production, not the particular commodity that is produced. In particular, it is assumed that the amount of scrap produced per *dollar* of output is the same for all commodities produced by a given sector of production. As a result,

$$A^{\circ I} = U^{\circ}[\hat{X}^{\circ I}]^{-1}V^{\circ}[\hat{X}^{\circ}]^{-1}, \quad l^{I} = L^{\circ}[\hat{X}^{\circ I}]^{-1}V^{\circ}[\hat{X}^{\circ}]^{-1} \quad \text{and}$$

$$k^{I} = K^{\circ}[\hat{X}^{\circ I}]^{-1}V^{\circ}[\hat{X}^{\circ}]^{-1},$$

where $X^{\circ I} = V^{\circ}\mathbf{1}$ and $X^{\circ} = V^{\circ T}\mathbf{1}$. Similarly, the scrap input coefficients are given by

$$a^{I}_{81.} = u_{81.}[\hat{X}^{\circ I}]^{-1}V^{\circ}[\hat{X}^{\circ}]^{-1}$$

[19]See Wolff (1985, eq. (7)) for details of the proof.

[20]Under the assumption that capital decays exponentially, total depreciation would equal total capital decay and hence the total value of scrap.

and scrap output coefficients by[21]

$$b^{\mathrm{I}} = v^{\mathrm{T}}_{.81}[\hat{X}^{\circ \mathrm{I}}]^{-1} V^{\circ}[\hat{X}^{\circ}]^{-1}[\hat{k}^{\mathrm{I}}]^{-1}.$$

We can now redefine π^{I}, the vector of sectoral rates of TFP growth in the industry model, as

$$\pi^{\mathrm{I}} = -[p\,\mathrm{d}A^{\mathrm{I}} + w\,\mathrm{d}l^{\mathrm{I}} + (\mathrm{d}k^{\mathrm{I}})(r - p_{81}\hat{b}^{\mathrm{I}}) - p_{81}(\mathrm{d}b^{\mathrm{I}})\hat{k}^{\mathrm{I}}]\hat{p}^{\circ -1}. \qquad (12')$$

Then, eq. (16) remains as before:

$$\rho = \pi^{\mathrm{I}} s^{\mathrm{I}} \beta + \theta, \qquad (16)$$

where, as before, $s^{\mathrm{I}} = \hat{p}(I - A^{\mathrm{I}})^{-1}\hat{p}^{-1}$, β is the commodity composition of final output, but now

$$\theta = [p^{\circ}(I - A^{\mathrm{I}}) - (wl^{\mathrm{I}} + rk^{\mathrm{I}} + p_{81}(a^{\mathrm{I}}_{81.} - b^{\mathrm{c}}\hat{k}^{\mathrm{c}}))]\,\mathrm{d}X^{\circ}/y. \qquad (17')$$

As before,

$$\rho = \pi^{\mathrm{c}} s^{\mathrm{c}} \beta^{\mathrm{c}} = \pi^{\mathrm{I}} s^{\mathrm{I}} \beta^{\mathrm{I}} + \theta \qquad (25)$$

and the comparison of the two models is identical to that presented in subsection 2.3.

5. The inclusion of international trade

The trade sector is modeled after Leontief (1941). Let non-competitive imports be arranged in a row vector, m. Competitive imports need no separate symbol, but are treated as a (negative) part of final demand.[22] To support the non-competitive imports, the trade sector needs some exports, say e, a column vector, where e could be called the vector of required or debt exports. Excess exports, on top of debt exports, need no separate symbol, but are treated as a (positive) part of final demand. The trade vector uses debt exports as inputs and yields non-competitive imports as output to be distributed over the other sectors. Total non-competitive imports are given by the scalar, $m\mathbf{1}$, which is simply the sum of the components of m. The augmented make table becomes

[21]This is essentially the same as the procedure recommended by the Bureau of Economic Analysis.

[22]Note that non-competitive imports are given by sector of purchase, but aggregated by commodity, while for competitive imports it is just the other way.

$$\tilde{V}=\begin{pmatrix} V & 0 \\ 0 & m\mathbf{1} \end{pmatrix}.$$

Non-competitive imports and debt exports are attached to the use table in the usual way:

$$\tilde{U}=\begin{pmatrix} U & e \\ m & 0 \end{pmatrix}.$$

The adjustment of final demand becomes automatic. Prior to the modeling of the trade sector, final demand was defined by

$$Y=(V^{\mathrm{T}}-U)\mathbf{1}.$$

That is, final demand is net output aggregated for each commodity across industries. It includes all exports and competitive imports. Non-competitive imports, m, are reported 'under the line', like a factor cost.

After this new treatment of the trade sector, the resulting mechanics remain the same. Final demand is net output aggregated over all sectors, including trade:

$$\tilde{Y}=(\tilde{V}^{\mathrm{T}}-\tilde{U})\mathbf{1}.$$

It is easy to check that substitution of the above expressions for $\tilde{V}$ and $\tilde{U}$ and of Y yields

$$\tilde{Y}=\begin{pmatrix} Y-e \\ 0 \end{pmatrix}.$$

In other words, not only non-competitive imports, but also debt exports are excluded from final demand in the model with endogenous trade. This completes the new accounting framework.

We can now analyze productivity growth. At the sectoral level, trade productivity growth is

$$\pi^{\mathrm{c}}_{\mathrm{trade}}=-p\,\mathrm{d}\tilde{A}^{\mathrm{c}}_{.\mathrm{trade}}/p_{\mathrm{trade}},$$

where p_{trade} is the price of the international trade sector and $\tilde{A}^{\mathrm{c}}$ is the commodity technology coefficients matrix of the augmented interindustry flow matrices:

$$\tilde{A}^{c} = \tilde{U}\tilde{V}^{-T} = \begin{pmatrix} U & e \\ m & 0 \end{pmatrix} \begin{pmatrix} V^{-T} & 0 \\ 0 & (m\mathbf{1})^{-1} \end{pmatrix} = \begin{pmatrix} A^{c} & e/m\mathbf{1} \\ mV^{-T} & 0 \end{pmatrix}.$$

The industry technology trade coefficients are the same, since this sector has no secondary products. Moreover, since no other sector of the economy produces trade 'output', the treatment of the trade sector is an issue independent of the choice of the model of secondary production. For this reason, the treatment of the trade sector is the same in the industry technology model.

Sectoral productivity growth of the international trade sector reduces to

$$\pi^{c}_{\text{trade}} = -p\,\mathrm{d}(e/m\mathbf{1})/p_{\text{trade}}.$$

In this expression, $e/m\mathbf{1}$ is the export/import ratio in physical units. Because of the negative sign, the change in this ratio, valued at fixed prices, is the change in the terms of trade. Hence trade productivity growth equals the change in the terms of trade. In other words, the productivity of the trade sector is given by the terms of trade, a result that agrees with one's intuition.

For the economy as a whole, total productivity growth is given by

$$\tilde{\rho} = (\tilde{p}\,\mathrm{d}\tilde{Y} - w\,\mathrm{d}\Lambda - r\,\mathrm{d}\kappa)/\tilde{Y}.$$

As before, a tilde refers to the augmented flow matrices. In the case of labor and capital (Λ and κ, respectively) it is immaterial, since the trade sector does not use them, and hence the tilde may be omitted. Note that excess exports, which is included in $\tilde{Y}$, contribute to total factor productivity. The opposite is true of debt exports, as they are merely an input requirement for non-competitive imports.

Since the coefficients we have specified for the augmented matrices are based on the commodity technology model, the alternative expression for total factor productivity growth holds:

$$\tilde{\rho} = -[\tilde{p}\,\mathrm{d}\tilde{A}^{c} + w\,\mathrm{d}(l,0) + r\,\mathrm{d}(k,0)]\tilde{X}/\tilde{Y}.$$

Once more, it is illumination to substitute the special structure of the trade sector. The expression becomes

$$\tilde{\rho} = -\left[(p, p_{\text{trade}})\,\mathrm{d}\begin{pmatrix} A^{c} & e/m\mathbf{1} \\ mV^{-T} & 0 \end{pmatrix} + w\,\mathrm{d}(l,0) + r\,\mathrm{d}(k,0) \right] \begin{pmatrix} X \\ m\mathbf{1} \end{pmatrix} \Big/ p(Y-e)$$

$$= -[(p\,\mathrm{d}A^{c} + p_{\text{trade}}\,\mathrm{d}(mV^{-T}),\ p\,\mathrm{d}(e/m\mathbf{1})) + w\,\mathrm{d}(l,0) + r\,\mathrm{d}(k,0)] \begin{pmatrix} X \\ m\mathbf{1} \end{pmatrix} \Big/ p(Y-e)$$

$$= -[p(\mathrm{d}A^{c})X + p_{\text{trade}}\,\mathrm{d}(mV^{-T})X + p\,\mathrm{d}(e/m\mathbf{1})m\mathbf{1} + w(\mathrm{d}l)X + r(\mathrm{d}k)X]/p(Y-e).$$

A comparison with the usual total factor productivity growth formula for ρ that neglects the trade sector yields two new terms,

$$-p_{\text{trade}}\,\mathrm{d}(mV^{-T})X - p\,\mathrm{d}(e/m\mathbf{1})m\mathbf{1}.$$

The latter term is basically π^{c}_{trade}, so that productivity growth of the international trade sector is additively separable from total factor productivity growth. This fact is due to the absence of circular flows within that sector. The first term is basically the factor productivity aspect of non-competitive imports. It is also separable, essentially since non-competitive imports are aggregated across commodities and a new physical dimension is created for this aggregate.

In many studies, non-competitive imports are modeled as a pure factor input without taking into account the exports needed to fund them. In such studies, only the first term arises. We prefer to include the productivity of the trade sector which turns out to be given by the terms of trade.

6. Productivity analysis

We begin the analysis by computing two measures of the overall rate of TFP growth in the economy. From expression (4), TFP growth consists of an amalgam of changes and weights. Changes of net outputs are added and changes of factor inputs are subtracted, each weighted by their respective relative prices. The formula holds exactly for continuous time estimates. However, the data, of course, are available only for discrete time periods, 1967–1972 and 1972–1977. Thus, an approximation to the formula must be made. A change over a period can be estimated only by taking the difference of the two observations made during the period, at the base year and at the end year. Thus, the problem of approximation is reduced to the choice of weights in the formula. The most common choice is to take the average of the base year value and the end year value of any weight. For any period, the ratios p/y, w/y, and r/y are approximated by the averages of their respective values at the base year and the end year. This constitutes the TFP growth measure based on the average relative price index.

Table 4
Annual rate of overall TFP growth.

	1967–1972	1972–1977	1967–1977	Change
1. Turnqvist–Divisia	0.73%	−0.26%	0.17%	−0.99%
2. Average period prices	0.74%	−0.24%	0.17%	−0.98%

This measure of TFP growth is the most natural one, based on the specification of changes and their weights, as given in expression (4). However, it is possible to transform the changes and the weights without altering the equation in continuous time. Then the same reasoning leads to another measure in discrete time. The most common transformation is to relative changes. If we define $\alpha = w\Lambda/y$ as the wage share in the national product, use rK/y as the profit share in view of eq. (1) after aggregation (postmultiplication by **1**), and recall that the definition of the value shares, $\beta = \hat{p}Y/y$, can be transformed into an equation for relative changes, then

$$\rho = \beta^{\mathrm{T}}\,\mathrm{d}(\ln Y) - \alpha\,\mathrm{d}(\ln \Lambda) - (1-\alpha)\,\mathrm{d}(\ln \kappa), \qquad (4')$$

where $\mathrm{d}(\ln Y)$ is the vector whose jth component is equal to $\mathrm{d}(\ln Y_j) = \mathrm{d}Y_j/Y_j$. If we now replace the differentials by finite differences and the weights by their respective averages over the period, we obtain the TFP growth measure based on the Tornqvist–Divisia index.

To streamline the presentation of our results, we present pairs of percentages, where the first component is based on the Tornqvist–Divisia index and the second component (in parentheses) on the average relative price index.[23] TFP growth over the 1967–1972 period is 0.73 (0.74) percent per year, while for the 1972–1977 period it averages −0.26 (−0.24) percent per annum (see table 4). Hence the change in annual TFP growth between the two periods is −0.99 (−0.98) percent. This result accords with previous studies that show about a one percentage point drop in annual productivity growth over this time span [see Wolff (1985a) for a survey]. Note also that the choice of index has a negligible influence on the measurement of TFP growth and its slowdown.

We next consider alternative decompositions of the change in overall TFP growth into its various effects. The first of these, from eq. (26a), is based on commodity-level measures of TFP growth computed from the commodity technology model. There are three components to this decomposition. The first of these is the sectoral TFP growth effect, resulting from the change in

[23]Under conditions of strictly-concave and continuously differentiable production functions, constant returns to scale, and perfect competition, the Tornqvist–Divisia index is the theoretically correct measure. However, if any of these conditions is violated, other measures may be preferred. [See Baumol and Wolff (forthcoming) for a discussion of this.]

Table 5

Percentage decomposition of the change in overall TFP growth between 1967–1972 and 1972–1977 into three effects (based on the commodity-level commodity technology model).[a]

	Percentage contribution				
	$\Delta\rho$	$(\Delta\pi^c)s^c\beta$	$\pi^c(\Delta s^c)\beta$	$\pi^c s^c(\Delta\beta)$	Sum
1. Turnqvist–Divisia	−0.99%	85.0%	3.1%	12.0%	100.0%
2. Average period prices	−0.98%	90.0%	−1.1%	11.1%	100.0%

[a]See eq. (26a) for decomposition.

Table 6

Primary and secondary product annual TFP growth, 1967–1977 and their percentage contribution to the change in overall TFP growth (all computations are based on the commodity technology model).[a]

	1967–1972	1972–1977	1967–1977	Change	Percentage contribution
1. Turnqvist–Divisia					
a. Primary product TFP	0.80%	−0.17%	−0.26%	−0.97%	94.5%
b. Secondary product TFP	−1.22%	−2.75%	−2.18%	−1.53%	5.9%
c. Secondary product weight	3.64%	3.50%	3.77%	−0.15%	−0.4%
d. Overall TFP growth	0.73%	−0.26%	0.17%	−0.99%	100.0%
2. Average period prices					
a. Primary product TFP	0.79%	−0.17%	0.27%	−0.96%	94.4%
b. Secondary product TFP	−0.67%	−2.28%	−2.02%	−1.61%	6.0%
c. Secondary product weight	3.64%	3.50%	3.77%	−0.15%	−0.3%
d. Overall TFP growth	0.74%	−0.24%	0.17%	−0.98%	100.0%

[a]See eq. (24) for decomposition.

sectoral rates of TFP. This accounts for 85.0% (90.0%) of the decline in overall TFP growth (see table 5). The second is the interindustry multiplier effect, from a change in matrix s. It is small, accounting for 3.1% (−1.1%) of the decline. The third is the final output or composition effect. It accounts for 12.0% (11.1%) of the slowdown. The composition effect is larger than those reported in Wolff (1985b) for the 1958–1976 period, even though the period under consideration here, 1967–1977, is shorter.[24]

The second decomposition of TFP growth, also based on the commodity technology model, involves separate results for primary output and secondary output (see table 6). Primary product TFP growth is 0.80% (0.79%) for the 1967–1972 period and −0.17% (−0.17%) for the 1972–1977 period, yielding a change of −0.97% (−0.96%). Secondary product TFP growth is

[24]Since the composition of final output tends to change slowly over time, the composition effect is usually greater the longer the period under consideration. These results suggest that the BEA transfer method for secondary output, which was used in Wolff (1985b), tends to bias downward the contribution of compositional shifts of final output to changes in overall productivity growth.

Table 7

Percentage decomposition of the change in overall TFP growth between 1967–1972 and 1972–1977 into three effects (based on the commodity-level industry technology model).[a]

	Percentage contribution					
	$\Delta\rho$	$(\Delta\pi^1)s^1\beta$	$\pi^1(\Delta s^1)\beta$	$\pi^1 s^1(\Delta\beta)$	$\Delta\theta$	Sum
1. Turnqvist–Divisia	−0.99%	85.4%	2.6%	11.5%	0.5%	100.0%
2. Average period prices	−0.98%	91.8%	−1.3%	10.7%	−1.1%	100.0%

[a]See eq. (26b) for decomposition.

−1.22% (−0.67%) for the first period and −2.75% (−2.28%) for the second, yielding a change of −1.53% (−1.61%). The most striking result is that productivity growth was considerably lower for secondary output than for primary output. Also, the decline in TFP growth was more severe for secondary output than for primary output. From eq. (24), the change in overall TFP growth is then decomposed into three effects. The first of these, from the change in primary product TFP growth, accounts for 94.5 (94.4) percent of the change in overall TFP growth – a result largely due to the fact that primary output comprises over 96 percent of total output, as the secondary product weights are 3.64% (3.64%) for the 1967–1972 period and 3.50% (3.50%) for the 1972–1977 period. The second, from the decline in secondary product TFP growth, accounts for the remaining 5.9 (6.0) percent. The third effect, from the change in the relative level and composition of secondary output, is of almost no importance: −0.4% (−0.3%). Thus, the change in overall TFP growth is dominated by the change in primary output TFP growth, because secondary output comprise a relatively small proportion of total output at this level of aggregation. Secondary product TFP growth, although starting at a negative level, declined further and thus contributed to the slowdown.

We next look to the bias that results from the use of the industry technology model. Eq. (26b) decomposes overall TFP growth into four effects. The relative importance of the effects is given by the following results: 85.4% (91.8%) for the sectoral TFP growth effect, 2.6% (−1.3%) for the interindustry multiplier effect, 11.5% (10.7%) for the final output or composition effect, and 0.5% (−1.1%) for the secondary bias effect (see table 7). The bias in computing the overall TFP slowdown from the industry technology model is insignificant. The distribution over the three other effects is not affected much either, as a comparison with the commodity technology model above shows. In short, the use of the industry technology model, though theoretically inferior to the commodity technology model for the decomposition of TFP change, is relatively harmless, at least for this level of aggregation and this period. The reason is that the relative level and composition of secondary output was stable over the period.

Table 8

Percentage decomposition of the change in overall TFP growth between 1967–1972 and 1972–1977 into two effects (based on the industry-level commodity technology model).[a]

	Percentage contribution					
	Δp	$\pi^c s^c(\Delta\beta)$	$\pi^c(\Delta s^c)\beta$	$(\Delta\psi)Ms^c\beta$	$\psi(\Delta M)s^I\beta$	Sum
1. Turnqvist–Divisia	−0.99%	12.0%	3.1%	82.1%	2.9%	100.0%
2. Average period prices	−0.98%	11.1%	−1.1%	86.9%	3.1%	100.0%

[a]See eqs. (26a) and (26c) for decomposition.

We next turn to the industry-level productivity growth effect. As was argued in the body of the text, the use of industry-level productivity growth rates leads to a further decomposition of the sectoral TFP growth effect into a market share effect and an industry-level productivity growth effect. Our result is that 97% (97%) of the sectoral TFP growth effect can be ascribed to the industry-level productivity growth effect, and the remainder to the market share shift effect (see table 8). Thus, in addition to the final output composition effect accounting for 12.0 (11.1) percent of the slowdown, another 2.9 (3.1) percent can be ascribed to changes of market shares among the industries. This result, in particular, indicates that so-called 'shift effects', embodying both final output compositional changes and shifts in industry market shares, were important in explaining the productivity slowdown of this period. Also, accounting for the interindustry multiplier effect, only 82.1 (86.9) percent of the overall productivity slowdown remains to be ascribed to the slowdown in industry-level productivity growth.

Finally, on the sectoral level, there are some rather interesting differences in the measurement of TFP growth based on commodity-level and industry-level indices derived from the commodity technology model. These are shown in table 9. Though most of the differences are small, there are several sectors in which the differences are quite large. The first of these is forestry and fisheries (sector 3), with a 1.7 percentage point difference in estimated rates of annual TFP growth; the second is agricultural services (4), with a difference of 0.7 percentage points; the third is plastics (28), also with a 0.7 percentage point difference; and the final set consists of chemical products (27), drugs and related products (29), and transportation and warehousing (65), each with a 0.3 percentage point difference. However, the mean square error over all 82 sectors is rather small, 0.1 percentage points.

The last column of table 9 shows the 'contribution' of each sector to overall TFP growth, where the contribution is defined as $\pi_j^c p_j X_j / y$ and is thus sectoral TFP growth multiplied by its normalized gross output weight. Sectors with large positive contributions are livestock (1), other agricultural products (2), transportation and warehousing (65), and wholesale and retail trade (69). Sectors with strong negative contributions are construction (11),

Table 9

Commodity-level and industry-level TFP growth by sector, 1967–1977 (based on the commodity technology model and Turnqvist–Divisia index).

	Commodity level TFP (π^c)	Industry level TFP (π^I)	Difference ($\pi^I - \pi^c$)	Weight ($p_j X_j/y$)	Contribution ($\pi_j^c p_j X_j/y$)
1. Livstock	2.08%	2.08%	0.00%	0.0164	0.034%
2. Agr prod	3.98	3.98	0.00	0.0125	0.050
3. For fish	−6.03	−4.34	1.69	0.0008	−0.005
4. Agr serv	−1.60	−0.87	0.73	0.0022	−0.003
5. Iron min	−3.58	−3.48	0.10	0.0006	−0.002
6. Nfer min	−0.66	−0.68	−0.02	0.0007	−0.000
7. Coal min	−6.08	−6.07	0.01	0.0019	−0.011
8. Gas petr	0.22	0.21	−0.01	0.0060	0.001
9. Ston min	3.14	2.85	−0.29	0.0009	0.003
10. Chm ming	−4.87	−4.71	0.17	0.0002	−0.001
11. New cons	−1.52	−1.52	0.00	0.0321	−0.049
12. Main&rep	−0.21	−0.21	0.00	0.0097	−0.002
13. Ordnance	−0.72	−0.58	0.14	0.0017	−0.001
14. Food pro	0.41	0.45	0.04	0.0379	0.016
15. Toba man	0.79	0.79	0.00	0.0015	0.001
16. Fabr&yrn	0.51	0.53	0.02	0.0061	0.003
17. Txt good	2.12	2.04	−0.09	0.0018	0.004
18. Apparel	1.16	1.15	0.00	0.0107	0.012
19. Misc txt	1.50	1.34	−0.16	0.0019	0.003
20. Lmb&wood	0.12	0.16	0.04	0.0060	0.001
21. Wood con	−2.36	−2.18	0.18	0.0002	−0.000
22. Hhld fur	1.09	1.08	−0.01	0.0022	0.002
23. Oth furn	0.47	0.50	0.03	0.0011	0.001
24. Papr&pro	0.20	0.21	0.01	0.0062	0.001
25. Papr con	1.16	1.14	−0.03	0.0023	0.003
26. Prnt&pub	0.28	0.28	0.00	0.0058	0.002
27. Chem pro	−2.11	−1.81	0.31	0.0094	−0.020
28. Plastics	2.48	1.82	−0.67	0.0036	0.009
29. Drugs et	2.02	1.77	−0.25	0.0040	0.008
30. Paint pr	0.63	0.59	−0.05	0.0010	0.001
31. Petr ref	−0.98	−0.94	0.04	0.0116	−0.011
32. Rbbr pro	0.12	0.18	0.06	0.0062	0.001
33. Leath in	2.23	2.21	−0.02	0.0004	0.001
34. Footwear	−0.01	0.01	0.02	0.0016	−0.000
35. Glass pr	−0.84	−0.80	0.04	0.0016	−0.001
36. Stn clay	−0.15	−0.16	0.00	0.0046	−0.001
37. Iron&stl	−1.18	−1.15	0.03	0.0109	−0.013
38. N-fr met	−0.75	−0.73	0.02	0.0061	−0.005
39. Met cont	−0.18	−0.17	0.01	0.0045	−0.000
40. Heat plb	0.42	0.40	−0.02	0.0045	0.002
41. Screw ma	0.89	0.85	−0.04	0.0032	0.003
42. Oth metl	−0.36	−0.37	−0.01	0.0044	−0.002

Table 9 (continued)

	Commodity level TFP (π^c)	Industry level TFP (π^I)	Difference ($\pi^I - \pi^c$)	Weight (p_jX_j/y)	Contribution ($\pi_j^c p_jX_j/y$)
43. Engines	0.47%	0.38%	−0.09%	0.0014	0.001%
44. Farm mag	1.36	1.27	−0.09	0.0016	0.002
45. C min&oi	−1.32	−1.21	0.11	0.0022	−0.003
46. Mat hndl	0.67	0.57	−0.10	0.0008	0.001
47. Met&wrk	0.08	0.09	0.01	0.0022	0.000
48. Spc ind	−0.76	−0.68	0.08	0.0015	−0.001
49. Gen ind	−0.35	−0.29	0.06	0.0024	−0.001
50. Maih sop	−0.34	−0.31	0.03	0.0014	−0.000
51. Offc mag	3.97	3.77	−0.20	0.0025	0.010
52. Serv ind	1.60	1.57	−0.03	0.0018	0.003
53. Elec ind	0.47	0.50	0.03	0.0030	0.001
54. Hhsld ap	2.47	2.37	−0.10	0.0017	0.004
55. Light&wi	0.71	0.71	0.00	0.0014	0.001
56. Radio&TV	0.16	0.20	0.04	0.0049	0.001
57. Elec com	3.41	3.17	−0.24	0.0028	0.010
58. Misc e m	0.52	0.55	0.03	0.0011	0.001
59. Motr veh	0.61	0.60	−0.01	0.0160	0.010
60. Aircrfts	−0.01	−0.01	0.00	0.0048	−0.000
61. Oth trns	0.65	0.64	−0.01	0.0034	0.002
62. Scientif	1.97	1.83	−0.15	0.0022	0.004
63. Opt phot	2.77	2.60	−0.17	0.0015	0.004
64. Misc man	1.43	1.39	−0.04	0.0034	0.005
65. Trnsp&wh	2.34	2.01	−0.33	0.0274	0.064
66. Communic	2.31	2.31	0.00	0.0110	0.025
67. Brodcast	0.00	0.00	0.00		0.000
68. Utility	−1.62	−1.72	−0.10	0.0312	−0.050
69. Trade-rt	1.73	1.72	−0.01	0.0849	0.147
70. Fin & in	0.18	0.17	−0.01	0.0225	0.004
71. Rl est r	0.33	0.21	−0.12	0.0140	0.005
72. Hotl rep	2.02	2.02	0.00	0.0140	0.028
73. Busn ser	0.16	0.23	0.07	0.0228	0.004
74. Auto rep	0.37	0.28	−0.08	0.0066	0.002
75. Amusemen	1.43	1.39	−0.04	0.0052	0.007
76. Med ed s	−0.48	−0.48	0.00	0.0383	−0.018
77. Fed govt	3.59	3.59	0.00	0.0039	0.014
78. State sr	−2.72	−2.71	0.00	0.0026	−0.007
79. Govt ind	−1.16	−1.16	0.00	0.0798	−0.093
80. Houshold	0.00	0.00	0.00		0.000
81. Scrap	0.00	0.00	0.00		0.000
82. Import/exp	−2.45	−2.45	0.00	0.0187	−0.046
83. Unwt ave	0.07	0.08	0.01		
84. Overall	0.17	0.17	0.00		0.172

utilities (68), and the government industry (79). The government sector shows a negative one percent per annum rate of TFP growth over the 1967–1977 period, largely due to the rapid growth in its capital stock. One sector in particular, the import–export sector (82), deserves special mention, since its 'rate of TFP growth' is equivalent to the annual rate of change in the terms of trade. The terms of trade deteriorated sharply against the U.S. over the 1967–1977 period, at an annual rate of 2.5 percent.

Table 10 shows calculations of the change in TFP growth between the 1967–1972 and the 1972–1977 periods based on the commodity-level and industry-level measures. Here, again, differences are generally small, with an overall mean square error of 0.12 percentage points. However, there are 13 sectors which show sizeable differences: forestry and fisheries (3), agricultural services (4), stone quarrying (9), ordnance (13), chemical products (27), plastics (28), drugs and related products (29), engine manufacturing (43), metal working machinery (47), specialized industrial machinery (48), miscellaneous machinery (50), service industry machinery (52), and business services (73).[25]

The fourth column of table 10 shows the 'contribution' of each sector to the change in overall TFP growth, where the contribution is defined as $(\Delta\pi)^c_j p_j X_j/y$ and is thus the change in sectoral TFP growth multiplied by its normalized gross output weight. There are no sectors with large positive contributions, except wholesale and retail trade (69). Sectors with strong negative contributions are construction (11), food processing (14), petroleum refining (31), and the government industry (79). The government sector shows an almost two percentage point decline in its rate of TFP growth between the 1967–1972 and the 1972–1977 period because of the rapid acceleration in the growth of its capital stock. The export–import sector (82) again deserves special mention. The results indicate that the terms of trade fell against the U.S. by 3.2 percentage points between the 1967–1972 and the 1972–1977 periods. Since non-competitive imports comprise about three percent of GDP, deterioration in the terms of trade between the two periods accounted for about a quarter (−0.0026/−0.0099) of the overall productivity slowdown.

7. Conclusion

By starting the productivity analysis with flow data of inputs and outputs,

[25]A sector-by-sector comparison of commodity-level TFP growth derived from the commodity technology model with that derived from the industry technology model shows a slightly higher degree of bias from the use of the latter. The mean square error over all 82 sectors in the computation of TFP growth over the 1967–1977 period from the two models is 0.20 percentage points, and that for the computation of the change in TFP growth between the 1967–1972 and the 1972–1977 periods is 0.33 percentage points.

Table 10

Change in commodity-level and industry-level TFP growth by sector between the 1967–1972 and the 1972–1977 periods (based on the commodity technology model and Turnqvist–Divisia index).

	Commodity level TFP ($\Delta\pi^c$)	Industry level TFP ($\Delta\pi^I$)	Difference ($\Delta\pi^I - \Delta\pi^c$)	Contribution ($\Delta\pi_j^c p_j X_j/y$)
1. Livstock	1.54%	1.54%	0.00%	0.11%
2. Agr prod	1.07	1.07	0.00	0.06
3. For fish	−3.72	−3.35	0.37	−0.01
4. Agr serv	2.76	2.36	−0.40	0.03
5. Iron min	−3.29	−3.30	−0.01	−0.01
6. Nfer min	−5.72	−5.70	0.02	−0.02
7. Coal min	0.06	0.05	−0.01	0.00
8. Gas petr	−4.76	−4.75	0.01	−0.12
9. Ston min	4.93	4.48	−0.45	0.02
10. Chm ming	3.75	3.65	−0.10	0.00
11. New cons	−2.25	−2.25	0.00	−0.31
12. Main&rep	−3.22	−3.22	0.00	−0.13
13. Ordnance	−2.22	−1.92	0.30	−0.02
14. Food pro	−1.15	−1.03	0.12	−0.19
15. Toba man	0.33	0.32	−0.01	0.00
16. Fabr&yrn	1.19	1.18	−0.01	0.03
17. Txt good	2.60	2.40	−0.20	0.02
18. Apparel	1.29	1.28	−0.01	0.06
19. Misc txt	0.99	1.03	0.04	0.01
20. Lmb&wood	−3.68	−3.61	0.07	−0.09
21. Wood con	−3.87	−3.80	0.07	−0.00
22. Hhld fur	1.54	1.50	−0.04	0.01
23. Oth furn	−0.32	−0.30	0.02	−0.00
24. Papr&pro	−1.03	−0.99	0.04	−0.03
25. Papr con	2.21	2.18	−0.03	0.02
26. Prnt&pub	1.76	1.73	−0.03	0.04
27. Chem pro	−4.12	−3.67	0.45	−0.16
28. Plastics	−1.13	−1.86	−0.73	−0.02
29. Drugs et	−0.56	−0.94	−0.38	−0.01
30. Paint pr	1.20	1.01	−0.19	0.01
31. Petr ref	−3.60	−3.64	−0.04	−0.18
32. Rbbr pro	−1.55	−1.49	0.06	−0.04
33. Leath in	2.27	2.25	−0.02	0.00
34. Footwear	1.32	1.33	0.01	0.01
35. Glass pr	2.04	1.99	−0.05	0.01
36. Stn clay	−0.87	−0.85	0.02	−0.02
37. Iron&stl	0.69	0.68	−0.01	0.03
38. N-fr met	1.38	1.34	−0.04	0.04
39. Met cont	2.92	2.82	−0.10	0.02
40. Heat plb	0.63	0.56	−0.07	0.01
41. Screw ma	−1.84	−1.66	0.18	−0.03
42. Oth metl	0.15	0.18	0.03	0.00

Table 10 (continued)

	Commodity level TFP ($\Delta\pi^c$)	Industry level TFP ($\Delta\pi^I$)	Difference ($\Delta\pi^I-\Delta\pi^c$)	Contribution ($\Delta\pi_j^c p_j X_j/y$)
43. Engines	−2.47%	−2.16%	0.31%	−0.02%
44. Farm mag	−1.26	−1.22	0.04	−0.01
45. C min&oi	−2.75	−2.64	0.11	−0.03
46. Mat hndl	−1.17	−1.14	0.03	−0.00
47. Met&wrk	2.41	2.07	−0.34	0.02
48. Spc ind	−3.98	−3.58	0.40	−0.03
49. Gen ind	−0.07	−0.11	−0.04	−0.00
50. Maih sop	3.49	3.29	−0.19	0.02
51. Offc mag	1.68	1.55	−0.13	0.02
52. Serv ind	−2.98	−2.56	0.42	−0.02
53. Elec ind	1.46	1.33	−0.13	0.02
54. Hhsld ap	1.27	1.03	−0.24	0.01
55. Light&wi	−0.80	−0.68	0.12	−0.00
56. Radio&TV	2.34	2.25	−0.09	0.05
57. Elec com	1.53	1.45	−0.08	0.02
58. Misc e m	−0.47	−0.44	0.03	−0.00
59. Motr veh	0.26	0.24	−0.02	0.02
60. Aircrfts	0.73	0.69	−0.04	0.01
61. Oth trns	0.68	0.64	−0.04	0.01
62. Scientif	0.46	0.43	−0.03	0.00
63. Opt phot	−1.73	−1.77	−0.04	−0.01
64. Misc man	1.18	1.12	−0.06	0.02
65. Trnsp&wh	0.07	−0.03	−0.10	0.01
66. Communic	1.50	1.50	0.00	0.07
67. Brodcast	0.00	0.00	0.00	0.00
68. Utility	−1.01	−0.90	0.11	−0.13
69. Trade-rt	0.64	0.63	−0.02	0.23
70. Fin & in	1.16	1.16	0.00	0.11
71. Rl est r	0.90	0.78	−0.12	0.05
72. Hotl rep	1.02	1.02	0.00	0.06
73. Busn ser	1.16	1.42	0.26	0.11
74. Auto rep	1.26	1.23	−0.03	0.04
75. Amusemen	2.64	2.58	−0.06	0.06
76. Med ed s	1.18	1.18	0.00	0.19
77. Fed govt	−1.76	−1.76	0.00	−0.03
78. State sr	−0.34	−0.33	0.01	−0.00
79. Govt ind	−1.83	−1.83	0.00	−0.62
80. Houshold	0.00	0.00	0.00	0.00
81. Scrap	0.00	0.00	0.00	0.00
82. Import/exp	−3.24	−3.24	0.00	−0.26
83. Unwt ave	−0.09	−0.10	−0.01	
84. Overall	−0.99	−0.99	0.00	−0.84

constructing input–output coefficients in the process, and setting up value relations simultaneously, we have shown that the presence of secondary products have both theoretical and empirical ramifications. With regard to the former, we have shown that in order to establish a theoretically correct relationship between sectoral and overall levels of productivity growth, we must adopt the so-called commodity technology model of secondary production in setting up the input–output relations. Since the literature has employed ready-to-use input–output coefficient matrices derived from the industry technology model, productivity growth decompositions based on them have been biased. We have proved that a decomposition of overall productivity growth into industry-level productivity growth rates involves changes not only in final demand and the Leontief inverse but also a matrix of market shares.

The empirical results indicate that, though the industry technology model bias is by itself insignificant, a portion of the sectoral TFP growth effect is captured by shifts in market shares. In particular, only 82.1 (86.9) percent of the overall productivity slowdown can be ascribed to the slowdown in industry-level productivity growth, particularly that of construction, food processing, petroleum refining, and the government industry, with the remaining 13 to 18 percent due to changes in the composition of final output and market shares, including the interindustry multiplier effect. This compositional effect is of the same order of magnitude as found in Wolff (1985) for a much longer period (that between 1947–1967 and 1967–1976). Though we were able to separate out the secondary product effect, little of the slowdown can be ascribed to changes in secondary product TFP growth rates, but the levels of secondary product TFP growth rates are extremely low throughout the period of analysis. Since our analysis allows a detailed commodity breakdown of these rates, the source of this problem can be identified as the high representation of some slow productivity growers among secondary products, particularly the following products: chemical products in the petroleum refining industry, non-ferrous metal products in the iron and steel industry, and business services provided by the printing and publishing industry.

Results on the sectoral level indicate that the bias from using industry-level measures of TFP growth instead of commodity-level indices, while small on average, is quite large for several sectors. Slightly larger biases were found on the sectoral level from using the industry technology model. Two special sectors in this study are the scrap sector and international trade. Inclusion of the scrap sector in our framework captures depreciation and the gains from recycling. In our modeling of international trade, its sectoral productivity growth is found to be identical to the change in the terms of trade, and non-competitive import savings in other sectors are captured as well. Changes in the terms of trade were found to be significant for the U.S. over the 1967–

1977 period and accounted for almost a fourth of the estimated slowdown in overall TFP growth.

Though the results reported in this paper do not indicate a major effect on overall TFP growth from changes in secondary output and composition, this may be due to the high order of aggregation. Even at the 85-sector order, this may not necessarily remain true in the future. In particular, the relative level and composition of secondary output may be changed more substantially over time, even at the 85-sector level. As a result, the model presented here may produce outcomes that differ more from standard factor productivity growth studies that ignore the correct specification of the input–output value relations between the sectors, including scrap and trade.

Finally, there are two major implications of our work for multiregional analysis. First, to avoid biased relationships between regional and national levels of productivity growth, we suggest the use of the commodity technology model in the construction of multiregional input–output models. Second, our accounting framework can be directly adapted to identify strong and weak regions in terms of productivity growth and, more particularly, to single out those areas of the country that contributed most to the productivity slowdown. We hope that such an analysis will be undertaken in the future.

References

Baumol, William J. and Edward N. Wolff, n.d., Three fundamental productivity concepts: Principles and measurement, in: R. Feiwel, ed., Joan Robinson and modern economic theory (Macmillan, London) forthcoming.

Carter, Anne P., 1970, Structural change in the American economy (Harvard University Press, Cambridge, MA).

Denison, Edward F., 1979, Explanations of declining productivity growth, Survey of Current Business 59, Aug. (Part 2) 1–24.

Denison, Edward F., 1984, Accounting for slower economic growth: An update, in: J. Kendrick, ed., International comparisons of productivity and the causes of the slowdown (Ballinger, Cambridge, MA).

Gorman, John A., John C. Musgrave, Gerald Silverstein and Kathy A. Comins, 1985, Fixed private capital in the United States, Survey of Current Business 65, no. 7, July, 36–59.

Kop Jansen, Pieter and Thijs ten Raa, 1989, The choice of model in the construction of input–output matrices, International Economic Review 31, no. 1, Jan., 213–227.

Leontief, Wassily, 1941, The structure of the American economy, 1919–1939 (Oxford University Press, New York).

Leontief, Wassily, 1953, Studies in the structure of the American economy (Oxford University Press, New York).

Ritz, Philip M., 1979, The input–output structure of the U.S. economy, 1972, Survey of Current Business 59, no. 2, Feb., 34–72.

Ritz, Philip M., Eugene P. Roberts and Paula C. Young, 1979, Dollar value tables of the 1972 input–output study, Survey of Current Business 59, no. 4, April, 51–72.

ten Raa, Thijs, Debesh Chakraborty and J. Anthony Small, 1984, An alternative treatment of secondary products in input–output analysis, Review of Economics and Statistics 66, no. 1, Feb., 88–97.

U.S. Interindustry Economics Division, 1974, The input–output structure of the U.S. economy: 1967, Survey of Current Business 54, no. 2, Feb., 24–56.
U.S. Interindustry Economics Division, 1984, The input–output structure of the U.S. economy, 1977, Survey of Current Business 64, no. 5, May, 42–84.
Viet, Vu Quang, 1987, Study of input–output tables: 1970–1980, Paper presented at the international conference on input–output techniques, Sapporo, Japan, July.
Wolff, Edward N., 1985a, The magnitude and causes of the recent productivity slowdown in the U.S., in: K. McClennan and W. Baumol, eds., Policies for the stimulation of U.S. productivity growth (Oxford University Press, New York).
Wolff, Edward N., 1985b, Industrial composition, interindustry effects and the U.S. productivity slowdown, Review of Economics and Statistics 67, May, 268–277.
Yuskavage, Robert E., 1985, Employment and employee compensation in the 1977 input–output accounts, Survey of Current Business 65, no. 11, Nov., 11–25.

Regional Science and Urban Economics 24 (1994) 75–92. North-Holland

Productivity measurement within an input–output framework

Edward N. Wolff*

Department of Economics, 269 Mercer Street, New York University, New York, NY 10003, USA

Received June 1991, final version received April 1992

Input–output provides features for the measurement and analysis of total factor productivity (TFP) growth. First, TFP growth can be measured using gross output and incorporating materials as an input. Second, a growth accounting framework can be developed to measure the effect of final output mix changes on aggregate productivity growth. Third, capital can be treated as a produced means of production. Fourth, measures of composite technical change can overcome difficulties engendered by the substitution of externally provided inputs for those previously provided by the firm. Fifth, TFP growth of secondary production can be analytically separated from that of primary output.

JEL classification: O47; C67

1. Introduction

The input–output (I-O) framework provides a powerful system for the measurement of productivity growth and the analysis of productivity trends. In many respects, the I-O system provides distinct methodological advantages over more standard productivity analysis based on industry gross product originating (GPO).

In this paper I consider five topics on the analysis of technical change within an I-O framework. The first is the measurement of sectoral (or industry) rates of productivity growth. The second is the use of an I-O growth accounting framework to measure so-called 'compositional effects' – that is, the effect of changes in the mix of final outputs on aggregate productivity growth. The third is the treatment of capital as a produced means of production. The fourth is the introduction of productivity measures that reflect changes in total (direct and indirect) factor requirements. The

Correspondence to: E.N. Wolff, Department of Economics, 269 Mercer Street, New York University, New York, NY 10003, USA.

*The author wishes to express appreciation to Thijs ten Raa and two anonymous referees for their comments and to the C.V. Starr Center for Applied Economics at New York University for financial support.

SSDI 0166-0462(93)05003-8

fifth topic is the treatment of secondary production within a productivity growth framework. The paper also provides some methodological comparisons of productivity measurement in an I-O system with GPO-based measures.

2. The accounting framework

Define:[1]

U = an input or 'use' commodity-by-industry flow matrix, where u_{ij} shows the total amount of commodity i consumed by industry j;

V = an output or 'make' industry-by-commodity flow matrix, where v_{ij} shows the total output of commodity j produced by industry i;[2]

$x = V^{\mathrm{T}}\mathbf{1}$ = (column) vector, showing the gross output of each commodity,

where a superscript T refers to the transpose of the indicated matrix, and $\mathbf{1}$ = vector with unit entries. Also, let:

$y = (V^{\mathrm{T}} - U)\mathbf{1}$ = (column) vector of final demand by commodity;

e = (row) vector, showing total employment by industry; and

k = (row) vector, showing total capital stock by industry.

To derive the corresponding technical coefficients, I will make use of the commodity technology model, where it is assumed that each commodity is produced by the same technology, irrespective of the industry of production. In this case, industries are considered independent combinations of outputs j, each with their separate input coefficients (a_{ij}). As shown in ten Raa et al. (1984), the commodity technology requirements (coefficient) matrix is given by

$$A = U[V^{\mathrm{T}}]^{-1} = \text{matrix of interindustry technical coefficients,}$$

where V is restricted to a square matrix (that is, there are as many industries as commodities).[3] Row vectors of labor and capital stock coefficients can be derived in analogous fashion:

$$\ell = e[V^{\mathrm{T}}]^{-1} = \text{(row) vector of labor coefficients}$$

[1]The time subscript is dropped for notational convenience.

[2]In the traditional one-matrix I-O framework, the V matrix is implicitly treated as a diagonal matrix.

[3]An alternative formulation is possible through the industry technology model, where it is assumed that each industry has the same input requirements per dollar of output for each commodity which it produces and that the market shares for each commodity are fixed among industries. Unfortunately, as documented in ten Raa et al. (1984) and ten Raa and Wolff (1991), the industry technology model is characterized by several serious analytical difficulties, so that I use only the commodity technology model here.

where

$$\kappa = k[V^{T}]^{-1} = \text{(row) vector of capital coefficents.}$$

In addition, let us define

p =(row) vector of commodity prices;
n =total employment (a scalar) in the economy;
c =total capital stock (a scalar) in the economy;
w =the annual wage rate (a scalar), assumed constant across industries; and
r =the rate of profit on the capital stock (a scalar), also assumed constant across industries.[4]

3. Measurement of sectoral productivity growth

In the I-O framework, sectoral output is measured by gross commodity output x (alternately called gross domestic output or GDO), while the inputs consist of employment, fixed capital, and materials (intermediate inputs). The rate of TFP (total factor productivity) growth for sector j is usually defined as

$$\pi_j \equiv -\left(\sum_i p_i \, \mathrm{d}a_{ij} + w\, \mathrm{d}\ell_j + r\, \mathrm{d}\kappa_j\right) \Big/ p_j, \tag{1}$$

where π is the corresponding row vector and 'd' refers to the differential. This measure is a continuous version of a measure of sectoral technical change proposed by Leontief (1953). Since for any variable z, $\mathrm{d}z = z\,\mathrm{d}\log z$, where log is the natural logarithm, sectoral TFP growth is also given by

$$\pi_j = -\sum_i \alpha_{ij}(\mathrm{d}\log a_{ij}) - \alpha_{Lj}(\mathrm{d}\log \ell_j) - \alpha_{Kj}(\mathrm{d}\log \kappa_j), \tag{2}$$

where $\alpha_{ij} = p_i a_{ij}/p_j$, $\alpha_{Lj} = w\ell_j/p_j$, and $\alpha_{Kj} = r\kappa_j/p_j$. These three terms give the current value shares of the respective inputs in the total value of output. Since productivity growth rates are measured over discrete time periods rather than instantaneously, the average value share of α_{ij}, α_{Lj}, and α_{Kj} over the sample period is normally used to measure π (the so-called Tornqvist–Divisia index). Tornqvist–Divisia estimates of I-O based TFP growth are provided in Wolff (1985) and Jorgensen et al. (1987).[5]

It might be helpful at this point to contrast this measure with one

[4]It is implicitly assumed that the government sector receives a shadow rate of return r on its capital stock.

[5]The U.S. Bureau of Labor Statistics has also produced multifactor measures of productivity growth in the United States. One series (the so-called 'KLEM' series) includes four inputs – capital, labor, energy, and materials. A second series adds a fifth input, services.

developed from the GPO framework. In the latter, output is measured as gross product originating, GPO (also referred to as value added or GDP), in constant dollars. GPO in constant dollars is measured by the so-called 'double deflation' method, in which gross output and intermediate inputs are each deflated by their own price indices and the difference is defined as GPO in constant dollars. There are typically two inputs in standard analysis: employment and fixed capital stock. In formal terms,

$$\mathrm{GPO}_j = x_j - \mathbf{1}a_{.j},$$

where $a_{.j}$ is the jth column of matrix A. TFP growth in this framework is then given by

$$\pi_j^* = \mathrm{d}\log \mathrm{GPO}_j - \alpha_{Lj}^*(\mathrm{d}\log e_j) - \alpha_{Kj}^*(\mathrm{d}\log k_j), \tag{2'}$$

where $\alpha_{Lj}^* = we_j/p_j\mathrm{GPO}_j$ and $\alpha_{Kj}^* = rk_j/p_j\mathrm{GPO}_j$.

Difficulties in the double deflation measure have been well documented [see, for example, Dalgaard (1988)]. First, the GPO output measure is itself difficult to interpret directly, since it corresponds to neither the physical output of the sector nor to the income generated within the sector. Second, weak separability must be assumed for the production function of each sector j for this to be a reliable index. In particular,

$$x_j = f(k_j, e_j, a_{.j}) = f(f^*(k_j, e_j); a_{.j}),$$

where f and f^* are algebraic functions. If the assumption is violated, then GPO as a measure of sectoral output may itself be contaminated by technical change, as reflected in changes in the interindustry coefficients.[6] Third, the double deflation method may lead to negative numbers for real GPO if relative price changes and/or changes in output or input structure are sufficiently great over the period of measurement. Fourth, since GPO is defined as the difference of two variables, the measurement error in GPO is equal to the sum of the measurement errors in the two components. Fifth, for the same reason, any measurement error in gross output will be amplified into a larger *percentage* error in GPO.

Despite these criticisms, measurements of TFP growth based on the GPO measure are, empirically, highly correlated with those based on gross output. Using 1963 and 1977 U.S. I-O data, I calculated both π and π^* for 76 sectors over this period (see table 1). The correlation coefficient between these two measures is 0.96,[7] and the corresponding rank correlation is 0.98. Thus,

[6] Also, see Woodland (1978) and Blackorby and Schworm (1988) for more discussion of the weak separability assumption and empirical tests.

[7] The correlation coefficients for the 52 manufacturing industries in the I-O data is also 0.95.

Table 1

Annual rate of total factor productivity growth in the United States, 1963–1977, computed from gross output and GPO[a] (%).

	Gross output (π)	GPO (π^*)
1 Livestock and Products	−0.49	−0.75
2 Other Agriculture Products	−1.16	−2.17
3 Forestry & Fishery Products	−1.57	−3.01
4 Agricultural Services	0.73	1.39
5 Iron & Feroalloy Mining	−1.73	−3.73
6 Non-ferrous Metal Mining	−1.47	−3.04
7 Coal Mining	−4.25	−7.75
8 Crude Petroleum & Gas	−0.47	−1.61
9 Stone & Clay Mining	1.54	2.16
10 Chemicals Mining	−2.34	−5.79
11 New Construction	−0.93	−2.04
12 Repair Construction	0.29	0.61
13 Ordnance & Accessories	0.29	0.42
14 Food & Kindred Products	0.58	2.46
15 Tobacco Manufactures	−0.11	−1.05
16 Fabrics, Yarn & Thread	0.96	3.33
17 Miscel. Textile Goods	2.96	13.24
18 Apparel	0.97	2.53
19 Fabricated Textiles	1.54	5.17
20 Lumber & Wood Products	0.01	0.13
21 Wooden Containers	0.76	2.30
22 Household Furniture	0.89	2.11
23 Other Furniture	0.68	1.56
24 Paper & Allied Products	0.27	0.71
25 Paperboard Containers	1.00	2.56
26 Printing & Publishing	0.96	2.08
27 Chemical Products	−1.27	−4.23
28 Plastics & Synthetics	2.68	8.73
29 Drugs & Cleaners	1.80	4.62
30 Paints & Allied Products	0.15	0.36
31 Refined Petroleum	−0.58	−4.29
32 Rubber & Allied Products	0.67	1.56
33 Leather Products	0.17	0.08
34 Footwear	0.42	1.01
35 Glass Products	0.06	0.20
36 Stone & Clay Products	−0.06	−0.08
37 Primary Iron & Steel	−0.72	−1.77
38 Primary Non-ferrous Metal	−0.38	−1.37
39 Metal Containers	0.09	0.35
40 Structural Metal Product	0.44	1.16
41 Screws, Bolts & Nuts	0.57	1.44
42 Other Fabricated Metal	0.07	0.03
43 Engines & Turbines	0.44	1.08
44 Farm Machinery	1.25	3.26
45 Construction, etc. Mach.	−0.80	−1.99
46 Materials Handling Equip.	0.80	1.97
47 Metalworking Machinery	0.61	1.04
48 Special Industrial Equip.	−0.33	−0.76
49 General Industrial Equip.	−0.05	−0.14
50 Machine Shop Products	0.48	0.85
51 Office Machines	2.21	4.70
52 Service Industry Machine	2.11	5.87

Table 1 (Continued)

	Gross output (π)	GPO (π^*)
53 Electrical Ind. Equip.	0.98	2.07
54 Household Applicances	2.71	8.38
55 Electric Lighting Equip.	0.40	0.86
56 Radio & TV Equip.	0.66	1.47
57 Electronic Components	4.55	11.35
58 Miscel. Electric Equip.	0.16	0.27
59 Motor Vehicles	0.62	2.09
60 Aircraft & Parts	0.34	0.77
61 Other Transport Equip.	0.88	2.31
62 Professional Instruments	1.39	2.76
63 Optical Equip.	2.88	5.08
64 Miscel. Manufacturing	0.90	2.09
65 Transport. & Warehousing	2.18	3.80
66 Communications	2.63	3.28
67 Radio & TV Broadcasting	−0.65	−1.21
68 Utilities	−0.56	−1.36
69 Wholesale & Retail Trade	0.45	0.67
70 Finance & Insurance	−0.02	−0.13
71 Real Estate & Rental	0.78	0.85
72 Personal & Repair Services	0.47	0.83
73 Business Services	−0.26	−0.87
74 Auto repair & Services	0.88	1.82
75 Amusements	0.28	0.63
76 Medical & Educational Serv.	−1.27	−1.56
Unweighted Average	0.42	1.08

[a]Own calculations from 1963 and 1977 U.S. input–output data. See eqs. (2) and (2′) for definitions of π and π^*.

standard measures of TFP growth appear to be reliable substitutes for I-O based measures.[8]

4. Composition effects

Composition effects on aggregate productivity movements can be incorporated into an I-O framework. The special advantage is that changes in final output composition – i.e. the mix of outputs which comprise the vector of final output – can be directly analyzed in relation to aggregate productivity growth. Compositional change can involve total final demand or particular components, such as household consumption.

[8]Interestingly, the correlation coefficient between corresponding measures of labor productivity growth (x_j/e_j and GPO_j/e_j) is lower, at 0.75. Also, it is interesting to note that TFP growth based on GPO is more than twice as great as that based on gross output (a mean of 1.08% per annum compared with 0.42% per annum). The difference is due to the fact that intermediate inputs account for about half of gross output and their coefficients change very little over time.

This can be formalized as follows. Let us first define aggregate TFP growth, ρ, as

$$\rho \equiv [p\,\mathrm{d}y - w\,\mathrm{d}n - r\,\mathrm{d}c]/py. \tag{3}$$

This measure is directly analogous to eq. (1), the index of sectoral TFP, except that intermediate inputs are netted out. Indeed, with further manipulation, ρ can be rewritten in the more usual form as the growth in output less the growth of labor and capital, each weighted by their respective value shares:

$$\rho \equiv \sum_i \beta_i(\mathrm{d}\log y_i) - \alpha_L(\mathrm{d}\log n) - \alpha_K(\mathrm{d}\log c), \tag{4}$$

where $\alpha_L = wn/py$, the wage share in total income; $\alpha_K = rc/py$, the capital share in total income; and $\beta_j = p_j y_j/py$, showing the share of final output j in the total value of final output.

Aggregate TFP growth can be related to changes in the interindustry coefficient matrix as follows. From the Leontief balance equation,

$$y = (I - A)x, \tag{5}$$

it follows that

$$\mathrm{d}y = (I - A)\,\mathrm{d}x - (\mathrm{d}A)x. \tag{6}$$

By definition,

$$\mathrm{d}n = \ell\,\mathrm{d}x + (\mathrm{d}\ell)x, \tag{7}$$

$$\mathrm{d}c = \kappa\,\mathrm{d}x + (\mathrm{d}\kappa)x. \tag{8}$$

Substituting (6), (7), and (8) into (3) yields

$$\rho = [p(I - A)\,\mathrm{d}x - p(\mathrm{d}A)x - w\ell\,\mathrm{d}x - w(\mathrm{d}\ell)x - r\kappa\,\mathrm{d}x - r(\mathrm{d}\kappa)x]/py. \tag{9}$$

Making use of the basic Leontief price equation

$$p(I - A) = w\ell + r\kappa, \tag{10}$$

and substituting (10) into (9), we obtain

$$\rho \equiv -(p\,\mathrm{d}A + w\,\mathrm{d}\ell + r\,\mathrm{d}\kappa)x/py. \tag{11}$$

Then, it follows from (1) and (11) that

$$\rho = \pi\hat{p}x/py, \tag{12}$$

where a caret refers to a diagonal matrix the diagonal of which is equal to the indicated vector.

Moreover, from (5), we have

$$x=(I-A)^{-1}y. \tag{13}$$

Substituting this into (12) yields

$$\rho=\pi\hat{p}(I-A)^{-1}y/py$$

$$=\pi\hat{p}(I-A)^{-1}(\hat{p}^{-1})\hat{p}y/py.$$

It then directly follows that

$$\rho=\pi S\beta, \tag{14}$$

where $S=\hat{p}(I-A)^{-1}\hat{p}^{-1}$, the Leontief (value) inverse coefficient matrix, showing the dollar value of each input used per dollar of output. From (14), we can derive directly:

$$\mathrm{d}\rho=\mathrm{d}\pi(S\beta)+\pi(\mathrm{d}S)\beta+\pi S(\mathrm{d}\beta). \tag{15}$$

It should be noted that this formula is similar to a growth accounting framework, which allows one to attribute various portions of the *change* in overall productivity growth to different factors.

This decomposition, in particular, allows us to separate the change in overall TFP growth into three effects, corresponding to the three terms on the right-hand side of (15). The first of these is the 'technical change effect', which shows the change in overall TFP growth that can be attributed solely to changes in sectoral rates of TFP growth. The second is the 'interindustry structure effect', which shows the change in overall TFP growth that stems from changes in the Leontief inverse matrix. This term reflects, in part, changes in linkage patterns among sectors. The third is the 'output shares' (or 'composition') effect, which shows how much overall TFP growth would have changed if sectoral technical change and the interindustry structure had remained constant over time but the (value) composition of final output changed as it did in actuality. This is the term of major interest here. However, it should be noted that β measures value shares, not real shares, and thus $\mathrm{d}\beta$ reflects, in part, relative price changes. Moreover, it is also apparent that the three effects isolated in Eq. (15) are *not* independent.[9] We shall return to these two points in section 5 below.

Results for the 1974–1976 period, based on U.S. Bureau of Economic Analysis (BEA) 85-order I-O tables, are shown in the first line of table 2

[9] I thank an anonymous referee for making this point.

Table 2
Decomposition of the change in overall TFP growth into three components: technical change, interindustry structure, and output shares effects.

		Percentage contribution			
	Overall	Technical change	Inter-industry structure	Output shares	Sum of three effects[a]
Periods and measures	$\Delta\rho$	$(\Delta\pi)S\beta$	$\pi(\Delta S)\beta$	$\pi S(\Delta\beta)$	Sum
A. 1947–1967/1967–1976					
1. Standard TFP model[b]	−0.0188	97.7	−5.4	6.3	98.6
2. Depreciation method[b]	−0.0211	86.7	−7.5	21.4	100.6
3. Harrod–Peterson[b]	−0.0201	93.3	−9.7	16.8	100.4
B. 1967–1972/1972–1977					
Standard TFP model[c]	−0.0099	85.0	3.1	12.0	100.0

[a]The sum of the three effects may not equal unity because of rounding error and the exclusion of second order terms.
[b]Results are based on eq. (16). The source is Wolff (1985, table 2).
[c]Results are based on eq. (16). The source is ten Raa and Wolff (1991, table 5).

(which I have labeled the 'standard TFP model', for reasons that will become apparent in the next section).[10] Calculations were performed with traditional single total flow I-O tables (that is, the V matrix is diagonal).[11] Since empirical work is based on time periods, rather than instantaneous change, I use the discrete approximation to (15):

$$\Delta\rho \cong \Delta\pi(S\beta) + \pi(\Delta S)\beta + \pi S(\Delta\beta), \tag{16}$$

where, for example, $\Delta\beta_t = \beta_t - \beta_{t-1}$ and second-order terms are ignored.[12] Between the 1947–1967 and the 1967–1976 periods, the overall rate of TFP growth declined from 1.64% per year to −0.24% per year, or by 1.88 percentage points. The change in final output value shares, β, accounted for 6% of the change. The value share effect was largely offset by the interindustry effect, which was negative and reflected the decreased value of

[10]In order to incorporate non-competitive imports into the analysis, an endogenous column of exports is added to the total flow matrix to balance the row of non-competitive imports. In this way, imports can also be thought of as being 'produced' domestically by the exports required to sell in exchange for them. Changes in the terms of trade are directly reflected in the rate of 'TFP growth' of this industry, since, if the terms of trade move against the United States, more resources are needed to produce the exports required to balance the more expensive imports. The final output vector, y, is correspondingly adjusted for this. See ten Raa and Wolf (1991) for more details on this adjustment.

[11]See Wolff (1985) for sources and methods.

[12]Also, since the decomposition is performed between two sub-periods, such as 1947–1967 and 1967–1976, I use the average value of π, S, and β in each sub-period in the actual calculations.

interindustry inputs per dollar of final output. As a result, the sectoral technical change effect almost equalled the total change in ρ.

Results for the 1967–1977 period are also shown in table 2 (Panel B). These are based on BEA 85-order make-and-use I-O tables for 1967, 1972, and 1977.[13] TFP growth over the 1967–1972 period was 0.73% per year, which for the 1972–1977 period it averaged −0.26% per year. The change in annual TFP growth between the two periods was thus −0.99 percentage points. Changes in sectoral rates of TFP accounted for 85.0% of the decline in overall TFP growth between the two sub-periods. The interindustry structure effect, from the change in matrix S, was small, accounting for 3.1% of the decline. The composition effect, from the change of final output shares, explained the remaining 12% of the slowdown in TFP growth.[14]

Composition effects can also be addressed within GPO-based productivity analyses, and many studies have done so [see, for example, Nordhaus (1972), Denison (1979, 1984), Norsworthy et al. (1979) and Bailey (1982)]. However, such studies rely on changes in the composition of GPO instead of shifts in final output composition. Final output shifts are usually held to be autonomous (or exogenous to the system), since they reflect changes in consumer tastes and demand patterns. In contrast, shifts in gross output are not exogenous and, instead, are derived from final output shifts as well as changes in the structure of intersectoral linkages. This follows directly from (5), the well-known Leontief inverse equation.

Changes in the composition of GPO are even more difficult to interpret since they reflect both changes in gross output and interindustry linkages. Thus, using a GPO-based productivity framework, it is not possible to provide a precise decomposition of the change in overall productivity growth into a technical change effect and one emanating from changes in the composition of exogenous output.[15]

5. Treatment of capital as a produced means of production

In standard TFP analysis, capital is treated as a primary factor of production. One can alternatively consider capital as a produced means of production, since capital, like intermediate inputs, is produced by one or

[13]See ten Raa and Wolf (1991) for details on sources and methods.

[14]In the industry technology model, introduced in footnote 3 above, it is not possible to analytically derive overall TFP growth as a weighted average of commodity-level rates of productivity growth. However, the bias is empirically very small, and results from the decomposition of overall TFP growth based on the industry technology model are quite similar to those from the commodity technology model. See ten Raa and Wolf (1991) for further details.

[15]Indeed, in the six studies cited above, the analysis were conducted in terms of changes in sectoral productivity *levels*, rather than changes in sectoral *rates* of productivity growth. See Baumol and Wolff (1984) for a discussion of some of the methodological problems associated with decompositions of productivity levels.

more sectors of the economy. The latter approach has the advantage of incorporating changes in the (primary) resource requirements of producing capital in the measurement of overall technical change.

The I-O framework allows the introduction of capital as a produced means of production. In order to treat capital as an endogenous input, a new (endogenous) industry is created, whose row is the capital stock replaced in each sector of the economy and whose column consists of the inputs required to produce the replacement capital stock. Final demand is valued net of replacement investment, and labor becomes the only primary factor of production. The accounting framework of the standard I-O model is then modified as follows:

g = row vector showing the amount of capital stock replaced per unit of sectoral output;

h = the column vector showing the interindustry inputs required to produce one unit of replacement capital stock;

$\tilde{A} = \begin{pmatrix} A & h \\ g & 0 \end{pmatrix}$, the augmented interindustry coefficient matrix;

$\tilde{y} = \begin{pmatrix} y - h(gx) \\ 0 \end{pmatrix}$, the vector of net final output;

$\tilde{x} = \begin{pmatrix} x \\ h(gx) \end{pmatrix}$, the modified vector of gross output.

Two methods are used here to value the capital stock consumed in each sector: (1) the vector g is set equal to depreciation per unit of output (the 'depreciation method'); and (2) the vector g is set equal to the actual increase in gross capital stock per unit of output in each sector. The latter will be referred to as the 'Harrod–Peterson' method, since it was suggested by Peterson (1979), who attributed the idea to Harrod. In both cases the vector h is set to the coefficients of the gross capital formation vector in final demand.[16]

Measures of sectoral TFP growth analogous to (1) can then be derived. In addition, a decomposition of the overall rate of TFP growth into three effects, analogous to that of eq. (15), can be developed for the augmented I-O system. Results are shown in lines 2 and 3 of Panel A of table 2. The decline in the annual rate of TFP growth between 1947–1967 and 1967–1976 computed from the two augmented systems is slightly greater than that using standard TFP measures. However, the main difference in results is that changes in final output shares now account for a much larger proportion of the decline in overall TFP growth, between 17 and 21%, while declines in

[16]Also, see Rymes (1971, 1972) for other treatments of capital as a produced means of production within an I-O setting.

sectoral rates of TFP growth are correspondingly less important. Thus, in these two frameworks, where capital is treated as a produced means of production, composition effects explain a substantial proportion of the changes (slowdown) in overall productivity growth. The reason is that shifts in the composition of net final output, $\tilde{y}$, are considerably greater than those of gross final output, y.

6. Total factor requirements

Another concept of productivity growth that can be developed in an I-O framework derives from the total factor requirements of a sector's (final) output. In this approach, based on the Leontief inverse, a sector's 'composite TFP growth' is measured by the rate of decline of its direct plus indirect labor and capital requirements. Formally, let us define the total (direct plus indirect) labor and capital requirements per unit of final output as

$$\lambda = \ell(I-A)^{-1} \quad \text{and} \quad \gamma = \kappa(I-A)^{-1}.$$

From (10) it follows that

$$p = w\lambda + r\gamma. \tag{17}$$

We can now define the rate of composite TFP growth as

$$\tilde{\pi}_j \equiv -(w\,\mathrm{d}\lambda_j + r\,\mathrm{d}\gamma_j)/p_j, \tag{18}$$

where $\tilde{\pi}$ is the corresponding row vector. This measure is analogous to the rate of (direct) TFP growth, shown in eq. (1), except that it reflects changes in total factor requirements instead of merely direct ones. In other words, the measure $\tilde{\pi}_j$ essentially shown the rate of technical progress that would occur in a composite sector j if all the sectors that contributed directly or indirectly to sector j's final output were fully integrated into that sector.[17]

We can now derive a relation between aggregate TFP growth, ρ, and sectoral rates of composite TFP growth, $\tilde{\pi}$. From (18) and (10) we obtain

$$\begin{aligned}\tilde{\pi} &= -[w\,\mathrm{d}[\ell(I-A)^{-1}] + r\,\mathrm{d}[\kappa(I-A)^{-1}]]\hat{p}^{-1}\\ &= -[(w\ell + r\kappa)\,\mathrm{d}[I-A)^{-1}] + (w\,\mathrm{d}\ell + r\,\mathrm{d}\kappa)(I-A)^{-1}]\hat{p}^{-1}\\ &= -[p(I-A)\,\mathrm{d}[(I-A)^{-1}] + (w\,\mathrm{d}\ell + r\,\mathrm{d}\kappa)(I-A)^{-1}]\hat{p}^{-1}.\end{aligned}$$

By the product rule,

[17]This notion is very similar to Pasinetti's (1977) concept of 'vertically integrated' sectors.

$$\mathrm{d}I = (I - A)\,\mathrm{d}[(I - A)^{-1}] + [\mathrm{d}(I - A)](I - A)^{-1},$$

so that

$$(I - A)\,\mathrm{d}[(I - A)^{-1}] = (\mathrm{d}A)(I - A)^{-1}.$$

Substituting, we obtain

$$\tilde{\pi} = -(p\,\mathrm{d}A + w\,\mathrm{d}\ell + r\,\mathrm{d}\kappa)(I - A)^{-1}\hat{p}^{-1}$$

$$= \pi S,$$

by (1). A comparison with (14) indicates that

$$\rho = \tilde{\pi}\beta. \tag{19}$$

In other words, each $\tilde{\pi}_i$ is a weighted average of the π_j, where the weights are determined by the dollar contribution of each sector j to a dollar of final output of sector i.

Eq. (19) leads to an alternative decomposition of aggregate productivity growth, given by

$$\mathrm{d}\rho = (\mathrm{d}\tilde{\pi})\beta + \tilde{\pi}\,\mathrm{d}\beta. \tag{20}$$

In this case there are two effects: the first from changes in composite sectoral TFP growth and the second, as before, from shifts in the composition of final output. This approach avoids the difficulty of (15), noted in section 3 above, that the technical change effect and interindustry structure effect are not independent, since they both depend on changes in the direct technical coefficients. However, eq. (20) still has the problem that changes in the composition of final output, $\mathrm{d}\beta$, reflect changes in relative prices and, therefore, from (10), changes in the technical coefficients.

We can overcome this latter difficulty by decomposing $\mathrm{d}\beta$ into a price effect and a 'real composition' effect. By definition

$$\beta = \hat{p}y/py$$

and, therefore,

$$\mathrm{d}\beta = \frac{\mathrm{d}(\hat{p}y)}{py} - \frac{\hat{p}y}{(py)^2}\,\mathrm{d}(py)$$

and

$$\mathrm{d}\beta = \left(\mathrm{d}\hat{p} - \frac{\hat{p}y}{py}\,\mathrm{d}p\right)\frac{y}{py} + \left(\hat{p} - \frac{\hat{p}y}{py}p\right)\frac{\mathrm{d}y}{py}.$$

Table 3

Decomposition of the change in overall TFP growth into three components: composite technical change, price, and real output shares effects.[a]

		Percentage contribution			
	Overall	(1) Composite technical change	(2) Price effect	(3) Total technical change	(4) Real output shares
Periods and measures	$\Delta \rho$	$[\Delta \tilde{\pi}]$	$[\Delta p]$	(1)+(2)	$[\Delta y]$
1947–1967/1967/1976					
1. Standard TFP model[b]	−0.0188	93.7	7.1	100.8	−0.8
2. Depreciation method[b]	−0.0211	78.5	16.2	94.7	5.3
3. Harrod–Peterson[b]	−0.0201	83.0	13.8	96.8	3.2

[a]Results are based on eq. (21).

The first term on the RHS of the last equation reflects only price changes and the second only changes in the real composition of final output. It is important to note that the first term reflects only *relative* price changes and the second only *compositional* changes in real output. This can be seen by respectively substituting cp for $\mathrm{d}p$ in the first term and cy for $\mathrm{d}y$ in the second, where c is a constant.[18]

From (20), we now obtain

$$\mathrm{d}\rho = (\mathrm{d}\tilde{\pi})\beta + \tilde{\pi}\left[\left(\mathrm{d}\hat{p} - \frac{\hat{p}y}{py}\mathrm{d}p\right)\frac{y}{py}\right] + \tilde{\pi}\left[\left(\hat{p} - \frac{\hat{p}y}{py}p\right)\frac{\mathrm{d}y}{py}\right]. \tag{21}$$

In (21), the change in overall TFP growth is separated into two exogenous effects. The first is from the change in technical coefficients, reflected in the composite technical change effect ($\mathrm{d}\tilde{\pi}$) and the price effect (from $\mathrm{d}p$), which together I will call the 'total technical changes effect' (I have kept them separate here for heuristic reasons). The second is the 'real composition' or 'real output share' effect (from $\mathrm{d}y$).

Table 3 shows the results of this decomposition for the 1947–1976 period.[19] In the standard TFP framework, 94% of the change in overall TFP growth between the 1947–1967 and 1967–1976 time periods was attributable to changes in the rate of composite TFP growth. Changes in relative prices, as reflected in the value composition of final output, explained another 7%, so that together they accounted fully for the slowdown of aggregate productivity growth. Indeed, the change in real output shares had a slightly negative effect, indicating that they shifted (slightly) toward sectors with

[18]I wish to thank Thijs ten Raa for this derivation, as well as the derivation of eq. (19).

[19]As before, I use average values for $\tilde{\pi}$, p^*, and y^* over the 1947–1967 and 1967–1976 sub-periods.

above-average rates of productivity growth. In the two non-standard frameworks, with capital treated as a produced means of production, the real output share effects were positive but remained small (at 5% and 3%). The price effects were relatively large (at 16% and 14%), indicating that the value composition effect (shown in table 2) is attributable almost entirely to changes in relative prices, rather than to shifts in real output composition. When the composite technical change and price effect are taken together, it now becomes clear that most of the slowdown in overall TFP growth over this period was due to changes in technical coefficients.

Aside from its use in decomposition analysis, the rate of composite technical change has the added advantage of avoiding the so-called 'contracting out' problem in productivity analysis. Certain activities that were once internal to a firm's operation may be subcontracted out after a certain point in time. Legal services are a case in point. During the early part of the postwar period, most corporate legal work was performed in-house. However, over the years, much of the work was shifted to law firms. Thus, instead of relying on in-house counsel, corporations contracted many of these legal services from other establishments – that is, directly from law firms. In I-O terms, legal services were shifted from a direct labor input to an intermediate purchase. This phenomenon also characterized many other business services, such as accounting and advertising. Whole divisions were eliminated as firms subcontracted out many of these services.[20]

In standard GPO-based productivity analysis, this type of change is very difficult to capture. Contracting out a relatively low productivity growth activity like legal services may show up as an acceleration of the industry's own productivity growth, even though there has been no change in the industry's technology (only the externalization of a formerly internal activity). However, in an I-O framework, this apparent inconsistency can be avoided by using measures of total factor requirements. This method generally produces consistent results, whether an establishment directly employs service employees or purchases their services from other sectors of the economy. Indeed, such a contracting-out phenomenon should, ceteris paribus, leave measures of *composite* technical change unaffected, since it represents only a substitution of indirect labor for direct labor.[21]

7. Secondary products

The I-O framework also allows one to explicitly model joint production. In particular, modern I-O tables provide both a 'use' and a 'make' matrix, the first of which shows the use of commodities by producing industry, and

[20] See, for example, Carter (1970) for a discussion of the growth of business services as an intermediate input.

[21] See Ten Raa and Wolff (1992) for more details.

the latter of which shows the quantities of each commodity made by each industry. As in most productivity data, industries are classified on the basis of the primary output of each establishment. Other products produced by an establishment are classified as 'secondary' outputs. In standard GPO-based productivity series, commodities are not separated and are collapsed into the primary output of the establishment. Output and input series are then built up on the basis of the primary output only. If there are significant differences in the productivity performance of primary and secondary outputs, then such standard productivity series can be biased.

In contrast, in an I-O framework, it is possible to explicitly model the technology of the secondary product. One can first define overall productivity growth for primary output as a weighted sum of the commodity-level productivity growth of primary output only. To do this, let the matrix V^{P} be the diagonal of the matrix V (primary products) and the matrix V^{S} be the off-diagonal elements (secondary products). Then, productivity growth of primary output is given by

$$\rho^{\mathrm{P}} = [\pi\hat{p}V^{\mathrm{P}}\mathbf{1}/pV^{\mathrm{P}}\mathbf{1}]\cdot(px/py), \tag{22}$$

where commodity rates of TFP growth are effectively weighted by the value share of primary output in the total value of primary output [and the last term is included as in (12)]. In analogous fashion, secondary product productivity growth is defined as

$$\rho^{\mathrm{S}} = \left[\sum_j \pi\hat{p}(V^{\mathrm{S}})^{\mathrm{T}}_{\cdot j}/p(V^{\mathrm{S}})^{\mathrm{T}}\mathbf{1}\right]\cdot(px/py), \tag{23}$$

where the weights are the value shares of secondary output in the total value of secondary output. Let $\omega^{\mathrm{P}} = pV^{\mathrm{P}}\mathbf{1}/px$, the value share of primary output in total output, and $\omega^{\mathrm{S}} = p(V^{\mathrm{S}})^{\mathrm{T}}\mathbf{1}/px = 1-\omega^{\mathrm{P}}$, the value share of secondary output in total output. Then

$$\rho = \omega^{\mathrm{P}}\rho^{\mathrm{P}} + \omega^{\mathrm{S}}\rho^{\mathrm{S}}. \tag{24}$$

Finally, the change in overall TFP growth can be decomposed into a primary product and secondary product effect, as follows:

$$\mathrm{d}\rho = \omega^{\mathrm{P}}\,\mathrm{d}\rho^{\mathrm{P}} + \omega^{\mathrm{S}}\,\mathrm{d}\rho^{\mathrm{S}} + \mathrm{d}\omega^{\mathrm{S}}(\rho^{\mathrm{S}} - \rho^{\mathrm{P}}), \tag{25}$$

where the first term shows the change in overall TFP growth attributable to the change in productivity growth among primary products, the second term the portion due to the change in productivity growth among secondary output, and the third term the portion due to the change of the share of secondary output in total output.

Table 4
Primary and secondary product TFP growth, 1967–1977, and their percentage contribution to the change in overall TFP growth[a]

	1967–1972 (% per year)	1972–1977 (% per year)	Change (% per year)	Percentage contribution
a. Primary product TFP	0.80	−0.17	−0.97	94.5
b. Secondary product TFP	−1.22	−2.75	−1.53	5.9
c. Change in secondary product weight (percentage points)	3.64	3.50	−0.15	−0.4
d. Overall TFP growth	0.73	−0.26	−0.99	100.0

[a]See eq. (25) for decomposition. The source is ten Raa and Wolf (1991, table 6).

As shown in table 4, TFP growth for primary output averaged 0.80% per year for the 1967–1972 periods and −0.17% per year for the 1972–1977 period, yielding a change of −0.97 percentage points. TFP growth for secondary production averaged −1.22% for the first period and −2.75% for the second, yielding a change of −1.53%. The most striking results is that productivity growth was considerably lower for secondary output than for primary output. Also, the decline in TFP growth was more severe for secondary output than for primary output. This suggests that standard GPO-based measures of TFP growth can be significantly biased for certain industries.

From eq. (25), the change in overall TFP growth is then decomposed into three effects. The first of these, from the change in primary product TFP growth, accounted for 94.5% of the change in overall TFP growth – a result largely due to the fact that primary output comprised over 96% of total output. The second, from the decline in secondary product TFP growth, explained 5.9%. The third effect, from the change in the relative level and composition of secondary output, was of almost no importance.

8. Concluding remarks

The I-O framework provides a number of powerful features for the measurement and analysis of productivity growth. First, TFP growth can be measured using gross output as the output measures and both primary factors and materials as inputs (avoiding many of the difficulties of GPO-based measures). Second, an I-O growth accounting framework can be developed to measure composition effects – that is, the effect of changes in the mix of final output on aggregate productivity growth. Third, capital can be incorporated into productivity analysis as a produced means of production, since capital, like intermediate inputs, is produced by one or more sectors of the economy. This approach has the advantage of embodying changes in the (primary) resource requirements of producing capital in the measurement of overall technical change.

Fourth, measures of composite technical change can be introduced to avoid difficulties in productivity measurement engendered by the substitution of externally provided inputs for services that were previously provided internally to the firm. This can be accomplished by the introduction of productivity measures that reflect changes in total (direct and indirect) factor requirements. Fifth, in an I-O system, secondary production can be explicitly modeled and its rate of technical change analytically separated from that of primary output.

References

Baumol, W.J. and E.N. Wolff, 1984, On interindustry differences in absolute productivity, Journal of Political Economy 92, no. 6, 1017–1134.

Bailey, M.N., 1982, The productivity growth slowdown by industry, Brookings Papers on Economic Activity 2, 423–454.

Blackorby, C. and W. Schworm, 1988, The existence of input and output aggregates in aggregate production functions, Econometrica 56, no. 3, 613–643.

Carter, A., 1970, Structural changes in the American economy (Harvard University Press, Cambridge, MA).

Dalgaard, E., 1988, Real value added, the double deflation method, and systems of national accounts, Mimeo.

Denison, E.F., 1979, Accounting for slower economic growth (Brookings Institution, Washington, DC).

Denison, E.F., 1984, Accounting for slower economic growth: An update, in: J.W. Kendrick, ed., International comparisons of productivity and causes of the slowdown (Ballinger, Cambridge, MA).

Jorgenson, D., F. Gollop and B. Fraumeni, 1987, Productivity and U.S. economic growth (Harvard University Press, Cambridge, MA).

Leontief, W., 1953, Studies in the structure of the American economy, 1919–1929 (Oxford University Press, New York).

Nordhaus, W.D., 1972, The recent productivity slowdown, Brookings Papers on Economic Activity 3, 493–536.

Norsworthy, J.R., J. Harper and K. Kunze, 1979, The slowdown in productivity growth: Analysis of some contributing factors, Brookings Papers on Economic Activity 2, 387–421.

Pasinetti, L.L., 1977, Lectures on the theory of production (Columbia University Press, New York).

Peterson, W., 1979, Toral factor productivity in the U.K.: A disaggregated analysis, in: K.D. Patterson and K. Schott, eds., The measurement of capital: Theory and practice (Macmillan Press, London).

Rymes, J.K., 1971, On concepts of capital and technical-change (Cambridge University Press, Cambridge).

Rymes, J.K., 1972, The measurement of capital and total factor productivity in the context of the Cambridge theory of capital, Review of Income and Wealth, Series 18, March.

ten Raa, T. and E.N. Wolff, 1991, Secondary products and the measurement of productivity growth, Regional Science and Urban Economics 21, no. 4, 581–615.

ten Raa, T. and E.N. Wolff, 1992, Productivity analysis when services are outsourced, Mimeo.

ten Raa, T., D. Chakraborty and J.A. Small, 1984, An alternative treatment of secondary products in input–output analysis, Review of Economics and Statistics 66, no. 1, 88–97.

Wolff, E.N., 1985, Industrial composition, interindustry effects, and the U.S. productivity slowdown, Review of Economics and Statistics 67, no. 2, 268–277.

Woodland, A.D., 1978, On testing weak separability, Journal of Econometrics 8, 383–398.

[4]

A neoclassical analysis of total factor productivity using input-output prices

Thijs ten Raa

1. Introduction

During one of our very last discussions Wassily Leontief asked me: "What are you doing these days?" I replied that I reconcile input-output analysis and neoclassical economics. He leant back, thought, looked me straight in the eyes, and said: "Should be easy."

Yet input-output analysis and neoclassical economics seem hard to mix. The resentment between the two schools of economics is a two-way affair. Neoclassical economists consider input-output analysis a futile exercise in central planning. The relationship between the delivery of a bill of final goods and its requirements in terms of gross output and factor inputs is considered mechanical, with little or no attention paid to the role of the price mechanism in the choice of techniques (Leontief, 1941). True, input-output analysis is used to relate prices to factor costs, but here too the analysis is considered mechanical as input-output coefficients are presumed to be fixed. To make things worse, the quantity and value analyses are perceived to be disjunct, with no interaction between supply and demand.

Conversely, input-output economists consider neoclassical economics a futile exercise in marginal analysis that fails to grasp the underlying structure of the economy. Firms supply up to the point that marginal revenue equals marginal cost and set the price accordingly. But does not marginal cost depend on all prices in the system, including the one of the product under consideration? And if the answer is yes, should not we take into account the interindustry relations, i.e. apply input-output analysis?

Many, including me, have been held captive by these perceptions. Yet they are misleading. Instead of criticizing the critiques – a meta-analysis that is doomed to have little input – I provide some shock therapy that turns the perceptions upside down by analyzing a concrete issue, namely productivity measurement. Why productivity? Well, the standard, neoclassical measure of productivity growth, the so-called "Solow residual" between output growth and input growth, employs market values of labor and capital to compute a weighted average of their input growth rates. Now, it can be shown that the Solow residual is equal to a weighted average of the growth rates of the real wage and the real rental rate of capital. (In other words, total factor productivity (TFP) growth is the sum of labor productivity growth and capital productivity growth.) By taking the wage rate and rental rate at market values in computing the Solow residual, neoclassical economists accept at face value what they are supposed to measure.

In this paper I adopt the methodological position of neoclassical economics, by which productivity is defined as the marginal contribution of factor inputs, but apply input-output analysis to determine its value. The analysis is framed in the orthodox general equilibrium model, which subsequently will be specified to accommodate growth accounting. I will recover the neoclassical formulas, such as the Solow residual, but the structure of the economy will be exploited to determine the values.

2. Earlier work

My first attempt to reconcile input-output and neoclassical economics is in the sequel papers ten Raa (1994) and ten Raa and Mohnen (1994). We maximized the value of final demand at world prices. Final demand for non-tradable commodities was simply fixed at the observed level. In short, we expanded final demand for tradable commodities, but not for non-tradable commodities. The model lacks a utility foundation. We rectified this in ten Raa (1995) and Mohnen et al. (1997), where we maximized the level of the entire domestic final demand vector, given its proportions. In ten Raa and Mohnen (2002) we investigated not only the frontier of the economy, but also the fluctuations of the observed economy about its frontier. All the aforementioned papers are about small, open economies with exogenous prices for the tradable commodities. The main contribution of this paper is that it lays out the theory for a closed economy. In other words, we make the step from partial to general equilibrium analysis.

Subsidiarily, I now present the theory from an orthodox mathematical economic perspective, say Debreu (1959). First and foremost, the two "practical" approaches of input-output analysis and growth accounting are clearly embedded in a unifying framework. Second, the general equilibrium framework endogenizes the value shares used in growth accounting exercises (such as Jorgenson and Griliches, 1967). Third, the exposition makes Debreu's framework accessible to applied economists.

3. Growth accounting

There are two sources of growth. The first is that economies produce more output simply because they use more input, such as labor. Of course, this is a mere size effect; there is no increase in the standard of living. The second source of growth is more interesting. Economies produce more output per unit of input because of technological progress. The classical exposition of these two sources of growth is Solow (1957). He demonstrates that the residual between output and input growth measures the second source of growth; that is, the shift of the production possibility frontier. In his analysis Solow makes two assumptions. First, the production function is macroeconomic, hence transforming labor and capital into a single output. Second, the economy must be perfectly competitive, so that factor inputs are priced according to their marginal productivities. By the first assumption, the output has a well-defined growth rate. The input growth rate, however, must be some weighted average of the labor growth and capital growth rates; the appropriate weights are shown to be the value shares of labor and capital in national income. The two assumptions are quite restrictive. The use of a single output requires aggregation of commodities and makes it difficult to compare sectors in terms of productivity performance. The notion of perfect competition is a far cry from most observed economies.

I will show how growth accounting can be freed from these assumptions. Basically, I will work in a multidimensional commodity model and calculate productivities without using observed value shares. The analysis is self-contained and serves as a nice refresher of mathematical economics. The main concepts of this branch of economics are equilibrium, efficiency, and the welfare theorems that interrelate equilibrium and efficiency. I will review all this in the next section. To make the theory operational I will then consider the linear case of the model, with constant returns to scale and non-substitutability in both production and household consumption. Efficiency is then the outcome of a linear program, and the Lagrange multipliers of the factor input constraints measure their productivities. Summing over endowments I obtain total factor productivities. The analysis is shown to be consistent with the aforementioned Solow residual. Moreover, input-output analysis will enable us to reduce TFP growth rates to sectoral productivity, and thus to pinpoint the strong and the weak sectors.

4. Equilibrium and efficiency

Denote the number of commodities in an economy by integer n. The commodity space is the n-dimensional Euclidian space, $\mathbb{R}^n$. A commodity bundle is a point in this space, say $\mathbf{y} \in \mathbb{R}^n$. Negative components represent inputs and positive components outputs. For example, in a Robinson Crusoe economy, where (labor) time is transformed into food, $(-1, 1)'$ is the bundle representing one hour of work and an ounce of food. A prime is used to indicate transposition. Denote the collection of all technically feasible commodity bundles by Y. Y is a subset of $\mathbb{R}^n$. It represents the production possibilities of the economy. I make two assumptions on Y. First, Y is convex. This means that, if $\mathbf{y}$ and $\mathbf{z}$ belong to Y, then so does $\lambda\mathbf{y} + (1 - \lambda)\mathbf{z}$ for any λ between 0 and 1. Although the assumption is always made in general equilibrium analysis, it is not innocent; it rules out increasing returns to scale. Second, Y is compact. In the context of our Euclidian commodity space this means that Y is bounded and closed. In the literature this assumption – namely the boundedness – is relaxed, but at the expense of uninteresting complications.

In a perfectly competitive economy producers pick the production plan that maximizes profit given the prices. Denote the commodity prices by vector $\mathbf{p}$ and let a prime denote transposition. The profit of any production plan $\mathbf{y}$ is then given by $\mathbf{p}'\mathbf{y}$ since inputs have negative signs in $\mathbf{y}$. $\mathbf{p}'\mathbf{y}$ is the inner product of $\mathbf{p}$ and $\mathbf{y}$: $\Sigma_{i=1}^n p_i y_i$. Here the positive terms represent revenue and the negative terms cost. Now maximize $\mathbf{p}'\mathbf{y}$ by choosing $\mathbf{y}$. The solution will depend on $\mathbf{p}$ and, therefore, is denoted $\mathbf{y}(\mathbf{p})$. Formally,

$$\mathbf{y}(\mathbf{p}) = \underset{\mathbf{y} \in Y}{\operatorname{argmax}}\ \mathbf{p}'\mathbf{y}$$

Given $\mathbf{p}$, producers "supply" $\mathbf{y}(\mathbf{p})$. Strictly speaking, only the positive components represent supply, while the negative components represent business demand, as for labor. I define "supply" as the mapping $\mathbf{y}(\bullet)$. This constitutes one side of equilibrium analysis.

Turn to consumers. For simplicity I assume there is only one utility function, u, so consumers have the same preferences. For a commodity bundle $\mathbf{y}$, the real number $u(\mathbf{y})$ represents the utility it yields to the consumers. Utility is essentially ordinal. Comparing commodity bundles $\mathbf{y}$ and $\mathbf{z}$, what matters is if $u(\mathbf{y}) > u(\mathbf{z})$, $u(\mathbf{y}) < u(\mathbf{z})$, or $u(\mathbf{y}) = u(\mathbf{z})$, but the absolute difference between the utility levels is immaterial. In fact, the entire analysis will be unaffected by a monotonic transformation of the utility function. I make three assumptions on u. First, u is continuous. This is an innocent, technical assumption, that can be shown to be implied by the other assumptions, using a monotonic transformation. The second assumption is that u is increasing. This means that more is preferred. Third, u is quasi-concave. This is defined by the condition that the preferred set, $\{\mathbf{y} \mid u(\mathbf{y}) \geq \text{constant}\}$, is convex. It means that consumers prefer convex combinations.

In a perfectly competitive economy consumers pick the commodity bundle that maximizes utility, subject to the budget constraint and given the prices. What is the budget constraint? For the moment ignore dividends, so that all income stems from labor. In the framework of Robinson Crusoe's economy, the question is when $\mathbf{y} = (-h, f)'$ is financially feasible. (Here h is hours worked and f is amount of food.) If p_2 is the price of the good and p_1 the price of labor time, then the answer is $p_2 f \leq p_1 h$, which can be written succinctly as $\mathbf{p}'\mathbf{y} \leq 0$. The budget constraint is basically zero, because the commodity bundle has a negative component that generates (labor) income. In a private enterprise economy, profit, $\mathbf{p}'\mathbf{y}(\mathbf{p})$, supplements the budget constraint and consumers solve the following optimization problem

$$\max_{\mathbf{y}} u(\mathbf{y}) \text{ subject to } \mathbf{p}'\mathbf{y} \leq \mathbf{p}'\mathbf{y}(\mathbf{p})$$

The commodity bundle that comes out of this is what consumers "demand." (The positive components represent demand, the negative components household supply, as of labor.) I define "demand" as the mapping from prices $\mathbf{p}$ to the commodity bundle that solves the consumers' problem.

Now we have all the building blocks and can proceed to define the main concepts of mathematical economics, namely equilibrium and efficiency. Conceptually, they are very different. Equilibrium requires a price system; it is defined by the equality between demand and supply. Since the latter are both mappings from prices to commodity bundles, "equilibrium" is defined formally as a price vector, $\mathbf{p}^*$, such that supply and demand assume a common value. Equilibrium is a positive concept, to describe what actually happens in market economies, without saying it is good or bad. Statements on the performance of an economy, however, are normative and require no price mechanism. Suppose we want to compare a centrally planned economy to a decentralized market economy. The centrally planned economy may have no price system at all. Still, we want to evaluate which one performs better. This is a matter of utility. We say one economy is better than another if it attains a higher utility level for the consumers. An economy is efficient if it obtains the maximum utility level that is technologically feasible. Since utility is defined on commodity bundles, "efficiency" is defined formally by a commodity bundle, $\mathbf{y}^*$, such that utility is maximized over Y

$$\mathbf{y}^* = \underset{\mathbf{y} \in Y}{\operatorname{argmax}}\, u(\mathbf{y})$$

Notice the conceptual difference between equilibrium and efficiency. The former is given by a price vector, the latter by a commodity bundle. An equilibrium equates supply and demand, but makes no statement on the level of utility. Efficiency promotes utility, but requires no price system.

Although the concepts are very different, there is a deep, close relationship for perfectly competitive economies. By definition, an economy is perfectly competitive if no producer or consumer can manipulate the prices, but considers them as given. It can be claimed that the commodity bundle generated by the equilibrium price vector is efficient. In short, an equilibrium is efficient. This statement is called the "first welfare theorem". I also claim that an efficient commodity bundle can be generated by an equilibrium price vector. In short, an efficient allocation is an equilibrium. This statement is called the "second welfare theorem". The two welfare theorems are deep and must be proved.

The proof of the first welfare theorem is relatively easy. We must show that an equilibrium, say $\mathbf{p}^*$, generates an efficient allocation, $\mathbf{y}(\mathbf{p}^*)$. The proof is by contradiction. Suppose $\mathbf{y}(\mathbf{p}^*)$ is not efficient. By definition of efficiency there exists $\mathbf{y} \in Y$ such that $u(\mathbf{y}) > u(\mathbf{y}(\mathbf{p}^*))$. By definition of demand it must be that $\mathbf{y}$ is too expensive: $\mathbf{p}^{*\prime}\mathbf{y} > \mathbf{p}^{*\prime}\mathbf{y}(\mathbf{p}^*)$. By definition of supply it must be that $\mathbf{y}$ is not feasible: $\mathbf{y} \notin Y$. This contradicts the definition of $\mathbf{y}$. The supposition that $\mathbf{y}(\mathbf{p}^*)$ is not efficient is therefore not tenable. This completes the proof that an equilibrium is efficient.

The proof of the second welfare theorem proceeds as follows. Let $\mathbf{y}^*$ be efficient, hence maximize $u(\mathbf{y})$ over Y. Then we must construct an equilibrium price system that generates it. Consider the feasible set, Y, and the preferred set, $\{\mathbf{y} \in \mathbb{R}^n \mid u(\mathbf{y}) > u(\mathbf{y}^*)\}$. By efficiency of $\mathbf{y}^*$, the sets do not intersect. By assumptions on production and utility, the two sets are convex. Now we invoke Minkowski's separating hyperplane theorem, by which two convex sets that do not intersect can be separated by a hyperplane. (See, for example, Rockafellar, 1970.) Hence there exists a row vector, say $\mathbf{p}^*$, such that

$$\mathbf{p}^{*\prime}\mathbf{y}_1 > \mathbf{p}^{*\prime}\mathbf{y}_2$$

holds for all $\mathbf{y}_1 \in \{\mathbf{y} \in \mathbb{R}^n \mid u(\mathbf{y}) > u(\mathbf{y}^*)\}$ and $\mathbf{y}_2 \in Y$. I claim $\mathbf{p}^*$ is an equilibrium. For this we must show that, given $\mathbf{p}^*$, $\mathbf{y}^*$ is supplied and demanded. First consider supply. Since utility is increasing, the above inequality yields for any $\boldsymbol{\varepsilon} > \mathbf{0}$ (in $\mathbb{R}^n$)

$$\mathbf{p}^{*\prime}(\mathbf{y}^* + \boldsymbol{\varepsilon}) > \mathbf{p}^{*\prime}\mathbf{y},\ \mathbf{y} \in Y$$

Hence $\mathbf{p}^{*\prime}\mathbf{y}^* \geq \mathbf{p}^{*\prime}\mathbf{y}$, hence $\mathbf{y}^*$ maximizes profit and, therefore, is supplied: $\mathbf{y}^* = \mathbf{y}(\mathbf{p}^*)$. Next consider demand. If $\mathbf{y}$ is superior to $\mathbf{y}^*$, $u(\mathbf{y}) > u(\mathbf{y}^*)$, then it is out of the budget, $\mathbf{p}^{*\prime}\mathbf{y} > \mathbf{p}^{*\prime}\mathbf{y}^* = \mathbf{p}^{*\prime}\mathbf{y}(\mathbf{p}^*)$. Hence $\mathbf{y}^*$ maximizes utility subject to the budget constraint and, therefore, is demanded. This completes the proof that an efficient allocation is an equilibrium.

So far, I have remained silent about existence. Does an equilibrium exist? The usual analysis to find an intersection point of supply and demand is by means of a so-called "fixed point theorem". This is difficult. We take a short cut. It is easy to see that an efficient allocation exists. All we have to do is maximize utility, u, over the feasible set, Y. Since u is continuous and Y is compact, a maximum exists, say $\mathbf{y}^*$. By the second welfare theorem it is an equilibrium, say $\mathbf{p}^*$. Hence an equilibrium exists.

In the literature all sorts of variations on the above analysis are found. More commodities, more products, more consumers – you name it. The basic structure, however, remains the same. Equilibrium is defined by the equality of supply and demand, efficiency by the impossibility of raising the utility level further, and the two are related by the first and second welfare theorems, provided convexity assumptions hold and agents are price takers. Then competitive prices can be analyzed by studying the efficiency problem, where utility is maximized over the feasible set. For example, the well-known statement that competitive economies reward factor inputs according to their productivities can be demonstrated. This will be done in the next section for linear economies.

5. Efficiency and productivity

The model of the last section is quite general, at least in terms of functional forms. I now add the flesh and blood of linear economics, including input-output analysis. Let there be m activities. Denote an $m \times n$-dimensional matrix of outputs by $\mathbf{V}$ and an $n \times m$-dimensional matrix of inputs by $\mathbf{U}$. Add an m-dimensional vector of capital inputs, $\mathbf{k} \geq \mathbf{0}$, and similarly for labor, $\mathbf{l} \geq \mathbf{0}$. Let the economy be endowed with a capital stock k and labor force l. Assume every activity i requires positive factor input (k_i and l_i not both zero). Let

$$Y = \{\mathbf{y} \in \mathbb{R}^n \mid \mathbf{y} \leq (\mathbf{V}' - \mathbf{U})\mathbf{s}, \mathbf{k}'\mathbf{s} \leq k, \mathbf{l}'\mathbf{s} \leq l, \mathbf{s} \geq \mathbf{0}\}$$

where $\mathbf{s} \in \mathbb{R}^m$ is the vector listing m activity levels. Then Y is an example of a production possibility set as we defined it in section 3. Y is the intersection of a number of half-spaces, which is obviously convex. The assumption that every activity requires factor input ensures that Y is compact.

The modeling of household consumption is similar. Denote an n-dimensional vector of consumption coefficients by $\mathbf{a} > \mathbf{0}$. Then, for $\mathbf{y} \geq \mathbf{0}$,

$$u(\mathbf{y}) = \min y_i / a_i$$

is the Leontief utility function. (I choose this utility function because it enables us to substitute observed consumption values in the TFP growth expression of the next section.) Basically, consumers want their bundle in the proportions of **a**, say $c\mathbf{a}$, where c is a scalar. It is easy to see that

$$u(\mathbf{y}) = \max_{c\mathbf{a}\leq\mathbf{y}} c$$

Proof. First we prove $u(\mathbf{y}) \geq \max_{c\mathbf{a}\leq\mathbf{y}} c$. For all $\mathbf{y} \geq c\mathbf{a}$, $u(\mathbf{y}) \geq u(c\mathbf{a}) = c$. Hence also $u(\mathbf{y}) \geq \max_{c\mathbf{a}\leq\mathbf{y}} c$. Next we prove the converse. At least one constraint in $\max_{c\mathbf{a}\leq\mathbf{y}} c$ is binding: $a_j c^* = y_j$ for some j, where c^* is the constrained maximum. Now $u(\mathbf{y}) = \min y_i/a_i \leq y_j/a_j = c^* = \max_{c\mathbf{a}\leq\mathbf{y}} c$. This completes the proof.

We have production and utility, so we can set up the efficiency problem,

$$\max_{\mathbf{y}\in Y} u(\mathbf{y})$$

Using the alternative formulation of the utility function, we can rewrite the efficiency problem as

$$\max_{\mathbf{s},\mathbf{y},c} c \text{ subject to } c\mathbf{a} \leq \mathbf{y} \text{ and } \mathbf{y} \in Y.$$

Notice that both the objective and the constraints are linear in the variables. The efficiency problem of a linear economy is a linear program. The linear program can be simplified slightly by eliminating one of the variables, **y**

$$\max_{\mathbf{s},c} c \text{ subject to } c\mathbf{a} \leq (\mathbf{V}' - \mathbf{U})\mathbf{s}, \mathbf{k}'\mathbf{s} \leq k, \mathbf{1}'\mathbf{s} \leq l, \mathbf{s} \geq \mathbf{0}$$

This linear program maximizes the level of final consumption subject to the material balance, the capital and labor constraints, and a nonnegativity constraint. Another, succinct formulation of the linear program is

$$\max(\mathbf{0}'\ 1)\begin{pmatrix}\mathbf{s}\\ c\end{pmatrix} \text{ subject to } \begin{bmatrix}\mathbf{U}-\mathbf{V}' & \mathbf{a}\\ \mathbf{k}' & 0\\ \mathbf{1}' & 0\\ -\mathbf{I} & 0\end{bmatrix}\begin{bmatrix}\mathbf{s}\\ c\end{bmatrix} \leq \begin{bmatrix}\mathbf{0}\\ k\\ l\\ \mathbf{0}\end{bmatrix}$$

In general, when we $\max f(\mathbf{x})$ subject to $g(\mathbf{x}) \leq b$, the first-order conditions are $\mathbf{f}' = \lambda\mathbf{g}'$, $\lambda \geq 0$. Here $\mathbf{f}'$ is the (row) vector of partial derivatives $\partial f/\partial x_i$ of f. If g is scalar valued, $\mathbf{g}'$ is also the row vector of partial derivatives $\partial g/\partial x_i$. If the constraints are given by $G(\mathbf{x}) \leq \mathbf{b}$, with G vector valued,

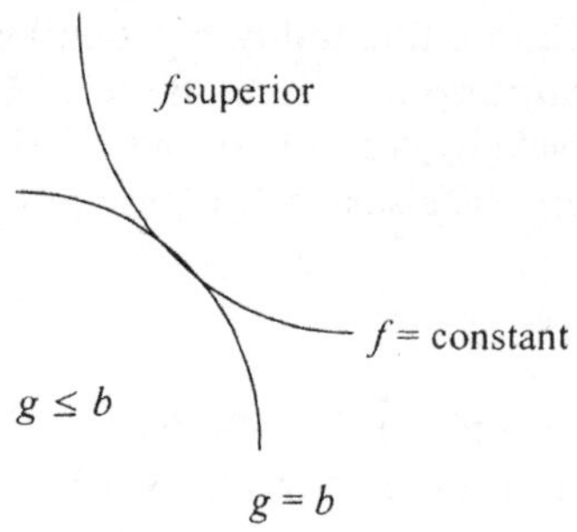

Figure 10.1 Isoquants of the objective and constraint functions

the first-order conditions are $\mathbf{f}' = \boldsymbol{\lambda}'\mathbf{G}$, $\boldsymbol{\lambda} \geq \mathbf{0}$, where $\mathbf{G}$ is the Jacobian matrix of partial derivatives (i.e. element g_{ij} of matrix $\mathbf{G} = \partial g_i(\mathbf{x})/\partial x_j$).

The first-order conditions reflect the tangency of the isoquants to the objective and constraint functions. In figure 10.1 f and g grow in the same direction (the north-east), hence $\lambda \geq 0$. If λ were negative, then f and g would grow in opposite directions and one could simply increase f by wandering into the feasible region (g would be reduced). λ is called the Lagrange multiplier. Because $\mathbf{f}' = \lambda\mathbf{g}'$, and $g(\mathbf{x}) \leq b$, λ measures the rate of change of the objective function with respect to the constraint. If b is relaxed by one unit, then f goes up by λ units. If G is vector valued, then each constraint has a Lagrange multiplier and $\boldsymbol{\lambda}$ is a vector of Lagrange multipliers.

In our linear program, $f\binom{\mathbf{s}}{c} = (\mathbf{0}'\ 1)\binom{\mathbf{s}}{c}$ and $\mathbf{f}' = (\mathbf{0}'\ 1)$. Also,

$$G\begin{pmatrix}\mathbf{s}\\ c\end{pmatrix} = \begin{bmatrix}\mathbf{U}-\mathbf{V}' & \mathbf{a}\\ \mathbf{k}' & 0\\ \mathbf{l}' & 0\\ -\mathbf{I} & \mathbf{0}\end{bmatrix}\begin{pmatrix}\mathbf{s}\\ c\end{pmatrix} \quad \text{and} \quad \mathbf{G} = \begin{bmatrix}\mathbf{U}-\mathbf{V}' & \mathbf{a}\\ \mathbf{k}' & 0\\ \mathbf{l}' & 0\\ -\mathbf{I} & \mathbf{0}\end{bmatrix}$$

The constraints are the material balance, the capital constraint, the labor constraint, and the non-negativity constraint. It is customary to denote the Lagrange multipliers by $\mathbf{p}$, r, w and $\boldsymbol{\sigma}$ respectively. The first-order conditions, $\mathbf{f}' = \boldsymbol{\lambda}'\mathbf{G}$, $\boldsymbol{\lambda} \geq \mathbf{0}$, read

$$(\mathbf{0}'\ 1) = (\mathbf{p}', r, w, \boldsymbol{\sigma}')\begin{bmatrix}\mathbf{U}-\mathbf{V}' & \mathbf{a}\\ \mathbf{k}' & 0\\ \mathbf{l}' & 0\\ -\mathbf{I} & \mathbf{0}\end{bmatrix}, \quad (\mathbf{p}', r, w, \boldsymbol{\sigma}') \geq \mathbf{0}'$$

The second component, $\mathbf{p}'\mathbf{a} = 1$, is a price normalization condition. The first component, $\mathbf{0}' = \mathbf{p}'(\mathbf{U} - \mathbf{V}') + r\mathbf{k}' + w\mathbf{l}' - \boldsymbol{\sigma}'$, can be rewritten as $\mathbf{p}'(\mathbf{V}' - \mathbf{U}) = r\mathbf{k}' + w\mathbf{l}' - \boldsymbol{\sigma}'$, $\boldsymbol{\sigma} \geq \mathbf{0}$, or

$$\mathbf{p}'(\mathbf{V}' - \mathbf{U}) \leq r\mathbf{k}' + w\mathbf{l}'$$

On the left-hand side we find value added and on the right-hand side factor costs for the respective activities.

$\mathbf{p}$, r and w are the perfectly competitive equilibrium prices. I am going to demonstrate this by means of the so-called "phenomenon of complementary slackness". Let me explain this phenomenon in terms of $\max f(\mathbf{x})$ subject to $G(\mathbf{x}) \leq \mathbf{b}$. The first-order conditions are $\mathbf{f}' = \boldsymbol{\lambda}'\mathbf{G}$, $\boldsymbol{\lambda} \geq \mathbf{0}$. The phenomenon says that, if a constraint is non-binding, $g_i(\mathbf{x}) < b_i$, then the Lagrange multiplier is zero, $\lambda_i = 0$. Hence g_i plays no role in the first-order condition. The phenomenon also says that, if a Lagrange multiplier is strictly positive, $\lambda_i > 0$, then the constraint is binding, $g_i(\mathbf{x}) = b_i$. A nice way to write the phenomenon of complementary slackness is

$$\boldsymbol{\lambda}'[G(\mathbf{x}) - \mathbf{b}] = 0$$

The left-hand side is the inner product of two non-negative vectors. It is zero if – and only if – each term of the inner product is zero: $\lambda_i[g_i(\mathbf{x}) - b_i] = 0$. This, indeed, is a short way of writing $g_i(\mathbf{x}) < b_i \Rightarrow \lambda_i = 0$ and $\lambda_i > 0 \Rightarrow g_i(\mathbf{x}) = b_i$.

Now I explain why the Lagrange multipliers are competitive prices. Suppose that, for some activity, value added is strictly less than factor costs. Then $\sigma_i > 0$. By the phenomenon of complementary slackness, $s_i = 0$. Hence the price system is such that negative profits signal activities that are inactive in the coefficient allocation. If the economy had this price system and producers were profit maximizers, they would undertake precisely those activities that we want them to do. Notice that profits would be zero. The unprofitable activities are inactive, and value added is everywhere less than or equal to factor costs.

There is another interesting consequence of the phenomenon of complementary slackness, namely the identity between national product and national income. If G is linear, $G(\mathbf{x}) = \mathbf{Gx}$ and the last equation becomes

$$\boldsymbol{\lambda}'\mathbf{Gx} = \boldsymbol{\lambda}'\mathbf{b}$$

By the first-order condition $\mathbf{f}' = \boldsymbol{\lambda}'\mathbf{G}$,

$$\mathbf{f}'\mathbf{x} = \boldsymbol{\lambda}'\mathbf{b}$$

If f is also linear, this reads

$$f(\mathbf{x}) = \boldsymbol{\lambda}'\mathbf{b}$$

In our linear program,

$$(0' \ 1)\begin{pmatrix} \mathbf{s} \\ c \end{pmatrix} = (\mathbf{p}', r, w, \boldsymbol{\sigma}')\begin{bmatrix} 0 \\ k \\ l \\ 0 \end{bmatrix}$$

or

$$c = rk + wl$$

This is the famous macroeconomic identity of the national product and national income. It confirms that Lagrange multipliers measure the rate of change of the objective function (consumption level c) with respect to the constraints (capital k and labor l). If the stock of capital is increased by a unit, then the contribution to the objective is r. Hence r measures the productivity of capital. Similarly, w measures the productivity of labor. r and w need not be the observed prices of capital and labor, but are the Lagrange multipliers of the efficiency program, also called shadow prices. For perfectly competitive economies, however, there is agreement.

6. Total factor productivity

Capital productivity is r and labor productivity is w, where r and w are the shadow prices of the linear program that maximizes consumption, subject to the material balance, the capital constraint, the labor constraint and the non-negativity constraint. Now let time elapse. Everything changes; not only the output levels, but also the technical coefficients and the consumption coefficients. The linear program changes; r and w change. Hence there is capital productivity growth, $\dot{r} = dr/dt$, and labor productivity growth, $\dot{w} = dw/dt$. All this is per unit of capital or labor. Total capital productivity growth is $\dot{r}k$ and total labor productivity growth is $\dot{w}l$. Adding and normalizing by the level, we obtain the nominal total factor productivity growth rate, $(\dot{r}k + \dot{w}l)/(rk + wl)$. To obtain it in real terms we must subtract the price increase of the consumption bundle, $p_{j(i)} - \mathbf{p}'\dot{\mathbf{a}}$. The real "total factor productivity growth rate" is

$$TFP = (\dot{r}k + \dot{w}l)/(rk + wl)$$

Here k and l are the factor constraints, and r and w their Lagrange multipliers. Although this productivity growth concept is grounded in the theory of mathematical programming (where Lagrange multipliers measure productivities of constraints), there is perfect consistency with the traditional Solow residual. By total differentiation of the macroeconomic identity of the national product and national income, $\dot{r}k + \dot{w}l = \dot{c} - r\dot{k} - w\dot{l}$, and dividing through by the identity itself we obtain

$$TFP = \dot{c}/c - r\dot{k}/p_{j(i)} - \mathbf{p}'\dot{\mathbf{a}}/(rk + wl) - w\dot{l}/(rk + wl)$$

If we use shorthand $\hat{c} = \dot{c}/c$ for a relative growth rate, we obtain

$$TFP = \hat{c} - \alpha_k\hat{k} - \alpha_l\hat{l}/p_{j(i)} - \mathbf{p}'\dot{\mathbf{a}}$$

where $\alpha_k = rk/(rk + wl)$, the competitive value share of capital, and $\alpha_l = wl/(rk + wl)$, the competitive value share of labor. The right-hand side of the last equation is precisely the Solow residual. Notice, however, that the competitive value shares are not necessarily the observed ones. For non-competitive economies, they must be calculated by means of the linear program of section 4; for an application see ten Raa and Mohnen (2002).

7. Input-output analysis of total factor productivity

By definition, positive TFP growth means that output grows at a faster rate than input and, therefore, that the output/input ratio or standard of living goes up. In this section I will explain the phenomenon in terms of technical change at the sectoral level.

The linear program selects activities to produce the required net output of the economy. In continuous time we may consider infinitesimal changes, and the pattern of activities that are actually used is locally constant (except in degenerate points where the linear program has multiple solutions). In this section we ignore the activities that are not used. Hence, activity vector $\mathbf{s}$ is and remains positive.

From the last section, recall that the numerator of the Solow residual is $\dot{c}/p_{j(i)} - \mathbf{p}'\dot{\mathbf{a}}c - r\dot{k} - w\dot{l}$. We are going to express c, k and l in terms of $\mathbf{s}$. By complementary slackness between $c\mathbf{a} \leq (\mathbf{V}' - \mathbf{U})\mathbf{s}$ and $\mathbf{p} \geq \mathbf{0}$ we have $c\mathbf{p}'\mathbf{a} = \mathbf{p}'(\mathbf{V}' - \mathbf{U})\mathbf{s}$, or, using the price normalization condition,

$$c = \mathbf{p}'(\mathbf{V}' - \mathbf{U})\mathbf{s}$$

Assume that capital and labor have positive productivity. Then, also by complementary slackness,

$$k = \mathbf{k}'\mathbf{s}, \quad l = \mathbf{l}'\mathbf{s}$$

Substitute in $\dot{c} - r\dot{k} - w\dot{l}$, and use $[x]^*$ for the rate of change $\dot{x}$ if x is the product of variables, then we obtain

$$\{[\mathbf{p}'(\mathbf{V}' - \mathbf{U})]^* - r\dot{\mathbf{k}}' - w\dot{\mathbf{l}}'\}\mathbf{s}/p_{j(i)} - \mathbf{p}'\dot{\mathbf{a}}c\,[\mathbf{p}'(\mathbf{V}' - \mathbf{U}) - r\mathbf{k}' - w\mathbf{l}']\dot{\mathbf{s}}$$

Since $\mathbf{s}$ remains positive, by complementary slackness, $\mathbf{p}'(\mathbf{V}' - \mathbf{U}) = r\mathbf{k}' - w\mathbf{l}'$, and the second term vanishes. It is customary to define TFP growth of sector i as output growth minus input growth, normalized by output

$$TFP_i = \frac{[\mathbf{p}'(\mathbf{V}' - \mathbf{U})]_i^* - r\dot{k}_i - w\dot{l}_i}{(\mathbf{p}'\mathbf{V}')_i}$$

It then follows that

$$\begin{aligned} TFP &= \sum_i (\mathbf{p}'\mathbf{V}')_i TFP_i s_i / [c + \dot{\mathbf{p}}'(\mathbf{V}' - \mathbf{U})\mathbf{s}/p_{j(i)} - \mathbf{p}'\dot{\mathbf{a}}c]/c \\ &= \sum_i d_i TFP_i \end{aligned}$$

where $d_i = (\mathbf{p}'\mathbf{V}')_i s_i / \mathbf{p}'(\mathbf{V}' - \mathbf{U})\mathbf{s}$. These weights are called Domar weights and sum to the gross/net output ratio of the economy, which is greater than one. The last step assumes that the material balance is binding.

To see the reduction of TFP growth as the reduction of input-output coefficients in the traditional sense, consider the case where sectors produce single outputs. Then

$$TFP_i = \left(p_i \dot{v}_{ij(i)} - \sum_j p_j \dot{u}_{ji} - r\dot{k}_i - w\dot{l}_i \right) \Big/ \left(p_i v_{j(i)} \right)$$

In this case input coefficients are defined by $a_{ji} = u_{ji}/v_{ij(i)}$, $\kappa_i = k_i/v_{ij(i)}$ and $\mu_i = l_i/v_{ij(i)}$. Substitution yields

$$\begin{aligned} TFP_i = \Bigg(& p_i \dot{v}_{ij(i)} - \sum_j p_j \left[a_{ji} v_{ij(i)} \right]^{\cdot} \\ & - r\left[\kappa_i v_{ij(i)} \right]^{\cdot} - w\left[\mu_i v_{ij(i)} \right]^{\cdot} \Bigg) \Big/ \left(p_{j(i)} v_{ij(i)} \right) \end{aligned}$$

By complementary slackness, $p_i v_{ij(i)} = \sum_j p_j a_{ji} v_{ij(i)} - r\kappa_i v_{ij(i)} - w\mu_i v_{ij(i)}$ and we obtain

$$TFP_i = \left(-\sum_j p_j \dot{a}_{ji} - r\dot{\kappa}_i - w\dot{\mu}_i \right) \Big/ p_{j(i)}$$

that is, sectoral cost reductions. With obvious matrix notation,

$$TFP = -\sum_i d_i (\mathbf{p}'\dot{\mathbf{a}}_i - r\dot{\boldsymbol{\kappa}} - w\dot{\boldsymbol{\mu}})$$

is reduced to a reduction in input-output coefficients. If there is only one sector producing each commodity, then $j(i) = i$. If sectors produce multiple outputs, then the result basically holds, but input-output coefficients are no longer obtained by simple scalar divisions.

8. Conclusion

For perfectly competitive economies there is an intimate relationship between efficiency and equilibrium. The marginal productivities of capital and labor that are the Lagrange multipliers to the efficiency program coincide with perfectly competitive equilibrium prices. For such economies one can measure TFP growth by means of the Solow residual, using the observed value share of the factor inputs. Most economies, however, are not perfectly competitive. Then, to measure productivities, one must find the shadow prices of the factor inputs by solving a linear program. In this paper I have proposed the linear program that maximizes Leontief utility subject to resource constraints. We have thus obtained a Solow residual measure for TFP without assuming that the economy is on its frontier. The flip side of the coin is that the numerical values we use in the residual reflect shadow prices instead of observed prices. The data required for the determination of TFP are input-output coefficients and constraints on capital and labor. These data capture the structure of the economy and are real rather than nominal. Our measure of TFP growth, firmly grounded in the theory of mathematical programming, admits a decomposition in sectoral contributions, allowing us to pinpoint the strong and the weak sectors of the economy.

We have freed neoclassical growth accounting from its use of market values of factor inputs in the evaluation of the Solow residual and, therefore, some circularity in its methodology. Perhaps surprisingly, we accomplished this by using input-output analysis to determine the values of factor inputs. Input-output analysis and neoclassical economics can be used fruitfully to fill gaps in each other. Contrary to perception, the gap in input-output analysis is not the interaction between prices and quantities but the concept of marginal productivity, and the gap in neoclassical economics is not the structure of the economy but the determination of value shares of factor inputs.

REFERENCES

Debreu, G. (1959) *Theory of Value* (New Haven, CT, Yale University Press).
Jorgenson, D., and Z. Griliches (1967) The explanation of productivity change, *Review of Economic Studies*, 34, 308–350.

Leontief, W. W. (1941) *The Structure of American Economy, 1919–1929* (Cambridge, MA, Harvard University Press).

Mohnen, P., T. ten Raa and G. Bourque (1997) Mesures de la croissance de la productivité dans un cadre d'équilibre général: l'économie du Québec entre 1978 et 1984, *Canadian Journal of Economics*, 30, 295–307.

ten Raa, T. (1994) On the methodology of input-output analysis, *Regional Science and Urban Economics*, 24, 3–25.

(1995) *Linear Analysis of Competitive Economies* (New York, Harvester Wheatsheaf).

ten Raa, T., and P. Mohnen (1994) Neoclassical input-output analysis, *Regional Science and Urban Economics*, 24, 135–158.

(2002) Neoclassical growth accounting and frontier analysis: a synthesis, *Journal of Productivity Analysis*, 18, 111–128.

Rockafellar, R. T. (1970) *Convex Analysis* (Princeton, NJ, Princeton University Press).

Solow, R. M. (1957) Technical change and the aggregate production function, *Review of Economics and Statistics*, 39, 312–320.

PART II

INTERNATIONAL TRADE AND PRODUCTIVITY GROWTH

[5]

Productivity Growth and Capital Intensity on the Sector and Industry Level: Specialisation among OECD Countries, 1970–1988

Edward N. Wolff

In a recently completed book, *Competitiveness, Convergence, and International Specialization*, David Dollar and I investigated the sources of the convergence of aggregate labour productivity observed among industrialised countries (see, for example, Maddison 1982; Abramovitz 1986; Baumol 1986; Baumol, Batey Blackman and Wolff 1989; Wolff 1991; and Barro 1991). The convergence phenomenon is usually attributed to the so-called 'advantages of backwardness', by which is meant the potential for the diffusion of technical knowledge from the leading economies to the more backward ones. The further an economy is from the technological frontier, the greater the rate of technical advance possible from such borrowing. Thus, countries further behind the leading economy in terms of labour productivity will tend to experience higher *rates* of productivity growth.

In our book, we considered two possibilities: (a) convergence of labour productivity in individual industries; and (b) specialisation of countries in industries that differ from one country to another, with modest leads in labour productivity in the country that specialises in them.[1] We first examined data for manufacturing industries and found that between the early 1960s and the early 1970s the first of these forms of development, productivity catch-up on the industry level, played the dominant role. However, after that, specialisation became the main vehicle of convergence. Indeed, after the early 1970s, convergence of labour productivity within industries slowed down considerably, and that of total factor productivity (TFP) essentially halted. There were also good reasons to believe that more rapid rates of technological advance might be associated with more rapid rates of capital formation. Our evidence supported the existence of a strong interaction effect (complementarities) between the growth in capital intensity and that of TFP.

We found remarkably similar results when we compared productivity levels of the major non-manufacturing sectors among the industrialised countries of the world. There was strong evidence of convergence in labour productivity levels for the total economy in these countries during the 1970s and early 1980s and a somewhat weaker trend at the sectoral level, but the dispersion in technology levels generally remained unchanged. Also, when looking across the ten major sectors, we found a much more varied pattern of sector leadership in the 1980s than among individual manufacturing industries, which the US still generally dominated.

We also found that variation in technology levels, capital intensity and labour productivity levels was consistently greater at the individual level than at the aggregate level. These results lend support to our hypothesis that specialisation of countries in different industries, particularly since the mid-1970s, played the critical role. The greater similarity in overall productivity levels than in those of the representative industry is attributable to the fact that countries excel in different industries, so that on average among countries aggregate productivity levels are closer than industry productivity levels. The same is true for capital intensity. We concluded that countries chose different industries for their main investment in new technology, which explains the convergence of labour productivity and TFP on the aggregate level.

In this paper, I update the results of our book using the latest (January 1992) version of the OECD International Sectoral Database (ISDB). The data run principally from 1970 to 1988. Four questions are addressed. First, has convergence continued on the aggregate level through 1988 (section 1)? Second, has country specialisation continued through the 1980s (section 2)? I also present a more formal test of the specialisation hypothesis: namely, that aggregate convergence continued after 1970 through the *uneven* development of industries in the individual OECD countries. Third, have countries invested more heavily in industries with rapidly growing TFP (section 2)? Fourth, has the interaction effect between capital investment and TFP growth continued through the 1980s (section 3)? Concluding remarks are made in section 4.

1. PATTERNS OF AGGREGATE PRODUCTIVITY GROWTH AND CAPITAL FORMATION

I will begin by presenting an overview of the aggregate performance of OECD countries from 1970 to 1990 with regard to labour productivity growth, total factor productivity and the growth in capital intensity (as defined by the capital–labour ratio). I confine the analysis to OECD countries, since I am not interested in establishing general patterns of convergence but in focusing on the role of individual sectors in this process.[2]

1.1 Labour Productivity

Table 8.1 presents results for the total economy on the basis of the January 1992 version of the OECD International Sectoral Database (ISDB). The data set covers the period from 1960 to 1989, though the period of greatest data availability is from 1970 to 1988. The data consist of GDP, already calculated in 1980 US dollar equivalents (on the basis of OECD purchasing power parity, or PPP, exchange rates), total employment (the sum of the number of employees and the number of self-employed), and gross capital stock, measured in 1980 US dollars equivalents.

I look at both catch-up, defined as the closure of the gap between follower countries and the leader in terms of productivity levels, and convergence, defined as decreasing dispersion in productivity levels among all countries in the sample. Catch-up is measured in two ways. The first index is the (unweighted) average productivity level of all countries excluding the US to that of the US (defined as 100). This measure climbed from 56 in 1970 to 75 in 1988, demonstrating substantial catch-up. The second, the ratio of the minimum productivity level to the maximum, also confirmed catch-up, as it increased from 40% to 56%. Convergence is measured by the coefficient of variation, defined as the ratio of the standard deviation to the mean, which fell from 0.26 to 0.15 over the period. This is the most direct indicator of convergence in productivity among OECD countries.[3]

The US led in terms of overall labour productivity throughout the period from 1970 to 1988. Its nearest rival in 1988 was The Netherlands, at 86% of the US level. Japan had the lowest average productivity level in 1970 but by 1988 it was ninth (out of 14), at 69% of the US level according to these data. Germany in 1988 was at 71% the US level.

The last two columns of Table 8.1 present rates of labour productivity growth over this period. A quick look at the data for the total economy suggests that those countries with lower productivity levels in 1970 (at the top of the table) experienced more rapid rates of labour productivity growth. This relation is confirmed by the correlation coefficient between the initial level of productivity and the rate of labour productivity growth (at the bottom of the table). A negative value indicates that more-backward countries grew faster. This coefficient was calculated to be –0.67 for 1970–1979 and –0.70 for 1979–1988.[4] Japan had the fastest rate of labour productivity growth in both periods and the US the lowest.

Labour productivity growth among OECD nations fell off by about

Table 8.1: Labour productivity levels relative to the US for the total economy among OECD countries, 1970–1988[a]

	Index number (US = 100)						Annual rate of lab. prod. growth (%)	
	1970	1973	1975	1979	1985	1988	1970–79	1979–88
Japan	40	46	47	55	64	69	4.18	3.37
Finland	41	44	47	52	57	63	3.34	2.93
Denmark	47	48	49	53	55	56	2.02	1.46
Norway	51	53	58	62	67	69	2.93	1.90
United Kingdom		54	53	56	60	64	1.83[b]	2.21
Sweden	52	54	55	56	58	60	1.52	1.63
France	55	59	62	69	74	78	3.30	2.13
Germany	56	58	60	67	69	71	2.91	1.45
Italy	57	60	61	69	70	74	2.79	1.61
Belgium	60	65	67	74	78	81	3.05	1.85
Australia	67	67	70	72	74	74	1.55	1.12
Netherlands	67	73	77	83	87	86	3.17	1.19
Canada	75	77	77	79	80	81	1.33	1.09
United States	100	100	100	100	100	100	0.78	0.80
Summary statistics for total economy								
Unweighted average								
(a) excluding US	56	58	60	65	69	71		
(b) including US							2.48	1.77
Coefficient of variation	0.26	0.23	0.22	0.19	0.17	0.15	0.38	0.39
Minimum/maximum	0.40	0.44	0.47	0.52	0.55	0.56		
Correlation with initial labour productivity[c]							–0.67	–0.70
Summary statistics for total industry[d]								
Unweighted average (excluding US)	54	57	59	66	71	74		
Coefficient of variation	0.26	0.23	0.22	0.18	0.15	0.14		
Minimum/maximum	0.37	0.43	0.44	0.52	0.59	0.60		

Notes

a Source: Own computations from OECD International Sectoral Database on diskettes (1992 version). Labour productivity is defined as the ratio of GDP in 1980 US dollars to total employment (persons engaged in production). Countries are ranked by their 1970 labour productivity level (1973 for the UK).

b UK figure for 1970–1979 based on total industry (see below).

c Correlation coefficient between annual rate of labour productivity growth and labour productivity level at the start of each period, across all OECD countries with available data.

d Total industry is defined as the total economy excluding producers of government services and other non-firm producers.

30% between 1970–1979 and 1979–1988. Comparisons with data from Maddison (1982) suggest that labour productivity growth peaked in the 1960–1970 period, fell in 1970–1979, and then again in the 1979–1988 period. Interestingly, the dispersion in labour productivity growth rates among countries (as measured by the coefficient of variation) showed no change between the 1970–1979 and 1979–1988 periods. This is a surprise since, according to the catch-up hypothesis, if labour productivity levels converge, so should rates of labour productivity growth, since they vary, by assumption, inversely with (initial) labour productivity levels.

Table 8.2 shows a similar set of statistics for total manufacturing. Here the results are quite different. Catch-up to the US level was considerably slower than for the total economy and confined to the 1970–1979 period, as average labour productivity in manufacturing relative to the US increased from 58 to 64%. Between 1979 and 1988, there was no further catch-up in labour productivity (and the ratio of minimum to maximum level actually declined). There was also modest convergence in manufacturing productivity levels between 1970 and 1979, as the coefficient of variation fell from 0.23 to 0.20. However, between 1979 and 1988, the coefficient of variation increased, from 0.20 to 0.23.

Results are also shown for labour productivity growth rates in manufacturing. During the 1970s, there was a clear inverse relation between initial productivity levels and productivity growth rates, with a correlation coefficient of −0.42. However, between 1979 and 1988, this relation failed to materialise. Indeed, there was *no* correlation between the two. Japan ranked first in terms of labour productivity growth in manufacturing in both 1970–1979 and 1979–1988. US labour productivity growth was slightly below average in the 1970–1979 period, but slightly above average in 1979–1988. As for the total economy, there was a significant fall-off in average labour productivity growth among OECD countries in manufacturing between the 1970s and 1980s, but, unlike the total economy, the dispersion in productivity growth rates was higher in the 1980s than the 1970s. Thus, it is clear that international performance in manufacturing was quite different than that from the total economy during the 1980s.[5]

1.2 Total Factor Productivity

I next present similar tabulations based on 'total factor productivity' or TFP. The TFP level for country *h* is measured using the Translog index:

$$\ln TFP^h = \ln Y^h - \bar{\alpha} \ln L^h - (1 - \bar{\alpha}) \ln K^h \tag{8.1}$$

where Y^h is the total output of country *h*, L^h is labour input, K^h is capital

Table 8.2: Labour productivity levels relative to the US for total manufacturing among OECD countries, 1970–1990[a]

	Index number (US = 100)						Annual rate of lab. OECD ISDB data		Prod. growth (%) BLS data[b]	
	1970	1973	1975	1979	1985	1988	1970–79	1979–88	1970–79	1979–90
Denmark	42	41	48	48	44	39	4.25	0.90	5.39	1.16
Japan	46	49	50	62	72	78	6.00	5.66	5.95	4.01
United Kingdom	54	53	53	52	52	56	2.15	4.18	2.69	4.32
Belgium	54	56	59	70	76	78	5.47	4.35	6.87	4.87
Finland	55	51	51	56	59	65	2.81	4.89		
Italy	57	57	58	69	72	76	4.67	4.37	5.69	3.83
Sweden	58	55	58	55	54	50	2.04	2.07	3.53	2.00
Norway	59	57	59	55	52	50	1.79	2.13	3.01	2.39
Netherlands	61	63	65	74	74	71	4.67	2.76	6.26	3.01
Germany	62	59	63	67	60	55	3.58	0.91	4.47	2.10
France	64	62	65	72	65	67	4.01	2.35	4.27	3.60
Australia	68	62	67	68	63	62	2.66	2.16		
Canada	81	80	82	81	76	72	2.57	1.89	3.33	1.45
United States	100	100	100	100	100	100	2.59	3.23	2.57	3.08
Summary statistics for total manufacturing										
Unweighted average										
(a) excluding US	58	57	60	64	63	63				
(b) including US							3.52	2.99	4.50	2.99
Coefficient of variation	0.23	0.23	0.21	0.20	0.21	0.23	0.37	0.48	0.32	0.38
Minimum/maximum	0.42	0.41	0.48	0.48	0.44	0.39				
Correlation with initial labour productivity[c]							–0.42	0.01		

Notes

a Source: Own computations from OECD International Sectoral Database on diskettes (1992 version). Labour productivity is defined as the ratio of GDP in 1980 US dollars to total employment (persons engaged in production). Countries are ranked by their 1970 labour productivity level in manufacturing.

b Source: Own computations from Bureau of Labor Statistics (1991), Table 1. Labour productivity is defined as output (GDP) in constant prices in each country per hour worked. No international level comparisons are available.

c Correlation coefficient between annual rate of labour productivity growth and labour productivity level at the start of each period, across all OECD countries with available data.

input, and $\bar{\alpha}$ is the international average wage share.[6]

Total factor productivity growth is based on the Divisia measure, ρ, defined as:

$$\rho^h = \hat{Y}^h - \bar{\alpha}\hat{L}^h - (1-\bar{\alpha})\hat{K}^h \tag{8.2}$$

where a superscript hat (^) indicates the rate of growth (see Gollop and Dale 1980, for a discussion of the Divisia index).[7]

The convergence in TFP levels for the total economy is even more marked than that in labour productivity levels (see Table 8.3).[8] Between 1970 and 1988, the coefficient of variation fell from 0.17 to 0.13 (com-

Table 8.3: Translog total factor productivity (TFP) levels relative to the US for the total economy and total manufacturing among OECD countries, 1970–1988[a]

	Results for the total economy					Results for total manufacturing				
	TFP levels[b]			TFP growth[c]		TFP levels[b]			TFP growth[c]	
	1970	1979	1988	1970–79	1979–88	1970	1979	1988	1970–79	1979–88
Finland	51	56	64	1.45	1.80	54	54	60	1.34	3.12
Denmark	57	61	65	1.01	1.15	49	52	44	2.22	0.11
Norway	63	68	71	1.33	0.84	57	50	42	0.00	-0.17
Sweden	63	63	66	0.43	0.98	59	52	49	0.17	1.26
United Kingdom		67	74	0.65[d]	1.38	58	53	56	0.49	2.49
Germany	70	77	78	1.36	0.57	71	73	62	1.83	0.10
France	73	82	87	1.69	1.07	69	74	65	2.22	0.57
Belgium	74	82	85	1.44	0.79	60	70	74	3.05	2.54
Netherlands	77	88	89	1.85	0.47	58	62	60	2.37	1.46
Australia	77	78	79	0.40	0.58	71	69	65	1.19	1.15
Japan	80	82	87	0.60	1.25	68	77	91[e]	2.78	3.71
Italy	84	87	88	0.71	0.52	65	68	72	2.00	2.48
Canada	85	86	83	0.52	–0.03	76	77	66[e]	1.65	0.25
United States	100	100	100	0.37	0.41	100	100	100	1.47	1.92
Summary statistics										
Unweighted average										
(a) excluding US	71	75	78			63	64	62		
(b) including US				0.98	0.84				1.63	1.50
Coefficient of variation	0.17	0.15	0.13	0.51	0.54	0.18	0.20	0.24	0.55	0.80
Minimum/maximum	0.51	0.56	0.64			0.49	0.50	0.42		
Correlation with initial TFP level				–0.96	–0.73				0.07	0.13

Notes

a Source: Own computations from OECD ISDB. TFP levels are computed according to eq. (8.1). Output is measured by GDP in 1980 US dollars, labour by total employment, and capital by gross fixed capital. Factor shares are based on the average ratio of employee compensation to GDP for the 12 countries over the 1970–1988 period. Countries are ranked by 1970 TFP level for the total economy.

b Index number, with US = 100.

c Average annual rates (in percent) based on the Tornqvist–Divisia index.

d The UK figure for 1970–1979 is based on total industry.

e 1987 is used instead of 1988.

pared to 0.15 for labour productivity). Average TFP in other countries grew from 71% of the US level to 78% (compared to 71% for labour productivity). As with labour productivity, those furthest behind had more rapid rates of growth in TFP, and the correlation coefficient between the two is –0.96 for 1970–1979 and –0.73 for 1979–1988.

The US maintained the highest level of TFP throughout the period, though Belgium, France, Italy, Japan and The Netherlands were all within

15% of the US by 1988. Japan's TFP growth was just about average (the difference with its labour productivity performance a reflection, as we shall see below, of its massive capital investment). The US had the lowest rate of TFP growth among these countries in the 1970–1979 period, and was second lowest during 1979–1988, at about half the average of all OECD countries. Average TFP growth among the countries in the sample fell off slightly between 1970–1979 and 1979–1988, though not nearly as much as labour productivity growth.

In manufacturing, the story was again different. There was rising dispersion in TFP levels, particularly between 1979 and 1988. The correlation between initial TFP level and TFP growth was slightly positive, at 0.07 in 1970–1979 and 0.13 in 1979–1988. The dispersion in TFP growth rates increased substantially between the 1970–1979 and the 1979–1988 periods. TFP growth in US manufacturing was 10% below average in the 1970s but 28% above average during the 1980s.

1.3 Capital Intensity

To complete the aggregate picture, we next present comparative results on capital–labour ratios among OECD countries in Table 8.4. According to the OECD data, the US remained the most capital-intensive country throughout the period between 1970 and 1988. However, the average capital–labour ratio among other countries increased from only 58% of the US level in 1970 to 81% in 1988. Japan is noteworthy in that its capital–labour ratio was only 20% of the US level in 1970 but reached 52% by 1988. There was general convergence in capital intensity among OECD countries, as the coefficient of variation fell from 0.29 to 0.16.

In terms of the growth in the capital–labour ratio, the results are even more telling. There was a significant inverse relation between initial capital–labour ratios and capital–labour growth, with correlation coefficients of –0.90 in the 1970–1979 period and –0.69 in the 1979–1988 period. Japan had the highest growth rate in both periods, while the US was last in 1970–1979 and second from last in 1979–1988. Average OECD growth in capital intensity also slowed down, by almost 40%, between the 1970–1979 and 1979–1988 periods. Japan also slowed down, with its rate of capital–labour growth almost falling by half between the 1970s and 1980s (from 8.5 to 4.8% points).

In manufacturing, the picture is again different. During the 1970s, there was modest convergence in capital intensity, with the coefficient of variation falling from 0.23 to 0.20, but this was followed by increasing dispersion during the 1980s. Japan had the highest capital–labour growth over the period, rising from 39% of the US level in 1970 to 69% in 1988. US capital–labour growth in manufacturing was the lowest among OECD

Table 8.4: Capital–labour ratios (K/L) *relative to the US and average annual growth rates for the total economy and manufacturing among OECD countries, 1970–1988*[a]

	Results for the total economy					Results for total manufacturing				
	K/L levels[b]			*K/L* growth[c]		*K/L* levels[b]			*K/L* growth[c]	
	1970	1979	1988	1970–79	1979–88	1970	1979	1988	1970–79	1979–88
Japan	20	38	52[d]	8.50	4.84[d]	39	60	69[d]	7.63	5.19[d]
Italy	40	57	66	4.93	2.59	74	103	116	6.35	4.48
France	52	67	77	3.82	2.51	83	96	106	4.25	4.22
United Kingdom	55	64	71	2.81	1.97	83	94	101	3.93	4.01
Germany	57	73	81	3.67	2.08	71	82	73	4.17	1.92
Finland	60	83	97	4.50	2.70	101	109	120	3.48	4.20
Belgium	61	78	90	3.84	2.52	78	102	114	5.72	4.30
Norway	62	80	92	3.79	2.51	107	123	152	4.23	5.45
Denmark	63	71	70	2.41	0.73	69	84	75	4.81	1.88
Sweden	65	75	80	2.59	1.56	97	113	102	4.45	1.92
Australia	71	83	86	2.73	1.28	90	97	91	3.48	2.39
Netherlands	72	87	94	3.14	1.73	117	150	150	5.46	3.08
Canada	75	81	93[d]	1.93	2.69[d]	118	113	121	2.18	3.89
United States	100	100	100	0.98	0.94	100	100	100	2.66	3.11
Summary statistics										
Unweighted average										
(a) excluding US	58	72	81			87	102	107		
(b) including US				3.55	2.19				4.49	3.57
Coefficient of variation	0.29	0.19	0.16	0.48	0.44	0.23	0.20	0.23	0.31	0.32
Minimum/maximum	0.20	0.38	0.52			0.33	0.40	0.46		
Correlation with initial TFP level				−0.90	−0.69				−0.69	0.01

Notes

a Source: Own computations from OECD International Sectoral Database on diskettes (1992 version). Labour is measured by total employment and capital by gross fixed capital. Countries are ranked according to their capital–labour ratio for the total economy in 1970.

b Index number, with US = 100.

c Average annual rates (in percent).

d 1987 is used instead of 1988.

countries in the 1970–1979 period, but close to average during the 1980s. Still, the US had switched from an above-average country in terms of capital intensity in 1970 (though not the highest) to a below-average one in 1988. During the 1970s, there was a significant inverse relation between initial capital–labour ratios and their growth, with a correlation coefficient of −0.69, but during the 1980s the correlation between the two was just about zero.

From equation (8.2), the relationship between labour productivity growth, TFP growth and capital–labour growth is given by

$$\hat{\Pi}^h = \rho^h + (1 - \bar{\alpha})\hat{k}^h \tag{8.3}$$

where $\hat{\Pi}^h$ is the rate of labour productivity growth in country h and $\hat{k}^h$ is the rate of growth of country h's capital–labour ratio (K^h/L^h). From the first four tables, it is apparent that the convergence in labour productivity levels for the total economy over the 1970–1988 period has been due to convergence in both TFP levels and capital intensity. However, in manufacturing, the dispersion in labour productivity levels and capital–labour ratios remained unchanged over the 1970–1988 period, while the dispersion of TFP levels actually increased. Moreover, the substantial fall-off in labour productivity growth observed between the 1970–1979 and 1979–1988 periods for both the total economy and manufacturing was due almost entirely to the slackening pace of capital investment, while the rate of TFP growth declined only slightly between the two periods.

2. PRODUCTIVITY AND CAPITAL FORMATION ON THE INDUSTRY LEVEL

I now turn to a consideration of the behaviour of productivity movements and capital accumulation at the individual sectoral and industry level. The OECD ISDB provides data on output, employment and capital stock for ten major sectors of the economy, and nine manufacturing industries. As before, the data run mainly from 1970 to 1988. The advantage of looking at the sectoral and industry level is that it may allow us to uncover the sources of productivity movements on the aggregate level. In particular, our focus here is on whether the catch-up process on the industry level has been even over time or more jagged in appearance.

A word of caution should be given at the outset regarding country comparisons of productivity levels at the industry or sector level. These are affected by the individual industry price deflators used in each country and the corresponding intercountry exchange rates, country conventions used to measure industry output and, most importantly, by the classification scheme used in each country to aggregate the detailed sub-industry or sub-sector data to the broader industry or sector level. As a result, it is difficult to place too much confidence in precise productivity comparisons for particular industries. However, considerable experience in such comparative work suggests that the general patterns are quite reliable, particularly measures of changes over time in productivity levels.

2.1 Labour Productivity

I begin with a consideration of relative labour productivity levels between OECD countries. I have divided the non-US countries into three groupings: Japan, Germany, and 'other OECD' countries. I have singled out Japan and Germany for special treatment since they, along with the US, constitute the three major economies of the world. We begin with a consideration of the major sectors of the economy.

If we first look at the performance of Japan relative to the US, it is clear that the 71% (69/40–1) catch-up in Japanese aggregate productivity relative to the US highlighted in the first line of Table 8.5 is also manifested for most *but not all* major sectors of the economy (also see Figure 8.1). Between 1970 and 1988, Japan made spectacular gains relative to the US in mining and quarrying (73%); manufacturing (69%); trade, restaurants and hotels (104%); and finance, insurance and real estate (119%). However, Japan made only modest relative advances in agriculture (12%); utilities (electricity, gas and water, 25%); transportation and communications (6%); and actually declined in relative terms in community, social, and personal services (a loss of 5%). By 1988, Japan had surpassed the US labour productivity level in utilities; finance, insurance and real estate; and government services, but, as noted above, had achieved only 78% of the US productivity level in total manufacturing, and was still very far behind in agriculture (18% of the US level); mining and quarrying (26% of the US level); and transportation and communications (47%). Thus, it is clear that Japanese productivity advances relative to the US was quite uneven over this period.

German performance relative to the US was not as spectacular as Japan's (see also Figure 8.2). Overall, Germany's labour productivity level advanced by 28% (71/56–1) on the US level. Its largest relative gains were recorded in agriculture (85%), utilities (49%), construction (82%); and finance, insurance and real estate (61%). Relative gains were modest in other sectors and, in fact, Germany fell back in mining and quarrying (29%) and in *manufacturing* (11%). By 1988, Germany had surpassed the US only in finance, insurance and real estate; and in community, social and personal services. It was still far behind the US in the other sectors, including manufacturing (55% of the US level).[9]

With respect to other OECD countries (see Figure 8.2), the record was again mixed. Major gains were found in only mining and quarrying (a result due almost entirely to The Netherlands' very high productivity in natural gas production) and construction. Modest gains occurred in agriculture, utilities, and finance, insurance and real estate. For the other major sectors, there were only modest relative gains (for government services, a modest relative loss). With the exception of mining and quarrying, and finance, insurance and real estate, the US was still considerably ahead of the other countries in terms of average labour productivity.

We can summarise these results in two ways. The first is to compute the coefficient of variation in productivity levels for each sector across countries. These are shown in the last three columns of panel A of Table 8.5. Two patterns emerge. First, the dispersion in labour productivity levels on the aggregate level shows a substantial decline between 1970 and 1988, with the coefficient of variation dropping over 40%, from 0.26 to 0.15. However, there are substantial declines in dispersion in only six of

Table 8.5: Labour productivity levels relative to the US, by major sector and manufacturing industry among OECD countries, 1970–1988[a]

	Productivity relative to US (Index number US = 100)						Coefficient of variation in productivity across all OECD countries		
	Japan		Germany		Other OECD				
	1970	1988	1970	1988	1970	1988	1970	1979	1988
A. Total economy[b]	40	69	56	71	57	71	0.26	0.19	0.15
Agriculture	16	18	22	41	41	55	0.52	0.39	0.36
Mining & quarrying[c]	10	26	14	10	32	160	1.06	1.83	1.17
Manufacturing	46	78	62	55	59	62	0.23	0.20	0.23
Utilities	86	107	44	65	52	70	0.42	0.31	0.29
Construction	43	64	41	75	46	84	0.35	0.20	0.22
Trade, restaurants[d]	34	69	55	64	62	71	0.27	0.24	0.20
Transp. & comm.[e]	45	47	50	58	49	55	0.31	0.29	0.24
Fin., insur., real est.[f]	73	159	81	131	77	100	0.28	0.21	0.29
Social, personal serv.[g]	67	63	136	161	85	87	0.49	0.45	0.29
Government services	77	101	70	72	70	68	0.25	0.25	0.26
Unweighted average:									
All industries							0.42	0.44	0.37
All industries except mining							0.35	0.28	0.28
B. All Manufacturing[h]	46	78	62	55	60	62	0.23	0.20	0.23
Basic metals	78	199	39	45	51	73	0.46	0.49	0.48
Chemicals[i]	83	170	69	59	51	66	0.35	0.42	0.43
Nonmetallic minerals[j]	56	58	58	65	60	75	0.29	0.27	0.27
Machinery & equip.[k]	33	78	60	47	58	55	0.27	0.25	0.32
Paper, print., publ.	55	95	52	61	67	77	0.24	0.21	0.23
Food, bev., tob.	56	35	68	54	62	67	0.28	0.27	0.35
Textiles	44	57	81	71	77	78	0.20	0.19	0.19
Wood & wood prod.[l]			72	54	70	77	0.26	0.18	0.23
Other industries[m]	45	46	54	41	61	62	0.64	0.53	0.71
Unweighted average:									
All industries							0.32	0.30	0.34

Productivity Growth and Capital Intensity on the Sector and Industry Level 197

C. Coefficient of variation of labour productivity levels relative to the US across industries by country

	10 major sectors			9 major sectors except mining			9 manufacturing industries		
	1970	1979	1988	1970	1979	1988	1970	1979	1988
Australia	0.35	0.26	0.23	0.33	0.27	0.22			
Belgium	0.39	0.33	0.34	0.25	0.17	0.19	0.36	0.25	0.18
Canada	0.15	0.16	0.23	0.15	0.17	0.23	0.17	0.11	0.22
Denmark	0.41	0.22	1.04	0.28	0.21	0.24	0.20	0.22	0.20
Finland	0.37	0.31	0.33	0.28	0.23	0.30	0.22	0.17	0.23
France	0.39	0.31	0.35	0.27	0.21	0.24	0.22	0.15	0.28
Germany	0.59	0.47	0.54	0.52	0.41	0.44	0.19	0.14	0.17
Italy	0.63	0.57	0.49	0.63	0.57	0.49	0.23	0.15	0.19
Japan	0.49	0.43	0.53	0.40	0.39	0.48	0.28	0.49	0.61
Netherlands	0.38	1.52	0.95	0.32	0.17	0.21	0.20	0.15	0.19
Norway	0.36	0.90	1.08	0.29	0.20	0.16	0.27	0.31	0.37
Sweden	0.36	0.30	0.35	0.25	0.21	0.28	0.33	0.32	0.34
United Kingdom	0.25	0.17	0.12	0.21	0.18	0.12	0.56	0.60	0.52
Average C.V.	0.39	0.46	0.51	0.32	0.26	0.28	0.27	0.25	0.29

Notes

a Source: Own computations from the OECD International Sectoral Database on diskettes (1992 version). Labour productivity is defined as the ratio of GDP in 1980 US dollars to total employment (persons engaged in production). Computations for other OECD countries are based on the unweighted average labour productivity of countries with available data.

Exceptions:

b UK figure for 1970 is based on total industry
c Excludes Italy, all years; UK, 1988
d Only wholesale and retail trade for Japan and The Netherlands
e Excludes The Netherlands in 1970 and 1979
f Excludes The Netherlands, all years; excludes UK, 1988; for Germany, includes finance and insurance only
g Excludes The Netherlands, 1970 and 1979
h Australia is included in total manufacturing but is excluded for all individual manufacturing industries
i Excludes The Netherlands in 1970 and 1979
j Excludes The Netherlands, 1970 and 1979; excludes Norway, all years
k Excludes The Netherlands in 1970 and 1979
l Excludes Japan, The Netherlands, and UK, all years
m Excludes The Netherlands, 1970 and 1979; excludes Norway, all years.

Key:

Agriculture: agriculture, forestry and fisheries
Mining and quarrying: includes oil and natural gas extraction
Manufacturing
  Basic metals: basic metal products
  Chemicals: includes petroleum, rubber and plastic products
  Nonmetallic minerals: nonmetallic mineral products
  Machinery & equip.: machinery and equipment, including fabricated metal products, industrial and transport machinery, office and data-processing equipment, and electrical and optical equipment
  Paper, print., publ.: paper, printing and publishing
  Food, bev., tob.: food, beverage and tobacco
  Textiles: includes wearing apparel and leather industries
  Wood & wood prod.: wood and wood products, including furniture
  Other industries: other manufactured products
Utilities: electrical, gas and water
Construction
Trade, restaurants: also includes hotels
Transp. & comm.: transportation, storage and communication
Fin., insur., real est.: finance, insurance and real estate
Social, personal serv.: community, social and personal services
Government services

Figure 8.1: Japanese labour productivity relative to the US by major sector, 1970 and 1988

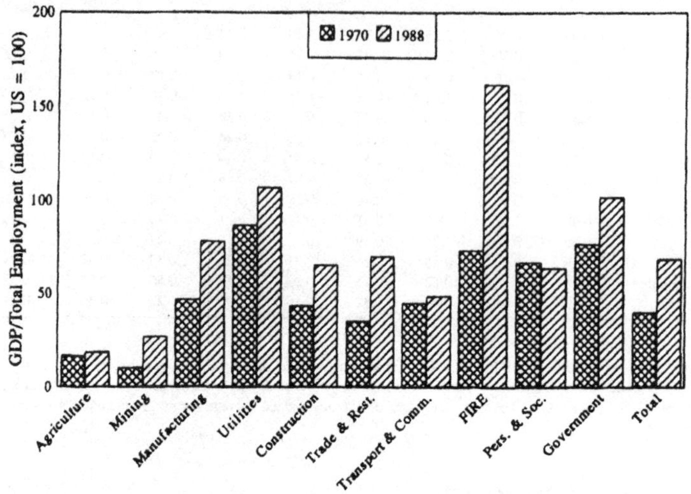

Figure 8.2: German and other OECD labour productivity relative to the US by major sector, 1970 and 1988

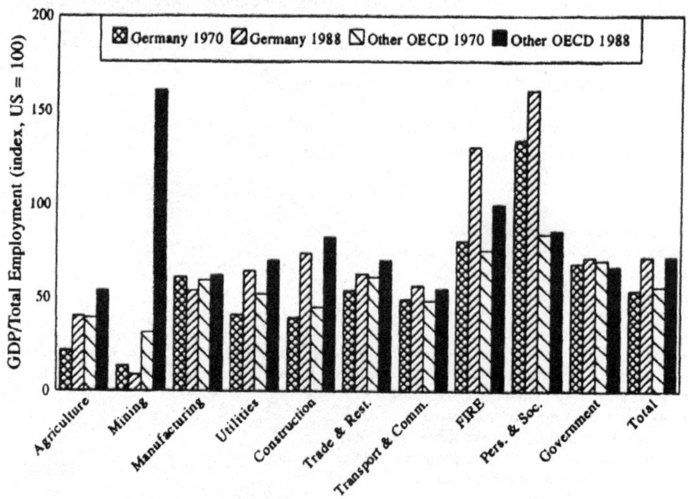

the ten sectors, and the average coefficient of variation (with or without mining) shows only a modest decline between 1970 and 1988. Second, the dispersion in productivity levels on the individual sector level, as measured by the average coefficient of variation, is substantially higher than that of the aggregate level (almost double in 1988).

The second summary approach is to compute the dispersion in sectoral productivity levels relative to the US level for each country across sectors. If sectors furthest behind the US level show the most rapid gain in productivity over time, then the dispersion in *relative* productivity levels across sectors should decline over time. Panel C of Table 8.5 shows that the coefficient of variation across all ten major sectors declines in seven out of the 13 countries between 1970 and 1988 and rises in five (and stays about the same in one). However, the average coefficient of variation increased substantially between 1970 and 1988. Since much of the variation is due to the mining sector, which in The Netherlands and Norway has extremely high labour productivity from natural gas or oil extraction, it is also useful to present the same statistics with that sector eliminated. In this case, the coefficient of variation declined in nine out of the 13 countries between 1970 and 1988, and its average value also shows a decline between 1970 and 1979 followed by a slight increase between 1979 and 1988.

Both sets of results indicate that the convergence in labour productivity observed on the aggregate level among OECD countries has been much more pronounced than at the individual sectoral level. This suggests uneven productivity developments within countries, with some sectors remaining quite backward (such as agriculture in Japan) and some modernising very quickly and even overtaking the US level (such as banking in Germany).

I next consider the individual manufacturing industries (bottom panel of Table 8.5 and Figures 8.3 and 8.4). Japan made its major gains in basic metals (157%), machinery and equipment (135%), and chemicals (106%). A substantial gain was also made in paper, printing and publishing (70%). However, relatively modest gains were recorded in nonmetallic minerals (3%), textiles (28%), and the catch-all group, other industries (2%), and in food, beverages and tobacco there was a substantial relative loss of 38 %. By 1988, Japan's labour productivity levels were far ahead of the US in basic metal products (99% greater) and chemicals (70% greater), and, indeed, in these two industries Japan had become the OECD leader in terms of productivity. However, the US led Japan in all the other industries, and, with the exception of paper, printing and publishing, Japan was still far behind the US in 1988. Indeed, according to the OECD data, in 1988 the US was still the OECD leader in food, beverages and tobacco; textiles; wood products; and machinery and equipment.

In Germany, there were no major gains. Of the nine manufacturing industries, Germany advanced relative to the US in only three and fell back in the other six. In 1988, the US was ahead of Germany in every industry. Other OECD countries made substantial gains on the US in basic metals, chemicals and nonmetallic minerals; remained at the same relative

Figure 8.3: Japanese labour productivity relative to the US by manufacturing industry, 1970 and 1988

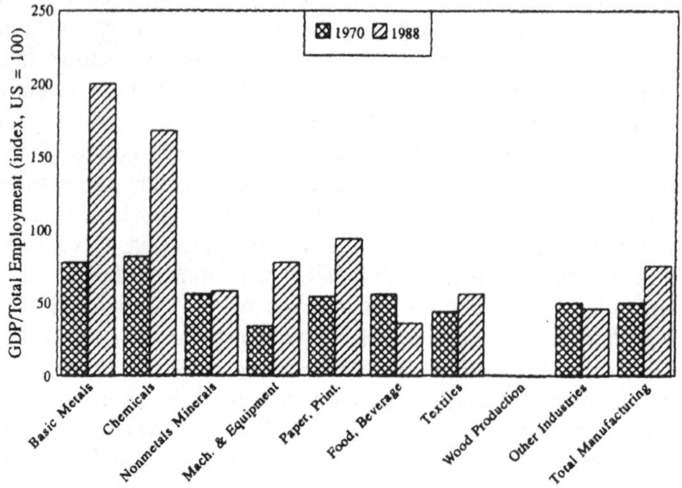

Figure 8.4: German and other OECD labour productivity relative to the US by manufacturing sector, 1970 and 1988

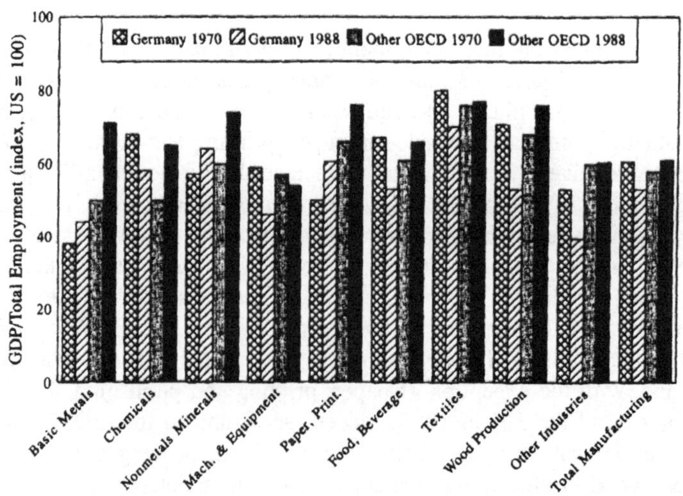

level with respect to the US in machinery and equipment, paper, printing and publishing, and food, beverages and tobacco; and actually fell further behind the US in textiles, wood, and other industries. By 1988, the US had a higher productivity level in all industries than the average of the other OECD countries. However, Finland was the OECD leader in paper, printing and publishing; and France in nonmetallic mineral products (including glass and ceramics).

The coefficient of variation of labour productivity levels across countries declined in five out of the nine manufacturing industries between 1970 and 1988 and increased in the other four. Its average value declined slightly, from 0.32 in 1970 to 0.30 in 1979, and then increased to 0.34 in 1988. The coefficient of variation of relative labour productivity levels across manufacturing industries declined in only four of the 13 countries and rose in four (remaining about the same in the others). Its average value also fell slightly between 1970 and 1979, from 0.27 to 0.25, and then increased to 0.29 in 1988. These results also give evidence of jagged productivity developments on the industry level within countries. Japan is particularly notable in both the increase of its coefficient of variation, from 0.28 in 1970 to 0.61 in 1988, and the size of the coefficient of variation in 1988. This finding, in particular, suggests intensive specialisation of Japanese manufacturing in particular industries and sub-industries.

2.2 Total Factor Productivity and Capital Intensity

Results on relative TFP levels among OECD countries by sector are, perhaps not surprisingly, similar to those for labour productivity (Table 8.6). Whereas the coefficient of variation in TFP for the total economy across countries declined from 0.17 to 0.13 between 1970 and 1980, dispersion in TFP across countries declined in only five of the ten major sectors (Panel A). The average coefficient of variation (with or without mining) shows only a modest decline between 1970 and 1988. Moreover, the average coefficient of variation is substantially higher than that of the aggregate level (more than double in 1988). The coefficient of variation in relative TFP across industries (excluding mining) by country shows a decline in nine countries (out of 13), and its average value falls modestly, from 0.33 to 0.29.

In manufacturing, the coefficient of variation in TFP levels across countries increased in eight out of the nine manufacturing industries between 1970 and 1988. The average coefficient of variation remained unchanged from 1970 to 1979, and then increased from 0.32 in 1979 to 0.36 in 1988. The coefficient of variation of relative TFP levels across manufacturing industries declined in only three countries and increased in four (remaining about the same in the other three). Its average value remained unchanged between 1970 and 1988. Japan again stands out in that its coefficient of variation increased from 0.31 in 1970 to 0.53 in 1988, suggesting intensive specialisation in Japanese manufacturing.

Results on capital–labour ratios are also shown in Table 8.6. On the aggregate level, as noted above, there was significant convergence in overall capital–labour ratios for the total economy, as the coefficient of variation fell from 0.29 in 1970 to 0.16 in 1988 (see Panel A). The same trend is reflected on the individual sectoral level, with the coefficient of variation declining in nine out of the ten major sectors, and remaining unchanged in the other. The average coefficient of variation also declined, from 0.53 to 0.45 for all ten sectors and from 0.48 to 0.40 for all except mining. Even so, its average value was considerably greater than the coefficient of variation for the total economy (over twice as great in 1988). Results are similar for the coefficient of variation of relative capital–labour ratios across sectors by country, declining in seven countries and rising in four. Its average value fell from 0.56 in 1970 to 0.52 in 1988.

In manufacturing, the coefficient of variation across countries fell in four manufacturing industries and rose in four. Its average value remained unchanged between 1970 and 1979, at 0.35, and then increased to 0.40 in

Table 8.6: TFP and capital–labour (K/L) *levels relative to the US, by major sector and manufacturing industry among OECD countries, 1970–1988*[a]

	Coefficient of variation across countries in relative TFP levels			Coefficient of variation across countries in relative *K/L* levels			Correlation coefficient between TFP and *K/L* growth	
	1970	1979	1988	1970	1979	1988	1970–79	1979–88
A. Total economy[b]	0.17	0.15	0.13	0.29	0.19	0.16	−0.10	0.37
Agriculture	0.28	0.29	0.38	0.45	0.33	0.26	−0.65	−0.63
Mining & quarrying[c]	0.63	1.00	0.76	1.00	1.04	0.87	0.49	0.76
Manufacturing	0.19	0.20	0.23	0.23	0.20	0.23	0.58	0.41
Utilities	0.59	0.39	0.35	0.39	0.33	0.34	−0.05	−0.05
Construction	0.31	0.24	0.27	0.43	0.36	0.39	−0.54	−0.30
Trade, restaurants[d]	0.25	0.22	0.20	0.32	0.32	0.31	0.43	−0.14
Transp. & comm.[e]	0.32	0.25	0.18	0.47	0.43	0.28	−0.54	−0.78
Fin., insur., real est.[f]	0.46	0.49	0.49	0.42	0.40	0.40	−0.34	−0.20
Social, personal serv.[g]	0.51	0.46	0.39	0.74	0.69	0.63	−0.77	−0.65
Government services	0.22	0.22	0.22	0.87	0.85	0.81	0.52	0.34
Unweighted average:								
(a) All sectors	0.38	0.38	0.35	0.53	0.50	0.45	−0.08	−0.12
(b) All except mining	0.35	0.31	0.30	0.48	0.44	0.40		
B. All manufacturing[h]	0.19	0.20	0.23	0.23	0.20	0.23	0.58	0.41
Basic metals	0.42	0.48	0.45	0.31	0.26	0.28	0.45	0.50
Chemicals[i]	0.36	0.37	0.39	0.33	0.33	0.36	0.02	0.04
Nonmetallic minerals[j]	0.24	0.24	0.26	0.34	0.28	0.28	−0.23	0.36
Machinery & equip.[k]	0.23	0.25	0.33	0.29	0.21	0.21	0.40	0.43
Paper, print., publ.	0.22	0.23	0.23	0.47	0.40	0.37	0.27	0.38
Food, bev., tob.	0.30	0.30	0.34	0.26	0.22	0.25	0.22	−0.20
Textiles	0.20	0.21	0.24	0.16	0.20	0.28	−0.36	0.32
Wood & wood prod.[l]	0.26	0.24	0.30	0.29	0.26	0.35	−0.03	−0.24
Other industries[m]	0.63	0.54	0.72	0.83	1.18	1.44	−0.10	−0.03
Unweighted average:	0.32	0.32	0.36	0.35	0.35	0.40	0.07	0.17

C. Coefficient of variation of TFP levels and capital–labour ratios relative to the US across industries by country

	Total factor productivity				Capital–labour ratio			
	9 sectors[n]		9 manuf. ind.		9 sectors[n]		9 manuf. ind.	
	1970	1988	1970	1988	1970	1988	1970	1988
Australia	0.31	0.22			0.72	0.56		
Belgium	0.21	0.25	0.42	0.21	0.68	0.40	0.37	0.36
Canada	0.23	0.30	0.12	0.20	0.85	0.65	0.26	0.29
Denmark	0.39	0.41	0.17	0.17	0.32	0.63	0.32	0.36
Finland	0.17	0.12			0.45	0.41		
France	0.23	0.21	0.27	0.14	0.45	0.59	0.66	0.40
Germany	0.74	0.72	0.15	0.15	0.59	0.66	0.24	0.33
Italy	0.51	0.44	0.24	0.27	0.57	0.63	0.59	1.23
Japan	0.44	0.37	0.31	0.53	0.49	0.45	0.36	0.53
Netherlands	0.23	0.19			0.49	0.36		
Norway	0.32	0.23	0.28	0.41	0.47	0.47	0.17	0.39
Sweden	0.15	0.18	0.29	0.21	0.36	0.36	0.43	0.53
United Kingdom	0.36	0.15	0.44	0.43	0.79	0.52	0.38	0.39
Average C.V.	0.33	0.29	0.27	0.27	0.56	0.52	0.38	0.48

D. Correlation coefficient between TFP growth and capital–labour growth across industries by country

	10 major sectors		9 manuf. industries	
	1970–79	1979–88	1970–79	1979–88
Australia	–0.08	0.45		
Belgium	0.42	–0.48	–0.32	–0.55
Canada	–0.62	–0.14	–0.13	0.28
Denmark	0.05	0.94	–0.17	–0.42
Finland	–0.24	0.43		
France	–0.70	–0.79	–0.20	0.73
Germany	–0.05	–0.06	0.24	0.22
Italy	–0.66	0.08	0.39	–0.54
Japan	–0.39	–0.56	0.23	0.83
Netherlands	0.61	0.68		
Norway	0.39	–0.43	–0.48	0.28
Sweden	–0.35	0.07	–0.16	0.32
United Kingdom	–0.82	0.02	0.04	0.95
United States	0.25	–0.28	0.34	–0.04
Average correl.	–0.16	–0.01	–0.02	0.19

Notes

a Source: Own computations from OECD International Sectoral Database on diskettes (1992 version). TFP levels are computed according to eq. (8.1). Output is measured by GDP in 1980 US dollars, labour by total employment and capital by gross fixed capital. Factor shares are based on the average ratio of employee compensation to GDP by individual sector and industry for the 12 countries over the 1970–1988 period.

Exceptions:

b UK figure for 1970 is based on total industry
c Excludes Italy, all years; UK, 1988
d Excludes Australia, all years; Denmark, 1988; only wholesale and retail trade for Japan and The Netherlands
e Excludes The Netherlands in 1970 and 1979
f Excludes Italy and The Netherlands, all years; excludes UK, 1988; for Germany, includes finance and insurance only
g Excludes The Netherlands, 1970 and 1979
h Australia, Finland and The Netherlands are included in total manufacturing but are excluded for all individual manufacturing industries
i Excludes The Netherlands in 1970 and 1979
j Excludes The Netherlands, 1970 and 1979; excludes Norway, all years
k Excludes The Netherlands in 1970 and 1979
l Excludes Belgium, Italy, Japan, The Netherlands and UK, all years
m Excludes The Netherlands, 1970 and 1979; excludes Norway, all years
n Mining and quarrying sector is excluded

Key: See notes to Table 8.5.

1988. However, there is an apparent problem with the other industry category (the capital–labour ratio seems unrealistically high for Italy). If we exclude this industry, then the average coefficient of variation declined from 0.31 in 1970 to 0.27 in 1979 and then increased to 0.30 in 1988. The coefficient of variation of relative capital–labour ratios across industry by country fell in only two countries and increased in seven between 1970 and 1988. Its average increased from 0.38 to 0.48. Here, again, the 1988 value for Italy appears affected by apparent errors in the data for the other industry category. If Italy is excluded, the average coefficient of variation still climbed, though from 0.35 to 0.40.

3. RELATION BETWEEN CAPITAL–LABOUR GROWTH AND TFP GROWTH

A cursory examination of Table 8.6 suggests that there may be a connection between countries and industries that did well in terms of TFP growth and those that had superior performance in capital–labour growth. It is, of course, not surprising that there is a strong positive relation between the rate of *labour productivity growth* and capital–labour growth. This is apparent from eq. (8.3). The rate of labour productivity growth is directly related to the rate of technological progress and the rate of capital–labour growth. The latter relation is usually referred to as 'capital deepening', meaning that more capital is put into the hands of each worker, thereby increasing their output (per hour worked).

However, what is not so apparent is that there may be a positive association between the rate of *technological progress* and the rate of growth in capital intensity. In previous work (my 1991 paper), I argued that there are several ways in which capital investment and technical change may be associated. First, it is likely that substantial investment is required to adopt new inventions (the so-called 'embodiment effect' or 'vintage effect'). A second avenue is that the introduction of new capital may lead to better organisation, management and the like. A third is through learning-by-doing. A fourth is that potential technological advance may stimulate capital formation, because the opportunity to modernise equipment promises a high rate of return to investment. A fifth is through the so-called Verdoorn effect, whereby investment growth may lead to a growth in demand and thereby to the maintenance of a generally favourable economic climate for investment. These possibilities do not lead to a specific functional relation between TFP growth and the rate of capital growth but do suggest a positive correlation between the two variables (see my 1991 paper for more details).

I first computed the simple correlation coefficient between the rate of TFP growth and the rate of growth in the capital–labour ratio, for both the 1970–1979 and the 1979–1988 periods. These are shown both across country within sector or industry (Panels A and B) and across sectors or industries within country (Panel D). Here the evidence of a positive relation between TFP growth and capital–labour growth is quite mixed. For the total economy, there is a positive correlation between the two in the 1979–1988 period (correlation coefficient of 0.37) but the correlation for the 1970–1979 period is slightly negative. However, among the major sectors, most of the correlation coefficients are negative. The notable exception is the manufacturing sector, which has positive correlations in both periods (0.58 and 0.41, respectively). This suggests that countries that were investing heavily in manufacturing were also experiencing greater than average TFP growth in manufacturing. However, an examination of the individual manufacturing industries again presents a mixed picture, though, on average, the correlations are slightly positive. Correlations across industries within country also show a mixed pattern, some countries with positive coefficients and others within negative ones. Perhaps, the notable exception is Japan, with a correlation coefficient of 0.83 among manufacturing industries in the 1979–1988 period, confirming its high investment and technological progress in certain targeted industries.

A more proper channel to test this relation is through a regression framework. I used the following specification:

$$RLTFPGRT_{it}^{h} = b_0 + b_1 RLKLGRT_{i,t-1}^{h} + b_2 RELTFP_{it}^{h} + \varepsilon_t^h \quad (8.4)$$

where $RLTFPGRT_{it}^{h}$ is the rate of (Divisia) TFP growth in sector (or industry) i in country h at time t relative to the corresponding US rate of TFP growth; $RLKLGRT^{h}{}_{i,t-1}$ is the rate of capital–labour growth in sector (or industry) i in country h at time $t-1$ relative to the corresponding US growth rate; $RELTFP_{it}^{h}$ is country h's TFP relative to the US at the start of each period; and ε is a stochastic error term. Both two-year and three-year averages are used for the growth variables to reduce random noise. The regression is performed on both the sample of nine manufacturing industries and the sample of ten major sectors. We treat each industry (or sector) in each country in each period as an observation. The US is excluded from this regression equation, since the value of the dependent variable is always unity.

The key variable of interest is *RLKLGRT*, since it provides a test of the 'interaction hypothesis'. This hypothesis suggests that the rate of growth of TFP will be positively correlated with the rate of growth of the capital–labour ratio. I use the lagged value of capital–labour growth in the regression for two reasons. First, in so far as causation may run both ways, there may be a 'simultaneity bias' introduced if we use the contemporaneous value of capital–labour growth. Second, there may also be costs of adjustment associated with the introduction of new capital. The coefficient of the contemporaneous value of *RLKLGRT* may thus reflect the negative influence of adjustment costs on (contemporaneous) productivity growth.

We also include the term *RELTFP* to control for the so-called 'catch-up effect', which states that industries and countries which lagged furthest behind the US in technological sophistication had the most opportunities to imitate and purchase advanced technology and hence should exhibit the fastest rate of technology advance. Taking each industry (sector) in each country as an observation, this hypothesis implies that the rate of growth of (relative) TFP should be inversely correlated with the level of (relative) TFP at the beginning of the period.

In some specifications, country and industry dummy variables are also included to control for country-specific effects, such as the degree of trade openness, culture and government policy; and industry-specific effects, such as market structure and diffusion patterns for new technology.

The results, shown in Tables 8.7 and 8.8, generally confirm the interaction hypothesis. For the manufacturing industry sample, there is a statistically significant relation between a country's (relative) rate of TFP growth and its (relative) rate of capital–labour growth, though the significance level varies from 10% to 1%. The results are strongest for the sample that uses three-year averages for the variables. For the major sector sample, all the regression forms show a highly significant effect of increasing capital intensity on TFP growth. The magnitudes of the coefficients are also interesting. Within manufacturing, a one percentage *point* increase in the annual rate of capital–labour growth is associated with about a 0.1 percentage point (the range is 0.07 to 0.12) increase in TFP growth. Across the major sectors, a one percentage point increase in the annual rate of capital–labour growth is associated with about a 0.3 percentage point (with a range from 0.24 to 0.37) increase in TFP growth.

The results also provide confirmation of the catch-up effect, showing a highly statistically significant inverse relation between the rate of TFP convergence by industry and country and its initial TFP level, relative to the US. However, the *size* of the coefficient is much lower than for relative capital–labour growth. A one percentage point increase in initial relative TFP level is associated with only about a (negative) 0.040 percentage point change in TFP growth for the total economy and about a 0.035 percentage point change in TFP growth in manufacturing.

Table 8.7: Regression of relative TFP growth on relative TFP level and growth in relative capital intensity[a] (manufacturing industry sample)

	Dependent variable: $RLTFPGRT^{h}_{it}$			
Independent variables	2-year average values			3-year averages
Constant	0.0037 (1.01)	−0.0131 (1.43)	−0.0509*** (4.28)	−0.0507*** (5.99)
$RLKLGRT^{h}_{i,t-1}$	0.0945** (6.16)	0.0742* (1.70)	0.0944** (2.22)	0.1151*** (2.86)
$RELTFP^{h}_{it}$	−0.0250*** (2.68)	−0.0362*** (3.53)	−0.0422*** (3.94)	−0.0358*** (4.14)
Country Dummies	Excluded	Included	Included	Included
Industry Dummies	Excluded	Excluded	Included	Included
R^2	0.023	0.074	0.154	0.332
$\bar{R}^2$	0.019	0.053	0.122	0.293
Std error	0.060	0.058	0.056	0.037
Sample size	550	550	550	364

Notes

a Results are based on two-year averages for *RLKLGRT* and *RLTFPGRT* (three-year averages in the last column). The sample covers the time period from 1970 to 1988, 13 countries (excluding the US), and 9 manufacturing industries. Lags are in terms of periods (for the two year average variables, the lag is two years). Estimated coefficients are shown next to the respective independent variable and the absolute value of the *t*-statistic is shown in parentheses. Industries and countries with missing data are excluded from the sample.

* Significant at the 0.10 level (two-tailed test)

** Significant at the 0.05 level (two-tailed test)

*** Significant at the 0.01 level (two-tailed test)

4. CONCLUDING REMARKS

An examination of aggregate statistics, based on the coefficient of variation, shows that convergence of labour productivity, TFP and capital intensity has continued over the period from 1970 to 1988 for the total economy among OECD countries. There is also clear evidence of catch-up, indicated by both rising average productivity and capital intensity of OECD countries relative to the United States and an inverse relation (negative correlation) between initial levels and rates of growth. However, there was no or little convergence in growth *rates* of productivity, which one would expect if productivity levels converged and advantages of backwardness held sway.

On the sectoral level, the coefficient of variation of labour productivity levels, TFP levels and capital intensity was much higher, on average, than that for the overall economy. Moreover, dispersion on the sectoral level shows only a very modest decline. The same pattern is evident for the

Table 8.8: Regression of relative TFP growth on relative TFP level and growth in relative capital intensity[a] *(major sector sample)*

	Dependent variable: $RLTFPGRT^{h}_{it}$			
Independent variables		2-year average values		3-year averages
Constant	−0.0068** (2.77)	−0.0164** (2.15)	−0.0083 (0.88)	−0.0033 (0.44)
$RLKLGRT^{h}_{i,t-1}$	0.3479*** (6.93)	0.3738*** (7.19)	0.3525*** (5.87)	0.2351*** (4.64)
$RELTFP^{h}_{it}$	−0.0369*** (7.08)	−0.0443*** (7.19)	−0.0464*** (6.59)	−0.0290*** (5.12)
Country dummies	Excluded	Included	Included	Included
Industry dummies	Excluded	Excluded	Included	Included
R^2	0.117	0.139	0.154	0.238
$\bar{R}^2$	0.115	0.0122	0.127	0.201
Std error	0.055	0.055	0.054	0.036
Sample size	743	743	743	494

Notes

a Results are based on two-year averages for *RLKLGRT* and *RLTFPGRT* (three-year averages in the last column). The sample covers the time period from 1970 to 1988, 13 countries (excluding the US), and 10 major sectors. Lags are in terms of periods (for the two-year average variables, the lag is two years). Estimated coefficients are shown next to the respective independent variable and the absolute value of the *t*-statistic is shown in parentheses. Industries and countries with missing data are excluded from the sample.

* Significant at the 0.10 level (two-tailed test)

** Significant at the 0.05 level (two-tailed test)

*** Significant at the 0.01 level (two-tailed test)

dispersion of productivity levels and capital–labour ratios relative to the United States across sectors within country. The simple correlation between TFP growth and capital–labour growth was virtually zero across sectors. However, the regression analysis, after controlling for differences in initial TFP, does show a strong positive relation between a sector's TFP growth and its rate of (lagged) capital–labour growth. Moreover, though the catch-up effect is statistically significant, about 50% of the growth of TFP from 1970 to 1988 was attributable to capital investment and only 10% to the catch-up effect, with the remainder due to other factors (results are calculated by substituting mean values of the independent variables into the regression equation results).

For total manufacturing, the convergence of productivity levels came to a halt by 1979 or so. There was a slight convergence of labour productivity levels and capital–labour ratios between 1970 and 1979, followed by a slight divergence between 1979 and 1988. On net, there was virtually no change between 1970 and 1988 in the dispersion of labour productivity levels and an actual increase in that of TFP. There is some evidence of catch-up in labour productivity levels and capital–labour ratios between 1970 and 1979 but none between 1979 and 1988. For TFP there was no catch-up in evidence either during the 1970–1979 period or the 1979–1988 period. Moreover, the coefficient of variation of growth rates of both labour productivity and TFP increased between the 1970–1979 period and the 1979–1988 period.

On the industry level, the coefficient of variation of labour productivity levels and capital–labour ratios declined slightly, on average, between 1970 and 1979 and increased somewhat between 1979 and 1988. The dispersion of TFP levels remained unchanged between 1970 and 1979 and then increased over the 1979–1988 period. The average dispersion of labour productivity, TFP and capital intensity was higher on the industry level than for total manufacturing.

As with the major sectors of the economy, there was virtually no correlation between TFP growth and capital–labour growth on the industry level. However, the regression analysis does show a strong positive relation between industry TFP growth and lagged capital–labour growth. Moreover, the catch-up effect is statistically significant in the regression analysis, though it fails to show up in the aggregate data. Additional calculations show that about 70% of the growth of TFP within manufacturing from 1970 to 1979 was attributable to capital investment and 10% to the catch-up effect and 80% to capital investment over the 1979–1988 period, with almost none of it stemming from the catch-up effect.

Perhaps the bottom line is that the simple advantages of backwardness argument as the explanation of *aggregate* convergence must be modified. The catch-up effect should show up, *if anywhere*, on the sectoral (or industry) level. This occurred very weakly among major sectors of the economy in the 1970s and 1980s and among manufacturing industries in the 1970s, but was virtually nonexistent during the 1980s within manufacturing. Instead, specialisation in particular industries in terms of investment, with its concomitant technological change, appears to be the main driving force over this period. This was particularly the case in manufacturing in the 1980s (Japan being an extreme example of this process). This has resulted in uneven or jagged productivity developments by sector and manufacturing industry within each country.

It also seems likely from other work that the advantages of backwardness effect was the primary mechanism of OECD growth from the 1950s up until the early 1970s. This might explain the high level of productivity growth among OECD countries during this period. However, as productivity levels converged, the advantages of backwardness exhausted themselves, as was particularly evident in manufacturing during the 1980s, and average productivity growth rates fell during the 1970s and again in the 1980s. Further productivity growth is now being achieved primarily through pushing out the technological frontier and, in many cases, overtaking the leader, a process that requires intense capital investment.

NOTES

1. A third possible mechanism was also considered – namely, that employment shifted over time towards industries with high productivity. We found that employment shifts played no role in the convergence of aggregate productivity.
2. See de Long (1988) and Baumol and Wolff (1988) for a discussion of the selectivity bias associated with the OECD sample.
3. Table 8.1 also shows summary statistics for total industry, defined as the total economy excluding producers of government services and other non-firm producers (such as domestic servants). The closest US concept is private GDP. Results for this series show slightly more rapid convergence and catch-up than the previous set for the total economy.
4. It should be stressed that the negative correlation coefficient does *not* by itself constitute a *test* of the convergence hypothesis but that it is indicative of such a relation. See Baumol (1986), de Long (1988), and Baumol and Wolff (1988) for further discussion.
5. The last two columns of Table 8.2 show productivity growth rates based on comparable international data from the US Bureau of Labor Statistics (1991). Results are similar to those from the OECD ISDB data.
6. I use the international factor shares in the computations throughout the paper. See Wolff (1991) for a discussion of the choice of the proper factor shares. The TFP measure is standardised by setting Y/L and Y/K to unity for the US in 1970 so that US TFP in 1970 is equal to one.
7. The Tornqvist approximation based on average period shares is employed.
8. It should be noted that differences in service life assumptions, retirement patterns, and capital prices among countries will lead to inconsistencies in (gross) capital stock estimates among countries and thus in TFP estimates.
9. The 55% figure may appear rather low, but it should be noted that productivity levels here are not adjusted for hours worked. With such an adjustment, GDP per hour worked in German manufacturing was 76% of the corresponding US level in 1988.

REFERENCES

Abramovitz, M. (1986), 'Catching Up, Forging Ahead, and Falling Behind', *Journal of Economic History*, 46, 385–406.

Barro, R.J. (1991), 'Economic Growth in a Cross Section of Countries', *Quarterly Journal of Economics*, 105, 407–443.

Baumol, W.J. (1986), 'Productivity Growth, Convergence, and Welfare: What the Long-Run Data Show', *American Economic Review*, 76, 1072–1085.

Baumol, W.J., Batey Blackman, S.A. and Wolff, E.N. (1989), *Productivity and American Leadership: The Long View*, Cambridge, MA: MIT Press.

Productivity Growth and Capital Intensity on the Sector and Industry Level 211

Baumol, W.J. and Wolff, E.N. (1988), 'Productivity Growth, Convergence, and Welfare: Reply', *American Economic Review*, 78, 1155–1159.

de Long, J.B. (1988), 'Productivity Growth, Convergence, and Welfare: Comment,' *American Economic Review*, 78, 1138–1154.

de Long, J.B. and Summers, L.H. (1991), 'Equipment Investment and Economic Growth', *Quarterly Journal of Economics*, 151, 445–502.

Dollar, D. and Wolff, E.N. (1993), *Competitiveness, Convergence, and International Specialization*, Cambridge, MA: MIT Press.

Gollop, F.M. and Dale W.J. (1980), 'US Productivity Growth by Industry, 1947–73', in J.W. Kendrick and B.N. Vaccara (eds), *New Developments in Productivity Measurement and Analysis*, Chicago: University of Chicago Press.

Maddison, A. (1982), *Phases of Capitalist Development*, Oxford: Oxford University Press.

Summers, R. and Heston, A. (1988), 'A New Set of International Comparisons of Real Product and Prices: Estimates for 130 Countries, 1950–1985', *Review of Income and Wealth*, 34, 1–26.

US Department of Labor, Bureau of Labor Statistics, Office of Productivity and Technology (1991), 'Output per Hour, Hourly Compensation, and Unit Labor Costs in Manufacturing, Twelve Industrial Countries, 1950–1990 and Unit Labor Costs in Korea and Taiwan, 1970–1990', December.

Wolff, E.N. (1991), 'Capital Formation and Productivity Convergence over the Long Term', *American Economic Review*, 81, 565–579.

[6]

COMMENT ON WOLFF

Thijs ten Raa

The initiator of the productivity convergence debate, Ed Wolff, who launched his empirical results early last decade, now takes us with yet another thought-provoking result. The total factor productivity convergence of the 1970s has continued in the 1980s, but the mechanism has changed. It is no longer a technological catch-up by less-developed countries, but the result of specialisation in high-growth sectors. Professor Wolff's diagnosis of convergence is in line with the trade liberalisation that we have witnessed recently.

Professor Wolff's results are still reassuring to the United States. Total factor productivity growth in Japan has not reached American levels yet. To some extent this result may be ascribed to his methodology, however. Total factor productivity growth is measured by the residual between the output growth rate and weighted input growth rates, where the weights are the value shares of the inputs. With an appeal to the theory of international trade, these value shares are equated across countries by taking international means. In this discussion, I am going to examine this methodology and its implication for the result that Japan is still lagging. I shall do so in the context of an example that is favourable to the adoption of the factor price equalisation theorem, namely a world with a common technology.

So let us consider a world economy with a CES production function,

$$F(L,K,\rho) = (\tfrac{1}{2}L^{-\rho} + \tfrac{1}{2}K^{-\rho})^{-1/\rho},$$

common to the US and Japan. Note that since the time argument does not appear on the right-hand side, technical change is absent. If factor inputs are valued by their marginal productivities, as they should be in total factor productivity growth analysis, the wage share is

$$\alpha = \tfrac{1}{2}(Y/L)^{\rho}.$$

For simplicity, let labour and capital grow exponentially in each country: $L = L_0e^{lt}$ and $K = K_0e^{kt}$, then the wage share reduces to

$$\alpha = \frac{e^{-\rho lt}}{e^{-\rho lt} + e^{-\rho kt}}.$$

The labour and capital growth rates may be different for the two countries. Professor Wolff pays attention to the higher growth rate of capital in Japan than in the US. The consequent abundance of capital depresses productivity. Let me stylise this fact by assuming balanced growth for the US ($k = l$), but unbalanced growth for Japan ($k > l$). Then the last expression shows that $\alpha = 1/2$ in the US, but $\alpha \to 1$ in Japan. In the latter country, capital gets so abundant that not only does its price go down, but even its value share does. (This is possible when the macroeconomic production function is CES rather than Cobb–Douglas.)

By averaging out with the US, Professor Wolff underestimates the wage share in Japan and overestimates the capital share. Since in the total factor productivity growth formula, the growth rate of capital dominates that of labour (and both are subtracted from the output growth rate), he underestimates total factor productivity growth in Japan. In other words, the high growth rate of Japanese capital may suppress total factor productivity growth, but the weight attached to it ought to be smaller than in the US and this off-setting effect is not taken into account when value shares are averaged out across countries. Japan may perform better than Professor Wolff's estimates suggest.

International trade theory may be employed to equate factor prices, but not factor shares, except possibly at the sectoral levels. One might build a case, using neoclassical paradigms, for equalisation of value shares between countries on a sector-by-sector basis. However, it is precisely the process of specialisation in sectors that may invalidate the equality of macroeconomic value shares between labour and capital across countries. It would be interesting to redo Professor Wolff's computations with the shares equalities inserted at the sectoral level, on which he builds his analysis anyway.

I am sceptical, however, as regards any use of the factor prices equalisation theorem. One of its assumptions is that at any point of time countries have access to a common technology. True, technical coefficients will differ, but only in response to scarcity conditions, not the state of technology, the book of blueprints of all conceivable techniques. In such a stylised world, any measure of total factor productivity growth that relates to technical change in Solow residual fashion ought to imply no divergence or convergence between countries, but a zero wedge. In other words, when there is access to a common technology, convergence is no issue.

In the final analysis the measurement of productivity growth and convergence is a matter of choosing factor input prices. Professor Wolff, like all leaders in the field, uses the ones based on market value shares. This may be appropriate for a pure competitive economy, but not for the real world. My preference would be to calculate the shadow prices of labour and capital through an appropriate linear program. There would be no need to assume a common technology or to equate value shares. The elasticities of substitution are endogenised by intersectoral shifts of economic activities.

The convergence field is exceptional in economics. Empirical results are ahead of methodology. It remains to be seen if my observations on the bias in Professor Wolff's work are significant. For the time being I accept his confirmation of American leadership and his diagnosis of convergence.

[7]

Economic Systems Research, Vol. 8, No. 4, 1996 391

Productivity Growth, Import Leakage and Employment Growth in Puerto Rico, 1967–87

ANGEL LUIS RUIZ & EDWARD N. WOLFF

(Received January 1996; revised July 1996)

ABSTRACT *Using Puerto Rican input–output data that cover the period 1967–87, we find that employment growth was led primarily by a rapid increase in final output—5.1% per year—although labor productivity growth was also substantial, at 3.7% per year. Import leakages also fell over this period, but had little impact on employment growth. Local absorption was more successful than exports in generating new jobs. Employment generated by local absorption grew by 35% and that from exports by 29%, even though exports increased almost four-fold, while local absorption only doubled. The difference reflects the greater labor intensity of industries that supply local absorption. There was also a notable shift in the occupational structure toward white-collar employment and away from blue-collar jobs. The primary reason for this was the shift in the composition of final demand toward industries that rely heavily on white-collar workers. A secondary reason was a bias in technological change, which favored white-collar over blue-collar workers.*

KEYWORDS: *Export-led growth, import substitution, productivity growth, decomposition analysis, Puerto Rico*

1. Introduction

The nature of the remarkable record of economic achievement in Puerto Rico makes input–output (IO) an even more indispensable tool that it is in other locations, for the design of rational plans for the island's future. The economic record of Puerto Rico is characterized by impressive success and crucial shortcomings. Perhaps its most notable accomplishment has been the growth in labor productivity which, in the period since World War II, has increased from the level of some of the world's most impoverished lands to an amount higher than that of any country in Latin America (see Baumol & Wolff, 1996). Even if that income

Angel Luis Ruiz, Interamerican University, Economic and Administrative Science Division, PO Box 191293, San Juan, Puerto Rico 00919. Edward N. Wolff (to whom correspondence should be addressed), New York University, Department of Economics, 269 Mercer Street, Room 700, New York, NY 10003, USA. The authors would like to express their gratitude to the Andrew W. Mellon Foundation for financial support, and to William Baumol, Jan Oosterhaven and two anonymous referees for their comments. An earlier version of this paper was presented at the 11th International Conference on Input–Output Techniques, New Delhi, India, 27 November–1 December 1995.

0953-5314/96/040391-23

level remains well below that of the US in an international comparison, on that criterion, Puerto Rico must be considered as one of the world's more prosperous areas. Direct observation supports the conclusion suggested by the data: while enormous problems remain, many of them critical, raising average per-capita income even further is not a matter of highest priority.

Instead, the highest priority is probably ascribable to what may be the greatest failure of the island's development programme, i.e. its inability to bring unemployment down to levels anywhere near those that would be considered normal in the US. Despite the general prosperity contributed by 'Operation Bootstrap' and its successors, and the tax incentives provided for the opening of manufacturing facilities on the island by Section 936 of the federal tax code, the unemployment rate was officially estimated at 16.4% in 1993. Not very long before, the figure was even higher (23.4% in 1983), and there are some who suggest that the figure today, corrected for disguised unemployment and other distorting influences, is well above 20%—a rate that prevailed in the US only during the Great Depression. This clearly means that the substantial rise that per-capita income underwent in Puerto Rico was most unevenly distributed. No doubt, a variety of social ills, such as a high crime rate, drug consumption and a number of others, are easily shown to be exacerbated by such unemployment rates, as is the migration to the US of a large body of Puerto Ricans with low incomes and records of low achievement in education and elsewhere.

The implication is that there may be general agreement that increased employment is an end sufficiently desirable in itself to be worth pursuing in the case of Puerto Rico, even if it entails some trade-off in economic efficiency and results in some sacrifice of further increases in per-capita income.

In this paper, we use IO data to investigate the record of Puerto Rico's productivity and employment growth over the period 1967–87 (the latest date for which the pertinent data are available). In particular, we analyze the effects of productivity growth, import leakage, and the level and composition of final demand, especially exports, on overall employment growth and on the occupational composition of employment in Puerto Rico.

We also draw some policy conclusions on ways in which employment may be stimulated on the island. The use of IO analysis for policy design is particularly appropriate here, because of the fulfilment of two conditions: (1) inputs (in this case, employment) as well as outputs directly enter society's objective function; (2) the economy in question is open, so that macro-economic policy is largely powerless to increase employment or to influence the use of other inputs. The only practical means to expand employment in Puerto Rico is to elicit increases in investment in labor-intensive activities, or a reallocation of the current capital stock in a similar direction. Even if markets were sufficiently perfect to permit full employment to be attained eventually through downward wage flexibility, the US minimum wage laws, which apply to Puerto Rico, would prevent it. In any event, the impediments to downward wage flexibility have been widely discussed in the literature.

However, to plan for such a programme, it is essential to determine which industries really are labor intensive, not only in the labor that they themselves employ, but also in the employment that their activities engender in the industries that serve them, and in the industries that serve those serving industries, and so on down the line. Of course, this is something that only IO analysis permits the investigator to find out. Once such a calculation has been carried out, one can begin to study what sort of incentive programme will be most effective in stimulating investment in industries that are truly labor intensive.

We find that, for this period at least, employment grew by 1.4% per year, i.e. somewhat greater than its post-World War II average of 1.1% per year. Employment growth was led primarily by a rapid increase in final output, amounting to 5.1% per year, over the period 1967–87, although labor productivity growth was also substantial, at 3.7% per year. Import leakages also fell over this period, but the impact of this on employment growth was relatively modest. Local absorption was more successful than exports in generating new jobs. Over the period 1967–87, employment generated by local demand grew by 35% and that from exports by 29%, even though exports increased almost four-fold, while local absorption only doubled. The difference is primarily because local absorption absorbs relatively labor-intensive output compared with exports. Between 1967 and 1982, there was also a notable shift in the occupational structure towards white-collar employment and away from blue-collar jobs. The primary reason for the change was the shift in the composition of final demand toward output produced by industries which relied heavily on white-collar workers. A secondary reason was a bias in technological change which favored white-collar over blue-collar workers.

Exports consist almost exclusively of manufacturing products, which have been promoted by the Puerto Rican government through a variety of incentives, including tax relief (Section 936 of the federal tax code), the provision of infrastructure and other subsidies. The result has been the development of US branch plants in Puerto Rico which still heavily rely on the US for inputs and an output market. We argue that a change is called for in development strategy which places greater emphasis on attracting more labor-intensive industries and industries that can rely on inputs produced in Puerto Rico.

In Section 2, we present a brief historical overview of macro-economic trends in Puerto Rico over the period 1947–93. Section 3 develops our accounting framework and model. Results are presented in Section 4, and Section 5 provides some concluding remarks.

2. Post-World War II Macro-economic Trends[1]

Before beginning the IO analysis, it is helpful to highlight the salient features of economic development in Puerto Rico since the end of World War II. There are five of note.

(1) The first is the rapid growth in per-capita income and, even more notably, aggregate labor productivity.
(2) The second is relatively low growth in employment over the period.
(3) The third is high (official) rates of unemployment.
(4) The fourth is the heavy reliance on export-led growth—comparable with the 'Four tigers' of Asia.
(5) The fifth is a limited degree of import substitution, particularly in manufacturing (which we will discuss further in Section 4).

Figure 1 shows the growth in output (gross domestic product (GDP) in constant US dollars), employment and labor productivity, defined as the ratio of GDP in constant dollars to employment. The growth in output has been spectacular: a ten-fold increase between 1947 and 1993. Labor productivity has also shown remarkable growth, increasing by more than six times over the period—or 5.0%

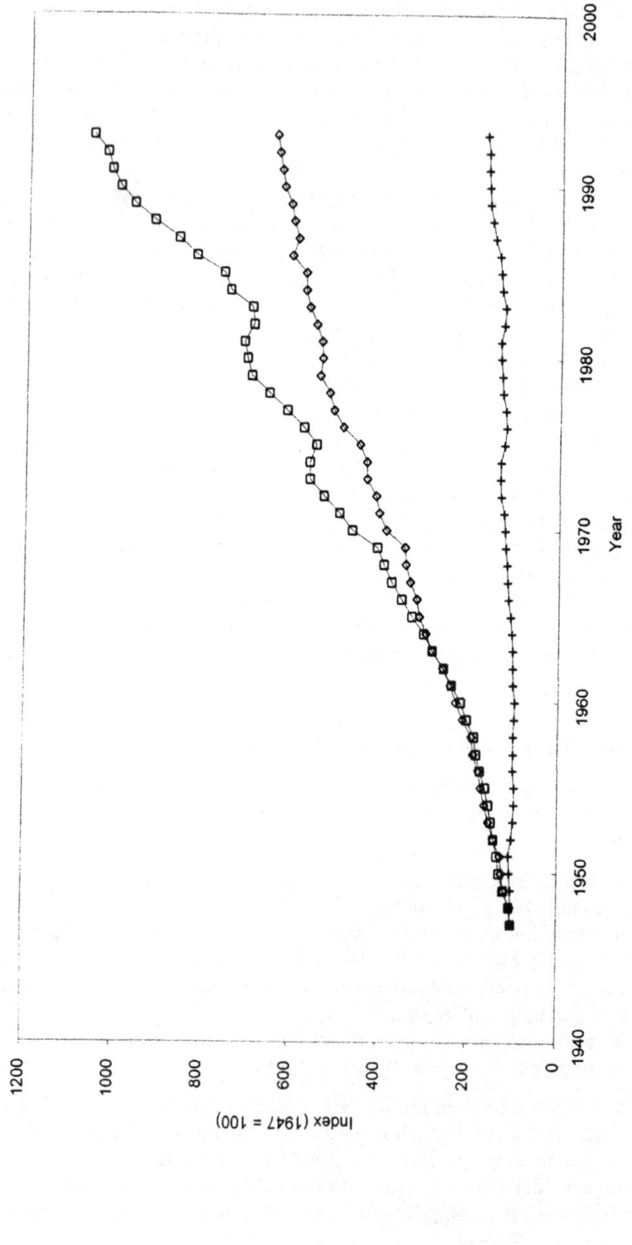

Figure 1. GDP (1954 dollars) (□), employment (+) and labor productivity (◇), with index, 1947 = 100.

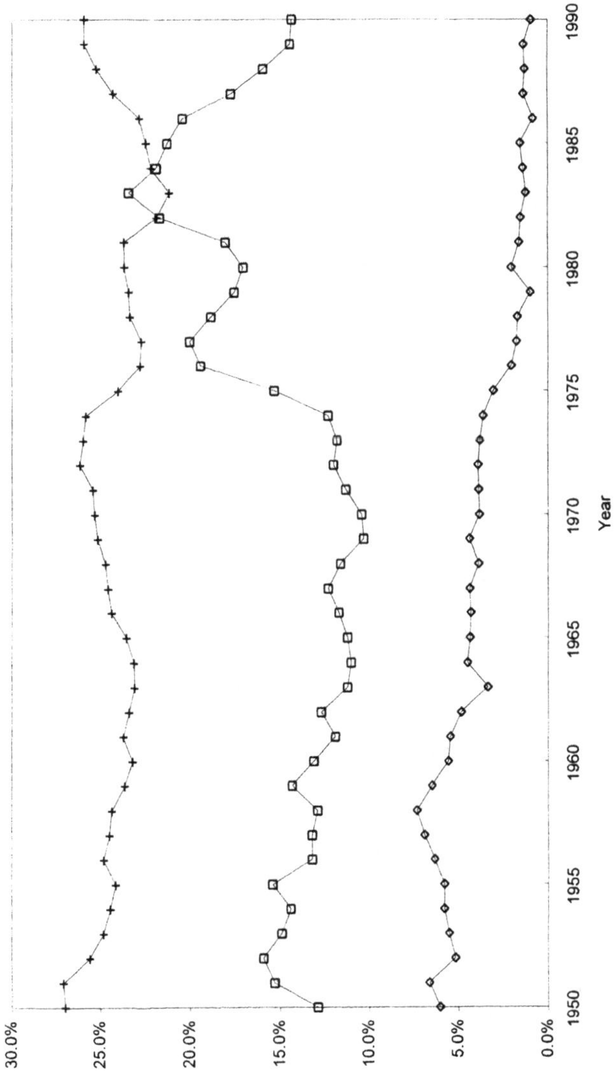

Figure 2. Unemployed rate (□), employment-to-population ratio (+) and annual productivity growth (5-year running average) (◇), 1950–90.

per year. However, employment has grown by only 65% or 1.1% per year. Puerto Rico has made exceptional achievements in both output growth and productivity, but has not been very succesful in generating new employment.

Figure 2 shows trends in annual labor productivity growth (a 5-year running average), the (official) unemployment rate and the ratio of employment to population. The productivity growth trend has been downwards from 5–6% per year during the 1950s, to 3–4% per year during the 1960s and 1970s, and further down to 1–2% per year during the 1980s. The unemployment rate generally followed a downward trend between 1950 and 1970 (from about 15% to 10%) but then turned sharply upward, topping 20% in the early 1980s, before retreating to 16% in the early 1990s. It is interesting that there is very little relation between productivity growth and the unemployment rate. Whereas productivity growth almost continuously followed a downward trend since the early 1950s, the unemployment rate has moved cyclically over the post-war period. The ratio of employment to population—another indicator of employment behavior—has also moved cyclically, first declining from 27% in the early 1950s, to 23% in the mid-1960s, rising to 26% in the early 1970s, then falling again to 21% in the early 1980s, before returning to 26% in the early 1990s. It seems clear that it is the structure of industry, rather than labor productivity growth, that has most affected employment.

The ratio of merchandise exports to GDP for Puerto Rico averaged 56% over the period 1960–90. This is the highest in Latin America and the Caribbean (at least for countries with the requisite data), except for the Bahamas (at 116%). This also compares with a figure of 35% for the Republic of Korea (i.e. South Korea) and 132% for Singapore (comparable figures are not available for Taiwan and Hong Kong). The ratio of exports plus imports to GDP averaged 121% in Puerto Rico over the period 1950–90. The comparable ratio is 45% for the Republic of Korea, 309% for Singapore and 64% for Taiwan. Both in terms of openness and export dependency, Puerto Rico ranks among the highest in the world.[2]

3. Accounting Framework and Model

The formal IO model can be introduced as follows.

$\mathbf{X}$ = 53-order vector of gross domestic output (GDO) by sector
$\mathbf{Y}_\mathrm{T}$ = 53-order vector of total final demand by sector
$\mathbf{Y}_\mathrm{D}$ = 53-order vector of domestic final demand by sector (equivalent to $\mathbf{C}_\mathrm{D} + \mathbf{I}_\mathrm{D} + \mathbf{G}_\mathrm{D} + \mathbf{E}_\mathrm{D}$ (consumption, investment, government expenditures and exports)
$\mathbf{A}_\mathrm{T}$ = 53-order matrix of total technical coefficients, where $a_{\mathrm{T}ij} = x_{\mathrm{T}ij}/x_j$
$\mathbf{A}_\mathrm{D}$ = 53-order matrix of domestic technical coefficients, where $a_{\mathrm{D}ij} = x_{\mathrm{D}ij}/x_j$
$\mathbf{L}$ = 53-order vector of total employment by industry
$\mathbf{l}$ = 53-order vector of labor coefficients, where $l_j = L_j/x_j$
N = total employment

All variables, unless otherwise indicated, are in constant dollars. Then, we have

$$\mathbf{X} = \mathbf{A}_\mathrm{D}\mathbf{X} + \mathbf{Y}_\mathrm{D} \qquad (1)$$

$$N = \mathbf{l}(\mathbf{I} - \mathbf{A}_\mathrm{D})^{-1}\mathbf{Y}_\mathrm{D} \qquad (2)$$

Define

B = 53-order matrix of domestic fulfilment of intermediate demand, where $b_{ij} = x_{Dij}/x_{Tij}$ (unity less the import leakage)

Then, we have

$$a_{Dij} = b_{ij} a_{Tij} \tag{3}$$

Define

$\mathbf{F}_T$ = 53 × 4 total final demand matrix (= ($\mathbf{C}_T$, $\mathbf{I}_T$, $\mathbf{G}_T$, $\mathbf{E}_T$))
$\mathbf{F}_D$ = 53 × 4 domestic final demand matrix (= ($\mathbf{C}_D$, $\mathbf{I}_D$, $\mathbf{G}_D$, $\mathbf{E}_D$))
G = 53 × 4 domestic fulfilment of final demand matrix, where $g_{ij} = f_{Dij}/f_{Tij}$ (unity less the import leakage)

For total final demand, we have

$\mathbf{G}^\star$ = 53-order vector of domestic fulfilment of total final demand, where $g_i^\star = y_{Di}/y_{Ti}$ (unity less the import leakage)
M = 10 × 53 manpower matrix, where m_{ij} shows employment of occupation i in industry j
E = 10 × 53 employment coefficient matrix, where $e_{ij} = m_{ij}/L_j$

Then, we have

$$\mathbf{D} = \mathbf{E}\hat{\mathbf{l}}(\mathbf{I} - \mathbf{A}_D)^{-1}\mathbf{Y}_D \tag{4}$$

where

D = 10-order vector that shows total employment by occupation

4. Results

We begin with statistics on employment multipliers by industry in 1987 (Table 1).[3] The first column in Table 1 shows the actual employment multipliers **λ**, based on the domestic coefficient matrix, i.e.

$$\boldsymbol{\lambda} = \mathbf{l}(\mathbf{I} - \mathbf{A}_D)^{-1}$$

There is considerable variation among sectors, from a high of 348 employees per million dollars (1967 prices) of output in sugar cane to a low of 12 employees per million dollars in petroleum refining. Of the major sectors, manufacturing had by far the lowest employment multiplier, i.e. 37 per million dollars (based on domestic final demand weights). The employment multiplier for transportation, communications and utilities (i.e. 68) is almost double that of manufacturing, and those for agriculture, mining and construction (102) and services (99) are about triple the manufacturing value.

The second column in Table 1 shows what the employment multipliers would be if there were complete import substitution, i.e. no imported intermediate inputs. This is given by

$$\boldsymbol{\lambda}_T = \mathbf{l}(\mathbf{I} - \mathbf{A}_T)^{-1}$$

The third column shows the percentage difference between $\boldsymbol{\lambda}_T$ and **λ**. A high value indicates the existence of considerable import leakage in the use of intermediate inputs. Here, too, there is considerable variation among sectors, from a high of 82% in petroleum refining (almost all intermediate inputs are imported) to a low of 3.9% for the commonwealth government (almost all inputs are produced

Table 1. Total (direct plus indirect) employment multipliers, 1987, and annual rate of change, 1967–87[a] (employees per million 1967 dollars of output)

Sector number and name		Employment multipliers			Annual rate of change, 1967–87 (%)		
		Domestic (λ)	Total (λ_T)	Per cent difference[b]	Domestic multiplier[c]	Total multiplier[d]	Per cent difference[e]
1	Sugar cane	348.1	387.1	10.1	0.51	0.33	− 54.9
2	Other agriculture, forestry and fishing	128.5	151.1	15.0	5.36	5.06	− 5.8
3	Mining	50.1	64.2	21.9	4.65	4.38	− 6.1
4	Construction	94.5	124.3	24.0	2.08	1.88	− 10.8
5	Meat and meat products	115.3	140.4	17.9	4.83	4.90	1.5
6	Milk and dairy products	92.4	128.3	28.0	5.16	4.40	− 17.3
7	Canned and preserved fruits and vegetables	59.0	112.5	47.5	5.11	3.83	− 33.5
8	Grain mill products	37.8	113.4	66.6	− 0.97	5.26	[f]
9	Bakery products	78.8	114.4	31.2	1.65	2.83	41.6
10	Sugar mills, refineries, and confectionery	61.8	86.3	28.4	7.68	6.40	− 20.1
11	Beer, malt and alcoholic beverages	19.1	27.2	29.6	5.05	4.55	− 11.0
12	Bottled and canned soft drinks	41.1	65.3	37.0	3.76	3.08	− 22.4
13	Miscellaneous food products	53.4	111.2	52.0	5.00	5.01	0.1
14	Tobacco products	33.1	44.2	25.1	6.22	8.74	28.9
15	Textile mill products and apparel	84.3	138.2	39.0	1.84	1.96	5.9
16	Furniture, lumber and wood products	92.2	150.8	38.9	1.59	0.96	− 65.8
17	Paper and allied products	49.2	86.0	42.7	1.41	1.71	17.2
18	Printing and publishing	66.5	102.8	35.3	2.61	1.81	− 44.5
19	Petrochemicals	26.9	50.5	46.7	3.95	3.91	− 1.1
20	Drugs and pharmaceuticals	17.7	29.1	39.1	3.75	2.97	− 26.3
21	Other chemical products	34.1	67.2	49.3	7.12	5.81	− 22.6
22	Petroleum refining	12.2	66.6	81.7	4.97	3.70	− 34.3
23	Other petroleum products	39.9	77.7	48.6	1.27	1.18	− 8.0
24	Rubber and plastic products	42.7	70.7	39.6	6.12	4.95	− 23.5
25	Leather and leather products	66.2	125.3	47.1	1.86	1.81	− 2.8
26	Cement, stone, clay, glass and concrete products	54.2	83.5	35.1	3.26	2.42	− 34.6

Table 1:—*continued*

Sector number and name	Employment multipliers: Domestic (λ)	Employment multipliers: Total (λ_T)	Employment multipliers: Per cent difference[b]	Annual rate of change, 1967–87 (%): Domestic multiplier[c]	Annual rate of change, 1967–87 (%): Total multiplier[d]	Annual rate of change, 1967–87 (%): Per cent difference[e]
27 Primary metal products	52.4	62.1	15.6	0.53	2.27	76.5
28 Fabricated metal products	48.5	84.7	42.7	3.35	2.96	−12.9
29 Machinery, except electrical	32.3	62.6	48.4	5.13	2.90	−76.9
30 Electrical and electronic machinery	39.9	61.0	34.5	4.85	4.66	−4.2
31 Transportation equipment	50.2	77.0	34.8	3.53	3.18	−11.1
32 Professional and scientific instruments	34.8	56.0	37.9	8.43	7.29	−15.7
33 Miscellaneous manufactures	42.4	74.4	43.0	3.23	3.32	2.8
34 Transportation	82.6	93.8	11.9	2.56	2.52	−1.6
35 Communications	36.7	42.4	13.4	4.54	4.46	−1.9
36 Electricity and irrigation services	40.2	58.1	30.9	0.97	1.32	27.0
37 Water and sewerage services	115.3	126.1	8.6	3.12	3.18	2.0
38 Wholesale and retail trade	109.5	116.2	5.8	1.80	1.68	−7.1
39 Finances	28.5	32.4	12.2	5.71	5.78	1.2
40 Insurance	61.4	71.9	14.7	4.60	4.81	4.2
41 Real estate	31.3	39.7	21.3	−2.47	−2.49	0.8
42 Hotels	188.9	204.4	7.6	−1.52	−1.46	−4.6
43 Personal services	110.0	130.4	15.7	6.40	5.86	−9.3
44 Business services	72.5	81.3	10.9	4.74	4.63	−2.4
45 Repair services, car rental and parking	19.4	27.1	28.5	10.10	9.06	−11.5
46 Amusement and recreation	155.3	178.2	12.8	1.43	1.59	9.9
47 Medical and hospital services	187.0	199.5	6.3	2.29	2.25	−1.7
48 Other services	113.4	120.1	5.6	0.61	0.38	−58.3
49 Commonwealth government	116.1	121.0	4.1	1.59	2.05	22.3
50 Municipal government	226.2	235.2	3.9	1.20	1.46	17.7
51 Federal government	75.0	84.2	11.0	−0.87	0.10	[f]
Unweighted average	73.0	97.3	25.0	3.37	3.29	−2.5

Table 1:—*continued*

Sector number and name	Employment multipliers			Annual rate of change, 1967–87 (%)		
	Domestic (λ)	Total (λ_T)	Per cent difference[b]	Domestic multiplier[c]	Total multiplier[d]	Per cent difference[e]
Average weighted by domestic final demand						
Agriculture, mining and construction	101.7	130.0	21.8	2.37	2.19	−8.4
Manufacturing	37.3	62.1	40.0	5.89	5.69	−3.6
Transportation, communications and utilities	67.6	78.4	13.8	2.80	2.85	1.8
Services	99.0	106.2	6.8	1.87	1.97	4.9
All sectors	66.0	83.5	20.9	3.63	3.70	1.8
Average weighted by gross domestic output						
Agriculture, mining and construction	106.1	133.5	20.5	3.51	3.16	−11.0
Manufacturing	38.3	64.5	40.7	5.54	5.37	−3.2
Transportation, communications and utilities	58.3	69.0	15.5	3.29	3.25	−1.1
Services	88.6	95.9	7.6	2.28	2.32	1.7
All sectors	65.2	82.1	20.6	3.78	3.84	1.6

[a] From $\boldsymbol{\lambda} = \mathbf{l}(\mathbf{I} - \mathbf{A}_D)^{-1}$ and $\boldsymbol{\lambda}_T = \mathbf{l}(\mathbf{I} - \mathbf{A}_T)^{-1}$.
[b] Given by $(\lambda_T - \lambda)/\lambda_T$.
[c] Given by $\ln(\lambda^{67}/\lambda^{87})/20$.
[d] Given by $\ln(\lambda_T^{67}/\lambda_T^{87})/20$.
[e] Given by $[\ln(\lambda_T^{67}/\lambda_T^{87})/20 - \ln(\lambda^{67}/\lambda^{87})/20]/\ln(\lambda_T^{67}/\lambda_T^{87})/20$.
[f] Signs differ between the two terms.

locally). Of the major sectors, the degree of import leakage is greatest for manufacturing (a 40% difference, based on domestic final demand weights), followed by agriculture, mining and construction (21%), transportation, communications and utilities (16%), and services (8%). Thus, manufacturing is the sector with the lowest (domestic) employment multiplier and the highest degree of import leakage.

Column four in Table 1 shows the annual rate of change of the inverse of λ between 1967 and 1987 (where we use the inverse to reduce the number of negative signs). Thus, a high positive value indicates a rapid reduction in the employment multiplier over time. Here, it is clear that manufacturing has had by far the most rapid reduction in its employment multiplier, at 5.9% per year on the basis of final demand weights (and 5.5% on the basis of gross output weights). This figure is more than 50% greater than the annual rate of reduction of the employment multiplier of transportation, communications and utilities (3.3%), more than double that for agriculture, mining and construction (2.4%), and more than three times as great as that for services (1.9%). For the economy as a whole, the employment multiplier declined by 3.6% per year on the basis of domestic final demand weights (and 3.8% per year on the basis of gross output weights).

The fifth column of Table 1 shows the same statistic for λ_T, which indicates what the annual rate of change of the inverse employment multipliers would be if there were no imported intermediate inputs. This figure is also a measure of the annual rate of growth of the total (direct plus indirect) labor productivity by sector.[4] Overall, labor productivity grew by 3.7% per year over the period 1967–87 (based on final demand weights). Manufacturing had the highest growth, at 5.7% per year, followed by transportation, communications and utilities (2.9%), agriculture, mining and construction (2.2%), and services (2.0%).

The difference between columns four and five is an indicator of whether or not the degree of intermediate import leakage has changed since 1967. A positive difference is indicative that, on net, import substitution has occurred; a negative difference indicates that import leakages have increased. For the economy as a whole, there was a modest degree of import substitution (1.8% difference on the basis of domestic final demand weights). Import substitution was relatively strong in the services sector (4.9% difference) and very modest in transportation, communications and utilities (1.8% difference). Manufacturing and (particularly) agriculture, mining and construction experienced increased intermediate import leakages between 1967 and 1987. Thus, the high rate of reduction of the domestic employment multiplier in manufacturing is primarily attributable to its high rate of total labor productivity growth, although increased intermediate import leakages also played a role.

4.1. Aggregate Employment

Table 2 shows the employment generated by each component of domestic final demand, derived from equation (2) for 1967, 1977 and 1987.[5] In 1967, for example, 41% of total employment was generated either directly or indirectly by personal consumption expenditures on domestically produced goods and services; 17% by investment; 15% by government spending; 24% by exports of goods and services; and 4% by visitor (tourist) spending in Puerto Rico (panel A). Between

Table 2. Employment generated by component of domestic final demand ($\mathbf{Y}_D$), 1967–87[a]

	Personal consumption expenditure	Investment	Government consumption	Exports: Goods and services	Exports: Visitor expenditures	Total domestic final demand $\mathbf{Y}_D$
(A) *Percentage composition of employment by component*						
1967	41.1	16.7	14.6	24.1	3.6	100.0
1977	46.3	10.0	22.7	17.2	3.8	100.0
1987	39.4	8.3	25.5	23.7	3.1	100.0
(B) *Average annual growth rate of employment by component (%)*						
1967–77	1.71	− 4.56	4.94	− 2.83	1.09	0.52
1977–87	0.75	0.44	3.48	5.53	0.49	2.34
1967–87	1.23	− 2.06	4.21	1.35	0.79	1.43
(C) *Employment generated per million dollars (1967 prices) of domestic final demand component*						
1967	141	141	153	118	153	137
1977	92	90	145	44	125	84
1987	75	85	125	36	99	66
Annual growth rate, 1967–87 (%)						
	− 3.13	− 2.51	− 1.02	− 5.95	− 2.17	− 3.63
Addendum: Average annual growth rate of domestic final output (1967 prices) by component (%)						
1967–77	6.01	− 0.03	5.53	7.07	3.08	5.44
1977–87	2.70	0.93	4.92	7.52	2.84	4.70
1967–87	4.36	0.45	5.23	7.29	2.96	5.07

[a]From equation (2), $N = \mathbf{l}(\mathbf{I} - \mathbf{A}_D)^{-1}(\mathbf{C}_D + \mathbf{I}_D + \mathbf{G}_D + \mathbf{E}_D)$.

1967 and 1977, the proportion of total employment generated by personal consumption increased from 41% to 46%, and then declined to 39% in 1987. The share generated by government expenditures increased dramatically over the years 1967 to 1987, rising from 15% to 26%. In contrast, the proportion attributable to domestic investment fell off very sharply, decreasing from 17% to only 8%. The share generated by direct exports also declined sharply, falling from 24% in 1967 to 17% in 1977, but then rebounded to 24% in 1987. The share attributable to tourism experienced a modest reduction between 1967 and 1987.

Panel B in Table 2 provides another way of looking at these changes, i.e. in terms of annual growth rates of employment. While overall employment grew by 1.4% per year between 1967 and 1987, the employment numbers generated by household consumption grew somewhat slower (1.2%), while employment from government expenditure rose much faster (4.2%). The total employment generated by investment actually declined over the period in absolute terms (by 34%). Employment generated by the export of goods and services increased at a pace slightly below average (1.35%), while tourist-generated employment rose by only 0.8% per year.

As is evident from equation (2), the change in the employment generated by final output arises from two sources: (1) changes in real output ($\mathbf{F}_D$) and (2) changes in the employment generated per real dollar of output, i.e. $[\mathbf{l}(\mathbf{I} - \mathbf{A}_D)^{-1}]$. Panel C in Table 2 shows statistics on the second of these effects. Here, it should be recalled that, strictly speaking, the term $[\mathbf{l}(\mathbf{I} - \mathbf{A}_D)^{-1}]$ is not an indicator of changes in total labor productivity, i.e. of the direct plus indirect labor required to produce one unit of output. The term also reflects the degree of import leakage in intermediate demand, i.e. the difference between the matrix **A** and the matrix $\mathbf{A}_D$.

There are striking differences in the level and changes in the employment generated per dollar among final demand components. In 1967, 153 jobs were generated per million dollars of government spending, as well as per million dollars of tourist spending. Personal consumption and investment generated slightly lower levels of employment, with both generating 141 jobs. Exports of goods and services generated by far the fewest, i.e. 118 jobs (14% lower than the total final demand).

Between 1967 and 1987, employment generated per million (1967) dollars of personal consumption expenditures fell by 47% (3.1% per year); employment generated by tourism and investment fell by slightly less, with levels of 35% and 40% respectively; while the number of jobs generated by a million dollars of government expenditure declined by only 18%, primarily reflecting the low productivity growth in this sector. In contrast, the number of jobs generated per million dollars of exports of goods and services fell by over 80%, or 6.0% per year. In 1987, jobs generated per dollar of direct exports amounted to less than half the number generated per dollar of personal consumption, investment and tourist spending.

The addendum to Table 2 shows the first effect, i.e. the growth in real domestic output by component. Over the years 1967–77, exports of goods and services had by far the fastest rate of growth, at 7.3% per year, compared with 5.2% per year for government consumption, 4.4% per year for personal consumption expenditures and only 0.5% per year for investment. Personal consumption grew very rapidly in the period 1967–77, at 6.0% per year, and then slowed down to 2.7% per year in the period 1977–87. Investment remained almost unchanged in real terms from 1967 to 1977, and then grew at 0.9% per year during 1977–87. The growth in government consumption was slightly higher between 1967 and 1977, at 5.5% per year, compared with 4.9% per year between 1977 and 1987. Export growth accelerated somewhat over the two periods, from 7.1% to 7.5% per year.

4.2. Decomposition of Changes in Employment

We next analyze the sources of employment growth by taking the differential of equation (2), i.e.

$$\Delta\mathbf{N} = \mathbf{l}(\mathbf{I} - \mathbf{A}_D)^{-1}\,\Delta\mathbf{Y}_D + \Delta[\mathbf{l}\ (\mathbf{I} - \mathbf{A}_D)^{-1}]\mathbf{Y}_D \qquad (5)$$

where a delta (Δ) indicates the change in the matrix over the period. We use average period weights to provide an exact decomposition of $\Delta\mathbf{N}$. The change in domestic final demand can be further decomposed into the change in the total final demand matrix, holding constant the final demand import leakage ratios, and into the change in the final demand import leakage ratios, holding constant the total final demand matrix, i.e.

$$\Delta\mathbf{F}_D = \mathbf{G}\star\Delta\mathbf{F}_T + \Delta\mathbf{G}\star\mathbf{F}_T$$

where the asterisk ($\star$) indicates term-by-term multiplication.

In a similar fashion, the change in the domestic interindustry coefficient matrix can be decomposed into the change in the total interindustry coefficient matrix, holding constant the interindustry import leakage ratios, and into the change in the interindustry coefficient leakage ratios, holding constant the total interindustry coefficient matrix, i.e.,

$$\Delta \mathbf{A}_D = \mathbf{B} \star \Delta \mathbf{A}_T + \Delta \mathbf{B} \star \mathbf{A}_T$$

We can isolate three terms in this decomposition. The first term, which we will call the 'final demand effect', is the change in total employment generated by the change in the total final demand matrix ($\Delta \mathbf{F}_T$) over the period, with technology and the import leakage ratios held constant. The second term, i.e. the 'technical change effect', shows the change in total employment generated by the change in technology ($\Delta[\mathbf{l}(\mathbf{I} - \mathbf{A}_T)^{-1}]$) over the period, with the final demand vector and the import leakage ratios held constant. The third term is the 'import leakage effect', which shows the change in employment that results from the change in the import leakage ratios ($\Delta \mathbf{B}$, $\Delta \mathbf{G}$), with technology and final demand held constant. The decomposition can be applied to each component of final demand. We do this for all components of final demand, except inventory change, which we leave unchanged in the decomposition.

The first effect can, in turn, be decomposed into two further effects. First, define $\phi_{ij} = F_{Tij}/\Sigma_i F_{Tij}$, where $\boldsymbol{\phi}$ is the coefficient matrix for final demand and shows the industrial composition of each component of final output. Also, let $\mathbf{H} = (\Sigma_i F_{Ti1}, \ldots, \Sigma_i F_{Ti4})$ be the four-order row vector that shows the total output of each component of final demand. Then, $\mathbf{Y}_T = \mathbf{H}\boldsymbol{\phi}$ and

$$\Delta \mathbf{Y}_T = \Delta \mathbf{H}\boldsymbol{\phi} + \mathbf{H}\Delta\boldsymbol{\phi} \tag{6}$$

The first term on the right-hand side, which we call the 'levels effect', shows the change in the vector of total final demand that is attributable to changes in the level of output of each component of final demand, holding constant the industrial composition of each component of final demand. The second term, which we call the 'composition effect', shows the change in the vector of total final demand that is attributable to changes in the composition of each component of final demand, holding constant the total level of final output by component.[6]

Results are shown in Table 3. Between 1967 and 1977, total employment increased by 35 000 workers, or 5% of the initial employment level. If technology and import leakages had remained constant, as well as the composition of each component of final demand, and total final demand had increased from its 1967 level to its 1977 level, then total employment would have increased by 56%. However, the composition of the final output shifted towards industries with lower employment multipliers, reducing employment by 13%, so that the net effect of the change in the final demand vector $\mathbf{Y}_T$ was a 43% increase in employment. If final demand and import leakages had remained constant, then the change in technology would have reduced employment by 43%. There was also some substitution of domestically produced products for imports, which increased employment by 5%. The net result was a 5% increase in total employment.

Total final demand grew slightly slower in the period 1977–87, increasing employment by 46%, in contrast to a 56% rise in the previous period. The composition effect was also weaker, decreasing employment by only 6%, so that the total effect of the change in final output was a 40% increase in total employment. Technological change slowed down quite sharply in the period 1977–87, reducing employment by only 12%. Changes in import leakages were negligible during this period, so that the net effect was a 26% gain in total employment.

Table 3. Sources of total employment growth by period: decomposition into a final demand effect, technical change effect and import leakage effect, 1967–87[a] (per cent of initial employment)

	Actual change in employment ΔN	Change in total final demand ΔY_T^b			Change in total coefficients (ΔA_T, ΔI)	Change in import leakages (ΔB, ΔG)
		Total effect	Levels effect	Composition effect		
(A) *Total final demand* (**Y**)						
1967–77	5	43	56	− 13	− 43	5
1977–87	26	40	46	− 6	− 12	− 1
1967–87	33	85	110	− 25	− 56	4
(B) *Local absorption* (**C** + **I** + **G**)						
1967–77	15	48	53	− 5	− 39	7
1977–87	16	33	35	− 2	− 14	− 3
1967–87	35	88	96	− 8	− 57	4
(C) *Exports, including tourism* (**E**)						
1967–77	− 22	37	66	− 29	− 57	− 2
1977–87	53	53	89	− 36	− 6	5
1967–87	29	77	131	− 54	− 52	5

[a]From equation (5), $\Delta N = \mathbf{l}(\mathbf{I} - \mathbf{A_D})^{-1}\Delta \mathbf{Y_D} + \Delta[\mathbf{l}(\mathbf{I} - \mathbf{A_D})^{-1}]\mathbf{Y_D}$, where $\mathbf{A_D} = \mathbf{A_T} \star \mathbf{B}$, $\mathbf{F_D} = \mathbf{F_T} \star \mathbf{G}$, and the asterisk (⋆) indicates term-by-term multiplication. The decomposition uses average period weights.

[b]From equation (6), $\Delta \mathbf{Y_T} = \Delta \mathbf{H}\phi + \mathbf{H}\Delta\phi$.

Over the entire period 1967–87, the growth in the level of total final demand added 110% to total employment, while the change in the composition of final demand reduced employment by 25% and technological change further reduced it by 56%. Reduced import leakage added 4% to total employment, of which the substitution of domestically produced intermediate inputs for imported inputs increased employment by 5%, while increased import leakage in final demand reduced employment by 1%.

We can now understand the sources of the change in employment growth between 1967 and 1987. Employment grew much slower during 1967–77 than in 1977–87. During the first period, rapid technological change and the shift in the mix of final output towards less labor-intensive industries completely offset the growth in the level of final output in generating new employment. However, import substitution was relatively strong, so that employment did manage to grow over these years, although only by 5%. During the period 1977–87, final output continued to increase at almost the same rate as in the previous period, but the rate of technological change fell off sharply and the final output composition effect decreased by half. With the degree of import leakage remaining almost unchanged over the period 1977–87, employment grew substantially, i.e. by 26%.

Patterns differ markedly between local absorption (personal consumption, investment and government spending) and exports. Panel B of Table 3 analyzes the contribution of local absorption to employment. The growth in employment generated by local absorption was 15% in 1967–77—much higher than total employment growth—and this was led by a substantial (48%) gain in jobs from the growth in real local absorption. Import substitution also played an important role, adding 7% to employment. Jobs generated by local absorption increased at almost the same rate during 1977–87, despite a slowing down of the growth in real local absorption. The main reason was that technological change reduced employment by only 14% in this period, in contrast to 39% during 1967–77. Import leakages also increased over the second period, causing a 3% reduction in employment. Shifts in the composition of local final output played a relatively minor role in explaining changes in employment.

The results for export-driven employment are quite different from those for local absorption. Jobs created by exports fell sharply in the first period, i.e. by 22%. Despite a very rapid growth in export demand (7.1% per year), the jobs generated from export growth alone amounted to only 37%, i.e. less than that from the growth in local absorption. The main reason was that shifts in export composition greatly favoured industries with relatively low employment multipliers (in particular, out of refined sugar and rum, and towards petrochemicals, drugs and pharmaceuticals, and electrical and electronic equipment), causing a 29% decline in employment. Moreover, productivity growth in export industries was very high, causing a 57% loss in jobs. Together with a moderate increase in import leakages, this was responsible for a tremendous loss of export-generated jobs.

In contrast, during 1977–87, employment generated by exports increased by a remarkable 53%. This was led by a 53% gain in employment that resulted from the growth in export demand (despite the fact that export demand grew only slightly faster in the period 1977–87 than in the previous period). By itself, the growth in the level of final demand would have increased employment by 89%. However, as in the previous period, this was offset by a continuing shift in the composition of exports toward less labor-intensive industries (particularly towards drugs and pharmaceuticals, electrical and electronic equipment, and professional and scientific instruments), which lowered employment by 36% in the later period.

Moreover, while the pace of technological change slowed down for the economy as a whole, it was particularly slow in the export industries, causing a 6% reduction in employment. This was particularly the case for the three major export industries (based on average export shares over the period 1977–87): drugs and pharmaceuticals, whose domestic employment multipliers (λ) increased over the period 1977–87 by 0.6% per year; electrical and electronic machinery, whose domestic employment multipliers remained constant; and textile mill products, whose domestic employment multipliers fell by 1.3% per year. There was also a substantial reduction in import leakages, adding another 5% to employment growth; together with the other two effects, this increased export-driven employment by 53% over the period 1977–87.

Interestingly, when we compare the records for local absorption and exports over the full period of 20 years, employment generated by local absorption increased more than that from export activity: 35% versus 29%. This difference results mainly from the greater final demand effect on employment: 88% from increasing local absorption compared with a 77% gain from export growth. The technical change effect was also slightly larger for the production of local absorption goods (57%) than export producers (52%). The leakage effect was quite similar for the two components: reduced import leakages added 4–5% to employment in the two cases.

Table 4. Percentage distribution of employment by major occupational group, 1967 and 1982

Occupational group	1967	1982	Annual growth rate of employment 1967–82 (%)
Executive, administrative and managerial occupations	8.3	8.7	1.24
Professional specialty occupations	9.3	11.8	2.46
Technicians and related support occupations	1.3	2.0	3.86
Administrative support occupations	12.0	15.2	2.43
Sales workers	7.8	10.7	2.97
Precision production, craft and repair occupations	12.8	10.4	−0.50
Operatives and fabricators	18.6	14.5	−0.76
Laborers except farm	6.1	5.5	0.10
Farm and fishery workers	12.5	4.7	−5.62
Service occupations	11.3	16.5	3.37
Total	100.0	100.0	0.88

4.3. *Employment by Occupational Group*

We next turn to changes in employment by occupation. Table 4 details changes in the composition of employment by major occupational group. As was also true for the US, Puerto Rico saw a sizable increase in the proportion of white-collar employment and a corresponding decline in blue-collar jobs over the period 1967–82.[7] Managerial jobs grew from 8.3% to 8.7% of total employment over this period; those employed in professional and speciality occupations grew from 9.3% to 11.8%; technical jobs and administrative support positions grew from 13.3% to 17.2%; and sales jobs grew from 7.8% to 10.7%.

Among the blue-collar occupations, a large relative loss—as well as an absolute decline—was experienced by craft jobs, falling from 12.8% to 10.4%; by operatives and fabricators, falling from 18.6% to 14.5%; and especially by farm workers, here falling from 12.5% to 4.7%. Non-farm laborers declined from 6.1% to 5.5% of total employment, although their number did rise slightly in absolute terms. The only blue-collar occupation that showed a relative increase was service jobs, which increased from 11.3% to 16.5% of total employment.

Table 5 shows employment by occupation as generated by the domestic final demand component in 1982 (see equation (4)). There are several interesting results. First, 19% of the jobs generated by personal consumption expenditures were in sales, and this component alone accounted for 76% of the sales jobs in the economy and 65% of farm jobs in 1982. Almost 31% of the jobs generated by investment were craft and skilled positions (mainly attributable to construction). Over one-third of the jobs generated by government expenditures were managerial and professional positions, and another 47% were administrative support and service jobs. Government spending accounted for almost one-third of all managerial jobs, 57% of all professional jobs, and over one-third of administrative support and service jobs. Over half of all jobs generated by exports of goods and services were skilled craft and operative jobs, and this component alone accounted

Table 5. Employment by occupational group, as generated by component of domestic final demand ($\mathbf{Y}_D$), 1982[a]

	Personal consumption expenditure	Investment	Government consumption	Exports: Goods and services	Exports: Visitor expenditures	Total domestic final demand $\mathbf{Y}_D$
(A) *Percentage of total employment generated by final demand component*						
Managerial	8.6	6.0	11.0	7.2	8.1	8.7
Professional	9.0	3.4	26.7	3.4	5.1	11.8
Technicians	2.4	1.6	2.0	1.8	0.8	2.0
Administrative support	14.4	8.7	21.9	11.3	11.5	15.2
Sales	18.5	8.7	0.8	6.2	14.2	10.7
Craft, repair	8.9	30.9	4.4	14.5	7.8	10.4
Operatives	10.3	15.4	4.5	35.8	13.5	14.5
Non-farm labor	5.2	16.3	2.4	6.0	4.8	5.5
Farm workers	6.9	1.8	1.7	4.4	6.8	4.7
Service	15.9	7.3	24.6	9.4	27.4	16.5
Total	100.0	100.0	100.0	100.0	100.0	100.0
(B) *Percentage of total employment of occupational group*						
Managerial	43.2	4.8	31.8	17.2	2.7	100.0
Professional	33.5	2.0	57.1	6.0	1.3	100.0
Technicians	51.0	5.4	24.4	17.8	1.2	100.0
Administrative support	41.9	4.0	36.5	15.4	2.2	100.0
Sales	76.3	5.7	2.0	12.1	3.9	100.0
Craft, repair	37.5	20.8	10.6	28.7	2.2	100.0
Operatives	31.4	7.5	7.8	51.1	2.7	100.0
Non-farm labor	42.4	21.0	11.2	22.9	2.6	100.0
Farm workers	64.7	2.7	9.1	19.4	4.2	100.0
Service	42.5	3.1	37.7	11.8	4.9	100.0
Total	44.1	7.0	25.2	20.7	2.9	100.0

[a]From equation (4), $\mathbf{D} = \mathbf{E}\hat{\mathbf{l}}(\mathbf{I} - \mathbf{A}_D)^{-1}\mathbf{Y}_D$.

for 51% of all operative jobs. Over one-quarter of the positions generated by tourist spending were service jobs.

Changes over time in the jobs generated by local absorption expenditure and exports also exhibit a sharp contrast, as shown in Table 6. Professional jobs generated by local absorption grew by 2.5% per year between 1967 and 1982, while professional jobs generated by exports increased by only 1.6% per year. Sales jobs generated by local absorption grew faster than those from exports (3.1% versus 2.2% per year), as did service jobs (3.7% versus 2.0% per year).

In contrast, technical jobs generated by exports rose faster than those generated by local absorption (5.4% versus 3.5% per year). Craft and skilled jobs that resulted from exports increased over time, rising 1.7% per year, but fell by 1.3%

Table 6. Employment by occupational group, as generated by local absorption and exports as a percentage of total employment generated by component, 1967 and 1982

	1967	1982	Annual growth rate of employment, 1967–82 (%)
(A) *Local absorption* (**C** + **I** + **G**)			
Managerial	9.2	9.1	1.15
Professional	11.8	14.3	2.53
Technicians	1.5	2.2	3.54
Administrative support	13.2	16.4	2.66
Sales	8.8	11.7	3.13
Craft, repair	13.8	9.4	− 1.30
Operatives	11.9	8.9	− 0.71
Non-farm labor	6.7	5.3	− 0.29
Farm workers	10.6	4.7	− 4.18
Service	12.4	18.0	3.69
Total	100.0	100.0	1.23
(B) *Exports, including tourism* (**E**)			
Managerial	5.6	7.3	1.59
Professional	2.8	3.6	1.57
Technicians	0.7	1.6	5.38
Administrative support	8.8	11.3	1.51
Sales	5.1	7.2	2.16
Craft, repair	10.3	13.7	1.69
Operatives	36.3	33.1	− 0.79
Non-farm labor	4.6	5.9	1.44
Farm workers	17.3	4.7	− 8.87
Service	8.3	11.6	2.02
Total	100.0	100.0	− 0.16

per year as a result of local absorption. The same pattern is evident for non-farm laborers. Farm jobs derived from both local absorption and exports fell between 1967 and 1982, but the rate of decline was twice as great for export-driven jobs. Indeed, in 1967, 17% of the jobs created by exports were farm jobs but, by 1982, this proportion had fallen to 5%, reflecting the replacement of manufactured exports for exports of agricultural products (particularly sugar-cane products).

The technique used to decompose the change in total employment into final demand, technology and linkage effects can also be applied to changes in occupational employment. The results, shown in Table 7 for the period 1967–82, allow us to understand some of the reasons for the shift of employment out of blue-collar positions into white-collar posts. The change in total final demand has favored white-collar jobs. By itself, it would have more than doubled technical jobs, almost doubled managerial, professional, administrative support and service jobs, and increased sales jobs by 71%. However, it would have raised the number of craft, operative, non-farm and farm labor jobs only in the range 35–61%.

Changes in technology acted to reduce employment in all occupational groups. The largest effects were on managerial, operative, non-farm labor and, especially, farm laborer jobs, where technological change alone would have reduced employment by 63–108%. Interestingly, other large effects are not confined to blue-collar jobs. Large negative effects are found for professional, technical, and administrat-

Table 7. Sources of total employment growth by occupational group, 1967–82: decomposition into a technical change effect, final demand effect and import leakage effects[a] (percentage of initial occupational employment)

	Actual change in employment ΔN	Change in total final demand $\Delta \mathbf{Y}_T$	Change in total coefficients $(\Delta \mathbf{A}_T, \Delta \mathbf{I}, \Delta \mathbf{E})$	Change in import leakages $(\Delta \mathbf{B}, \Delta \mathbf{G})$
Managerial	21	87	−69	3
Professional	45	98	−49	−5
Technicians	78	124	−47	1
Administrative support	44	92	−48	1
Sales	56	71	−20	5
Craft, repair	−7	35	−46	4
Operatives	−11	59	−76	6
Non-farm labor	1	61	−63	4
Service	66	85	−16	−3
Farm workers	−57	39	−108	12
Total	14	78	−68	4

[a]From equations (4) and (5), we have $\Delta \mathbf{D} = \mathbf{E}\hat{\mathbf{I}}(\mathbf{I} - \mathbf{A}_D)^{-1} \Delta \mathbf{Y}_D + \Delta[\mathbf{E}\mathbf{I}(\mathbf{I} - \mathbf{A}_D)^{-1}]\mathbf{Y}_D$ where $\mathbf{A}_D = \mathbf{A}_T \star \mathbf{B}$, $\mathbf{F}_D = \mathbf{F}_T \star \mathbf{G}$ and an asterisk ($\star$) indicates term-by-term multiplication. The decomposition uses average period weights.

ive support positions, as well as craft jobs. The effect is relatively small for sales and service jobs.

Import substitution for intermediate inputs and final output increased employment in all occupations except professionals and service workers. The effect was particularly strong for farm labor, where the substitution of locally produced agricultural products for imported products helped to raise employment by 12%. Other large effects are observed for operatives (6%), sales workers (5%), and craft workers and non-farm labor (4% for each group). In contrast, imports over the period substituted for local products that relied heavily on professional workers, reducing their employment by 5%; this also affected service workers, reducing their employment by 3%.

5. Concluding Remarks

Over the years 1967–87, employment grew by 1.4% per year—slightly greater than its historical average of 1.1% per year over the period 1947–93. Employment growth was led primarily by a rapid increase in final output which amounted to 5.1% per year over the period 1967–87. Holding constant technology and import leakages, the overall output growth would have increased employment by 85% over the two decades. In addition, a modest reduction in import leakages (holding constant final demand and technology) would have increased jobs by another 4%. Labor productivity growth was also substantial over these years, amounting to 3.7% per year. Technological change (holding constant final demand and import leakages) would have reduced employment by 56%.

There are marked differences between the two decades 1967–77 and 1977–87. Employment growth was feeble during the earlier period, amounting to only 0.5% per year, despite a vigorous growth of output of 5.4% per year. However, overall labor productivity grew rapidly, i.e. by 4.2% per year, and the technology effect almost exactly offset the employment growth induced by rising final demand. Import substitution occurred over the period 1967–77 and added 5% to job growth, accounting for the net gain in jobs over these years.

Between 1977 and 1987, employment increased by a substantial 2.3% per year, despite a modest slowing of output growth to 4.7% per year. The primary reason was a sharp slowing down of productivity growth, which averaged only 2.9% over these years. The import leakage effect was negligible over this period.

Between 1967 and 1982, there was also a notable shift in the occupational structure towards white-collar employment (managerial, professional, technical, clerical and sales) and away from blue-collar jobs (craft, operative, labor and service). White-collar jobs grew from 39% to 48% of total employment—or by 2.4% per year—over the period, and blue-collar jobs fell from 61% to 52% of total employment, or by −0.3% per year. The primary reason for the rapid growth in white-collar positions was the shift in the composition of final demand towards output produced by industries that relied heavily on white-collar workers, and away from those industries that were intensive in their use of blue-collar employees (88% increase for the predominantly white-collar industries compared with a 47% increase for the predominantly blue-collar industries). A secondary reason was a bias in technological change, which favored white-collar over blue-collar workers (a 46% reduction in white-collar employment compared with a 55% reduction in blue-collar employment). On the other hand, import leakage reductions slightly favored blue-collar over white-collar jobs (a 4% increase versus a 1% increase respectively).[8]

Local absorption was more successful than export demand (including tourist spending) in generating new jobs. Over the period 1967–87, employment generated by local demand grew by 35% and that from exports by 29%, despite the fact that exports grew by a factor of 3.8, while local absorption increased by a factor of only 2.0. The difference is primarily because local absorption relied on goods and services produced by more labor-intensive sectors than did export-oriented industries. A secondary reason is that the composition of exports has continued to shift toward industries with relatively low employment multipliers, whereas the composition of local demand has remained relatively unchanged over time. By itself, the growth in the level of final demand would have increased employment by 96% for local absorption and 131% for exports. However, changes in the composition of final output reduced employment by 54% for exports and by only 8% for local consumption. The technology effect was slightly greater in absolute value for local absorption than for exports (−57% versus −52%), while the import leakage effects were similar for the two components.

Local absorption and exports played similar roles in accounting for the greater growth in white-collar jobs than in blue-collar jobs over time. Between 1967 and 1982, white-collar employment generated by local demand grew by 37%, while blue-collar jobs that emanated from local demand remained virtually unchanged. White-collar jobs that resulted from exports increased by 28% over the same period, while blue-collar jobs declined by 14%.

The fact that export demand failed to keep up with local absorption in generating employment growth over the period 1967–87 calls into question the wisdom of the particular industrialization course pursued in Puerto Rico. In earlier work (Weisskoff & Wolff, 1975, 1977), we called attention to the 'enclave-like' nature of Puerto Rico's export industries, which rely heavily on the US for inputs and an output market, and which generate substantial import leakages. The earlier analysis was carried out for the Puerto Rican economy over the period 1948–63. We find here that the situation has not changed much since then. The export industries still operate basically as branch plants of their US owners, and have yet to be fully integrated into the local economy of Puerto Rico.

Much of the development of this type of economy can be attributed to a conscious development strategy embarked on by the Puerto Rican government. Through a variety of incentives, including tax relief (Section 936 of the federal tax code), the provision of infrastructure and other subsidies, the government has deliberately promoted manufacturing industries.[9] Exports (including tourist spending) consist almost entirely of manufactured products (93% of total exports in 1987, up from 82% in 1967), and almost half of the manufactures produced in Puerto Rico (49% in 1987, which was down slightly from 51% in 1967) are exported. Moreover, over half of the intermediate inputs used in manufactures are imported (54% in 1967 and 52% in 1987).

As a result, manufacturing industries in Puerto Rico have remained isolated from the rest of the local economy and have generated few jobs. They are characterized by high import leakages and low employment multipliers. This remains true despite a modest degree of import substitution of inputs in the production of export products between 1967 and 1987. Moreover, manufactured goods have undergone by far the most rapid growth in (total labor) productivity (5.7% per year over the period 1967–87). Although this is beneficial for overall growth in per-capita income and for the international competitiveness of Puerto Rican industries, it does not help very much in the creation of new jobs.

A change is called for in development strategy, to one which places greater emphasis on attracting more labor-intensive industries and industries that can rely on inputs produced in Puerto Rico. Which industries are the prime candidates? We see possibilities for the development of exportable services, such as finance, insurance and business services, as well as health services. As Ruiz and Castaner (1993) noted, the Caribbean basin, including Mexico, Central America, Colombia and Venezuela, now appears poised to undergo a rapid state of growth. Because of the high level of education of the Puerto Rican citizenry (see Baumol and Wolff (1996) for more details), it would make sense to promote the development of these high-end services for the Caribbean market. These services are all characterized by relatively high employment multipliers (see also Green (1996) for similar arguments).

Moreover, both tourism and agriculture have languished over the last several decades. Hotel services, agriculture and its associated manufactured food products all rely heavily on local inputs, and have high employment multipliers. Here, too, a reorientation of trade towards the surrounding Caribbean basin in the provision of these products might also reap rewards in terms of growth and employment.

Notes

1. See Baumol and Wolff (1996) for the sources and methods used for the data cited in this section.
2. Also, see Weisskoff (1985) for another, somewhat more critical treatment of Puerto Rico's post-World War II economic history.
3. A set of 51-order IO matrices for 1967, 1972, 1977, 1982 and 1987, as well as employment coefficient and sectoral price deflators, were obtained on either worksheets or computer tape from the Puerto Rico Planning Board (see Table 1 for sector names). Manpower matrices of 31 industries by 10 major occupational groups are based on decennial Census data for Puerto Rico for 1970 and

1980. The 1970 manpower matrix is aligned to the 1967 IO table, and the 1980 manpower matrix is aligned to the 1982 IO table.

4. Technically speaking, this is not exactly true, because a measure of total labor productivity would require some additional treatment of non-competitive imports. See Wolff (1985, 1994) for more details.
5. We concentrate our analysis on these three years, because both 1972 and 1982 were recession years.
6. As before, we use average period weights to provide an exact decomposition of $\Delta \mathbf{Y}_T$. See also Oosterhaven *et al.* (1995) for a related application of this decomposition.
7. The occupational data are based on the 1970 and 1980 Census of Population, aligned to the IO tables of 1967 and 1982 respectively. Unfortunately, data from the 1990 Census are not yet available, to permit estimates that correspond to the 1987 IO table.
8. Using a similar type of IO-based decomposition analysis, Han (1995) reports similar results for the Japanese economy over the period 1975–85.
9. See Melendez and Blum (1996) and Ruiz and Melendez (1996) for further discussion of Section 936 of the federal tax code. Interestingly, estimates of the elasticity of investment by Section 936 corporations to a dollar change in federal tax credits is only of the order of 15–20 cents during the first year after the tax change, and about 25–30 cents over 5 years. As a result, it is safe to conclude that other factors, such as an educated workforce, played crucial roles in the industrialization of the Puerto Rican economy.

References

Baumol, W. J. & Wolff, E. N. (1996) Catching up in the postwar period: Puerto Rico as the fifth 'tiger'?, *World Development*, 24, pp. 869–885.

Green, C. (1996) Industrial policy for Puerto Rico and the implications of political status, in: E. Melendez & A. L. Ruiz (eds) *Economic Implications of Puerto Rico's Status Options* (Westport, CT, Grenwood).

Han, X. (1995) Structural change and labor requirement of the Japanese economy, *Economic Systems Research*, 7, pp. 47–65.

Melendez, E. & Blum, J. (1996) Tax elasticity of Section 936 investment in Puerto Rico, in: E. Melendez & A. L. Ruiz (eds) *Economic Implications of Puerto Rico's Status Options* (Westport, CT, Greenwood).

Oosterhaven, J., Hoen, A. R. & van der Linden, J. A. (1995) Technology, trade and real value added growth of EC countries, 1975–1985, Paper presented at the *Eleventh International Conference on Input–Output Techniques*, New Delhi, India.

Ruiz, A. L. & Castaner, J. (1993) Economic impact in Puerto Rico of its exports to the Caribbean: an input–output analysis, in: I. Tirado (ed.) *Trade Issues in the Caribbean* (New York, Gordon and Breach).

Ruiz, A. L. & Melendez, E. (1996) The potential impact of the repeal of Section 936 on Puerto Rico's economy, in: E. Melendez & A. L. Ruiz (eds) *Economic Implications of Puerto Rico's Status Options* (Westport, CT, Greenwood).

Weisskoff, R. (1985) *Factories and Food Stamps* (Baltimore, MD, Johns Hopkins University Press).

Weisskoff, R. & Wolff, E. N. (1975) Development and trade dependence: the case of Puerto Rico, 1948–1963, *Review of Economics and Statistics*, 57, pp. 470–477.

Weisskoff, R. & Wolff, E. N. (1977) Linkages and leakages: industrial tracking in an enclave economy, *Economic Development and Cultural Change*, 25, pp. 607–628.

Wolff, E. N. (1985) Industrial composition, interindustry effects, and the US productivity slowdown, *Review of Economics and Statistics*, 67, pp. 268–277.

Wolff, E. N. (1994) Productivity measurement within an input–output framework, *Regional Science and Urban Economics*, 24, pp. 75–92.

Journal of Productivity Analysis, 18, 111–128, 2002

Neoclassical Growth Accounting and Frontier Analysis: A Synthesis

THIJS TEN RAA tenRaa@uvt.nl
Tilburg University, Box 90153, 5000 LE Tilburg, The Netherlands

PIERRE MOHNEN P.Mohnen@MERIT.unimaas.nl
Université du Québec à Montréal, CIRANO, University Maastricht and MERIT

Abstract

The standard measure of productivity growth is the Solow residual. Its evaluation requires data on factor input shares or prices. Since these prices are presumed to match factor productivities, the standard procedure amounts to accepting at face value what is supposed to be measured. In this paper we estimate total factor productivity growth without recourse to data on factor input prices. Factor productivities are defined as Lagrange multipliers to the program that maximizes the level of domestic final demand. The consequent measure of total factor productivity is shown to encompass not only the Solow residual, but also the efficiency change of frontier analysis and the hitherto slippery terms-of-trade effect. Using input-output tables from 1962 to 1991 we show that the source of Canadian productivity growth has shifted from technical change to terms-of-trade effects.

JEL classification: O47

Keywords: total factor productivity growth, efficiency change, terms-of trade effect, growth accounting, data envelopment analysis

1. Introduction

In this paper, we synthesize two strands of productivity analysis, namely neoclassical growth accounting and a frontier approach, known as data envelopment analysis (DEA).[1] In either branch of literature, productivity is essentially the output-input ratio and, therefore, productivity growth the residual between output growth and input growth. The difficulty is to implement these concepts when there is more than one output or input. Neoclassical analysis weights them by value shares, a procedure that requires data on factor input shares or prices. Since the latter are presumed to match factor productivities, the procedure amounts to accepting at face value what is supposed to be measured. Solow (1957) has justified this for competitive economies, where inputs are rewarded on the basis of their marginal productivities and outputs according to their marginal revenues, so that the residual measures the shift of the production function. DEA analysis considers the output and input proportions observable in activities (representing various economies and/or various years) and determines for instance how much more output could be produced if the inputs were processed by an optimal combination of all observed activities.

Although each approach tracks changes in the output-input ratio of an economy, the constructions are quite distinct. Neoclassical growth accounting attributes productivity growth to the inputs, say labor and capital. Indeed, Jorgenson and Griliches (1967) have shown that the total factor productivity (TFP-) growth residual equals the growth of the real factor rewards, summed over endowments. In this sense, the residual equals total factor productivity growth. The frontier approach decomposes productivity growth into a movement of the economy towards the frontier and a shift of the latter. Productivity growth is efficiency change plus technical change. The alternative decompositions inherit the advantages and disadvantages of their respective methodologies. Neoclassical growth accounting imputes productivity growth to factors, but cannot distinguish a movement towards the frontier and a movement of the frontier. This is the contribution of the frontier approach, which, however, is not capable of imputing value to factor inputs.

The two approaches differ not only in methodology, but also in focus. The overwhelming majority of empirical studies of economic growth (whether "old" or "new" growth papers) are based on the Solow model or some variant of it. Alternatively, the overwhelming majority of DEA papers deal with micro issues. In fact, the technique is used primarily for benchmarking within firms or industries (e.g., the burgeoning use of DEA in financial service industries). Our paper breaks common ground by applying all the tools to a national economy with a multitude of sectors. The issue is macro-growth, but the model is more micro in flavor. Basically, we will decompose productivity growth into frontier productivity growth and efficiency change. DEA practitioners restrict the first term to technical efficiency, but we take into account allocative efficiency. The frontier is obtained not by some best practice, but by efficient allocation of resources across sectors. Neoclassical growth accountants overlook the efficiency change term.

Some practitioners of the two approaches are aware of each others' work and sometimes report correlations between the alternative productivity measures (Perelman, 1995). What is missing, however, is a theoretical framework that encompasses the two approaches. That is the main purpose of our paper. We reproduce the neoclassical TFP growth formulas, but in a framework that is DEA in spirit. Unlike Färe, Grosskopf, Lovell and Zhang (1994), we do not determine an economy's frontier by benchmarking the production of a macro-aggregate on other economies, but by reallocating resources domestically so as to maximize the level of domestic final demand (that is excluding net exports) given input and output proportions and subject to a set of feasibility constraints. The shadow prices of the factor constraints measure the individual factor productivities. Our model is a general equilibrium activity analysis model with multiple inputs and outputs, and intermediate inputs, where the frontier is determined by an economic criterion and not a mechanical expansion factor. A first attempt to model intermediate inputs was made by Färe and Grosskopf (1996).

Our starting point is the Solow residual between output and input growth. We derive the equality of the Solow residual with the growth rates of the factor productivities by differentiating not the national income identity, but the related formula of the main theorem of linear programming applied to the aforementioned frontier program. By the same token, we capture the movement towards the frontier, or efficiency change, in addition to the standard Domar decomposition of TFP, involving technical change at the sectoral levels. A further contribution is the identification of the terms-of-trade effect in productivity analysis. It is well-known that an improvement in the terms of trade is tantamount to technical progress, but the treatment of this effect has been ad hoc so far. For example, Diewert and Morrison (1986) classify commodities a priori as exports or imports. In our frontier program net exports are appropriately endogenous.

We model trade by inclusion of a constraint on net imports. For balanced trade, the value of net imports, assessed at world prices, must be nonpositive. The model will select resource extensive commodities for exports and resource intensive commodities for imports, all relative to the world prices. If the price of an export item goes up, the net imports constraint is less tight and potential output is increased, in the same way as in response to an input-coefficient reduction. This is the terms-of-trade effect. The economic system that maps factor inputs into domestic final demand has two components: production and trade. The contributions to TFP-growth in the primal representation are given by the sectoral Solow residuals and the terms-of-trade effect, respectively, which can be considered shift effects. On top of this we must accommodate the empirical fact that trade is not always balanced. The economy may run a deficit, which we enter on the right hand side of our net imports constraint. This modification, however minor, adds a conventional input aspect to trade. We do not endogenize the year-to-year deficit of the economy, but, given the value of the deficit, the commodity composition of the trade vector will be determined along with the efficient allocation of resources. This is the input effect of debt which emerges in the dual decomposition of TFP, alongside the factor input productivities. The terms-of-trade effect will be an important source of growth, but the deficit effect will prove insignificant in the empirical part of this study.

Although we reproduce the formulas of neoclassical growth accounting and frontier analysis in a consistent way, there are some subtle differences. Compared to traditional growth accounting, the input value shares that enter our Solow residual are no longer the observed ones, but those based on the shadow prices of the frontier program. In perfectly competitive economies, where inputs are rewarded according to their marginal productivities and outputs according to their marginal revenues, it is perfectly legitimate to use the observed value shares in aggregating inputs or outputs. But, observed economies are not perfectly competitive and are not even on their production possibility frontiers. Hence the Solow residual based on observed value shares does not isolate technical change, but also captures variations of the economy about the competitive benchmark, such as changes in market power, returns to scale, disequilibrium in factor holdings, and suboptimal capacity utilization. The possibility of disequilibrium in factor holdings has preoccupied economists for a long time. In the early studies, the capital stock was corrected for variations in estimated capacity utilization or variations in electricity use to remove the effect of cyclical fluctuations from productivity growth. Berndt and Fuss (1986) proposed an alternative measure of capacity utilization, casted in terms of prices, rather than quantities. The degree of capacity utilization was measured and interpreted as the gap between observed and shadow prices (those at which the observed quantities would be optimal). There was an obvious link to be made with the q-theory of investment (Hayashi, 1982) that predicted the capital stock to be optimal when the ratio of the market price to the purchase price of capital is equal to unity at the marginal. If capital is only one quasi-fixed input and if the marginal q equals the average, q, the shadow price of capital could be measured by the market value. Morrison (1986) generalized the disequilibrium analysis to multiple inputs and recommended the estimation of shadow prices for total factor productivity measurement.

The shadow prices can be estimated using a temporary equilibrium model with some quasi-fixed factors. Caves, Christensen and Swanson (1981) estimated the shadow prices without specifying the source of disequilibrium in factor holdings. Alternatively, it is possible to estimate the shadow prices by specifying the source of inefficiencies in factor holdings or output supplies. The input demands, as well as the output supplies, may not be at their optimal values with respect to the observed prices because of adjustment costs, regulatory constraints, uncertainty, non-maximizing behavior, or imperfect competition. The gap between the observed and the shadow prices may be due to marginal adjustment costs (e.g., Morrison, 1988), regulatory distortions (Sickles, Good and Johnson, 1986), the value of the option to invest (Dixit and Pindyck, 1994), price-mark-ups related to demand elasticities (Bernstein and Mohnen, 1991). The Solow residual has been corrected for such departures from perfect competition, estimating mark-ups over marginal cost, scale elasticities and shadow prices, and modifying the formula for the residual (Morrisson, 1988; and Hall, 1990). The econometric literature is in the realm of partial equilibrium analysis.

We, however, endogenize commodity and factor prices by finding the frontier of the economy subject to its fundamentals, namely endowments, technology, and preferences. This general equilibrium approach goes back to Debreu (1959) who pursued it in a micro-economic model. Our model is at a medium level of disaggregation, but could conceivably be disaggregated further. Endowments are represented by the labor force, the accumulated stocks of capital and the trade deficit. They constrain the economy-wide allocation, but not the sectors in isolation. Technology is given by the combined inputs and outputs of the various sectors of the economy. Preferences are represented by the commodity proportions of domestic final demand.[2]

The paper is organized as follows. In the next section, we set up an activity analysis model to determine an economy's frontier. Then we define TFP-growth in the spirit of Solow (1957) and decompose it into frontier productivity growth and efficiency change. In Section 3, frontier productivity growth is further decomposed into technical change and a terms-of-trade effect. In Section 4 we measure TFP-growth and its various components for the Canadian economy over the period 1962–1991. Section 5 concludes and the data are described in an appendix.

2. TFP-Growth as the Sum of Frontier Productivity Growth and Efficiency Change

Figure 1 explains our model for an open economy with two commodities. Net output is given by vector y. Trade moves it to the domestic final consumption vector, f. (Domestic final demand is consumption plus investment, but not net exports. Note that commodity 1 is exported and commodity 2 imported.) Trade is a means to align domestic final consumption with the preferences. Assuming a Leontief welfare function, the optimum is attained by expanding vector f in its own direction, up to fc, where c is the expansion vector. In Figure 1 this is achieved by three things. Production y is pushed to the production possibility frontier (the curved line), reallocated in favor of output 2, yielding point y^*, and the pattern of trade is changed (exporting commodity 2 and importing commodity 1). The frontier of domestic final consumption, fc, is attained by the elimination of slack and the reallocation

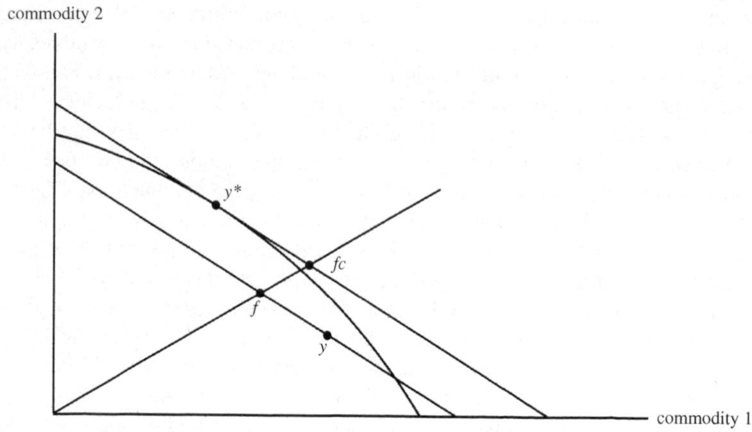

Figure 1. The production possibility frontier with actual and optimal net outputs (y and y^*, respectively) and domestic final demands (f and fc, respectively). The straight lines are budget lines in world trade.

of resources across sectors. Expansion vector c is a negative measure for efficiency. If $c = 1$, the economy is already at its optimum. If $c = 1.1$, the economy's potential is 10% more than actual performance.

Now consider the next period. For simplicity, assume that the factor inputs remain fixed. Any improvement, or TFP, shows an increase in domestic final demand, f. One extreme case is a movement from f to fc in Figure 1, without any structural change in the production possibility frontier or the terms of trade (the slope of the straight lines). Then all TFP is ascribed to efficiency change. Another extreme case is where f stays put, but the production possibility frontier moves out. Then the new fc would be greater. The increase in c signals a negative efficiency change which, however, is offset by the positive technical change.

We consider an open economy endowed with labor N, capital M (decomposed into various types) and an allowable trade deficit D. The economy is subdivided into a number of sectors, each producing a vector of commodities. Part of the commodities are used as intermediate inputs and the rest flows to final demand (either domestic final demand or exports). The frontier of the economy is defined as the maximal expansion of its vector of domestic final demand f, keeping the relative composition of that vector as fixed. The composition reflects preferences. The frontier of the economy can be reached by an optimal allocation of inputs (primary and intermediate) and production across sectors and by optimal commodity trade with the rest of the world.

The *frontier* of the economy is defined by the primal program,

$$\begin{aligned} &\max_{s,c,g} e^{\mathsf{T}} fc \text{ subject to} \\ &(V^{\mathsf{T}} - U)s \geq fc + Jg = F \\ &\qquad Ks \leq M \\ &\qquad Ls \leq N \\ &\quad -\pi g \leq -\pi g^{t} = D \quad s \geq 0. \end{aligned} \tag{1}$$

The variables (s, c, g) and parameters (all other) are the following [with dimensions in brackets]

s activity vector [# of sectors]
c level of domestic final demand [scalar]
g vector of net exports [# of tradeable commodities]
e unit vector of all components one
T transposition symbol
f domestic final demand [# of commodities]
V make table [# of sectors by # of commodities]
U use table [# of commodities by # of sectors]
J 0–1 matrix placing tradeables [# of commodities by of tradeables]
F final demand [# of commodities]
K capital stock matrix [# of capital types by # of sectors]
M capital endowment [# of capital types]
L labor employment row vector [# of sectors]
N labor force [scalar][3]
π U.S. relative price row vector [# of tradeables]
g^t vector of net exports observed at time t [# of tradeables]
D observed trade deficit [scalar].

We discuss the objective and the constraints, respectively. The objective is the expansion of the level of domestic final demand, c. Domestic final demand comprises consumption and investment. Investment is merely a means to advance consumption, albeit in the future. We include it in the objective function to account for future consumption. In fact, Weitzman (1976) shows that for competitive economies domestic final demand measures the present discounted value of consumption.[4]

Preserving the proportions of domestic final demand, f, we expand its level by letting the economy produce fc, where scalar c is the expansion factor. $c = 1$ is feasible (as it reflects the status quo), but $c > 1$ represents a movement towards the frontier of the economy. The model maximizes c. This is equivalent to the maximization $e^{\mathsf{T}} fc$, where e is the unit vector (with all entries equal to one), T the transposition sign, and f is the given domestic final demand vector. It is important to understand that f is not a variable but an exogenous vector. The positive multiplicative factor in the objective, $e^{\mathsf{T}} f$, will control the nominal price level.

The preservation of domestic final demand in finding the frontier of the economy in each year amounts to imposing a Leontief preference structure (fixed consumption pattern). It should be noted that the ray output expansion typical in multi-output DEA (the Farrell (1957) measure of efficiency) implicitly assumes fixed output proportions. It should also be noted that the Leontief specification of production and preferences that we adopt admits a great deal of substitutability as trade is free and, therefore, acts as a valve for factor imbalances between endowments and factor contents of domestic final demands. The economy may even mimic a Cobb-Douglas behavior, as demonstrated in ten Raa (1995). The main reason we opt for the Leontief specification is that the productivities associated with program (1) (in the sense of Lagrange multipliers) combine to TFP expressions which have exactly the same form as the ones in growth accounting. The imposition of fixed proportions ensures that optimal, frontier proportions are the same as the observed ones, while level differences (between the optimum and actual allocations) are a wash in productivity growth analysis. If we would have used a different production function, then the frontier allocation of the economy would feature different input-output proportions than the observed ones and there is no hope that measures for technical change look like the familiar ones of growth accounting.

The first constraint of the linear program (1) is the material balance: net output must cover domestic final demand plus net exports. Then follow the capital and labor constraints.[5] The next to last constraint is the trade balance: net imports valued at world prices may not exceed the existing trade deficit. Finally, sector activity levels must be nonnegative. The linear program basically reallocates activity so as to maximize the level of domestic final demand. Final demand also includes net exports, but they are considered not as an end, but rather as a means to fulfill the objective of the economy.[6] This endogenization of trade explains the role of the terms-of-trade in TFP analysis, as we shall see in Section 3.

The theory of mathematical programming teaches us that the Lagrange multipliers corresponding to the constraints of the primal program measure the competitive values or marginal products of the constraining entities (the commodities and factors) at the optimum. We will use the Lagrange multipliers in defining productivity growth. They are p (a row vector of commodity prices), r (a row vector of capital productivities), w (a scalar for labor productivity), and ε (a scalar for the purchasing power parity). They are determined by the dual program associated with (1),

$$\begin{aligned} &\min_{p,r,w,\varepsilon \geq 0} \; rM + wN + \varepsilon D \text{ subject to} \\ &p(V^{\mathsf{T}} - U) \leq rK + wL \\ &\qquad pf = e^{\mathsf{T}} f \\ &\qquad pJ = \varepsilon \pi. \end{aligned} \tag{2}$$

Factor costs are minimized subject to price constraints.[7] The first dual constraint defines competitive shadow prices of the commodities. Value added must be less than or equal to factor costs in each sector. (If it is less than factor costs, the sector will be inactive according to the phenomenon of complementary slackness.) The second dual constraint normalizes the prices.[8] Our commodities are measured in base-year prices and hence observed prices are one. The optimal competitive prices from the linear program will be slightly off, but we maintain the overall price level. The third and last dual constraint aligns the prices of the tradeable commodities with their opportunity costs: the relative U.S. prices. In free trade, the law of one price must hold (in the absence of transaction costs and imperfect information).

Following Solow (1957) we define total factor productivity growth as the residual between the final demand growth and aggregate-input growth, where each of them is a weighted average of component growth rates and the weights are competitive value shares. The growth rate of domestic final demand for commodity i is $\hat{f}_i = \dot{f}_i / f_i$, where $\dot{}$ denotes the time derivative. The competitive value shares are $p_i f_i / (\Sigma p_i f_i) = p_i f_i / (pf)$. Hence overall output growth amounts to

$$\Sigma[p_i f_i/(pf)]\hat{f}_i = \Sigma p_i \dot{f}_i/(pf) = p\dot{f}/(pf). \tag{3}$$

Inputs are aggregated in the same vein. The growth rate of labor is $\hat{N}$ and its competitive value share is $\beta = wN/(rM + wN + \varepsilon D)$. Likewise, denote the competitive value shares of capital by α (a row vector) and of the trade deficit by γ (a scalar). Then overall input growth can be written as

$$\alpha \hat{M} + \beta \hat{N} + \gamma \hat{D} \tag{4}$$

where each of the terms can be rewritten in time derivatives as we have done for outputs. For example, $\beta \hat{N} = [wN/(rM + wN + \varepsilon D)]\hat{N} = w\dot{N}/(rM + wN + \varepsilon D)$. *Total factor productivity growth* is defined as the residual between (3) and (4):

$$\begin{aligned} TFP &= p\dot{f}/(pf) - (\alpha \hat{M} + \beta \hat{N} + \gamma \hat{D}) \\ &= p\dot{f}/(pf) - (r\dot{M} + w\dot{N} + \varepsilon \dot{D})/(rM + wN + \varepsilon D). \end{aligned} \tag{5}$$

In the growth accounting literature it is customary to assume that the economy is perfectly competitive. Unfortunately this assumption is seldom fulfilled. Observed prices are not perfectly competitive and the economy need not be on its frontier. Also notice that p is not a device to convert nominal values to real values, but the endogenous price vector that sustains the optimal allocation of resources in the linear program.

In the spirit of Nishimizu and Page (1982) and further frontier analysis, such as DEA, for example Färe et al. (1994), we will decompose *TFP* in a shift of the frontier and a movement towards the frontier:

$$TFP = FP + EC \tag{6}$$

where *FP* if frontier productivity growth and *EC* is efficiency change. We will now define each of them.

By the theory of Lagrange multipliers, real shadow prices measure the marginal products of the factors at the optimum. Hence *frontier productivity growth* is the growth rates of the shadow prices of the factors (weighted by relative costs and recalling that capital is multi-dimensional) minus the growth rate of the commodity prices.[9]

$$FP = (\dot{r}M + \dot{w}N + \dot{\varepsilon}D)/(rM + wN + \varepsilon D) - \dot{p}f/(pf) \tag{7}$$

Frontier productivity growth so defined corresponds to the dual expression of TFP-growth for perfectly competitive economies elaborated by Jorgenson and Griliches (1967). It imputes productivity growth to factor inputs, which is beyond the scope of standard frontier analysis. The latter, however, is capable of accounting for efficiency change. Inefficiency is measured by the degree to which the economy can be expanded towards its frontier, c. A reduction in c signals an efficiency gain and, therefore, *efficiency change* is defined by

$$EC = -\hat{c}(= -\dot{c}/c) \tag{8}$$

We must now demonstrate that frontier productivity growth and efficiency change sum to total factor productivity growth. In other words, we must prove equation (6), given definitions (5), (7) and (8). Now, by the main theorem of linear programming, (1) and (2) have equal solution values, or, substituting the price normalization constraint of (2),

$$pfc = rM + wN + \varepsilon D. \tag{9}$$

The left hand side is the value of optimal domestic final demand and the right hand side is factor income. Thus, (9) is essentially the macro-economic identity of the national product and income. Differentiating totally, we obtain by the product rule

$$\dot{p}fc + p\dot{f}c + pf\dot{c} = \dot{r}M + r\dot{M} + \dot{w}N + w\dot{N} + \dot{\varepsilon}D + \varepsilon\dot{D} \tag{10}$$

or, rearranging terms,

$$p\dot{f}c - r\dot{M} - w\dot{N} - \varepsilon\dot{D} = \dot{r}M + \dot{w}N + \dot{\varepsilon}D - \dot{p}fc - pf\dot{c} \tag{11}$$

Now divide the first term on the left hand side and the last two terms on the right hand side of (11) by the left hand side of (9). Notice that c cancels out everywhere, except in the last term on the right hand side. Divide the remaining three terms on either side of (11) by the right hand side of (9). Then we obtain

$$\begin{aligned} &p\dot{f}/(pf) - (r\dot{M} + w\dot{N} + \varepsilon\dot{D})/(rM + wN + \varepsilon D) \\ &\quad = (\dot{r}M + \dot{w}N + \dot{\varepsilon}D)/(rM + wN + \varepsilon D) - p\dot{f}/(pf) - \dot{c}/c \end{aligned} \tag{12}$$

By definitions (5), (7) and (8), (12) reduces to (6). The noted cancellation of the expansion factor except in one term, enabled us to separate the efficiency change term from the frontier productivity growth term.

3. Frontier Productivity Growth Decomposition into Technical Change and the Terms-of-Trade Effect

In the previous section we decomposed TFP into frontier productivity growth and efficiency change. This section provides the further decomposition of frontier productivity growth into technical change and terms-of-trade effects. The latter is not an add-on, but emerges naturally from our linear programming model of TFP. It should not come as a surprise that terms-of-trade and sectoral technical changes arise simultaneously. The trade sector is like a production sector, with multiple inputs (namely exports) and outputs (namely imports). Like all sectors, productivity goes up when more output (import) is obtained per input (export), in other words, when the terms of trade improve. The specification of the function that maps inputs into outputs is different. In production we have the Leontief function. In trade we have the balance of payments, which is a linear function. From a formal point of view, the functions feature perfect complementarity and perfect substitutability, respectively, where the marginal rate of substitution is given by the terms of trade. The structures of production and trade (input-output proportions and terms of trade) may shift and thus cause TFP-growth. These are the Solow residual and the terms-of-trade effect, which we will spell out in this section. As always, *TFP*-growth accrues to factor income additions, to capital, labor, and debt supply, though the latter is typically very small and even zero when payments are balanced.

Our point of departure is *TFP* as defined in (5). Focus on the numerator of (5), by multiplying with the denominator, or (9). Then we obtain the following *TFP* numerator,

$$p\dot{f}c - r\dot{M} - w\dot{N} - \varepsilon\dot{D}. \tag{13}$$

By definition of F, see (1), the first term is $p\dot{F} - pJ\dot{g} - pf\dot{c}$. If the factor constraints are binding, then $M = Ks$, $N = Ls$ and $\varepsilon\dot{D} = -\varepsilon\pi\dot{g} - \varepsilon\dot{\pi}g$. The second subterm of the first term, $-pJ\dot{g}$, cancels against the first subterm of the last term, $-\varepsilon\pi\dot{g}$, (because of the third constraint of (2)) and (10) reduces to

$$[p\dot{F} - r(Ks)^{\cdot} - w(Ls)^{\cdot}] + \varepsilon\dot{\pi}g - pf\dot{c}. \tag{14}$$

Dividing by the denominator of *TFP*, or (9), we reobtain *TFP*, but now in the following three-way form:[10]

$$TFP = SR + TT + EC \tag{15}$$

where *SR* is the *Solow residual,*

$$SR = [p\dot{F} - r(Ks)^{\cdot} - w(Ls)^{\cdot}]/(rM + wN + \varepsilon D) \tag{16}$$

TT is the *terms-of-trade effect,*

$$TT = \varepsilon\dot{\pi}g/(rM + wN + \varepsilon D) \tag{17}$$

and *EC* is the efficiency change, defined earlier in (8). Comparison of *TFP* decompositions (12) and (6) reveals that effectively we have decomposed the structural change term, frontier productivity growth *FP*, into the technical change and terms-of-trade effects,

$$FP = SR + TT. \tag{18}$$

In discrete time, the expressions involving differentials are approximated using the identity $x_t y_t - x_{t-1}y_{t-1} = \hat{x}\overline{x_t y_t} + \hat{y}\overline{x_t y_t}$, where discrete time $\hat{x}_t = (x_t - x_{t-1})/\bar{x}_t$ and $\bar{x}_t = (x_t + x_{t-1})/2$, and similarly for $\hat{y}_t$ and $\bar{y}_t$.

4. Application to the Canadian Economy

To illustrate our methodology, we examine productivity growth in the Canadian economy during the period from 1962 to 1991 at the medium level of disaggregation, which comprises 50 industries and 94 commodities. The linear program was solved for each year from 1962 to 1991 yielding the optimal activity levels and shadow prices for the TFP-expressions.

Table 1 contains the shadow prices of labor (in 1986 \$/hour), of the three types of capital (building, equipment and infrastructure), and of the trade deficit (the latter four are rates of return) from 1962 to 1991. Labor was worth at the margin \$16.13 in 1986 prices in 1962. Its productivity followed an increasing trend until 1982 and then a bumpy road ending at \$46.13 in 1991. The rate of return on buildings followed a downward trend, dropping to zero in 1982, sharply rebounded in 1984, and then dropped again to reach zero from 1988 on. In other words, there were excess buildings in 1982 and in 1988–1991. Equipment was not fully utilized until 1983 and again in 1988, 1990 and 1991. Comparing the evolutions of their shadow prices, labor seems to be a substitute to building and equipment. Infrastructure had an increasing rate of return until 1974, much greater than the other two types of capital, and then a declining productivity until the end of our period. On average over the 1962–1991 period, a dollar increase in the trade deficit allowed a 64 cents increase in final demand.[11]

Table 1. Factor productivities (shadow prices).

Year	Labor	Buildings	Equipment	Infrastructure	Trade Deficit
1962	16.13	0.32	0.00	0.20	0.71
1963	16.50	0.33	0.00	0.19	0.71
1964	17.46	0.26	0.00	0.22	0.69
1965	17.86	0.28	0.00	0.18	0.69
1966	18.28	0.28	0.00	0.18	0.69
1967	19.31	0.20	0.00	0.18	0.68
1968	20.38	0.21	0.00	0.17	0.67
1969	20.91	0.17	0.00	0.18	0.67
1970	20.40	0.19	0.00	0.23	0.68
1971	21.78	0.14	0.00	0.24	0.66
1972	22.44	0.08	0.00	0.28	0.66
1973	22.96	0.05	0.00	0.32	0.65
1974	23.24	0.01	0.00	0.47	0.61
1975	22.70	0.05	0.00	0.45	0.64
1976	23.61	0.12	0.00	0.37	0.64
1977	24.52	0.08	0.00	0.34	0.65
1978	24.83	0.07	0.00	0.31	0.65
1979	24.85	0.06	0.00	0.32	0.65
1980	24.60	0.07	0.00	0.28	0.66
1981	24.31	0.10	0.01	0.25	0.69
1982	29.66	0.00	0.00	0.18	0.57
1983	12.07	0.62	0.83	0.15	0.82
1984	12.22	0.49	1.03	0.11	0.81
1985	23.11	0.24	0.22	0.16	0.73
1986	20.09	0.18	0.83	0.05	0.72
1987	20.76	0.11	0.99	0.03	0.70
1988	44.11	0.00	0.00	0.01	0.31
1989	22.41	0.00	1.21	0.00	0.63
1990	44.33	0.00	0.00	0.01	0.32
1991	46.13	0.00	0.00	0.01	0.29

Labor productivity is in 1986$ per hour. The shadow prices of capital (buildings, equipment and infrastructure) and the trade deficit are rates of return.

Table 2. Frontier productivity growth (*FP*) and efficiency change (*EC*) (equations (4) and (8), annualized percentages).

	1962–1974	1974–1981	1981–1991
FP	2.4	−0.8	3.6
EC	−0.6	0.9	−3.7
TFP	1.8	0.1	−0.1

Its shadow price was pretty stable until 1981 and more volatile and somewhat lower after 1981.

Table 2 shows the decomposition of TFP-growth into a shift of the frontier (frontier productivity growth FP) and a movement towards the frontier (efficiency change *EC*). The healthy TFP-growth in the period 1962–1974 reflects frontier productivity growth. The

Table 3. Frontier productivity growth (*FP*) by factor input (equation (7), annualized percentages).

	1962–1974	1974–1981	1981–1991
Buildings	−0.9	0.4	−0.3
Equipment	0.0	0.1	0.3
Infrastructure	1.1	−1.5	−1.2
Capital, total	0.2	−1.0	−1.1
Labor	2.4	0.5	5.0
Deficit	−0.0	0.0	−0.1
Price	−0.2	−0.3	−0.2
FP	2.4	−0.8	3.6

frontier slowed down, in fact contracted, in the period 1974–1981, but this was compensated by efficiency change, yielding a tiny TFP-growth rate. The period 1981–1991 showed no recovery, but an interesting reversal of the components. The frontier moved out, but this effect was nullified by a deterioration in efficiency change. The economy became healthy, but there were severe adjustment problems. The shift of the frontier displays the well-known pattern of the golden 1960s, the slowdown in the 1970s, and the structural recovery of the 1980s.[12]

Table 3 accounts for frontier productivity growth by factor input. The bulk of FP-growth is attributed to labor, next to nothing to the trade deficit, and the remainder to capital. In the first period FP and labor productivity both grow by 2.4%. The 0.2% capital productivity growth is distributed very unevenly over the three types of capital, with infrastructure picking up 1.1%, equipment none, and buildings plummeting by 0.9%. The slowdown in the second period is ascribed to both labor (dropping to 0.5% a year) and capital (turning −1.0% a year). As in the first period, infrastructure is decisive, now explaining all of the negative productivity growth in the second period. The successful FP-growth in the last period is again a labor story. Labor productivity grew at a dramatic 5.0% a year, offsetting a reduction in capital productivity growth of 1.1% a year. Again, the latter is determined by the productivity of infrastructure. The price correction term reflecting a change in final demand composition played a minor role. Demand has always tended to shift towards commodities requiring scarce resources, decreasing, but not by much, the positive effects of individual factor productivities on frontier productivity growth.

While Table 3 shows the composition of FP-growth by factor input, Table 4 decomposes it into the two sources of frontier shift, namely technical change and the terms-of-trade effect.

Table 4. Frontier productivity growth (*FP*) by Solow residual and terms-of-trade effect (equations (12)–(14), annualized percentages).

	1962–1974	1974–1981	1981–1991
SR	1.7	−1.3	−0.3
TT	0.7	0.5	3.8
FP	2.4	−0.8	3.6
SR at observed prices and activity levels	1.4	0.5	0.2

In the first period the bulk of FP-growth (2.4%) is caused by technical change (the Solow residual at shadow prices is 1.7%). The FP-slowdown in the second period is also ascribed to a downturn in technology. The recovery in the last period, however, is due not only to a Solow residual (at shadow prices) increase of one percent, but above all to an improvement in the terms-of-trade effect from 0.5 to 3.8% annually. It might look strange to have some negative Solow residuals, albeit at shadow prices. How can technology regress? There are at least two serious explanations to it. First, technical progress does not show in the statistics right away. This is the argument advanced by David (1990) to explain the productivity paradox of computers. It takes time to absorb the new information technology and to use it to its maximal efficiency, just as it took time to adjust to electricity at the beginning of the century. Second, the negative productivity growth is due to infrastructure, where the benefit might show up in the long run, and not in the short run because of adjustment costs.

It is interesting to contrast our measure of technical change (Table 4, line 1) with the traditional Solow residual, which we have added to Table 4. The main distinction of our productivity measures is the endogeneity of value shares. Prices are marginal productivities and quantities reflect frontier allocations. The Solow residual is a Domar weighted average of sectoral productivity growth rates, see equation (18), but our Domar weights are different, say from Wolff (1985), by the use of competitive activity levels for sectors and supporting prices for commodities and factor inputs. Table 4 reveals quite dramatic differences. A possible explanation of the large price effect is the excess supply of some factor inputs in some years, as noted in the discussion of Table 1. The observed-price based Solow residual is fairly unbiased in the period 1962–1974, but overstates the role of technical change in the periods 1974–1981 and 1981–1991. The terms-of-trade effect was far more important in explaining total factor productivity growth, particularly in the 1980s.

The intended contribution of this paper is to demonstrate that, at least in principle, productivity can be measured without recourse to factor shares or prices. The main reason for this disclaimer is that our model is fairly macro-economic in nature, featuring only one type of labor and three types of capital, with perfect mobility across sectors. More detailed specifications would affect the shadow prices and hence measured TFP. For example, if some type of capital is sector specific, then its constraint separates and each sector yields its own rate of return.

5. Conclusion

The standard procedure of measuring TFP-growth amounts to accepting at face value what is supposed to be measured: factor input prices. We have demonstrated that factor productivities can be determined as the Lagrange multipliers to a program that maximizes the level of domestic final demand. The consequent measure of total factor productivity growth encompasses not only the Solow residual, but also the terms-of-trade and the efficiency change effects.

We have applied our new measure of TFP-growth to the Canadian economy in the period from 1962 to 1991. Canadian TFP grew by 1.8% yearly in the 1960s, dropped in the 1970s to 0.1% and stayed put in the 1980s. The healthy TFP-growth in the 1960s reflects an outward shift of the frontier. The frontier then contracted in the 1970s, but this was offset by efficiency change. The 1980s shows a reversal of the two components. The frontier moved again, but efficiency change was negative, reflecting adjustment problems. The shift of the frontier tells the story of the golden 1960s, the slowdown of the 1970s, and the structural recovery of the 1980s. It appears that the bulk of this movement in frontier productivity can be attributed to labor productivity growth. We also find that the infrastructure component of the capital stock is the key driving force of capital productivity. The healthy factor productivity growth in the 1960s and the slowdown in the 1970s were both caused by technical change, but the recovery in the 1980s was due almost wholly to an improvement in the terms of trade.

The Solow residual measures the shift of the production possibility frontier of an economy that is presumed to be on its frontier. In this paper, we have shown that when this assumption if not valid, the frontier can be traced using input-output statistics. The Lagrange multipliers to the program that determines potential GDP measure the factor productivities. The expansion factor of the program is an inverse measure of the efficiency of the economy. By the main theorem of linear programming, factor productivity growth and efficiency change sum to TFP-growth.

The significance of this paper to applied researchers is that it demonstrates how to combine neoclassical growth accounting and frontier analysis, in order to account for technical change and efficiency change in TFP. The latter refers not only to "catching up" with best practice, but also to the broader notion of optimal allocation across sectors, including with respect to trade.

Appendix: Data

The constant price input-output tables obtained from Statistics Canada are expressed in 1961 prices from 1962–1971, in 1971 prices from 1971–1981, in 1981 prices from 1981–1986, and in 1986 prices from 1986–1991. All tables have been converted to 1986 prices using the chain rule. For reasons of confidentiality, the tables contain missing cells, which we have filled using the following procedure. The vertical and horizontal sums in the make and use tables are compared with the reported line and column totals, which do contain the missing values. We select the rows and columns where the two figures differ by more than 5% from the reported totals, or where the difference exceeds $250 million. We then fill holes or adjust cells on a case by case basis filling in priority the intersections of the selected rows and columns, using the information on the input or output structure from other years, and making sure the new computed totals do not exceed the reported ones.

There are three capital types, namely buildings, equipment, and infrastructure.[13] The gross capital stock, hours worked and labor earnings are from the KLEMS database of Statistics Canada, described in Johnson (1994).[14] In particular, corrections have been made to include in labor the earnings of the self-employed, and to separate business and non-business labor and capital. The total labor force figures are taken from Cansim (D767870) and converted in hours using the number of weekly hours worked in manufacturing (where it is the highest). Out of the 50 industries, no labor nor capital stock data exist for sectors 39, 40, 48, 49, 50, and no capital stock data for industry 46. The capital stock for industry 46 has been constructed using the capital/labor ratio of industry 47 (both industries producing predominantly the same commodity).

The international commodity prices are approximated by the U.S. prices, given that 70% of Canada's trade is with the United States. We have used the U.S. producer prices from the U.S. Bureau of Labor Statistics, Office of Employment Projection. The 169 commodity classification has been bridged to Statistics Canada's 94 commodity classification. As the debt constraint in (1) is given in Canadian dollars, we convert U.S. prices to Canadian equivalents. We have used, whenever available, unit value ratios, (UVRs, which are industry specific) computed and kindly provided to us by G. de Jong (1996). The UVRs are computed using Canadian quantities valued at U.S. prices. For the other commodities, we have used the purchasing power parities (PPP) computed by the OECD (which are based on final demand categories). The UVRs establish international price linkages for 1987, the PPPs for 1990 in terms of Canadian dollars per U.S. dollar. Hence, we require two additional transformations. First, U.S. dollars are converted to Canadian dollars using the exchange rates taken from Cansim (series 0926/133400). Second, since the input-output data are in 1986 prices, we need the linkage for 1986, which is computed by using the respective countries' commodity deflators: the producer price index for the U.S. (see above) and the total commodity deflator from the make table (except for commodities 27, 93 and 94, for which we use the import deflator from the final demand table) for Canada. Finally, international commodity prices are divided by a Canadian final demand weighted average of international commodity prices to express them in real terms.

The absence of trade in the input-output tables for most of the sample period renders the following commodities non-tradeable: services incidental to mining, residential construction, non-residential construction, repair construction, retail margins, imputed rent from owner occupied dwellings, accommodation & food services, supplies for office, laboratories & cafeterias, and travel, advertising & promotion.

The structure of some non-tradeability constraints implies the equality of the activity levels of "construction" and final demand, "owner-occupied dwellings" and final demand, and "printing and publishing" and "travel, advertising and promotion." We have forced the activity level of industry 39 (government royalties on natural resources, which essentially pertains to oil drigging in Alberta) to follow industry 5 (crude petroleum and natural gas) to ensure there are no such royalties without oil drigging. A more detailed documentation of the data and their construction is available from the authors upon request.

We do not claim that the data were measured without error. Particularly UVRs can be imprecise, according to Lichtenberg and Griliches (1989) and Siegel (1994). For a sensitivity analysis we refer to ten Raa (1995).

Acknowledgments

We thank Nathalie Viennot and Sofiane Ghali for their dedicated research assistance and René Durand, Jean-Pierre Maynard, Ronald Rioux and Bart van Ark for their precious cooperation in constructing the data. We thank editor Catherine Morrison and a referee for incisive suggestions. We acknowledge the financial support of the Social Sciences and Humanities Research Council of Canada (SSHRC), CentER, The Netherlands Foundation for the Advancement of Research (NWO), and the Association for Canadian Studies in The Netherlands.

Notes

1. In the frontier literature, there is a distinction between deterministic and stochastic frontiers. The former are obtained by linear programming methods such as DEA, the latter are estimated by econometric methods. See Coelli et al. (1998).
2. This is in the spirit of Mohnen, ten Raa and Bourque (1997) who, however, stay in the realm of neoclassical growth accounting and, therefore, do not capture efficiency changes nor the terms-of-trade effect.
3. Labor could also be decomposed into various types, but we have not done so in the empirical part.
4. In principle, our methodology could accommodate endogenous investment and the determination of the intertemporal production possibility frontier as in Hulten (1979), but we have not pursued this approach.
5. Actually, there is also non-business capital and labor, proportional to the activity level of the non-business sector, that is c. We have included their levels in the capital and labor constraints and their factor rewards in the coefficient of c in the objective function. For reasons of clarity in the exposition, we have not indicated these additional terms related to the non-business sector in (1).
6. We make no distinction between competitive and non-competitive imports. (Non-competitive imports are indicated by zeros in the make table.)
7. Since the commodity constraint in the primal program has zero bound, p does not show up in the objective function of the dual program. For details of the derivation see, for example, ten Raa (1995).
8. Remember from footnote 4 that there are two more constraint terms featuring c, namely non-business capital and labor. To preserve the price normalization, we have also included in the objective function of the primal program, (1), the base-year expenditure on non-business capital and labor which also shows up on the right-hand side of the second dual constraint.
9. Since prices are normalized at unity by the second dual constraint, see (2), the price correction term is a sheer compositional effect. If the composition of domestic final demand, f, is constant, then pf is also constant, by (2), and it follows that $p(f)^{\cdot} = \dot{p}f$ is zero. Otherwise the price correction term corrects marginal factor productivity growth rates for an inflationary effect, which does not reflect a change in the price level (since everything is already specified in real prices) but only a compositional effect.
10. If the factor constraints are not binding, a fourth term accounts for slack changes. Notice that all components, including the Solow residual, account for the value of trade balance in the numerator. This minor departure from the standard expression in the literature (including Mohnen, ten Raa and Bourque, 1997) is a consequence of our unifying framework that encompasses terms-of-trade effects. The Solow residual is a sum of terms, one for each sector, consistent with the Domar decomposition, see Hulten (1978). The terms reflect the observed factor inputs, K and L, by choice of Leontief specification in program (1). The presence of allocation vector s only affects the sectoral weights in the Solow residual.
11. Final demand does not increase by the full dollar because of the need to produce locally nontradeable commodities for a given commodity composition of final demand.
12. According to Bergeron, Fauvel and Paquet (1995), Canada hit a recession from January 1975 to March 1975, from May 1980 to June 1980, from August 1981 to November 1982, and from April 1990 to March 1991. We chose the breakpoints before the slump years 1975 and 1982 to compare productivity performances as much as possible over comparable phases of the business cycles.
13. Statistics Canada calls them "building constructions," "equipment" and "engineering constructions." Alternatively we could have modeled capital as being sector-specific, the so-called putty-clay model. We prefer the present hypothesis of sectoral mobility of capital within each group for three reasons. First, to let the economy expand, we would have needed capacity utilization rates which are badly measured and unavailable for a number of service sectors. Second, to relieve a numerical collinearity problem, we would have to relieve the capital constraint on the non-business sector. Third, the combination of 11 non-tradeables and sector-specific capacity expansion limits is too stringent. It would lead to a high shadow price on construction commodities and zero shadow prices almost anywhere else.

14. The intermediate inputs (among which energy, materials and services) are taken directly from the input-output tables at the medium level of disaggregation.

References

Berndt, E. and M. Fuss. (1986). "Productivity Measurement with Adjustments for Variations in Capacity Utilization, and Other Forms of Temporary Equilibrium." *Journal of Econometrics* 33, 7–29.

Bernstein, J. I. and P. Mohnen. (1991). "Price Cost Margins, Exports and Productivity Growth: With an Application to Canadian Industries." *Canadian Journal of Economics* 24, 638–659.

Bergeron, L., Y. Fauvel et A. Paquet. (1995). "L'indicateur synthétique avancé de l'économie canadienne selon la méthode de Stock et Watson." Mimeo, Centre de recherche sur l'emploi et des fluctuations économiques, UQAM.

Carter, A. P. (1970). *Structural Change in the American Economy*. Cambridge, MA: Harvard University Press.

Caves, D. W., L. R. Christensen and J. A. Swanson. (1981). "Productivity Growth, Scale Economies, and Capacity Utilization in U.S. Railroads, 1955–1974." *American Economic Review* 71, 994–1002.

Coelli, T., D. S. P. Rao and G. Battese. (1998). *An Introduction to Efficiency and Productivity Analysis*. Boston: Kluwer Academic Publishers.

David, P. (1990). "The Dynamo and the Computer." *American Economic Review,* Papers and Proceedings, 80(2), 355–361.

Debreu, G. (1959). *Theory of Value*. New Haven, CT: Yale University Press.

Diewert, W. E. and C. Morrison. (1986). "Adjusting Output and Productivity Indexes for Changes in the Terms of Trade." *Economic Journal* 96, 659–679.

Dixit, A. and R. Pindyck. (1994). *Investment under Uncertainty*. Princeton: Princeton University Press.

de Jong, G. (1996). "Canada's Postwar Manufacturing Performance: A Comparison with the United States." Research Memorandum, Groningen Growth and Development Center, GD-32.

Färe, R., S. Grosskopf, C. A. K. Lovell and Z. Zhang. (1994). "Productivity Growth, Technical Progress and Efficiency Changes in Industrialised Countries." *American Economic Review* 84, 66–83.

Färe, R. and S. Grosskopf. (1996). "Productivity and Intermediate Products: A Frontier Approach." *Economics Letters* 50, 65–70.

Farrell, M. (1957). "The Measurement of Productive Efficiency." *Journal of the Royal Statistical Society, Series A, General* 120(3), 253–282.

Hall, R. (1990). "Invariance Properties of Solow's Residual." In P. Diamond (ed.), *Growth/Productivity/-Employment,* Cambridge, MA: MIT Press, 71–112.

Hayashi, F. (1982). "Tobin's Marginal *q* and Average *q*: A Neoclassical Interpretation." *Econometrica* 50, 213–224.

Hulten, C. R. (1978). "Growth Accounting with Intermediate Inputs." *Review of Economic Studies* 45(3), 511–518.

Hulten, C. R. (1979). "On the Importance of Productivity Change." *American Economic Review* 65, 956–965.

Johnson, J. (1994). "Une base de données KLEMS décrivant la structure des entrées de l'industrie canadienne." Statistique Canada, Division des Entrées-Sorties, Cahier Technique #73F.

Jorgenson, D. and Z. Griliches. (1967). "The Explanation of Productivity Change." *Review of Economic Studies* 34(3), 308–350.

Lichtenberg, F. R. and Z. Griliches. (1989). "Errors of Measurement in Output Deflators." *Journal of Business and Economic Statistics* 1–9.

Mohnen, P., Th. ten Raa and G. Bourque. (1997). "Mesures de la croissance de la productivité dans un cadre d'équilibre général: L'économie du Québec entre 1978 et 1984." *Canadian Journal of Economics* 30(2), 295–307.

Morrison, C. (1986). "Productivity Measurement with Non-Static Expectations and Varying Capacity Utilization: An Integrated Approach." *Journal of Econometrics* 33, 51–74.

Morrison, C. (1988). "Quasi-Fixed Inputs in U.S. and Japanese Manufacturing: A Generalized Leontief Restricted Cost Function Approach." *Review of Economics and Statistics* 70(2), 275–287.

Nishimizu, M. and J. M. Page Jr. (1982). "Total Factor Productivity Growth, Technological Progress and Technical Efficiency Change: Dimensions of Productivity Change in Yugoslavia, 1965–1978." *Economic Journal* 92, 920–936.

Perelman, S. (1995). "R&D, Technological Progress and Efficiency Change in Industrial Activities." *Review of Income and Wealth* 41(3), 349–366.

Sickles, R., D. Good and R. Johnson. (1986). "Allocative Distortions and the Regulatory Transition of the U.S. Airline Industry." *Journal of Econometrics* 33(1/2), 143–163.

Siegel, D. (1994). "Errors in Output Deflators Revisited: Unit Values and the PPI." *Economic Inquiry* 32(1), 11–32.

Solow, R. (1957). "Technical Change and the Aggregate Production Function." *Review of Economics and Statistics* 39(3), 312–320.

ten Raa, Th. (1995). *Linear Analysis of Competitive Economies.* LSE Handbooks in Economics, Prentice Hall-Harvester Wheatsheaf, Hemel Hempstead.

Weitzman, M. (1976). "On the Welfare Significance of National Product in a Dynamic Economy." *Quarterly Journal of Economics* 90, 156–162.

Wolff, E. (1985). "Industrial Composition, Interindustry Effects, and the U.S. Productivity Slowdown." *Review of Economics and Statistics* 67, 268–277.

SKILLS AND CHANGING COMPARATIVE ADVANTAGE

Edward N. Wolff*

Abstract.—Using U.S. input-output data for the period 1947–1996 and *Dictionary of Occupational Titles* skill scores, I find that U.S. exports have a high content in cognitive and interactive skills relative to imports, and a low content in motor skills. Moreover, the skill gap between exports and imports has widened over time. Imports are more capital- and equipment-intensive than exports, but the difference has fallen over time. By 1987 exports were more computer-intensive than imports. In contrast, though exports were more R&D-intensive than imports in 1958, they were slightly lower in 1996. Labor productivity also rose faster in export than in import industries, and the unit labor cost of exports declined relative to imports.

I. Introduction

THIS paper considers the relation between the changing skill base of the U.S. labor force and the country's shifting comparative advantage in the international arena. Standard trade theory predicts that a country will export those products that intensively use those endowments in which it is favored relative to the other countries of the world and import products which are intensive in endowments that are scarce in that country. It was generally believed, for example, that the U.S. exported capital-intensive goods and imported labor-intensive ones, but empirical work showed that U.S. exports tended to be human-capital-intensive, and imports capital-intensive (the so-called *Leontief paradox*).

In this paper, I investigate the skill composition of exports and imports. Does the U.S. tend to export products that embody high-skill labor and import those that embody low-skill labor? How have these trade patterns changed over time? Do they reflect the changing skill composition of the U.S. labor force, which has shifted in favor of cognitive and interactive skills and away from motor skills? With the growth of the information economy (assuming that we are in the forefront of the world in that dimension as well), is the U.S. comparative advantage shifting in that direction as well?

A related issue regards the R&D intensity of U.S. trade. During the 1960s and 1970s the major export strength of the U.S. lay in industries whose research was heavily subsidized by the U.S. government (particularly, the Department of Defense), including aircraft, armaments, mainframe computers, and medical equipment (see Dollar & Wolff, 1993). Is the U.S. still exporting R&D-intensive products?

The data analysis is based on U.S. input-output data covering the period 1947 to 1996, and on U.S. Census of Population data on employment by occupation and industry, education, and skills for decennial Census years 1950, 1960, 1970, 1980, and 1990. I present statistics on the skill and educational content of U.S. exports and imports over the period from 1950 to 1990. Calculations are also provided of the share of information workers "embodied" in trade over the same period. Statistics are provided on the total capital, equipment, computer, and R&D content of U.S. trade flows over the years 1947 to 1996, as well as on the relative labor costs and productivity performance of U.S. exports and imports. On the basis of input-output data, it will be possible to compute both the direct and indirect content of trade.

I find that comparative advantage in U.S. international trade has been in industries high in cognitive and interactive skills and low in motor skills, and the skill gap between exports and imports has widened over time. U.S. exports also have a high content of knowledge workers and a low content of goods workers relative to imports, and the gap has grown over time as well. The results also show that imports are more capital- and equipment-intensive than exports but in this case the difference has fallen over time. Moreover, by 1987 exports were more intensive in office, computing, and accounting equipment (OCA) than imports. In contrast, whereas in 1958 the R&D intensity of U.S. exports was much greater than that of imports, by 1996 the R&D intensity of imports was slightly greater than that of exports. I also find that labor productivity rose faster in export than in import industries and the unit labor cost of export industries relative to import industries declined almost steadily over time.

Section II of this paper reviews the previous literature on the skill composition of trade. Section III develops the accounting framework used in the analysis. Section IV presents descriptive statistics on the composition of U.S. trade over the period from 1947 to 1996. The factor content of trade is analyzed in Section V. Concluding remarks are made in Section VI.

II. Review of Previous Literature

A. *The Heckscher-Ohlin Model*

There are two distinct approaches used to explain why different countries will specialize in different industries with regard to trade patterns. The first is the Heckscher-Ohlin model with factor-price equalization (see Heckscher [1919] 1949; Ohlin, 1933). The key assumption in the model is that all countries face the same technology but differ in the relative abundance of factors of production, from which it can be shown that factor prices will be equalized across countries. In the original Heckscher-Ohlin formulation, the proof is based on a two-good, two-factor model. Vanek (1968) extended the model to the multigood, multifactor case. The model is now referred to as the Heckscher-Ohlin-Vanek (or HOV) model. The model was further generalized by Deardorff (1982). The main implication of this model is that trade specialization is dictated by relative factor abundance. In particular, a country will export products that use

Received for publication February 25, 2000. Revision accepted for publication July 24, 2001.

* New York University and the National Bureau of Economic Research.

The Review of Economics and Statistics, February 2003, 85(1): 77–93 intensively those factors in which it is relatively abundant and import products that use intensively those factors which are relatively scarce in it.

This prediction has been subjected to a long series of studies. There are two types. The first involves comparing the resource content of exports with that of the domestic substitutes for imported products in a single country. This is legitimate because by the assumptions of the HOV model, the technology used in a country to produce products which are imported is the same as that used in other countries to produce these products. Moreover, the factor prices faced in the countries are the same, so that relative costs are identical.

The most widely known tests of the effects of relative factor endowments on trade patterns were conducted by Leontief (1956, 1964) using input-output data for the United States. The main finding is that despite the fact that the United States was then the most capital-intensive country in the world, it exported goods that were relatively labor-intensive and imported goods that were relatively capital-intensive. This phenomenon became known as the Leontief paradox. Many explanations were offered for it. These include (1) R&D differences among countries, (2) skill differentials, (3) differences in educational attainment and other human capital attributes; and (4) relative abundance of land and other natural resources (see Caves (1960) for more discussion). The first three factors will be examined in section IV.

The second type of test involves comparing trade patterns between two or more countries and relating these patterns to differences in factor abundance. One of the earliest of these studies was by MacDougall (1951, 1952), who compared British and American exports to see whether the British share of capital-intensive exports was smaller than the American share, as the model would predict due to the higher capital-labor ratio in the United States. He did not find any systematic evidence to support this prediction.

In a much more comprehensive study, Leamer (1984) examined trade patterns for over a hundred economies and found that actual patterns could be explained fairly well by an endowment-based model with ten factors, including capital, several types of natural resources and land, and three skill classes of labor. However, Leamer did not test for correspondence between the factor content of trade and the relative abundance of these factors within a country. In a later study, Bowen, Leamer, and Sveikauskas (1987) computed the amount of each of twelve factors of production embodied in the net exports of 27 countries in 1967 on the basis of the U.S. input-output matrix of total input requirements for that year. These factor contents were then compared with the relative factor abundance of the 27 countries. Using regression tests, they failed to find any correspondence between the two (in contradiction to the HOV model).

Trefler (1993, 1995) used another technique to investigate the Leontief paradox. Like Bowen et al. (1987), he first computed both the labor and the capital requirement of the net exports of a set of countries on the basis of the technology matrix of a single country (the United States). He then compared the labor and capital requirements with the national endowments of both labor and capital to determine whether the Leontief paradox held. This was generally confirmed. He then relaxed the assumption of factor-price equalization and showed that cross-country differences in factor prices could account for the fact that more capital-abundant countries had net exports that were labor intensive, and vice versa.

B. The Technology Gap Model

The second approach for analyzing trade patterns among countries derives from Ricardian trade theory, which emphasizes intercountry differences in technology and factor prices. The modern variant of the Ricardian approach is the technology gap model, whose central premise is that technology gaps and differences in innovativeness between countries will be a major source of trade flows (see, for example, Posner (1961) or Fagerberg (1988)). Whereas the HOV model is essentially a static model, the technology gap model emphasizes technical change as the key source of (changing) comparative advantage.

Empirical analysis of this model relies on using cross-national data to compare trade patterns and technology indicators. Dosi, Pavitt, and Soete (1990), using data for 40 manufacturing industries over the 1963–1977 period, found that patenting activity was a significant determinant of export share among OECD countries, with the exception of several resource-based industries and several in which patents are not a reliable indicator of innovative activity. Other variables that generally proved significant were labor productivity and capital intensity.

In later work, Amable and Verspagen (1995) reported that patents proved to be a significant determinant of export share in a majority of eighteen manufacturing industries for five countries covering the period 1970 to 1991. Wage costs were significant in a third of the sectors, and investment played a role in only a few sectors. Verspagen and Wakelin (1997) also discovered a significant effect of R&D intensity on net exports among a sample of nine OECD countries over the period 1970–1988 for 11 of 22 manufacturing industries.

Other trade economists emphasize the role of relative unit labor costs in international competitiveness. Fagerberg (1988) found that a country's relative unit labor costs were statistically significant as a determinant of a country's trade balance but that the effect was much weaker than that from technological variables. Dosi, Pavitt, and Soete (1990) also reported a much stronger effect of labor productivity than of unit labor costs on exports of total manufacturing.

Wolff (1995), using data for the five major OECD countries over the period 1870 to 1987 and controlling for country size, found that aggregate export performance was significantly related to relative productivity growth, the growth in capital intensity, R&D intensity, and capital vintage. Wolff (1997) used Balassa's (1965) revealed comparative advantage (RCA) index, which measures a country's share of a given export commodity in total world exports of that commodity as a ratio to a country's share of manufacturing exports in total world manufacturing exports, as an indicator of trade specialization. A similar index (RPA) was used for total production (output) shares by industry. On the basis of data for thirteen manufacturing industries in fourteen OECD countries over the period 1970–1992, the results showed that total factor productivity (TFP) growth was a powerful predictor of the change in RPA. It was also significantly related to the change in RCA for 1982–1992 but generally not for 1970–1982. On the other hand, the change in relative labor costs was generally negatively related to the change in RCA and in RPA for 1970–1982 but was not significant for 1982–1992.

In a follow-up study, Wolff (1999) found that improvement in relative labor productivity was a powerful predictor of the change in RPA among 33 manufacturing industries in 14 OECD countries over the period 1970–1993. The rate of capital formation also played an important role in the determination of RPA among low-tech industries but was less significant for medium-tech industries and not significant for high-tech ones. The results also showed that higher unit labor costs generally reduced competitiveness and hence RPA among low-tech industries.

C. *The Skill Content of Trade*

A few studies have examined the skill content of trade. Keesing (1965) used U.S. data for five occupational groups and fifteen industries to classify workers into a skilled and an unskilled category. Comparisons of the skill content of exports were made among nine OECD countries in 1957. Keesing found that relative to other countries' U.S. exports were the most skill-intensive, followed by West Germany, Sweden, and the United Kingdom. Japan ranked last in this group. Engelbrecht (1996) looked at the skill content of German exports and imports in 1976, 1980, and 1984. Using detailed occupational data, he concluded that comparative advantage resulted more from specialization in particular skill types than from the overall human capital endowment of a country. German exports, for example, were strongly endowed with labor from skilled manual occupations (such as metalworkers, toolmakers, and mechanics) and engineers.

Most recently, Lee and Schluter (1999) looked at the skill content of U.S. trade over the period 1972–1992. They constructed a dichotomous variable for skilled and unskilled workers on the basis of nine major occupational groups and found that the ratio of high-skilled to low-skilled workers was greater for exports than for imports, but the difference in the ratios remained nearly unchanged over this period.

III. Accounting Framework and Skill Measures

The input-output model can be introduced as follows, where all vectors and matrices are of order 45 and in constant (1992) dollars, unless otherwise indicated (see the Data Appendix for sources and methods):

X = column vector of gross output by sector,
E = column vector of exports by sector,
M = column vector of imports by sector,[1]
D = column vector of domestic consumption by sector (household consumption, investment, and government expenditures),
$Y = D + E - M$ = column vector showing the final output by sector.
A = square matrix of interindustry input-output coefficients.

Then

$$X = AX + Y. \tag{1}$$

Also, let

e = column vector of export coefficients, where $e_i = E_i/\Sigma E_i$,
m = column vector of import coefficients, where $m_i = M_i/\Sigma M_i$,
L = row vector of labor coefficients, showing employment per unit of output,
K = row vector of capital coefficients, showing total capital per unit of output,
R = row vector showing R&D expenditures as a percentage of net sales by industry,
S = row vector showing average skill scores of workers by industry,
W = row vector showing average employee compensation in 1992 dollars by industry,
N = 267×45 employment matrix, where N_{ij} shows the total employment of occupation i in industry j and where $L_j = \Sigma_i N_{ij}$,
n = 267×45 employment coefficient matrix, showing employment by occupation per unit of output, where $n_{ij} = N_{ij}/X_j$,
B = order-267 column vector of total employment by occupation, where $B_i = \Sigma_j N_{ij}$.
I = identity matrix.

[1] Technically, there are two types of imports recorded within the U.S. input-output framework. The first, called *competitive* or *comparable* imports, are ones for which there are direct domestic substitutes, such as Japanese cars. These are recorded in the row in which there are domestic substitutes and are summed in the import column in final demand. It is not possible to identify the destination of these imports by industry or final user. The second, called *noncompetitive, transferred,* or *noncomparable* imports, are ones for which there are no direct domestic substitutes, such as rubber. These are recorded in a separate row in the interindustry matrix by sector of destination. The calculations of skill or capital embodied in imports are performed only for competitive imports.

Then

$$B = nX = n(I - A)^{-1}Y. \quad (2)$$

The fourth (1977) edition of the *Dictionary of Occupational Titles* (DOT) is used to construct skill measures. For some 12,000 job titles, it provides a variety of alternative measures of job skill requirements based upon data collected between 1966 and 1974. This probably provides the best source of detailed measures of skill requirements covering the period 1950 to 1990. On the basis of this source, three measures of workplace skills are developed for each of 267 occupations, as follows (see Wolff (1996) for more details):

1. *Substantive complexity* (SC) is a composite measure of skills derived from a factor-analytic test of DOT variables. It was found to be correlated with general educational development, specific vocational preparation (training time requirements), data (synthesizing, coordinating, analyzing), and three worker aptitudes—intelligence (general learning and reasoning ability), verbal, and numerical.
2. *Interactive skills* (IS) can be measured, at least roughly, by the DOT *People* variable, which, on a scale of 0–8, identifies whether the job requires mentoring (8), negotiating (7), instructing (6), supervising (5), diverting (4), persuading (3), speaking-signaling (2), serving (1), or taking instructions (0). For comparability with the other measures, this variable is rescaled so that its value ranges from 0 to 10.
3. *Motor skills* (MS), another factor-based variable scaled from 0 to 10, reflects occupational scores on motor coordination, manual dexterity, and job requirements that range from setting up machines and precision working to feeding machines and handling materials.

Average industry skill scores are computed as a weighted average of the skill scores of each occupation, with the occupational employment mix of the industry as weights. Computations are performed for 1950, 1960, 1970, 1980, and 1990, on the basis of consistent occupation, by industry employment matrices for each of these years constructed from decennial Census data. There are 267 occupations and 45 industries.

4. *Mean years of schooling*. These are derived directly from decennial Census of Population data for years 1950, 1960, 1970, 1980, and 1990.

IV. The Composition of U.S. Trade

The percentage composition of exports is shown in Table 1.[2] In 1996, the most important U.S. export was (nonelectrical) industrial machinery, which made up 12.6% of all exports. This category includes OCA. In 1996, OCA by itself comprised 5.1% of all exports. The second most important export was electrical and electronic equipment, accounting for 9.3%, followed by shipping and other transportation services (8.2%), motor vehicles and parts (6.9%), chemicals and chemical products (5.6%), other transportation equipment such as aircraft (5.4%), and wholesale and retail trade (4.8% and 4.6%, respectively). Altogether, industrial machinery, electrical and electronic and transportation equipment, and chemicals made up almost 40% of all exports.

There have been some very striking changes in export composition over the half century. In 1947, the most important U.S. export (excluding transportation services) was processed food products, at 10.9%, followed by agriculture, forestry, and fishing (9.5%), (nonelectrical) industrial machinery (9.2%), primary metal products such as steel (9.0%), motor vehicles and parts (5.7%), and textile mill products such as fabrics (5.5%).[3] Since 1947, agriculture and food exports have steadily declined in relative importance, from 20.3% to 6.5% in 1996, as did exports of primary metal products, from 9.0% to 1.9%. Textile mill products plummeted from 5.5% to 0.8%. Both industrial machinery and motor vehicles remained high over the half century, actually increasing their share. The biggest gains were made by electrical and electronic equipment, from 3.2% to 9.3%.

As shown in table 2, the three leading imports in 1996 were motor vehicles and parts (14.2%), nonelectrical industrial machinery (14.1%), and electric and electronic equipment (13.2%). Together, this group constituted 41.5% of all imports. (It is also of note that these three industries were among the top four industries in exports.) In a somewhat distant fourth place in imports was oil and natural gas (8.4%), followed by apparel and other textiles (6.7%) and chemicals and chemical products (5.8%).

There were even more dramatic changes in import composition than in exports over the period from 1947 to 1996. In 1947 the leading import sector was, by far, processed foods and food products, accounting for 29.0% of all imports. This was followed by agricultural, forestry, and fishing products (15.4%), paper and paper products (14.5%), primary metal products such as steel (10.3%), and metal mining, including iron and copper (7.1%). Agriculture, food

[2] Exports and imports are valued at market prices. This valuation procedure is dictated by data availability. However, it may create some difficulties for products such as software and pharmaceuticals whose marginal cost is close to zero and, in particular, may lead to an overstatement of their importance in the trade flows relative to the use of marginal-cost pricing.

[3] Some distortion may have been introduced by the choice of 1947 as the initial year, in that the structure of U.S. trade may have been unduly influenced by the Marshall Plan and the requirements of European reconstruction. However, changes in the composition of both exports and imports have been fairly gradual over time. The correlation is 0.91 between 1947 and 1958 export composition, and 0.82 between 1947 and 1958 import composition. Using 1958 (or 1960) as a starting point instead of 1947 (or 1950) would not alter the main conclusions derived from tables 3–9.

TABLE 1.—PERCENTAGE COMPOSITION OF U.S. EXPORTS, WITH INDUSTRIES RANKED BY 1996 EXPORTS

	Fraction (%)					
Industry	1947	1958	1967	1977	1987	1996
Industrial machinery except electrical	9.2	12.7	14.3	12.8	10.9	12.6
Electrical and electronic equipment	3.2	4.5	5.4	6.5	7.4	9.3
Shipping and other transport services	13.0	12.0	10.6	6.7	8.8	8.2
Motor vehicles and equipment	5.7	4.8	5.5	7.9	7.6	6.9
Chemicals and allied products	3.8	5.3	6.0	5.3	5.9	5.6
Other transportation equipment	2.4	4.5	5.5	5.8	7.4	5.4
Retail trade	2.9	3.7	3.6	4.4	4.4	4.8
Wholesale trade	2.9	3.7	3.6	4.4	4.2	4.6
Real estate	0.3	1.3	1.6	2.6	3.4	4.6
Instruments and related products	1.1	1.4	2.4	2.4	4.0	4.1
Agriculture, forestry, and fishing	9.5	9.8	9.0	9.2	4.5	3.7
Food and kindred products	10.9	6.7	5.2	5.1	3.8	3.5
Rubber and plastic products	1.6	2.9	2.7	2.2	2.6	3.0
Fabricated metal products	2.2	2.9	3.6	4.0	3.4	2.4
Insurance	0.2	0.1	0.1	0.2	2.4	2.1
Banking, credit, and investment companies	0.2	0.1	0.1	0.2	2.4	2.1
Primary metal products	9.0	5.0	4.4	2.6	1.7	1.9
Paper and allied products	1.7	1.6	2.0	1.8	2.1	1.8
Petroleum and coal products	3.1	3.4	2.1	2.3	2.1	1.5
Business and repair services, except auto	0.2	0.7	0.6	1.0	0.7	1.1
Professional services and nonprofits	0.2	0.6	0.6	1.0	0.7	1.1
Apparel and other textile products	1.8	0.8	0.7	0.7	0.5	1.1
Lumber and wood products	1.0	0.6	1.0	1.4	1.2	0.9
Tobacco products	1.3	2.3	1.6	1.2	0.8	0.9
Amusement and recreation services	0.7	1.3	0.9	0.3	0.4	0.8
Textile mill products	5.5	1.3	0.9	1.2	0.8	0.8
Printing and publishing	0.4	0.5	0.7	1.0	0.7	0.7
Miscellaneous manufactures	1.0	0.6	0.9	0.9	0.9	0.7
Stone, clay, and glass products	1.0	0.9	0.9	0.8	0.6	0.6
Telephone and telegraph	0.2	0.3	0.4	0.7	1.1	0.6
Oil and gas extraction	1.2	0.2	0.3	0.2	0.5	0.6
Coal mining	2.1	1.7	0.8	1.5	0.8	0.3
Correlation with 1996 export composition:	0.64	0.83	0.89	0.91	0.97	1.00

Exports are in current dollars. Industries are classified according to a 45-sector aggregation. Only industries which account for one percent or more of exports in any year are listed.

products, and primary metal products were also among the leading four exports in 1947.

Between 1947 and 1996, processed foods and food products declined steadily from 29.0% to 3.4% of all imports, agriculture from 15.4% to 2.6%, paper and paper products from 14.5% to 2.0%, and metal mining products from 7.1% to 0.0%. The share of primary metal products in total imports, after doubling from 10.3% to 20.5% between 1947 and 1967, tailed off to 4.3% in 1996. In contrast, the import share of nonelectrical industrial machinery rose steadily between 1947 and 1996, from 1.2% to 14.1%, as did that of electrical and electronic equipment, from almost zero to 13.2%, and apparel, from 0.4% to 6.7%. Imports of motor vehicles and parts were volatile, first increasing from virtually zero in 1947 to 6.0% in 1958, dropping to 3.3% in 1967, expanding to 18.9% by 1987 (a reflection of the surge in Japanese car imports), and then diminishing to 14.2% in 1996. The other notable change is that oil imports swelled from 5.1% of all imports in 1947 to 23.8% in 1977, reflecting the steep oil price increases of the mid-1970s, and then abated to 8.4% in 1996.

Overall, import composition changed much more than export composition. The correlation between 1947 and 1996 import shares is a meager 0.13. The correlation rises to only 0.28 between 1958 and 1996 import shares, then to 0.49 between 1967 and 1996 shares, then to 0.70 between 1977 and 1996 shares, and finally to 0.96 between 1987 and 1996 shares. In contrast, the correlation between 1947 and 1996 export shares is a fairly high 0.64, and the correlation between 1958 and 1996 export shares reaches 0.83. In sum, while the composition of U.S. exports has remained fairly constant since the late 1950s, import composition has stabilized only since the late 1980s.

V. The Factor Content of U.S. Exports and Imports

I next turn to the skill content of U.S. exports and imports. The analysis is based on the total (direct plus indirect) labor requirements of exports and of the domestic substitutes for imports (see equation (2)).[4] It should be

[4] An alternative calculation is based on the direct labor requirements of each industry. The vectors nE and nM give the direct labor requirements by occupation to produce the exports and the same array of domestic goods that correspond to the imports of a given year, respectively. The results are quite similar, though differences in factor content between exports and imports, as expected, are somewhat larger. The similarity in results may reflect the high level of aggregation (45 sectors), which is necessitated, in turn, by the use of industry data from different sources. However, Feenstra and Hanson (2000) do not find that the level of

TABLE 2.—PERCENTAGE COMPOSITION OF U.S. IMPORTS, WITH INDUSTRIES RANKED BY 1996 IMPORTS

	Fraction (%)					
Industry	1947	1958	1967	1977	1987	1996
Motor vehicles and equipment	0.2	6.0	3.3	12.2	18.9	14.2
Industrial machinery except electrical	1.2	2.9	7.6	5.2	10.9	14.1
Electrical and electronic equipment	0.1	1.3	6.7	7.6	11.5	13.2
Oil and gas extraction	5.1	11.4	6.0	23.8	7.2	8.4
Apparel and other textile products	0.4	0.4	0.3	4.1	6.5	6.7
Chemicals and allied products	3.1	3.7	4.3	3.6	4.9	5.8
Primary metal products	10.3	12.8	20.5	8.1	4.5	4.3
Instruments and related products	1.8	1.8	2.0	2.0	4.0	3.9
Miscellaneous manufactures	2.2	2.4	3.2	2.5	3.8	3.5
Food and kindred products	29.0	12.4	7.5	5.5	4.5	3.4
Rubber and plastic products	0.4	0.7	1.9	2.1	2.9	3.2
Agriculture, forestry, and fishing	15.4	8.4	5.7	1.9	1.7	2.6
Fabricated metal products	0.3	1.7	3.1	2.0	2.8	2.5
Other transportation equipment	0.3	1.2	1.8	1.5	2.4	2.1
Leather and leather products	0.5	0.5	0.5	1.8	2.3	2.0
Paper and allied products	14.5	9.6	7.2	2.6	2.5	2.0
Petroleum and coal products	2.7	6.2	5.5	7.6	3.3	1.8
Lumber and wood products	4.5	4.9	4.6	2.4	1.6	1.6
Transportation	0.3	0.1	0.6	0.2	0.6	1.3
Stone, clay, and glass products	0.9	1.6	1.6	1.2	1.6	1.3
Furniture and fixtures	0.0	0.0	0.2	0.5	1.3	1.2
Textile mill products	3.4	5.5	4.8	1.1	1.2	0.9
Banking, credit, and investment	1.1	0.2	0.2	0.2	0.4	0.3
Insurance	1.0	0.2	0.2	0.2	0.4	0.3
Mining products of nonmetallic minerals	2.9	1.9	1.1	0.4	0.2	0.2
Tobacco products	2.9	0.3	0.1	0.2	0.2	0.1
Metal mining products	7.1	7.0	4.9	1.3	0.3	0.0
Correlation with 1996 import composition:	0.13	0.38	0.49	0.70	0.96	1.00

Imports are in current dollars. Industries are classified according to a 45-sector aggregation. Only industries which account for one percent or more of imports in any year are listed.

stressed that, as in previous studies, the subsequent analysis of comparative advantage is based on a comparison of the factors of production needed to produce exports with those needed to produce the domestic equivalent of imports. The technique receives theoretical justification in the HOV model by the assumption that technology is the same among countries that trade with one another. Another limitation of this kind of analysis is that a large part of trade is intra-industry. With the available data, we cannot distinguish between low-end and high-end imports or exports, and it is necessary to assume that the factor content of exports from an industry is the same as the factor content of the domestic substitutes of the imports.[5]

Both the export and the import vector include retail and wholesale trade margins and transportation margins.[6] The former represents the value added of domestic wholesale and retail activities involved in the sales of the exports, and the latter represents the shipping costs borne by American-based shippers. Since retail, wholesale, and shipping inputs will accompany any set of exports (and imports), they are not really indicative of comparative advantage. It makes sense to exclude these margins when analyzing comparative advantage, which I do in the tables that follow. Calculations were also performed for total exports and imports and for exports and imports excluding retail and wholesale trade margins only, but are not shown here. The pattern of results are, by and large, very similar to those shown in the tables.

A. *Skill Composition*

Results are shown in table 3 for the total skill content of U.S. trade. The average skill content of exports is given by $S\lambda^0 E/\gamma E$, where $\lambda = L(I - A)^{-1}$ shows the direct plus indirect labor requirements per unit of output, a superscript zero indicates a diagonal matrix with the indicated vector on the diagonal, and S is a row vector showing average skill levels by industry. The average skill content of imports is given by $S\lambda^0 M/\lambda M$.

The main result is that comparative advantage in U.S. international trade has been in industries intensive in both cognitive and interactive skills. Moreover, the comparative advantage in industries requiring high cognitive and interactive skills has been rising over time.

aggregation (two-digit versus four-digit SIC) affected the proportion of production to nonproduction worker content of U.S. manufacturing exports. Another variant is to include industry investment flows as part of the matrix A, as, for example, in Trefler and Zhu (2000). Unfortunately, investment flow matrices are not available on a consistent basis over the 1947–1996 period and so cannot be incorporated here. Trefler and Zhu do not report that the incorporation of investment flows materially affects the estimates of the relative factor content of exports and imports.

[5] A further limitation, as noted in footnote 1 above, is that noncompetitive imports cannot be included in the analysis, since, by definition, such imports do not have domestic substitutes. However, this is a relatively small share of total imports—only 12% in 1996.

[6] Technically, the wholesale and retail margins also include the value added of the rest-of-the-world sector. In the case of imports, these margins appear as negative entries, since imports generally generate domestic value added in American retailing, wholesaling, and transport industries.

TABLE 3.—AVERAGE SKILL CONTENT OF U.S. EXPORTS AND IMPORTS, 1950–1990

Skill Type	Level					Change, 1950–1990 (%)
	1950	1960	1970	1980	1990	
			A. Substantive Complexity (SC)			
Exports	3.44	3.59	3.76	3.92	4.15	20.5
Imports	3.39	3.42	3.59	3.73	3.84	13.3
Difference	0.05	0.16	0.18	0.19	0.30	
Total economy	3.75	3.81	4.07	4.23	4.38	16.9
			B. Interactive Skills (IS)			
Exports	1.45	1.55	1.63	1.74	1.94	34.3
Imports	1.45	1.46	1.51	1.61	1.74	20.2
Difference	0.00	0.09	0.12	0.13	0.20	
Total economy	2.19	2.21	2.27	2.31	2.37	8.0
			C. Motor Skills (MS)			
Exports	5.37	5.37	5.39	5.38	5.25	−2.3
Imports	5.28	5.34	5.43	5.42	5.32	0.9
Difference	0.09	0.04	−0.03	−0.04	−0.08	
Total economy	5.11	5.13	5.17	5.10	5.01	−1.9
			D. Mean Educational Attainment			
Exports	9.26	10.14	11.00	12.14	12.82	38.5
Imports	9.00	9.97	10.91	12.00	12.57	39.7
Difference	0.26	0.17	0.10	0.13	0.25	
Total economy	9.40	10.30	11.50	12.50	13.00	38.3
			E. Residual of Regression of Educational Attainment on SC			
Exports	−0.50	−0.50	−0.22	−0.07	−0.03	—
Imports	−0.69	−0.49	−0.14	−0.04	−0.04	—
Difference	0.19	−0.01	−0.09	−0.03	0.01	
Total economy	0.00	0.00	0.00	0.00	0.00	—

Exports and imports exclude wholesale and retail trade and transportation margins. The average direct plus indirect skill content of exports and imports is given by $S\lambda^0 E/\lambda E$ and $S\lambda^0 M/\lambda M$, respectively.

In 1950, the average SC content of exports was 3.44, compared to an average SC score of 3.39 for imports—a difference of 0.05 (panel A of table 3). By 1990, the average SC level of exports grew by 21% to 4.15 and that of imports by 13% to 3.84, so that the gap increased sixfold to 0.30.

Another interesting comparison is that between the cognitive skill content of exports and imports and the average cognitive skill content of all output. At first blush, the results are surprising—the average SC content of both exports and imports is lower than that of the total economy. However, the reason is that the highest SC scores are found in services such as finance, insurance, real estate, business services, and the government, which are to a large extent nontradables.

Results for interactive skills (IS) are quite similar to those for cognitive skills (panel B). The IS content of total exports is greater than that of total imports, and the gap has widened over time, in this case from a difference of 0.00 in 1950 to 0.20 in 1990. Here, too, both exports and imports have a lower IS content than the whole economy, because the industries with an especially high IS content are finance, insurance, real estate, business services, and the government, which primarily serve the domestic market.

The results for motor skills (MS) are just the opposite of those for SC and IS. In 1950, exports were more MS-intensive than imports. However, by 1970 the average MS of imports were higher, and by 1990 the gap had enlarged to −0.08. In this case, the MS content of both exports and imports is greater than that of the total economy, because of the high concentration of blue collar workers in goods-producing industries, which are more heavily involved in international trade than services.

The results for actual educational attainment are a bit of a surprise. They do show that workers in export industries have a higher mean schooling level than those employed in import industries, but the gap was about the same in 1990 as in 1950.

Table 4 shows a decomposition of the change in the average skill levels of exports and imports into two effects. This is derived as follows. The change in the average skill level generated by exports is given by

$$\frac{1}{2}\left[\left(\frac{S^1\lambda^{01}e^2}{\lambda^1 e^2}-\frac{S^1\lambda^{01}e^1}{\lambda^1 e^1}\right)+\left(\frac{S^2\lambda^{02}e^2}{\lambda^2 e^2}-\frac{S^2\lambda^{02}e^1}{\lambda^2 e^1}\right)\right] + \frac{1}{2}\left[\left(\frac{S^2\lambda^{02}e^1}{\lambda^2 e^1}-\frac{S^1\lambda^{01}e^1}{\lambda^1 e^1}\right)+\left(\frac{S^2\lambda^{02}e^2}{\lambda^2 e^2}-\frac{S^1\lambda^{01}e^2}{\lambda^1 e^2}\right)\right], \qquad (3)$$

where a superscript 1 indicates period 1 and a superscript 2 indicates period 2. The first term (the *trade effect*) measures how much the average skill content of exports would have grown from the change in the composition of exports over the period (from e^1 to e^2), while holding technology constant. The second term (the *industry effect*) measures how

TABLE 4.—DECOMPOSITION OF THE CHANGE IN SKILL LEVELS INTO TRADE AND INDUSTRY EFFECTS, 1950–1990

	Change			Percentage Decomposition		
Skill Type	Trade Effect	Industry Effect	Total	Trade Effect	Industry Effect	Total Change
			A. Substantive Complexity (SC)			
Exports	0.15	0.55	0.70	22	78	100
Imports	−0.01	0.47	0.45	−3	103	100
Difference	0.17	0.09	0.25	66	34	100
			B. Interactive Skills (IS)			
Exports	0.05	0.44	0.50	11	89	100
Imports	−0.10	0.40	0.29	−36	136	100
Difference	0.16	0.05	0.20	77	23	100
			C. Motor Skills (MS)			
Exports	0.06	−0.18	−0.12	−44	144	100
Imports	0.17	−0.12	0.05	349	−249	100
Difference	−0.11	−0.06	−0.17	64	36	100
			D. Mean Educational Attainment			
Exports	−0.07	3.64	3.56	−2	102	100
Imports	−0.24	3.81	3.57	−7	107	100
Difference	0.16	−0.17	−0.01	−1706	1806	100
			E. Residual of Regression of Educational Attainment on SC			
Exports	0.08	0.38	0.47	18	82	100
Imports	0.39	0.26	0.64	60	40	100
Difference	−0.30	0.13	−0.18	171	−71	100

Exports and imports exclude wholesale and retail trade and transportation margins. See equation (3).

much the average skill content of exports would have increased from the changes in both industry skill levels and interindustry and labor coefficients over the period, while holding export composition constant. Coefficient changes may reflect both changes in technology and shifts in factor supplies and relative prices of inputs. A similar decomposition can be used for the change in average skill levels of imports.[7]

Between 1950 and 1990, exports shifted toward industries with relatively high SC levels, such as industrial machinery, electrical equipment, and chemicals. This shift would have raised the average SC content of exports by 0.15 (see panel A). Both changes in (total) labor coefficients and changes in average SC levels within industry would have raised the average SC score of exports by another 0.55 points, for a total change in SC of 0.70 over the period. Over the same period, imports shifted slightly away from higher-cognitive-skill industries, while changes in technology and other industry effects advanced the average SC level by 0.47, a smaller amount than for exports. As a result, of the 0.25 increase in the difference of average SC levels between exports and imports over the four decades, 66% was due to changes in export and import composition and the other 32% to differences in changes of technical and occupational coefficients between export industries and their suppliers on the one hand and importers and their suppliers on the other hand.

Over the 1950–1990 period, exports moved slightly in favor of industries with higher IS levels, while imports shifted in favor of lower-IS industries. The industry effect was somewhat stronger for exports than imports, so that over three-fourths of the widening gap in IS levels between exports and imports was due to the trade effect.

The average MS level in export industries declined by 0.12 between 1950 and 1990, while it rose by 0.05 in import industries. Interestingly, both imports and exports shifted in favor of higher-MS industries, but the shift was much stronger among imports (particularly in 1950–1970). Coefficient changes had a relatively small effect on MS in 1950–1970, but a strong negative effect in the two decades after, causing a greater reduction in motor skills among exporters than among import industries. As a result, 64% of the 0.17-point decline in the difference in average MS between exports and imports over the four decades was due to a stronger shift of imports to high-MS industries, and the other 36% was due to the greater decline in MS among exporters and their suppliers than among import industries and their suppliers.

The pattern for mean educational attainment is quite different. During the 1950–1990 period, both exports and imports shifted away from industries with higher schooling levels, and the effect was larger for imports.[8] The industry effect was strong for both export and import industries,

[7] I use average weights to measure the two effects in order to provide an exact decomposition.

[8] In contrast, on the basis of direct labor requirements only, both exports and imports shifted slightly in favor of industries with higher schooling levels (the latter, in particular, due to the rapid decline in imports of agricultural and processed food products, both low-schooling industries). The difference in results between the direct and total labor requirements reflects the absorption of inputs from agriculture, mining, primary metals, and textiles, all low-schooling sectors, in both export and import industries.

TABLE 5.—EMPLOYMENT OF INFORMATION AND GOODS WORKERS AS A PERCENTAGE OF TOTAL EMPLOYMENT GENERATED BY EXPORTS AND IMPORTS: DIRECT PLUS INDIRECT LABOR INPUT, 1950–1990

	Fraction (%)					
Class of Worker	1950	1960	1970	1980	1990	Change 1950–1990 (percentage points)
			A. Knowledge Workers			
Exports	5.2	6.5	9.0	10.7	13.9	8.7
Imports	4.4	5.7	8.2	9.8	11.5	7.1
Difference	0.8	0.7	0.8	0.9	2.4	1.6
Total economy	7.5	8.0	9.6	11.0	12.9	5.4
			B. Data Workers			
Exports	18.9	21.0	25.7	30.4	32.4	13.5
Imports	16.5	19.3	24.7	28.8	28.5	12.0
Difference	2.4	1.6	1.0	1.6	3.9	1.5
Total economy	29.2	34.2	39.6	41.5	41.9	12.7
			C. Goods Workers			
Exports	71.4	65.4	57.8	50.6	44.9	−26.6
Imports	75.4	69.4	61.2	54.9	53.3	−22.2
Difference	−4.0	−4.0	−3.4	−4.3	−8.4	−4.4
Total economy	51.7	43.5	36.0	31.4	29.0	−22.7

Exports and imports exclude wholesale and retail trade and transportation margins. The total (direct plus indirect) employment by occupation generated by exports and imports is given by $n(I - A)^{-1}E$ and $n(I - A)^{-1}M$, respectively.

reflecting primarily the rising levels of educational attainment among workers in all sectors, but again slightly stronger for imports. As a result, the trade and industry effects offset each other, leading to virtually no change in the difference in mean education between exports and imports over this period.

Further analysis reveals why the results differ between educational attainment and cognitive skills. Cross-industry regressions were first performed of mean schooling on a constant term and SC for 1950, 1960, 1970, 1980, and 1990. Though schooling and SC are strongly correlated (the R^2 statistic ranges from 0.72 to 0.82, and the t-statistic on SC from 10.4 to 14.0), they are not perfectly correlated. In the second step, the skill content of exports and imports was computed using the residual of the regression of schooling on SC as the index of skill. In 1950, the residual content of both exports and imports was highly negative—that is, tradables had a lower schooling content relative to their SC content than that of the entire economy (see panel E of table 3). This result reflects the concentration of exports in processed food products (a residual of −0.35), industrial machinery (−0.21), primary metal products (−0.05), and textile products (−0.14) in 1950 and the concentration of imports in food products (−0.35), agriculture (−2.41), paper products (−0.52), and primary metal products (−0.05). However, the residual content of imports was more negative than that of exports because of its large share of agricultural products.

By 1990, the residual content of both exports and imports had closed to virtually zero. In the case of exports, this trend primarily reflected the elimination of the residual among export industries (the industry effect); among imports it was mainly due to the shift of import composition to industries where the residual was low (see panel E of table 4). Overall, the fact that the gap in cognitive skill content between exports and imports rose during 1950–1990 while the gap in educational attainment remained unchanged was almost exclusively attributable to the shift of imports to industries with relatively small differences in their schooling and SC content. This was offset, in part, by the greater reduction in the gap between schooling and SC content among export industries.

C. *Information Workers*

Workers are divided into four groups: knowledge, data, service, and goods workers. Information workers are the sum of knowledge and data workers. The overall results show that exports are more intensive in their use of information workers than imports and less intensive in their employment of goods-producing workers, and the difference has widened dramatically over time.

The basic data are from the U.S. Decennial Censuses of 1950, 1960, 1970, 1980, and 1990. In the classification schema, professional and technical workers are generally classified as knowledge or data workers, depending on whether they are producers or users of knowledge. Management personnel are taken to perform both data and knowledge tasks, since they produce new information for administrative decisions and also use and transmit this information. Clerical workers are classed as data workers for obvious reasons. I classify as goods-processing workers all those who transform or operate on materials or physical objects. These include craft workers, operatives (including transportation workers who move physical goods), and unskilled workers. The remaining group is made up of the service workers, who, primarily, perform personal services.

(See Baumol, Blackman, and Wolff (1989, Chapter 7) for more details on the classification scheme.)

The results, shown in table 5, are based on the total employment by occupation generated by exports (λE) and imports (λM). In 1950, exports were slightly more intensive in their use of knowledge workers than imports. The employment of knowledge workers generated by exports was 5.2% of the total employment generated by exports in 1950, compared to 4.4% for imports. The share of knowledge workers employed in the production of exports rose from 5.2% to 13.9% between 1950 and 1990—a gain of 8.7 percentage points. In contrast, the share of knowledge workers producing import substitutes expanded from 4.4% to 11.5%—an increase of only 7.1 percentage points. As a result the gap between the shares of knowledge workers employed in export and in import production widened from 0.8 to 2.4 percentage points over the four decades. It is also of note that the knowledge worker intensity of exports was below the economy-wide average from 1950 to 1980. However, by 1990 it exceeded the overall figure of 12.9%.

The pattern is quite similar for data workers. Exports are more intensive in their use of data workers than imports. While data workers as a share of the total workers producing exports climbed from 19% to 32% between 1950 and 1990, the share producing import substitutes rose from 17% to 29% (see panel B). As a result, the difference in the data worker share between exports and imports increased from 2.4 to 3.9 percentage points. Altogether, the gap between exports and imports in the share of information workers swelled from 3.2 to 6.3 percentage points over the four decades.

Whereas exports are intensive in their use of information workers, imports are relatively intensive in goods producing workers, as shown in panel C. It is of note first that both exports and import substitutes absorb a much higher share of goods workers than the overall economy—a reflection of the heavy bias of international trade toward manufactures. In 1950, 75.4% of the employment generated by import substitutes was goods-producing workers, compared to 71.4% for export producers—a difference of 4.0%. As for the whole economy, the proportion of goods workers generated by both exports and imports declined over time. For exports, the share fell from 71.4% to 44.9%, a drop of 26.5 percentage points; for imports, the share fell less, by 22.1 percentage points, from 75.4% to 53.3%. As a result, the difference between imports and exports in the share of goods workers more than doubled between 1950 and 1990, from 4.0 to 8.4 percentage points. The evidence clearly shows that U.S. exports are becoming more intensive in their use of information workers over time, while imports are becoming more intensive in their use of blue collar workers.

The decompositions shown in table 6 identify some of the reasons for the changes in the relative share of information and goods workers in export and import industries. The

TABLE 6.—DECOMPOSITION OF THE CHANGE IN PERCENTAGE SHARE OF INFORMATION AND GOODS WORKERS IN TOTAL EMPLOYMENT INTO TRADE AND INDUSTRY EFFECTS, 1950–1990

	Decomposition			Percentage Decomposition		
Class of Work	Trade Effect	Industry Effect	Total Change	Trade Effect	Industry Effect	Total Change
A. Knowledge workers:						
Exports	1.9	6.8	8.7	22	78	100
Imports	1.8	5.2	7.0	26	74	100
Difference	0.1	1.5	1.6	5	95	100
B. Data workers:						
Exports	3.8	9.7	13.5	28	72	100
Imports	4.7	7.3	12.0	40	60	100
Difference	−1.0	2.5	1.5	−65	165	100
C. Goods workers:						
Exports	−6.1	−20.5	−26.6	23	77	100
Imports	−7.0	−15.1	−22.2	32	68	100
Difference	0.9	−5.3	−4.4	−22	122	100

Exports and imports exclude wholesale and retail trade and transportation margins. See equation (4).

change in the share of employment of a given class of worker generated by exports is given by

$$\frac{1}{2}\left[\left(\frac{p^1\lambda^{01}e^2}{\lambda^1e^2}-\frac{p^1\lambda^{01}e^1}{\lambda^1e^1}\right)+\left(\frac{p^2\lambda^{02}e^2}{\lambda^2e^2}-\frac{p^2\lambda^{02}e^1}{\lambda^2e^1}\right)\right] + \frac{1}{2}\left[\left(\frac{p^2\lambda^{02}e^1}{\lambda^2e^1}-\frac{p^1\lambda^{01}e^1}{\lambda^1e^1}\right)+\left(\frac{p^2\lambda^{02}e^2}{\lambda^2e^2}-\frac{p^1\lambda^{01}e^2}{\lambda^1e^2}\right)\right], \quad (4)$$

where p is a row vector showing employment of a given class of worker (such as knowledge workers) as a share of industry employment. The first term (the trade effect) shows the effect of changes in export composition on employment shares, and the second term (the industry effect) shows the effect of changes in both interindustry and occupational coefficients on employment shares. A similar decomposition can be used for the share of employment, by class of worker, generated by imports.

Between 1950 and 1990, both exports and imports shifted toward industries with a higher share of knowledge and data workers and a lower share of goods workers. The trade effect for knowledge workers was about the same for exports and imports, but for both data and goods workers the trade effect was stronger for imports than for exports. The industry effects for both exports and imports were positive for knowledge and data workers and negative for goods workers, but here the effects were considerably larger among export industries. Moreover, the industry effects dominated the trade effects for both exports and imports. As a result, of the 1.6-percentage-point difference in the change of the share of knowledge workers generated by exports and imports, 95% was attributable to the faster growth of knowledge intensity among export industries and their suppliers than among import industries and their suppliers. Likewise, more than 100% of the 1.5-percentage-point increase in the

TABLE 7.—CAPITAL AND R&D INTENSITY OF U.S. EXPORTS AND IMPORTS: DIRECT PLUS INDIRECT LABOR AND R&D INPUT, 1947–1996

Quantity	Value						Ratio of 1996 to 1947
	1947	1958	1967	1977	1987	1996	
A. Ratio of total net capital (1,000s of 1992 dollars) to employment							
Exports	29.4	51.0	63.5	87.2	93.7	103.8	3.53
Imports	34.6	71.0	81.7	129.2	102.1	114.1	3.29
Ratio	0.85	0.72	0.78	0.67	0.92	0.91	
Total economy	54.7	65.8	76.9	83.5	87.7	95.6	1.75
B. Ratio of net equipment (1,000s of 1992 dollars) to employment							
Exports	9.4	17.5	23.1	34.7	38.9	46.2	4.91
Imports	10.5	20.3	26.4	39.0	40.7	47.5	4.51
Ratio	0.89	0.86	0.87	0.89	0.96	0.97	
Total economy	14.7	16.5	19.9	22.2	25.2	29.5	2.01
C. Ratio of OCA (100s of 1992 dollars) to employment[a]							
Exports	0.5	0.9	0.9	1.7	10.8	40.5	78.26
Imports	0.9	1.1	0.8	1.7	9.0	34.6	37.98
Ratio	0.57	0.87	1.01	1.01	1.20	1.17	
Total economy	0.9	1.2	1.1	1.6	9.2	33.9	39.64
D. Ratio of R&D expenditures to net sales (%)[b]							
Exports	—	1.77	1.91	1.51	2.61	2.15	1.21
Imports	—	0.89	1.18	1.37	2.55	2.17	2.44
Difference		0.88	0.73	0.14	0.07	−0.03	
Total manufacturing	—	2.70	2.92	2.27	3.40	3.03	1.12

Exports and imports exclude wholesale and retail trade and transportation margins. The total employment and capital generated by exports are given by $L(I - A)^{-1}E$ and $K(I - A)^{-1}E$, respectively. The total employment and capital generated by imports are given by $L(I - A)^{-1}M$ and $K(I - A)^{-1}M$, respectively.

[a] The government sector is not included.

[b] R&D data are available only for manufacturing. The total (direct plus indirect) R&D intensities of exports and imports are given by $R(I - A)^{-1}E/\mathbf{1}(I - A)^{-1}E$ and $R(I - A)^{-1}M/\mathbf{1}(I - A)^{-1}M$, respectively, where **1** is a row vector of ones. The ratios are for 1996 to 1958.

gap in the share of data workers was due to the higher growth of data worker intensity among exporters than importers, whereas imports shifted more toward data-intensive industries than exports. Similarly, more than 100% of the 4.4-percentage-point decline in the difference in the share of goods workers between exports and imports was ascribable to the slower contraction of goods-worker intensity among import industries than among export industries, whereas the shift in import composition led to a larger decline in the share of goods workers than did the shift in export composition.

D. *Capital Intensity of Exports and Imports*

Panel A of table 7 shows the capital intensity of exports and import. This comparison forms the basis of the Leontief paradox. The total net capital (in thousands of 1992 dollars) per worker in exports and imports is given by $K(I - A)^{-1}E/L(I - A)^{-1}E$ and $K(I - A)^{-1}M/L(I - A)^{-1}M$, respectively. The results show a pronounced and continuous rise in the capital intensity of exports from 1947 to 1996. In contrast, the capital intensity of imports rose steeply between 1947 and 1977 and then slipped from 1977 to 1997. The reason is the tremendous increase of oil imports during the 1970s (see table 2); oil is a very capital-intensive industry. Another finding is that the capital intensity of both exports and imports was below the overall capital-labor ratio of the economy in 1947 but equal to or above it in 1996. Imports, in fact, exceeded the overall capital-labor ratio by 1958 and remained above it through 1996, whereas exports exceeded it beginning in 1977. This indicates a shifting of both exports and imports toward more capital-intensive industries (primarily durable manufacturing).

The results show that, in fact, imports have been more capital-intensive than exports (the Leontief paradox). However, what is more telling is that the capital intensity of exports relative to imports, after falling between 1947 and 1977 from a ratio of 0.85 to 0.67, climbed to 0.91 in 1996. The capital intensity of exports rose by a factor of 3.5 between 1947 and 1996, compared to a 3.3-fold increase for imports. These results indicate a gradual shifting of U.S. comparative advantage back toward capital-intensive goods since 1977.

Panel B shows results for total net stocks of equipment per worker. Again, we find a continuous rise in the equipment intensity of both exports and imports between 1947 and 1996. In 1947, both exports and imports were less equipment-intensive than the overall economy, but by 1958 imports and by 1967 exports had exceeded the economy-wide ratio of equipment to employment. The results also show the equipment intensity of exports rising faster than that of imports over the years 1947 to 1996—a ratio of 4.9 compared to 4.5. As a result, the equipment intensity of exports relative to imports grew from a ratio of 0.89 in 1947 to 0.97 in 1996, with most of the gain occurring after 1977. Here, too, the U.S. comparative advantage is clearly shifting back toward industries with a high equipment-to-worker ratio.

TABLE 8.—DECOMPOSITION OF THE CHANGE IN CAPITAL AND R&D INTENSITY INTO TRADE AND INDUSTRY EFFECTS, 1947–1997

	Decomposition			Percentage Decomposition		
Quantity	Trade Effect	Industry Effect	Total Change	Trade Effect	Industry Effect	Total Change
A. Ratio of total net capital (1,000s of 1992 dollars) to employment:						
Exports	−9.5	83.9	74.4	−13	113	100
Imports	−42.9	122.4	79.5	−54	154	100
Ratio	0.12	−0.06	0.06	207	−107	100
B. Ratio of net equipment (1,000s of 1992 dollars) to employment:						
Exports	−6.3	43.1	36.8	−17	117	100
Imports	−16.8	53.8	37.0	−45	145	100
Ratio	0.18	−0.10	0.08	228	−128	100
C. Ratio of OCA (100s of 1992 dollars) to employment:						
Exports	5.6	34.4	40.0	14	86	100
Imports	17.1	16.6	33.7	51	49	100
Ratio	−1.81	2.41	0.60	−301	401	100
D. Ratio of R&D expenditures to net sales (percentage points)[a]:						
Exports	0.50	−0.12	0.38	132	−32	100
Imports	1.26	0.02	1.28	98	2	100
Ratio	−0.77	−0.14	−0.91	85	15	100

Exports and imports exclude wholesale and retail trade and transportation margins. See equation (5).
[a] R&D data are available only for manufacturing. The decomposition covers years 1958 to 1996 only.

The results are even more dramatic for OCA per worker (see panel C). The OCA intensity of exports grew twice as fast as that of imports between 1947 and 1996. Moreover, while imports were more intensive in OCA than exports in 1947, the situation reversed in 1967, and by 1996 the OCA intensity of exports relative to imports reached 1.17. U.S. comparative advantage now lies in industries that intensively use office and computing equipment.

The decompositions in Table 8 highlight some of the reasons for this remarkable turnaround in the capital intensity of exports relative to imports. The change in the capital-labor ratio generated by exports is given by

$$\frac{1}{2}\left[\left(\frac{\gamma^1 e^2}{\lambda^1 e^2}-\frac{\gamma^1 e^1}{\lambda^1 e^1}\right)+\left(\frac{\gamma^2 e^2}{\lambda^2 e^2}-\frac{\gamma^2 e^1}{\lambda^2 e^1}\right)\right] + \frac{1}{2}\left[\left(\frac{\gamma^2 e^1}{\lambda^2 e^1}-\frac{\gamma^1 e^1}{\lambda^1 e^1}\right)+\left(\frac{\gamma^2 e^2}{\lambda^2 e^2}-\frac{\gamma^1 e^2}{\lambda^1 e^2}\right)\right], \quad (5)$$

where, as before, the first bracketed term is the trade effect and the second is the industry effect, and $\gamma = K(I - A)^{-1}$, showing the direct plus indirect capital requirements per unit of output. A similar decomposition can be used for imports.

As shown in panel A, the ratio of total net capital per worker generated by exports increased by $74,400 (in 1992 dollars) between 1947 and 1977. Of this, $83,900 (or 113%) was accounted for by the rising capital intensity of export industries. The changes in export composition favored labor-intensive industries, but the effect was small. The change in technical coefficients in import industries had an even stronger effect on the increase in the capital-labor ratio generated by imports in this period, accounting for $122,400 (or 154%) of the total gain of $79,500. However, imports shifted away from capital-intensive industries (mainly agriculture and primary metal products) toward non-capital-intensive ones (primarily industrial machinery, electrical equipment, and motor vehicles), accounting for a $42,900 decline in the capital-labor ratio of import industries. As a result, the growth in the capital intensity of exports relative to imports was entirely due to changes in export and import composition (mainly the latter), which was partially offset by changes of technology in export and import industries and their suppliers.

Results are even stronger for equipment per worker (panel B). In this case, the ratio of the equipment intensity of exports relative to imports rose from 0.89 in 1947 to 0.97 in 1996. The change of $36,800 in the equipment-to-employment ratio generated by exports was due to the rising capital intensity of export industries, which was offset in part by shifts in export composition toward non-equipment-intensive industries. Likewise, the rise in the equipment intensity of imports, amounting to $37,000, was due to both the rising capital intensity of import industries and the negative effects of changing import composition. As with total capital intensity, the growth of the ratio in equipment intensity between exports and imports over this period emanated entirely from the trade effect (mainly changes in import composition), counterbalanced, in part, by the industry effect.

The pattern is different for OCA per worker. The ratio of OCA intensity of exports to imports increased from 0.57 in 1947 to 1.17 in 1996. The evidence here indicates that the composition of exports shifted toward industries that were intensive in their use of computers and office machinery, accounting for 14% of the total growth of OCA per worker of $4,000 over the 1947–1996 period. The other 86% was due to the rising investment in OCA per worker in export industries and their suppliers. Imports likewise shifted toward computer-intensive industries, particularly after 1977. Over the full 1947–1996 period, 51% of the overall gain of $3,370 in OCA per worker among import industries was attributable to changes in import composition, and the other 49% to increases in OCA intensity in import industries and their suppliers. Over the half century, imports shifted more strongly toward computer-intensive industries than exports, while computer intensity rose much faster in export industries than import industries. As a result, the rise in the ratio of OCA intensity in exports relative to imports over this period was due entirely to the faster growth of OCA per worker in export industries than in import industries, whereas shifts in export and import composition had a negative effect on this ratio.

E. *R&D Intensity of Exports and Imports*

Panel D of Table 7 shows both R&D expenditures generated by exports and imports as a percentage of net sales. Direct plus indirect R&D expenditures as a percentage of net sales of exports are given by $R(I - A)^{-1}E/\mathbf{1}(I - A)^{-1}E$, where $\mathbf{1}$ is a row vector of ones; direct plus indirect R&D expenditures as a percentage of net sales of imports are given by $R(I - A)^{-1}M/\mathbf{1}(I - A)^{-1}M$.

The results are surprising. The R&D intensity of U.S. exports in 1958 was almost twice as great as that of imports. The R&D intensity of both exports and imports increased between 1958 and 1987 and then fell off somewhat in 1996. However, over the 1958-to-1996 period, R&D intensity rose much faster for imports than for exports—a factor of 2.4 versus 1.2. As a result, by 1996, the R&D intensity of imports was slightly greater than that of exports. Interestingly, neither exports nor imports were as R&D-intensive as overall manufacturing.

The decomposition shown in panel D of table 8 indicate some of the reasons behind the falling R&D intensity of export industries relative to import industries. The decomposition of the change in the R&D expenditures as a ratio to net sales generated by exports is given by

$$\frac{1}{2}\left[\left(\frac{\rho^1 e^2}{q^1 e^2} - \frac{\rho^1 e^1}{q^1 e^1}\right) + \left(\frac{\rho^2 e^2}{q^2 e^2} - \frac{\rho^2 e^1}{q^2 e^1}\right)\right] + \frac{1}{2}\left[\left(\frac{\rho^2 e^1}{q^2 e^1} - \frac{\rho^1 e^1}{q^1 e^1}\right) + \left(\frac{\rho^2 e^2}{q^2 e^2} - \frac{\rho^1 e^2}{q^1 e^2}\right)\right],$$

where $\rho = R(I - A)^{-1}$ shows the direct plus indirect R&D requirements per unit of output, and $q = \mathbf{1}(I - A)^{-1}$. The first term is the trade effect, and the second term (the industry effect) shows the average effect of changes in industry R&D coefficients on overall R&D intensity. A similar decomposition can be used for the R&D intensity of imports.

The effects of the changing composition of exports and imports explain almost the entirety of the decline in the R&D intensity of exports relative to imports. Between 1958 and 1996, both exports and imports shifted toward more R&D-intensive industries, but the shift effect was more than twice as great for imports. Export growth was particularly strong in electrical and electronic equipment and scientific instruments, while imports gained share in motor vehicles, electrical and electronic equipment, chemicals, scientific instruments, and especially industrial machinery. Moreover, overall R&D expenditures in manufacturing, after declining from 2.70% of net sales in 1958 to 2.27% in 1977, increased to 3.03% in 1996. On net, the change in R&D coefficients (the industry effect) essentially washed out between the two periods. The fact that the trade effect was much stronger for imports than exports accounts for 85% of the elimination of the gap in R&D intensity between exports and imports.

F. *Labor Costs and Labor Productivity of Exports and Imports*

The final part of the analysis considers the average labor costs of both exports and imports. According to Ricardian trade theory, a country will export those products whose cost is relatively low and import those products whose cost is relatively high. Though the relevant comparison is with other trading countries, it might still be expected that a country will export the products of those industries that pay relatively low wages and import the products of industries with high wages.

The results, shown in Table 9, are a bit surprising. Average wages generated directly and indirectly by exports are given by $W(I - A)^{-1}E/L(I - A)^{-1}E$, where W is a row vector showing average employee compensation per full-time equivalent employee (FTEE) in 1992 dollars by industry. Average wages generated by imports are given by $W(I - A)^{-1}M/L(I - A)^{-1}M$. The unit labor cost of industry i is defined here as the ratio of average employee compensation per FTEE (in 1992 dollars) in industry i to labor productivity (the ratio of GDP in 1992 dollars to FTEE) in industry i. The average unit labor cost generated by exports is given by $W(I - A)^{-1}E/\mathbf{1}(I - A)^{-1}E$, and the average unit labor cost generated by imports is given by $W(I - A)^{-1}M/\mathbf{1}(I - A)^{-1}M$.

Export industries and their suppliers were paying 9% more than import industries and their suppliers in 1947, but 2% less by 1977 (panel A). Between 1977 and 1996, the situation reversed and average wages among exporters rose relative to import industries. By 1996, export industries were paying 4% more than import industries. It is also of note that both export and import industries paid wages lower than the economy-wide average wage in 1947, but higher than average in 1996. Panel B shows another measure of labor costs, employee compensation plus half of proprietors' income per person engaged in production (PEP). The results are almost identical. By this measure,

TABLE 9.—LABOR COSTS OF U.S. EXPORTS AND IMPORTS: DIRECT PLUS INDIRECT LABOR INPUT, 1947–1996

Labor Cost Component	Value						Ratio of 1996 to 1947
	1947	1958	1967	1977	1987	1996	
A. Employee compensation per FTEE (1,000s of 1992 dollars):							
Exports	15.6	21.4	27.8	35.5	38.4	39.4	2.53
Imports	14.3	20.8	27.9	36.2	37.9	37.8	2.65
Ratio	1.09	1.03	1.00	0.98	1.01	1.04	
Total economy	15.8	21.5	27.0	32.6	34.7	34.8	2.20
B. Employee compensation plus half proprietors' income per PEP (1,000s of 1992 dollars):							
Exports	15.8	21.5	27.6	35.4	37.9	39.2	2.48
Imports	14.7	20.8	27.7	36.3	37.4	37.2	2.53
Ratio	1.08	1.03	1.00	0.98	1.01	1.05	
Total economy	15.0	20.4	26.3	31.7	33.1	33.7	2.25
C. Output (GDP) per FTEE (1,000s of 1992 dollars):							
Exports	24.1	31.8	41.7	48.1	59.4	70.7	2.94
Imports	25.6	33.2	42.1	51.9	55.6	67.2	2.62
Ratio	0.94	0.96	0.99	0.93	1.07	1.05	
Total economy	30.1	38.1	46.3	53.1	57.5	61.1	2.03
D. Unit labor cost:							
Exports	0.65	0.67	0.67	0.74	0.65	0.56	0.86
Imports	0.56	0.63	0.66	0.70	0.68	0.56	1.01
Difference	0.09	0.05	0.00	0.04	−0.04	−0.01	
Total economy	0.53	0.56	0.58	0.61	0.60	0.57	1.08

Exports and imports exclude wholesale and retail trade and transportation margins. FTEE: Full-time equivalent employee. PEP: Person engaged in production.

exporters paid 8% higher wages than import industries in 1947, and 5% higher wages in 1996.[9]

Between 1947 and 1996, labor productivity grew faster in export than in import industries: 2.2% versus 2.0% per year (panel C). In 1947, output per FTEE was 6% higher in import industries than in export industries, but in 1996, it was 5% higher for exporters. Labor productivity also grew faster among both exports and imports than in the total economy over the 49-year stretch, because of the heavy concentration of manufactured goods in trade.

Changes in unit labor cost reflect both changes in worker compensation and labor productivity. In 1947 export industries had higher unit labor cost than import industries (panel D), a reflection of their higher wages. However, in this case we see an almost continuous decline in the unit labor cost of export industries relative to import industries between 1947 and 1996. The reason is the higher productivity growth of export industries relative to import industries, not the declining relative wages of export industries. By 1996, unit labor costs of exports were slightly below those of import industries.

VI. Conclusions

The composition of both exports and imports has changed considerably over the postwar period. In 1947, the most important U.S. exports in rank order (excluding wholesale and retail trade and transportation services) were food products, agricultural products, industrial machinery, primary metal products, motor vehicles, and textiles. Of this group, only industrial machinery could be considered high-tech, and only motor vehicles medium-tech. By 1996, industrial machinery exports ranked first, followed by electrical and electronic equipment, motor vehicles, chemicals, and other transportation equipment such as aircraft. These are all high-tech or medium-tech industries.

In 1947 the leading import was, by far, processed foods and food products, followed by agricultural products, paper and paper products, primary metal products, and metal mining. These were all low-tech industries. In 1996, the three leading imports were motor vehicles, industrial machinery, and electric and electronic equipment, all medium- or high-tech. So, while U.S. exports shifted over time away from low-tech industries and toward medium- and high-tech ones, the shift was even more pronounced for U.S. imports.

The principal finding is that U.S. comparative advantage lies in cognitive- and interactive-skill-intensive products, and the comparative advantage in cognitive and interactive skills increased between 1950 and 1990. The finding of a higher skill content of exports than imports is consistent with the results of Lee and Schluter (1999), though they did not find that the gap widened over time. With the exception of 1950, imports have been more motor-skill-intensive than exports, and the difference has also widened over this period. Workers employed in export industries have had a higher mean schooling level than those in import industries, but the gap remained unchanged. The widening gap in cognitive, interactive, and motor skills between exports and imports was due primarily to changes in the composition of exports and imports. Changing trade composition also fa-

[9] A third measure, wages and salaries per FTEE, also shows almost exactly the same pattern (results not shown).

vored exports over imports in terms of mean schooling, but this effect was almost exactly offset by the industry effect, which favored imports. The fact that the cognitive skill content widened between exports and imports while their schooling content remained unchanged was traced to the shift of imports towards industries whose cognitive skill and schooling levels were in balance.

The results also show that exports are more intensive in their use of knowledge and data workers than imports and less intensive in their employment of goods-producing workers, and these differences have widened over time. The dominant factor explaining these trends is the greater absorption of information workers and the greater displacement of goods workers among export producers than import industries, rather than shifts in the composition of trade.

The results here provide new confirmation that imports are more capital-intensive than exports. However, in this case the capital intensity of exports relative to imports has been climbing since 1977. The results also show that while imports are more equipment intensive than exports, the equipment intensity of exports rose faster than that of imports over these years. The OCA intensity of exports has also grown much faster than that of imports, and by 1987 exports were more OCA-intensive than imports. These results thus indicate a gradual shifting of U.S. comparative advantage back toward capital-intensive goods since 1977, particularly toward industries with a high equipment and OCA intensity.

All the growth in the total capital and equipment intensity of exports relative to imports over the years 1947 to 1996 was due to changes in export and import composition (mainly the latter), partially offset by a greater rise in capital intensity among import industries. In contrast, the increase in the OCA intensity of exports relative to imports over this period was due entirely to the faster growth of OCA per worker in export industries than in import industries, while shifts in export and import composition had a negative effect on the ratio.

Although the R&D intensity of U.S. exports was almost twice as great as that of imports in 1958, it was slightly higher in import industries in 1996. Almost the entirety of the growth in R&D intensity in imports relative to exports is explained by changes in trade composition—particularly, growing imports of motor vehicles, industrial machinery, electrical equipment, chemicals, and scientific instruments over these years.

There is no indication that average wages or employee compensation grew faster in import than in export industries, as might be expected from the Ricardian theory of comparative advantage. However, labor productivity rose faster in export than import industries between 1947 and 1996. As a result, the unit labor cost of export industries declined almost steadily relative to import industries between over this period, as Ricardian theory would predict.

In sum, we find that the United States exports cognitive and interactive skills and imports motor skills. It also substitutes information for blue collar workers. Moreover, the gap in skill and information content between exports and imports has been widening over time. These results implicitly suggest that the occupational structure of the American workforce has been shifting faster into high-cognitive-skill knowledge jobs and away from motor-skill-intensive blue collar jobs than those of other advanced industrial countries (which is consistent with the findings of Engelbrecht (1996) with regard to Germany).

American exports embody a higher level of schooling than do its imports, but in this case the gap has not changed over time. The likely reason is that other OECD countries have experienced a rapid catch-up in educational attainment. Evidence of this is provided in Wolff (2000). It is also possible that schooling levels among our trading partners have increased faster than the cognitive skill content of their exports to the United States. This hypothesis would be consistent with the finding that U.S. imports have shifted towards industries with a higher cognitive skill content relative to their average schooling levels.

The gradual loss of comparative advantage in R&D-intensive products also reflects a catch-up in R&D by other OECD countries. According to National Science Board (1998), Japan's R&D intensity (the ratio of R&D expenditures to GDP) has steadily grown since 1980 and by 1995 was 2.78%, compared to 2.52%, in the U.S., 2.28%, in Germany, 2.34% in France, and 2.05% in the United Kingdom).

While the United States no longer has the edge in R&D and may lose it in education, it has taken the lead in another aspect of high-tech production, computer intensity, and is gradually reclaiming its advantage in total capital and equipment intensity.[10] This is likely a reflection of the gradual erosion in the human capital advantage of the United States vis-à-vis other OECD countries. For the moment, complementarities between OCA and both cognitive skills and knowledge worker jobs (see Wolff, 1996) may account for the lower overall capital intensity of exports than of imports.

The trends also suggest that the Leontief paradox may be overturned in the near future. However, this may create a new paradox, since the U.S. is no longer the most capital-abundant country in the world (according to the OECD International Sectoral Database, in 1995 the U.S. ranked behind Germany, the Netherlands, and Belgium in overall capital intensity).

The results on productivity and labor costs are consistent with my earlier studies (Dollar and Wolff, 1993; Wolff,

[10] Some researchers equate these various dimensions of high-tech production. However, as shown in table 10, the cross-industry correlation of R&D intensity with equipment intensity, OCA intensity, and workers skill is very low. Equipment intensity also has a low correlation with workers' skill levels, while OCA intensity has a correlation of about 0.5.

TABLE 10.—CORRELATION COEFFICIENTS BETWEEN DIFFERENT DIMENSIONS OF HIGH-TECH PRODUCTION, 1990

	R&D/Sales	SCIENG	Equip/PEP	OCA/PEP	SCHOOL	SC	Knowledge
1. R&D/Sales	1.00						
2. SCIENG	0.93	1.00					
3. Equip./PEP	−0.06	0.00	1.00				
4. OCA/PEP	0.11	0.20	0.49	1.00			
5. SCHOOL	−0.01	−0.01	0.12	0.46	1.00		
6. SC	0.02	0.04	0.15	0.55	0.89	1.00	
7. Knowledge	0.16	0.22	0.12	0.45	0.69	0.76	1.00

Correlation coefficients are computed from industry data (44 industries, excluding the government sector). Key: 1. R&D/Sales: the ratio of R&D expenditures to total industry net sales. 2. SCIENG: scientists and engineers engaged in R&D per FTEE. 3. Equip./PEP: the stock of machinery and equipment per PEP. 4. OCA/PEP: the stock of office, computing, and accounting equipment per PEP. 5. SCHOOL: Mean years of schooling in industry. 6. SC: Mean substantive complexity in industry. 7. Knowledge: knowledge workers as a percentage of total industry employment.

1995, 1997, 1999), which found on the basis of cross-national evidence that changes in industry net exports were positively related to industry productivity growth and negatively related to changes in unit labor cost. They also provide support to the technology-gap model of trade. On the other hand, these results, together with the findings on capital and R&D intensity, are hard to reconcile with the standard (and static) HOV model. However, they do appear consistent with the Trefler-HOV model, which allows for factor price and unit labor cost differences across countries.

REFERENCES

Amable, B., and Bart Verspagen, "The Role of Technology in Market Share Dynamics," *Applied Economics* 27 (1995), 197–204.

Balassa, Bela, "Trade Liberalization and 'Revealed' Comparative Advantage," *The Manchester School* 33 (May 1965), 99–123.

Baumol, William J., Sue Anne Batey Blackman, and Edward N. Wolff, *Productivity and American Leadership: The Long View* (Cambridge, MA: MIT Press, 1989).

Bowen, Harry P., Edward E. Leamer, and Leo Sveikauskas, "Multicountry, Multifactor Tests of the Factor Abundance Theory," *American Economic Review* 77:5 (1987), 791–809.

Caves, Richard E., *Trade and Economic Structure: Models and Methods* (Cambridge, MA: Harvard University Press, 1960).

Deardorff, A. V., "The General Validity of the Heckscher-Ohlin Theorem," *American Economic Review* 72 (1982), 683–694.

Dollar, David, and Edward N. Wolff, *Competitiveness, Convergence, and International Specialization* (Cambridge, MA: MIT Press, 1993).

Dosi, Giovanni, Keith Pavitt, and Luc Soete, *The Economics of Technical Change and International Trade* (London: Harvester Wheatsheaf, 1990).

Engelbrecht, Hans-Jurgen, "The Composition of the Human Capital Stock and the Factor Content of Trade: Evidence from West(ern) Germany," *Economic System Research* 8:3 (1996), 271–297.

Fagerberg, Jan E., "International Competitiveness," *Economic Journal* 98 (June 1988), 355–374.

Feenstra, Robert C., and Gordon H. Hansen, "Aggregation Bias in the Factor Content of Trade: Evidence from U.S. Manufacturing," *American Economic Review Papers and Proceedings* 90:2 (2000), 155–160.

Heckscher, Eli, "The Effect of Foreign Trade on the Distribution of Income," reprinted in H. S. Ellis and L. A. Metzler (Eds.), *Readings in the Theory of International Trade* (Homewood, IL: Richard D. Irwin, Inc., [1919] 1949), 272–300.

Keesing, Donald B., "Labor Skills and International Trade: Evaluating Many Trade Flows with a Single Measuring Device," *Review of Economics and Statistics* 47:3 (1965), 287–294.

Lawson, Anne M., "Benchmark Input-Output Accounts for the U.S. Economy, 1992," *Survey of Current Business* 77:11 (1997), 36–83.

Leamer, Edward E., *Sources of International Comparative Advantage* (Cambridge, MA: MIT Press, 1984).

Lee, Chinkook, and Gerald Schluter, "Effect of Trade on the Demand for Skilled and Unskilled Workers," *Economic System Research* 11:1 (1999), 49–65.

Leontief, Wassily, "Factor Proportions and the Structure of American Trade: Further Theoretical and Empirical Analysis," *Review of Economics and Statistics* 38:4 (1956), 386–407.

——— "International Comparisons of Factor Cost and Factor Use," *American Economic Review* 54 (1964), 335–345.

MacDougall, G. D. A., "British and American Exports: A Study Suggested by the Theory of Comparative Costs, Part I," *Economic Journal* 61 (December 1951), 697–724.

——— "British and American Exports: A Study Suggested by the Theory of Comparative Costs, Part II," *Economic Journal* 62 (September 1952), 487–521.

National Science Board, *Science & Engineering Indicators—1998*, NSB 98-1 (Arlington, VA: National Science Foundation, 1998).

Ohlin, Bertil, *Interregional and International Trade* (Cambridge, MA: Harvard University Press, 1933).

Posner, M., "International Trade and Technical Change," *Oxford Economic Papers* 13:3 (1961), 323–341.

Trefler, Daniel, "International Factor Price Differences: Leontief Was Right!" *Journal of Political Economy* 101 (1993), 961–987.

——— "The Case of Missing Trade and Other Mysteries," *American Economic Review* 85 (1995), 1029–1046.

Trefler, Daniel, and Susan Chun Zhu, "Beyond the Algebra of Explanation: HOV for the Technology Age," *American Economic Review Papers and Proceedings* 90:2 (2000), 145–149.

Vanek, J., "The Factor Proportions Theory: The *N*-Factor Case," *Kyklos* 21:4 (1968), 749–756.

Verspagen, Bart, and Wakelin, K., "Trade and Technology from a Schumperterian Perspective," *International Review of Applied Economics* 11:2 (1997), 181–194.

Wolff, Edward N., "Technological Change, Capital Accumulation, and Changing Trade Patterns over the Long Term," *Structural Change and Economic Dynamics* 6:1 (1995), 43–70.

——— "Technology and the Demand for Skills," *OECD Science, Technology and Industry Review* 18 (1996), 96–123.

——— "Productivity Growth and Shifting Comparative Advantage on the Industry Level" (pp. 1–19), in Jan Fagerberg, Par Hansson, Lars Lundberg, and Arne Melchior (Eds.), *Technology and International Trade* (Edward Elgar Publishing Ltd, 1997).

——— "Specialization and Productivity Performance in Low-, Medium-, and High-Tech Manufacturing Industries" (pp. 419–452), in Alan Heston and Robert E. Lipsey (Eds.), *International and Interarea Comparisons of Prices, Income, and Output*, Studies of Income and Wealth 61 (Chicago: Chicago University Press (NBER), 1999).

——— "Human Capital Investment and Economic Growth: Exploring the Cross-Country Evidence," *Structural Change and Economic Dynamics* 11:4 (2000), 433–472.

DATA APPENDIX

1. *NIPA employee compensation:* Figures are from the National Income and Product Accounts (NIPA), available on the Internet. Employee compensation includes wages and salaries and employee benefits. Proprietors' income is net income to self-employed persons, including partners in businesses and owners of unincorporated businesses.

2. *NIPA employment data:* The number of full-time equivalent employees (FTEEs) equals the number of employees on full-time schedules

plus the number of employees on part-time schedules converted to a full-time basis. The number of FTEEs in each industry is the product of the total number of employees and the ratio of average weekly hours per employee for all employees to average weekly hours per employee on full-time schedules. The number of persons engaged in production (PEPs) equals the number of full-time and part-time employees plus the number of self-employed persons. Unpaid family workers are not included.

3. *Capital stock figures* are based on chain-type quantity indexes for net stock of fixed capital in 1992 dollars, year-end estimates. Source: U.S. Bureau of Economic Analysis, CD-ROM NCN-0229, "Fixed Reproducible Tangible Wealth of the United States, 1925–97."

4. *Research and development expenditures* performed by industry, including company, federal, and other sources of funds. Company-financed R&D performed outside the company is excluded. Industry series run from 1957 to 1997. Source: National Science Foundation, Internet. For technical details, see National Science Foundation, *Research and Development in Industry,* NSF96-304 (Arlington, VA: National Science Foundation, 1996).

5. The original input-output data are 85-sector U.S. input-output tables for years 1947, 1958, 1963, 1967, 1972, 1977, 1982, 1987, 1992, and 1996 (see, for example, Lawson (1997) for details on the sectoring). The 1947, 1958, and 1963 tables are available only in single-table format. The 1967, 1972, 1977, 1982, 1987, 1992, and 1996 data are available in separate make and use tables. These tables have been aggregated to 45 sectors for conformity with the other data sources. The 1950, 1960, 1970, 1980, and 1990 input-output tables are estimated from the benchmark U.S. input-output tables. The 1950 table is interpolated from the 1947 and 1958 input-output tables; the 1960 table is interpolated from the 1958 and 1963 input-output tables; the 1970 table is interpolated from the 1967 and 1972 input-output tables; the 1980 table is interpolated from the 1977 and 1982 input-output tables; and the 1990 table is interpolated from the 1987 and 1992 input-output tables.

6. *Imports and exports.* Sources for the industry-level data are U.S. input-output data for years 1947, 1958, 1963, 1967, 1972, 1977, 1982, 1987, 1992, and 1996. The data are interpolated for years 1950, 1960, 1970, 1980, and 1990.

PART III

OUTSOURCING AND PRODUCTIVITY SPILLOVERS

Journal of Productivity Analysis, 16, 149–165, 2001.

Outsourcing of Services and the Productivity Recovery in U.S. Manufacturing in the 1980s and 1990s

THIJS ten RAA tenRaa@kub.nl
Tilburg University, Box 90153, 5000 LE Tilburg, The Netherlands, Phone 011-31-13-4662365, Fax 011-31-13-4663280

EDWARD N. WOLFF Edward.Wolff@nyu.edu
Department of Economics, New York University, 269 Mercer Street, New York, N.Y. 10003, Phone 1-212-998-8917, Fax 1-212-995-4186

Abstract

Manufacturing productivity growth recovered during the 1980s and 1990s, while other sectors, particularly services, did not. In the same period U.S. manufacturing has engaged in the "outsourcing" or "contracting-out" of service functions. Has the recovery of manufacturing been accomplished by industrial reorganization—sloughing off sluggish services—rather than technical progress? We analyze this question by reducing service inputs to their consituent elements of material inputs. Service productivity growth is thus imputed to the goods sectors, reducing the recovery of manufacturing productivity growth in the 1980s by one fifth. The recovery lasted through the 1990s, when high productivity performers in manufacturing have been relatively successful at outsourcing sluggishservices.

JEL classification: 047, 051, C67

Keywords: productivity, services, outsourcing

1. Introduction

The motivation for this study comes from two recent phenomena that have received considerable attention. The first is that manufacturing productivity growth recovered during the 1980s and 1990s, after a protracted period of slowdown during the 1970s, while other sectors, particularly services, did not recover. Statistics calculated from input-output data and shown in Table 1 illustrate this point. Average annual total factor productivity (TFP) growth, defined as the price-weighted sum of changes in input-output coefficients, increased from 0.04 percent over the 1967–77 period to 0.87 percent over the 1977–87 period and 0.72 percent over the 1987–96 period. Construction was the only other major sector which showed a similar recovery over the 1977–87 period but then experienced a relapse in the 1987–96 period. Utilities and other services both underwent a slight recovery in the 1987–96 period.

Table 1. Sectoral total factor productivity growth by major sector, 1947–1996[a] (percent per annum).

	1947–1958	1958–1967	1967–1977	1977–1987	1987–1996	1947–1996
Agriculture	1.82	0.87	1.78	1.36	1.42	1.47
Mining	−0.95	0.12	−1.75	−2.42	1.19	−0.82
Construction	0.08	0.92	−0.85	0.58	−0.43	0.05
Manufacturing	0.96	1.14	0.04	0.87	0.72	0.74
Transportation	−0.22	3.29	2.62	1.34	1.10	1.57
Communication	2.09	1.94	2.31	−1.35	0.10	1.04
Utilities	3.32	1.61	−1.11	−1.16	0.36	0.64
Wholesale and Retail Trade	0.34	1.25	1.58	1.74	1.14	1.19
Finance, Insurance Real Estate	1.61	0.65	2.28	−2.23	−0.59	0.38
Other Services	−0.09	−0.21	−0.22	−0.33	0.40	−0.10
Weighted Average[b]	0.73	0.93	0.39	0.33	0.53	0.58
GDP[c]	1.41	1.77	0.71	0.58	0.96	1.08

[a]Periodization and calculations are based on U.S. input-output data. See equation (5) for the definitions of sectoral TFP growth.
[b]Weighted average of sectoral rates of TFP growth, where current dollar gross output (GDO) by sector is used as the weight.
[c]Economy-wide TFP growth is computed by weighting sectoral TFP growth by GDO/GDP (as GDP represents current dollar net output only).

The second is that since the 1980s U.S. manufacturing has engaged in the "outsourcing" or "contracting-out" of service functions. This process refers to the process of replacing in-house services, such as legal, advertising, accounting, and related business services with services purchased from outside the firm (see, for example, Postner, 1990 for a discussion of this issue from an accounting point of view).[1]

Anne Carter in her 1970 book noted early on the rapid increase in total service requirements per unit of manufacturing output between 1947 and 1967. Studies of the U.K. economy indicate that this phenomenon has continued in more recent years. Using U.K. input-output data, Barker (1990) reported that about 20 percent of the growth in service (gross) output between 1979 and 1984 was attributable to changes in manufacturing intermediate demand, and Barker and Forssell (1992) calculated that 22 percent of the growth of business services over the same period was associated with change in input-output coefficients in manufacturing.

Our own calculations from input-output data, presented in Table 2, do suggest that the outsourcing of services has accelerated during the 1980s and 1990s. There was a gradual increase in the share of total service inputs in gross output (in both current and constant dollars) between 1947 and 1977, with the proportion rising from 9.6 to 13.4 percent in current dollars and from 12.0 to 16.7 percent in constant dollars. Between 1977 and 1982, total service inputs jumped from 13.4 to 16.3 percent of gross output in current dollars and increased from 16.7 to 17.7 percent in constant dollars. Between 1982 and 1996, there was a further rise in the service share in total output, from 16.3 to 18.4 percent in current dollars and from 17.7 to 18.4 percent in constant dollars.

Table 2. Ratio of service inputs to gross output in U.S. manufacturing, 1947–1996.[a]

	All Service Inputs[b]		All Service Inputs Except Trade		All Service Inputs Except Trade & Utilities	
Year	Ratio in Current $	Ratio in 1992 $	Ratio in Current $	Ratio in 1992 $	Ratio in Current $	Ratio in 1992 $
1947	0.096	0.120	0.071	0.099	0.064	0.088
1958	0.119	0.150	0.085	0.120	0.076	0.104
1963	0.113	0.138	0.084	0.113	0.073	0.095
1967	0.122	0.150	0.093	0.125	0.082	0.106
1972	0.139	0.161	0.099	0.126	0.088	0.107
1977	0.134	0.167	0.091	0.124	0.075	0.102
1982	0.163	0.177	0.110	0.120	0.086	0.095
1987	0.154	0.162	0.103	0.110	0.085	0.093
1992	0.181	0.181	0.121	0.121	0.102	0.102
1996	0.184	0.184	0.118	0.123	0.103	0.109

[a]Calculations are based on U.S. input-output data. See Section 3 for a discussion of data sources and methods.
[b]Service inputs are defined as (sector numbers refer to the standard 85-sector BEA classification scheme): (65) transportation and warehousing: (66) communications; (67) broadcasting; (68) utilities; (69) wholesale and retail trade; (70) finance and insurance; (71) real estate and rentals; (72) hotels and repair services; (73) business service; (74) eating and drinking establishments; (75) auto services and repairs; (76) amusements and entertainment; (77) medical and educational services; (78) federal government enterprises; (79) state and local government enterprises; (82) government industry.

Results are also shown for the share of total services inputs excluding wholesale and retail trade in gross output and the share of total services except trade and utilities in total output. The time trends in these series are quite similar to those for the share of total services in output. One of the most notable changes was in the proportion of business service and finance and insurance inputs in total gross output, which almost tripled between 1947 and 1966 in current dollar terms (from 1.8 to 4.9 percent) and doubled in constant dollar terms (from 3.6 to 7.3 percent).

Our speculation is that part of the recovery of manufacturing productivity growth may be a consequence of the outsourcing of services from manufacturing. The argument is that if these services have lower productivity growth rates than the production of goods within manufacturing, then the outsourcing of previously internally provided services will increase measured productivity growth within manufacturing. Siegel and Griliches (1992) find a correlation coefficient of .13 (significant at .01 level) between acceleration in TFP and the average ratio of purchased services to output. It is of direct interest to determine how much of the change in measured productivity growth in manufacturing is due to changes in intermediate demand for services.

It should be emphasized at the outset that we do not have any direct data about the degree of outsourcing that takes place. This would require information on the firm level of the amount of inputs devoted to internally provided services (such as accounting or advertising) and the replacement of these inputs with externally provided services. However, the degree of increase in intermediate inputs of services used in manufacturing, particularly in constant dollars, during the 1980s is suggestive that contracting-out was a major factor explaining its rise.[2] Indeed, Abraham (1990) and Abraham and Taylor (1993) find that market mediated work arrangements associated with business service employment increased substantially over the period 1975–1990.

Our analytical technique is based on a consolidation framework initiated by Leontief (1967). In this approach, service inputs into manufacturing are essentially reduced to their constituent elements of labor, capital, and goods inputs. This consolidation framework will allow us to decompose the change in TFP growth within manufacturing into effects emanating from the purchases of services and from the rate of material productivity growth in manufacturing. Services productivity growth is imputed to the consuming sectors. If the recovery of TFP growth in manufacturing during the 1980s is due largely to outsourcing of services, then the increase in the rate of TFP growth computed with this consolidated measure should be smaller than the rate of TFP growth computed from only the direct coefficients.

The strengths of input-output analysis are its capacity to organize sectoral data in a consistent framework and to interrelate quantitative changes, as in manufacturing and the services. The weaknesses are the insensitivity of techniques with respect to input prices and the assumption of constant returns-to-scale.

Our approach avoids many of the problems of measurement normally accounted in measuring the output of service industries (Griliches, 1992). In traditional measures of TFP growth within manufacturing, service inputs are treated in analogous fashion to inputs of goods industries, labor, and capital. Difficulties in measuring service outputs may seriously distort measures of TFP within manufacturing. On the other hand, input measures are quite adequate in service sectors, as in other industries within the economy. Labor, capital, and material inputs are easily identifiable and measurable in services, and are, in principle, no different than in other industries.

The basic data sources for this study are U.S. 85-order input-output tables for 1947, 1958, 1967, 1977, 1987, and 1996. The use-make framework will be exploited in the analysis for the last three tables. The next section develops the model. A description of the data sources and methods is given in Section 3, the results are discussed in Section 4, and concluding remarks and interpretations are made in the last section.

2. Productivity Analysis of Services

Carter (1970) found an increase in the total requirements of service output over the 1947–67 period in the U.S., but could not decompose it into a real interindustry effect of greater specialization and a specious effect from the reclassification of such service activities from sectors where they are secondary output to sectors where they constitute primary output. By introducing the use-make activity framework, ten Raa and Wolff (1991) showed that many establishments which produced services in addition to their primary output during the 1960s sloughed off this production during the 1970s. In this paper we want to assess the implication of this process by decomposing total growth of the goods sectors into an own component and a service component.

A main problem is that service output is not tangible. In other words, how do we measure the output of services required for nonservice production and how do we impute factor inputs to this output? The idea proposed in this paper is to circumvent the problem by relating the inputs of services to the outputs of the sectors that use those services. We will do so by elimination of the intermediate services, where the elimination is to be understood in a mathematical sense.

Since outsourced services are intermediate inputs and we want to relate them to manufacturing outputs, we need an input-output framework. The strengths of this approach are the capacity to impute service TFP growth to the goods producing sectors and, more generally, to decompose macro TFP growth into sectoral technical changes. The weaknesses are the implicit identification of activities and outputs and the use of exogenous factor prices. To overcome the former element we distinguish commodities from sectors and admit secondary products.

We partition the n commodities of the economy in (1) m goods and (2) $n - m$ services. Goods can be dropped on your feet and services are anything else. Goods include manufactures, but also agricultural and other produce. The measurement of TFP growth requires the following data for sector i, $i = 1, \ldots, n$: commodity outputs v_{ij}, $i = 1, \ldots, n$, commodity inputs u_{ji}, labor employment L_i and capital employment K_i. We also need the wage rate w and the rental rate r. Obvious matrix notation for the flows is V, U, L, and K. Although V and U are both $n \times n$-dimensional, V is of dimension sector $\times$ commodity and U commodity $\times$ sector, adhering to the System of National Accounts convention (see Kop Jansen and ten Raa, 1990). L and K are n-dimensional row vectors. w and r are scalars.

The basic idea exposed in this paper is to impute the gross output and the productivity of the services to the goods by relating the goods inputs into the services to the goods outputs of the service consuming sectors. The idea is applicable to the services used in the production of goods (business services), but not to the services which feed final demand (personal services). We therefore define **standard TFP growth** as the relative real rate of change of the net output of goods to the required factor inputs ratio,

$$\frac{p^1 dy^1}{p^1 y^1} - \frac{w dL^* + r dK^*}{w L^* + r K^*}$$

Here y^1 is the m-dimensional subvector of goods components of n-dimensional net output $y = (V^T - U)e$, where e is the unit vector with all entries equal to one. Similarly, p^1 collects the goods components of the row vector of competitive prices, which is defined by $p(V^T - U) = wL + rK$. The amount of labor required for the production of the net output of goods is

$$L^* = \ell(I - A)^{-1} \begin{pmatrix} y^1 \\ 0 \end{pmatrix} \tag{1}$$

where input-output coefficients are $A = U(V^T)^{-1}$ and labor coefficients are $\ell = L(V^T)^{-1}$ (see Kop Jansen and ten Raa, 1990). L^* includes labor employment in the service sectors needed for the fulfilment of intermediate demand in the goods sectors. $\ell(I - A)^{-1}$ is the $n \times n$-dimensional row vector of total labor coefficients, measuring the labor contents of units of goods and services. The amount of capital required for the production of the net output of goods is defined similarly.

Our strategy is to evaluate the labor and capital contents in the lower dimensional space of goods, using the Leontief inverse of consolidated input-output coefficients,

$m \times m$-dimensional matrix A^*, and consolidated labor and capital coefficients, m-dimensional row vectors ℓ^* and k^*. In the appendix (statement A) we show that

$$L^* = \ell^*(I - A^*)^{-1}y^1 \tag{2}$$

where A^* is Leontief's (1976) matrix of consolidated input-output coefficients,

$$A^* = A_{11} + A_{12}(I - A_{22})^{-1}A_{21} \tag{3}$$

and consolidated labor coefficients (as well as capital coefficients) are defined similarly,

$$\ell^* = \ell^1 + \ell^2(I - A_{22})^{-1}A_{21} \tag{4}$$

The m-dimensional subvector of labor coefficients for the goods, ℓ^1, is augmented by a row vector that features the direct service requirements of goods, A_{21}, transformed to total service requirements by the Leontief inverse of services own coefficients, A_{22}, and further to labor contents by the services labor coefficients, ℓ^2.

There are two ways to decompose standard TFP growth. As a preliminary, we show in the appendix (statement B) that the denominators in the expression for goods TFP growth are equal: $p^1y^1 = wL^* + rK^*$. Now the first way is a direct Wolff (1985) decomposition into **sectoral TFP growth rates,**

$$\pi_i = -\left(\sum_{j=1}^{n} p_j da_{ji} + wd\ell_i + rdk_i\right) \Big/ p_i \tag{5}$$

where index i runs through the goods and the services. Standard TFP growth is a weighted average of all the sectoral TFP growth rates. The weights are proportional to the competitive value shares of the gross outputs of goods and services that sustain the final demand for goods. The weights sum to the gross-to-net-output competitive value ratio by the Domar aggregation rule.[3]

The second way is a similar decomposition into **consolidated TFP growth rates,**

$$\pi_i^* = -\left(\sum_{j=1}^{m} p_j da_{ji}^* + wd\ell_i^* + rdk_i^*\right) \Big/ p_i \tag{6}$$

where i runs through the goods only. Standard TFP growth is a weighted average of the consolidated TFP growth rates over goods. The weights remain $(p_i x_i^*)/(px^*)$, where x^* is the goods subvector of the full Leontief inverse of $\binom{y^1}{0}$, or, equivalently, the consolidated Leontief inverse of y^1. The equivalence is demonstrated in the appendix (statement C). In this paper we analyze sectoral TFP growth rates, particularly for manufacturing. **Manufacturing consolidated TFP growth** is the weighted average of the manufacturing π_i^*'s, where the weights are the competitive value shares of consolidated manufacturing output, $(p_i x_i^*)/(px^*)$. Note that comparison with macro-economic TFP growth would require inflation of our measures by the Domar factor.

A first decomposition of consolidated TFP growth rates (6) is obtained by separating the consolidated coefficient reductions according to (3) and (4) and sorting out the leading and following terms:

$$\pi_i^* = \rho_i + \sigma_i \tag{7}$$

where

$$\rho_i = -\left(\sum_{j=1}^{m} p_j da_{ji} + w d\ell_i + r dk_i\right) \Big/ p_i \tag{8}$$

and σ_i is defined similarly, capturing the reductions in the following terms of (3) and (4). ρ_i measures the reduction in direct materials, labor, and capital inputs. σ_i measures the reduction in indirect materials, labor, and capital inputs, as embodied in the service inputs. ρ_i is not a standard sectoral TFP growth rate, for the summation is through m only, ignoring the service inputs, $m+1, \ldots, n$. However, it is not difficult to forge the relationship. It amounts to a further decomposition.

For this purpose, return to the decomposition of standard TFP growth using (5). Ignoring the Domar factor, standard TFP growth amounts, using (5) and (8),

$$\begin{aligned}
&\sum_{i=1}^{n} \frac{p_i x_i^*}{px^*}\pi_i \\
&= \sum_{i=1}^{n} \frac{p_i x_i^*}{px^*}\pi_i + \sum_{i=m+1}^{n} \frac{p_i x_i^*}{px^*}\pi_i \\
&= -\sum_{i=1}^{n} \frac{p_i x_i^*}{px^*}\left(\sum_{j=1}^{n} p_j da_{ji} + w d\ell_i + r dk_i\right) \Big/ p_i + \sum_{i=m+1}^{n} \frac{p_i x_i^*}{px^*}\pi_i \\
&= \sum_{i=1}^{n} \frac{p_i x_i^*}{px^*}\left(\rho_i - \sum_{j=m+1}^{n} p_j da_{ji}/p_i\right) + \sum_{i=m+1}^{n} \frac{p_i x_i^*}{px^*}\pi_i
\end{aligned} \tag{9}$$

Comparison with (7) shows that the service components of consolidated TFP growth, σ_i, pick up not only the reductions of the service inputs, which we denote by

$$\sigma_i^1 = -\sum_{j=m+1}^{n} p_j da_{ji}/p_i \tag{10}$$

but also services TFP growth, π_{m+1} through π_n, the last terms of (9). The amount of services TFP growth imputed to good i is denoted by σ_i^2 and is determined residually by

$$\sigma_i = \sigma_i^1 + \sigma_i^2 \tag{11}$$

This equation amounts to the further reduction of consolidated TFP growth, (7). A rearrangement of terms is illuminating. For this purpose, note that the terms under the first summation sign on the right hand side of (9) contain the standard TFP growth rates,

$$\pi_i = \rho_i + \sigma_i^1 \tag{12}$$

It follows from equations (7), (11), and (12) that consolidated TFP growth equals standard goods TFP growth plus imputed services TFP growth,

$$\pi_i^* = \pi_i + \sigma_i^2 \tag{13}$$

If some standard TFP growth rate is great, but the corresponding consolidated TFP growth is modest, it must be that σ_i^2 is negative. The sector performs well, but service productivity drag is imputed to it. Such a sector looks "smart" in the sense that outsourced and external services productivity drag does not show in its sectoral TFP growth rate. Here we model outsourcing by imputing all services to the goods, even when they were not provided in-house by manufacturing originally. This model does not lay claim to outsourcing as a historic process, but reduces the services "superstructure" to the materials "substructure."

Does manufacturing look "smart"? In other words, has the recovery of manufacturing productivity been accomplished by industrial reorganization—sloughing off sluggish services—rather than technical progress? A macro answer is given by the sign of services TFP growth imputed to manufacturing, that is the manufacturing σ_i^2's weighted by value shares. If it is negative, then outsourcing of services is a source of manufacturing productivity growth. A micro answer is provided by the correlation between imputed service TFP growth, σ_i^2, and standard TFP growth, π_i, across manufacturing sectors. If it is negative, good performers are imputed a relatively large service drag and outsourcing would be a determinant of the distribution of TFP growth within manufacturing.

3. Data Sources and Methods

Our basic data source consists of U.S. input-output dollar flow tables, which were originally obtained from the Bureau of Economic Analysis on the 87-sector level for years 1947, 1958 and 1967 in single-table format, and on the 85-sector level for years 1967, 1977, 1987, and 1996 in the dual use-make table format. The single-table format relies on the so-called BEA transfer method. In this method, the transaction matrix is constructed on an industry by industry basis. A secondary product produced by industry i which is primary to industry j is recorded as a purchase made by industry j from industry i. The actual sales of the secondary product produced in i are then "transferred" to the sales row of industry j.[4]

The 1967, 1977, 1987, and 1996 data are available in separate make and use tables.[5] The 1977 and 1987 tables use the same accounting conventions. However, there are four important changes between the 1967 tables and those of the later years. First, two dummy sectors, business travel and entertainment and office supplies, are present in the 1967 table but were eliminated in the 1977, 1987, and 1996 tables. We follow the later convention and distribute the output of the two dummy sectors to the appropriate using industries. Second, in the 1977, 1987, and 1996 tables, the restaurant sector was separated from the trade sector, while in the 1967 table the two are aggregated into a single sector. It was not possible to separate the restaurant sector from the trade sector in the 1967 data. As a result, we have aggregated the two sectors in the 1977, 1987, and 1996 data for consistency with the earlier year.[6]

Third, in the 1967 table, a portion of the wholesale and retail trade activity and real estate (rental) activity engaged in by the various sectors were recorded as a secondary product of these sectors, whereas in the later years these transactions were recorded as primary to the trade and real estate sectors, respectively. For consistency with the later years, we transferred these secondary outputs to their primary sector.[7] Fourth, in the 1967 table, comparable imports are recorded as if purchased by the industry producing the comparable domestic commodity and then added to that industry's output for distribution to the actual purchasing industries. In the later tables, comparable imports are recorded as directly purchased by the using industry from the comparable domestic industry. We follow the later convention in our work.

Charles Bowman of the U.S. Bureau of Labor Statistics graciously provided us with a consistent set of labor coefficients, capital coefficients, and sectoral price deflators through 1996. The labor and output data are an updated version of the Bureau of Labor Statistics' Historical Output and Employment Data Series.[8] The capital stock data are derived from the U.S. Bureau of Economic Analysis' net stocks of plant and equipment by industry series through 1996. Capital stock figures are based on chain-type quantity indexes for net stock of fixed capital in 1992$, year-end estimates. For technical details, see Katz and Herman (1997).

Five sectors—research and development, business travel and office supplies, scrap and used goods, and inventory valuation adjustment—appeared in some years but not in others (the earlier years for the first three sectors and the later years for the last two sectors). In order to make the accounting framework consistent over the years of analysis, we eliminated these sectors from both gross and final output. This was accomplished by distributing the inputs used by these sectors proportional to either the endogenous sectors which purchased the output of these five sectors or to final output.[9]

One additional refinement, suggested by Leontief (1941), was made. Instead of treating noncompetitive imports as exogenous, an endogenous column of exports was incorporated in the A matrix to balance the row of noncompetitive imports. In this way, imports can also be thought of as being "produced" domestically by the exports required to sell in exchange for them. The final output vector was adjusted for this. (See Wolff, 1985, and ten Raa and Wolff, 1991, for more details.)

All matrices were deflated to 1992 dollars using the sectoral price deflators.[10] Productivity growth rates for 1947–1958 and 1958–1967 are calculated using the single-table basic framework (and making use of the 1967 single table data). Productivity growth rates for 1967–1977 and 1977–1987, and 1987–1996 are calculated using the use-make framework (and relying on the 1967 dual table data). Because of alignment difficulties between the various input-output years (several industries are collapsed in the 1987 and 1996 tables, in particular) and with the employment and capital stock data, productivity growth estimates are available for only 51 industries, including 29 manufacturing industries.

We divided the original 85 industries into two groups, goods and services. The goods industries include: agriculture (1–4),[11] mining (5–10), construction (11–12), manufacturing (13–64), transportation (65), communications (66–67), and utilities (68). Services include: trade (69), finance, insurance, and real estate (70–71), government services (78, 79, and 82), and all other services (72–77).

4. Results

Table 3 shows our central results, on the decomposition of manufacturing TFP growth into a material inputs component and a service inputcomponent. Line 1 shows the trend in standard commodity TFP growth in manufacturing, which falls from 1.14 percent per year in 1958–1967 to 0.04 in 1967–1977 and then recovers to 0.87 in 1977–1987, and 0.72 in 1987–1996.

Table 3. Decomposition of manufacturing TFP growth into material inputs and service inputs, 1947–1996 (Average annual growth in percentage points).

	1947–1958	1958–1967	1967–1977	1977–1987	1987–1996
1. Standard TFP Growth [π]	0.96	1.14	0.04	0.87	0.72
2. Consolidated TFP Growth [π^*]	0.94	1.20	0.16	0.81	0.81
a. Change in Material Inputs [ρ]	1.05	1.05	0.26	0.91	0.88
b. Change in Consolidated Service Inputs [σ]	−0.11	0.15	−0.09	−0.10	−0.07
1. Change in Use of Service Inputs [σ^1]	−0.08	0.09	−0.22	−0.03	−0.16
2. Change in TFP of Service Industries [σ^2]	−0.02	0.06	0.13	−0.06	0.09

Line 2 presents results on TFP growth for the consolidated manufacturing industries, π^*, which incorporates both the direct productivity growth of the manufacturing industries as well as the productivity growth of service industries supplying the manufacturing sectors.

The figures also show a fall-off in consolidated TFP growth between the 1958–1967 and 1967–1977 periods, from 1.20 to 0.16 percent per year, and then a recovery in the 1977–1987 period to 0.81 percent per year which was maintained in the 1987–1996 period. These results clearly support the central premise of the paper that the recovery in standard manufacturing TFP growth between 1967–1977 and 1977–1987 (0.83 percentage points) was greater than the recovery in consolidated TFP growth (0.65 percentage points). These findings are consistent with the argument that the outsourcing of services was partly responsible for the recovery of productivity growth in manufacturing during the 1980s.

A decomposition is shown of consolidated manufacturing TFP growth, π^*, into ρ, TFP growth in these industries attributable to a reduction in direct materials, labor, and capital inputs; and into σ, TFP growth in goods industries attributable to a reduction in indirect materials, labor, and capital inputs as embodied in the service inputs into goods industries. The main contributor to consolidated TFP growth was the reduction in the use of direct material inputs within manufacturing (including labor and capital). The average annual rate of change in ρ was 1.05 percent over the 1947–1958 and 1958–1967 periods, 0.26 percent over the 1967–1977 period, 0.91 percent over the 1977–1987 period, and 0.88 over the 1987–1996 period. Though the time path is similar for ρ as for π^*, the changes between periods are smaller for ρ than for π^*. Even in the productivity slowdown period, 1967–1977, TFP growth from the change in direct material inputs was still proceeding at a respectable 0.3 percent per year.

The major difference was in the time trend of σ, the rate of TFP growth due to the material inputs embodied in direct manufacturing service inputs. During the 1958–1967 period, this component added 0.15 percentage points per year to consolidated TFP growth in manufacturing. However, during the 1967–1977, 1977–1987, and 1987–1996 periods, σ was negative, at a steady −0.1 percent per year. These results indicate that while (direct) materials, labor, and capital inputs per unit of output in manufacturing industries fell over the three time periods, their indirect materials, labor, and capital inputs (as embodied in their service inputs) per unit of output increased over both the 1967–1977 and 1977–1987 periods, thus creating a drag on productivity growth within the manufacturing industries. Manufacturing was more successful in reducing its direct material, labor, and capital inputs than in decreasing its indirect inputs from the service sectors. The U.S. economy suffered from the Baumol (1967) disease, that is the low productivity growth of the service sectors.

In Section 2, we break down σ into σ^1, productivity growth in the consolidated goods industries emanating from a reduction in direct service inputs, and σ^2, productivity growth in the consolidated goods industries emanating from technical change in the service industries which supply the goods industries, is again revealing. During the 1947–1958 period, of the 0.11 percentage points decrease in σ, almost all was due to the increased use of direct service inputs into manufacturing ($\sigma^1 = -0.08$). During the 1958–1967 period, of the 0.15 percentage points increase in σ, 0.09 percentage points came from a reduction in direct service inputs into manufacturing and 0.06 percentage points from positive TFP growth within the service industries. Between 1967 and 1977, of the −0.09 percentage points change in σ, −0.22 percentage points was attributable to the increased use of direct service inputs in manufacturing (σ^1) and 0.13 percentage points to the modest gains of TFP growth within the service industries. Over the 1977–1987 period, of the −0.10 percentage points change in σ, −0.03 percentage points came from increased use of service inputs and −0.06 percentage points from the negative TFP growth of the service industries supplying manufacturing.

The results show that the TFP growth of service industries which supply manufacturing declined from 0.13 percent per year in the 1967–1977 period to −0.06 percent per year in the 1977–1987 period. This decline of intermediate services TFP growth indicates that manufacturing kept the Baumol disease at bay in the 1977–1987 period. A manufacturing firm looks "smart" in terms of TFP growth if it outsources these stagnant service activities and concentrates its activities on high productivity fabrication and assembly operations. During the 1980's, part of the recorded gains in TFP growth in manufacturing is thus attributable to the outsourcing of services. Table 4 shows that "smart" sectors in the recovery period of 1977–1987 are printing and publishing ($\pi_i = 0.52$ but $\sigma_i^2 = -0.16$), drugs, cleaning & toilet preparations ($\pi_i = 1.52$, $\sigma_i^2 = -0.36$), and aircraft and parts ($\pi_i = 0.41$ and $\sigma_i^2 = -0.18$).

To examine the relationship between TFP growth in manufacturing and the supplying service industries, we compute the correlation between standard TFP growth π_i and σ_i^2, the TFP growth of the supplying services. A negative correlation means that goods sectors with rapid rates of standard TFP growth are more likely, on average, to purchase services from sectors with low productivity growth. This is an indirect indication that these manufacturing industries have been successful in outsourcing services with low productivity growth.

The correlation coefficients, shown in the last line of Table 4, indicate that this selection mechanism was not the driving force behind the manufacturing recovery in the 1977–87 period (0.039), but in fact happened in the recent 1987–96 period (−0.483). The latter period is the period of major outsourcing of U.S. manufacturing indeed. It is interesting to notice that high productivity performers have been relatively successful at outsourcing sluggish services. The industrial reorganization of the economy between manufacturing and services is a new factor that explains the continuation of the manufacturing productivity recovery.

A related study by Siegel and Griliches (1992) looked at the relation between manufacturing productivity growth in 1973–1979 and 1979–1986 and the outsourcing of services, measured as the average ratio of purchased services within manufacturing to manufacturing output in 1977 and 1982. They found very weak correlations between the latter measure

Table 4. Standard TFP growth (π) and TFP growth of service industries supplying manufacturing industries (σ^2) by manufacturing industry, 1958–1987 (average annual growth in percentage points).

	1947–1958		1958–1967		1967–1977		1977–1987		1987–1996	
	π_i	σ_i^2	π_i	σ_i^2	π_i	σ_i^2	π_i	σ_i^2	π_i	σ_i^2
Ordance and Accessories	−2.15	−0.18	0.94	0.06	−0.20	0.12	2.48	−0.10	−0.16	0.11
Food and Kindred Products	1.17	−0.00	0.81	0.06	0.25	0.11	0.59	−0.07	0.49	0.10
Tobacco Manufactures	0.54	−0.10	0.41	0.05	−0.46	0.12	−1.13	−0.22	−2.39	0.17
Textile Mill Products	1.58	−0.01	1.42	0.04	0.86	0.09	1.32	−0.03	0.61	0.08
Apparel and Other Textile Products	2.18	−0.00	1.20	0.05	0.95	0.09	1.35	−0.03	2.93	0.03
Paper and Allied Products	0.91	−0.02	0.95	0.05	0.05	0.12	0.42	−0.02	0.39	0.08
Printing and Publishing	−0.68	−0.12	0.90	0.06	−0.24	0.31	0.52	−0.16	0.17	0.09
Industrial Chemicals, Agricultural Fertilizers and Chemicals	2.36	−0.03	1.34	0.04	−1.75	0.13	1.15	−0.10	−1.14	0.10
Plastics and Synthetic Materials	3.13	−0.07	2.34	0.02	1.77	0.11	1.04	−0.07	0.72	0.09
Drugs, Cleaning & Toilet Preparations	4.27	−0.17	1.76	0.15	1.96	0.29	1.52	−0.36	−3.31	0.25
Paints and Allied Products	1.37	−0.03	−0.45	0.08	0.48	0.17	1.81	−0.06	−0.25	0.09
Petroleum and Coal Products	1.73	−0.03	1.69	0.02	−2.04	0.07	1.77	−0.04	−0.78	0.05
Rubber and Miscellaneous Products	0.91	0.06	1.78	0.07	−0.32	0.12	0.95	−0.08	1.60	0.08
Leather and Leather Products	1.50	−0.05	0.03	0.05	0.07	0.15	−0.09	−0.06	−0.16	0.07
Lumber and Wood Products	−1.29	−0.03	1.83	0.06	−1.07	0.10	0.80	−0.01	−0.33	0.09
Furniture and Fixtures	0.67	−0.03	0.53	0.08	0.81	0.15	0.79	−0.09	0.97	0.12
Stone, Clay, and Glass Products	0.05	−0.04	0.96	0.05	−0.49	0.11	0.51	−0.08	1.80	0.06
Primary Metal Industries	0.47	−0.01	1.06	0.04	−1.48	0.11	−0.02	−0.03	1.68	0.11
Fabricated Metal Products	0.07	−0.03	0.83	0.05	−0.32	0.13	0.32	−0.04	1.01	0.10
Industrial Machinery and Equipment, Except OCA	0.18	−0.03	1.00	0.07	0.98	0.14	3.11	−0.03	0.69	0.11
Computer and Office Equipment	1.33	−0.06	0.50	0.11	5.20	0.16	6.82	−0.07	6.36	0.09
Other Electronic and Electric Equipment	1.11	−0.06	1.65	0.08	1.08	0.16	0.65	−0.07	1.27	0.13
Audio, Video, and Communication Equipment	2.77	−0.06	3.10	0.06	0.14	0.19	2.00	−0.08	0.79	0.12
Electronic Components and Accessories	2.29	−0.08	2.86	0.07	2.80	0.14	2.63	−0.06	3.33	0.09
Motor Vehicles—Cars & Trucks	0.59	−0.05	1.22	0.06	0.51	0.09	−1.38	−0.02	0.21	0.10
Aircraft and Parts	1.88	−0.04	0.64	0.04	−0.13	0.16	0.41	−0.18	2.01	0.06
Other Transportation Equipment	−0.49	−0.02	1.51	0.06	0.37	0.14	−0.46	0.00	1.53	0.09
Instruments and Related Products	0.95	−0.06	0.51	0.08	1.87	0.15	2.56	−0.12	0.96	0.11
Miscellaneous Manufacturing Industries	0.30	−0.01	1.15	0.09	0.83	0.18	0.21	−0.20	1.97	0.14
Correlation[a] Between π and σ^2	0.003		−0.088		0.243		0.039		−0.483	

[a]Correlation across 29 manufacturing sectors. This is a pure number.

and manufacturing productivity growth in each of the two periods as well as the change in productivity growth between these two periods across 392 manufacturing industries. We obtain similar results for the 1977–1987 and 1987–1996 periods (correlations of 0.00 and 0.10, respectively).

5. Concluding Remarks

The results of this paper support our major hypothesis that the recovery of standard TFP growth in manufacturing in the 1977–1987 period was related to an increased use of inputs purchased from service industries. TFP growth in manufacturing, after falling from 1.14 percent per year in the 1958–1967 period to 0.04 in the 1967–1977 period, jumped to 0.87 percent per year in the 1977–1987 period and 0.72 percent per year in the 1987–1996 period. Over the same period, the share of total service inputs in gross output in constant dollars increased moderately, from 15.0 percent in 1958 to 16.7 percent in 1977 and 18.4 percent in 1996.

Our most compelling evidence in support of our hypothesis is that the recovery in annual manufacturing TFP growth between 1967–1977 and 1977–1987 (0.83 percentage points) was greater than the increase in consolidated TFP growth (0.65 percentage points). In other words, if we include the material inputs embodied in the services purchased by manufacturing in the manufacturing industry's input structure, the measured increase in TFP growth is smaller than conventionally measured TFP growth, in fact by one fifth in the 1977–1987 period. The U.S. economy suffered from the Baumol (1967) disease. The recovery lasted in the 1987–1996 period, when high productivity performers in manufacturing have been relatively successful at oursourcing sluggish services.

Both sets of findings are consistent with the argument that the outsourcing of services was partly responsible for the recovery of conventionally measured TFP growth in manufacturing during the 1980s. The results also support the argument that manufacturing industries have been successful at externalizing the slow productivity growth service activities.

It is difficult to say whether the increased service inputs into manufacturing industries were due strictly to outsourcing—that is, the **substitution** of externally produced output for internally provided inputs—since we have no way of assessing the production of intermediate services within the industry. However, the increase of service inputs within manufacturing during the 1977–1996 period was probably a result of a combination of outsourcing and the substitution of service activities in general for material inputs.

What is clear is that service inputs into manufacturing industries have increased in importance over time and have created an increasingly large drag on both their consolidated productivity growth and even their direct productivity growth. Manufacturing industries have been much more successful in reducing their direct material, labor, and capital inputs per unit of output than in reducing their service inputs.

Appendix

First let us collect the statements in Section 2 that remain to be proved:

A. $L^* = \ell^*(I - A^*)^{-1}y^1$

B. $p^1y^1 = wL^* + rK^*$

C. $(I\ 0)(I - A)^{-1}\begin{pmatrix} y^1 \\ 0 \end{pmatrix} = (I - A^*)^{-1}y^1$

We will do so using

LEMMA

$$(I - A)^{-1}\begin{pmatrix} I \\ 0 \end{pmatrix} = \begin{pmatrix} I \\ (I - A_{22})^{-1}A_{21} \end{pmatrix}(I - A^*)^{-1},$$

where in $\binom{I}{0}$, *the entries are the unit and zero matrices of dimensions* m *and* $n - m$, *respectively.*

Proof of Lemma. It suffices to show that

$$(I - A)\begin{bmatrix} I \\ (I - A_{22})^{-1}A_{21} \end{bmatrix}(I - A^*)^{-1} = \begin{pmatrix} I \\ 0 \end{pmatrix}$$

Now the left hand side is

$$\begin{pmatrix} I - A_{11} & -A_{12} \\ -A_{21} & I - A_{22} \end{pmatrix}\begin{pmatrix} I \\ (I - A_{22})^{-1}A_{21} \end{pmatrix}(I - A^*)^{-1}$$

$$= \begin{pmatrix} I - A_{11} - A_{12}(I - A_{22})^{-1}A_{21} \\ -A_{21} + (I - A_{22})(I - A_{22})^{-1}A_{21} \end{pmatrix}(I - A^*)^{-1}$$

$$= \begin{pmatrix} I - A^* \\ 0 \end{pmatrix}(I - A^*)^{-1}$$

which is the right hand side indeed. ■

Proof of A. By definition of L^*, (1), and the lemma,

$$L^* = \ell(I - A)\begin{pmatrix} y^1 \\ 0 \end{pmatrix} = \ell(I - A)^{-1}\begin{pmatrix} I \\ 0 \end{pmatrix}y^1$$

$$= (\ell^1 \quad \ell^2)\begin{pmatrix} I \\ (I - A_{22})^{-1}A_{21} \end{pmatrix}(I - A^*)^{-1}y^1$$

$$= [\ell^1 + \ell^2(I - A_{22})^{-1}A_{21}](I - A^*)^{-1}y^1 = \ell^*(I - A^*)^{-1}y^1$$

by definition of ℓ^*, (4).

■

Proof of B. Competitive prices are defined by

$$p(V^T - U) = wL + rK$$

Division by V^T yields

$$p(I - A) = w\ell + rk$$

Hence

$$p^1 y^1 = p\begin{pmatrix} I \\ 0 \end{pmatrix} y^1 = (w\ell + rk)(I - A)^{-1}\begin{pmatrix} I \\ 0 \end{pmatrix} y^1$$

$$= (w\ell + rk)(I - A)^{-1}\begin{pmatrix} y^1 \\ 0 \end{pmatrix} = wL^* + rK^*$$

by definition of L^*, (1), and similar for capital. ■

Proof of C. The left hand side equals

$$(I \quad 0)(I - A)\begin{pmatrix} I \\ 0 \end{pmatrix} y^1 = (I \quad 0)(I - A^*)^{-1} y^1$$

by the lemma. ■

Acknowledgments

We would like to express our gratitude to the C.V. Starr Center for Applied Economics at New York University, CentER at Tilburg University, and the Alfred P. Sloan Foundation which provided financial support for this work. We also acknowledge useful suggestions by two anonymous referees.

Notes

1. Actually, in the modern literature this idea can be traced back to Stigler (1951), who defined "externalization" or "unbundling" as referring to the portion of intermediate demand for services which is supplied by service firms, rather than in the production unit itself.
2. If the increasing share of service inputs in gross output was due only to the rising relative prices of services (relative to goods), then we would expect that the service share would increase in current dollar terms but remain unchanged in constant dollar terms. Since the service share rises in constant dollars as well, this reflects a real shift in input structure, rather than a change in relative prices. Quality adjustment would reinforce this observation.
3. According to this rule, standard TFP growth amounts $\sum_{i=1}^{n} \frac{p_i x_i^*}{p^1 y^1} \pi_i$. For a derivation see Wolff (1985). The weights sum to $\frac{px^*}{p^1 y^1}$, the Domar factor. The calculus of TFP growth holds for non-constant returns to scale, provided that the index of returns to scale is constant. For an analysis see ten Raa (1995, chapter 12).
4. See, for example, U.S. Industry Economics Division (1974), for a discussion of methodology and for a listing of the sectors. This method creates artificial transactions. A formula for the transfer based input-output coefficient is given by Kop Jansen and ten Raa (1990) who also show that the method distorts the material and financial balance equations of input-output analysis. As a result, the method can distort the measurement of productivity growth in both industries i and j. Moreover, it can also affect the measurement of linkages between sectors. The bias in TFP growth associated with alternative coefficients constructions is small in ten Raa and Wolff (1991), where the nature of the distortions is exposed.
5. A description of the 1967 tables can be found in U.S. Interindustry Economics Division (1974); of the 1977 tables in U.S. Interindustry Economics Division (1984), and of the 1987 tables in Lawson and Teske (1994). The 1967 data were not published as separate make and use tables, but the raw data for them are available on computer tape, which Paula Young of BEA graciously supplied to us. No published documentation is yet available for the 1996 tables.
6. We refer to the aggregated sector as the trade sector.

7. To balance the flow tables, we adjusted the value added of the trade sector so that its total inputs equalled its new output total and adjusted both the value added of the real estate sector and the real estate input row so that the value of total output and inputs of the real estate sector matched.
8. Data on hours worked by sector, though the preferable measure of labor input to employment, are not available by sector and year and therefore could not be incorporated.
9. The allocation of the scrap sector was handled differently in the make-use framework of the 1967, 1977, 1987, and 1996 tables. See ten Raa and Wolff (1991) for details.
10. In addition, the deflator for transferred imports was calculated from the NIPA import deflator, that for the Rest of the World industry was calculated as the average of the NIPA import and export deflator, and the deflator for the inventory valuation adjustment was computed from the NIPA change in business inventory deflator. The source is Council of Economic Advisers (1999).
11. Sector numbers refer to the standard BEA 85-sector classification scheme. See, for example, U.S. Interindustry Economics Division (1984) for details. Although transportation, communications, and utilities are traditionally classified as services, their output is more easily measurable than that of other services and their productivity performance over time more closely mirrors that of the other goods industries rather than the other services. See Baumol, Blackman and Wolff (1989), Chapter 6, for further discussion.

References

Abraham, K. G. (1990)."Restructuring the Employment Relationship: The Growth of Market Mediated Work Arrangements." In K. G. Abraham and R. B. McKersie (eds.), *New Developments in the Labor Market.* Cambridge, Mass.: MIT Press.

Abraham, K. G. and S. K. Taylor. (1993). "Firms' Use of Outside Contractors: Theory and Evidence." NBER Working Paper No. 4468, Cambridge, Mass.

Barker, T. (1990). "Sources of Structural Change for the UK Service Industries 1979–84." *Economic Systems Research* 2(2), 173–183.

Barker, T. and O. Forssell. (1992). "Manufacturing, Services and Structural Change, 1979–1984." In C. Driver and P. Dunne (eds.), *Structural Change in the UK Economy*. Cambridge: Cambridge University Press.

Baumol, W. J. (1967). "Microeconomics of Unbalanced Growth: The Anatomy of Urban Crisis." *American Economic Review* 57(3), 415–426.

Baumol, W. J., S. A. B. Blackman and E. N. Wolff. (1989). *Productivity and American Leadership: The Long View*. Cambridge, Mass.: MIT Press.

Carter, A. P. (1970). *Structural Change in the American Economy*. Cambridge, Mass.: Harvard University Press.

Council of Economic Advisers. (1999). *Economic Report of the President*. Washington, D.C.: U.S. Government Printing Office.

Griliches, Z. (ed.). (1992). *Output Measurement in the Service Sectors*, NBER Studies in Income and Wealth, Vol. 56. Chicago: University of Chicago Press.

Katz, A. J. and S. W. Herman. (1997). "Improved Estimates of Fixed Reproducible Tangible Wealth, 1929–95." *Survey of Current Business*, May, 69–92.

Kop Jansen, P. and T. ten Raa. (1990). "The Choice of Model in the Construction of Input-Output Coefficients Matrices." *International Economic Review* 31(1), 213–227.

Lawson, A. M. and D. A. Teske. (1994). "Benchmark Input-Output Accounts for the U.S. Economy, 1987." *Survey of Current Business* 74(4), 73–115.

Leontief, W. (1941). *The Structure of the American Economy*, 1919–1939. New York: Oxford University Press.

Leontief, W. (1967). "An Alternative to Aggregation in Input-Output Analysis and National Accounts." *Review of Economics and Statistics* 49(3), 412–419.

Postner, H. H. (1990). "The Contracting-Out Problem in Service Sector Analysis: Choice of Statistical Unit." *Review of Income and Wealth* Series 36(2), 177–186.

Ritz, P. M. (1979). "The Input-Output Structure of the U.S. Economy, 1972, 11." *Survey of Current Business* 59(2), 34–72.

Ritz, P. M., E. P. Roberts and P. C. Young. (1979). "Dollar Value Tables of the 1972 Input-Output Study." *Survey of Current Business* 59(4), 51–72.

Siegel, D. and Z. Griliches. (1992) "Purchased Services, Outsourcing, Computers, and Productivity in Manufacturing." In Z. Griliches (ed.), *Output Measurement in the Service Sectors*, NBER Studies in Income and Wealth, Vol. 56. Chicago: University of Chicago Press.

Stigler, G. J. (1951). "The Division of Labor is Limited by the Extent of the Market." *Journal of Political Economy* 59.

ten Raa, T. (1995). *Linear Analysis of Competitive Economies*. Hemel Hempstead: Harvester Wheatsheaf/Prentice Hall.

ten Raa, T. and E. N. Wolff. (1991). "Secondary Products and the Measurement of Productivity Growth." *Regional Science and Urban Economics* 21(4), 581–615.

U.S. Bureau of Economic Analysis. (1991). "Benchmark Input-Output Accounts for the U.S. Economy, 1982." *Survey of Current Business* 71(7), 30–71.

U.S. Interindustry Economics Division. (1974). "The Input-Output Structure of the U.S. Economy: 1967." *Survey of Current Business* 54(2), 24–56.

U.S. Interindustry Economics Division. (1984). "The Input-Output Structure of the U.S. Economy, 1977." *Survey of Current Business* 64(5), 42–84.

Wolff, E. N. (1985). "Industrial Composition, Interindustry Effects and the U.S. Productivity Slowdown." *Review of Economics and Statistics* 67, May, 268–77.

Yuskavage, R. E. (1985). "Employment and Employee Compensation in the 1977 Input-Output Accounts." *Survey of Current Business* 65(11), 11–25.

ELSEVIER

Structural Change and Economic Dynamics 11 (2000) 473–489

STRUCTURAL CHANGE AND ECONOMIC DYNAMICS

www.elsevier.nl/locate/strueco

Engines of growth in the US economy

Thijs ten Raa [a,*], Edward N. Wolff [b]

[a] *Department of Economics, Tilburg University, Box 90153, NL-5000 LE Tilburg, Netherlands*

[b] *Department of Economics, New York University, 269 Mercer Street, New York, NY 10003, USA*

Received 1 November 1999; received in revised form 1 July 2000; accepted 29 August 2000

Abstract

There is good reason to believe that R&D influences on TFP growth in other sectors are indirect. For R&D to spill over, it must first be successful in the home sector. Indeed, observed spillovers conform better to TFP growth than to R&D in the upstream sectors. Sectoral TFP growth rates are thus inter-related. Solving the intersectoral TFP equation resolves overall TFP growth into sources of growth. The solution essentially eliminates the spillovers and amounts to a novel decomposition of TFP growth. The top 10 sectors are designated 'engines of growth' led by computers and office machinery. The results are contrasted with the standard, Domar decomposition of TFP growth. © 2000 Elsevier Science B.V. All rights reserved.

JEL classification: O30; O41; O51; L86; D57

Keywords: Input–output; Sources of growth; Spillovers

1. Introduction

Spillovers of technical change are known to drive a wedge between private and social rates of return to research and development (R&D). What is less known, is that spillovers render total factor productivity (TFP) growth in some sectors more critical than in others. While it is true by growth accounting that we may decompose macro TFP growth into sectoral components and thus identify the progressive sectors, this procedure amounts to a neutral addition of sectoral TFP growth rates. The contribution of a sector's TFP growth is determined by the value

* Corresponding author. Tel.: + 31-13-4662365; fax: + 31-13-4663280.

E-mail addresses: tenraa@kub.nl (T. ten Raa), edward.wolff@nyu.edu (E.N. Wolff).

PII: S0954-349X(00)00029-1

share of the sector in the total economy, without one sector being more critical than another. The picture changes slightly, but no more than that, when we regress TFP growth on R&D in a panel of sectors. Here, too, R&D may turn out to be more influential when spent in some sectors, but the mechanics of growth accounting remain the same, and TFP growth is not more critical in those sectors.

The story takes a twist when R&D influences TFP growth in other sectors not directly, but indirectly, that is, only after it has been proven successful in the sector where it has been spent. If this is the case, then spillovers inter-relate sectoral TFP growth rates and we may expect multiplier effects. The multipliers will depend on the spillover relationships, and these need not be equal to the structure of the material balances in the economy. Hence, TFP multiplier effects are not given by the standard multiplier matrix, the Leontief inverse.

There is good reason to believe that R&D influences on TFP growth in other sectors are indirect. For R&D to spill over, it must first be successful in the home sector. Indeed, observed spillovers conform better to TFP growth than to R&D in the upstream sectors, as noted in Wolff (1997). Hence it is of utmost interest to determine which sectors transmit technical change more strongly. These sectors are the engines of growth. Engines of growth need not feature high R&D, but once they move in terms of own TFP growth, they push the entire economy.

The interdependence of sectoral TFP growth rates is given by a system of equations that account for the spillover effects. In this paper we solve the spillover equations for TFP growth rates. The reduced form of the TFP growth rates shows their dependence on sectoral R&D expenditures, and the coefficients measure total returns to R&D, including the spillover effects. Observed sectoral TFP growth rates are thus ascribed to sources of growth.

Direct sectoral decompositions of TFP growth impute little to automation. As Bob Solow noticed: "You can see the Computer Age everywhere but in the productivity statistics." Our solution of the spillover structure will reveal computers as a primary engine of growth.

In the next section we review some of the literature. In Section 3 we present the general equilibrium analysis of TFP spillovers. We decompose TFP growth not only by sectoral TFP growth in an accounting fashion, but also by sources of growth. We do so by solving the TFP equation for its multiplier structure. Engines of growth are defined formally. Then, in Section 4, we describe the data set we use. Results for the US economy are presented in Section 5 and Section 6 concludes.

2. Review of the literature

R&D spillovers refer to the direct knowledge gains of customers from the R&D of the supplying industry (see Griliches, 1979). There have been several approaches to measuring R&D spillovers. Brown and Conrad (1967) base their measure of borrowed R&D on input–output trade flows (both purchases and sales) between industries. Terleckyj (1974, 1980) and Goto and Suzuki (1989) provided measures of the amount of R&D embodied in customer inputs on the basis of interindustry material and capital purchases made by one industry from supplying industries. Scherer (1982), relying on Federal Trade Commission line of business data, used product (in contradistinction to process) R&D, aimed at improving output quality, as a measure of R&D spillovers.

Another approach is to measure the 'technological closeness' between industries, even if they are not directly connected by interindustry flows. For example, if two industries use similar processes (even though their products are very different or they are not directly connected by interindustry flows), one industry may benefit from new discoveries by the other industry. Such an approach is found in Jaffe (1986), who used patent data to measure technological closeness between industries. The patent approach to spillovers has been continued by Evenson and Johnson (1997), Kortum and Putnam (1997), Verspagen (1997) and Verspagen and Los (2000).

Bernstein and Nadiri (1989) use as a measure of intra-industry R&D spillovers total R&D at the two-digit SIC level and apply this measure to individual firm data within the industry. Mairesse and Mohnen (1990) report similar results by comparing R&D coefficients based on firm R&D with those based on industry R&D. If there are intra-industry externality effects of firm R&D, then the coefficients of industry R&D should be higher than those of firm R&D. However, their results do not show that this is consistently the case. (Also see Mohnen, 1992a and Griliches, 1992 for reviews of the literature.)

A different approach was followed by Wolff and Nadiri (1993), who used as their measure of embodied technical change a weighted average of the TFP growth of supplying industries, where the weights are given by the input–output coefficients of an industry. This formulation assumed that the knowledge gained from a supplying industry is in direct proportion to the importance of that industry in a sector's input structure. Wolff (1997) updated these earlier results using US input–output data for the period 1958 to 1987, and found strong evidence that industry TFP growth is significantly related to the TFP performance of supplying sectors, with an elasticity of almost 60 percent. The results also indicated that direct productivity spillovers were more important than spillovers from the R&D performed by suppliers.

A substantial number of studies, perhaps inspired by Solow's quip, have also examined the linkage between computerization or information technology (IT) in general and productivity gains. The evidence is mixed. Most of the earlier studies failed to find any excess returns to IT, over and above the fact that these investments are normally in the form of equipment investment. These include Bailey and Gordon (1988), who examined aggregate productivity growth in the US and found no significant contribution of computerization; Loveman (1988), who reported no productivity gains from IT investment; Parsons et al. (1993), who estimated very low returns on computer investments in Canadian banks; and Berndt and Morrison (1995), who found negative correlations between labor productivity growth and high-tech capital investment in US manufacturing industries. One of the few exceptions in these earlier studies is Bresnahan (1986), who did estimate positive and significant spillovers from mainframe computers in financial services.

The later studies generally tend to be more positive. Both Siegel and Griliches (1992) and Steindel (1992) estimated a positive and significant relationship between computer investment and industry-level productivity growth. Lau and Tokutso (1992) estimated that about half of real output growth in the United States could be attributed directly or indirectly to IT investment. Oliner and Sichel (1994) reported a significant contribution of computers to aggregate US output growth. Lichtenberg (1995) estimated firm-level production functions and found an excess return to IT equipment and labor. Siegel (1997), using detailed industry-level manufacturing data for the US, found that computers are an important source of quality change and that, once correcting output measures for quality change, computerization had a significant positive effect on productivity growth. Brynjolfsson and Hitt (1996, 1998) found a positive correlation between firm-level productivity growth and IT investment over the 1987–1994 time period, particularly when accompanied by organization changes. Lehr and Lichtenberg (1998) used data for US federal government agencies over the 1987–1992 period and found a significant positive relation between productivity growth and computer intensity. Lehr and Lichtenberg (1999) investigated firm-level data among service industries over the 1977–1993 period and also reported evidence that computers, particularly personal computers, contributed positively and significantly to productivity growth.

Two studies looked, in particular, at R&D spillovers embodied in IT investment. Bernstein (1995) found a positive and highly significant influence of R&D linked (both embodied and disembodied) in communication equipment on the TFP growth of industries using this equipment. van Meijl (1995) also estimated a positive and significant effect of R&D embodied in IT investment in general on TFP growth in other sectors. Both, moreover, found that the spillover effect was increasing rapidly over time.

Technological sources of growth have been documented by economic historians (Landes, 1969) and modeled by Amable (1993) and many others, but it is only fairly recently that attempts have been made to pinpoint sources of growth in a micro-economic or at least multi-sectoral framework. The term 'engines of growth' has been coined by Bresnahan and Trajtenberg (1995). Their central notion is that a handful of 'general purpose technologies' bring about and foster generalized productivity gains throughout the economy. The productivity of R&D in a downstream sector increases as a consequence of innovation in the general purpose technology. Bresnahan and Trajtenberg (1995) proceed to construct a partial equilibrium model of an upstream sector and a downstream sector, and then examine the welfare consequences of a simple one-step innovation game. Our model, however, is general equilibrium; the interaction between sectors is circular and there is no presumed engine of growth. While the terminology of Bresnahan and Trajtenberg (1995) is suggestive and useful indeed, it remains to identify the engines of growth given the body of input–output data that represent the structure of a national economy.

Caselli (1999) and Helpman and Rangel (1999) stress the educational requirements of the new information technology. These requirements slow down productivity growth, at least initially, and create wage inequality, at least in equilibrium, with workers recouping their training costs. The invention of the new technology is exogenous and its spread is determined by the mechanics of utility maximization in a dynamic economy with a single output. These authors take the source of the new technology for granted and examine its propagation and productivity effects. We start at the other end, the sectoral productivity growth rates, and try to trace back the sources of growth, in terms of sectoral R&D activities. We do so by solving the spillover structure for its reduced form. Unlike Caselli (1999) and Helpman and Rangel (1999), we were not motivated by the information technology revolution, but by the sheer theoretical challenge to pinpoint sources of growth in a general equilibrium input–output framework.

3. Productivity analysis of spillovers

Our point of departure is the Solow residual definition of total factor productivity (TFP) growth, Π:

$$\Pi = (pdy - wdL - rdK)/(py) \tag{1}$$

Here y is the final demand vector, L is labor input, K is capital input, w and r their respective prices, and p is the row vector of production prices, reflecting zero profits:

$$p(I-A) = v = wl + rk \tag{2}$$

where A is the matrix of the intermediate input coefficients and v, l and k are the raw vectors of value-added, labor and capital coefficients. As Solow (1957) showed, the zero profit condition is needed to let the residual measure technical change. More precisely, the numerator of residual Eq. (1) becomes

$$\begin{aligned} &pd[(I-A)x] - wd(lx) - rd(kx) \\ &= (-pdA - wdl - rdk)x + [p(I-A) - wl - rk]dx \end{aligned} \tag{3}$$

where the last term vanishes only if we use the production prices of Eq. (2). Then TFP growth defined by Eq. (1) reduces to

$$\Pi = -(pdA + wdl + rdk)x/(py) = \pi\hat{p}x/(py) \tag{4}$$

where

$$= -(pdA + wdl + rdk)\hat{p}^{-1} \tag{5}$$

is the row vector of sectoral TFP growth rates and $\hat{p}x/(py)$ is the column vector of Domar weights.

Important determinants of sectoral TFP growth are R&D and spillovers. As we have seen in the previous section, a prominent way to model spillovers is a weighted average of R&D in supplying sectors, where the weights are direct or total input coefficients, with the diagonal set to zero to avoid double counting of R&D. We, however, measure spillovers as a weighted average of TFP growth in supplying sectors. We have three reasons to do so. First, for R&D to spill over into TFP growth of other sectors it must first be successful in the home sector, and this success is measured by its effect in terms of TFP growth. Second, we wish to endogenize the general equilibrium transmission of spillovers. Instead of putting in total input coefficients (the standard Leontief inverse) into the equation (as do Sakurai et al., 1997), we want to obtain them by solving the equation. Third, TFP growth based spillovers yield the best fit, according to Wolff (1997).

We distinguish four sources of sectoral TFP growth, π_j, an autonomous source, α, R&D in sector j per dollar of gross output, denoted by

$$\rho_j = RD_j/(p_j x_j) \tag{6}$$

a direct productivity spillover $\Sigma(p_i a_{ij}/p_j)\pi_i$, and a capital embodied spillover $\Sigma(p_i b_{ij}/p_j)\pi_i$, where b_{ij} is the investment coefficient of capital good i in sector j, per unit of output. We first regress sectoral TFP growth as follows (denoting the vector with all entries equal to one by e):

$$\pi = \alpha e^{\mathrm{T}} + \beta_1 \rho + \beta_2 \pi \hat{p} A \hat{p}^{-1} + \beta_3 \pi \hat{p} B \hat{p}^{-1} + \varepsilon \tag{7}$$

where α, β_1, and β_2 are coefficients and ε is a stochastic error term (Wolff, 1997). The weights of the sources are assumed to be constant across sectors. If we denote the spillover matrix by

$$C = \beta_2 \hat{p} A \hat{p}^{-1} + \beta_3 \hat{p} B \hat{p}^{-1} \tag{8}$$

then Eq. (7) reads, ignoring the error term

$$\pi = \alpha e^{\mathrm{T}} + \beta_1 \rho + \pi C \tag{9}$$

To interpret the regression coefficient as a return to R&D (Mohnen, 1992b), we relate TFP growth to R&D both directly and indirectly, that is through the spillovers. The direct effect is obtained by substituting Eqs. (6) and (9) into Eq. (4):

$$\begin{aligned} \Pi &= [\alpha e^{\mathrm{T}} + \beta_1 RD(\hat{p}\hat{x})^{-1} + \pi C]\hat{p}x/(py) \\ &= \alpha DR + \beta_1 RDe/(py) + \pi C\hat{p}x/(py) \end{aligned} \tag{10}$$

where RD is the row vector with elements RD_j given by Eq. (6) and $DR = (px)/(py)$, the Domar ratio, and RDe is the total R&D expediture, summed over sectors. There are two, equivalent interpretations of β_1. First, since Π is a growth rate, β_1 measures the *rate of return to R&D intensity*, where the latter is taken with respect to the value of net output or GDP. Second, since the denominator in the definitions of Π, see Eq. (1), is also py, the equality of the numerators in Eq. (10) reveals that β_1 measures the *return to R&D*, in terms of output value per dollar expenditure. β_1 measures the direct rate of return to R&D intensity or, equivalently, the direct return to R&D. Now notice that the last term of Eq. (10), the intermediate inputs and embodied TFP growth rates, features the row vector of sectoral TFP growth rates, π, and, therefore, reinforces the effect of R&D on productivity through the spillovers.

The total return to R&D is obtained by taking into account the spillover effects. This is done by solving regression Eq. (9) for π, that is by taking the Leontief inverse of matrix C. Thus we define multiplier matrix M by

$$M = (I - C)^{-1} = I + C + C^2 + \cdots \tag{11}$$

Sakurai et al. (1997) model indirect spillover effects by putting the standard Leontief inverse directly into the TFP regression equation. We, however, model the direct spillovers and determine the indirect ones by general equilibrium analysis of the transmission mechanism, solving Eq. (9) using Eq. (11):

$$\pi = (\alpha e^{\mathrm{T}} + \beta_1 \rho)M \tag{12}$$

The direct rate of return to R&D was based on $\beta_1\rho$. The total rate of return is obtained by inflation through multiplier matrix M in Eq. (11). Here I reproduces the direct rate of return, C, specified in Eq. (8), produces the direct spillover effect, and $C^2 + \cdots$ the indirect spillover effects. The TFP growth expression in Eq. (4) becomes

$$\Pi = \pi\hat{p}x/(py) = (\alpha e^{\mathrm{T}} + \beta_1\rho)M\hat{p}x/(py) \tag{13}$$

Eq. (13) reduces TFP growth not only to sectoral TFP growth rates, but also to autonomous TFP growth and sectoral R&D expenditures. The middle expression in Eq. (13) is the usual Domar decomposition of TFP growth, Eq. (4). The right-hand side of Eq. (13) is an alternative, novel decomposition:

$$\Pi = [(\alpha + \beta_1\rho_1)\sum_j m_{1j}p_jx_j + \cdots + (\alpha + \beta_1\rho_n)\sum_j m_{nj}p_jx_j]/(py) \tag{14}$$

Again, there are two, equivalent measures for the productivity effect of R&D. The *total rate of return to R&D intensity* ρ_i amounts to $\beta_1(\Sigma_j m_{ij}p_jx_j)/(py)$. Here β_1 is deflated by multipliers m_{ij} because of the spillover effects and also by gross/net output ratios as the sectoral R&D intensities ρ_i are defined as the R&D/gross output ratios (which are small because of the denominators).

Once more, the second interpretation is derived from the observation that either side of Eq. (14) has py as denominator. Hence the *total return to R&D*, in terms of output value per dollar expenditure in sector i, amounts to $\beta_1(\Sigma_j m_{ij}p_jx_j)/(p_ix_i)$ using Eq. (6). Notice that the direct return to R&D, β_1, is inflated by the factor $(\Sigma_j m_{ij}p_jx_j)/(p_ix_i)$ because of the spillover effects stemming from sector i. Notice also that some sectors have stronger spillover effects than others, as determined by the rows of the multiplier matrix. The factors $(\Sigma_j m_{ij}p_jx_j)/(p_ix_i)$ reinforce the returns to R&D and are, therefore, *spillover multipliers.* Spillover multipliers are related to the standard forward multipliers of input–output analysis (the row totals of the standard Leontief inverse), but there are two differences. First, spillover multipliers are based on the Leontief inverse of spillover matrix C rather than technology matrix A. Second, spillover multipliers are not straight row sums, but weighted by output value ratios $(p_jx_j)/(p_ix_i)$. We shall compare spillover multipliers to standard forward multipliers for the US economy. Spillover multipliers account for the ratio of the total to the direct return to R&D and, therefore, measure the external effect of sectoral R&D.

Eq. (14) shows that the contribution of a sector to TFP growth can be high for two reasons. First, the intensity of R&D can be high. Second, the spillover factor $\Sigma_j m_{ij}p_jx_j$ may be high. Decomposition Eq. (14) reduces overall TFP growth to sources of growth, $\alpha + \beta_1 \rho_1$ for sector 1 to $\alpha + \beta_1 \rho_n$ for sector n, aggregated by the (forward) linkages, $\Sigma_j m_{1j} p_j x_j$ for sector 1 to $\Sigma_j m_{nj} p_j x_j$ for sector n. Whereas the first decomposition, Eq. (4), is a TFP growth accounting identity, the second decomposition, Eq. (14), imputes TFP growth to sources of growth taking into account the general equilibrium spillover effects. Sectors that pick up much TFP growth in decomposition Eq. (14) are the *engines of growth*. The greatest engine of growth is the sector, say i, with the greatest value of $(\alpha + \beta_1 \rho_i)\Sigma_j m_{ij} p_j x_j$. Whereas sectors with high TFP growth can be identified by direct growth accounting in the sense of Domar, engines of growth reveal themselves only after solving the intersectoral TFP growth rates equation for spillover effects to its reduced form, Eq. (13).

4. Data sources

The basic data are 85-sector US input–output tables for years 1958, 1967, 1977, and 1987.[1] Labor coefficients were obtained from Bureau of Labor Statistics' Historical Output and Employment Data Series (obtained on computer diskette).[2]

Capital stock by input–output industry for 1967 and 1977 was calculated directly from the net stocks of plant and equipment by input–output industry provided on computer tape by the US Bureau of Industry Economics (the BIE Capital Stocks Data Base as of January 31, 1983). These series ran through 1981 for manufacturing industries and through 1980 for the other sectors. They were updated to 1987 on the basis of the growth rate of constant dollar net stock of fixed capital between 1980 (or 1981) and 1987 calculated from the National Income and Product Accounts (NIPA).[3]

Sectoral price indices were calculated from the Bureau of Labor Statistics' Historical Output Data Series (obtained on computer diskette) on the basis of the current and constant dollar series.[4]

[1] Details on the construction of the input–output tables can be found in the following publications: 1967, US Interindustry Economics Division (1974); US Interindustry Economics Division (1984); and 1987, Lawson and Teske (1994). We aggregate sectors 1–4, 5&6, 9&10, 11&12, 20&21, 22&23, 33&34, 44&45 and delete 74 and 80–85. Thus we partition the US economy in 68 sectors.

[2] Data on hours worked by sector, though the preferable measure of labor input to employment, are not available by sector and year and therefore could not be incorporated.

[3] The source is Musgrave (1992). Since there are fewer industries in the NIPA breakdown than in the input–output data, we applied the same percentage growth rate across all input–output industries falling within a given NIPA classification. Data on government-owned capital stock for all years were obtained from Musgrave (1992).

[4] In addition, the deflator for transferred imports was calculated from the NIPA import deflator, that for the Rest of the World industry was calculated from the NIPA import and export deflator, and the deflator for the inventory valuation adjustment was computed from the NIPA change in business inventory deflator. The source is US Council of Economic Advisers (1992), Tables B-1, B-2 and B-3.

Five sectors — research and development, business travel and office supplies, scrap and used goods, and inventory valuation adjustment — appeared in some years, but not in others (the earlier years for the first three sectors and the later years for the last two sectors). In order to make the accounting framework consistent over the four years of analysis, we eliminated these sectors from both gross and final output. This was accomplished by distributing the inputs used by these sectors proportional to either the endogenous sectors which purchased the output of these five sectors or the final output.[5]

Data on the ratio of R&D expenditures to GDP were obtained from the National Science Foundation, *Research and Development in Industry*, various years, for 32 manufacturing industries covering the period 1958 to 1987. We were able to allocate these figures to 48 manufacturing industries in the input–output data.[6]

5. Results

Table 1, upper panel, shows the standard forward multipliers for the 68 industries in each of the four years. In 1987, not surprisingly, wholesale and retail trade is the sector with the highest forward linkage, since, by construction, it supplies almost all industries in the economy. The second most important supplier is the business service sector, followed by primary iron and steel, transportation, utilities, and industrial chemicals. On the bottom of the list are the consumer-oriented sectors, including tobacco products, ordinance (that is, armaments), household appliances, and footwear and leather products. Cross-industry correlations in forward linkages are very high, though they tend to attenuate over time. The correlation coefficient between the 1987 and 1977 forward linkages is 0.96, compared with a correlation of 0.92 between the 1958 and 1987 linkages; the respective rank correlations are 0.97, 0.96, and 0.90.

We next compute the new forward linkages based on matrix C. Results on forward linkage multipliers based on Eq. (7) with $\alpha = 0.003$, $\beta_1 = 0.106$, $\beta_2 = 1.101$ and $\beta_3 = 0.753$ (following Wolff, 1997) are shown in Table 1, lower panel. There are now some interesting differences between these new multipliers and the standard forward linkage multipliers. On the basis of the 1987 multipliers, the trade sector ranks first and the construction sector ranks second, which is not unexpected since new investment is incorporated in the multiplier calculation. Business services

[5] The allocation of the scrap sector was handeled differently in the make-use framework of the 1967, 1977 and 1987 tables. See ten Raa and Wolff (1991) for details.

[6] This was calculated in two steps. First Company R&D from the Federal Trade Commission Line of Business Data was averaged over 1974, 1975 and 1976 and then divided by the average of industry GDP over the same 3 years. Second, using the National Science Foundation data, we computed the average ration R&D expentitures to net sales at the 32-industry level for the 1958–1987 period and adjusted the first set of R&D to gross output ratios accordingly. It should be noted that the R&D data at this level of detail are not available prior to 1958, which prevented us from aldso including the 1947–1958 period in the regression analysis. The net sales are net of intra-company sales.

Table 1
Ranks and values of forward linkage multipliers based on $\hat{p}A\hat{p}^{-1}$ (traditional) and matrix C spillovers, 1958–1987, with sectors ranked by 1987 multipliers (top 10 only)

		1987		1958		1967		1977	
Traditional									
59	Trade, restaurants	1:	5.71	2:	4.79	3:	4.18	1:	5.08
63	Business services	2:	4.77	4:	3.40	2:	4.32	3:	3.89
28	Primary iron and steel	3:	3.55	1:	4.83	1:	4.79	2:	4.41
55	Transportation	4:	3.35	3:	3.77	5:	3.37	5:	3.31
58	Utilities	5:	3.19	10:	2.34	8:	2.52	7:	3.07
19	Industrial chemical	6:	3.19	6:	3.09	6:	3.28	6:	3.30
61	Real estate	7:	2.95	5:	3.31	4:	3.88	10:	2.74
6	Construction	8:	2.59	12:	2.26	11:	2.30	11:	2.69
4	Crude petroleum and gas	9:	2.57	13:	2.21	16:	2.06	4:	3.37
29	Primary non-ferrous metals	10:	2.51	7:	2.78	7:	2.87	9:	2.79
Correlations with 1987 forward linkages				0.917		0.929		0.956	
Rank correlations with 1987 forward linkages				0.903		0.957		0.973	
Matrix C spillovers									
59	Trade, restaurants	1:	8.22	2:	6.93	3:	6.06	2:	7.72
6	Construction	2:	8.11	1:	7.83	1:	7.16	1:	8.44
63	Business services	3:	6.44	5:	4.35	4:	5.54	4:	5.12
28	Primary iron and steel	4:	4.33	3:	6.35	2:	6.10	3:	5.69
55	Transportation	5:	4.21	4:	4.85	6:	4.30	6:	4.25
61	Real estate	6:	3.93	6:	4.23	5:	4.96	9:	3.72
58	Utilities	7:	3.83	11:	2.77	9:	2.97	8:	3.75
19	Industrial chemicals	8:	3.75	7:	3.66	7:	3.85	7:	3.95
4	Crude petroleum and gas	9:	3.07	12:	2.62	17:	2.40	5:	4.27
29	Primary non-ferrous metals	10:	2.94	8:	3.39	8:	3.51	11:	3.42
Correlations with 1987 forward linkages				0.938		0.945		0.966	
Rank correlations with 1987 forward linkages				0.909		0.944		0.952	
Correlations with traditional forward linkage multiplier		0.905		0.880		0.903		0.898	
Rank correlations with traditional forward linkage multiplier		0.963		0.916		0.927		0.890	

now rank third, followed by primary iron and steel and transportation. The correlation coefficients between the new forward linkage multipliers and the standard forward linkage multipliers are now around 0.9, and the rank correlations range from 0.89 to 0.96. Cross-industry correlations in these new forward linkages are high and increase over time. The correlation coefficient between the 1987 and 1958 forward linkages is 0.94, that between the 1987 and 1967 multipliers is 0.95; and that between the 1987 and 1977 multipliers is 0.97; the corresponding rank correlations are 0.91, 0.94, and 0.95.

We next look at the major spillover sectors over the 1958–1987 period. These are defined as sectors i with high spillover terms $\pi_i(c_{i1} \ldots c_{in})$ which reflect both the strength of their forward linkages and their TFP growth. These sectors, shown in Table 2, are the ones which contributed most to the overall TFP growth of the economy. Over the whole 1957–1987 period, the most important source of overall growth was the trade sector, reflecting its very high forward linkage value. The second most important sector was computer and office equipment, a reflection of its very high TPF growth. Indeed, in the 1977–1987 period, it made by far the greatest contribution to embodied TFP growth. The third most important sector over the 1958–1987 period was electronic components, followed by transportation and plastics and synthetics. At the bottom of the list are the low (actually negative) TFP growth sectors, including crude petroleum and gas, finance and insurance, business services, radio and TV broadcasting, and metallic mining.

It is also of interest that there is very little correlation over time in the rank order (or values) of sectors in terms of πC. The correlation coefficient between the 1958–1967 and the 1977–1987 values is 0.27 and the rank correlation is 0.22; the corresponding figures between the 1967–1977 and 1977–1987 values are −0.03 and 0.12. This is a reflection of the fact that sectoral TFP growth is very variable over time.

Our final step is to decompose overall TFP growth into sectoral contributions. The decomposition is based on Eq. (14) and the figures are percentages of the positive growth contributions only, to avoid engines of growth making more than 100%. The results are shown in the bottom panel of Table 3. The results are quite striking. Over the full 1958–1987 period, the computer and office equipment industry was directly or indirectly responsible for over one fifth of the positive contributions to TFP growth of the economy. It was the leading sector in both the 1967–1977 and the 1977–1987 subperiods. Indeed, in the 1977–1987 period, it accounted for one fifth of the positive contributions to overall TFP growth. A reason for this large effect is that TFP growth in computers and office equipment averaged 9.94% per year during this period. The next largest growth rates during this period were for electronic components and accessories, at 3.88% per year, and non-metallic minerals mining, at 3.70% per year. It is also of interest that annual TFP growth in computers and office equipment accelerated from 1.22% in the 1958–1967 period to 2.58% in 1967–1977 and 9.94% in 1977–1987. The next leading

Table 2
Embodied total factor productivity growth rates, based on $\pi_i(c_{i1} \ldots c_{in})$ in Eq. (9), 1958–1987, with sectors ranked by 1958–1987 values (top 10 only, figures in percent per annum)

		1958–1987		1958–1967		1967–1977		1977–1987	
59	Trade, restaurants	1:	7.9	4:	5.9	3:	7.4	2:	8.9
41	Computer and office equipment	2:	6.4	50:	0.7	7:	3.5	1:	14.5
47	Electronic components	3:	5.7	9:	4.0	5:	4.7	3:	7.6
55	Transportation	4:	5.1	1:	10.0	2:	7.6	58:	−1.9
20	Plastics and synthetics	5:	5.1	6:	4.9	4:	5.3	6:	4.8
61	Real estate	6:	4.9	3:	6.5	1:	12.9	62:	−2.9
1	Agriculture	7:	3.1	29:	2.0	6:	4.0	11:	3.0
53	Ophthalmic and photographic equipment	8:	2.5	18:	3.1	10:	2.8	25:	2.0
10	Fabrics, yarn and thread mills	9:	2.4	17:	3.1	23:	1.4	12:	2.9
24	Rubber, miscellaneous plastics	10:	2.4	14:	3.2	43:	0.3	9:	3.7
Correlations with 1977–1987 values				0.274		−0.028			
Rank correlations with 1977–1987 values				0.222		0.120			

Table 3
Percentage decomposition of overall TFP growth by sector, based on Eq. (4) (Domar) and Eq. (14) (sources of growth), with sectors ranked by 1958–1987 values (top 10 only, figures in percent per annum, with denominator the sum of positive elements only)

		1958–1987		1958–1967		1967–1977		1977–1987	
Domar									
59	Trade, restaurants	1:	21.6	2:	11.4	2:	16.0	1:	19.1
61	Real estate	2:	16.5	1:	11.9	1:	30.6	66:	−8.3
1	Agriculture	3:	8.6	6:	4.1	4:	7.8	4:	5.5
55	Transportation	4:	7.3	3:	9.0	3:	8.4	59:	−1.8
8	Food products	5:	5.5	5:	5.1	5:	3.5	5:	3.6
41	Computer and office equipment	6:	3.6	52:	0.2	14:	1.5	2:	8.2
12	Apparel	7:	2.9	16:	1.8	11:	1.9	7:	3.1
21	Drugs and cleaning products	8:	2.4	19:	1.4	10:	2.0	11:	2.5
47	Electronic components	9:	2.3	23:	1.1	12:	1.7	6:	3.1
56	Communications	10:	2.2	12:	2.2	6:	3.1	58:	−1.4
Rank correlations with 1977–1987 values				0.31		0.11			
Engines of growth									
41	Computer and office equipment	1:	18.0	19:	0.8	1:	14.3	1:	19.2
47	Electronic components	2:	9.2	8:	3.6	3:	11.8	2:	5.9
20	Plastics and synthetics	3:	5.7	6:	4.2	4:	9.2	5:	1.9
52	Scientific and control instruments	4:	4.3	68:	−0.5	8:	3.8	3:	3.6
50	Aircraft and parts	5:	4.2	1:	15.3	62:	−0.5	55:	0.0
46	Audio, video and communications equipment	6:	3.8	4:	6.9	13:	2.3	6:	1.8
21	Drugs and cleaning products	7:	3.7	11:	2.2	5:	5.9	8:	1.5
49	Motor vehicles	8:	3.2	3:	7.2	2:	13.0	68:	−4.8
24	Rubber, miscellaneous plastics	9:	2.5	12:	1.8	19:	1.2	7:	1.8
44	Household appliances	10:	2.3	9:	2.9	7:	4.5	14:	0.4
Rank correlations with 1997–1987 values				0.400		0.231			
Rank correlations with Domar values		0.812		0.691		0.809		0.807	

sector was electronic components, which accounted for 14% of the positive contributions of overall TFP growth over the full 1958–1987 period and for 6% in 1977–1987. Plastics and synthetics ranked third over the three decades, followed by scientific and control equipment and then aircraft and parts. Together, the top five industries were responsible for 41% of the positive contributions of overall TFP growth over the full 1958–1987 period and for 31% in 1977–1987. It is also notable that the top 10 industries are all manufacturing industries.

There is very little correlation over time in the rank order of sectors in terms of their contribution to overall TFP growth. The rank correlations between the 1958–1967 and the 1977–1987 values is 0.40 and that between the 1967–1977 and 1977–1987 values is 0.23. This again is a reflection of the fact that sectoral TFP growth in the US economy can change radically over time. It also suggests that the engines of growth in the US economy can change radically over time. In the real estate sector, for example, annual TFP growth, after rising from 1.42% in the 1958–1967 period to 2.97% in 1967–1977, plummeted to −0.76% in 1977–1987. This, together with its linkages to other industries in the economy, also accounts for its very low ranking in the 1977–1987 period.

A comparison with the standard decomposition of overall TFP growth based on Domar factors (Eq. (4)) is also instructive (see the top panel of Table 3). Here, the top four industries, in rank order, over the 1958–1987 period are wholesale and retail trade (including restaurants), real estate, agriculture, and transportation. Computers and office equipment rank only sixth, compared with their top rank on the basis of matrix C. Like the engines of growth, there is a positive but low correlation in rank order of these industries over time, because of the high variability of TFP growth between periods. However, overall, the Domar rankings are similar to those based on matrix C, with rank correlations of 0.8 or so for most periods and for the entire 1958–1987 period. This result reflects the fact that industry-level TFP growth is the main determinant of the contribution of an industry to overall TFP growth.

6. Conclusion

Because of spillovers of technical change, sectoral productivity growth rates depend on each other. Solving this interdependence, by taking the Leontief inverse of the spillover matrix, amounts to imputation of total factor productivity growth to sectoral sources. The decomposition is not that of standard growth accounting, because productivity growth is not counted in the sector where it occurs, but in the sectors that trigger it. The sectors to which most productivity growth is imputed are computers and office equipment and electronic components. In the standard growth accounting decomposition they rank 6 and 9 only. Productivity spillovers explain their status as leading engines of growth.

Acknowledgements

We are grateful to the C.V. Starr Center for Applied Economics at New York University and to CentER at Tilburg University for visitorships. A referee provided very useful suggestions.

References

Amable, B., 1993. Catch-up and convergence: a model of cumulative growth. International Review of Applied Economics 7 (1), 1–25.

Bailey, M., Gordon, R., 1988. The productivity slowdown, measurement issues, and the explosion in computer power. Brookings Papers on Economic Activity 2, 347–432.

Berndt, E.R., Morrison, C.J., 1995. High-tech capital formation and economic performance in US manufacturing industries. Journal of Econometrics 69, 9–43.

Bernstein, J.I., Nadiri, M.I., 1989. Research and development and intra-industry spillovers: an empirical application of dynamic duality. Review of Economic Studies 56, 249–269.

Bernstein, J.I., 1995. The Canadian communication equipment industry as a source of R&D spillovers and productivity growth. Paper presented at the Conference of Implications of Knowledge-Based Growth for Micro-Economic Policies, March 30–31, Ottawa, Ontario, Canada.

Bresnahan, T., 1986. Measuring the spillovers from technical advance: mainframe computers in financial services. American Economic Review 74 (4), 743–755.

Bresnahan, T.F., Trajtenberg, M., 1995. General purpose technologies engines of growth. Journal of Econometrics 65 (1), 83–108.

Brown, M., Conrad, A., 1967. The influence of research on CES production relations. In: Brown, M. (Ed.), The Theory and Empirical Analysis of Production. In: Studies in Income and Wealth, vol. Vol. 3. Columbia University Press for the NBER, New York.

Brynjolfsson, E., Hitt, L., 1996. Computers and productivity growth: firm-level evidence. Mimeo, MIT Sloan School, July.

Brynjolfsson, E., Hitt, L., 1998. Information technology and organizational design: evidence from micro data. Mimeo, MIT Sloan School, January.

Caselli, F., 1999. Technological revolutions. American Economic Review 89 (1), 78–102.

Evenson, R.E., Johnson, D., 1997. Introduction: invention input–output analysis. Economic Systems Research 9 (2), 149–160.

Goto, A., Suzuki, K., 1989. R&D capital, rate of return on R&D investment and spillover of R&D in Japanese manufacturing industries. Review of Economics and Statistics 71 (4), 555–564.

Griliches, Z., 1979. Issues in assessing the contribution of research and development to productivity growth. Bell Journal of Economics 10, 92–116.

Griliches, Z., 1992. The search for R&D spillovers. Scandinavian Journal of Economics 94, 29–47.

Helpman, E., Rangel, A., 1999. Adjusting to a new technology: experience and training. Journal of Economic Growth 4(4), 359–383.

Jaffe, A.B., 1986. Technology opportunity and spillovers of R&D: evidence from firms' patents, profits, and market value. American Economic Review 76, 984–1001.

Kortum, S., Putnam, J., 1997. Assigning patents to industries: tests of the Yale Technology Concordance. Economic Systems Research 9 (2), 161–176.

Landes, D., 1969. The Unbound Prometheus. Cambridge University Press, Cambridge.

Lau, L., Tokutso, I., 1992. The impact of computer technology on the aggregate productivity of the United States: an indirect approach. Mimeo, Stanford University Department of Economics.

Lawson, A.M., Teske, D.A., 1994. Benchmark input–output accounts for the US economy, 1987. Survey of Current Business 74, 73–115.

Lehr, W., Lichtenberg, F., 1998. Computer use and productivity growth in US Federal Government Agencies, 1987–92. Journal of Industrial Economics 44 (2), 257–279.

Lehr, W., Lichtenberg, F., 1999. Information technology and its impact on productivity: firm-level evidence from government and private data sources, 1977–1993. Canadian Journal of Economics 32 (2), 335–362.

Lichtenberg, F.R., 1995. The output contribution of computer equipment and personnel: a firm level analysis. Economics of Innovation and New Technology 3 (4), 201–217.

Loveman, G.W., 1988. An assessment of the productivity impact of information technologies. In: Management in the 1990s. MIT Press, Cambridge, MA.

Mairesse, J., Mohnen, P., 1990. Recherche-developpment et productivite: un sorvoi de la litterature econometrique. Economie et Statistique 237/238, 99–108.

Mohnen, P., 1992a. New technology and interindustry spillovers. Science/Technology/Industry Review 7, 131–147.

Mohnen, P., 1992b. The relationship between R&D and productivity growth in Canada and other major industrialized countries, Canada Communications Group, Ottawa, Canada.

Musgrave, J.C., 1992. Fixed reproducible tangible wealth in the United States, revised estimates. Survey of Current Business 72, 106–137.

National Science Foundation, Research and Development in Industry, Government Printing Office, Washington, DC, various years.

Oliner, S., Sichel, D., 1994. Computers and output growth revisited: how big is the puzzle? Brookings Papers on Economic Activity 2.

Parsons, D.J., Gotlieb, C.C., Denny, M., 1993. Productivity and computers in Canadian banking. Journal of Productivity Analysis 4, 91–110.

Sakurai, N., Papaconstantinou, G., Ioannides, E., 1997. Impact of R&D and technology diffusion on productivity growth: empirical evidence for 10 OECD countries. Economic Systems Research 9 (1), 81–109.

Scherer, F.M., 1982. Interindustry technology flows and productivity growth. Review of Economics and Statistics 64, 627–634.

Siegel, D., Griliches, Z., 1992. Purchased services, outsourcing, computers, and productivity in manufacturing. In: Griliches, Z. (Ed.), Output Measurement in the Service Sector. University of Chicago Press, Chicago.

Siegel, D., 1997. The impact of computers on manufacturing productivity growth: a multiple-indicators, multiple-causes approach. Review of Economics and Statistics, 68–78.

Solow, R.M., 1957. Technical change and the aggregate production function. Review of Economics and Statistics 39 (3), 312–320.

Steindel, C., 1992. Manufacturing productivity and high-tech investment. Federal Reserve Bank of New York Quarterly Review 17, 39–47.

ten Raa, T., Wolff, E.N., 1991. Secondary products and the measurement of productivity growth. Regional Science and Urban Economics 21 (4), 581–615.

Terleckyj, N.W., 1974. Effects of R&D on the productivity growth of industries: an exploratory study, National Planning Association, Washington, DC.

Terleckyj, N.W., 1980. Direct and indirect effects of industrial research and development on the productivity growth of industries. In: Kendrick, J.W., Vaccara, B. (Eds.), New Developments in Productivity Measurement. National Bureau of Economic Research, New York.

US Council of Economic Advisers, 1992. Economic Report of the President, US Government Printing Office, Washington, DC.

US Interindustry Economics Division, 1974. The input–output structure of the US economy, 1967. Survey of Current Business 54, 24–56.

US Interindustry Economics Division, 1984. The input–output structure of the US economy, 1977. Survey of Current Business 64, 42–84.

van Meijl, H., 1995. Endogenous technological change: the influence of information technology, theoretical considerations and empirical results. Ph.D. Thesis, Maastricht.

Verspagen, B., 1997. Measuring intersectoral technology spillovers: estimates from the European and US patent office databases. Economic Systems Research 9 (1), 47–66.

Verspagen, B., Los, B., 2000. R&D spillovers and productivity: evidence from US manufacturing microdata. Empirical Economics 25 (1), 127–148.

Wolff, E.N., Nadiri, M.I., 1993. Spillover effects, linkage structure, and research and development. Structural Change and Economic Dynamics 4, 315–331.

Wolff, E.N., 1997. Spillovers, linkages, and technical change. Economic Systems Research 9 (1), 9–23.

Economic Systems Research, Vol. 9, No. 1, 1997 9

Spillovers, Linkages and Technical Change

EDWARD N. WOLFF

(Received January 1996; accepted June 1996)

ABSTRACT *Using US input–output data for the period 1958–87, I find strong evidence that industry total factor productivity (TFP) growth is significantly related to the TFP performance of the supplying sectors, with an elasticity of almost 60%. R&D intensity is also found to be a significant determinant of industry TFP growth, with an estimated return of about 10–13% and the return to embodied R&D is estimated at 43%. Direct productivity spillovers, from the technological progress made by supplying sectors, appear to be more important than spillovers from the R&D performed by suppliers. They also play a key role in explaining changes in manufacturing TFP growth over time. Changes in the contribution made by direct productivity spillovers to TFP growth account for almost half of the slowdown in TFP growth in manufacturing from 1958–67 to 1967–77, and for 20% of the TFP growth recovery in this sector from 1967–77 to 1977–87. Changes in R&D intensity and embodied R&D are relatively unimportant in explaining movements in manufacturing TFP growth over these three periods.*

KEYWORDS: *Embodied R&D, embodied total factor productivity growth, productivity, linkages, USA*

1. Introduction

In previous work (Wolff & Nadiri, 1993), we used US input–output (IO) data for the period 1947–77 to analyze the relationship between R&D, technical change and intersectoral linkages. Our most novel finding was that, among manufacturing industries, an industry's rate of technological progress is positively and significantly related to that of its supplying sectors. As in most previous studies, we also found a statistically significant relationship between the R&D intensity of a sector and its rate of productivity growth. The results also showed the presence of spillover effects of R&D embodied in intermediate inputs within manufacturing. The results were statistically significant for private R&D embodied in intermediate inputs, but not for total embodied R&D.

Edward N. Wolff, Department of Economics, 269 Mercer Street, New York University, New York, NY 10003, USA. E-mail: ewolff@fasecon.econ.nyu.edu. I would like to thank Pierre Mohnen and an anonymous referee for their valuable suggestions. I would also like to express my gratitude to the Alfred P. Sloan Foundation and the C.V. Starr Center for Applied Economics, for their financial support.

0953-5314/97/010009-15

Table 1. TFP growth by major sector, 1958–87[a]

	TFP growth (per cent per year)			
	1958–67	1967–77	1977–87	1958–87
Agriculture	0.70	1.48	1.20	1.14
Mining	0.18	−1.02	−0.18	−0.36
Construction	0.76	−1.53	0.18	−0.23
Manufacturing	1.05	0.10	0.80	0.64
Transportation	2.18	1.77	−0.44	1.13
Communication	0.69	1.51	−1.47	0.22
Utilities	1.10	−3.33	1.59	−0.26
Wholesale and retail trade	0.91	1.07	1.12	1.04
Finance, insurance and real estate	0.58	2.00	−1.22	0.45
Other services	−0.89	0.52	−1.16	−0.50
Total[b]	0.68	0.35	0.11	0.37

[a]Calculations are based on US IO data. See equation (1) for the definition of TFP growth.
[b]Total TFP growth is defined as a weighted average of sectoral rates of TFP growth, where current dollar gross domestic output (GDO) by sector is used as the weight.

This paper follows up our previous work on the subject. The data analysis is now extended to 1987 (but it begins in 1958, instead of 1947), and the number of manufacturing industries is expanded from 19 to 48. This study will also focus particular attention on the resurgence of productivity growth in manufacturing during the 1980s. This is documented in Table 1, where the periodization is chosen to conform to the years for which IO tables are available. In manufacturing, total factor productivity (TFP) growth—defined as the price-weighted sum of changes in IO coefficients—fell from 1.1% per year in 1958–67 to 0.10% in 1967–77, but then strongly rebounded to 0.80% per year in the period 1977–87. Utilities represented the only other major sector that showed a similar pattern in TFP growth over the three periods.

Was the recovery of productivity growth in manufacturing a consequence of greater spillovers among sectors? Were there changes in linkage structure that contributed to greater spillovers? Were there greater spillovers between manufacturing and non-manufacturing sectors? These are some of the issues to be investigated in this paper. I also look further at the spillovers of R&D and technical change that occur among industries in the economy.

The remainder of the paper is organized into five parts. Section 2 provides a brief review of some of the pertinent literature on interindustry spillover effects. Section 3 develops the basic accounting framework. Section 4 provides the regression results on the spillover effects of R&D and sectoral technical change. Section 5 analyzes the factors responsible for the recovery of TFP growth in manufacturing in the period 1977–87. Concluding remarks are presented in the final section.

2. Review of Previous Literature

R&D spillovers refer to the direct knowledge gains of customers from the R&D of the supplying industry (see Griliches, 1979).[1] There have been several approaches to measuring R&D spillovers. Brown and Conrad (1967) base their measure of borrowed R&D on IO trade flows (purchases and sales) between industries.

Terleckyj (1974, 1980) provides measures of the amount of R&D embodied in customer inputs on the basis of interindustry material and capital purchases made by one industry from supplying industries. Scherer (1982), relying on Federal Trade Commission line of business data, uses product (as distinct from process) R&D, aimed at improving output quality, as a measure of R&D spillovers.

Another approach is to measure the 'technological closeness' between industries. For example, if two industries use similar processes (even though their products are very different, or they are not directly connected by interindustry flows), then one industry may benefit from new discoveries by the other industry. Such an approach is found in Jaffe (1986), where patent data are used to measure technological closeness between industries.

Bernstein and Nadiri (1989) use total R&D at the two-digit Standard Industrial Classification (SIC) level as a measure of intra-industry R&D spillovers and apply this measure to individual firm data within the industry. Mairesse and Mohnen (1990) report similar results, by comparing R&D coefficients based on firm R&D with those based on industry R&D. If there exist intra-industry externality effects of firm R&D, then the coefficients of industry R&D should be higher than those of firm R&D. However, the results of Mairesse and Mohnen do not show that this is consistently the case.

There have been a host of studies which have followed one of these approaches for estimating the spillover effects of R&D (see Mohnen (1990, 1992), Nadiri (1991) and Griliches (1992) for reviews of the literature). In contrast, the literature on direct productivity spillovers is more sparse. Some of the earlier literature on the subject is quite suggestive. For the German economy, Oppenlander and Schulz (1981) calculate that only about one-third of new products are derived from new technology (i.e. process innovation). The remainder are 'market innovations', which are used to open up new markets for the products. Pavitt (1984) estimates that, out of 2000 innovations introduced in the UK, only about 40% were developed in the sector using the innovation. The remaining innovations were borrowed from new technologies developed in other sectors.

The work of Nelson and Winters (1982) illustrates another approach. In their evolutionary model, spillovers in technology among firms may occur as firms search or sample from their environment to develop new production techniques. Moreover, Rosenberg (1982) and Rosenberg and Frischtak (1984) suggest the existence of clusters of innovations in industries that occupy a strategic position in the economy in terms of both forward and backward linkages. They speculate that there are certain intra-industry flows of new equipment and materials that have generated a vastly disproportionate level of technological change and productivity growth in the economy.

A paper by Bartelsman *et al.* (1991) is also highly suggestive. Using regression analysis, they relate the growth in an industry's output to a weighted average of the growth in the total outputs of the supplying industries, where the weights are proportional to the industry's inputs coefficients. They conclude that the linkage between an industry and its suppliers appears to be the dominant factor in accounting for long-term growth-oriented externalities. However, they do not directly relate an industry's own productivity growth to the R&D of its suppliers, or to its suppliers' rate of productivity growth.

Wolff and Nadiri (1993) provide one of the first direct investigations of productivity spillovers. As their measure of embodied technical change, they use a weighted average of the TFP growth of the supplying industries, where the weights are given by the technical IO coefficients of an industry. This formulation assumes that the knowledge gained from a supplying industry is in direct proportion to the importance of that industry in a sector's input structure. I intend to follow this approach in this paper.

3. Accounting Framework and Model

My model is based on an IO accounting framework. Let us define the following:

$\mathbf{X}_t$ = (column) vector of gross output by sector at time t.
$\mathbf{Y}_t$ = (column) vector of final demand by sector at time t.
$\mathbf{A}_t$ = square matrix of interindustry technical coefficients a_{ij} at time t.
$\mathbf{L}_t$ = (row) vector of labor coefficients ℓ_{it} at time t, showing employment per unit of output.
$\mathbf{K}_t$ = (row) vector of capital stock coefficients k_{ij} at time t, showing the capital of each type required per unit of output.
$\mathbf{P}_t$ = (row) vector of prices at time t, showing the price per unit of output of each industry.

Unless otherwise indicated, all variables are in real terms. In addition, let us define the following scalars:

w_t = the annual wage rate.
i_t = the rate of profit on the capital stock at time t.

Following Leontief (1953), I define the rate of TFP growth for sector j in period T, i.e. TFPGRT_{jT} or π_{jT}, by

$$\text{TFPGRT}_{jT} \equiv \pi_{jT} = -\left(\sum_i \bar{p}_{iT}\Delta a_{ijT} + \bar{w}_T \Delta \ell_{jT} + \bar{i}_T \Delta k_{jT}\right)/p_{jt0} \quad (1)$$

where Δ refers to the change-over period T, $\bar{p}_{iT}$ is the average price over period T, $\bar{w}_T$ is the average wage over period T, $\bar{i}_T$ is the average rate of profit over period T, and p_{jt0} is sector j's price at the beginning of the period (t_0).

R&D intensity is introduced into the model as follows. Let

$$\text{RDGDP}_{jt} \equiv r_{jt} = \text{RD}_{jt}/\text{GDP}_{jt} \quad (2)$$

which shows the amount of R&D expenditure (RD) in constant US dollars per constant dollar of GDP in sector j.

Forward spillovers from R&D are estimated on the basis of trade flows between sectors. I use two different formulations of R&D spillovers. The first assumes that the amount of information gained from supplier i's R&D is proportional to its importance in sector j's input structure (i.e. the magnitude of a_{ij}) and to sector i's R&D intensity:

$$\text{RDIND}_{jt} \equiv \sum_i a^0_{ijt}\text{RD}_{it}/\text{GDP}_{jt} \quad (3)$$

where $\mathbf{A}^0$ is identical to the matrix $\mathbf{A}$, except that the diagonal is set to zero to prevent double-counting of R&D expenditure. For period T, the average values of a^0_{ij} and r_j over the period are used.

The second approach assumes that the amount of R&D that spills over from sector i to sector j is proportional to the amount of output that sector i sells to sector j. This approach is used by Terleckyj (1974, 1980). Define the sales coefficient b_{ijt} as

$$b^0_{ijt} \equiv a^0_{ijt}x_{jt}/x_{it} \quad (4)$$

which shows the percentage of sector *i*'s output that is sold to sector *j*. Then, the alternative measure of indirect R&D (RDINDA) is given by[2]

$$\mathrm{RDINDA}_{jt} = \sum_i b^0_{ijt}\mathrm{RD}_{it}/\mathrm{GDP}_{jt} \tag{5}$$

A similar approach is used by Scherer (1982), except that his measure of indirect R&D is distributed proportionally to the number of patents issued by sector *i* which fall in sector *j*'s industrial classification.[3]

It is also possible to construct estimates of direct productivity spillovers in an analogous fashion to the approach for R&D spillovers. This is given by

$$\mathrm{TFPIND}_{jt} \equiv \sum_i a^0_{ijt}\pi_{it} \tag{6a}$$

which is a measure of sector *j*'s indirect knowledge gain from technological change in its supplying sectors. In this case, it is assumed that the information gained from supplier *i*'s TFP is proportional to its importance in sector *j*'s input structure. An alternative measure is given by

$$\mathrm{TFPINDA}_{jt} = \sum_i b^0_{ijt}\pi_{it} \tag{6b}$$

where it is assumed that the knowledge gain in sector *j* from sector *i*'s TFP growth is proportional to the percentage of sector *i*'s output that is sold to sector *j*.

4. Data Sources and Regression Results

The basic data are 85-sector US IO tables for the years 1958, 1967, 1977 and 1987.[4] Labor coefficients for 1958 were obtained from Peter Petri of the Brandeis Economic Research Center; those for 1967 were calculated from US Bureau of Labor Statistics (1979); and those for 1977 were directly available in Yuskavage (1985). Sectoral employment for 1987 was estimated by first calculating the growth rates of employment by IO industry on the basis of the Bureau of Labor Statistics *Historical Output and Employment Data Series* (obtained on computer diskette) and then applying these growth rates to the 1977 IO sectoral employment totals to update to 1987.[5]

Capital stock by IO industry for 1967 and 1977 was calculated directly from the net stocks of plant and equipment by IO industry provided on computer tape by the US Bureau of Industry Economics (1983). These series ran through 1981 for manufacturing industries and through 1980 for the other sectors. They were updated to 1987 on the basis of the growth rate of constant dollar net stock of fixed capital between 1980 (or 1981) and 1987, calculated from the National Income and Product Accounts (NIPA).[6]

Sectoral price indices for the years 1958 and 1967 were provided by the Brandeis Economic Research Center, and those for 1977 were obtained from the Bureau of Economic Analysis worksheets. Deflators for 1987 were calculated from the Bureau of Labor Statistics *Historical Output Data Series* (obtained on computer diskette) on the basis of the current and constant dollar series.[7]

Five sectors—R&D, business travel, office supplies, scrap and used goods, and inventory valuation adjustment—appeared in some years but not in others (the earlier years for the first three sectors, and the later years for the last two sectors). To make the accounting framework consistent over the 4 years of analysis, I eliminated these sectors from both gross and final output. This was accomplished by distributing the inputs used by these sectors proportional to the endogenous sectors which purchased the output of these five sectors, or to final output.[8]

Table 2. Regressions of R&D intensity, embodied R&D and embodied TFP growth on sectoral TFP growth (TFPGRT)[a]

Independent variable	Specification (1)	(2)	(3)	(4)	(5)
Constant	0.004*	0.002	− 0.001	0.002	0.004
	(1.84)	(0.62)	(0.37)	(0.67)	(1.62)
RDGDP	0.126***	0.101**	0.112***	0.102**	0.124***
	(3.32)	(2.50)	(3.00)	(2.51)	(3.28)
RDIND		0.429*			
		(1.76)			
TFPIND			1.300***		
			(2.80)		
RDINDA				0.408*	
				(1.66)	
TFPINDA					0.146
					(0.91)
DUM6777	− 0.003	− 0.003	0.002	− 0.003	− 0.003
	(1.10)	(0.89)	(0.48)	(0.91)	(0.99)
DUM7787	0.000	0.001	0.004	0.001	0.000
	(0.06)	(0.32)	(1.19)	(0.29)	(0.07)
R^2	0.060	0.074	0.096	0.073	0.064
$\bar{R}^2$	0.046	0.056	0.078	0.054	0.045
Standard error σ	0.0168	0.0167	0.0166	0.0168	0.0168
Sample size	204	204	204	204	204

[a]Estimated coefficients are shown next to the respective independent variables and the absolute value of the *t*-statistic is shown in parentheses. The White procedure for a heteroscedasticity-consistent covariance matrix is used in the estimation.

*Significant at the 0.10 level (two-tailed test); **significant at the 0.05 level (two-tailed test); ***significant at the 0.01 level (two-tailed test).

Data on the ratio of R&D expenditures to GDP were obtained from the National Science Foundation's *Research and Development in Industry* for 32 manufacturing industries, covering the period of 1958–87. I was able to allocate these figures to 48 manufacturing industries in the IO data.[9] All told, productivity growth estimates could be made for 68 IO industries.[10]

4.1. Regression Results

I use two specifications to estimate the direct return to R&D, as well as the spillover effects of R&D and technological change. These are

$$\text{TFPGRT}_{jT} = b_0 + b_1\,\text{RDGDP}_{jT} + b_2\,\text{RDIND}_{jT} + \sum_k c_k D_{kT} + \varepsilon_{jT} \qquad (7a)$$

$$\text{TFPGRT}_{jT} = b_0 + b_1\,\text{RDGDP}_{jT} + b_2\,\text{TFPIND}_{jT} + \sum_k c_k D_{kT} + \varepsilon_{jT} \qquad (7b)$$

where b_0, b_1, b_2, b_3 and c_k are coefficients, and ε_{jT} is stochiastic error term. In both cases, the sample is a pooled cross-section time-series data set that consists of 68 industries and three time periods (1958–67, 1967–77 and 1977–87). From Mansfield (1980) and Griliches (1980), the coefficient b_1 is interpreted as the rate

Table 3. Mean values (in percentage points) of TFP growth, R&D intensity, embodied R&D and embodied TFP growth by period for manufacturing and non-manufacturing sectors

	1958–67	1967–77	1977–87
(A) TFPGRT: annual rate of TFP growth			
Manufacturing	1.05	0.10	0.80
Non-manufacturing	0.52	0.60	−0.25
Total[a]	0.68	0.35	0.11
(B) RDGDP: R&D as a per cent of GDP by industry			
Manufacturing	2.67	2.41	2.87
Non-manufacturing	0.00	0.00	0.00
Total	1.09	0.97	1.05
(C) RDIND: R&D embodied in inputs			
Manfacturing	0.64	0.53	0.54
Non-manufacturing	0.26	0.21	0.20
Total	0.41	0.34	0.32
(D) TFPIND: TFP growth embodied in inputs			
Manufacturing	0.44	0.10	0.20
Non-manufacturing	0.25	0.11	−0.04
Total	0.33	0.10	0.05

[a]Total TFP growth is defined as a weighted average of sectoral rates of TFP growth, where current dollar gross domestic output (GDO) by sector is used as the weight.

of return of R&D, under the assumption that the (average) rate of return to R&D s equalized across sectors. Time dummies D_{kT} (for the periods 1967–77 and 1977–87) are introduced to allow for period-specific effects on productivity growth that are not attributable to R&D. We assume that the ε_{jt} terms are independently distributed but may not be identically distributed. The regression results reported n Tables 3 and 4 use the White procedure for a heteroscedasticity-consistent covariance matrix.[11]

Table 4. Decomposition of the change (in percentage points) in embodied R&D and embodied TFP growth into a supply and linkage effect

	1967–77/1958–67			1977–87/1967–77		
	Total	Supply	Linkage	Total	Supply	Linkage
(A) Δ(RDIND): R&D embodied in inputs[a]						
Manufacturing	−0.11	−0.01	−0.10	0.01	0.05	−0.04
Non-manufacturing	−0.05	−0.03	−0.02	−0.02	−0.01	−0.01
Total	−0.07	0.05	−0.13	−0.02	−0.01	−0.01
(B) Δ(TFPIND): TFP growth embodied in inputs[b]						
Manufacturing	−0.34	−0.33	−0.01	0.11	0.09	0.02
Non-manufacturing	−0.14	−0.12	−0.02	−0.15	−0.13	−0.02
Total	−0.22	−0.20	−0.02	−0.06	−0.04	−0.01

[a]From equation (8), we have
$\Delta(\mathrm{RDIND}_j) = \Sigma_i\, \bar{a}_{ij}^0\, \Delta r_i$ [supply effect] + $\Sigma_i\, \Delta a_{ij}^0\, \bar{r}_i$ [linkage effect].
[b]From equation (9), we have
$\Delta(\mathrm{TFPIND}_j) = \Sigma_i\, \bar{a}_{ij}^0\, \Delta \pi_i$ [supply effect] + $\Sigma_i\, \Delta a_{ij}^0\, \bar{\pi}_i$ [linkage effect].

However, because of data limitations, a contemporaneous IO framework is used to analyze the relations between R&D, technical change and intersectoral linkages—it should be stressed that these three relations are necessarily dynamic and may occur with considerable lags. Moreover, the use of synchronic time periods—in this case, 1958–67, 1967–77 and 1977–87—allows us to capture long-term effects of R&D on productivity.

Regression results on R&D and technology spillovers are shown in Table 2. R&D intensity is significantly related to sectoral TFP growth at the 1% significance level in three out of the five specifications, and at the 5% level in the other two specifications. The estimated direct return to R&D ranges from 10.1% to 12.6%. These estimates are slightly low compared with previous work on the subject (see Nadiri (1991) or Mohnen (1992), for example, for a review of previous estimates). There are two possible reasons. First, my TFP growth figures are based on gross output and three inputs, i.e. intermediate inputs, labor and capital, instead of value added and two inputs—labor and capital—so that my estimates of sectoral TFP growth are about one-half of those based on value added.[12] Second, because of data limitations, I do not net out the inputs used in the R&D activity of each industry to avoid double-counting, as suggested by Schankerman (1981). This will cause a downward bias in the estimated return to R&D.

When RDIND is included with RDGDP in the equation, the return to embodied R&D is estimated to be 43% (specification (2)). This estimate is about average compared with previous work on the subject (Nadiri, 1991; Mohnen, 1992). The coefficient estimate is significant at the 10% level. By adding together the coefficients of RDGDP and RDIND, we obtain estimates of the total or social rate of return to R&D of 53%.

When TFPIND is included with RDGDP in the estimating equation (specification (3)), the spillover effects of technical change are found to be very strong. The coefficient of TFPIND has a value of 1.3 and is significant at the 1% level. To interpret the coefficient value, note from equation (6) that TFPIND is a weighted average of the TFP growth of supplying sectors, with the value of intermediate inputs as weights, multiplied by the ratio of the total value of intermediate inputs to total output. This ratio averages 0.433 over the four sample years. As a result, an increase of one percentage point in the TFP growth of supplying sectors would be associated with a 0.57 (0.433×1.30) percentage point increase in the sector's own TFP growth.

Specifications (4) and (5) show related results when the alternative forms, i.e. RDINDA and TFPINDA, are used. The results for RDINDA are very similar to those for RDIND. However, TFPINDA has much lower coefficient values than those for TFPIND and the variable is not statistically significant. The results rather forcefully suggest that the strength of direct spillovers of productivity, such as from the computer industry to the insurance industry, depends on the relative importance of computers in the technology of the insurance industry, rather than on the share of computers sold by the computer industry to the insurance sector.

The time dummy variables (DUM6777 and DUM7787) are not significant, despite the apparent slowdown in productivity growth between 1958–67 and 1967–77. The R^2 statistic ranges from 0.06 to 0.10, which is typical for this type of cross-industry regression. Specification (3), which includes TFPIND, has the best fit, as measured by the standard error of the regression and the adjusted R^2 statistic.

5. Sources of Productivity Recovery in Manufacturing in 1977–87

Here, we investigate sources of the resurgence of TFP growth in manufacturing in the period 1977–87. On the basis of the framework used in this analysis, there may have been three contributing factors to the recovery. First, the R&D intensity (RDGDP) may have increased during 1977–87. Second, the R&D embodied in inputs (RDIND) may have risen in this period, either because the R&D intensity of the supplying industries rose or because industries purchased a higher share of their inputs from R&D-intensive industries. Third, technical change embodied in inputs (TFPIND) may have risen in the period 1977–87, either because the TFP growth rate of the supplying industries rose or because industries purchased a higher share of their inputs from industries with higher rates of productivity growth.

Table 3 shows the mean values of each of the key variables for the periods 1958–67, 1967–77 and 1977–87. The evidence does indicate a recovery of R&D intensity in manufacturing in the third period. The average R&D intensity declined from 2.7% in 1958–67 to 2.4% in 1967–77, and then rebounded to 2.9% in 1977–87. However, there was no recovery in embodied R&D in the third period. The average R&D embodied in manufacturing inputs (RDIND) fell from 0.64% in the first period to 0.53% in the second, and remained at almost the same level in the third period. The pattern was similar for RDIND in non-manufacturing, but it was different for TFP embodied in inputs. The average TFPIND in manufacturing fell precipitously from 0.44% in 1958–67 to 0.10% in 1967–77, and then rose to 0.20% in 1977–87, which was still less than half of its 1958–67 level. For non-manufacturing, TFPIND fell from 0.25% in the first period to 0.11% in the second period, and then declined further to −0.04% in the third period.

Further analysis allows us to decompose changes in embodied R&D into two effects: changes in the R&D intensity of supplying sectors (supply effect), and a change in the interindustry coefficient matrix (linkage effect). From equation (3), the change in RDIND between periods T_0 and T_1 is given by

$$\Delta(\text{RDIND}_j) \equiv \text{RDIND}_{jT1} - \text{RDIND}_{jT0} = \sum_i \bar{a}_{ij}^0 \Delta r_i + \sum_i \Delta a_{ij}^0 \bar{r}_i \qquad (8)$$

where $\bar{a}_{ij}^0$ is the average value of coefficient a_{ij} in periods T_0 and T_1; $\bar{r}_i$ is the average value of R&D intensity in periods T_0 and T_1; Δr_i is the change in R&D intensity between periods T_0 and T_1; and Δa_{ij}^0 is the change in coefficient a_{ij} between periods T_0 and T_1. Likewise, we have

$$\Delta(\text{TFPIND}_j) \equiv \text{TFPIND}_{jT1} - \text{TFPIND}_{jT0} = \sum_i \bar{a}_{ij}^0 \Delta \pi_i + \sum_i \Delta a_{ij}^0 \bar{\pi}_i \qquad (9)$$

Results of the decomposition are shown in Table 4. Between 1958–67 and 1967–77, almost all the reduction in R&D embodied in inputs used by the manufacturing industries (RDIND) results from a shift in their input structure away from R&D-intensive industries and towards industries which spent less on R&D. The linkage effect alone accounts for a reduction by 10 percentage points in RDIND out of a total reduction of 11 points. In the non-manufacturing sectors, the reduction in RDIND of five percentage points comes about equally from a reduction in the R&D intensity of their supplying industries and a shift in inputs towards less R&D-intensive industries.

Between 1967–77 and 1977–87, manufacturing industries continued to shift their input structure away from R&D-intensive industries. However, the R&D intensity of their supplying industries also increased between the two periods. The supply effect essentially cancels out the linkage effect, resulting in almost no net change in RDIND within manufacturing. In non-manufacturing, the input structure again shows a modest shift away from the more R&D-intensive sectors, and the R&D intensity of their supplying sectors also declines slightly, resulting in a modest overall decrease in RDIND between these two periods.

In contrast, almost all the change in embodied technical change (TFPIND) is explained by changes in the TFP growth of supplying sectors. The sharp decline in TFPIND in manufacturing industries, i.e. 0.33 percentage points, between 1958–67 and 1967–77 is almost entirely the result of the slowdown in productivity growth of their supplying industries. The same is true for the non-manufacturing sector over this period. Likewise, the increase in TFPIND over the periods 1967–77 and 1977–87 is almost completely the result of the recovery in TFP growth of the input industries. The continued decline in TFPIND in non-manufacturing is again largely the result of a continued decline in TFP growth of the industries that sell to non-manufacturing sectors.

The final part of the analysis presents a decomposition of the change in TFP growth between periods into components. The first three columns of Table 5 show the contribution of each variable—defined as the coefficient value multiplied by the average value of the variable—to TFP growth by period. Tabulations are made separately for specification (2) (which includes RDIND) and specification (3) (which includes TFPIND), and for manufacturing and non-manfacturing. On the basis of specification (2), R&D intensity (RDGDP) and embodied R&D (RDIND) make about equal contributions to manufacturing TFP growth in 1958–67, i.e. 0.27 percentage points. The residual (the unexplained portion) is 0.34 percentage points.

Between 1958–67 and 1967–77, the contribution of RDGDP declines slightly, i.e. from 0.27 to 0.24 percentage points, as does that of RDIND, i.e. from 0.27 to 0.23 percentage points. The fourth column shows the sources of the productivity slowdown between these two periods, computed as the difference in the contributions of each component in 1967–77 and 1958–67. The modest decreases in RDGDP and RDIND account for 3% (−0.03/−0.94) and 5% (−0.05/−0.94), respectively, of the slowdown in TFP growth between these two periods. With this specification, over 90% of the productivity slowdown is not explained by these variables.

Between 1967–77 and 1977–87, the contribution of RDGDP shows a modest increase from 0.24 to 0.29 percentage points, while that of embodied R&D shows no change. Of the rather substantial upsurge in TFP growth in manufacturing of 0.70 percentage points per year between these two periods, the gain in RDGDP accounts for 7%. However, over 90% of the change in TFP growth again remains unexplained (i.e. is accounted for by the change in the contributions of the time dummies and the residual).

In the non-manufacturing sector, the contribution of embodied R&D (RDIND) to TFP growth declines over time, changing from 0.11 percentage points in 1958–67 to 0.09 percentage points in 1967–77, and then to 0.08 percentage points in 1977–87. The decline in the contribution of RDIND between the periods 1967–77 and 1977–87 explains only 1% of the drop of 0.85 percentage points in TFP growth. Moreover, while the contribution of RDIND also falls between the periods 1958–67 and 1967–77, TFP growth actually increases slightly. Most of the change in TFP growth in non-manufacturing is again picked up by the time dummies and the residual.

Table 5. Decomposition of the change in TFP growth between periods into effects from the change in R&D intensity, embodied R&D and embodied TFP growth

	Contribution of each factor to TFP growth by period[a] (per cent per year)			Decomposition of the change in TFP growth between periods[b] (per cent per year)	
	1958–67	1967–77	1977–87	1967–77/1958–67	1977–87/1967–77
(I) Specification (2) (including RDIND)					
(A) Manufacturing					
Constant	0.16	0.16	0.16	0.00	0.00
RDGDP	0.27	0.24	0.29	− 0.03	0.05
RDIND	0.27	0.23	0.23	− 0.05	0.00
Time dummies	0.00	− 0.26	0.09	− 0.26	0.35
Residual	0.34	− 0.27	0.03	− 0.61	0.30
TFPGRT[c]	1.05	0.10	0.80	− 0.94	0.70
(B) Non-manufacturing					
Constant	0.16	0.16	0.16	0.00	0.00
RDGDP	0.00	0.00	0.00	0.00	0.00
RDIND	0.11	0.09	0.08	− 0.02	− 0.01
Time dummies	0.00	− 0.26	0.09	− 0.26	0.35
Residual	0.25	0.60	− 0.59	0.36	− 1.19
TFPGRT[c]	0.52	0.60	− 0.25	0.08	− 0.85
(II) Specification (3) (including TFPIND)					
(A) Manufacturing					
Constant	− 0.11	− 0.11	− 0.11	0.00	0.00
RDGDP	0.30	0.27	0.32	− 0.03	0.05
TFPIND	0.57	0.13	0.26	− 0.44	0.14
Time dummies	0.00	0.16	0.37	0.16	0.21
Residual	0.29	− 0.35	− 0.05	− 0.64	0.30
TFPGRT[c]	1.05	0.10	0.80	− 0.94	0.70
(B) Non-Manufacturing					
Constant	− 0.11	− 0.11	− 0.11	0.00	0.00
RDGDP	0.00	0.00	0.00	0.00	0.00
TFPIND	0.33	0.14	− 0.06	− 0.19	− 0.19
Time dummies	0.00	0.16	0.37	0.16	0.21
Residual	0.30	0.41	− 0.46	0.11	− 0.86
TFPGRT[c]	0.52	0.60	− 0.25	0.08	− 0.85

[a]Defined as the coefficient value multiplied by the average value of the variable by period. Coefficients are from specification (2) or (3) in Table 2. Key: TFPGRT, annual rate of TFP growth; RDGDP, R&D intensity; RDIND, R&D embodied in inputs; TFPIND, TFP growth embodied in inputs.

[b]Defined as the difference between the coefficient value multiplied by the average value of the second period and that of the first period.

[c]TFPGRT is equal to the sum of components.

Results from specification (3) are much more telling. In 1958–67, embodied technical change (TFPIND) alone accounts for over one-half of manufacturing TFP growth (0.57 out of 1.05 percentage points per year). Between 1958–67 and 1967–77, the contribution of TFPIND falls from 0.57 to 0.14 percentage points. The decline in TFPIND by itself accounts for 47% (− 0.44/ − 0.94) of the slowdown in TFP growth between these two periods. As with specification (2), the modest reduction in RDGDP explains another 3% of the slowdown in TFP growth, leaving about one-half not explained by these two variables.

Between 1967–77 and 1977–87, the contribution of embodied TFP growth shows a marked gain from 0.13 to 0.26 percentage points. Of the increase in TFP growth in manufacturing of 0.70 percentage points between these two periods, the gain in TFPIND accounts for 20% (0.14/0.70) and that of RDGDP for 7%. However, most of the productivity recovery again remains unexplained.

In the non-manufacturing sector, embodied TFP growth (TFPIND) has a marked effect on TFP growth in 1958–67, i.e. 0.33 percentage points, but its contribution falls off to 0.14 percentage points in 1967–77 and to − 0.06 percentage points in 1977–87. The decline in the contribution of TFPIND between the periods 1967–77 and 1977–87 amounts to 0.19 percentage points, which accounts for 22% of the fall of 0.85 percentage points in annual TFP growth in this sector. However, while the contribution of TFPIND also falls by 0.19 percentage points between the first two periods, TFP growth increases by 0.08 percentage points.

6. Conclusions

I find strong evidence that industry TFP growth is significantly related to the TFP performance of supplying sectors, with an elasticity of almost 60%. The relation now holds for all sectors of the economy, instead of manufacturing alone, as was found by Wolff and Nadiri (1993). The difference in results probably results from the inclusion here of the period 1977–87 in the regression analysis (and the exclusion of data for 1947–58). In fact, in the earlier paper (Wolff & Nadiri, 1993), we had speculated that intersectoral technology spillovers might be heightened during the 1980s, because of the paradigmatic shift from electromechanical automation to information technologies, and the widespread use of computers in non-manufacturing sectors. These new results appear to confirm that speculation.

R&D intensity is also found to be a highly significant determinant of sector TFP growth. The estimated return to R&D is 10–13%. The return to embodied R&D is estimated to be 43%.

In an analysis of the sources of the change in TFP growth in manufacturing between 1958 and 1987, changes in direct productivity spillovers appear to play a key role. Between 1958–67 and 1967–77, TFP growth in manufacturing falls by 0.91 percentage points per year. The contribution of productivity spillovers declines from 0.57 to 0.13 percentage points between these two periods, so accounting for 47% of the productivity slowdown. Between 1967–77 and 1977–87, TFP growth in manufacturing increases by 0.70 percentage points per year. The contribution of embodied TFP growth also shows a marked gain, i.e. from 0.13 to 0.26 percentage points, explaining 20% of the productivity recovery in this sector. Changes in R&D intensity and embodied R&D are relatively unimportant in explaining movements in manufacturing TFP growth over these three periods.

It is also found that the decline in productivity spillovers in manufacturing between 1958–67 and 1967–77 comes almost entirely from the slowdown in the TFP growth of supplying sectors; changes in linkage structure play almost no role. Similarly, the increase in productivity spillovers between 1967–77 and 1977–87 results almost completely from the recovery in TFP growth of the supplying industries.

In contrast, between 1958–67 and 1967–77, the reduction in embodied R&D in manufacturing results almost exclusively from a shift in its input structure away from the more R&D-intensive industries and towards the less R&D-intensive industries. Between 1967–77 and 1977–87, manufacturing industries continued to shift their input structure away from R&D-intensive industries. However, the R&D intensity of their supplying industries also increased, resulting in almost no net change in embodied R&D. The shift in manufacturing inputs away from R&D-intensive industries may seem surprising, in light of the growing computerization within manufacturing. However, it primarily reflects the increasing relative share of services in the manufacturing input structure and the declining share of inputs from other manufacturing industries.

These results point towards the importance of direct productivity spillovers among closely connected industries. Such agglomeration effects have been discussed by others (see, for example, Rosenberg, 1982), but this paper supplies strong additional evidence of technological change in one sector affecting TFP growth in purchasing sectors. The new results presented here strongly suggest that, within manufacturing at least, a decline in TFP growth in one industry can pull down the technological growth of associated industries, leading to a cascading effect of technological change between supplying industries and their users. Similarly, the recovery of TFP growth in one industry can pull up that of its customers. This result also provides support to the notion of knowledge spillovers among industries that has been resurrected in the new growth theory.

Notes

1. Griliches also identifies a second interpretation of spillovers; namely, that inputs purchased from an R&D-performing industry may embody quality improvements that are not fully appropriated by the supplier. It should be emphasized at the outset that, while these two notions of spillovers are quite distinct, they cannot be distinguished statistically in this work.
2. Matrix $\mathbf{A}^0$ is used again to avoid double-counting of industry *j*'s own R&D.
3. Wolff and Nadiri (1993) also introduced another measure of borrowed R&D, which is the amount of R&D embodied in new investment. This variable was estimated on the basis of capital flow data by industry. Unfortunately, a capital flow matrix is not yet available for 1987 to allow a similar computation.
4. Details on the construction of the IO tables can be found in the following publications: 1967—US Interindustry Economics Division, 1974; 1977—US Interindustry Economics Division, 1984; 1987—Lawson & Teske, 1994.
5. Data on hours worked by sector, although the preferable measure of labor input to employment, are not available by sector and year, so could not be incorporated.
6. The source is Musgrave (1992). Because there are fewer industries in the NIPA breakdown than in the IO data, I applied the same percentage growth rate across all IO industries that fall within a given NIPA classification. Data on government-owned capital stock for all years were obtained from Musgrave (1992).
7. In addition, the deflator for transferred imports was calculated from the NIPA import deflator; that for the rest-of-the-world industry was calculated as the average of the NIPA import and export deflator; and the deflator for the inventory valuation adjustment was computed from the NIPA change in business inventory deflator. The source is US Council of Economic Advisers (1992, Tables B-1, B-2 and B-3).
8. The allocation of the scrap sector was handled differently in the make–use framework of the 1967, 1977 and 1987 tables. See ten Raa and Wolff (1991) for details.
9. This was calculated in two steps. First, company R&D from the Federal Trade Commission Line of Business Data was averaged over 1974, 1975 and 1976, before being divided by the average of industry GDP over the same three years. Second, using the National Science Foundation data, I computed the average ratio of R&D expenditures to GDP at the 32-industry level for the period 1958–87 and adjusted the first set of R&D-to-GDP ratios accordingly. It should be noted that, although it would be preferable to use the ratio of R&D to industry sales in this analysis, the National Science Foundation provides a consistent time series only on the ratio of R&D to industry GDP. Moreover, the R&D data at this level of detail were not available prior to 1958, which prevented me from also including the period 1947–58 in the regression analysis.
10. The sectoring followed the standard 85-order Bureau of Economic Analysis (BEA) classification scheme, with the following exceptions: agriculture (1–4); metallic ores mining (5–6); non-metallic

minerals mining (9–10); construction (11–12); lumber and wood products (20–21); furniture and fixtures (22–23); footwear, leather and leather products (33–34); farm, construction and mining machinery (44–45).

11. It should be noted that, because $TFPGRT_{jT}$ is a function of $RDGDP_{jT}$, a specification bias would be introduced by including both $RDIND_{jT}$ and $TFPIND_{jT}$ in the same specification (because $TFPIND_{jT}$ is then a function of $RDIND_{jT}$). I thank an anonymous referee for pointing this out.
12. Terleckyj (1980) supports this conjecture. With a two-factor TFP index, the coefficient on direct (private) R&D is 0.27; with a three-factor TFP index, the coefficient is 0.20 (Terleckyj, 1980, Table 6.6, p. 375).

References

Bernstein, J. I. & Nadiri, M. I. (1989) Research and development and intra-industry spillovers: an empirical application of dynamic duality, *Review of Economic Studies*, 56, pp. 249–269.

Brown, M. & Conrad, A. (1967) The influence of research on CES production relations, in: M. Brown (ed.) *The Theory and Empirical Analysis of Production, Studies in Income and Wealth*, Vol. 3 (New York, Columbia University Press for the NBER).

Bartelsman, E. J., Cabbalero, R. J. & Lyons, R. K. (1991) Short and long run externalities, *NBER Working Paper 3810*, August.

Griliches, Z. (1979) Issues in assessing the contribution of research and development to productivity growth, *Bell Journal of Economics*, 10, pp. 92–116.

Griliches, Z. (1980) R&D and the productivity slowdown, *American Economic Review*, 70, pp. 343–348.

Griliches, Z. (1992) The search for R&D spillovers, *Scandinavian Journal of Economics*, 94, pp. 29–47.

Jaffe, A. B. (1986) Technology opportunity and spillovers of R&D: evidence from firms' patents, profits, and market value, *American Economic Review*, 76, pp. 984–1001.

Lawson, A. M. & Teske, D. A. (1994) Benchmark input–output accounts for the US economy, 1987, *Survey of Current Business*, 74, pp. 73–115.

Leontief, W. (1953) *Studies in the Structure of the American Economy, 1919–29* (New York, Oxford University Press).

Mairesse, J. & Mohnen, P. (1990) Recherche-developpment et productivite: un sorvoi de la litterature econometrique, *Economie et Statistique*, 237-238, pp. 99–108.

Mansfield, E. (1980) Basic research and productivity increase in manufacturing, *American Economic Review*, 70, pp. 863–873.

Mohnen, P. (1990) New technology and interindustry spillovers, *Science/Technology/Industry Review*, 7, pp. 131–147.

Mohnen, P. (1992) *The Relationship between R&D and Productivity Growth in Canada and Other Major Industrialized Countries* (Ottawa, Canada Communications Group).

Musgrave, J. C. (1992) Fixed reproducible tangible wealth in the United States, revised estimates, *Survey of Current Business*, 72, pp. 106–137.

Nadiri, M. I. (1991) Innovations and technological spillovers, *mimeo*.

National Science Foundation (Various years) *Research and Development in Industry* (Washington, DC, Government Printing Office).

Nelson, R. R. & Winters, S. G. (1982) *An Evolutionary Theory of Economic Change* (Cambridge, MA, Harvard University Press).

Oppenlander, K. M. & Schulz, L. (1981) Innovation test: a new survey of the IFO institute, paper presented at the *15th CIRET Conference*, Athens.

Pavitt, K. (1984) Sectoral patterns of technical change: towards a taxonomy and theory, *Research Policy*, 13, pp. 343–373.

ten Raa, T. & Wolff, E. N. (1991) Secondary products and the measurement of productivity growth, *Regional Science and Urban Economics*, 21, pp. 581–615.

Rosenburg, M. (1982) *Inside the Black Box: Technology and Economics* (Cambridge, Cambridge University Press).

Rosenburg, M. & Frischtak, C. R. (1984) Technological innovation and long waves, *Cambridge Journal of Economics*, 8, pp. 7–24.

Schankerman, M. (1981) The effects of double-counting and expensing on the measured returns to R&D, *Review of Economics and Statistics*, 63, pp. 454–457.

Scherer, F. M. (1982) Interindustry technology flows and productivity growth, *Review of Economics and Statistics*, 64, pp. 627–634.

Terleckyj, N. W. (1974) *Effects of R&D on the Productivity Growth of Industries: an Exploratory Study* (Washington, DC, National Planning Association).

Terleckyj, N. W. (1980) Direct and indirect effects of industrial research and development on the productivity growth of industries, in: J. W. Kendrick & B. Vaccara (eds) *New Developments in Productivity Measurement* (New York, National Bureau of Economic Research).

US Bureau of Industry Economics (1983) *Capital Stocks Database as of January 31, 1983.*

US Bureau of Labor Statistics (1979) *Time series data for input–output industries, Bulletin 2018.*

US Council of Economic Advisers (1992) *Economic Report of the President* (Washington, DC, US Government Printing Office).

US Interindustry Economics Division (1974) The input–output structure of the US economy: 1967, *Survey of Current Business*, 54, pp. 24–56.

US Interindustry Economics Division (1984) The input–output structure of the US economy, 1977, *Survey of Current Business*, 64, pp. 42–84.

Wolff, E. N. & Nadiri, M. I. (1993) Spillover effects, linkage structure, and research and development, *Structural Change and Economic Dynamics*, 4, pp. 315–331.

Yuskavage, R. E. (1985) Employment and employee compensation in the 1977 input–output accounts, *Survey of Current Business*, 65, pp. 11–25.

PART IV

LABOR AND CAPITAL PRODUCTIVITY

[13]

Labor Quality and Productivity Growth in the United States: An Input–Output Growth-Accounting Framework

EDWARD N. WOLFF and DAVID R. HOWELL

Much recent research has focused on the productivity slowdown that has afflicted most of the industrialized world since the late 1960s (see Maddison, 1982, 1987). In spite of this effort, there has been limited success in developing a comprehensive and convincing explanation for the slowdown (see, for example, Denison, 1979, 1984; Wolff, 1985a, 1985b). The post-1967 period is also characterized by a slowdown in output growth, an intensifying international competition, and rapid changes in production technology—most notably toward the use of programmable automation in both factories and offices. The consequences of these changes for the labor force have been immense, with much higher than normal unemployment rates, a reduction in job security, an increase in part-time work, and changes in the skill requirements of work. This chapter focuses on the last of these—changes in skill requirements—and explores its significance for the productivity slowdown.

The measure and explanation of productivity growth should take into account changes in the quality of inputs over time. In the case of labor, change in quality will reflect the evolution of both the skill content of jobs and the mix of jobs. If changes in skill content and job mix result in an upgrading (downgrading) of skill requirements, effective labor input per hour worked will increase (decrease). Thus, the quality of labor employed (and the way quality is measured) can have, at least potentially, a major effect on the measured rate of productivity growth. In previous productivity studies, labor input has been measured by the use of undifferentiated quantities (hours or employees) of labor. In some recent studies, these quantities have been adjusted using an index of relative earnings. Only under extremely strong assumptions, however, will earnings offer a reliable guide to the quality (skill levels) of employed labor. In the analysis presented in this chapter, we replace relative earnings with alternative measures of job-skill requirements derived from the Dictionary of Occupational Titles (U.S. Department of Labor, 1977).

In prior work (Wolff, 1985b), a standard input–output accounting system was modified in order to analyze the effects of changes in final output composition on overall productivity growth in the economy. A growth-accounting framework was developed whereby changes in overall productivity growth could be decomposed into various sources. In Wolff (1985b), three sources were considered: (1) changes in the rate of technical changes on the sectoral level, (2) changes in the Leontief inverse matrix, and (3) changes in the sectoral composition of final demand. In this chapter, we extend the framework to incorporate changes in the skill composition of the labor force.

This chapter consists of three primary sections. In the first, we develop a growth-accounting framework from a standard input–output system to analyze three sources of overall productivity growth in the U.S. economy: sectoral technical change, changes in the composition of final output, and changes in the skill composition of the labor force.

In the second section, we consider some issues surrounding the measurement of labor skills and describe our approach. At the end of this section, we present results on changes in skill requirements for the U.S. economy and for each of 10 large industry sectors.

In the third section, we present results on the sources of productivity growth in the United States from 1958 to 1977. This analysis is distinguished by the use of alternative measures of both productivity growth (unadjusted for labor quality) and labor input (reflecting various measures of skill requirements). Particular attention is paid to the sources of the productivity slowdown that occurred after 1967.

GROWTH-ACCOUNTING FRAMEWORK

Because we are primarily interested in skill changes and their effect on productivity growth, we develop a growth-accounting framework for labor productivity growth,[1] beginning with a standard input–output accounting framework. Unless otherwise noted, all components are in constant dollar terms. Let

X_t = (column) vector of gross output by sector at time t.
Y_t = (column) vector of final demand by sector at time t.
a_t = matrix of interindustry technical coefficients at time t.
l_t = (row) vector of labor coefficients at time t, showing employment per unit of output.
p_t = (row) vector of prices at time t, showing the price per unit of output of each industry.

In addition, let us define the following scalars:

$$y_t = p_t Y_t = \text{total final output valued at current prices } p.$$
$$L_t = l_t X_t = \text{total employment at time } t.$$

Furthermore, let us also introduce the technical inverse coefficient matrix q as[2]

$$q = (I - a)^{-1} \tag{11-1}$$

and define the total labor requirements vector λ as

1. See Wolff (1985b) for the derivation of an analogous growth-accounting framework for total factor productivity growth.

2. It should be noted that we are treating depreciation as exogenous in this framework. See Wolff (1985b) for the case in which depreciation is treated as endogenous and, more generally, in which capital is treated as a produced means of production.

$\lambda = lq$ = (row) vector, showing the direct plus indirect labor requirements per unit of output.

It follows directly that in the case in which labor is the only factor of production, the vector λ is also the vector of relative prices:

$$p_t = \lambda_t \tag{11-2}$$

We can now define the rate of growth of overall or economy-wide unadjusted labor productivity, ρ, in conventional fashion as

$$\rho \equiv pdY/y - dL/L \tag{11-3}$$

On the sectoral level, we introduce an analogous concept, the rate of unadjusted "total labor productivity" (TLP) growth, defined as

$\pi_j \equiv -d\lambda_j/p_j = -d\lambda_j/\lambda_j$ = rate of unadjusted TLP growth in sector j.

It then follows directly that[3]

$$\rho = \pi\hat{p}Y/y \tag{11-4}$$

We can now introduce a labor-quality index into the framework as follows. Let

m_t = matrix of occupational coefficients by industry, such that $\sum m_{ij} = 1$.

Then, define

σ_t = (row) vector showing the skill score of each occupation i at time t (each skill index will lead to a different vector σ).

Then

$s_t = \sigma_t m_t$ = (row) vector, showing the average skill level of each industry j at time t.

Skill-adjusted labor input can now be defined as

$l^* = (\sigma m)\hat{l} = s\hat{l}$ = (row) vector of quality-adjusted direct labor coefficients by industry, showing direct quality-adjusted employment per unit of output.

3. This can be shown as follows.

$$\begin{aligned}\pi\hat{p}Y/y &= -(d\lambda)Y/y \\ &= -[ldq + (dl)q]Y/y\end{aligned}$$

since, by definition, $\lambda = lq$. Then,

$$\begin{aligned}\pi\hat{p}Y/y &= [-l(dq)Y - (dl)X]/y \\ &= \{-l(dq)Y + ldX - [ldX + (dl)X]\}/y \\ &= [-l(dq)Y + ldX - dL]/y\end{aligned}$$

since $L = lX$. Moreover, since $X = qY$,

$$\begin{aligned}\pi\hat{p}Y/y &= [-l(dq)Y + l(dq)Y + lqdY - dL]/y \\ &= (\lambda dY - dL)/y\end{aligned}$$

But $p_t = \lambda_t$. Hence, $y_t = p_t Y_t = \lambda_t Y_t = L_t$, and

$$\pi\hat{p}Y/y = pdY/y - dL/L$$

This completes the proof.

Total quality-adjusted labor input, L^*, is then given by

$$L^* = l^*X \tag{11-5}$$

We can now derive quality-adjusted rates of labor productivity growth. First, define

$\lambda^* = s\hat{l}q = s\hat{\lambda} =$ (row) vector of total (direct plus indirect) quality-adjusted labor requirements per unit of output.

Then,

$\pi_j^* = -d\lambda^*{}_j/\lambda_j^* =$ rate of quality-adjusted total labor productivity (TLP) growth for each sector j.

But, by definition,

$$\pi_j^* = -d\lambda_j/\lambda_j - ds_j/s_j$$

Define

$\theta_j \equiv ds_j/s_j =$ rate of increase of average skill requirements in sector j.

Then,

$$\pi_j^* = \pi_j - \theta_j \tag{11-6}$$

A growth-accounting framework can now be developed from this approach. Because we are interested in identifying the sources of change in conventionally measured labor productivity growth, we first take the discrete time differential of Equation (11-4). If we ignore second-order terms, then the change in the rate of growth of overall unadjusted labor productivity is given by

$$\Delta\rho \cong \pi(\Delta\beta) + (\Delta\pi)\beta \tag{11-7}$$

where $\beta_j \equiv p_jY_j/y =$ the value share of sector j in total final output. From Equation (11-6), it now follows that

$$\Delta\rho \cong \pi(\Delta\beta) + (\Delta\pi^*)\beta + (\Delta\theta)\beta \tag{11-8}$$

This decomposition allows us to separate the change in overall unadjusted labor productivity growth into three effects, corresponding to the three terms on the right-hand side of Equation (11-8). The first is the final output composition effect, which shows the change in overall productivity growth that would occur if sectoral rates of productivity growth remained unchanged over time but final output shares shifted as they did in actuality. Here, β measures value shares, not real shares, and $\Delta\beta$ reflects, in part, relative price changes. The second is the technical change effect, which shows the change in overall labor productivity that would occur if final output shares remained constant over time but sectoral rates of TLP growth, adjusted for changes in labor quality, changed as they had in actuality. The third is the skill effect, which shows the effect of changes in average skill levels by industry on the change in overall TFP growth, assuming that all other factors remained constant. This last term is of particular interest for the post-1967 period, because it will indicate what portion (if any) of the slowdown in overall labor productivity growth is attributable to changes in the quality of the labor force.

MEASUREMENT OF LABOR QUALITY

Several recent studies (Gollop and Jorgenson, 1980; Chinloy, 1980, 1981) have developed measures of labor input that reflect the relative compensation received by workers. This standard approach is based on the view that, as Gollop and Jorgenson (1980) stated, "A worker's average compensation per hour provides a good approximation to the worker's marginal productivity" (p. 48). In a competitive labor market, earnings differentials among individuals will reflect relative skills, effort, and job attractiveness. Using this approach, Darby (1984, p. 303) computes the quality of an hour of labor by females under the age of 25 as 41 percent of an hour of male workers over 25. The relative quality of female labor rises to 57 percent for women in the over 25 age group.

Virtually every analyst who conducted a major productivity study that adjusted labor hours for changes in quality has adopted this marginal productivity approach. Yet, it requires some very strong assumptions about the character of the postwar United States economy. For example, production must be characterized by neither increasing nor decreasing returns; the effects of monopoly power in product markets (employer ability to pay high wages), union power, regulation, and discriminatory behavior must be negligible, and workers and firms must be well-informed maximizers whose decisions ensure that current wages reflect only the current (rather than future) provision of labor services. Only if these (and other) assumptions are good approximations can we rely on current wage differentials to reflect the current quality of labor inputs.

The consistent findings in wage studies of significant wage effects of capital intensity, concentration, firm size, union status, race, and gender raise substantial doubts about this reliability (Krueger and Summers, 1987). For instance, the standard earnings-based approach suggests that an hour of an unskilled automobile assembly-line worker's labor (typically male) is about three times the quality of a sewing machine operator's hour (typically female), a result that is manifestly open to question. Should the ratio of assembly-line workers to sewing machine operators increase, the work force as a whole will appear to be undergoing an upgrading of skills. With no change in output or employment, productivity growth will appear to have slowed as more labor inputs (skill units) appear to be used in production.

Years of schooling and experience are alternative labor-embodied measures of skills. Like relative earnings, the reliability of these measures is problematic: the quality of schooling varies greatly over time and among regions, and there may have been inflationary trends in credential and certification requirements. Concerning experience, there is the problem of the conflation of skills developed on the job with years of experience. Does a janitor with 15 years of experience have three times the skills of a janitor with 5 years of experience?

Because of these difficulties with labor-embodied skill measures, we have chosen to adjust labor input by direct job-based measures of labor-skill requirements. These are measures of the skills required for adequate performance of tasks, not measures of the skill residing in a given worker independently of the job.

Job-Based Measures of Skill Requirements

The development of such job-related skill measures for industries was accomplished by weighting occupational employment by occupation skill requirements. The analysis of changes in skill levels over several decades required Census employment data, and because occupation and industry classifications change with every decennial Census, a major part of this project involved the development of consistent occupation by industry employment matrices for 1960, 1970, 1980 and 1985. Thus, our industry skill measures are based on employment matrices at the 267 occupation and 64 industry level.

The best sources of detailed, economy-wide measures of the skill requirements of jobs for the postwar period are the second (1949), third (1965), and fourth (1977) editions of the Dictionary of Occupational Titles (DOT). Based on over 75,000 on-site visits between 1966 and 1974, the fourth edition provides a variety of measures of job content, including the required levels of General Educational Development (GED), Specific Vocational Preparation (SVP), Data (intelligence, verbal and numerical), and Temperament (adaptability to performing repetitive work) that are required. Roos and Treiman (Miller et al., 1980) reclassified the DOT occupations to 591 1970 Census occupations and calculated the values of a number of DOT variables for each of these Census occupations.

Our measures of job-skill requirements capture three fundamental dimensions of skills: cognitive, interactive, and motor. Two variables are used to measure cognitive skills: general educational development (GED) and substantive complexity (SC). GED is employed in part because it has been the most frequently used DOT variables in past studies of skill change. It also serves as a check for the SC measure. SC is derived from a factor analytic test of a large number of DOT variables. Using the 4th edition scores for 1970 Census occupations, Roos and Treiman (Miller et al., 1980, Appendix F) conducted a factor analysis of 46 DOT variables to determine whether an underlying factor might be identified as "substantive complexity." The results provided strong support for the existence of such a factor: it was highly correlated with GED, Specific Vocational Preparation, Data (synthesizing, coordinating, and analyzing), and other measures of cognitive skills (p. 339).[4]

Interactive skills are measured by the DOT "People" variable, which, on a scale of 0–8, identifies whether the job requires mentoring (0), negotiating (1), instructing (2), supervising (3), diverting (4), persuading (5), speaking–signaling (6), serving (7), or taking instructions (8). For comparability with the other measures, we reversed the order of this scale to run from low to high skills.

Motor skills (MS) can be represented by another factor-based variable (Miller et al., 1980, p. 339). High MS scores reflect job requirements such as setting up machines, precision working, and operating/controlling. Lower scores reflect tending and feeding machines and handling materials.

A final measure, Total (TOT) Skills, can be created to capture all three fundamental dimensions of job skills by summing the Substantive Complexity, People (scaled to a 0–10 range), and Motor Skills measures.

Skill Change, 1960–1985

Table 11-1 presents the percentage change in job-based skill levels for both total employees and nonsupervisory workers for 1960–1970, 1970–1980, and 1980–1985.

4. A strong case for the use of factor-based scales is made by Miller et al. (1980). They conducted a series of reliability tests and concluded that "the more reliable indicators of the features of occupations tapped by the worker traits and worker functions variables could be created by developing factor-based multiple-item scales to represent the various dimensions revealed by factor analysis. Such scales would have the advantage of greater internal reliability and consistency than single indicators" (p. 188).

TABLE 11-1 Percentage Change in Economy-Wide Skill Levels, 1960–1985

Skill Measure	*1960–1970* (%)	*1970–1980* (%)	*1980–1985* (%)
SC	7.1	4.7	1.2
	(4.3)[a]	(1.9)	(0.6)
GED	3.6	2.2	0.6
	(1.9)	(0.6)	(0.3)
PS	2.6	2.2	0.0
	(0.7)	(1.0)	(0.0)
MS	0.7	−1.7	−0.6
	(2.0)	(−0.4)	(0.2)
TOT[b]	4.7	2.5	0.3
	(3.2)	(1.3)	(0.3)

[a]Figures for nonsupervisory personnel are in parentheses.
[b]The measure TOT is defined as TOT = SC + PS + MS.

As noted earlier, our measures of job-embodied skill requirements are based upon data collected between 1966 and 1974. As a result, changes in industry skill levels from 1960 to 1985 reflect only changes in employment among our 267 occupations within each industry. This table shows negligible or small changes for Motor Skills (MS) and People Skills (PS), but larger changes for the cognitive skills variables (SC and GED) for all three periods. For both SC and GED, the percentage increase in total employee skill levels in the 1970–1980 decade was only about two-thirds as large as the change between 1960 and 1970. If the 1980–1985 figures are doubled to get rough decade-equivalent figures, the increase in these skill measures was again considerably smaller (about half) than the previous decade.

For nonsupervisory (NS) workers, defined as all occupations except professional, technical, and kindred workers and managers and administrators, the change in SC and GED for both the 1960–1970 and the 1970–1980 periods was substantially lower than the change for total employees. Further, the percentage decline between the growth in SC levels in the 1960s and the growth in the 1970s for NS workers (from 4.3 to 1.9, a decline of about 56 percent) was much larger than the decline for all workers (from 7.1 to 4.7, a decline of about 34 percent). The results for GED requirements are similar. Thus, our indices of cognitive skills increased more slowly for the least skilled both within and between each of these decades.

Table 11-2 presents mean SC and people skill (PS) levels for 10 large industry groups in 1970 and the percentage change in these levels over the 1960s and the 1970s. The highest skill levels in 1970, by both measures, were recorded in other services (business, professional, medical, and educational) and FIRE (finance, insurance, and real estate). The nondurable manufacturing sector had the lowest SC level in 1970, whereas the lowest PS levels were recorded in the construction and durable manufacturing sectors. During the 1960s, the largest increases in SC levels occurred in three relatively low-skill sectors—mining, nondurable manufacturing, and durable manufacturing—as well as in other services, a high-skill sector. Mining and the two manufacturing sectors also had substantially larger increases in PS requirements over

TABLE 11-2 Mean SC and PS Skill Levels by Major Industry Group and Percentage Change over Time, 1960–1980

	Substantive Complexity (SC)			*People Skills (PS)*		
	SC Level 1970	*Change 1960–1970 (%)*	*Change 1970–1980 (%)*	*PS Level 1970*	*Change 1960–1970 (%)*	*Change 1970–1980 (%)*
1. Agriculture	3.85	−1.00	0.0	1.85	0.14	0.51
2. Mining	3.93	13.80	5.60	1.63	20.93	13.01
3. Construction	4.20	5.50	2.70	1.44	9.35	6.08
4. Nondurable manufacturing	3.39	8.33	4.75	1.54	8.26	11.01
5. Durable manufacturing	3.84	7.37	1.93	1.45	13.00	8.02
6. Transportation, communications, utilities	3.68	6.17	3.60	1.95	3.83	6.26
7. Trade	4.01	0.85	4.72	2.20	−3.83	4.90
8. Finance, insurance, real estate	5.24	4.02	1.14	3.01	6.66	2.37
9. Other services	4.86	7.44	3.96	3.53	7.38	1.90
10. Government	4.44	3.90	4.24	2.54	2.05	9.81

the 1960–1980 period than the other sectors. These results suggest an inverse relationship between skill levels and skill change, a hypothesis that is supported by correlation analysis.

Our data also suggest a negative relationship between skill change and employment growth. Thus, although the service sectors (numbers 6 through 10 in Table 11-2) have seen the most rapid increases in employment, average skill increases have been moderate. This may be accounted for by evidence that a large portion of service sector employment growth has occurred among low-skilled occupations. In contrast, although the goods-producing sectors have shown much slower employment growth, they have had major changes in occupation mix, as low-skilled production workers are eliminated and managers, professionals, and technical workers increase their share of employment.

SOURCES OF PRODUCTIVITY GROWTH, 1958–1977

We begin the analysis with a comparison of alternative measures of overall labor productivity growth from 1958 to 1977.[5] In deriving the growth-accounting framework, we used the total labor requirements vector λ as the relative price vector, thus as the weights for the sectoral components of final output to arrive at total final output, y. This was necessary to arrive at Equation (11-4). However, this is a somewhat unconventional choice of prices to compute total final output. As a check, we compared more conventional measures of overall labor productivity growth with those computed using λ.

The results are shown in Table 11-3. The first line shows estimates of annual rates of overall unadjusted labor productivity growth. Economy-wide labor productivity growth averaged 2.6 percent per year over the 1958–1967 period, 1.2 percent per year from 1967 to 1977, and 1.9 percent per year over the whole 1958–1977 period. The change in labor productivity growth between 1958–1967 and 1967–1977 was −1.4 percentage points. The second line shows similar calculations using current market prices (p_m). Productivity growth estimates are higher for both periods, but the change in productivity growth between the two periods is almost the same as in line 1.

Constant sectoral market prices are used in lines 3 and 4. The results are very similar to those using λ. In line 5, we use the average market price in each period to weight the components of final demand. This index produces the largest decline in labor productivity growth between the two periods. Lines 6 and 7 use constant total labor requirement price indices, and the results are quite similar to those of line 1. In the last line, we use the average value of λ over the period as the price index, and the resulting decline in labor productivity growth between the two periods is somewhat higher than that of line 1.

Summary measures for the eight price indices are presented at the bottom of

5. See Wolff (1985b) for details on sources and methods for the input–output data. The occupation-by-industry matrices were merged with the input–output tables on a 47-industry level. The concordance between the 87-sector Bureau of Economic Analysis (BEA) industry classification scheme for the input–output data and the 64-industry classification scheme used for the occupation-by-industry matrices can be obtained from the authors. Because the occupation-by-industry matrices were for different years than the input–output data, geometric interpolation of the industry skill scores for the Census years was used to impute industry skill scores to the input–output data.

TABLE 11-3 Alternative Estimates of the Annual Rate of Growth of Overall Unadjusted Labor Productivity Growth, 1958–1977

Price Index	*1958–1967* (%)	*1967–1977* (%)	*1958–1977* (%)	*Change from 1958–1967 to 1967–1977* (%)
1. Current lambda (λ_t)	2.59	1.23	1.92	−1.36
2. Current market price (p_{mt})	2.97	1.70	2.34	−1.27
3. Constant 1972 prices	2.69	1.27	1.95	−1.42
4. Constant prices, 1958–1977 average	2.74	1.24	1.95	−1.50
5. Average price for period $[(p_{mt} + p_{mt-1})/2]$	2.82	1.16	1.90	−1.66
6. Constant 1967 lambda	2.47	1.15	1.77	−1.32
7. Constant lambda, 1958–1977 average	2.46	1.09	1.73	−1.37
8. Average lambda for period $[(\lambda_{mt} + \lambda_{mt-1})/2]$	2.51	0.98	1.68	−1.53
Average of eight measures (%)	2.66	1.23	1.90	−1.43
Standard deviation of the eight measures (%)	0.17	0.20	0.19	0.12
Ratio of standard deviation to average	0.065	0.162	0.100	−0.083

Table 11-3. The variation among the eight indices is small relative to the average value of these indices. Thus, measures of overall productivity growth appear to be insensitive to the particular price indices employed to weight the final output components. Moreover, estimates of labor productivity growth using our measure λ fall almost in the midpoint of this range of estimates, suggesting considerable reliability for this index.

Table 11-4 presents results on total labor productivity growth (TLP) for 10 large industry groups using unadjusted labor hours (π) and skill-adjusted labor hours (π^*). It is, perhaps, helpful to begin with the last line of the table, which shows the overall measures. As noted above, overall unadjusted TLP grew by 2.6 percent per year between 1958 and 1967. The average skill level of the labor force, as measured by GED, increased by 0.4 percent per year over this period. As a result, TLP, adjusted by GED level, grew by 2.2 percent per year (2.6–0.4 percent). Likewise, the average skill level of the employed labor force, as measured by SC scores, increased by 0.7 percent per year, and SC-adjusted TLP growth increased at 1.9 percent per year, 0.7 percentage points less than unadjusted labor productivity growth.

Both unadjusted and adjusted TLP growth declined between 1958–1967 and 1967–1977. The unadjusted measure fell from 2.6 to 1.2 percent per year. GED-adjusted TLP grew by 1.0 percent per year in the second period, compared to 2.2 percent in the 1958–1967 period, whereas SC-adjusted TLP grew by 0.8 percent per year, down from 1.9 percent in the first period. The rate of increase in the average skill level of the work force also declined between the two periods. The GED-weighted skill level slowed from an annual rate of increase of 0.4 percent in 1958–1967 to 0.2 percent

TABLE 11-4 Annual Rates of Total Labor Productivity Growth, by Sector and Period, Using Unadjusted and Adjusted Labor Hours

	1958–1967 (%)			*1967–1977 (%)*			*1958–1977 (%)*			*Change from 1958–1967 to 1967–1977 (%)*		
Sector	*Unadjusted*	*GED*	*SC*	*Unadjusted*	*GED*	*SC*	*Unadjusted*	*GED*	*SC*	*Unadjusted*	*GED*	*SC*
1. Agriculture	3.47	3.37	3.35	4.23	4.02	3.89	3.85	3.70	3.62	0.76	0.65	0.54
2. Mining	0.76	0.43	0.09	−1.90	−2.22	−2.50	−0.57	−0.89	−1.21	−2.66	−2.65	−2.59
3. Construction	3.54	3.26	3.08	−0.40	−0.57	−0.74	1.57	1.34	1.17	−3.94	−3.83	−3.82
4. Nondurable manufacturing	4.05	3.80	3.59	1.30	1.02	0.74	2.68	2.41	2.16	−2.75	−2.78	−2.85
5. Durable manufacturing	3.81	3.55	3.31	0.72	0.56	0.38	2.27	2.05	1.85	−3.09	−2.99	−2.93
6. Transportation, communication, utilities	3.94	3.67	3.41	2.30	2.16	1.94	3.12	2.92	2.68	−1.64	−1.51	−1.47
7. Trade	2.69	2.63	2.58	0.30	0.34	0.28	1.49	1.48	1.43	−2.39	−2.29	−2.30
8. Finance, insurance, real estate	2.50	2.20	1.99	3.05	2.74	2.44	2.77	2.47	2.22	0.55	0.54	0.45
9. Other services	2.08	1.69	1.33	−0.20	−0.35	−0.60	0.94	0.67	0.37	−2.28	−2.04	−1.93
10. Government	0.52	0.34	0.17	−0.31	−0.50	−0.72	0.10	−0.08	−0.27	−0.83	−0.84	−0.89
Overall	2.59	2.24	1.91	1.23	1.02	0.77	1.92	1.63	1.34	−1.36	−1.22	−1.13

in 1967–1977, whereas the annual rate of increase in the SC-weighted skill level slowed from 0.7 to 0.4 percent.

In our accounting, the crucial variable is the *change* over time in the *difference* between the skill-weighted and the unadjusted rates of labor productivity growth (cf. Equation 11-8). This difference narrowed between the two periods, from 0.35 in 1958–1967 to 0.21 in 1967–1977 for the GED-based measure and from 0.68 to 0.46 for the SC-based index (see the last row of Table 11-4). As a result, overall skill-adjusted TLP growth fell *less* than unadjusted TLP growth between the 1958–1967 and the 1967–1977 periods. Unadjusted TLP growth fell by 1.36 percentage points between the two periods, whereas GED-adjusted TLP growth fell by 1.22 percentage points and SC-adjusted TLP growth fell by 1.13 percentage points. The direct implication of this is that part of the slowdown in overall unadjusted TLP growth is the result of the slowdown in the rate of growth in employee skill levels. In terms of Equation (11-8), the $\Delta\theta$ term is negative.

Results are similar on the industry level. Because average skill scores increased in all industries from 1958 to 1967, rates of skill-adjusted TLP growth are correspondingly lower than unadjusted TLP growth in every sector. The differences are quite substantial in all sectors except agriculture and trade. Similar results are apparent for 1967–1977. Skill-adjusted rates of TLP growth were uniformly smaller than the unadjusted rates, with the exception of the GED-adjusted index in the trade sector. With the exception of the trade sector, differences between the unadjusted and adjusted TLP growth rates were again fairly large.

As Table 11-4 shows, the annual rate of unadjusted TLP growth fell between 1958–1967 and 1967–1977 in all sectors except agriculture and FIRE. In construction and durable manufacturing, unadjusted TLP growth fell by more than three percentage points, and in mining, nondurable manufacturing, trade, and other services by more than two percentage points between these periods. Among the eight sectors with lower productivity growth in 1967–1977 than 1958–1967, unadjusted TLP growth fell by more than GED-adjusted TLP growth in each except nondurable manufacturing and government, and fell by more than SC-adjusted TLP growth in each except nondurable manufacturing. The sectoral results indicate that for most, but not all, sectors, the slowdown in skill growth helped account for part of the sectoral slowdown in unadjusted TLP growth.

Table 11-5 shows the decomposition of the change in overall unadjusted TLP growth into three sources: (1) final output composition effect, (2) sectoral technical change effect, and (3) skill change effect. The decomposition is based directly on Equation (11-8) and was performed at the 47-sector level. About 10 percent of the slowdown in overall productivity growth was the results of changes in the composition of final output. This estimate is consistent with the earlier estimates reported in Wolff (1985b). The skill-change effect varies considerably depending on the skill measure used. On the basis of the substantive complexity (SC), motor skill (MS), and composite (TOT) indices, about one-sixth of the productivity slowdown was accounted for by the slowdown in the growth of skill requirements and about three-fourths by the slowdown in the rate of sectoral technical change. Based on GED, skill changes accounted for about 10 percent of the productivity slowdown, whereas on the basis of the people skill (PS) index, skill changes explained virtually none of the productivity slowdown.

TABLE 11-5 Percentage Decomposition of Change in Overall Unadjusted Labor Productivity Growth between 1958–1967 and 1967–1977[a]

Measure and Weights	*Final Output Effect* (%)	*Technical Change Effect* (%)	*Skill Change Effect* (%)	*Sum Of Three Effects* (%)
1. SC measure				
a. First period weights	11.4	70.2	16.1	97.7
b. Average period weights	10.0	76.3	15.2	101.5
2. GED measure				
a. First period weights	11.4	77.1	9.6	98.1
b. Average period weights	10.0	82.3	9.1	101.5
3. PS measure				
a. First period weights	11.4	84.3	2.8	98.5
b. Average period weights	10.0	88.8	2.6	101.5
4. MS measure				
a. First period weights	11.4	69.2	17.1	97.7
b. Average period weights	10.0	75.3	16.1	101.5
5. TOT measure				
a. First period weights	11.4	71.3	15.1	97.8
b. Average period weights	10.0	77.2	14.2	101.5

[a]The three effects may not sum to unity because of the exclusion of second-order terms and rounding errors.

CONCLUSION

To explore the changes in the skill content of labor inputs and to determine the implications of these changes for the measurement and analysis of productivity growth, we have employed a variety of measures of job-skill requirements from the Dictionary of Occupational Titles. These measures were chosen to capture the cognitive, interactive, and motor skills dimensions of job requirements.

Based upon changes in occupation mix alone, our results indicate a general upgrading of the skill content of labor inputs from 1960 to 1985, with the greatest increases occurring from 1960 to 1970. Although these results are broadly consistent with earlier studies using DOT data (Rumberger, 1981; Spenner, 1983), ours apply to a more recent period. More importantly, our employment matrices have enabled us to calculate these changes for individual industries.

The productivity analysis produced three principal results. First, the growth in skill requirements accounts for a substantial portion of the growth in unadjusted TLP from 1958 to 1977. Thus, unadjusted TLP growth averaged 1.92 percent per year, whereas GED-adjusted TLP growth was 1.63 percent and SC-adjusted TLP growth was just 1.34 percent. At the 10-sector level, skill-adjusted TLP growth was lower than the unadjusted rate for each sector. The differences were quite substantial, except for trade. This indicates that skill upgrading was responsible for a considerable portion of the productivity gains of each of the major sectors except trade.

Second, overall productivity growth fell by over one percentage point between 1958–1967 and 1967–1977. Moreover, TLP growth slowed down in all sectors of the economy, except agriculture and trade. In seven sectors, unadjusted TLP growth declined by more than two percentage points. The data also show that the rate of increase in skill levels fell between the two periods. As a result of the slowdown in growth of skill requirements, the gap between the skill-adjusted and unadjusted rates narrowed between 1958–1967 and 1967–1977 in 8 of the 10 sectors. In equivalent terms, the contribution of skill growth to sectoral productivity growth fell between the two periods in almost all industries.

Third, on the basis of our input–output growth-accounting framework, we find that the slowdown in the rate of increase in job-skill requirements helps account for a portion of the slowdown in overall labor productivity growth between 1958–1967 and 1967–1977. For three of five of our skill indices, about one-sixth of the productivity slowdown of the 1970s is attributable to the decline in the rate of increase in skill requirements of workers. This is a rather significant finding, particularly in light of previous literature on the sources of the productivity slowdown in the United States, which have failed to consider the effects of changes in direct measures of labor quality. Studies that have used indirect measures of labor quality, such as education and age (Denison, 1979a), have failed to attribute a significant portion of the productivity slowdown to changes in labor quality.

ACKNOWLEDGMENTS

An earlier version of this chapter was presented at the Eighth International Conference on Input–Output Techniques in Sapporo, Japan, in August 1986. We would like to thank those present at the conference for their comments. We would particularly like to acknowledge Karen R. Polenske for her comments and suggestions, Wayne Farel for his able research assistance, and the C. V. Starr Center for Applied Economics for its financial support of this work.

REFERENCES

Chinloy, Peter. 1980. "Sources of Quality Change in Labor Input." *American Economic Review*. Vol. 70, pp. 108–119.

Chinloy, Peter. 1981. *Labor Productivity*. Cambridge, MA: Abt Books.

Darby, Michael R. 1984. "The U.S. Productivity Slowdown: A Case of Statistical Myopia." *American Economic Review*. Vol. 74, pp. 301–322.

Denison, Edward F. 1979. "Explanations of Declining Productivity Growth." *Survey of Current Business*. Vol. 59, pp. 1–24.

Denison, Edward F. 1984. "Accounting for Slower Economic Growth: An Update." In *International Comparisons of Productivity and the Causes of the Slowdown*, edited by John Kendrick. Cambridge, MA: Ballinger Publishing Co.

Gollop, Frank M., and Dale W. Jorgenson. 1980. "U.S. Productivity Growth by Industry, 1947–73." In *New Developments in Productivity Measurement and Analysis*, edited by John Kendrick and Bea Vaccara. Chicago: University of Chicago Press.

Krueger, Alan B., and Lawrence H. Summers. 1987. "Reflections on the Interindustry Wage Structure." In *Unemployment and the Structure of Labor Markets*, edited by Kevin Lang and Jonathan S. Leonard. New York: Basil-Blackwell, pp. 17–47.

Maddison, Angus. 1982. *Phases of Capitalist Development*. Oxford: Oxford University Press.

Maddison, Angus. 1987. "Growth and Slowdown in Advanced Capitalist Economies: Techniques of Quantitative Assessment." *Journal of Economic Literature*. Vol. 25, pp. 649–698.

Miller, Ann R., Donald J. Treiman, Pamela S. Cain, and Patricia A. Roos. 1980. Work, Jobs and Occupations: A Critical Review of the Dictionary of Occupational Titles. Washington, D.C.: National Academy Press.

Rumberger, Russell W. 1981. "The Changing Skill Requirements of Jobs in the U.S. Economy." *Industrial and Labor Relations Review*. Vol. 34, pp. 578–591.

Spenner, Kenneth I. 1983. "Deciphering Prometheus: Temporal Changes in Work Content." *American Sociological Review*. Vol. 48, pp. 824–837.

U.S. Department of Labor. 1977. "Dictionary of Occupational Titles." 4th ed. Washington, D.C.: U.S. Government Printing Office.

Wolff, Edward N. 1985a. "The Magnitude and Causes of the Recent Productivity Slowdown in the U.S." In *Productivity Growth and U.S. Competitiveness*, edited by Kenneth McClennan and William Baumol. New York: Oxford University Press.

Wolff, Edward N. 1985b. "Industrial Composition, Interindustry Effects, and the U.S. Productivity Slowdown." *Review of Economics and Statistics*. Vol. 67, pp. 268–277.

Economic Systems Research
Vol. 18, No. 3, 221–255, September 2006

Routledge
Taylor & Francis Group

The Growth of Information Workers in the US Economy, 1950–2000: the Role of Technological Change, Computerization, and Structural Change

EDWARD N. WOLFF

Department of Economics, New York University, USA

(Received May 2005; revised April 2006)

ABSTRACT *Using data from the decennial US Censuses of 1950, 1960, 1970, 1980, 1990, and 2000, I construct matrices of employment by 267 occupations and 64 industries and then aggregate the occupations into four categories: (i) knowledge producers; (ii) data processors; (iii) service workers; and (iv) goods-processing workers. I find that information workers (the sum of the first two categories) increased from 37% of the workforce in 1950 to 59% in 2000. Then, using an input–output decomposition analysis, I find that the growth in information workers was driven not by a shift in tastes toward information-intensive goods and services (as measured by the composition of final demand) but rather by a roughly equal combination of the substitution of information workers for goods and service workers within the structure of production of industries and the unbalanced growth effect (from differential rates of industry productivity growth). Finally, on the basis of regression analysis, I find that R&D expenditures and computer investment are positively associated with the growth in knowledge workers but negatively associated with the growth of data workers.*

KEY WORDS: Information workers, input–output, R&D, computerization, productivity

1. Introduction

Fritz Machlup's classic 1962 book, *The Production and Distribution of Knowledge in the United States*, found that with the growth of clerical occupations at the turn of the century,

---

Correspondence Address: Edward N. Wolff, Department of Economics, 269 Mercer Street, Room 700, New York University, New York, NY 10003, USA. Email: Edward.wolff@nyu.edu

0953-5314 Print/1469-5758 Online/06/030221–35 © 2006 The International Input–Output Association
DOI: 10.1080/09535310600844193

'the ascendancy of knowledge-producing occupations has been an uninterrupted process... a movement from manual to mental, and from less to more highly trained labor' (Machlup, 1962, pp. 396–397). Since the book's appearance, several studies, including Porat (1977), Beniger (1986), Rubin and Huber (1986), Baumol *et al.* (1989), and Reich (1991) have documented the growth in the relative size of the information economy. Baumol *et al.* (1989, Chapter 7), in particular, found that information workers increased from about 42% of the workforce in 1960 to 53% in 1980.

In this paper, I document the growth of information workers in the US economy over the postwar period and analyze the sources of their growth. The paper is divided into five parts. In the next section, I review the pertinent literature on skill-biased technological change and the effects of international trade on skill composition. Particular attention is paid to the role of Information Technology (IT) on skill change. I also include a model derived from Autor *et al.* (2003) on the effects of IT on occupational composition.

The third section updates the statistics on the composition of the workforce between information and non-information jobs to 2000. Particular interest is focused on the post-1980 period, which has seen a tremendous growth in the use of computers in production and which Freeman (1987) and others have termed a new 'techno-economic paradigm,' based on computer-driven information technology. For this analysis, I rely on matrices of employment by occupation and industry derived from the decennial US Censuses of 1950, 1960, 1970, 1980, 1990, and 2000. The occupations are aggregated into four categories: (i) knowledge producers; (ii) data processors; (iii) service workers; and (iv) goods-processing workers.

I find that information workers (the sum of the first two categories) increased from 37% of the workforce in 1950 to 59% in 2000, with the rate of increase for knowledge-producing workers peaking in the 1960s and 1970s and then slowing down somewhat, while that of data workers peaked in the 1960s and then tapered off after that. Yet, all in all, most of the growth in information employment did not take place among high-skilled, high-paid professionals and managers but rather among moderate-skilled, relatively low-paid clerical and sales workers. Another interesting finding is that, while in 1950, over half of total employment was found in blue-collar jobs, this proportion slipped to under a quarter by 2000. As Machlup predicted, we have moved from a society in which we work with our hands to one in which we work with our mind.

The fourth section uses an input–output decomposition analysis to break down the changes in the information workers' share of the labor force into three parts: (i) the substitution of information labor for labor of other types within the production process – that is, the change in the proportion of information workers in each industry's labor force; (ii) the change in each industry's share of the economy's total output; and (iii) the change associated with relative variations in labor productivity of the different industries.

The first of these three components indicates the extent to which the composition of the labor force in a typical industry has become more information-intensive (assuming all other things remain the same). The second element relates to different industries' shares of the economy's final output and is pertinent in determining the extent to which the expansion in information-related employment is attributable to an increase in the economy's demand for products with a high information content. The third component plays the part in testing the role of unbalanced growth in the information explosion – that is, the extent to which growth in the number of information workers can be attributed to relatively lower productivity growth in industries using more information.

I find that the growth in the number of information workers was driven not by a shift in tastes toward information-intensive goods and services (as measured by the composition of final demand) but rather by a roughly equal combination of the substitution of information workers for goods and service workers within the structure of production of industries and the unbalanced growth effect.

The fifth section relies on econometric analysis to analyze the sources of growth of information workers on the industry level. The dependent variables are the changes in knowledge and data workers as a percentage of total employment in the industry over the period. Independent variables include (1) total factor productivity (TFP) growth, (2) expenditures on research and development, (3) investment in new equipment, (4) investment in office, computer and accounting machinery (OCA), and (5) the degree of international competitiveness of an industry.

R&D expenditures is the most significant factor that contributes to the growth in knowledge workers and it is negatively associated with the growth of data workers. Investment in OCA also exerts a positive effect on the knowledge worker employment and a strong negative effect on the employment of data workers. Concluding remarks are made in the final section of the paper.

2. Review of Related Literature

A considerable literature has now accumulated on factors that might have caused changes in the occupational distribution, particularly since the early 1970s in the US. In particular, much of this literature maintains that IT and organizational changes over this period have led to changes in labor demand that favor more skilled workers. Here I review some of the pertinent literature on the role of technological change, information technology, and international trade.

2.1. Skill-biased Technological Change

The most prevalent view on changes in skill composition is biased technological change, due to the introduction of computers and the general diffusion of IT. The argument is that the last 30 years have witnessed a major technological revolution led by widespread computerization and the consequent diffusion of IT. This change has skewed the income distribution by placing a high premium on college-educated and skilled labor while reducing the demand for semi-skilled and unskilled workers. One important piece of evidence is that the rate of return to a college education (the wage premium paid to a college graduate relative to a high school graduate) almost doubled over the decades of the 1980s and 1990s.

This argument has been made by Bound and Johnson (1992) and Berman *et al.* (1994), who identify the declining ratio of production to non-production workers *within industry* as the major determinant of changes in relative wages between skilled and unskilled workers. The fact that both the employment share and relative wages shifted in favor of non-production workers is evidence of biased technological change.

Davis and Haltiwanger (1991), using data on production and non-production workers in US manufacturing plants from 1963 to 1986, provided some of the early evidence to support this hypothesis They found that the employment shift toward non-production workers occurred disproportionately in large plants between 1977 and 1986, and this was accompanied by a sharp upgrading of worker education and occupational skill levels. Katz and Murphy (1992) developed a model that accounted for changes in both the demand and supply of unskilled and skilled labor. Using CPS data over the period 1963 to 1987, they concluded that while the supply of college graduates fluctuated over time, there was a steady increase in the demand for skilled labor in the US over the period.

Berman *et al.* (1994), using data from the Annual Survey of Manufactures over the period 1979 to 1987 for 450 manufacturing industries, found that over two-thirds of the increase in the ratio of non-production to production workers within manufacturing was due to the increased use of non-production workers within industry, and less than one third to a reallocation of labor between industries. They inferred from this the existence of skill biased technological change. Berman *et al.* (1998) also provided evidence that the increase in the share of skilled (non-production) workers in total employment occurred across a wide range of OECD countries. Yet, they also found that the trend decelerated in almost all OECD countries during the 1980s (with the notable exception of the United States). Machin and van Reenen (1998), using data for seven OECD countries, found that R&D intensity was positively linked to the relative growth of high skilled workers. Allen (2001) also concluded that technology variables accounted for 30% of the increase in the college wage premium over the period from 1979 to 1989.

2.2. *The IT 'Revolution'*

Two relatively early papers have called the rapid introduction and diffusion of computers and associated Information Technology (IT) a 'technological revolution.' Christopher Freeman, writing in 1987, termed this transformation as a new 'techno-economic paradigm,' based on microprocessor driven information technology. According to Freeman (1987, p. 51), information technology has 'emerged in the last couple of decades as a result of the convergence of a number of inter-related radical advances in the field of microelectronics, fibre optics, software engineering, communications and computer technology.' He defined IT 'both as a new range of products and services, and as a technology which is capable of revolutionizing the processes of production and delivery of all other industries and services.' David (1991) referred to 'the paradigmatic shift' from electromechanical automation to information technologies and argued that the shift to information technologies might entail major changes in the organizational structure of companies.

One result of this technological revolution is a transformation of the skills required in the labor market. According to Freeman (1987, p. 66), the results of extensive research conducted by the Science Policy Research Unit (SPRU) of the University of Sussex showed that information technology 'reduces the requirements for inspection and lower management (and clerical) employees, but increases the requirement for skilled systems designers and engineers and the level of responsibility for skills for maintenance...' There is also some suggestion from the case study literature that with the introduction of new information technologies there is a growing demand for various professional, technical and skilled production occupations, while the shares of lower and middle level managers and supervisors, inspectors, semi-skilled operatives and many clerical occupations decline. Strong support for this pattern was found by Milkman and Pullman (1991) in their study on employment restructuring at a GM auto assembly plant. Osterman (1986) found that a 10% increase in company computing power led to a 1% reduction in managerial employment. Zuboff (1988, pp. 284, 358–359) in a study of several manufacturing plants concluded that lower and middle managers were particularly 'vulnerable' to deskilling and displacement by the introduction of information technologies.

Leontief and Duchin (1986) used US input–output to analyze the effects of computer-driven automation on employment in four sectors – manufacturing, office work, education, and health care. Taking account of the increased need for workers in the production of computer-based equipment, the authors concluded that automation will not cause serious displacement of workers if the economy is able to achieve a smooth transition from the old to new technologies.

In my own work, I also presented evidence on the transformative effects of computerization on the labor market and the consequent structural adjustments that have ensued. In Wolff (2002), I used employment data for 267 occupations and 44 industries that were obtained from the decennial Census of Population for years 1960, 1970, 1980, and 1990 (see the section on Technology and the Growth in Information Employment, below). I constructed an index of occupational dissimilarity that measures how much occupational composition had shifted within industry over three time periods (1960–70, 1970–80, and 1980–90). The econometric results indicated that the coefficient of computerization as measured by the rate of growth of OCA per worker is statistically significant at the 1% level and that computerization is strongly and positively associated with the degree of occupational restructuring within industry over time.

Several other papers have looked at the effects of computer usage or IT on earnings. Reich (1991) argued that American workers are divided into two distinct groups – 'symbolic analysts' who produce knowledge and new Information Technology, and ordinary clerical and production workers, who are outside the IT revolution. Globalization has rewarded the first group of workers with increased earnings but depressed the earnings of the second group.

Krueger (1993) argued that pronounced declines in the cost of personal computers caused their widespread adoption in the workplace and shifted the production function in ways that favored more skilled workers. He also estimated the rate of return to computer usage at 15 to 20%. This finding was later challenged by DiNardo and Pischke (1997), who estimated, using German household data, a similar return to the use of pencils. They argued that computer use *per se* was not causing workers to earn a premium but, rather, was associated with unmeasured skills that were being rewarded in the workplace. However, in later work, Autor *et al.* (1998) supplied new evidence that there was a substantial and increasing wage premium associated with computer use, despite a large growth in the number of workers with computer skills.

Dunne *et al.* (2004), using manufacturing establishment data for the US, concluded that a substantial portion of the rising dispersion in wages is due to increases in wage differentials between establishments. The latter, in turn, are attributable to plant-level productivity differences and are correlated with both computer intensity and overall capital intensity. In similar fashion, Bartel *et al.* (2003) used plant level data for the valve manufacturing industry in the US and found evidence of a strong correlation between IT use and skill demand on the plant level. In particular, more IT-intensive plants demanded more computer programming and math skills, as well as a broader range of problem-solving skills.

Some recent theoretical literature has also laid the ground work toward understanding the relation between skill demand and IT. Bresnahan and Trajtenberg (1995) and Helpman and Trajtenberg (1998) introduced the notion of a 'General Purpose Technology' (GPT).

They argued that at any given time, there are typically a few technologies that play a far-reaching role in generating technical change in a wide range of user sectors. One example is the steam engine during the first industrial revolution. A second is the role of electrification in the early 20th century, as well as automotive technology. A third is the diffusion of computers, micro-electronics, and information technology in the last two or three decades of the 20th century. Such GPTs may be responsible for causing sustained and pervasive productivity gains throughout a wide number of industries in the economy.

A GPT has the following three characteristics. (1) It is used as inputs by a wide range of industries in the economy. This results from the fact that the GPT performs some general function, such as continuous rotary motion in the case of the steam engine or binary logic in the case of micro-electronics. (2) A GPT has the potential for continuous technical advances, which manifests itself *ex post* in the form of continuous advances in productivity. (3) A GPT has complementarities with the user sectors, especially in manufacturing.

In this regard, a GPT plays an important role as an 'engine of growth.' As an improved GPT becomes available, it is adopted by an increasing number of user industries and it fosters complementary advances that make it more attractive to adopt in the future. These two effects lead to an increase in the demand for the GPT, which in turn induces further technological advances in the GPT, and additional advances in the using sector (through its complementarity with the technologies of the using sector). This 'virtuous circle' leads to further technological advances, and as the use of the GPT spreads throughout the economy its effects show up as increased productivity growth at the aggregate level of the economy.

Helpman and Trajtenberg (1998) developed a GPT-based growth model to analyze the long-run dynamics that result from the introduction of new GPTs within fixed time intervals. Their theoretical analysis predicts a two-phase effect from the introduction and diffusion of a GPT. During the first phase, output and productivity decline in absolute terms. However, during the second phase, the benefits of a more advanced GPT come into play, after a sufficient number of complementary inputs are developed. During the latter phase, there is a spell of growth, with both output and productivity rising. The implication of this model is that it may explain the behavior of productivity arising from the introduction of Information Technology, with very slow productivity growth during the 1970s and 1980s, followed by a burst of productivity growth in the latter half of the 1990s. They argue that the first phase can be quite long – 25 or 30 years in the case of electrification or IT.

Helpman and Trajtenberg (1998) also extended their model to consider the case of two types of workers – skilled and unskilled. In their model, skilled labor is considered complementary to GPT (in our case, Information Technology) and R&D, while unskilled labor is assumed to be a substitute. Over time, their model predicts that the relative demand for unskilled labor will fall and that for skilled labor will rise during phase one. However, during the second phase, relative demand shifts toward unskilled workers. It is probably safe to assume that the period from 1970–2000, covered in this paper, is still part of the first of the two technological phases in the Helpman–Trajtenberg model.

Bresnahan *et al.* (2002) provide evidence of a positive relation between IT and the demand for skilled level. Analyzing data for about 400 large US firms over the period 1987–1994, they found evidence that IT is complementary to a new workplace organization which includes broader responsibilities for line workers, greater decentralized decision-making, and more self-managing teams. In turn, both IT and the new organizational structures are complements with worker skills measured in a variety of dimensions, including cognitive skill requirements.

Autor *et al.* (2002, 2003) provided empirical evidence of complementarity between computerization and skilled labor. Autor *et al.* (2002) investigated the effects of computerization in the form of the introduction of image processing of checks on the demand for two types of labor in a large bank. In the deposit processing department, image processing led to the substitution of computers for relatively low skilled (high-school educated) workers. In the exceptions processing department, which requires conceptual and problem-solving skills and employs primarily college-trained workers, the introduction of image processing led to an increase in the demand for workers with these particular skills.

Autor *et al.* (2003) provided a more general analysis of the effects of computerization on skill demand. They considered different skill types in their exploration. They found that computers substitute for a limited set of skills – in particular, those involving routine or repetitive cognitive and manual tasks. Conversely, computerization is complementary with tasks involving non-routine problem solving and interactive tasks. Using data on job skill requirements from the Department of Labor Dictionary of Occupational Titles over the period from 1960 to 1998, they found evidence of a positive correlation between the degree of computerization and the relative shift in skill demand within industries, occupations, and educational groups toward more skilled (that is, more non-routine) jobs and away from less skilled (that is, less routine jobs).

They also developed a pertinent model whose main elements I summarize here (more details can be found in their paper). Their assumptions are as follows. (i) There are two types of tasks or skills – 'routine' R and 'non-routine' N. (ii) Computer technology is more substitutable for routine than non-routine skills. (iii) Routine and non-routine tasks are themselves imperfect substitutes. (iv) Greater intensity of routine inputs increases the marginal productivity of non-routine inputs. (v) The aggregate production function is a constant returns to scale Cobb–Douglas production function of the form:

$$q = R^{1-\beta} N^{\beta} \quad (1)$$

where $0 < \beta < 1$ and where q is output, which sells at price one. Further assumptions are: (vi) computer capital, C, and workers are perfect substitutes in carrying out routine tasks, R; (vii) computer capital is supplied elastically at market price P per efficiency unit; (viii) P is falling exogenously over time due to technical advances; (ix) on the labor supply side, the authors assume that each worker i can be characterized according to his (her) relative efficiency in routine and non-routine tasks by $\alpha_i = N_i/R_i$, where $\alpha_i > 0$. It then follows from the perfect substitutability of computers and routine skills that the wage per efficiency unit W_R is given by:

$$W_R = P \quad (2)$$

Workers choose their occupation to maximize their earnings. As a result, the marginal worker with relative efficiency units α^* is indifferent between working in an R or an N occupation when

$$\alpha^* = W_R / W_N \quad (3)$$

Workers with $\alpha_i < \alpha^*$ supply routine labor and those with $\alpha_i \geq \alpha^*$ supply non-routine labor. Let $g_1(\alpha)$ and $g_2(\alpha)$ denote the functions that give the population endowment in efficiency units of routine and non-routine tasks, respectively, as a function of α. Then

$$R^* = \int_0^{\alpha^*} g_1(x)\,\mathrm{d}x \quad \text{and} \quad N^* = \int_{\alpha^*}^{\infty} g_2(x)\,\mathrm{d}x$$

where R^* is the supply of routine labor and N^* is the supply of non-routine labor.

Define $\theta = (C^* + R^*)/N^*$, the ratio of routine (including computer) tasks to non-routine tasks inputs in production. It follows that if factors are paid their marginal product, then

$$W_R = \partial q/\partial R = (1-\beta)\theta^{-\beta} \quad \text{and} \quad W_N = \partial q/\partial N = \beta\theta^{1-\beta} \tag{4}$$

Thus, factors that raise the relative intensity of routine task input (that is, increase θ) lower the wage per efficiency unit of routine task input and raise the wage paid to non-routine task input. From equation (2) and the first-order condition for W_R it follows that:

$$\partial(\ln W_R)/\partial(\ln P) = 1 = -\beta\,\partial(\ln\theta)/\partial(\ln P) \tag{5}$$

so that $\partial(\ln \theta)/\partial(\ln P) = -1/\beta$. As a result, a decline in computer prices will reduce the wage per efficiency unit of routine tasks and increase the relative intensity of routine tasks in production. Since, by assumption, routine and non-routine tasks are complementary inputs,

$$\partial(\ln W_N)/\partial(\ln P) = (\beta - 1)/\beta \tag{6}$$

In other words, a decline in computer prices will increase the wages of non-routine tasks. From equations (3), (5) and (6), it follows that:

$$\partial(\ln \alpha^*)/\partial(\ln P) = 1/\beta \tag{7}$$

A decrease in computer prices and a rise in IT investment will therefore decrease the *relative labor supply* to routine tasks and increase the *relative labor supply* to non-routine ones. These categories line up fairly well with two occupational groupings that I develop below. The first is knowledge workers, which corresponds to non-routine labor, and the second is data workers, which corresponds to routine labor. As will be seen in the fifth section, the predictions of this model are borne out very well.

2.3. *International Trade and Skill Composition*

A large literature has also accumulated on the effects of international trade on wage differentials. The main approach derives from the factor content of the trade model, which puts primary emphasis on the effective supplies of less skilled and more skilled labor (see, for example, Berman *et al.*, 1994). Imports embody both unskilled and skilled labor, which when added to the domestic supply of these two factors, determines their effective supply. Because imports to the US are generally less skill intensive than domestic production, the opening of the domestic economy to imports augments the relative effective supply of low skilled workers and lowers that of high skilled workers and thereby puts downward pressure on the wages of the former relative to the latter.

These studies generally conclude that increased trade had a minimal effect on skill composition. The reason is that US international trade is just too small to have much impact on wages or employment. Almost all of these studies estimated that the rising volume of imports in the United States accounted for no more than 20% of the shift in demand between low skilled and high skilled workers. Borjas *et al.* (1992) estimated that rising trade flows explained at most 15% of the increase in the earnings differential between college graduates and high school graduates between 1980 and 1988. Bound and Johnson (1992), Krugman and Lawrence (1994), Berman *et al.* (1994), and Richardson (1995) also found very little effect of international trade on the divergence in compensation between more skilled and less skilled workers. However, Krugman and Lawrence (1994) did find that imports from developing countries significantly reduced employment of unskilled production workers in developed countries. Moreover, Wood (1994, 1998) found large effects, with international trade accounting for as much as half of the decreased demand for low skilled workers (see Freeman, 1995, for a review of these studies).

3. Growth of Information Employment

The basic data are from the US Decennial Censuses of 1950, 1960, 1970, 1980, 1990, and 2000. In the calculations, the figures in the Census tables of employment by occupation and industry are first aggregated, in conformity with an internally consistent classification scheme, into 267 occupations and 64 industries (see the Data Appendix for details). The occupations are aggregated once more into six categories: (i) knowledge production; (ii) data processing; (iii) supply of services; (iv) goods production; (v) a hybrid class including both knowledge and data activities; and (vi) a second hybrid class including both data and service activities.

In the classification schema, professional and technical workers are generally classified as knowledge or data workers, depending on whether they are producers or users of knowledge (see Appendix Table A1 for details). The line is somewhat arbitrary at points, and judgment calls have been made. Moreover, in some cases, professional workers are classified as data-service workers. For example, doctors and nurses are treated in this way, since they use information and also perform a personal service. Management personnel are taken to perform both data and knowledge tasks, since they produce new information for administrative decisions and also use and transmit this information. Clerical workers are classed as data workers for obvious reasons. I classify as goods-processing workers all labor that transforms or operates on materials or physical objects. These include craft workers, operatives (including transportation workers who move physical goods), and unskilled labor. The remaining group is made up of the service workers, who, primarily, perform personal services.

I then (somewhat arbitrarily) classify half of those that fall into the hybrid knowledge/data category as knowledge workers and the other half as data workers. In similar fashion, I split the hybrid data/service category half into data and half into service workers. The resulting groups are referred to as the 'total knowledge', 'total data', and 'total service' categories. Information workers are then defined as the sum of (total) knowledge and (total) data workers. The non-information category is composed of the residual – including (total) service and goods-processing workers.[1]

Table 1 gives a breakdown of total employment by type of worker from 1950 to 2000, the corresponding growth rates in each category, and the percentage composition.[2] Over the five decades, knowledge workers were the fastest growing group, increasing 3.1% per year. They were followed by data workers and service workers, at 2.5% per year and 2.4% per year, respectively. In contrast, goods producers increased their number by only 0.2% per year. Altogether, employment of information workers grew 2.6% per year (one percentage point above average), while non-information workers increased 0.8% per year (about one point below average).

The developments differ by decade. Between 1950 and 1960, the fastest growing group was service workers, followed by data workers, and knowledge workers. Goods producers declined in absolute number. In the next decade, knowledge workers led the way, followed by data workers, and service workers. The number of goods producers again fell in absolute terms.

The decade of the 1970s again saw knowledge workers with the highest growth rate, in this case followed by data and service workers, and goods-processing workers, whose employment increased in absolute terms. During the decade of the 1980s knowledge workers again led all groups, followed by data and service workers, and goods-processing workers. The 1990s again saw knowledge workers in the lead, followed by data and service workers, and goods-producing workers again declined in absolute terms.

The last panel of Table 1 provides another way of viewing the growth of the information sector. In 1950, 8% of total employment consisted of knowledge workers and 29% of data workers. Altogether, 37% of the employed labor force was made up of information workers. Goods workers formed a majority of total employment, at 52%, while service workers constituted only 10% of total employment. By 2000, the proportion of information workers in total employment had increased to 59% of the total. The number of knowledge workers had risen to 15% and that of data workers to 44% of total employment. Service workers were up to 14% and goods producers dramatically down to 24%.

In sum, knowledge workers grew as a share of total employment in each of the five decades and was the fastest growing group in all but the 1950s. However, its biggest increase in relative terms occurred during the 1980s and 1990s, when its share of total employment increased by about two percentage points in each decade. Data workers enjoyed their largest growth in relative terms during the 1950s and 1960s. There was a marked slowdown in the increase of their share of total employment in the 1970s, and during the 1980s there was virtually no change in their share. The share of service workers in total employment rose quite rapidly in the 1950s and much slower thereafter. The share of goods producers in total employment fell in every decade, and in the 1950s, 1960s, and 1990s its number declined in absolute terms as well.

4. Industry Changes in Information Employment

Since our subsequent analysis depends substantially on comparative shifts in the share of information workers among industries, we first examine the relative information-intensity of the major sectors of the economy. As shown in Table 2, in 2000 the finance, insurance, and real estate sector had the highest percentage of knowledge workers in their employment, about 22%, followed by business and other services and the government sector in a virtual tie, at about 19%. Mining (largely geologists and engineers), manufacturing, and transportation, communications, and utilities followed in a second group. At the

Table 1. Employment growth and percentage composition of employment by type of worker, 1950–2000

Type of worker	1950	1960	1970	1980	1990	2000
	Total employment (in millions)					
1. Knowledge	2.2	2.8	4.8	6.8	9.4	13.9
2. Data	14.2	19.0	26.9	34.7	41.1	49.1
3. Knowledge/data	4.5	5.0	5.4	8.2	11.9	14.0
4. Data/services	1.7	2.0	3.0	4.9	5.4	7.2
5. Services	6.0	8.4	10.2	13.5	16.5	19.5
6. Goods	30.4	28.6	28.3	31.2	34.4	33.2
7. Total knowledge	4.4	5.3	7.5	10.9	15.3	20.9
8. Total data	17.2	22.5	31.1	41.2	49.8	59.7
9. Total information	21.7	27.8	38.6	52.1	65.1	80.6
10. Total non-information	37.2	38.0	40.0	47.2	53.6	56.3
11. Total employment	58.9	65.8	78.7	99.3	118.8	136.9
	Annual rate of growth of employment (in percent)					
	1950–60	1960–70	1970–80	1980–90	1990–2000	1950–2000
Total knowledge	1.7	3.5	3.7	3.4	3.1	3.1
Total data	2.7	3.3	2.8	1.9	1.8	2.5
Total services	3.4	1.9	2.8	2.0	1.7	2.4
Goods	−0.6	−0.1	1.0	1.0	−0.4	0.2
Total information	2.5	3.3	3.0	2.2	2.1	2.6
Total non-information	0.2	0.5	1.6	1.3	0.5	0.8
Total	1.1	1.8	2.3	1.8	1.4	1.7
	Percent distribution of employment					
	1950	1960	1970	1980	1990	2000
Total knowledge	7.5	8.0	9.6	11.0	12.9	15.2
Total data	29.2	34.2	39.6	41.5	41.9	43.6
Total services	10.2	12.8	13.0	13.6	13.9	14.2
Goods	51.7	43.5	36.0	31.4	29.0	24.3
Total information	36.8	42.2	49.1	52.5	54.8	58.9
Total non-information	63.2	57.8	50.9	47.5	45.2	41.1
Total	100.0	100.0	100.0	100.0	100.0	100.0

Note: The total for knowledge workers (line 7) is given by the sum of line 1 and half of line 3. The total for data workers (line 8) is given by the sum of line 2, half of line 3, and half of line 4. The total for information workers (line 9) is defined as the sum of line 7 and line 8. The total for non-information workers (line 10) is the residual.

bottom were agriculture, construction, and trade. All told, service industries had a slightly higher share of knowledge workers than goods-producing sectors – 15.6 versus 14.4%.

There is more variation in the share of data workers among sectors. In 2000, the finance, insurance, and real estate sector led the way at 66%, and it was also the most information-intensive: about 87% of its employees were knowledge or data workers. The trade sector

Table 2. Knowledge and data workers as a percent of total employment by major industry, 1950–2000

Sector	1950	1960	1970	1980	1990	2000
A. Knowledge Workers						
Agriculture	0.5	0.9	2.3	3.4	3.6	9.7
Mining	4.5	7.6	10.5	12.6	14.8	13.4
Manufacturing	5.9	7.0	9.3	9.8	11.9	17.8
Construction	4.9	7.2	7.7	7.6	10.1	8.4
Transportation, communications, and utilities	5.8	6.7	7.8	9.5	11.3	14.5
Trade	10.6	7.9	7.0	9.3	10.7	6.0
Finance, insurance, and real estate	9.2	10.6	10.6	12.1	15.4	21.7
Business and other services	12.0	11.1	12.5	13.7	15.6	18.7
Government	12.4	11.8	13.9	15.5	16.1	18.6
Total goods	4.4	6.1	8.3	9.0	10.9	14.4
Total services	11.2	9.9	10.5	12.2	14.0	15.6
Total	7.5	8.0	9.6	11.0	12.9	15.2
B. Data Workers						
Agriculture	0.7	1.4	3.9	6.2	7.2	13.7
Mining	11.2	17.3	23.4	26.3	28.5	24.3
Manufacturing	21.8	22.9	25.9	27.3	27.1	28.3
Construction	7.8	12.2	17.5	19.8	19.2	22.6
Transportation, communications, and utilities	32.4	31.9	35.7	37.1	36.1	39.0
Trade	51.9	54.5	52.9	51.6	53.0	60.8
Finance, insurance, and real estate	69.2	79.1	80.3	79.3	75.8	65.5
Business and other services	31.1	35.1	43.5	45.1	45.0	45.3
Government	53.7	54.2	52.9	51.1	48.2	37.5
Total goods	16.0	19.7	24.4	26.1	25.8	28.3
Total services	45.0	48.2	51.0	51.2	50.9	50.2
Total	29.2	34.2	39.6	41.5	41.9	43.6

Note: Calculations are shown for total knowledge workers and total data workers. The goods sector consists of agriculture, mining, manufacturing, construction, and transportation, communications, and utilities. The service sector includes trade; finance, insurance, and real estate; business and other services; and government.

was next in line, at 61%, followed by business and other services, at 45%, and transportation, communications, and utilities, at 39%, and the government sector, at 38%. In agriculture, mining, construction, and manufacturing, data workers comprised between 14 and 28% of total employment. The share of data workers in total employment was almost twice as high in services as in goods industries.

There are also marked differences in time trends between goods-producing sectors and services. In the former, there was an almost steady rise in both knowledge workers and data workers as a share of total industry employment between 1950 and 2000. In manufacturing, in particular, information workers constituted 46% of total employment by 2000, up from 28% in 1950, and blue-collar production workers made up 52%, down from 70% in 1950 (service workers constituting the remainder). This result confirms the growing 'white-collarization' of manufacturing in the US, often alluded to in the press.

Among service industries, there was generally a fall-off in the percentage of knowledge workers in employment between 1950 and 1960 (1970 in one case), followed generally by a steady rise through 2000 (with the trade sector an exception). In contrast, data workers increased relative to total employment in all four service sectors between 1950 and 1960. In the trade sector, the share of data workers held steady from 1960 to 1990 and then climbed in 2000; in finance, insurance, and real estate, the share remained relatively constant between 1960 and 1980 and then declined from 1980 to 2000; in business and other services, the share increased from 1960 to 1980 and then remained constant from 1980 to 2000; and in the government sector, there was a gradual decline in the share of data workers in total employment from 1960 to 2000. All told, between 1950 and 2000, information workers increased in number relative to non-information workers in all major sectors except the government.

The growth in the overall share of information workers in total employment is due to two proximate causes. The first is technological change on the industry level, which may favor information workers relative to non-information workers. This may be attributable to the increasing sophistication and complexity of productive techniques, which requires more producers, manipulators, and transmitters of knowledge. The second is shifts in the industrial composition of employment. In particular, industries more intensive in their use of information workers may have grown in terms of employment relative to industries that rely more heavily on service and goods-processing workers.

The second, in turn, can be further decomposed into two additional effects. The first of these is from changes in the composition of final output. In particular, an increasingly educated population may be demanding products with an ever-increasing information content over time. The second of these may arise from differential movements in industry labor productivity. In particular, from the unbalanced growth hypothesis, employment in activities with relatively slower rates of productivity growth must increase relative to employment in high productivity growth activities, even with constant output proportions (see, for example, Baumol, 1967, or Baumol *et al.*, 1989, Chapter 7). There may be some presumption that information-intensive industries, such as business services and the government, may suffer form relatively stagnant productivity growth.

We can address this issue formally through the use of an input–output model. First, define the following matrix and vector components, where all variables are in constant (2000) dollars, unless otherwise indicated, $\mathbf{x}$ is the 64×1 column vector showing the total output (gross domestic output) by sector, $\mathbf{y}$ the 64×1 column vector showing the final output by sector, $\mathbf{E}$ the 267×64 employment matrix, where e_{ij} shows the total employment of occupation i in industry j, $\mathbf{h}$ the 1×64 row vector showing total employment by industry, where $h_j = \Sigma_i e_{ij}$, and $\mathbf{b}$ the 267×1 column vector of total employment by occupation, where $b_i = \Sigma_j e_{ij}$.

Let us now define the following coefficients: $\mathbf{A}$ is the 64×64 matrix of inter-industry input–output coefficients, where a_{ij} indicates the amount of input i (in 2000 dollars) required per unit of output j (in 2000 dollars); $\mathbf{z}$ the 64×1 column vector showing the percentage distribution of total final output by sector, where $z_i = y_i/\Sigma_i y_i$; $\mathbf{F}$ the 267×64 employment coefficient matrix, showing employment by occupation per unit of output, where $f_{ij} = e_{ij}/x_j$; $\mathbf{C}$ the 267×64 employment distribution matrix, showing the percentage distribution of employment by occupation within each sector, where $c_{ij} = e_{ij}/h_j$; and $\boldsymbol{\mu}$ the 64×1 vector of labor coefficients showing total employment per unit of output, where $\mu_j = h_j/x_j$. To derive the basic relationship, I start with the basic Leontief identity

$$\mathbf{x} = (\mathbf{I} - \mathbf{A})^{-1}\mathbf{y} \tag{8}$$

It then follows that

$$\mathbf{b} = \mathbf{Fx} = \mathbf{F}(\mathbf{I} - \mathbf{A})^{-1}\mathbf{y} = \mathbf{C}\hat{\boldsymbol{\mu}}(\mathbf{I} - \mathbf{A})^{-1}\mathbf{y} = \mathbf{C}\boldsymbol{\Psi}\mathbf{y}$$

where $\boldsymbol{\Psi} = \hat{\boldsymbol{\mu}}(\mathbf{I} - \mathbf{A})^{-1}$, which shows the direct plus indirect labor requirements per unit of final output and a circumflex (or 'hat') connotes a diagonal matrix whose elements are those of the associated vector. Then, for a given percentage final output vector $\mathbf{z}$,

$$\mathbf{b_z} = \mathbf{C}\boldsymbol{\Psi}\mathbf{z} \tag{9}$$

where $\mathbf{b_z}$ shows employment by occupation generated by the final output vector $\mathbf{z}$. We then have:

$$\Delta\mathbf{b_z} = (\Delta\mathbf{C})\boldsymbol{\Psi}\mathbf{z} + \mathbf{C}(\Delta\boldsymbol{\Psi})\mathbf{z} + \mathbf{C}\boldsymbol{\Psi}(\Delta\mathbf{z}) \tag{10}$$

where the symbol Δ indicates change over the period. Two decompositions are used. Following the work of Dietzenbacher and Los (1998), I use average period weights in the first to yield an approximate decomposition as follows:

$$\Delta\mathbf{b} \approx \frac{1}{4}(\Delta\mathbf{C})(\boldsymbol{\Psi}_0 + \boldsymbol{\Psi}_1)(\mathbf{z}_0 + \mathbf{z}_1) + \frac{1}{4}(\mathbf{C}_0 + \mathbf{C}_1)(\Delta\boldsymbol{\Psi})(\mathbf{z}_0 + \mathbf{z}_1)$$
$$+ \frac{1}{4}(\mathbf{C}_0 + \mathbf{C}_1)(\boldsymbol{\Psi}_0 + \boldsymbol{\Psi}_1)(\Delta\mathbf{z}) \tag{10a}$$

These results are shown in Table 3. The second is based on two exact polar decompositions, as follows:

$$\Delta\mathbf{b} = (\Delta\mathbf{C})\boldsymbol{\Psi}_1\mathbf{z}_1 + \mathbf{C}_0(\Delta\boldsymbol{\Psi})\mathbf{z}_1 + \mathbf{C}_0\boldsymbol{\Psi}_0(\Delta\mathbf{z}) \tag{10b}$$
$$\Delta\mathbf{b} = (\Delta\mathbf{C})\boldsymbol{\Psi}_0\mathbf{z}_0 + \mathbf{C}_1(\Delta\boldsymbol{\Psi})\mathbf{z}_0 + \mathbf{C}_1\boldsymbol{\Psi}_1(\Delta\mathbf{z}) \tag{10c}$$

From Dietzenbacher and Los (1998), the average of the last two polar decompositions yields a Fisher-type index and I show these results in Table 4.

Equation (10) decomposes the change in the occupational composition of employment into three parts. The first term corresponds to the change in the employment shares of different occupations within industry. In other words, this term reflects the extent to which production processes within industries have changed their techniques so as to substitute information labor for labor of other types. This term is referred to as the *substitution effect.*

The second term involves the change in the vector of quantities of direct plus indirect labor per unit of output, by industry – that is, the change in the reciprocal of each industry's 'total' labor productivity. This approach derives from the work of Pasinetti (1973), who first introduced the concept of a vertically integrated industry (that is, incorporating direct and indirect coefficients). The total labor productivity approach has also been used by Wolff (1985) and Dietzenbacher *et al.* (2000). This term also captures the unbalanced growth effect – that is, the fact that (total) labor productivity grows at different rates in different industries. I call this the *productivity effect.*[3] The final term reflects changes in

Table 3. Decomposition of the change in employment composition by type of worker into a substitution, productivity, and output effect using average period weights, 1950–2000

Type of work	Decomposition in percentage points				Percent decomposition			
	Substitution effect	Productivity effect	Output effect	Total change	Substitution effect	Productivity effect	Output effect	Total change
1. Knowledge Workers								
1950–60	−0.32	0.86	−0.03	0.49	−65.8	175.5	−6.1	103.5
1960–70	0.80	0.64	0.02	1.53	52.5	41.8	1.3	95.6
1970–80	1.10	0.21	0.08	1.42	77.7	14.8	5.6	98.1
1980–90	1.50	0.33	0.06	1.94	77.2	17.0	3.1	97.3
1990–00	1.69	0.77	0.03	2.33	72.6	33.0	1.3	107.0
1950–00	4.77	3.01	0.17	7.70	62.0	39.2	2.2	103.4
2. Data Workers								
1950–60	1.59	3.36	0.03	4.91	32.3	68.4	0.6	101.3
1960–70	2.01	4.14	−0.57	5.40	37.2	76.7	−10.6	103.3
1970–80	0.65	1.35	0.02	1.97	32.9	68.6	1.0	102.5
1980–90	0.04	0.34	0.09	0.40	9.3	84.3	22.3	115.9
1990–00	0.78	0.81	0.02	1.69	46.1	47.7	1.3	95.1
1950–00	5.06	9.89	−0.41	14.38	35.2	68.8	−2.9	101.1
3. Service Workers								
1950–60	1.11	1.24	0.38	2.76	40.1	44.9	13.8	98.7
1960–70	−0.61	0.84	0.27	0.57	−105.6	146.3	47.0	87.7
1970–80	0.13	0.58	0.48	1.18	10.9	49.0	40.6	100.5
1980–90	−0.69	0.11	0.69	0.08	—	—	—	—
1990–00	−0.13	0.87	0.10	0.71	−18.0	122.7	14.8	119.5
1950–00	−0.19	3.72	1.82	5.31	−3.6	70.1	34.2	100.7

(*Table continued*)

Table 3. *Continued*

Type of work	Decomposition in percentage points				Percent decomposition			
	Substitution effect	Productivity effect	Output effect	Total change	Substitution effect	Productivity effect	Output effect	Total change
4. Goods-processing Workers								
1950–60	−2.32	−5.26	−0.59	−8.16	28.4	64.4	7.2	100.1
1960–70	−2.27	−4.61	−0.74	−7.50	30.2	61.5	9.9	101.6
1970–80	−1.87	−1.30	−1.41	−4.57	41.0	28.4	30.8	100.2
1980–90	−0.80	−1.28	−0.37	−2.42	33.1	52.9	15.3	101.2
1990–00	−1.99	−2.49	−0.04	−4.73	42.0	52.7	0.8	95.5
1950–00	−9.25	−15.12	−2.97	−27.38	33.8	55.2	10.8	99.8

Note: Calculations are shown for total knowledge workers, total data workers, total service workers, and goods producers. Average period weights are used in all cases. The substitution, productivity, and output effects refer, respectively, to the three terms of equation (10).

Table 4. Decomposition of the change in employment composition by type of worker into a substitution, productivity, and output effect using Fisher-type weights, 1950–2000

	Decomposition in percentage points				Percent Decomposition			
Type of worker	Substitution effect	Productivity effect	Output effect	Total change	Substitution effect	Productivity effect	Output effect	Total change
1. Knowledge Workers								
1950–60	−0.40	0.92	−0.03	0.49	−83.1	189.3	−6.2	100.0
1960–70	0.79	0.71	0.03	1.53	51.7	46.6	1.6	100.0
1970–80	1.11	0.24	0.08	1.42	77.8	16.6	5.6	100.0
1980–90	1.49	0.39	0.06	1.94	76.8	20.0	3.3	100.0
1990–00	1.47	0.82	0.03	2.33	63.3	35.3	1.4	100.0
1950–00	4.45	3.08	0.17	7.70	57.8	40.0	2.2	100.0
2. Data Workers								
1950–60	1.57	3.31	0.03	4.91	32.0	67.4	0.6	100.0
1960–70	1.89	4.08	−0.57	5.40	35.0	75.5	−10.5	100.0
1970–80	0.63	1.32	0.02	1.97	31.9	67.0	1.1	100.0
1980–90	−0.03	0.35	0.09	0.40	−8.5	87.0	21.5	100.0
1990–00	0.91	0.76	0.02	1.69	53.8	44.9	1.3	100.0
1950–00	4.97	9.82	−0.41	14.38	34.6	68.3	−2.9	100.0
3. Service Workers								
1950–60	1.14	1.29	0.33	2.76	41.4	46.7	11.9	100.0
1960–70	−0.54	0.92	0.20	0.57	−94.6	159.7	34.9	100.0
1970–80	0.13	0.61	0.45	1.18	10.7	51.6	37.8	100.0
1980–90	−0.69	0.08	0.69	0.08	—	—	—	—
1990–00	−0.29	0.96	0.04	0.71	−41.4	136.3	5.1	100.0
1950–00	−0.26	3.87	1.70	5.31	−4.9	72.8	32.1	100.0

(Table continued)

Table 4. *Continued*

Type of worker	Decomposition in percentage points				Percent Decomposition			
	Substitution effect	Productivity effect	Output effect	Total change	Substitution effect	Productivity effect	Output effect	Total change
4. Goods-processing Workers								
1950–60	−2.32	−5.31	−0.54	−8.16	28.4	65.0	6.6	100.0
1960–70	−2.14	−4.69	−0.67	−7.50	28.6	62.5	8.9	100.0
1970–80	−1.86	−1.33	−1.38	−4.57	40.7	29.2	30.1	100.0
1980–90	−0.77	−1.34	−0.31	−2.42	31.9	55.5	12.6	100.0
1990–00	−2.18	−2.58	0.03	−4.73	46.1	54.5	−0.6	100.0
1950–00	−9.28	−15.25	−2.86	−27.38	33.9	55.7	10.4	100.0

Note: Calculations are shown for total knowledge workers, total data workers, total service workers, and goods producers. The results are based on the average of two decompositions. The first uses first period weights for the first two terms and second period weights for the third term. In the second decomposition, the weighting is reversed. The substitution, productivity, and output effects refer, respectively, to the three terms of equation (10).

the composition of final output among different industries, which I call the (final) *output effect*.[4]

If the last term turns out to be significant and substantial in an empirical calculation, this will imply that the growth in information employment is indeed attributable to an information revolution. This is because a large third term indicates that buyers are typically turning increasingly to outputs whose production has a large information content. The same may also be true, in part, of a large first term, which may indicate that a typical production process has increased in reliance on information labor. However, if the second term turns out to be substantial and significant it will suggest that a corresponding portion of the increase in the share of information labor is attributable not to an upsurge in information use, but rather to unbalanced growth – the shift of labor out of activities whose productivity growth is atypically large.

The primary data source consists of US standard 87-order (benchmark) Bureau of Economic (BEA) analysis input–output tables for years 1947, 1958, 1963, 1967, 1972, 1977, 1982, 1987, and 1992, and the 'annual' BEA input–output table for 2000, which are used to compute the vector of final demand and the vector that shows the direct and indirect labor requirements (see the Data Appendix for details on sources and methods for the input–output data.) These data are aggregated to 64 sectors to align with the occupation by industry matrices already described above.[5]

On the basis of average period weights, the substitution effect gained continuing strength over time as a source of growth of employment for knowledge workers (Panel 1 of Table 3). During the 1950s, in fact, the effect was negative, indicating that industries substituted other types of workers for knowledge workers in their industry employment. During the 1960s, this effect contributed 0.8 percentage points to the increase in the share of knowledge workers in total employment; in the 1970s, 1.1 percentage points; and in the 1980s and the 1990s, 1.5 percentage points.

In contrast, the productivity effect was a generally diminishing source of growth for knowledge workers between 1950 and 1980, accounting for 0.9 percentage points in the period 1950–1960, 0.6 percentage points in 1960–1970, and 0.2 percentage points in 1970–1980, and then picking up to 0.3 percentage points in 1980–1990 and 0.8 percentage points in the 1990s. Differences in productivity growth between information-intensive industries and other industries fell considerably between the first two decades of the period and the second two, a reflection mainly of the sharp drop in overall labor productivity growth between the two 20-year periods (from 1.8 to 1.0% per year on the basis of GDP per fulltime equivalent employee), and then widened in the last decade, as overall productivity growth rebounded (to 1.5% per year).

Changes in (final) output composition played virtually no role at all in the growth of the share of knowledge workers in the labor force. All told, about three-fifths of the growth in this share over the half century was attributable to the substitution of knowledge workers for other types of workers within industry and the other two-fifths or so to the unbalanced growth effect.

Results for data workers differ with those for knowledge workers. The substitution effect was much stronger in the decades of the 1950s and 1960s than the 1970s and 1980s. In fact, the substitution effect fell from 1.6 percentage points in the 1950s to virtually zero in the 1980s. However, as with knowledge workers, the productivity effect shows a diminishing influence over time, falling from 3.4 percentage points in the period 1950–60 to 0.3 percentage points in 1980–90, though it did rebound to

0.8 percentage points in the 1990s. Changes in the composition of final output did play a modest role on changes in the share of data workers in total employment in the 1960s, although the effect was negative (−0.6 percentage points). In the other decades, the effect was very small. Over the entire five decades, output changes had only a very minor bearing on the growth of data workers in total employment. The dominant effect was uneven productivity growth, which accounted for about two-thirds of the increase in its share of total employment, while the substitution effect contributed the other one third or so.

For service worker employment, the substitution effect was positive and relatively strong in the 1950s, contributing 1.1 percentage points to the growth in their share of total employment. However, the effect was very weak thereafter, and during the 1960s, 1980s, and 1990s the effect was actually negative, indicating that information workers were substituted for service employees. The unbalanced growth effect was also strong in the 1950s, 1.2 percentage points, gradually lessened over time, reaching 0.1 percentage points in the 1980s, but then climbing to 0.9 percentage points in the 1990s. Changes in output composition had a positive effect on the employment of service workers. It generally increased over time, from 0.4 percentage points in the 1950s to 0.7 percentage points in the 1980s, reflecting primarily the increased demand for medical, educational, social, and personal services, but then tailing off to virtually zero in the 1990s. Over the entire 1950–2000 period, the principal source of growth in the share of service employment in total employment was the productivity effect, which accounted for about 70% of its growth, followed by changes in output composition, which accounted for 34%, and, lastly, the substitution effect, which accounted for only about −4%.

The story for goods-processing workers is very different from that for the other types of workers. All three effects were strongly negative, and each played a role in the decline in the share of goods-processing workers in total employment. The strongest influence was the differential productivity effect, which accounted for over half its total decrease between 1950 and 2000. The effect was extremely strong in the 1950s and 1960s – −5.3 and −4.6 percentage points, respectively – and accounted for over 60% of the relative decline of goods workers in those two decades. In the 1970s and 1980s, the effect had fallen to −1.3 percentage points, although, here too, strengthened in the 1990s, to −2.5 percentage points. The substitution effect explained another third of the decrease in the share of goods-processing workers in total employment over the entire half century. The effect gradually diminished over time, from −2.3 percentage points in the 1950s to −0.8 percentage points in the 1980s, although once again picked up to −2.0 percentage points in the 1990s. Changes in output composition also played a role, accounting for 11% of its overall decline as a share of total employment over the entire period. The effect was particularly strong in the 1970s, when it contributed −1.4 percentage points or 31% of the drop in its share.

Results on the basis of the average of the two polar decompositions, shown in Table 4, are very close to those of Table 3. Over the five decades, the substitution effect is slightly weaker and the productivity effect slightly stronger for knowledge workers on the basis of the Fisher-type weights. For service workers, the substitution effect is slightly more negative and the productivity effect slightly stronger on the basis of the Fisher-type weights.

In sum, on the production side of the economy, a large contribution was made by technological change within each industry which substituted information labor for other types of labor. The substitution component explained almost three-fifths of the growth in the share of knowledge workers and over a third of the growth in the share of data workers. It also accounted for over a third of the decline in the share of goods-processing workers, although none of the growth in the percentage of service workers in total employment.

The unbalanced productivity component was the strongest of the three effects. The absorption of workers from industries whose productivity grew relatively slowly explained almost two-fifths of the increase in the share of knowledge workers in total employment, two thirds of the increase in the share of data workers, over 70% of the rising share of service workers, and over half of the decline in the share of goods-processing workers. The output composition effect contributed almost nothing to the growth of information employment but accounted for almost a third of the growth in the share of service workers in total employment and 10% of the decline in the share of goods-processing workers.

These results also imply that the so-called 'information explosion' is almost entirely a consequence of unbalanced growth and the substitution of information labor within production. Demand shifts towards heavily information-using products did not play a role in the growth of information workers.

5. Technology and the Growth in Information Employment

Although about half of the growth in information employment has resulted from the less rapid productivity growth of the more information-intensive industries in the economy, the other half has also arisen from changes in employment patterns within industry. This section uses econometric methods to analyze the sources of growth of information workers on the industry level. I use three sets of independent variables: (i) measures of technological activity; (ii) investment, including computerization; and (iii) indices of international competitiveness.

According to the literature reviewed in the second section as well as the model developed in this section, we should expect to find a positive relation between the growth of the share of knowledge workers in total employment and the pace of technological change and a corresponding negative relation between the growth of the share of data workers and the pace of technological change. As a result, both TFP growth and R&D intensity, which are indicators of the development of new technology, should be positively correlated with the growth in the share of knowledge workers and negatively correlated with the change in the share of data workers.

Likewise, a positive relation should be expected between the growth of the share of knowledge workers in total employment and the intensity of IT investment and a corresponding negative relation between the growth of the share of data workers and IT investment. Predictions are ambiguous for the shares of service and goods workers in employment since these jobs represent a combination of routine and non-routine tasks.

With regard to non-IT equipment investment, the dominant view is the capital-skills complementarity hypothesis. Greater investment in equipment should be associated with a greater demand for knowledge workers and a reduced demand for the other types of workers. As indicated in the first section, international competitiveness may also affect the rate of change in the employment of information workers. Greater international trade should be associated with an increased share of knowledge workers and a reduced share of data workers.

The regression analysis uses pooled cross-section time-series data, covering 44 industries in three ten-year time periods, 1960–1970, 1970–1980, and 1980–1990, and 32 industries for the 1990–2000 time period.[6] I use a fixed effect model, with industry dummy variables, as follows:

$$\begin{aligned}\text{KNOWSHAR}_{jt} = \beta_0 + \beta_1 \ln(\text{TFP}_{jt}) + \beta_2\text{RDKGDP}_{jt} + \beta_3 \ln(\text{EQPKXPEP}_{jt})\\ + \beta_4 \ln(\text{OCAKPEP}_{jt}) + \beta_5\text{EXPGDP}_{jt} + \beta_6\text{IMPGDP}_{jt}\\ + \Sigma_{43}\gamma_j\text{INDDUM}_{jt} + u_{jt}\end{aligned}$$

where for industry j at time t, KNOWSHAR_{jt} is the share of knowledge workers, TFP_{jt} is the TFP level, RDKGDP_{jt} is the ratio of R&D capital stock to GDP, EQPKXPEP_{jt} is the total net stock of equipment and machinery less OCA per worker (PEP), OCAKPEP_{jt} is the net stock of OCA per worker, EXPGDP_{jt} is the ratio of exports to GDP, IMPGDP_{jt} is the ratio of imports to GDP, INDDUM_{jt} is a set of 43 industry dummy variables[7] and γ_j are the corresponding coefficients, and u_{jt} is a stochastic error term. First-differencing (over time) yields:

$$\begin{aligned}\Delta\text{KNOWSHAR}_{jT} = \beta_0 + \beta_1\text{TFPGRT}_{jT} + \beta_2\text{RDGDP}_{jT} + \beta_3\text{EQPXPEPGRT}_{jT}\\ + \beta_4\text{OCAPEPGRT}_{jT} + \beta_5\Delta\text{EXPGDP}_{jT} + \beta_6\Delta\text{IMPGDP}_{jT}\\ + v_{jT} \qquad (12)\end{aligned}$$

where, industry j over the period T (from $t-1$ to t), $\Delta\text{KNOWSHAR}_{jT}$ is the change in the share of knowledge workers, TFPGRT_{jT} is TFP growth, RDGDP_{jT} is the average ratio of R&D expenditures to GDP in period T, EQPXPEPGRT_{jT} is the growth in the total net stock of equipment and machinery less OCA per worker (PEP), OCAPEPGRT_{jT} is the growth of the net stock of OCA per worker, ΔEXPGDP_{jT} is the change in the ratio of exports to GDP, ΔIMPGDP_{jT} is the change in the ratio of imports to GDP, and v_{jT} is a stochastic error term. I also include period dummy variables. Moreover, although in principle the industry dummy variables zero out in the first-differencing, I also include a set of these in order to capture any unobserved heterogeneity of industry characteristics on changes over time. In addition, as alternatives to OCAPEPGRT and EQPXPEPGRT, I have also used INVOCAPEP and INVEQPXPEP, investment in OCA and non-OCA equipment per worker. A similar set of specifications is used for $\Delta\text{DATASHAR}_{jT}$, the change in the share of data workers.[8]

Results are reported in Table 5. In the two specifications without industry dummy variables, the strongest effect on the growth of knowledge workers comes from R&D investment (the ratio of R&D expenditures to industry output). Its coefficient is positive and highly significant (at the 1% level).[9] Its coefficient is negative for the growth in data workers and also significant, although at the 5% level. These results are consistent with the hypothesis that new technology increases the need for highly skilled workers relative to less skilled workers.

Computerization has a positive and marginally significant effect on gains in knowledge employment and a highly significant negative effect (at the 1% level) on the growth in data workers.[10] These results are consistent with the hypothesis that computerization increases the demand for high-skilled workers relative to lower-skilled ones

Table 5. Regressions of the share of information workers in total employment on technology and other variables using industry level data, 1960–2000

Independent variables	Dependent variable: Change in the employment share of knowledge workers		Change in the employment share of data workers	
Constant	0.027 (3.59)**	0.053 (3.06)**	0.054 (4.85)**	0.020 (0.81)
TFP growth	−0.042 (0.47)	−0.102 (0.92)	−0.093 (0.71)	−0.023 (0.15)
Ratio of R&D expenditures to total output	0.264 (2.78)**	0.313 (2.89)**	−0.342 (2.11)*	−0.316 (0.94)
Investment in equipment less OCA (in 1000s, 2000$) per worker	0.062 (1.45)	0.029 (0.35)	0.074 (1.14)	0.199 (1.62)
Investment in OCA (in 1000s, 2000$) per worker	1.794 (1.91)#	1.926 (2.16)*	−13.275 (9.74)**	−13.537 (8.46)**
Change in the ratio of imports to total output	0.034 (1.27)	0.027 (0.68)	−0.002 (0.06)	−0.035 (0.62)
Change in the ratio of exports to total output	0.309 (2.24)*	0.051 (1.29)	0.329 (1.59)	0.297 (1.20)
Time dummies	YES	YES	YES	YES
Industry dummies	NO	YES	NO	YES
R^2	0.14	0.37	0.44	0.63
Adjusted R^2	0.09	0.07	0.41	0.46
Standard error	0.0292	0.0296	0.0439	0.0422
Sample size	164	164	164	164

Note: The sample consists of pooled cross-section time-series data, with observations on each of the 44 industries in 1960–1970, 1970–1980 and 1980–1990 (sector 45, public administration, is excluded because of a lack of appropriate capital stock data), and 32 industries in 1990–2000. The coefficients are estimated using use the White procedure for a heteroskedasticity-consistent covariance matrix. The absolute value of the t-statistic is in parentheses below the coefficient. See the Data Appendix for sources and methods. Significance levels: # – 10%; * – 5% level; ** – 1% level.

(skills that are substitutes for IT). Investment in total equipment excluding OCA per worker has a positive but statistically insignificant effect on the change in the share of knowledge workers. Its effect on the change in the proportion of data workers is also positive but again not significant.

The other variables used in the regression analysis, TFP growth and changes in trade intensity, are not statistically significant except for the change in export intensity in the case of the growth of knowledge workers. Its coefficient is positive and significant at the 5% level. The direction of causation is not clear. On the one hand, these results may suggest that export-oriented industries require knowledge workers for the development of new products, product design and styling, and process innovation (increasing efficiency in the production of existing products). On the other hand, it may be the case that knowledge-intensive industries are better positioned for the export market.

Dummy variables for time periods 1960–1970, 1970–1980, and 1980–1990 are significant for the growth of both knowledge and data workers (results not shown). One other point of interest is that the goodness of fit is much stronger in the case of data workers than knowledge workers. The high R-square for the former is primarily attributable to the extremely significant (and negative) effects of OCA investment on the employment of data workers (a t-ratio of almost 10).

The introduction of the industry dummy variables causes two of the results to change. The coefficient on the change in export intensity in the regression on the change in the share of knowledge workers remains positive but now become statistically insignificant, and the coefficient on R&D intensity in the regression on the change in the share of data workers remains negative but becomes insignificant. These results suggest that these two effects may have resulted from unobserved heterogeneity of industry characteristics. On the other hand, the coefficients on R&D intensity and investment in OCA per worker in the former regression actually become stronger and their t-values rise. The coefficient on OCA investment per worker in the latter equation retains its very significant, negative coefficient.

6. Conclusion

This paper documents the rapid growth of information workers in the US economy. Information workers as a group grew from 37% of total employment in 1950 to 59% in 2000. However, the time patterns are quite different for knowledge-producing and data workers, with the increase in the share of the former accelerating from 0.5 percentage points during the 1950s to 2.3 percentage points in the 1990s and that of the latter slowing down from 5.0 to 1.7 percentage points.

About two-fifths of the growth in the share of knowledge workers in total employment and two-thirds of the increase in the share of data workers over the period from 1950 to 2000 is attributable to differential rates of productivity movements among the industries of the economy. However, the unbalanced growth effect diminished over the first four decades, a reflection of the general slowdown in overall productivity growth between the 1950s and 1960s and the ensuing two decades, although it did pick up in the 1990s, as overall productivity growth rebounded.

On the production side of the economy, the substitution component explained almost three-fifths of the growth in the share of knowledge workers over the five decades and about a third of the growth in the share of data workers. The substitution effect increased in importance over time in the case of knowledge workers (from −0.4 percentage points in the 1950s to 1.5 percentage points in the 1990s) but generally diminished over time for data workers (from 1.6 to 0.0 percentage points in the 1980s but then up to 0.9 percentage points in the 1990s). It also accounted for a third of the decline in the share of goods-processing workers.

In contrast, demand shifts towards heavily information-using products contributed virtually nothing to the growth of information employment. In other words, the relative growth in information workers has come through changes in production technology, not through the substitution of information-intensive products for others among final consumers.

The results of the regression analysis reveal that R&D expenditures had the strongest influence on the growth of knowledge workers. These results are in accord with those of Machin and van Reenen (1998). OCA investment also exerted a positive effect.

On the other hand, investment in OCA exerted a strong depressing effect on the growth in data workers. These results are in accord with the Autor *et al.* (2003) model described in the second section. TFP growth and investment in equipment other than OCA per worker were not significant factors in the growth of either knowledge or data workers. The change in export intensity was found to be significantly related to the growth of knowledge workers but this effect was washed out when industry dummy variables were introduced.

Notes

[1]Other ratios were used to split the hybrid groups (such as one-third and two-thirds), with little effect on the results of the data analysis. I also modified the original classification schema by 'upgrading' several occupations, with little difference in results. In particular, medical doctors (occupations 27–29, 31–33), therapists (36), and clergymen (38) were upgraded from 'Data/Service' workers to 'Knowledge/Service' workers; and insurance agents, brokers, and underwriters (84), real estate agents and brokers (86), and stock and bond salesmen were upgraded from 'Data' workers to 'Knowledge/Data' workers. By the original classification scheme, the share of total knowledge workers in total employment rose from 7.5 to 15.2% from 1950 to 2000 or by 7.7 percentage points. By the new classification scheme, the share increased from 8.3 to 16.4% or by 8.1 percentage points.

[2]I have made some minor changes in the classification scheme used in earlier work so that the results reported here differ slightly from those reported in Baumol *et al.* (1989, Chapter 7).

[3]Like other standard output series and deflators, the standard input–output framework is not well equipped to handle product innovations because of the assumption of homogenous outputs (they are much better at capturing process innovation). As a result, measures of productivity growth in the input–output framework are likely to be biased downward because of the failure of adequately capturing quality improvements in products.

[4]The output effect also captures changes in both the relative share and the composition of investment demand. In principle, this can also be considered a technology-related effect, since investment demand is at least partly determined by technological factors just like the demand for intermediate inputs included in the productivity effect. The incorporation of this added effect would require a full series of US capital stock matrices, which are, unfortunately, not available for the time span covered in this analysis.

[5]Since the occupation-by-industry matrices are for different years than the input–output data, geometric interpolation of industry employment for the input–output data was used to align industry employment in the input–output data with the Census years from 1950 to 2000.

[6]See Appendix Table A2 for details on the industry classification. The public administration sector is excluded because of a lack of OCA capital stock data. Also, because of the adoption of the North American Industrial Classification System (NAICS) in 1997, only 33 industries in the 1990–2000 period could be constructed that were compatible with earlier years (the public administration sector is again excluded because of a lack of OCA capital stock data). The 1950–1960 period is also excluded because of a lack of industry-level R&D data for this period.

[7]Only 31 industry dummies for 1990–2000.

[8]Because of the heterogeneous nature of both service and goods-producing workers, no clear predictions are possible regarding the factors that affect the change in their employment shares, so that these equations are not estimated. The White procedure for a heteroskedasticity-consistent covariance matrix is also used in the estimation (see White, 1980).

[9]Part of this result reflects the fact that about half of R&D expenditures are on R&D labor, which almost by definition consists primarily of knowledge workers such as scientists and engineers.

[10]Investment of OCA per worker has somewhat stronger effects than the growth of OCA per worker.

References

Allen, S.G. (2001) Technology and the wage structure, *Journal of Labor Economics*, 19, pp. 440–483.

Autor, D.H., Katz, L.F. and Krueger, A.B. (1998) Computing inequality: how computers changed the labor market?, *Quarterly Journal of Economics*, 113, pp. 1169–1214.

Autor, D.H., Levy, F. and Murnane, R.J. (2002) Upstairs, downstairs: computers and skills on two floors of a bank, *Industrial and Labor Relations Review*, 55, pp. 432–447.

Autor, D.H., Levy, F. and Murnane, R.J. (2003) The skill content of recent technological change: an empirical exploration, *Quarterly Journal of Economics*, 118, pp. 1279–1334.

Bartel, A., Ichniowski, C. and Shaw, K. (2003) The effects of technological change on skill demand: an analysis using direct intra-industry data, unpublished manuscript, available at http://www.gsb.columbia.edu/faculty/abartel/research.html.

Baumol, W.J. (1967) Macroeconomics of unbalanced growth: the anatomy of urban crisis, *American Economic Review*, 57, pp. 415–426.

Baumol, W.J., Blackman, S.A.B. and Wolff, E.N. (1989) *Productivity and American Leadership: The Long View* (Cambridge, MA: MIT Press).

Beniger, J.R. (1986) *The Control Revolution: Technological and Economic Origins of the Information Society* (Cambridge, MA: Harvard University Press).

Berman, E., Bound, J. and Griliches, Z. (1994) Changes in the demand for skilled labor within U.S. manufacturing: evidence from the annual survey of manufactures, *Quarterly Journal of Economics*, 109, pp. 367–398.

Berman, E., Bound, J. and Machin, S. (1998) Implications of skill-biased technological change: international evidence, *Quarterly Journal of Economics*, 113, pp. 1245–1279.

Borjas, G.J., Freeman, R.B. and Katz, L.F. (1992) On the labor market effects of immigration and trade, in: G.J. Borjas and R.B. Freeman (Eds) *Immigration and the Workforce: Economic Consequences for the United States and Source Areas* (Chicago: University of Chicago Press).

Bound, J. and Johnson, G.E. (1992) Changes in the structure of wages in the 1980s: an evaluation of alternative explanations, *American Economic Review*, 82, pp. 371–392.

Bresnahan, T.F., Brynjolfsson, E. and Hitt, L.M. (2002) Information technology, workplace organization, and the demand for skilled labor: firm-level evidence, *Quarterly Journal of Economics*, 117, pp. 339–376.

Bresnahan, T.F. and Trajtenberg, M. (1995) General purpose technologies: engines of growth?, *Journal of Econometrics*, 65, pp. 83–108.

David, P.A. (1991) Computer and dynamo: the modern productivity paradox in a not-too-distant Mirror, in: *Technology and Productivity: The Challenge for Economic Policy*, pp. 315–348 (Paris: OECD).

Davis, S.J. and Haltiwanger, J. (1991) Wage dispersion between and within U.S. manufacturing plants, 1963–86, *Brookings Papers on Economic Activity: Microeconomics*, pp. 115–180.

Dietzenbacher, E. and Los, B. (1998) Structural decomposition techniques: sense and sensitivity, *Economic Systems Research*, 10, pp. 307–323.

Dietzenbacher, E., Hoen, A.R. and Los, B. (2000) Labour productivity in Western Europe (1975–1985): an intercountry, interindustry analysis, *Journal of Regional Science*, 40, pp. 425–452.

DiNardo, J.E. and Pischke, J.-S. (1997) The returns to computer use revisited: have pencils changed the wage structure too?, *Quarterly Journal of Economics*, 112, pp. 291–303.

Dunne, T., Foster, L., Haltiwanger, J. and Troske, K. (2000) Wage and productivity dispersion in U.S. manufacturing: the role of computer investment, *Journal of Labor Economics*, 22, pp. 397–429.

Freeman, C. (1987) Information technology and the change in techno-economic paradigm, in: C. Freeman and L. Soete (Eds) *Technical Change and Full Employment* (Oxford: Basil Blackwell).

Freeman, R.B. (1995) Are your wages set in Beijing?, *Journal of Economic Perspectives*, 9, pp. 15–32.

Helpman, E. and Trajtenberg, M. (1998) A time to sow and a time to reap: growth based on general purpose technologies, in: E. Helpman (Ed.) *General Purpose Technologies and Economic Growth* (Cambridge, MA: MIT Press).

Katz, L.F. and Murphy, K.M. (1992) Changes in relative wages, 1963–1987: supply and demand factors, *Quarterly Journal of Economics*, 107, pp. 35–78.

Krueger, A.B. (1993) How computers have changed the wage structure: evidence from microdata, *Quarterly Journal of Economics*, 108, pp. 33–60.

Krugman, P.A. and Lawrence, R.J. (1994) Trade, jobs and wages, *Scientific American*, pp. 44–49.

Lawson, A.M. (1997) Benchmark input-output accounts for the U.S. economy, 1992, *Survey of Current Business*, 77, pp. 36–83.

Leontief, W. and Duchin, F. (1986) *The Future Impact of Automation on Workers* (New York: Oxford University Press).

Machin, S. and van Reenen, J. (1998) Technology and changes in skill structure: evidence from seven OECD countries, *Quarterly Journal of Economics*, 113, pp. 1215–1244.

Machlup, F. (1962) *The Production and Distribution of Knowledge in the United States* (Princeton, NJ: Princeton University Press).

Milkman, R. and Pullman, S. (1991) Technological change in an auto assembly plant: the impact on workers' tasks and skills, *Work and Occupations*, 18, pp. 123–147.

Osterman, P. (1986) The impact of computers on the employment of clerks and managers, *Industrial and Labor Relations Review*, 39, pp. 163–189.

Pasinetti, L. (1973) The notion of vertical integration in economic analysis, *Metroeconomica*, 24, pp. 1–29.

Porat, M.U. (1977) *The Information Economy: Definition and Measurement*, Office of Telecommunications Special Publication 77-12, US Department of Commerce (Washington, DC: US Government Printing Office).

Reich, R. (1991) *The Work of Nations: Preparing Ourselves for 21st Century Capitalism* (New York: Alfred Knopf).

Richardson, D.J. (1995) Income inequality and trade: how to think, what to conclude?, *Journal of Economic Perspectives*, 9, pp. 33–55.

Rubin, M.R. and Huber, M.T. (1986) *The Knowledge Industry in the United States, 1960–1980* (Princeton, NJ: Princeton University Press).

White, H. (1980) A heteroskedasticity-consistent covariance matrix estimator and a direct test for heteroskedasticity, *Econometrica*, 48, pp. 817–838.

Wolff, E.N. (1985) Industrial composition, interindustry effects, and the U.S. productivity slowdown, *Review of Economics and Statistics*, 67, pp. 268–277.

Wolff, E.N. (2002) Computerization and structural change, *Review of Income and Wealth*, 48, pp. 59–75.

Wood, A. (1994) *North-South Trade, Employment, and Inequality: Change Fortunes in a Skill-Driven World* (NewYork: Oxford University Press).

Wood, A. (1998) Globalization and the rise in labour market inequalities, *Economic Journal*, 108, pp. 1463–1482.

Zuboff, S. (1988) *In The Age of the Smart Machine: The Future of Work and Power* (New York: Basic Books).

Data Appendix

1. NIPA employment data: Figures are from the National Income and Product Accounts (NIPA), available on the Internet [http://www.bea.gov/bea/dn2/home/annual_industry.htm]. Persons engaged in production (PEP) equals the number of full-time and part-time employees plus the number of self-employed persons. Unpaid family workers are not included.
2. Capital stock and investment figures are based on chain-type quantity indexes for net stock of fixed capital and investment in 2000$, year-end estimates. Source: US Bureau of Economic Analysis, CD-ROM NCN-0229, 'Fixed Reproducible Tangible Wealth of the United States, 1925-97' and the Internet [http://www.bea.gov/bea/dn/home/fixedassets.htm].
3. Research and development expenditures performed by industry include company, federal, and other sources of funds. Company-financed R&D performed outside the company is excluded. Industry series on R&D and full-time equivalent scientists and engineers engaged in R&D per full-time equivalent employee run from 1957 to 2002. Sources: National Science Foundation, Internet. For technical details, see National Science Foundation, *Research and Development in Industry*, (Arlington, VA: National Science Foundation), NSF96-304, 1996; and the Internet [http://www.nsf.gov/sbe/srs/nsf01305/htmstart.htm].
4. The original input–output data are 85-sector US input–output tables for years 1947, 1958, 1963, 1967, 1972, 1977, 1982, 1987, 1992, and 2000 (see, for example, Lawson, 1997, for details on the sectoring). The 1947, 1958, and 1963 tables are available only in single-table format. The 1967, 1972, 1977, 1982, 1987, 1992, and 2000

data are available in separate make and use tables. These tables have been aggregated to 45 sectors for conformity with the other data sources. The 1950, 1960, 1970, 1980, and 1990 input–output tables are interpolated from the benchmark U.S. input–output tables. The 2000 input–output table is provided directly by the BEA as part of their annual input–output series. The source is the Internet [http://www.bea.gov/bea/dn2/i-o_annual.htm]. Import and export data by industry are also derived from the input–output data.

5. The formula for the average annual growth in total factor productivity is: $TFPGRTH_t = (dY_t)/Y_t - \alpha(dL_t)/L_t - (1-\alpha)(dK_t)/K_t$, where Y_t is GDP at time t, L_t is the total labor input, K_t is the capital input, and α is the average wage share in over the period. The labor input is measured by PEP and the capital input by the fixed non-residential net capital stock (in 2000 dollars). The wage share is measured as the ratio of employee compensation to GDP, both in current dollars, averaged over the relevant time period. Since the data are for discrete time periods, the Tornq-vist–Divisia measure, based on average period shares, is used in the actual estimation.

Appendix

Table A1. Classification of occupations into knowledge, data, service and goods workers

Occupation		
Number	Occupation name	Information group category
1	Accountants	Knowledge
2	Architects	Knowledge
3	Computer programmers	Knowledge
4	Computer systems analysts	Knowledge
5	Computer specialists, nec	Knowledge
6	Aero- and aeronautical engineers	Knowledge
7	Chemical engineers	Knowledge
8	Civil engineers	Knowledge
9	Electrical and electronic engineers	Knowledge
10	Industrial engineers	Knowledge
11	Mechanical engineers	Knowledge
12	Metal, material, mining and petro-chemical engineers	Knowledge
13	Sales engineers	Data
14	Engineers, nec	Knowledge
15	Farm management advisers, foresters, conservationists and home mgmt. advisers	Knowledge
16	Judges	Knowledge
17	Lawyers	Knowledge
18	Librarians, archivists, and curators	Knowledge
19	Actuaries, statisticians, and operation research analysts	Knowledge
20	Mathematicians	Knowledge
21	Agricultural scientists	Knowledge
22	Biological scientists	Knowledge
23	Chemists	Knowledge
24	Geologists, physicists, and astronomers	Knowledge
25	Life and physical scientists, nec	Knowledge

(*Table continued*)

Table A1. *Continued*

Occupation		
Number	Occupation name	Information group category
26	Personnel and labor relations workers	Data/Services
27	Chiropractors	Data/Services
28	Dentists	Data/Services
29	Optometrists	Data/Services
30	Pharmacists	Data
31	Physicians, medical and osteopathic	Data/Services
32	Veterinarians	Data/Services
33	Podiatrists, and health practitioners, nec	Data/Services
34	Dietitians	Data/Services
35	Registered nurses	Data/Services
36	Therapists	Data/Services
37	Health technologists and technicians	Data
38	Clergymen	Data/Services
39	Religious workers, nec	Data/Services
40	Social scientists	Knowledge
41	Social workers	Data/Services
42	Recreation workers	Data
43	Teachers, college and university	Knowledge
44	Adult education teachers	Data
45	Elementary and secondary teachers	Data
46	Pre- and kindergarten teachers	Data
47	Teachers, except college and university, nec	Data
48	Agricultural, biological, and chemical technicians	Data
49	Draftsmen	Data
50	Electrical engineering technicians	Data
51	Engineering and science technicians, nec	Data
52	Airplane pilots	Data/Services
53	Air traffic controllers	Data
54	Flight Engineers	Data
55	Tool programmers, numerical control	Data
56	Technicians, nec, including radio operators	Data
57	Vocational and educational counselors	Data/Services
58	Designers	Knowledge
59	Editors and reporters	Knowledge
60	Writers, artists, and entertainers, nec	Knowledge
61	Research worker, not specified	Knowledge
62	Bank officers and financial managers	Knowledge/Data
63	Buyers & shippers: farm, wholesale, retail	Data
64	Credit men	Data
65	Funeral directors and embalmers	Data/Services
66	Health administrators	Knowledge/Data
67	Construction inspectors, public admin.	Data
68	Inspectors, except construction, pub. admin	Data
69	Managers and superintendents, buildings	Data/Services
70	Office Managers, nec	Data
71	Ship officers, pilots, and pursers	Knowledge/Data
72	Administrators, public admin., nec	Knowledge/Data
73	Officials of lodges, societies, and unions	Knowledge/Data

(*Table continued*)

Table A1. *Continued*

Occupation		
Number	Occupation name	Information group category
74	Postmasters and mail superintendents	Knowledge/Data
75	Purchasing agents and buyers, nec	Data
76	Railroad conductors	Data
77	Restaurant, cafeteria and bar managers	Data/Services
78	Sales managers & department heads, retail	Knowledge/Data
79	Sales managers, except retail trade	Knowledge/Data
80	School admin., college, elementary, secondary	Knowledge/Data
81	Managers and administrators, nec	Knowledge/Data
82	Advertising agents and salesmen	Data
83	Auctioneers, demonstrators, hucksters,	Data
84	Insurance agents, brokers, & underwriters	Data
85	Newsboys	Data
86	Real estate agents and brokers	Data
87	Stock and bond salesmen	Data
88	Sales representatives, manufacturing and wholesale	Data
89	Sales clerks, retail; salesmen	Data
90	Bank tellers	Data
91	Bookkeepers	Data
92	Cashiers	Data
93	Collectors, bills and accounts	Data
94	Dispatchers and starters, vehicles	Data
95	File clerks	Data
96	Insurance adjusters and examiners	Data
97	Library attendants and assistants	Data
98	Mail carriers, post office	Data
99	Messengers and office boys	Data
100	Miscellaneous clerical workers	Data
101	Office machine operators	Data
102	Payroll and timekeeping clerks	Data
103	Postal clerks	Data
104	Real estate appraisers	Data
105	Receptionists	Data
106	Secretaries	Data
107	Shipping and receiving clerks	Data
108	Statistical clerks	Data
109	Stenographers	Data
110	Stock clerks and storekeepers	Data
111	Teacher aides, except school monitors	Data
112	Telegraph operators	Data
113	Telephone operators	Data
114	Ticket station and express agents	Data
115	Typists	Data
116	Bakers	Goods
117	Blacksmiths	Goods
118	Boilermakers	Goods
119	Brick, stonemasons, and tile setters	Goods
120	Bulldozer, excavating, grading operators	Goods
121	Cabinetmakers	Goods

(Table continued)

Table A1. *Continued*

Occupation Number	Occupation name	Information group category
122	Carpenters and apprentices	Goods
123	Cement and concrete finishers	Goods
124	Compositors, typesetters & apprentices	Goods
125	Cranemen, derrickmen, hoistmen	Goods
126	Decorators and window dressers	Goods
127	Electricians and apprentices	Goods
128	Electric power linemen and cablemen	Goods
129	Electro- and stereotypers, and engravers	Goods
130	Foremen, nec	Data
131	Forgemen and hammermen	Goods
132	Painters	Goods
133	Glaciers	Goods
134	Heat Treaters, annealers,and temperers	Goods
135	Inspectors nec, scalers, and graders	Goods
136	Jewelers and watchmakers	Goods
137	Job and die setters, metal	Goods
138	Locomotive engineers and firemen	Goods
139	Machinists and apprentices	Goods
140	Air conditioning, heating and refrigeration repairmen	Goods
141	Aircraft mechanics	Goods
142	Machinery mechanics and repairmen, nec	Goods
143	Household appliance mechanics	Goods
144	Loom fixers	Goods
145	Office machine mechanics and repairmen	Goods
146	Radio and television repairmen	Goods
147	Railroad and car shop mechanics	Goods
148	Miscellaneous mechanics and repairmen	Goods
149	Millers of grain, flour, and feed	Goods
150	Millwrights	Goods
151	Metal molders and apprentices	Goods
152	Motion picture projectionists	Goods
153	Opticians, lens grinders and polishers	Goods
154	Pattern and model makers, except paper	Goods
155	Photoengravers and lithographers	Goods
156	Plasterers and apprentices	Goods
157	Plumbers, pipe fitters and apprentices	Goods
158	Power station operators	Goods
159	Pressmen, plate printers, and apprentices	Goods
160	Rollers and finishers, metal	Goods
161	Roofers and slaters	Goods
162	Sheetmetal workers and tinsmiths	Goods
163	Shipfitters	Goods
164	Shoe repairmen	Goods
165	Stationary engineers	Goods
166	Structural metal craftsmen	Goods
167	Tailors	Goods
168	Phone installers, repairmen, and linemen	Goods
169	Tool and die makers and apprentices	Goods

(*Table continued*)

Table A1. *Continued*

Occupation Number	Occupation name	Information group category
170	Upholsterers	Goods
171	Craftsmen and kindred workers, nec	Goods
172	Asbestos and insulation workers	Goods
173	Assemblers	Goods
174	Blasters and powdermen	Goods
175	Bottling and canning operatives	Goods
176	Chainmen, rodmen, and axmen: surveying	Goods
177	Checkers, examiners and inspectors: manufacturing	Goods
178	Clothing ironers and pressers	Goods
179	Cutting operatives, nec	Goods
180	Dressmakers and seamstresses, except factory	Goods
181	Drillers: earth	Goods
182	Dry wall installers and lathers	Goods
183	Dyers	Goods
184	Filers, polishers, sanders, and buffers	Goods
185	Furnacemen, smeltmen and pourers	Goods
186	Garage workers and gas station attendants	Goods
187	Graders and sorters: manufacturing	Goods
188	Produce graders and packers, nec	Goods
189	Heaters: metal	Goods
190	Laundry and dry cleaning operatives, nec	Goods
191	Meat cutters and butchers	Goods
192	Packers and wrappers, except produce	Goods
193	Metal platers	Goods
194	Mine operatives, nec	Goods
195	Mixing operatives	Goods
196	Oilers and greasers, except automotive	Goods
197	Painters: manufactured articles	Goods
198	Photographic process workers	Goods
199	Drill press operatives	Goods
200	Lathe and milling machine operatives	Goods
201	Precision machine operatives, nec	Goods
202	Punch and stamping press operatives	Goods
203	Riveters and fasteners	Goods
204	Sailors and deckhands	Goods
205	Sawyers	Goods
206	Sewers and stitchers	Goods
207	Shoemaking machine operatives	Goods
208	Solderers	Goods
209	Stationary firemen	Goods
210	Carding, lapping, and combing operatives	Goods
211	Knitters, loopers, and toppers	Goods
212	Spinners, twisters, and winders	Goods
213	Weavers	Goods
214	Textile operatives, nec	Goods
215	Welders and flame-cutters	Goods
216	Winding operatives, nec	Goods
217	Machine operatives, misc. specified	Goods

(*Table continued*)

Table A1. *Continued*

Occupation Number	Occupation name	Information group category
218	Miscellaneous operatives	Goods
219	Transportation operatives	Goods
220	Fork lift and tow motor operatives	Goods
221	Motormen: mine, factory, logging camp, etc.	Goods
222	Parking attendants	Goods
223	Railroad brakemen	Goods
224	Railroad switchmen	Goods
225	Taxicab drivers and chauffeurs	Goods
226	Truck drivers	Goods
227	Animal caretakers, except farm	Goods
228	Construction laborers	Goods
229	Fishermen and oystermen	Goods
230	Freight and materials handlers	Goods
231	Garbage collectors	Service
232	Gardeners and groundskeepers, except farm	Service
233	Longshoremen and stevedores	Goods
234	Lumbermen, raftsmen, and woodchoppers	Goods
235	Stock handlers	Goods
236	Teamsters	Goods
237	Vehicle washers and equipment cleaners	Goods
238	Warehousemen, nec	Goods
239	Miscellaneous laborers	Goods
240	Not specified laborers	Goods
241	Farmers and farm managers	Goods
242	Farm foremen and farm labor	Goods
243	Cleaning service workers	Service
244	Food service workers except private household	Service
245	Cooks except private household	Service
246	Waiters	Service
247	Health aides (including dental assistants and trainees)	Service
248	Nursing aides, Orderlies, and Attendants	Service
249	Practical nurses including lay midwives	Service
250	Airline stewardesses	Service
251	Attendants: recreation and amusement	Service
252	Attendants: personal service, nec	Service
253	Barbers	Service
254	Boarding and lodging house keepers	Service
255	Bootblacks	Service
256	Child care workers except private household	Service
257	Elevator operators	Service
258	Hairdressers and cosmetologists	Service
259	Housekeepers except private household	Service
260	School monitors and ushers (recreation)	Service
261	Welfare service aides	Service
262	Crossing guards and bridge tenders	Service
263	Firemen and fire protection workers	Service
264	Guards, watchmen, marshals, and constables	Service
265	Policemen and detectives	Service
266	Sheriffs and bailiffs	Service
267	Private household workers	Service

Table A2. Concordance among the various industrial classification schemes used in this paper

45- Sector Classification Number	Name	1970 Census Codes[a]	BEA 85-Order Codes[b]	1987 SIC Codes	64-Order Scheme	10-Order Scheme
1	Agriculture, forestry, and fishing	017–029	1–4	01–09	1	1
2	Metal mining	47	5–6	10	2	2
3	Coal mining	48	7	11,12	3	2
4	Oil and gas extraction	49	8	13	4	2
5	Mining of nonmetallic minerals, except fuels	57,058	9–10	14	5	2
6	Construction	067–078	11,12	15–17	6	3
7	Food and kindred products	268–298	14	20	7–10	4
8	Tobacco products	299	15	21	11	4
9	Textile mill products	307–309, 317–318	16–17	22	12	4
10	Apparel and other textile products	329,327	18–19	23	13	4
11	Lumber and wood products	108,109	20–21	24	14–15	4
12	Furniture and fixtures	118	22–23	25	16	4
13	Paper and allied products	328–337	24–25	26	17	4
14	Printing and publishing	338,339	26	27	18	4
15	Chemicals and allied products	347–349, 357–359	27–30	28	19–21	4
16	Petroleum and coal products	377,378	31	29	22	4
17	Rubber and miscellaneous plastic productsc	379,387	32	30	23	4
18	Leather and leather products	388–397	33–34	31	24	4
19	Stone, clay, and glass products	119, 127–128,	35–36	32	25–28	5
20	Primary metal products	139,147–149	37–38	33	29–30	5
21	Fabricated metal products, including ordnance	157–159,167–169 258	13,39–42	34	31–32	5
22	Industrial machinery and equipment, exc. electrical	177–179, 187–189 197–198	43–52	35	33–35	5

23	Electric and electronic equipment	199,207–209	53–58	36	36	5
24	Motor vehicles and equipment	219	59	371	37	5
25	Other transportation equipment	227–229, 237–238	60–61	37	38–40	5
26	Instruments and related products	239,247–249	62–63	38	41	5
27	Miscellaneous manufactures	259	64	39	42	4
28	Transportation	407–429	65	40–42, 44–47	43	6
29	Telephone and telegraph	448–449	66	481,482,489	44	6
30	Radio and TV broadcasting	447	67	483,484	45	6
31	Electric, gas, and sanitary services	467–79	68	49	46	6
32	Wholesale trade	507–599	69A	50–51	47	7
33	Retail trade	600–699	69B,74	52–59	48	7
34	Banking; credit and investment companies	707–709	70A	60–62,67	49	8
35	Insurance	717	70B	63–64	50	8
36	Real estate	718	71B	65–66	51	8
37	Hotels, motels, and lodging places	777,778	72A	70	52	9
38	Personal services	769,779–799	72[part]	72	53,62[c]	9
39	Business and repair services except auto	727–748,758–767	73C,72[part]	73,76	54,62[c]	9
40	Auto services and repair	749,757	75	75	55	9
41	Amusement and recreation services	807–817	76	78–79	56	9
42	Health services, including hospitals	828–848	77A	80	57–58	9
43	Educational services	857–868	77B[part]	82	59	9
44	Legal and other professional services and non-profit org.	849,869–897	73A,73B, 77B[part]	81,83,84,86 87,89	60–61	9
45	Public Administration	907–947	78,79,84	43[d]	63–64	10

(a) 1970 Census of Population industry classification scheme.
(b) Bureau of Economic Analysis 85-sector industrial classification system for input-output data (1987 version).
(c) Business and Personal Services n.e.c. (Census codes 728–48, 758–67, 779, 789–799 and 64-sector code 62) split proportionately between two sectors.
(d) US postal service only.

ELSEVIER

Structural Change and Economic Dynamics
17 (2006) 306–328

STRUCTURAL CHANGE AND ECONOMIC DYNAMICS

www.elsevier.com/locate/econbase

The vintage effect in TFP-growth: An analysis of the age structure of capital

Maury Gittleman [a], Thijs ten Raa [b], Edward N. Wolff [c,*]

[a] *Bureau of Labor Statistics, Postal Square Building, 2 Massachusetts Ave. NE Rm 4130, Washington, DC 20212, USA*

[b] *Department of Economics, Tilburg University, Box 90153, 5000 LE Tilburg, The Netherlands*

[c] *Department of Economics, New York University, 269 Mercer Street, New York, NY 10003, USA*

Received June 2004; received in revised form February 2005; accepted May 2005
Available online 1 August 2005

Abstract

The age structure of capital plays an important role in the measurement of productivity. It has been argued that the slowdown in the 1970s can be ascribed to the aging of the stock of capital. In this paper, we incorporate the age structure in productivity measurement. One proposition proves that Nelson's [Nelson, R.R., 1964. Aggregate production functions and medium-range growth projections. American Economic Review 54 (September), 575–605] formula is only an approximation. Our final proposition shows that inclusion of the vintage effect prompts an upward correction of measured productivity growth in times of an aging stock of capital. Here capital ages if the investment/capital ratio falls short of the inverse of the capital age, as a first proposition shows. The analysis rests on a rigorous accounting for vintages. We translate the Bureau of Economic Analysis' age of capital data into a measure of rates of obsolescence. Empirically, the correction of productivity growth for the vintage effect requires an estimate of the obsolescence and depreciation parameters on the basis of age data. The results indicate that the use of capital stock in efficiency units does cause some smoothing of total factor productivity growth over time. In the 1950s, when investment accelerated, the vintage-adjusted capital growth rate well exceeded the BEA growth rate, and vintage-adjusted

* Corresponding author. Tel.: +1 212 998 8917; fax: +1 212 995 4186.
E-mail addresses: Gittleman_M@bls.gov (M. Gittleman), tenRaa@UvT.nl (T. ten Raa), Edward.Wolff@NYU.edu (E.N. Wolff).

doi:10.1016/j.strueco.2005.05.002

TFP-growth is significantly lower than unadjusted TFP-growth. The measured productivity slowdown of the 1970s is somewhat ameliorated.

JEL classification: O30; O47; E22

Keywords: Investment; Capital vintage; Productivity

1. Introduction

An important source of technological advance is through new technology embodied in investment goods (see, for example, Solow, 1960; Jorgenson, 1966). It is also consistent with the "vintage effect," which states that new capital is more productive than old capital per (constant) dollar of expenditure.[1] If the capital stock data do not correct for vintage effects, then a negative correlation should be observed between the rate of technological gain and the change in the average age of capital.

Several papers have attempted to measure the contribution of the vintage effect to U.S. productivity growth, particularly as a factor in explaining the productivity slowdown of the 1970s. A number of different approaches have been used over the years. We discuss five of them below. First, Kendrick (1980) relied on a growth accounting approach. Using the average age of capital goods as an indicator of the rate of diffusion of new technology, he found that between 1948 and 1966, the average age declined by 3 years, contributing 0.25 percentage points to the overall productivity growth rate. Between 1966 and 1973 the decline in average age slowed to 1 year and between 1973 and 1978 there was no decline in the average age of capital stock. Clark (1979), also using growth accounting methods and assuming that new capital stock is 1% more productive than last year's capital stock, estimated a somewhat smaller vintage effect than Kendrick did. He estimated that of the 0.66-point decline in the labor productivity growth rate between 1948–1965 and 1965–1973, the vintage effect explained 0.09 points; of the 1.17-point decline between 1965–1973 and 1973–1978, the vintage effect accounted for 0.10 points.

Hulten (1992) employed a second approach, measuring capital not in physical units, but in efficiency units. Using data on quality-adjusted investment flows of capital goods purchased by manufacturing industries, he estimated that about 20% of total quality-adjusted technical change in U.S. manufacturing over the period 1949–1983 could be ascribed to embodied technical change in machinery and equipment. However, he found very little difference in the contribution of embodied technical change to total technical change between the periods 1949–1973 and 1974–1983, the slowdown period. Nonetheless, Hulten's methodology is powerful. Correct accounting for units of capital reveals the vintage effect on total factor productivity (TFP) growth explicitly, as our paper will show.

[1] We will estimate rates of obsolescence for physical capital; for knowledge capital see Bosworth (1978) and Pakes and Schankerman (1984). As Ben Eden pointed out to one of us, this is an aggregation issue. Indeed, we will estimate the stock of capital in efficiency units. For a recent review of capital measurement, see Diewert and Lawrence (2000).

Third, Hulten and Wykoff (1992) used the price of used capital goods to estimate the obsolescence rate of capital. These estimates were based on used asset prices for numerous individual asset classes. Based on these estimates, the economists inferred rates of depreciation for all asset classes in the U.S. Another natural source of information is scrapping data, as we will discuss later.

A fourth approach is exemplified by Harper (2002), who proposed a new technique for estimating the vintage effect based on the contemporaneous marginal product of each asset. His measure of quality adjustment assumes that durable goods prices reflect marginal products—in contradistinction to the standard neoclassical assumption that prices reflect the discounted stream of future rents. Harper used his model to develop a new method of aggregating different vintages of capital.

A fifth approach was used by Wolff (1991, 1996). Using Nelson's method for econometrically estimating the vintage effect (see below), Wolff (1991) found a very significant vintage effect, estimated by the change in the average age of the capital stock, for Canada, France, Germany, Japan, Italy, the U.K., and the U.S. over the period 1880–1979. These results suggested that embodied technical change played a significant role in the productivity fall-off of the 1970s. Using more recent data for these countries, Wolff (1996) estimated that the vintage effect explained on average about two-fifths of the post-1973 productivity slowdown among these countries.

We make interrelated contributions to the theory and the empirics of the vintage effect. Three propositions show that Nelson's (1964) formula for the capital stock (in efficiency units) as a function of age is only an approximation and offer exact formulas, one for the aging of capital as a function of the investment ratio and one for the vintage effect on TFP-growth. We estimate rates of obsolescence using age-of-capital data and the consequent vintage effect in TFP.

One has to be careful. Obsolescence and depreciation are hard to distinguish (Hulten and Wykoff, 1992) and depreciation rates may be used to construct age data. Indeed, our theory will confirm that only combined rates of depreciation and obsolescence feature in the measurement of the (efficiency units) stock and the economic lifetime of capital. The major question is whether our age data of the Bureau of Economic Analysis (BEA) contain independent information. Now according to the BEA's technical documentation, estimates of the age of capital are based on estimated lifetimes of each type of capital and, as a result, do not directly capture expected obsolescence of the capital. In the past BEA used information on scrapping to produce estimates of what it called "gross capital" and "discards" (see Katz and Herman, 1997). In the new *net* capital stock data used here, BEA no longer directly uses scrapping information to obtain its depreciation estimates but it still uses information on scrapping indirectly in its service life estimates.[2] We exploit this source to estimate rates of obsolescence. The remainder of the paper is organized as follows. Section 2 provides some theoretical background on the measurement of the vintage effect, including Nelson's formula. Section 3 introduces our model of the vintage effect and Section 4 provides a theoretical discussion of the relationship between the age of capital

[2] The depreciation schedule used for each asset reflects, in part, the assumed service life of the asset. The service life estimates in the new BEA capital stock series are, with a few exceptions, unchanged from the older BEA capital stock data. These, in turn, are based on discard data (see Katz and Herman, 1997, p. 74).

and investment. Sections 5–7 provide estimates of the obsolescence rate of capital by type of capital, vintage-adjusted net capital stock, and the vintage effect on TFP-growth for the U.S. Economy over the 1947–1997 period. Concluding remarks are made in Section 8.

2. Background on the vintage effect

The age structure of capital plays an important role in the measurement of productivity. When investment is low, the stock of capital ages and, therefore, the units not only perish, but also become obsolete from a technological point of view: capital is no longer state of the art. This mechanism has a negative contribution to measured productivity; in the absence of technical change, the Solow residual will be negative. Such an outcome is paradoxical, because the residual has been claimed to account for the shift of the production possibilities frontier (Solow, 1957) and knowledge does not contract, but expands.

At least conceptually, the paradox is resolved when capital is measured not in physical units, but in efficiency units (Hulten, 1992). Then, continuing our discussion of the low investment example, the higher obsolescence of capital will show up in a negative contribution to the growth of capital in terms of efficiency units. Since the Solow residual measure of productivity is the difference between the output growth rate and a weighted average of the labor and capital growth rates, the lower measure of capital growth (as capital is measured in efficiency units) yields more productivity. In other words, the conventional measure of productivity would understate the role of technical change in times of an aging stock of capital.

The econometric analysis of the vintage effect in productivity measurement goes back to Nelson (1964). Suppose that this year's capital investment is $s\%$ more productive than last year's, with the obsolescence parameter s constant over time. As Erwin Diewert noted, obsolescence could be interpreted as anticipated price decline, i.e., the expected inflation rate of a new asset is negative. Denote the capital stock measured in natural units (constant prices) by K, and the capital stock in "efficiency units" by K^s. The greater the obsolescence parameter, the smaller will be the capital stock in efficiency units. In other words, K^s will be decreasing in s. In fact, Nelson (1964) has postulated

$$K^s = K\ \exp(-s\bar{A}) \tag{1}$$

where $\bar{A}$ is the average age of the capital stock. This formula simply states that the capital stock existing at time t is, on average, less efficient by a factor of $s\bar{A}$ than the capital goods produced at time t. One of the contributions of this paper is that the Nelson (1964) specification is shown to be an approximation at best (for small values of $s\bar{A}$) and improvable by a full fledged vintage analysis. Since Wolff (1996) employed the formula, his ascription of the productivity slowdown to the vintage effect should be reinvestigated. This paper sets up a rigorous framework of vintage capital that is amenable to estimation.

Although the functional form used in formula (1) will be shown to be untenable, the fact that a higher rate of obsolescence effectively diminishes the volume of capital is true and has a simple implication for the measurement of productivity. The explanation begins with a general definition of TFP-growth by means of a Solow residual that features an arbitrary obsolescence parameter, s:

$$\mathrm{TFP}^{s\wedge} = \hat{Y} - \alpha L^{\wedge} - \beta K^{s\wedge} \tag{2}$$

where $\hat{Y} = (p\,\mathrm{d}y/\mathrm{d}t)/py$ (with p the commodity price vector and y the net output vector), $\alpha = wL/py$ (with w the wage rate and L labor employment), $\hat{L} = (\mathrm{d}L/\mathrm{d}t)/L$, $\beta = rK^s/py$ (with r the rental rate of capital).

When capital obsolescence is ignored, $s = 0$, $K^s = K$, and $\mathrm{TFP}^{\hat{s}} = \mathrm{TFP}\hat{}$. Otherwise, measured productivity growth is corrected. A result of this paper is that the correction must be upward (downward) if capital ages (becomes younger). The measurement of capital in terms of efficiency units and the consequent adjustment of measured productivity require an estimate of the obsolescence parameter, s. This will be obtained by an analysis of age data.[3]

3. The model

Consider a unit of investment at time t, the *vintage* of this piece of capital, and the stream of services that it will yield at later times $t' > t$. The initial level of the capital service is $\exp(st)$, where s is the obsolescence parameter; future capital is more productive. Thereafter, for $t' > t$, depreciation takes its toll at a rate σ and the level of capital service goes down to $\exp(st)\exp[-\sigma(t' - t)]$, where σ is the depreciation parameter. We assume that the obsolescence and depreciation parameters are constant over time, but may vary by *type of capital*.

The exponential decay of capital is the most common specification and the depreciation parameter admits an easy interpretation in terms of lifetime. For illustration consider a unit of investment at time 0. It yields a stream of capital services $\exp(-\sigma t)$ at times $t > 0$. What is the expected lifetime? At time t the amount of capital that depreciates is $-\mathrm{d}/\mathrm{d}t \exp(-\sigma t) = \sigma \exp(-\sigma t)$. This density function sums to unity over $t > 0$. The expected lifetime is

$$\int t\sigma \exp(-\sigma t)\,\mathrm{d}t = \frac{1}{\sigma}\int t\sigma \exp(-\sigma t)\,\mathrm{d}\sigma t = \frac{1}{\sigma} \tag{3}$$

Here $\int$ is the integral from 0 to ∞. *This notation holds throughout this paper.* Expression (3) shows that a rate of depreciation of for example 5% implies a lifetime of 20 years.

Change the perspective by looking backward from time t. Let I denote investment. In natural units (constant prices), the stock of capital at time t is

$$K(t) = \int I(t - t')\exp(-\sigma t')\,\mathrm{d}t' \tag{4}$$

Depreciation (at the rate σ) refers to the *physical deterioration* of capital goods. For example, internal combustion engines lose efficiency over time as fissures develop between the piston and cylinder.[4] Obsolescence, on the contrary, refers to *economic deterioration*. For example, a matrix printer may still function well, but now it pales in comparison to a laser printer.[5]

---

[3] For other vintage models, see Böhm-Bawerk (1959), Tatom (1979), Wolff (1991), or Abramovitz (1994).

[4] Another example is a baseball pitcher, whose throwing speed will generally decline as he ages.

[5] An obsolescence rate may be negative. First class train service is not what it used to be.

In current efficiency units, invoking obsolescence parameter s, the stock of capital at time t is

$$K^s(t) = \int I(t - t') \exp(-st') \exp(-\sigma t')\,dt' \tag{5}$$

Equation (5) shows that in terms of efficiency units only the combined rate of depreciation and obsolescence matters, that is $s+\sigma$. As equation (3) showed that the physical lifetime of capital is $1/\sigma$, the economic lifetime is only $1/(s+\sigma)$. Differentiating with respect to t and integrating by parts,

$$\frac{dK^s}{dt} = I - (s + \sigma)K^s \tag{6}$$

Substituting (6) into (2),

$$\mathrm{TFP}^{s\wedge} = \hat{Y} - \alpha L^{\wedge} - \beta\left[\frac{I}{K^s} - (s + \sigma)\right] \tag{7}$$

where K^s is given by (5) and also features s in combination with σ only. Formula (7) shows that TFP-growth equals net output growth minus labor growth, minus the investment rate, and minus the sum of obsolescence and depreciation. From an economic point of view, it does not matter if capital deteriorates because of physical or technological aging—that is depreciation (σ) or obsolescence (s). Empirically, the obsolescence parameter is hard to get. For this purpose we will analyze age data.

Suppose we invested one unit of capital last year and one unit this year. The average age of the stock of capital is less than 0.5, because last year's unit has depreciated. For example, if the rate of depreciation is 10%, we have 0.9 unit of last year and 1 unit of this year, so that the average age is 0.45. In terms of efficiency units, the average age is even less. For example, if the rate of obsolescence is also 10%, the average goes down to 0.40. Obviously, the average age of the stock depends on the rate of obsolescence we employ. Formally, it is defined by

$$\bar{A}^s(t) = \frac{\int I(t - t') \exp[-(s + \sigma)t']t'\,dt'}{\int I(t - t') \exp[-(s + \sigma)t']\,dt'} \tag{8}$$

The numerator accounts for each unit of capital by its age, t', and the denominator is the total number of units, or $K^s(t)$ of (4). When capital obsolescence is ignored, $s=0$ and $\bar{A}s(t) = \bar{A}(t)$. An important question is whether the average age of capital has risen or lessened over time. The answer depends on the time derivative of (8), which is presented in the next section.

4. The relationship between the age of capital and investment

Investment adds young units to the stock of capital. It contributes to the age reduction of capital. On the other hand, there is the autonomous aging of capital. To beat this, investment must be strong enough to lower the average age of capital. The change in the age of capital is given by the following proposition:

Proposition 1.

$$\frac{d\bar{A}^s}{dt} = 1 - \left(\frac{I}{K^s}\right)\bar{A}^s.$$

Proof. The derivative of the numerator of (8) becomes, integrating by parts, $\int I(t-t')\{\exp[-(s+\sigma)t'] - (s+\sigma)\exp[-(s+\sigma)t']t'\}\,dt' = K^s(t)[1-(s+\sigma)\bar{A}^s(t)]$. The derivative of the denominator of (8) is given by (6). It follows, by the quotient rule and the fact that the numerator can be written as $\bar{A}^s(t)K^s(t)$ in view of (8) and (5), that $d\bar{A}^s(t)/dt = \{K^s(t)\cdot K^s(t)[1-(s+\sigma)\bar{A}^s(t)] - \bar{A}^s(t)K^s(t)[I(t)-(s+\sigma)K^s(t)]\}/K^s(t)^2$. This simplifies into $1-[I(t)/K^s(t)]\bar{A}^s(t)$. □

An alternative proof, in discrete time, has been given to us by Erwin Diewert and is presented in Appendix B. Proposition 1 is quite intuitive. It states that if the investment ratio is the inverse of the age of capital, then the age will be preserved. If the investment ratio is higher (lower) than the inverse of the age of capital, then capital will become younger (older). Though intuitive, Proposition 1 has an important ramification.

Proposition 2. *Formula* (1) *is not exact.*

Proof. Suppose (1) is exact. Differentiation with respect to time yields, $dK^s/dt = dK/dt\cdot\exp(-s\bar{A}) - K\cdot s\exp(-s\bar{A})\cdot d\bar{A}/dt$. By (6) and (1), the left hand side is $I-(s+\sigma)K^s = I-(s+\sigma)K\cdot\exp(-s\bar{A})$. Multiplying through by $\exp(s\bar{A})$ we obtain $\exp(s\bar{A})\cdot I-(s+\sigma)K = dK/dt - K\cdot s\cdot d\bar{A}/dt$. On the right hand side, using (6) with $s=0$, the first term is $I-\sigma K$ and, using Proposition 1 with $s=0$, the second term is $-K\cdot s\cdot[1-(I/K)\bar{A}]$. The terms sK and σK cancel, respectively. Dividing by I we obtain $\exp(s\bar{A}) = 1+s\bar{A}$. This non-linear equation is approximately true for small values of $s\bar{A}$, but exact only for $s\bar{A}=0$. □

The upshot of Proposition 1 is that simple replacement of $K(t)$ by $K^s(t)$ on a yearly basis amounts to an approximate modification of TFP-growth for obsolescence (s) at best. A more exact procedure reconstructs $K^s(t)$ on the basis of past investment.

5. Estimation of obsolescence and of the growth in the capital stock

Instead of using Nelson's formula (1) in a regression analysis (Wolff, 1996), we will go back to basics—namely equation (8), the definition of capital age. Since we assume that the obsolescence and depreciation parameters are constant over time, the equation cannot exactly meet the data and, therefore, we must attach an error term:[6]

$$\bar{A}^s(t) = \frac{\int I(t-t')\exp[-(s+\sigma)t']t'\,dt'}{\int I(t-t')\exp[-(s+\sigma)t']\,dt'} + \varepsilon_t(s+\sigma) \tag{9}$$

[6] Robert Inklaar has suggested that the rate of obsolescence has accelerated and could be made period specific.

On the left hand side we enter the Bureau of Economic Analysis' age of capital (by type of capital) and implicitly assume that the weights of vintages are in terms of efficiency units.[7] There are 57 types of capital goods (see Table 1 for a listing) and the series runs from 1947 to 1997.[8] We use annual time-series data, so that we effectively replace the integral in equation (9) with a sum.

On the right hand side, we enter investment data. These are also obtained from the Bureau of Economic Analysis fixed reproducible capital series. There are also 57 types of investment goods (corresponding to the 57 capital types) and the series runs from 1901 to 1997. Since the right hand side features the expression $s+\sigma$, the error term will depend on the sum, as indicated in equation (9). Now let $\varepsilon_t(s+\sigma)$ have density function f with mean zero and unknown variance. The likelihood of our observations is the product $\ldots \cdot f[\varepsilon_t(s+\sigma)] \cdot \ldots \cdot f[\varepsilon_0(s+\sigma)]$. Maximization of the log likelihood, which is a series, yields an estimate of $s+\sigma$. If the error term is normally distributed, estimation via non-linear least squares (NLLS) is equivalent to maximum likelihood estimation, so in that case NLLS will provide consistent and asymptotically efficient estimates (Amemiya, 1985).

Equation (9) was estimated using NLLS, with a separate regression performed for each capital type to arrive at type-specific rates of obsolescence and depreciation. The results are shown in Table 1. In light of the rapid rate of technological innovation in the computer industry, it is no surprise that the rates of obsolescence and depreciation are highest for computer-related equipment. The estimates suggest that, on average, more than half (0.521) of the efficiency units of mainframe computers and computer tape drives was lost each year during the period to obsolescence and depreciation, with the rates for computer storage devices (0.457) and computer printers (0.452) only somewhat slower. The personal computers rate of obsolescence and depreciation, 0.256, is equivalent to a lifetime of 4 years, see equation (3).[9] To put these rates in perspective, an annual rate of obsolescence and depreciation of 0.067 is obtained if one restricts this parameter to be the same for all capital types combined. On the other end of the spectrum are buildings and other structures, which tend to have longer lives than other types of capital. For example, the combined rate of depreciation and obsolescence for commercial warehouses is 0.023, that for amusement and recreational buildings is 0.025, and that for hospitals and other institutional buildings is only 0.019. In the middle is a variety of industrial, transportation, and miscellaneous equipment, such as aircraft (0.103), agricultural machinery (0.115), and construction machinery (0.051).

We next compare rates of growth of our newly estimated net stocks of capital with those of the BEA both by type of capital and by industry. It should be noted that while the BEA does adjust capital stock each year for depreciation, it does not generally adjust the capital stock figures for technological obsolescence. The major exception is computer equipment, which is adjusted each year on the basis of a hedonic regression that captures

[7] The Bureau of Economic Analysis does not disentangle annual rings of capital and, therefore, we cannot test this implicit assumption. As Nelson (1964, footnote 13) points out, the issue is the measurement of capital in physical versus value terms. Our inclusion of the obsolescence effect is tantamount to assuming that values are used for the weights in the capital age calculation. This seems reasonable.

[8] The source is: U.S. Bureau of Economic Analysis, CD-ROM NCN-0229, "Fixed Reproducible Tangible Wealth of the United States, 1925–1997."

[9] According to Elsa Fontainha this agrees with the accounting rules, at least in Portugal.

Table 1
Rates of obsolescence and depreciation by capital type

	Capital type	Parameter	Standard error	*t*-Statistic
1.	Mainframe computers	0.521	0.005	99.1
2.	Personal computers	0.256	0.005	54.5
3.	Direct access storage devices	0.176	0.024	7.5
4.	Computer printers	0.452	0.007	63.7
5.	Computer terminals	0.355	0.007	53.0
6.	Computer tape drives	0.521	0.147	3.6
7.	Computer storage devices	0.457	0.005	87.4
8.	Other office equipment	0.340	0.003	124.5
9.	Communication equipment	0.116	0.001	101.5
10.	Instruments	0.140	0.001	106.1
11.	Photocopy and related equipment	0.195	0.001	144.0
12.	Nuclear fuel rods	0.413	0.000	[a]
13.	Other fabricated metal products	0.091	0.001	123.6
14.	Steam engines	0.050	0.001	71.3
15.	Internal combustion engines	0.222	0.007	30.5
16.	Metalworking machinery	0.119	0.003	37.6
17.	Special industry machinery, n.e.c.	0.100	0.003	33.8
18.	General industrial, including materials handling, equipment	0.107	0.003	42.9
19.	Electrical transmission, distribution, and industrial apparatus	0.049	0.000	126.6
20.	Trucks, buses, and truck trailers	0.205	0.003	68.7
21.	Autos	0.192	0.006	32.5
22.	Aircraft	0.103	0.002	47.8
23.	Ships and boats	0.059	0.002	32.1
24.	Railroad equipment	0.060	0.002	25.5
25.	Household furniture	0.145	0.002	64.7
26.	Other furniture	0.127	0.001	182.1
27.	Farm tractors	0.155	0.002	78.0
28.	Construction tractors	0.180	0.002	112.2
29.	Agricultural machinery, except tractors	0.115	0.003	37.9
30.	Construction machinery, except tractors	0.151	0.003	43.3
31.	Mining and oilfield machinery	0.159	0.001	161.8
32.	Service industry machinery	0.166	0.001	115.2
33.	Household appliances	0.175	0.003	62.6
34.	Other electrical equipment, n.e.c.	0.195	0.002	128.6
35.	Other non-residential equipment	0.156	0.001	122.3
36.	Industrial buildings	0.031	0.001	49.2
37.	Office buildings	0.023	0.002	13.5
38.	Mobile structures	0.060	0.004	16.2
39.	Commercial warehouses	0.023	0.002	15.5
40.	Other commercial buildings, n.e.c.	0.026	0.001	18.7
41.	Religious buildings	[b]	[b]	[b]
42.	Educational buildings	0.188	0.216	0.9
43.	Hospital and institutional buildings	0.019	0.001	13.6
44.	Hotels and motels	0.035	0.007	5.0
45.	Amusement and recreational buildings	0.025	0.004	5.7
46.	Other non-farm buildings	0.024	0.001	22.7
47.	Local transit buildings	[b]	[b]	[b]
48.	Railroad structures	−0.004	0.000	[a]
49.	Railroad track replacement	0.021	0.000	[a]
50.	Telecommunications	[b]	[b]	[b]

Table 1 (*Continued*)

	Capital type	Parameter	Standard error	t-Statistic
51.	Electric light and power	0.022	0.000	[a]
52.	Gas	0.023	0.000	[a]
53.	Petroleum pipelines	0.020	0.000	[a]
54.	Farm-related buildings and structures	0.016	0.003	6.2
55.	Petroleum and natural gas exploration	0.057	0.000	[a]
56.	Other mining exploration	0.044	0.001	76.4
57.	Other non-farm structures	0.016	0.002	6.9

[a] Standard error is zero (capital type has only one observation), so t-statistic cannot be computed.
[b] Estimation did not converge. We do not adjust the BEA stocks.

such features of computers as speed and memory. The comparisons are shown in Tables 2 and 3.

Table 2 shows the annualized growth rates of net capital stock by capital type. We have aggregated the types from the original 57 to 28 because many of the series have zeroes in the early years of the period (for example, computer equipment and nuclear fuel rods). If the vintage parameter s is positive, then a rising ratio of investment to net capital stock over a period will cause the vintage-adjusted capital growth rate to exceed the BEA capital growth rate. Conversely, if the investment to net capital stock ratio is declining over a period (and s is positive), then the vintage-adjusted capital growth rate will be less than the BEA capital growth rate.

Over the full 1947–1997 period, there was very little difference between the BEA and the vintage-adjusted growth rate of the total capital stock—only 0.09 percentage points. Differences are quite small for most of the capital types. There are a few exceptions. The vintage-adjusted annual growth rate of other office equipment exceeded the BEA growth rate by 0.36 percentage points, as did the vintage-adjusted growth rate of petroleum and natural gas exploration equipment. In contrast, the annual growth rate of the BEA net stock of automobiles exceeded the vintage-adjusted growth rate by 1.04 percentage points. The last line of the table shows the correlation coefficient between the two sets of growth rates across the 28 capital types. Over the full 1947–1997 period, the correlation is extremely high (0.99).

Results also vary by 10-year period. The vintage-adjusted annual growth rate for total capital exceeded the BEA growth rate by 0.39 percentage points in the 1947–1957 period and by 0.10 percentage points in the 1957–1967 period but fell short of it by 0.10 percentage points in the 1987–1997 period. The biggest differences are recorded for computer equipment. In the 1967–1977 period, the difference between the BEA and the vintage-adjusted growth rate (2.70 percentage points) was a reflection of the rapid acceleration in computer equipment investment over the period. The difference was −1.99 percentage points in the 1977–1987 period, but virtually zero in the 1987–1997 period. Other large differences in the two growth rates are observed for autos as well as railroad structures and track. However, by and large, the correlation in the two sets of capital growth rates is very high by 10-year period—ranging from 0.983 to 0.998.

The BEA capital stock data are also available for 62 individual industries (see Table A.1 for a listing). In Table 3, we show the results for 11 major sectors. Differences in the

Table 2

Annual rate of growth of net capital stock by capital type and period, 1947–1997 (figures are in percentage points)

Capital type[a]	1947–1997			1947–1957			1957–1967			1967–1977			1977–1987			1987–1997		
	BEA	Vintage	Diff.	BEA	Vintage	Diff.	BEA	Vintage	Diff.	BEA	Vintage	Diff.	BEA	Vintage	Diff.	BEA	Vintage	Diff.
Computer equipment (1–7)	–	–	–	–	–	–	–	–	–	26.39	29.08	−2.70	30.69	32.68	−1.99	21.22	21.18	0.05
Other office equipment (8 and 11)	7.01	7.37	−0.36	7.87	8.96	−1.09	7.02	7.52	−0.50	10.03	10.30	−0.27	8.20	8.10	0.10	1.94	1.98	−0.04
Communication equipment (9)	8.08	8.11	−0.03	10.15	10.13	0.02	9.62	9.63	0.00	7.32	7.33	−0.02	8.69	8.70	−0.01	4.64	4.76	−0.13
Instruments (10)	6.24	6.28	−0.04	10.43	10.48	−0.04	2.50	2.55	−0.05	7.96	7.92	0.04	5.82	5.84	−0.02	4.48	4.60	−0.13
Fabricated metal products (12 and 13)	3.60	3.68	−0.08	7.12	7.17	−0.05	2.58	2.65	−0.08	7.17	7.15	0.01	1.08	1.25	−0.16	0.07	0.18	−0.11
Engines and industrial machinery (14–19)	3.32	3.43	−0.11	5.18	5.40	−0.22	3.70	3.80	−0.10	3.37	3.45	−0.08	2.35	2.36	−0.01	2.01	2.15	−0.14
Trucks, buses, and truck trailers (20)	4.48	4.42	0.05	4.98	4.66	0.32	4.84	4.89	−0.05	5.92	6.12	−0.20	2.27	2.08	0.19	4.37	4.36	0.01
Autos (21)	5.12	4.08	1.04	9.61	7.42	2.19	2.66	0.40	2.26	5.65	7.49	−1.84	4.49	4.09	0.40	3.18	1.00	2.18
Aircraft (22)	6.68	6.36	0.32	7.70	7.51	0.18	13.66	13.17	0.48	6.63	5.96	0.67	3.53	3.35	0.18	1.89	1.83	0.06
Ships and boats (23)	1.10	1.02	0.08	1.14	0.84	0.30	1.29	1.03	0.26	5.01	4.88	0.13	0.58	0.65	−0.07	−2.54	−2.31	−0.22
Railroad equipment (24)	0.46	0.38	0.07	2.49	2.59	−0.10	0.31	0.33	−0.02	1.00	1.04	−0.04	−1.39	−1.34	−0.05	−0.13	−0.72	0.58
Furniture (25 and 26)	4.37	4.38	−0.01	4.69	4.85	−0.16	4.10	4.08	0.02	3.27	3.21	0.06	5.84	5.84	0.00	3.96	3.94	0.02
Agricultural, construction, mining, and service industry machinery (27–32)	2.55	2.67	−0.12	5.61	6.03	−0.42	2.61	2.65	−0.05	4.63	4.55	0.08	−0.30	−0.23	−0.07	0.22	0.37	−0.14
Appliances and other equipment (33–35)	5.77	5.86	−0.09	5.39	5.77	−0.38	7.34	7.38	−0.04	6.76	6.77	−0.01	5.70	5.72	−0.02	3.67	3.69	−0.02
Industrial and commercial buildings (36–40)	3.46	3.67	−0.21	2.78	3.23	−0.45	4.37	4.65	−0.28	3.80	3.95	−0.15	4.07	4.15	−0.09	2.29	2.39	−0.10
Educational and institutional buildings (41–43)	4.06	4.29	−0.24	5.45	6.00	−0.55	5.95	6.19	−0.24	3.56	3.56	0.00	2.65	3.02	−0.37	2.67	2.70	−0.03
Hotels and motels (44)	4.37	4.43	−0.07	2.11	2.14	−0.04	7.63	8.02	−0.39	3.80	3.71	0.09	5.10	5.19	−0.09	3.19	3.10	0.09
Recreational buildings (45)	1.91	2.01	−0.10	0.79	1.06	−0.27	3.84	3.81	0.03	1.01	1.20	−0.20	1.22	1.35	−0.13	2.67	2.63	0.04
Other non-farm buildings (46)	2.39	2.73	−0.34	3.24	4.05	−0.81	6.74	7.30	−0.55	−0.25	−0.31	0.06	1.58	1.76	−0.18	0.65	0.87	−0.22
Local transit buildings (47)	−2.47	−2.47	0.00	−1.89	−1.89	0.00	−3.16	−3.16	0.00	−2.46	−2.46	0.00	−2.43	−2.43	0.00	−2.43	−2.43	0.00
Railroad structures and track (48 and 49)	−0.87	0.34	−1.20	−0.69	0.68	−1.36	−1.19	0.13	−1.32	−0.91	0.29	−1.20	−0.67	0.39	−1.06	−0.89	0.20	−1.08
Telecommunications (50)	4.08	4.08	0.00	4.94	4.94	0.00	4.27	4.27	0.00	5.07	5.07	0.00	3.93	3.93	0.00	2.19	2.19	0.00

Table 2 (*Continued*)

Capital type[a]	1947–1997			1947–1957			1957–1967			1967–1977			1977–1987			1987–1997		
	BEA	Vintage	Diff.	BEA	Vintage	Diff.	BEA	Vintage	Diff.	BEA	Vintage	Diff.	BEA	Vintage	Diff.	BEA	Vintage	Diff.
Electric light and power and gas (51 and 52)	2.68	2.67	0.01	4.78	4.82	−0.04	2.99	2.97	0.02	3.11	3.12	−0.01	1.76	1.72	0.04	0.74	0.71	0.03
Petroleum pipelines (53)	0.78	1.23	−0.45	1.29	2.01	−0.72	0.11	0.63	−0.53	3.76	4.13	−0.37	−0.83	−0.47	−0.36	−0.45	−0.17	−0.28
Farm-related buildings and structures (54)	2.08	1.90	0.18	3.32	3.31	0.00	3.47	2.91	0.56	3.68	2.56	1.12	0.50	0.99	−0.50	−0.59	−0.29	−0.30
Petroleum and gas exploration (55)	2.62	2.98	−0.36	6.26	6.27	−0.01	2.42	2.45	−0.03	1.41	1.57	−0.16	4.20	4.92	−0.73	−1.21	−0.34	−0.87
Other mining exploration (56)	3.14	3.15	−0.01	1.61	1.65	−0.04	3.27	3.25	0.02	6.55	6.47	0.08	4.12	4.16	−0.03	0.15	0.23	−0.08
Other non-farm structures (57)	2.66	2.93	−0.28	−0.53	0.11	−0.64	1.71	2.13	−0.42	3.63	3.75	−0.12	4.67	4.75	−0.08	3.80	3.92	−0.12
Total	3.05	3.13	−0.09	3.13	3.51	−0.39	3.21	3.30	−0.10	3.44	3.45	−0.01	2.99	3.02	−0.04	2.48	2.38	0.10
Correlation between BEA and vintage growth rates[b]			0.989			0.983			0.985			0.994			0.998			0.992

Note: BEA figures are for non-residential net stocks, real-cost valuation (1992 Dollars). Governmental capital stock is excluded.

[a] The numbers in parentheses refer to the capital type classification scheme in Table 1.

[b] Computer equipment is excluded because of zero values for the computation of correlation coefficients for 1947–1997, 1947–1957, and 1957–1997.

Table 3

Annual rate of growth of net capital stock by major sector and period, 1947–1997 (figures are in percentage points)

Sector[a]	1947–1997			1947–1957			1957–1967			1967–1977			1977–1987			1987–1997		
	BEA	Vintage	Diff.	BEA	Vintage	Diff.	BEA	Vintage	Diff.	BEA	Vintage	Diff.	BEA	Vintage	Diff.	BEA	Vintage	Diff.
Agriculture (1 and 2)	2.15	2.08	0.08	4.23	4.11	0.12	2.87	2.59	0.28	4.01	3.37	0.64	−0.44	−0.04	−0.40	0.09	0.35	−0.27
Mining (3–6)	2.63	2.88	-0.25	4.82	4.92	-0.09	3.03	3.07	−0.04	2.14	2.26	−0.12	4.22	4.63	−0.41	−1.07	−0.47	−0.60
Construction (7)	2.33	2.53	−0.19	4.10	4.85	−0.74	3.52	3.53	−0.01	4.30	4.21	0.09	−0.41	−0.40	−0.02	0.16	0.44	−0.28
Manufacturing non-durables (19–28)	2.56	2.62	−0.06	2.58	2.75	−0.17	2.97	3.07	−0.10	3.61	3.70	−0.10	1.66	1.67	−0.01	1.96	1.91	0.05
Manufacturing durables (8–18)	3.02	3.25	−0.24	4.37	5.00	−0.63	3.59	3.85	−0.26	3.37	3.56	−0.19	2.14	2.19	−0.04	1.61	1.67	−0.06
Transportation (29–35)	0.23	0.79	−0.56	0.05	0.99	−0.93	−0.24	0.53	−0.77	0.71	1.15	−0.44	0.25	0.65	−0.40	0.36	0.64	−0.28
Communications (36 and 37)	5.56	5.55	0.01	7.07	7.02	0.05	6.07	6.04	0.02	5.96	6.01	−0.05	5.10	5.11	0.00	3.60	3.55	0.04
Utilities (38–40)	3.18	3.27	−0.09	5.24	5.51	−0.28	3.16	3.24	−0.08	3.61	3.69	−0.09	2.68	2.69	0.00	1.22	1.23	−0.01
Trade (41 and 42)	4.51	4.44	0.06	3.44	3.32	0.12	5.15	5.10	0.04	4.47	4.62	−0.15	4.87	4.79	0.08	4.60	4.38	0.22
Finance, insurance, and real estate (43–49)	4.55	4.78	−0.23	4.16	4.68	−0.52	5.50	5.76	−0.26	4.00	4.09	−0.10	5.25	5.62	−0.37	3.82	3.73	0.09
Other services[b] (50–62)	5.21	5.08	0.13	5.82	5.81	0.00	6.50	6.43	0.07	5.20	5.12	0.09	3.56	3.41	0.15	4.96	4.64	0.32
Total	3.05	3.13	−0.09	3.13	3.51	−0.39	3.21	3.30	−0.10	3.44	3.45	−0.01	2.99	3.02	−0.04	2.48	2.38	0.10
Correlation of growth rates across 62 industries (scalar)		0.952			0.973			0.887			0.941			0.987			0.989	

Note: BEA figures are for non-residential net stocks, real-cost valuation (1992 Dollars).

[a] The numbers in parentheses refer to the industry classification scheme shown in Appendix A.

[b] Non-governmental services only.

annual growth rates of the two capital stock series over the full 1947–1997 period are relatively small for the total capital stock and for most sectors, with the notable exception of transportation, with a difference of 0.56 percentage points between the vintage-adjusted and the BEA series. The correlation in capital growth rates over the 1947–1997 period across the 62 individual industries is 0.95, somewhat lower than the correlation coefficient across capital types.

Differences in capital growth rates between the two series are more marked for the individual 10-year periods than for the full 50-year period. In the 1947–1957 period, large differences are found for durables manufacturing, transportation, and the combined sector, fire, insurance, and real estate; in the 1957–1967 period, for transportation; in the 1967–1977 period, for both agriculture and transportation; in the 1977–1987 period, for agriculture, mining, transportation, and finance, insurance, and real estate; and in the 1987–1997 period, for mining.[10]

6. Estimation of implied TFP-growth

Substitution of our estimate of the total obsolescence and depreciation rate in formula (7) yields TFP-growth corrected for vintage effects. Estimates of TFP-growth based on BEA capital and on efficiency units (that is, vintage-adjusted capital stock) are shown in Table 4 for the major sectors and the total non-governmental economy. The output measure is real gross domestic product in chained 1992 Dollars; the labor input is persons engaged in production (PEP); the capital input is non-residential net stocks, real-cost valuation (1992 Dollars); and the labor share is the ratio of employee compensation to net national product.[11] Due to differences in industry classification between the two sources, we use 58 industries instead of 62 (see Table 5).

Over the full 1947–1997 period, overall TFP grew slightly faster (0.04 percentage points per year) on the basis of the BEA capital stock data than on the basis of the vintage-adjusted capital stock in efficiency units. This is a reflection of the slightly slower growth in BEA capital stock than capital stock in efficiency units. Differences are also quite small for the 11 major sectors. The largest difference in annual TFP-growth is recorded for the finance, insurance, and real estate sector—a 0.18 percentage points difference between the BEA and the vintage-adjusted measures. The correlation in TFP-growth rates over the 1947–1997 period across the 58 individual industries is 0.90.

Differences in TFP-growth rates between the two series are somewhat more marked for the individual 10-year periods than for the full 50-year period. In the 1947–1957 period, large differences in annual TFP-growth are found for finance, insurance, and real estate (0.39 percentage points), transportation (0.21), construction (0.20), and for the overall economy (0.16); in the 1957–1967 period, for agriculture (−0.21), transportation (0.17), and finance, insurance, and real estate (0.20 percentage points); in the 1967–1977 period, for agriculture (−0.49); in the 1977–1987 period, for agriculture (0.30), mining (0.22), and finance,

[10] The correlation coefficients in capital growth rates across the 62 industries by ten-year period range from a low of 0.89 in the 1957–1967 period to a high of 0.99 in the 1987–1997 period.

[11] The source for all data except the capital stock data is: http://www.bea.doc.gov/bea/dn2.htm.

Table 4
Annual rate of growth of total factor productivity by major sector and period, 1947–1997 (figures are in percentage points)

Sector	1947–1997			1947–1957			1957–1967			1967–1977			1977–1987			1987–1997		
	BEA	Vintage	Diff.	BEA	Vintage	Diff.	BEA	Vintage	Diff.	BEA	Vintage	Diff.	BEA	Vintage	Diff.	BEA	Vintage	Diff.
Agriculture	0.71	0.77	−0.06	−1.70	−1.61	0.09	−1.24	−1.03	−0.21	−1.73	−1.24	−0.49	4.89	4.59	0.30	3.35	3.15	0.20
Mining	1.08	0.95	0.13	1.17	1.12	0.05	2.21	2.19	0.02	−0.58	−0.65	0.06	−1.26	−1.47	0.22	3.86	3.55	0.31
Construction	−0.20	−0.25	0.05	2.84	2.64	0.20	1.12	1.12	0.00	−4.39	−4.36	−0.02	−0.78	−0.78	0.00	0.21	0.14	0.07
Manufacturing non-durables	1.84	1.82	0.02	2.13	2.08	0.05	2.43	2.40	0.03	2.28	2.25	0.03	1.76	1.75	0.00	0.59	0.60	−0.02
Manufacturing durables	2.55	2.51	0.05	1.86	1.74	0.12	2.15	2.10	0.05	1.82	1.78	0.04	2.19	2.18	0.01	4.75	4.74	0.01
Transportation	1.17	1.05	0.13	0.17	−0.04	0.21	2.90	2.73	0.17	1.00	0.90	0.10	0.52	0.43	0.09	1.26	1.20	0.06
Communications	2.54	2.54	−0.01	2.19	2.21	−0.02	3.45	3.46	−0.01	2.85	2.83	0.02	2.45	2.45	0.00	1.73	1.75	−0.02
Utilities	2.74	2.68	0.06	4.60	4.43	0.17	3.57	3.53	0.05	4.08	4.02	0.05	−1.25	−1.25	0.00	2.69	2.69	0.01
Trade	0.74	0.77	−0.03	1.67	1.72	−0.05	1.17	1.19	−0.02	−0.75	−0.81	0.06	0.38	0.41	−0.03	1.24	1.33	−0.09
Finance, insururance, and real estate	−0.29	−0.47	0.18	1.65	1.26	0.39	−0.18	−0.38	0.20	0.06	−0.02	0.07	−1.94	−2.22	0.28	−1.05	−0.99	−0.07
Other services[a]	−0.24	−0.20	−0.04	−0.09	−0.09	0.00	0.26	0.28	−0.02	0.33	0.35	−0.03	−0.56	−0.51	−0.05	−1.14	−1.04	−0.10
Total	1.12	1.08	0.04	1.90	1.74	0.16	1.87	1.83	0.04	0.53	0.52	0.01	0.33	0.31	0.02	0.95	0.99	−0.04
Correlation of growth rates across 58 industries (scalar)		0.898			0.992			0.961			0.992			0.998			0.999	

Note: The output measure is real gross domestic product in chained 1992 Dollars; the labor input is persons engaged in production (PEP); the capital input is non-residential net stocks, real-cost valuation (1992 Dollars), and the labor share is the ratio of employee compensation to net national product.

[a] Non-governmental services only.

Table 5
Annual rate of growth of total factor productivity by industry and period, 1947–1997 (figures are in percentage points)

	Industry	BEA Capital stock estimates						Vintage capital stock in efficiency units					
		1947–1967	1967–1987	1987–1997	1967 Slowdown	1987 Recovery	Five period std. dev.	1947–1967	1967–1987	1987–1997	1967 Slowdown	1987 Recovery	Five period std. dev.
1	Farms	1.06	2.59	3.83	1.54	1.24	1.97	1.14	2.64	3.69	1.50	1.05	1.85
2	Agricultural services, forestry, and fishing	−1.55	1.06	0.84	2.61	−0.22	1.95	−1.54	1.12	0.83	2.66	−0.29	1.94
3	Metal mining	2.07	1.80	7.26	−0.27	5.46	4.59	2.01	1.78	7.21	−0.23	5.43	4.58
4	Coal mining	3.30	0.76	9.85	−2.53	9.08	4.59	3.24	0.81	9.78	−2.43	8.97	4.56
5	Oil and gas extraction	0.22	−1.94	2.83	−2.16	4.77	2.25	0.21	−2.15	2.39	−2.36	4.54	2.36
6	Non-metallic minerals, except fuels	2.59	3.17	2.48	0.58	−0.69	0.42	2.48	3.15	2.37	0.67	−0.78	0.46
7	Construction	1.98	−2.58	0.21	−4.56	2.80	2.41	1.88	−2.57	0.14	−4.45	2.71	2.36
8	Lumber and wood products	1.22	2.29	−2.49	1.07	−4.78	2.92	1.15	2.27	−2.49	1.12	−4.76	2.93
9	Furniture and fixtures	3.51	1.89	1.06	−1.62	−0.82	1.74	3.50	1.89	1.06	−1.62	−0.83	1.73
10	Stone, clay, and glass products	1.44	1.45	2.20	0.01	0.76	0.56	1.46	1.46	2.14	0.00	0.68	0.57
11	Primary metal industries	2.79	0.25	2.63	−2.54	2.38	1.81	2.56	0.24	2.62	−2.32	2.39	1.74
12	Fabricated metal products	−1.48	1.71	1.84	3.19	0.13	2.83	−1.45	1.72	1.87	3.17	0.14	2.83
13	Industrial machinery and equipment	1.71	4.10	7.80	2.39	3.70	2.58	1.73	4.09	7.81	2.37	3.72	2.58
14	Electronic and other electric equipment	3.70	2.80	9.90	−0.91	7.10	2.75	3.71	2.79	9.90	−0.92	7.11	2.75
15	Motor vehicles and equipment	3.26	1.96	−0.51	−1.30	−2.47	2.32	3.26	1.94	−0.44	−1.32	−2.38	2.31
16	Other transportation equipment	3.39	0.34	−2.90	−3.04	−3.25	2.51	3.39	0.34	−2.89	−3.05	−3.23	2.52
17	Instruments and related products	2.54	2.63	4.68	0.09	2.05	0.87	2.56	2.64	4.69	0.08	2.05	0.86
18	Miscellaneous manufacturing industries	2.72	2.87	1.03	0.15	−1.84	0.88	2.72	2.86	0.98	0.15	−1.88	0.90
19	Food and kindred products	2.01	2.58	0.17	0.57	−2.41	1.04	1.98	2.56	0.16	0.58	−2.40	1.06
20	Tobacco products	0.57	−5.64	−2.91	−6.21	2.72	4.05	0.71	−5.65	−3.00	−6.36	2.65	4.20
21	Textile mill products	4.18	4.81	2.94	0.63	−1.87	1.22	4.17	4.80	2.93	0.63	−1.87	1.23
22	Apparel and other textile products	1.63	3.20	3.19	1.56	−0.01	0.78	1.63	3.19	3.22	1.55	0.04	0.79
23	Paper and allied products	1.50	2.49	0.70	0.99	−1.80	1.28	1.49	2.48	0.69	0.99	−1.79	1.28
24	Printing and publishing	1.33	−0.21	−1.98	−1.55	−1.77	1.30	1.33	−0.21	−1.95	−1.54	−1.74	1.28
25	Chemicals and allied products	3.89	3.31	1.26	−0.58	−2.05	1.07	3.89	3.29	1.32	−0.60	−1.98	1.06
26	Petroleum and coal products	3.66	2.51	0.01	−1.15	−2.50	2.66	3.51	2.49	−0.01	−1.03	−2.50	2.71
27	Rubber and miscellaneous plastics products	1.23	2.36	3.99	1.12	1.63	1.76	1.22	2.34	4.08	1.12	1.74	1.80
28	Leather and leather products	0.55	2.47	3.66	1.91	1.19	1.46	0.54	2.47	3.65	1.93	1.19	1.47

Table 5 (*Continued*)

	Industry	BEA Capital stock estimates						Vintage capital stock in efficiency units					
		1947–1967	1967–1987	1987–1997	1967 Slowdown	1987 Recovery	Five period std. dev.	1947–1967	1967–1987	1987–1997	1967 Slowdown	1987 Recovery	Five period std. dev.
29	Railroad transportation	3.32	2.99	6.46	−0.33	3.47	3.63	3.06	2.76	6.24	−0.29	3.47	3.64
30	Local and interurban passenger transit	−3.82	−1.19	−2.28	2.63	−1.08	1.61	−3.82	−1.15	−2.29	2.67	−1.14	1.62
31	Trucking and warehousing	3.29	−0.27	−0.39	−3.56	−0.12	2.34	3.28	−0.24	−0.25	−3.52	−0.02	2.31
32	Water transportation	−1.25	2.18	0.52	3.44	−1.66	2.04	−1.20	2.18	0.50	3.38	−1.68	2.04
33	Transportation by air	5.66	1.01	1.83	−4.65	0.83	2.96	5.68	1.07	1.79	−4.61	0.72	2.94
34	Pipelines, except natural gas	7.71	2.04	3.24	−5.67	1.20	3.01	7.57	1.97	3.20	−5.61	1.23	2.99
35	Transportation services	0.16	1.13	−0.24	0.97	−1.37	2.41	0.17	1.13	−0.21	0.96	−1.34	2.41
36	Telephone and telegraph	3.00	2.81	2.07	−0.20	−0.74	0.97	3.02	2.80	2.09	−0.22	−0.71	1.02
37	Radio and television	0.55	1.68	0.68	1.13	−1.00	2.54	0.57	1.69	0.74	1.12	−0.95	2.53
38	Electric, gas, and sanitary services	4.08	1.41	2.69	−2.67	1.28	2.39	3.98	1.39	2.69	−2.59	1.30	2.13
39	Wholesale trade	0.68	−0.78	2.07	−1.46	2.85	1.27	0.68	−0.80	2.23	−1.49	3.03	1.36
40	Retail trade	1.47	0.14	0.77	−1.32	0.63	0.59	1.50	0.12	0.80	−1.37	0.68	0.73
41	Banking	−0.70	−1.71	−3.05	−1.01	−1.34	1.04	−0.69	−1.65	−2.86	−0.97	−1.21	1.06
42	Non-depository institutions	1.13	−3.80	−6.04	−4.92	−2.25	3.12	1.31	−3.84	−5.78	−5.15	−1.94	3.30
43	Security and commodity brokers	0.63	0.23	8.65	−0.39	8.42	3.34	0.60	0.26	8.77	−0.34	8.51	3.40
44	Insurance carriers	0.38	−1.94	2.91	−2.33	4.86	3.34	0.40	−1.94	3.00	−2.34	4.94	3.85
45	Insurance agents, brokers, and service	0.86	−1.21	0.22	−2.07	1.43	1.35	0.84	−1.14	0.45	−1.98	1.59	1.90
46	Real estate	1.56	−0.26	0.30	−1.82	0.56	1.00	1.28	−0.41	0.31	−1.69	0.71	0.96
47	Holding and other investment offices	3.13	1.15	−0.45	−1.98	−1.60	2.49	−0.67	−0.56	−0.78	0.11	−0.23	2.36
48	Hotels and other lodging places	0.12	−0.51	2.49	−0.63	3.01	1.94	0.07	−0.50	2.54	−0.57	3.04	1.97
49	Personal services	0.07	−1.00	−0.41	−1.06	0.59	0.51	0.09	−0.98	−0.33	−1.07	0.66	0.65
50	Business services	0.35	−0.48	−0.97	−0.83	−0.49	0.35	0.40	−0.41	−0.89	−0.81	−0.48	0.84
51	Auto repair, services, and parking	−0.65	−0.30	−1.32	0.35	−1.02	1.51	−0.55	−0.26	−1.04	0.29	−0.79	2.11
52	Miscellaneous repair services	−0.36	−0.42	−4.19	−0.07	−3.77	1.68	−0.36	−0.43	−4.27	−0.07	−3.84	1.77
53	Motion pictures	−2.45	1.56	−2.26	4.01	−3.81	2.27	−2.43	1.60	−2.13	4.03	−3.72	2.27
54	Amusement and recreation services	0.88	0.51	−0.04	−0.37	−0.55	1.14	0.85	0.54	0.08	−0.31	−0.46	1.09
55	Health services	−1.11	−0.68	−3.15	0.43	−2.47	1.36	−1.10	−0.69	−3.12	0.41	−2.43	1.41
56	Legal services	−0.50	−2.56	−1.29	−2.05	1.27	2.10	−0.46	−2.50	−1.00	−2.05	1.50	2.07
57	Educational services	−1.04	−1.30	−2.16	−0.26	−0.86	0.96	−1.01	−0.54	−2.03	0.47	−1.49	0.98
58	Other services, n.e.c.	−4.51	2.60	−1.91	7.11	−4.52	4.26	−4.48	2.60	−1.83	7.08	−4.43	4.26
	Total	1.88	0.43	0.95	−1.46	0.52	0.66	1.79	0.42	0.99	−1.37	0.58	0.62

Note: See notes to Table 4 for technical details on TFP estimation. The government sector is not included.

insurance, and real estate (0.28); and in the 1987–1997 period, for agriculture (0.21) and mining (0.31).[12]

7. Aging capital and the vintage effect on TFP

The effect of the incorporation of the rate of obsolescence on TFP-growth is shown to depend on the aging of the stock of capital. In fact, there is a straight proportionality between aging and the vintage effect:

Proposition 3.

$$\frac{\mathrm{dTFP}^{s\wedge}}{\mathrm{d}s} = \frac{\beta \mathrm{d}\bar{A}^s}{\mathrm{d}t}.$$

Proof. Differentiate (7) with respect to s, using (5) and (8): $\mathrm{dTFP}^{s\wedge}/\mathrm{d}s = -\beta\,\mathrm{d}[I/K^s - (s+\sigma)]/\mathrm{d}s = -\beta[-I/K^{s2}(\mathrm{d}/\mathrm{d}s)\int I(t-t')\exp(-st')\exp(-\sigma t')\mathrm{d}t' - 1] = -\beta\,[-I/K^{s2}\int I(t-t')\exp(-st')(-t')\exp(-\sigma t')\mathrm{d}t' - 1] = -\beta[(I/K^s)\bar{A}^s - 1] = \beta\,\mathrm{d}\bar{A}^s/\mathrm{d}t$ by Proposition 1. □

The message of this proposition is clear. In times when capital becomes older, measured TFP-growth increases as obsolescence, s, is taken into account. Conversely, in times when capital becomes younger, measured TFP-growth decreases as obsolescence, s, is taken into account. Thus, the incorporation of obsolescence may well remove some of the cyclicality of TFP-growth. Let us explain.

In an upswing of the business cycle the investment/capital ratio tends to be high. This means, by Proposition 1, that capital becomes younger and, therefore, by Proposition 3, that the incorporation of the vintage effect in TFP measurement amounts to a downward correction. By the same token, in a downswing of the business cycle capital grows older and the incorporation of the vintage effect amounts to an upward correction. In short, the vintage effect is expected to be counter-cyclical.

TFP-growth itself, however, is known to be pro-cyclical, which is considered an awkward finding, as it is supposed to measure the shift of technology rather than the business cycle (see, for example, Gordon, 1979). As the vintage effect is expected to be counter-cyclical, it may have a smoothing impact. In short, the vintage effect may throw light on productivity puzzles such as the pro-cyclical behavior of TFP-growth and the slowdown of productivity in the 1970s.

The results displayed in Table 5 are interesting. The left panel displays standard TFP-growth figures, based on BEA capital stock estimates. The right panel displays our vintage-adjusted TFP-growth rates. In each panel, the first three columns show the annual rate of TFP-growth during the high productivity growth period of 1947–1967, the slow productivity

[12] The correlation coefficients in capital growth rates across the 58 industries by ten-year period range from a low of 0.96 in the 1957–1967 period to a high of 1.00 in the 1987–1997 period.

growth period of 1967–1987, and then the recovery period 1987–1997.[13] The differences between the figures in the first two columns indicate the 1967 slowdown and are listed in the fourth columns. Similarly, the differences between the figures in the second and third columns indicate the 1987 recovery and are listed in the fifth columns. The sixth and final column in either panel shows the standard deviations of the TFP-growth rates over the five 10-year period (1947–1957, 1957–1967, 1967–1977, 1977–1987, and 1987–1997).

There are three questions of interest. First, does the use of capital measured in efficiency units reduce the measured slowdown between the 1947–1967 and the 1967–1987 periods? Second, does the use of capital in efficiency units increase the measured recovery after 1987 (that is to say, does it cause TFP-growth in the 1987–1997 period to return more closely to its long-term average performance)? Third, does the use of capital in efficiency units reduce disparities in measured TFP-growth across the five 10-year period? The answer to the three questions is generally "yes."

First, for the overall economy, the slowdown in annual TFP-growth after 1967 is 1.46 percentage points on the basis of BEA capital stock but only 1.37 percentage points on the basis of vintage-adjusted capital stock. The measured slowdown is also reduced in 31 of the 58 detailed industries. Second, for the overall economy, the recovery in annual TFP-growth is 0.52 points on the basis of BEA capital stock and 0.58 points on the basis of capital stock in efficiency units. The measured recovery is also increased in 40 of the 58 detailed industries. Third, the standard deviation of TFP-growth for the overall economy over the five 10-year period is 0.66 on the basis of BEA capital stock and 0.62 on the basis of capital measured in efficiency units. The standard deviation is also lower on the basis of the vintage-adjusted capital stock in 33 of the 58 industries.

8. Conclusion

TFP-growth is known to be pro-cyclical, an awkward finding, as it is supposed to measure the shift of technology rather than the business cycle. If the age of capital is counter-cyclical, then the vintage effect is also counter-cyclical by Proposition 3, a neutralizing effect. In short, the vintage effect throws theoretical light on productivity puzzles such as the slowdown in the 1970s and the pro-cyclicality of productivity growth.

The results indicate that the use of capital stock in efficiency units does cause some smoothing of TFP-growth over time. The productivity growth slowdown of the 1970s – known from studies that do not take into account the age structure of capital – is reduced on the basis of these new capital stock data. The reason is that capital became older over this period. The relationship between the aging of capital and the sign of the vintage effect has

[13] We have decided to use 1967 as the demarcation of the beginning of the slowdown period instead of the more standard 1973 because of peculiarities associated with the year 1973 (such as the beginning of the oil crisis in the U.S. and the end of Bretton Woods). In Table 5, '1967 slowdown' and also '1987 recovery' should be understood as representing differences between the two surrounding 10-year period in each case rather than single-year events.

a theoretical foundation. While our vintage correction of TFP-growth over the slowdown has the right sign, the magnitude is small.

Based on our new method, we find that the vintage effect accounted for 0.06 percentage points of the 1.34 percentage points decline in overall TFP-growth between the 1957–1967 and the 1967–1977 periods or about 5% of the productivity slowdown. This is about the same order of magnitude as Kendrick (1980) and Clark (1979), though much lower than Wolff (1996). The difference in the findings here from those of Wolff (1996) appears to stem from methodological differences in the two techniques. Wolff (1996) used regression analysis to estimate *indirectly* the contribution of the vintage effect to productivity growth on the basis of the Nelson (1964) formulation. Using a sample of six OECD countries over the period 1950–1989, TFP-growth was regressed on the relative TFP at the beginning of the period, the growth in the capital stock, and the change in the average age of capital in each country. Here, we *directly* estimate the vintage effect for each asset type. Though Wolff (1996) did control for other factors, such as the change in human capital within each country, it is likely that the very strong vintage effect that he estimated is due to the omission of other pertinent variables that explain technological change.

For the manufacturing sector, the vintage effect explained 40% of the (very modest) 0.15 percentage points productivity slowdown in non-durable manufacturing and 27% of the 0.33 percentage points slowdown in durable manufacturing between the 1957–1967 and the 1967–1977 periods. This result is larger than that estimated by Hulten (1992). However, whereas Hulten estimated that the vintage effect accounted for about 20% of the total quality-adjusted technical change in manufacturing over the years 1949–1983, we estimate that it accounted for only about 5% over the 1947–1997 period.

Perhaps, our most significant results are for the 1950s (the 1947–1957 period), when investment in the economy accelerated and the vintage-adjusted capital growth rate well exceeded the BEA growth rate (3.51 and 3.13%, respectively).[14] As a result vintage-adjusted TFP-growth is 8.4% lower than unadjusted TFP-growth for the whole economy (with the figures for the construction sector and the finance, insurance and real estate sector 7 and 34% lower).

Acknowledgements

We thank participants at the International Input–Output Association conference in Montreal, Canada, at a seminar at Vanderbilt University, and at the NBER productivity workshop, particularly the paper's discussant, Erwin Diewert, for their helpful comments. The views expressed herein are those of the authors and not necessarily those of the Bureau of Labor Statistics.

[14] We are grateful to Bob Margo for this observation.

Appendix A

Table A.1
Listing of detailed industries for BEA capital stock data

1	Farms
2	Agricultural services, forestry, and fishing
3	Metal mining
4	Coal mining
5	Oil and gas extraction
6	Non-metallic minerals, except fuels
7	Construction
8	Lumber and wood products
9	Furniture and fixtures
10	Stone, clay, and glass products
11	Primary metal industries
12	Fabricated metal products
13	Industrial machinery and equipment
14	Electronic and other electric equipment
15	Motor vehicles and equipment
16	Other transportation equipment
17	Instruments and related products
18	Miscellaneous manufacturing industries
19	Food and kindred products
20	Tobacco products
21	Textile mill products
22	Apparel and other textile products
23	Paper and allied products
24	Printing and publishing
25	Chemicals and allied products
26	Petroleum and coal products
27	Rubber and miscellaneous plastics products
28	Leather and leather products
29	Railroad transportation
30	Local and interurban passenger transit
31	Trucking and warehousing
32	Water transportation
33	Transportation by air
34	Pipelines, except natural gas
35	Transportation services
36	Telephone and telegraph
37	Radio and television
38	Electric services
39	Gas services
40	Sanitary services
41	Wholesale trade
42	Retail trade
43	Federal reserve banks
44	Other depository institutions
45	Non-depository institutions
46	Security and commodity brokers
47	Insurance carriers
48	Insurance agents, brokers, and service

Table A.1 (*Continued*)

49	Real estate
50	Non-financial holding and investment offices
51	Financial holding and investment offices
52	Hotels and other lodging places
53	Personal services
54	Business services
55	Auto repair, services, and parking
56	Miscellaneous repair services
57	Motion pictures
58	Amusement and recreation services
59	Health services
60	Legal services
61	Educational services
62	Other services, n.e.c.

Appendix B. Discrete time analysis of capital aging

Proposition 1 links the aging of capital to the investment/stock ratio. Erwin Diewert provided the following discrete time proof.

Eq. (5) reads

$$K^s(t) = I(t) + (1-s-\sigma)I(t-1) + (1-s-\sigma)^2 I(t-2) + \cdots \tag{10}$$

Defining the number of years embodied in this stock by

$$N^s(t) = 1 \cdot I(t) + 2(1-s-\sigma)I(t-1) + 3(1-s-\sigma)^2 I(t-2) + \cdots \tag{11}$$

Eq. (8) reads

$$\bar{A}^s(t) = \frac{N^s(t)}{K^s(t)} \tag{12}$$

Substituting $N^s(t) = K^s(t) + (1-s-\sigma)\, N^s(t-1)$, a consequence of (11), (12) reads $\bar{A}^s(t) = 1 + (1-s-\sigma)N^s(t-1)/K^s(t) = 1 + (1-s-\sigma)\bar{A}^s(t-1)K^s(t-1)/K^s(t)$. Now substituting $K^s(t) = (1-s-\sigma)\ K^s(t-1) + I(t)$, which follows from (10), just like (6) from (5): $\bar{A}^s(t) = 1 + \bar{A}^s(t-1)[K^s(t) - I(t)]/K^s(t) = 1$ or $\bar{A}^s(t) - \bar{A}^s(t-1) = 1 - [I(t)/K^s(t)]\bar{A}^s(t-1)$. This is Proposition 1 in discrete time.

References

Abramovitz, M., 1994. Catch-up and convergence in the postwar growth boom and after. In: Baumol, W.J., Nelson, R.R., Wolff, E.N. (Eds.), Convergence of Productivity: Cross-National Studies and Historical Evidence. Oxford University Press, New York, pp. 86–125.

Amemiya, T., 1985. Advanced Econometrics. Harvard University Press, Cambridge, MA.

Bosworth, B., 1978. The rate of obsolescence of technical knowledge—a note. Journal of Industrial Economics 26 (3), 273–279.

von Böhm-Bawerk, E., 1959. Positive theory of capital. tr. George Huncke, Hans Sennholz, Capital & Interest, vol. 2, Libertarian Press, Grove City, PA.

Clark, P.K., 1979. Issues in the analysis of capital formation and productivity growth. Brookings Papers on Economic Activity 2, 423–431.
Diewert, W.E., Lawrence, D.A., 2000. Progress in measuring the price and quantity of capital. In: Lau, J.L. (Ed.), Econometrics, vol. 2. Econometrics and the Cost of Capital: Essays in Honor of Dale W. Jorgenson. The MIT Press, Cambridge, pp. 273–326.
Gordon, R.J., 1979. The end of expansion phenomenon in short-run productivity behavior. Brookings Papers on Economic Activity 2, 447–461.
Harper, M.J., 2002. Technology and the theory of vintage aggregation. Paper Presented at the Joint NBER-CRIW Measurement Workshop, Cambridge, MA, July 29–31.
Hulten, C.R., 1992. Growth accounting when technical change is embodied in capital. American Economic Review 82 (September), 964–980.
Hulten, C.R., Wykoff, F.C., 1992. The measurement of economic depreciation. In: Hulten, C.R. (Ed.), Depreciation, Inflation, and the Taxation of Income from Capital. The Urban Institute Press, Washington, pp. 81–125.
Jorgenson, D.W., 1966. The embodiment hypothesis. Journal of Political Economy 74 (February), 1–17.
Katz, A.J., Herman, S.W., 1997. Improved estimates of fixed reproducible tangible wealth, 1929–95. Survey of Current Business (May) 77, 69–92.
Kendrick, J.W., 1980. Productivity trends in the United States. In: Maital, S., Meltz, N.M. (Eds.), Lagging Productivity Growth. Ballinger Publishing Co., Cambridge, pp. 9–31.
Nelson, R.R., 1964. Aggregate production functions and medium-range growth projections. American Economic Review 54 (September), 575–605.
Pakes, A., Schankerman, M., 1984. An exploration into the determinants of research intensity. In: Griliches, Z. (Ed.), Patents, R&D and Productivity. The University of Chicago Press, Chicago, pp. 73–88.
Solow, R.M., 1957. Technical change and the aggregate production function. Review of Economics and Statistics 39 (3), 312–320.
Solow, R.M., 1960. Investment and technical progress. In: Arrow, K.J., Karlin, S., Suppes, P. (Eds.), Mathematical Models in the Social Sciences, 1959. Stanford University Press, Stanford, pp. 89–104.
Tatom, J.A., 1979. The productivity problem. Federal Reserve Bank of St. Louis Monthly Review (September) 61, 3–16.
Wolff, E.N., 1991. Capital formation and productivity convergence over the long-term. American Economic Review 81 (June), 565–579.
Wolff, E.N., 1996. The productivity slowdown: the culprit at last? American Economic Review 86 (December), 1239–1252.

ELSEVIER

Journal of Economic Behavior & Organization
Vol. 65 (2008) 573–584

JOURNAL OF
Economic Behavior
& Organization

www.elsevier.com/locate/econbase

Competition and performance: The different roles of capital and labor

Thijs ten Raa [a,*], Pierre Mohnen [b]

[a] *Department of Econometrics, University of Tilburg, P.O. Box 90153, 5000 LE Tilburg, The Netherlands*
[b] *University of Maastricht, MERIT and CIRANO, The Netherlands*

Received 4 February 2005; accepted 12 December 2005
Available online 16 October 2006

Abstract

Neoclassical economists argue that competition promotes efficiency, but Schumpeter argues that it is monopoly rents that help entrepreneurs to invest in R&D. We investigate the overall effect of competition on total factor productivity growth (TFP) growth. We use rent, defined as the factor reward above its perfectly competitive value, as a negative measure of competition. Our main finding is that performance is positively associated with rents on capital but not with rents on labor. Neoclassical economists and Schumpeter may both be right, but the mechanisms differ.

JEL classification: L16; O41; C67

Keywords: Competition; Rent; TFP; Schumpeter hypothesis

1. Introduction

Is competition good for performance? Yes, say neoclassical economists, arguing that it eliminates slack and hence promotes static efficiency. No, say Schumpeter and others, pointing out that monopoly rents induce entrepreneurs to invest in R&D and thus promote dynamic efficiency. The mechanisms alluded to are quite different, and the overall effect of competition becomes an empirical issue. Nickell (1996) finds some support for the view that competition improves performance, but the evidence is not overwhelming. Aghion et al. (2001, 2002) and Boone (2001)

* Corresponding author. Tel.: +31 13 466 2365; fax: +31 20 420 6502.
E-mail addresses: tenRaa@UvT.nl (T. ten Raa), p.mohnen@merit.unimaas.nl (P. Mohnen).

0167-2681/$ – see front matter © 2006 Elsevier B.V. All rights reserved.
doi:10.1016/j.jebo.2005.12.007

argue that the relationship between competition and innovation is non-monotonic. Griffith (2001) finds that product market competition improves performance in principal-agent type firms. We will review the argument in some detail and then pitch our approach.

If a market is more competitive, the stakes of sweeping it by winning an innovation contest are greater, as the scope is wider. On a product-by-product basis, however, margins are lower in a more competitive market. Aghion et al. (2001) combine the two countervailing effects in a single model, where industries are duopolies engaged in price (Bertrand) competition. 'Competition' is measured by the elasticity of substitution between the duopolists' products. A higher degree of substitutability boosts the reward to an innovation winner among leveled firms (the neoclassical effect), but reduces the (marginal) reward to non-leveled firms (the Schumpeterian effect). A level field will become less leveled and the new equilibrium is less congenial for innovation; followers face low rents to gain when demand is more elastic, while leaders do not distance themselves further as technological knowledge is assumed to spill over anyway after a single period. Industries become less leveled and the rent dissipation effect overtakes the contest effect. Competition and innovation have an inverted U relationship as a result. In a Hotelling-style example of three vendors Boone finds a U relationship and notes that "basically anything can happen," but Aghion et al. (2002) find empirical support for the inverted U relationship between competition and innovation.

Since Aghion et al. (2001, 2002) measure competition by means of the elasticity of substitution, both the neoclassical and the Schumpeterian effects are channelled through the product markets. This is also the market studied by Griffith, who suggests, however, that agency costs play a role in the scope for performance. We want to analyze the role of factor markets. Do neoclassical economists not argue that competition is good because it keeps managers sharp? And does Schumpeter not argue that monopoly profits are good because they fund R&D? Labor and capital may play conflicting roles in terms of the relationship between competition and performance. This conflict may explain why there is no simple relationship between the two.

Rather than relating rents to elasticities of demand in a neoclassical model of price competition, we decompose rents into factor components in a classical input–output framework and investigate whether the opposing effects of competition operate through different markets. A natural thought seems to be that competition in the labor market may be good, but competition in the capital market may be bad, both in terms of performance. In other words, neoclassical and Schumpeterian economists may both be right, but rather than combining the opposing effects in some non-linear relationship, we point to different factor markets. The potential policy conclusions would be vastly different. The aforementioned literature may suggest an optimal level of product market competition at best. We say at best, because competition is modeled as a shift in consumers' preferences (more substitutability) and firms are assumed to (Bertrand) price compete throughout. In this paper, however, departures from competition are modeled directly as rents and factor markets are targeted.

What do we mean by competition and performance? The measurement of performance is relatively straightforward. Solow (1957) has demonstrated for perfectly competitive economies that the shift of the production possibility frontier, which is the ultimate determinant of the standard of living, is measured by total factor productivity growth (TFP). TFP is also the relevant measure for the standard of living in non- or less competitive economies, where it measures not only the shift of the frontier, but also the change in efficiency (Nishimizu and Page, 1982). In short, we let performance be measured by TFP.

The measurement of competition is trickier. The industrial organization literature provides a number of indices. Perhaps concentration indices are the most popular ones, but we will not employ them. We believe that industries with a low number of firms may well be competitive. In the tradition of Lerner (1934) we measure market power more directly by the extent that price has been raised over cost (i.e. by rent). Indeed, Nickell finds that rent is the most important determinant in the assessment of the influence of competition on performance, but rent is hard to measure. Nickell takes the difference between the rates of return on company capital and treasury bonds and admits this merely measures capital rent, and even as such is only a rough proxy; neoclassical economists point out that competition stamps out labor rent.

In the spirit of Nickell we take rent as the (negative) measure of competition and define it by the difference between actual and perfectly competitive rewards. Actual rewards are given by value-added and perfectly competitive rewards by factor costs at shadow prices. To determine the latter we need a general equilibrium model, which may have been the main obstacle in assessing the role of competition in the performance of an economy. We do so by analyzing Canadian input–output data over the period 1962–1991. Rent and TFP are determined at a level of aggregation that is more macro- than micro-economic.

Section 2 presents the model we employ to determine competitive valuations. Then, in Section 3, we define rent and impute it to capital and labor. Section 4 investigates the relationship between competition and performance (as measured by rent and TFP, respectively).

2. The productivity model

Both competition and performance are related to productivity. For performance the connection to productivity is straightforward, as it is measured by TFP, the growth of (total factor) productivity. The connection between competition and rent is slightly more indirect. Competition is (negatively) measured by rent. Rent is the difference between actual and perfectly competitive rewards where the latter are essentially marginal productivities.

The standard approach to productivity is neoclassical TFP analysis, where output and input components are combined into indices using value shares as weights. The acceptance of value shares at face value is equivalent to taking factor rewards for granted, and this procedure has been justified for perfectly competitive economies (Solow, 1957; Jorgenson and Griliches, 1967). We, however, are interested in the difference between observed and competitive rewards and, therefore, cannot apply the standard procedure, but must derive productivities from the real input and output data of the economy.

We follow Nishimizu and Page in letting total factor productivity growth be the composition of a shift of the best-practice frontier (true technological progress) and a change in technical efficiency, and in using linear programming techniques to identify the frontier and the resulting level of efficiency. Nishimizu and Page use sectoral panel data to estimate a time-shifting translog production frontier for every sector and sectoral levels of technical efficiency in each period, but ignore the input balance constraints. We estimate instead a general equilibrium model with different sectoral levels of activity in each period and an overall level of technical efficiency for the whole economy in each period.

Our model is input–output in spirit, but we admit different numbers of industries and of commodities, as in activity analysis. Industries transform factor inputs and intermediate inputs into outputs, and the net output commodity vector feeds domestic final demand and net exports. The marginal productivities of the factor inputs are the shadow prices associated with the factor constraints of the program that maximizes welfare. Now if we assume that producers use Leontief technologies and end users of the commodities have Leontief preferences, then the formulas governing these shadow prices are perfectly consistent with neoclassical growth accounting and, moreover, capture the efficiency change effect of frontier analysis; see ten Raa and Mohnen (2002).

The model maximizes the level of domestic final demand, given its commodity proportions and subject to material balances, factor constraints, and balance of payments:

$$\begin{aligned} &\max_{s,c,g} e^{\mathrm{T}} fc \text{ subject to} \\ &(V^{\mathrm{T}} - U)s \geq fc + Jg =: F \\ &Ks \leq M \\ &Ls \leq N \\ &-\pi g \leq -\pi g' =: D \\ &s \geq 0. \end{aligned} \tag{1}$$

The variables (s, c, g) and parameters (all other) are the following [with dimensions in brackets]:

s	activity vector [# of industries]
c	level of domestic final demand [scalar]
g	vector of net exports [# of tradable commodities]
e	unit vector with all components equal to one
T	transposition symbol
f	domestic final demand [# of commodities]
V	make table [# of industries by # of commodities]
U	use table [# of commodities by # of industries]
J	0 1 matrix placing tradable [# of commodities by # of tradables]
F	potential final demand [# of commodities]
K	capital stock matrix [# of capital types by # of industries]
M	capital endowment [# of capital types]
L	labor employment row vector [# of industries]
N	labor force [scalar]
π	U.S. relative price row vector [# of tradable]
g^t	vector of net exports observed at time t [# of tradable]
D	observed trade deficit [scalar].

In (1), the observed allocation corresponds to $s = e$ and $c = 1$. This is feasible. The optimal value of expansion factor c will be greater than one. It measures the ratio of potential to actual domestic absorption. Domestic absorption is GDP except net exports; it is also called domestic GDP. We denote the shadow prices associated with the constraints of program (1) by p (a row vector of commodity prices), r (a row vector of capital productivities), w (a scalar for labor productivity), ε (a scalar for the purchasing power parity), and σ (a row vector of slacks for the sectors). Then the dual program reads

$$\begin{aligned} &\min_{p,r,w,\sigma \geq 0} rM + wN + \varepsilon D \text{ subject to} \\ &p(V^{\mathrm{T}} - U) = rK + wL - \sigma \\ &pf = e^{\mathrm{T}} f \\ &pJ = \varepsilon\pi. \end{aligned} \tag{2}$$

The first dual constraint equates value added to factor costs for active industries (which have zero slack according to the theory of linear programming), all at shadow prices. The second dual constraint normalizes the level of commodity prices by the multiplicative constant we entered in the objective function of (1). The third dual constraint aligns the prices of the tradable commodities with the terms-of-trade.

The primal (1) and dual (2) programs have equal value by the main theorem of linear programming. In view of the price normalization constraint of (2) the identity reads

$$pfc = rM + wN + \varepsilon D \tag{3}$$

The *level* of total factor productivity is given by the ratio of actual output to optimally weighted factor input, $e^{\mathrm{T}} f/(rM + wN + \varepsilon D)$. According to Eq. (3) the level of total factor productivity is $1/c$, which is essentially Debreu's coefficient of resource allocation (ten Raa, 2003). *Total factor productivity growth* is the rate of growth of the level of total factor productivity at *fixed* price weights[1]:

$$TFP = \frac{p\dot{f}}{pf} - \frac{rM + wN + \varepsilon\dot{D}}{rM + wN + \varepsilon D}. \tag{4}$$

Total factor productivity growth has been shown to be the sum of the Solow residual,

$$SR = \frac{[p\dot{F} - r(K\dot{s}) - w(L\dot{s})]}{rM + wN + \varepsilon D}, \tag{5}$$

the terms-of-trade effect,

$$TT = \frac{\varepsilon\dot{\pi}g}{rM + wN + \varepsilon D}, \tag{6}$$

and the efficiency change,

$$EC = -\frac{\dot{c}}{c}, \tag{7}$$

in ten Raa and Mohnen. The Solow residual is a Domar weighted average of industry Solow residuals (Mohnen and ten Raa, 2000):

$$SRi = \frac{p(V^{\mathrm{T}} - \dot{U})_{.i} - r\dot{K}_i - w\dot{L}_i}{pV_i}. \tag{8}$$

with weights

$$\frac{pV_i \cdot s_i}{pfc}. \tag{9}$$

The industry Solow residuals measure the dynamic performance of the economy. The static performance is measured by the efficiency change. The latter, see formula (8), measures the growth rate of the actual/potential GDP ratio because c measures the ratio of potential to actual domestic GDP. Here, efficiency change is driven by reallocations of the factor inputs, capital and labor, between industries. It could be imputed to the industries following ten Raa (2003), but these efficiency changes would still measure inter-industry allocative gains rather than intra-industry catching up with best practices. Input–output analysis implicitly identifies technical coefficients with observed input–output proportions. sectoral productivity growth rates, see (8), capture technical change, intra-firm efficiency changes and inter-firm allocative efficiency changes

[1] *Warning*: We use *TFP* for TFP growth. No symbol is needed for the level of TFP. As usual, a dot denotes differentiation with respect to time.

(ten Raa, 2005). It would be interesting to make this further decomposition, but that requires access to and use of the establishment data underlying the use and make tables.

3. Rent

In a broad sense, rent comprises all payments made to factor inputs for the provision of their services. The owner of a building collects rent from the businesses that use the space, and a worker receives compensation for the labor provided. This broad concept of rent includes not only the opportunity costs of the services but also the bonuses that reflect distortions such as market power. The narrow concept of rent, however, is limited to these bonuses and, therefore, consists of the excess payments over and above the opportunity cost. It is the latter concept of rent that we use to measure departures from competition.

The first dual constraint of (2) is the value relationship between value-added and factor costs when prices are competitive. It has its counterpart for observed prices, which we denote by p^{o}, r^{o}, and w^{o} for commodities, capital, and labor, respectively, where the superscript indicates 'observed.' Thus,

$$p^{\text{o}}(V^{\text{T}} - U) = r^{\text{o}}K + w^{\text{o}}L + \sigma^{\text{o}}. \tag{10}$$

Here σ^{o} is defined residually and represents profits.[2]

We define *rent* as the difference between observed value-added, given by row vector $p^{\text{o}}(V^{\text{T}} - U)$, and competitive value-added, given by row vector $v = p(V^{\text{T}} - U)$. The row vector of differences defines rent by sector. We can impute rent (in each sector) to the factor suppliers. Subtracting the first dual equation in program (2) from Eq. (10) we obtain

$$Rent = (r^{\text{o}} - r)K + (w^{\text{o}} - w)L + (\sigma^{\text{o}} + \sigma). \tag{11}$$

In words, rent is the sum of capitalists' rent, workers' rent, and excess profits. Often capitalists' rent and excess profits are pooled to define *K-rent*, $(r^{\text{o}} - r)K + (\sigma^{\text{o}} + \sigma)$. Similarly denoting workers' rent $(w^{\text{o}} - w)L$ by *L-rent*, Eq. (11) is consolidated as follows:

$$Rent = K\text{-}rent + L\text{-}rent. \tag{12}$$

Notice that each term in Eq. (12) is a row vector of industry rents. The consolidation of profits into capital rent is apt for economies where profits accrue to shareholders rather than workers (i.e. capitalism). All the rent terms represent excess payments, over and above competitive values, so that rent is a negative measure for competitiveness. This is in the spirit of Nickell, who captures capital rent by putting r = treasury bills rates and $\sigma = 0$, and who misses labor rent. We fill the gaps by letting our general equilibrium model determine the shadow prices.

Although we are able to dissociate capital from labor rents, we admit that we face some aggregation problems. There are more than three types of capital: often software, hardware, telecommunication equipment and inventories are measured as separate pieces of the aggregate capital stock, and the separation of R&D from value added is presently under discussion in

[2] Given that the make matrix V is in producer prices and the use matrix U (and the final demand vector F) is in consumer prices, there is a discrepancy due to various types of margins. The Canadian input–output tables contain a separate table of seven types of margins. We have assimilated the margins to final demand, which is computed residually from the U, V and net trade (g) data. The margins are most likely included in our residual measure of observed capital rents, obtained by subtracting observed labor payments from observed value added.

statistical offices. There is certainly more than one type of labor. Actually, data on labor by type of occupation exist for Canada, but not for the whole period that we are analyzing.[3] Therefore, we have not separated out labor into different types. Given the different compositions by type of labor and capital across industries, our assumption of uniform competitive factor payments across sectors is certainly debatable, and we will do this in the next section.

4. Competition and performance

The standard approach to measuring the impact of competition on performance is to regress the Solow residual (representing performance) on rent (representing the departure from competition):

$$SR_{it}=\alpha+\beta Rentit-1+\varepsilon_{it}, \quad \varepsilon_{it}=\mu_i+\lambda_t+v_{it};\ i=1,\ldots,45,\ t=1963,\ldots,1991. \tag{13}$$

A positive role of competition would be signaled by a negative value of β. Coefficient α represents technological progress. The *data* underlying our panel of growth rates for 45 Canadian sectors and 29 time periods are described in Appendix in Supplementary Material. In order to control for industry specific and time-specific effects on productivity, we model a two-way error component model: μ_i represents the sector effect and is distributed i.i.d. with mean zero and standard deviation σ_μ, λ_t represents the time effect, distributed i.i.d. with mean zero and standard deviation σ_t, and v_{it} is the idiosyncratic effect, distributed i.i.d. with mean zero and standard deviation σ_v. A generalized least-squares estimation produces consistent estimates if there is no correlation between the composite error term and the rent. If $\sigma_\mu=\sigma_v=0$, we have a fixed sectoral and time effects model. In Eq. (13) we have instrumented rent by its one-period lagged value to avoid a possible simultaneity bias.[4]

We have first tested whether we cannot pool the data. The Chow test rejects pooling of different industries (a test statistic of 1.56 above the tabulated value of a $\chi^2_{44,1303}$). When, however, we allow for different β's over time or over time and sectors, we cannot reject homogeneity ($0.50<\chi^2_{28,1303}$ and $1.16<\chi^2_{72,1303}$, respectively). Next, we have estimated Eq. (13) using sector, time and sector/time dummies (i.e. exploiting, respectively, deviations from the industry means, from the year means, and the double deviations from time and industry means). We have estimated the model once using total rent, and once with rent split into labor and capital components. Since labor and capital rents may influence performance in different ways, it is interesting to investigate their separate effects. The results are tabulated in Table 1. In all cases we reject the absence of sector-specific or time-specific fixed effects. We see that the effect of total rents on TFP is always positive, although in the most preferred specification (with time and industry dummies) it is significant only at 6.7 percent level of confidence. Splitting rents, we find that the labor components are generally insignificant and that the capital components consistently have positive effects, significant at the 5 percent level as soon as we control for time effects.

---

[3] Canadian data on skill levels, based on the national occupational classification (NOC) or the standard occupational classification exist continuously only from 1980 onwards. Gera et al. (2001) have used those data and constructed two sets of four skill levels (based on occupations, however, and not on qualifications) using the NOC classification and a skill classification proposed by Baumol and Wolff (1989) and updated by Wolff (2006). We have preferred to work with a longer dataset spanning 30 years without distinguishing labor by type of skills.

[4] It should be mentioned that the causality between rent and TFP may also flow the other way. Rents may be the result of ex-post successful innovations. By inverting the lag structure one could try to identify the direction of causality.

Table 1
Within regression of TFP on rents (percentage points increases per billion Canadian dollars, p-values in parentheses)

Regressors	Standard: total rent				Separate labor and capital rents			
	1	2	3	4	5	6	7	8
Total rent	0.023 (0.154)	0.037 (0.166)	0.026 (0.091)	0.047 (0.067)	–	–	–	–
Labor rent	–	–	–	–	0.0161 (0.406)	0.059 (0.065)	−0.051 (0.786)	−0.003 (0.920)
Capital rent	–	–	–	–	0.028 (0.114)	0.024 (0.399)	0.052 (0.004)	0.084 (0.004)
Dummies	None	Industry	Time	Both	None	Industry	Time	Both
SSR	2.02191	1.79794	1.84367	1.61900	2.02119	1.79566	1.83093	1.61009
d.f.	1303	1259	1275	1231	1302	1258	1274	1230
F-test		3.28^{**}	4.10^{**}	3.60^{**}		3.30^{**}	4.38^{**}	3.67^{**}

The dependent variable is the industry Solow residual; SSR is the sum of squared residuals; d.f. is degrees of freedom; the F-test tests the joint significance of the dummy coefficients; **significance at the 5 percent level.

Table 2
One-way and two-way random effects regression of TFP on rents (percentage points increases per billion Canadian dollars, *p*-values in parentheses, except where indicated)

	One-way	One-way	Two-way
Labor rent	0.037 (0.152)	0.000 (0.998)	0.007 (0.795)
Capital rent	0.025 (0.288)	0.058 (0.009)	0.057 (0.016)
σ_μ	0.0112 (0.0017)*	–	0.0111 (0.0016)*
σ_t	–	0.0108 (0.0018)*	0.0111 (0.0018)*
Hausman test of exogeneity of rents	2.64 (0.267)	7.83 (0.020)	4.09 (0.129)

*Standard errors in parentheses. The dependent variable is the industry Solow residual.

The interesting result is thus that rents in the hands of capital but not rents in the hands of labor yield higher TFP. The estimates indicate the need to control for time-specific effects (although the test of pooling reveals no heterogeneity over time). Remember that the sectoral TFP figures are obtained jointly by the resolution of pairs of linear programs. By the general equilibrium property year-specific shocks are transmitted to all sectors. Thus, we have good reasons to believe that time effects are important indeed.

In Table 2 we estimate a random effects specification of heterogeneity for the model with both types of factor rents. The sector and year error components have standard deviations that are significantly different from zero. According to the Hausman test, there is no correlation between the factor rents and the error terms, except when sector effects are not controlled for. We therefore prefer the random effects estimates, since under that hypothesis they are more efficient. Labor rent is never significant. Capital rent, however, boosts TFP. A billion dollar increase in capital rents, which corresponds on average to roughly 30 percent of the total capital rents per sector, increases sectoral TFP growth by 0.06 percent. The magnitude of the lack of competition effect is not tremendous, but the sign agrees with the Schumpeterian perspective.

The conflict between neoclassical and Schumpeterian economists on the role of competition has never been resolved by the evidence. Our disaggregation of rent into capital and labor components throws some dim light on the issue. Both Schumpeter and the neoclassical economists may be right, but their mechanisms are channeled through different markets, namely the capital and labor markets, respectively. In hindsight this should not come as a surprise. Schumpeter's argument, that departures from competition may yield positive contributions to dynamic efficiency, was built on the role of R&D, particularly the way it is financed. The neoclassical argument, that competition is good, has been built on the insight that it eliminates slack, particularly managerial laziness. Upon closer inspection, the arguments point at different factor markets and may both apply. We obtain evidence in favor of a Schumpeterian effect that operates through the capital market, but no evidence of a neoclassical effect that would operate through the labor market. At this junction we wish to recall that our data set does not allow for differences in labor quality. A referee's hunch is that sectors with a preponderance of high quality labor would exhibit higher TFP. Because labor 'rent' is high in these sectors when not corrected for quality, correcting for quality will lead to a more negative coefficient of labor rent on TFP, resurrecting the neoclassical effect.[5]

[5] The issue of disentangling capital rents from higher return requirements is also difficult. For example, in cyclical sensitive sectors, one would expect a higher return to capital, and not call this rent. Also, in sectors where large intangible investments are made (media, pharma), high rents may just reflect measurement error in capital services. Luckily, any systematic, non-time varying effect of these will be soaked up by the fixed effects.

Table 3
Effects of net R&D expenditures on rents

	Sector heterogeneity		Time heterogeneity		Sector and time heterogeneities	
	Fixed effects	Random effects	Fixed effects	Random effects	Fixed effects	Random effects
Labor rent	−0.319 (0.568)	−0.279 (0.614)	1.190 (0.049)	0.994 (0.096)	0.238 (0.671)	0.148 (0.787)
Capital rent	1.336 (0.008)	1.308 (0.009)	−0.067 (0.907)	0.182 (0.747)	0.641 (0.211)	0.764 (0.125)
σ_μ	–	104.177 (11.141)*	–	–	–	103.72 (11.08)*
σ_t	–	–	–	17.42 (4.87)*	–	22.42 (3.54)*
Hausman test		1.030 (0.598)		7.46 (0.024)+		2.18 (0.340)+

Fixed and random effects models, with sector and/or time as sources of heterogeneity (*p*-values in parentheses, except where otherwise indicated). *Notes*: the dependent variable is the industry Solow residual. *Standard errors in parentheses. +The Hausman test of exogeneity of rents is not very reliable as it is based on a non-positive definite difference in the variance–covariance matrices of the respective estimates.

In Table 3 we double-check the hypothesis of a Schumpeterian effect from capital rent on productivity, knowing that there is a large consensus that R&D earns a positive rate of return and hence has a positive effect on TFP. We regress by ordinary least squares the pooled data of R&D stock on capital rent and labor rent, again lagged by one period. We present the estimates of both the fixed effects and the random effects models, with one and two sources of heterogeneity. The Hausman test is only reliable for the sector heterogeneity, where it accepts the exogeneity of the regressors with respect to the error terms. In any case, the fixed and random effects estimates tell the same story. When we control for the greatest source of heterogeneity (sectoral effects), the capital rent is positively correlated with the R&D expenditures, as hypothesized by Schumpeter, but not with labor rent. When we control for time effects, surprisingly it is labor rent that is positively correlated with R&D expenditures, whereas capital rent is not significant. The deviations over time of R&D expenditures with respect to industry means are positively correlated with deviations in capital rents from industry means. The sectoral deviations with respect to yearly means across all sectors seem to be correlated with the same kind of deviations in labor rents. The story could still be consistent with a neoclassical view, in the sense that excess labor rent stimulates attempts to reduce cost through process R&D. (This interpretation would require additional verification. We do not at this stage have R&D split into process and product R&D.) If we control for both sources of heterogeneity, no factor rent is significant, although at the margin (if we accept a 12.5 percent level of confidence) we would accept the Schumpeter hypothesis.

5. Conclusion

We have investigated the influence of competition on performance. Performance is measured by Solow residuals derived from a general equilibrium model that maximizes the standard of living. The factor rewards are shadow prices, which are not necessarily equal to the observed rewards. In fact, the difference is rent, which we take as the (negative) measure of competition.

The weak evidence we have found can be summarized as follows. Total rent exerts a positive influence on productivity performance, and it is significant at the 7 percent level, even if we control for business cycle and technological opportunity effects by using time and sector dummies. Capital rents dominate the total effect. When capital and labor rents enter the equation separately, labor rents become insignificant, but capital rents continue to have a strong positive sign. Schumpeter and the neoclassical economists may both be right, but their mechanisms are channeled through different factor markets, namely the capital and labor markets, respectively. Indeed, the use of rent as a source of funding for R&D applies to capital, and the argument that rent yields slack pertains to labor. The Schumpeter hypothesis is also backed by R&D regressions on capital rent.

If capital rent is positive for performance, the policy issue emerges of how to promote technological progress without skewing the income distribution too much. An intelligent policy suggestion would be to reallocate the Schumpeterian advantages of capital rents to workers by providing them with stock options. This practice is spreading in the Western world and may indeed reconcile the different roles of capital and labor competition in performance.

Acknowledgments

We gratefully acknowledge Duncan Foley's suggestion to consider including efficiency in our measure of performance. We thank two anonymous referees for their insightful comments. The second author thanks CentER for its hospitality.

Appendix A. Supplementary data

Supplementary data associated with this article can be found, in the online version, at doi:10.1016/j.jebo.2005.12.007.

References

Aghion, P., Harris, C., Howitt, P., Vickers, J., 2001. Competition, imitation and growth with step-by-step innovation. Review of Economic Studies 68, 467–492.

Aghion, P., Bloom, N., Blundell, R., Griffith, R., Howitt, P., 2002. Competition and innovation: an inverted-U relationship. NBER Working Paper 9269.

Baumol, W., Wolff, E., 1989. Sources of postwar growth of information activity in the United States. In: Osberg, L., Wolff, E., Baumol, W. (Eds.), The Information Economy: The Implications of Unbalanced Growth. Institute for Research on Public Policy, Halifax, pp. 17–46.

Boone, J., 2001. Intensity of competition and the incentive to innovate. International Journal of Industrial Organization 19, 705–726.

Gera, S., Gu, W., Lin, Z., 2001. Technology and the demand for skills: an industry-level analysis. Canadian Journal of Economics 34, 132–148.

Griffith, R., 2001. Product market competition, efficiency and agency costs: an empirical analysis. The Institute for Fiscal Studies WP01/12.

Jorgenson, D., Griliches, Z., 1967. The explanation of productivity change. Review of Economic Studies 34, 308–350.

Lerner, A., 1934. The concept of monopoly and the measurement of monopoly power. Review of Economic Studies 1, 157–175.

Mohnen, P., ten Raa, Th., 2000. A general equilibrium analysis of the evolution of Canadian service productivity. Structural Change and Economic Dynamics 11, 491–506.

Nickell, S., 1996. Competition and corporate performance. Journal of Political Economy 104, 724–746.

Nishimizu, M., Page Jr., J.M., 1982. Total factor productivity growth, technological progress and technical efficiency change: dimensions of productivity change in Yugoslavia, 1965–78. Economic Journal 92, 920–936.

Solow, R., 1957. Technical change and the aggregate production function. Review of Economics and Statistics 39, 312–320.

ten Raa, Th., 2003. Debreu's coefficient of resource utilization, the Solow residual, and TFP: the connection by Leontief preferences. CentER Discussion Paper 111.

ten Raa, Th., 2005. Aggregation of productivity indices: the allocative efficiency correction. Journal of Productivity Analysis 24, 203–209.

ten Raa, Th., Mohnen, P., 2002. Neoclassical growth accounting and frontier analysis: a synthesis. Journal of Productivity Analysis 18, 111–128.

Wolff, E., 2006. The growth of information workers in the U.S. economy: the role of technological change, computerization, and structural change. Economic Systems Research 18, 221–255.

Further reading

de Jong, G., 1996. Canada's postwar manufacturing performance: a comparison with the United States. Groningen Growth and Development Center Research Memorandum GD-32.

Johnson, J., 1997. A KLEMS database: describing the input structure of Canadian industry. Statistics Canada Aggregate Productivity Measures 15-204^{E}, pp. 19–32.

Statistics Canada, 2005. CANSIM Time Series Data Base—Data Usage Charge.

Statistics Canada, 2006. Industrial Research and Development, Catalogue 88-202.

PART V

PRODUCTIVITY AND EFFICIENCY ANALYSIS: SYNTHESIS

Journal of Productivity Analysis, 24, 203–209, 2005

Aggregation of Productivity Indices: The Allocative Efficiency Correction

THIJS TEN RAA tenRaa@UvT.nl
Tilburg University, 5000 LE Tilburg, The Netherlands

Abstract

Aggregation of productivity indices is known to be consistent under very restrictive conditions only. This paper quantifies the aggregation inconsistency.

JEL Classifications: O47, C43

Keywords: aggregation, productivity, allocative efficiency

1. Introduction

Firms' productivity indices do not sum to the industry productivity index, except when production is linear in the sense that marginal rates of substitution and marginal rates of transformation are constant and these constants are common to the firms (Blackorby and Russell, 1999). The trouble is that industry productivity is influenced not only by the performance of firms, but also by the allocation of resources between the firms. In an attempt to salvage the aggregation of productivity, Färe and Primont (2003) show that if all firms are allocatively efficient and their technologies admit time-invariant quadratic approximations, then the productivity indices can be aggregated. Unfortunately, the Färe–Primont conditions are also prohibitively restrictive. To me the bottom line seems to be that the determination of industry productivity requires not only the aggregation of firm productivities, but also the inclusion of some allocative efficiency terms. Indeed, in a recent growth accounting study, Jorgenson et al. (2003) aggregate industry productivities to total productivity growth and capture allocative efficiency changes in their formula (53). Johansen (1972) offers a simple but powerful framework that I will use for a back-of-the-envelop theory that encompasses the different strands of the productivity aggregation literature and quantifies the aggregation inconsistency.

Unfortunately, the literature is loaded with formulas. Part of the blame can be put on the mix of conceptual and approximation issues. A conceptual issue is the definition of productivity. Roughly speaking, it is the output/input ratio, but input and output are multi-dimensional objects. An approximation issue is at which level to meter rates of changes. It makes a difference if one approximates the time derivative of an input or the time derivative of the logarithm of the input. Respective measures are the Fisher ideal and the Törnqvist indices. This difference dissolves in the continuous time framework, which I henceforth use for analytical convenience. I also simplify the concept of a productivity indicator. Färe and Primont (2003) use the Luenberger indicator, which is based on the distance to the frontier along some direction in commodity space; they remain silent about the choice of direction. I suggest that, at least for single-output industries, the appropriate Luenberger direction is along output. In this case the production structure is quasi-linear in output. Now Woertman and ten Raa (2004) argue that for quasi-linear functions the direction is determined by the linear commodity component, as in that case Luenberger's measure is equal to both the compensating and the equivalent variations. In the context of consumption theory this is the direction of the numerair commodity and in the context of production theory it is the direction of output. This observation reduces the distance function to the output gap and, as we shall see, the derived productivity indicator to the Solow residual. It makes the analysis so crisp that the extension to multi-output industries becomes obvious.

2. Indices

Let me introduce the formalities. Single-output firm k maps input vector $x_k(t)$ in output scalar $y_k(t) \leq F_k(x_k(t), t)$, where $F_k(\bullet, t)$ is its production function at time t. (Parameter t shifts the production function, or what is called technical change.) In this one-dimensional output case Luenberger's output-based distance function is given by

$$D_k(x_k(t), y_k(t)t) = F_k(x_k(t)) - y_k(t) \tag{2.1}$$

and measures the *output gap* (Färe and Grosskopf, 2004, p. 107). In general, even without the quasi-linear structure of (2.1), the distance function measures *in*efficiency. *Efficiency change* is therefore defined by *minus* the change in the distance function:

$$\mathrm{EC}_k = -\frac{dD_k}{dt}. \tag{2.2}$$

The distance to the frontier may grow without any change in inputs or outputs, simply because the frontier shifts out. This is called *technical change*. It is defined by the partial derivative of the distance function with respect to time:

$$\mathrm{TC}_k = \frac{\partial D_k}{\partial t}. \tag{2.3}$$

The sum of efficiency change and technical change defines *productivity change*:

$$\mathrm{PC}_k = \mathrm{EC}_k + \mathrm{TC}_k. \tag{2.4}$$

Application of the chain rule to (2.2) and addition of (2.3) transforms (2.4) into

$$\mathrm{PC}_k = -\frac{\partial D_k}{\partial x_k}\dot{x}_k(t) - \frac{\partial D_k}{\partial y_k}\dot{y}_k(t). \tag{2.5}$$

Here, as usual, a dot denotes the derivative of a function of time and the derivatives with respect to the input and output vectors are row vectors (so that the terms on the right hand side are inner products which can be denoted without dot). The discrete time approximation of (2.5) is what Chambers, et al. (1996) call the Luenberger productivity index. That index is the point of departure of Färe and Primont's (2003) aggregation analysis. In case of the quasi-linear structure of (2.1), expression (2.5) simplifies quite dramatically into

$$\mathrm{PC}_k = \dot{y}_k(t) - \frac{\partial F_k}{\partial x}(x_k(t), t)\dot{x}_k(t). \tag{2.6}$$

In other words, productivity change is equal to firm k's *Solow residual* between its output change and input changes, where the latter are weighted by their marginal product values.

3. Aggregation

The more standard Solow residual is at the macro level, or, in the context of the present literature, the industry level. For this I need the *industry* distance function or output gap. Following Johansen (1972), potential industry output is a function of *total input*, $x(t) = \sum x_k(t)$, determined by the following constrained maximization problem:

$$\max \sum F_k(\xi_k, t) : \sum \xi_k = x(t). \tag{3.1}$$

Since the optimal allocation depends on time (through the constraint and the objective function), let me denote it by $\xi_k = x_k^*(t)$. In my view the (negative) aggregation results of Blackorby and Russell (1999) and Färe and Primont (2003) reflect the condition that attainment of the optimal industry output requires not only a push of the firms to their respective frontiers, from $y_k(t)$ to $F_k(\cdot, t)$, but also a reallocation of resources between them, that is from $x_k(t)$ to $x_k^*(t)$. The benefit of the latter reallocation is simply missed when firm efficiency indices are aggregated, without correction. The missing element is the potential allocative efficiency gain; it will be derived next.

It is important to realize that potential industry output does *not* depend on the allocation of the actual inputs, $(x_k(t))$, and *not even* on the allocation of the optimal inputs, $(x_k^*(t))$. Potential industry output depends *only* on *total* input, $x(t) = \sum x_k(t)$. True, the solution to (3.1) can be written $\sum F_k(x_k^*(t), t)$, but the $x_k^*(t)$'s are functions of $x(t)$. In short, program (3.1) maps *one* input vector, $x(t)$, in potential output. Symbol F denotes the mapping.

Potential industry output is $F(x(t), t)$ and, therefore, the industry output gap of (2.1) becomes

$$D(x(t), y(t), t) = F(x(t), t) - y(t), \tag{3.2}$$

where the last term is defined by $y(t) = \sum y_k(t)$. The productivity analysis of the firm can now be applied to the industry. The data are now inputs $x(t)$, outputs $y(t)$, and production function $F(\bullet, t)$. Subjection to (2.6) yields the following expression for industry productivity change:

$$\mathrm{PC} = \dot{y}(t) - \frac{\partial F}{\partial x}(x(t), t)\dot{x}(t) \tag{3.3}$$

The "aggregation problem" consists of interrelating the micro-and macro-productivity changes (2.6) and (3.3), respectively. This boils down to an analysis of the industry production function, F, which is the solution to (3.1).

Denote the Lagrange multipliers of the (vector) constraint in (3.1) by (row) vector w. Since Lagrange multipliers measure the sensitivity of the objective function, F, with respect to the bounds in the constraints, $x(t)$, I obtain

$$w(t) = \frac{\partial F}{\partial x}(x(t), t). \tag{3.4}$$

Now the first-order condition of (3.1) with respect to ξ_k reads, in the optimum,

$$\frac{\partial F_k}{\partial x}(x_k^*(t), t) = w(t). \tag{3.5}$$

This is the well-known result that efficiency implies the equalization of marginal productivities. Substitution of (3.5) in (3.4) and subsequently in (3.3) yields

$$\mathrm{PC} = \sum \left[\dot{y}_k(t) - \frac{\partial F_k}{\partial x}(x_k^*(t), t)\dot{x}_k(t) \right]. \tag{3.6}$$

Comparison of this result with (2.6) shows that aggregation is perfect, in the sense that PC_k sum to PC, if

$$\frac{\partial F_k}{\partial x}(x_k^*(t), t) = \frac{\partial F_k}{\partial x}(x_k(t), t). \tag{3.7}$$

This condition is indeed fulfilled if marginal productivities are constant, an observation that confirms the sufficiency part of the result of Blackorby and Russell (1999). The condition is also fulfilled if the mixes of the observed input vectors are right, i.e., if the observed inputs $x_k(t)$ are collinear with the optimal $x_k^*(t)$, and returns to scale are constant, an observation that confirms the result of Färe and Primont (2003). If none of these conditions are fulfilled, a correction must be made. In fact, the connection between (2.6) and (3.6) is:

$$\mathrm{PC} = \sum \mathrm{PC}_k + \sum \left[\frac{\partial F_k}{\partial x}(x_k(t), t) - \frac{\partial F_k}{\partial x}(x_k^*(t), t) \right] \dot{x}_k(t). \tag{3.8}$$

It is interesting that the correction consists of a sum of terms, one for each firm. For each firm the correction measures the excess marginal productivities (over and above the competitive, economy-wide ones), weighted by the changes in inputs. The difference in brackets is the excess rate of return, or the difference between the private and social values of inputs.

It is not difficult to understand the correction expression. Suppose firm k is under endowed with input 1. Then input 1 is relatively scarce at firm 1, hence will carry a high marginal product or supernormal private value. But the latter is used as a weight in the Solow residual of firm k, where the input change contributes *negatively*. In short, the scarcity of input 1 causes a downward bias in the Solow residual of firm k when the private value weight is used instead of the social value. The positive correction term (the excess rate of return times the change in the input at firm k) offsets the bias.

The aggregation bias of productivity changes can go either way. In terms of efficiency *levels*, however, it goes one way, a fact that is exceedingly simple to demonstrate. The solution to (3.1) exceeds the value without reallocations:

$$F(x(t),t) \geq \sum F_k(x(t)t). \tag{3.9}$$

In view of (2.1) and (3.2) it follows that

$$D\left(\sum x_k(t), \sum y_k(t), t\right) \geq \sum D_k(x_k(t), y_k(t), t). \tag{3.10}$$

This inequality, noted by Färe and Grosskopf (2004, p. 108), states that industry inefficiency exceeds aggregate firms' inefficiency. The difference is the allocative inefficiency. The salient contribution of this paper is to *quantify* the aggregation inconsistency: the second term on the right-hand side of formula (3.8).

4. Generalizations

I have derived this result for quasi-linear output gaps, $F(x(t),t) - y(t) \geq 0$. The extension to general production structures, $F(x(t), -y(t); t) \geq 0$, is obvious. If I redefine $(x(t), -y(t))$ as net input vector $x(t)$, I may simply drop $\dot{y}_k(t)$ from productivity changes (2.6) and (3.3). Since (3.8) does not display output $y(t)$, decomposition formula (3.8) remains valid for general *net* input vectors $x(t)$!

The formula does not even seem to depend on the direction in commodity space along which Luenberger's distance function is measured. It is implicit, however. The appropriate direction is given by the gradient of the general industry production structure. However, in this general setting the optimal input allocation, where the gradient is to be evaluated, depends on the desired mixed of outputs and for the latter we need a criterion. If the industry is a price-taker (e.g., exposed to world competition), then that price vector (e.g., the terms of trade) specifies the Luenberger direction. In general, the direction should be determined by the perfectly competitive equilibrium prices.

Strictly speaking, the program defining the industry production function should feature nonnegativity constraints. The incorporation of these constraints is a straightforward application of the Kuhn–Tucker conditions. First-order condition (3.5) is replaced by the following complementary slackness condition:

$$\frac{\partial F_k}{\partial x}(x_k^*(t),t) \leq w(t), \left[w(t) - \frac{\partial F_k}{\partial x}(x_k^*(t),t)\right] x^*(t) = 0. \tag{4.1}$$

In view of equations (3.3) and (3.4) the optimal marginal productivity in formula (3.8) must be replaced by $w(t)$:

$$\mathrm{PC} = \sum \mathrm{PC}_k + \sum \left[\frac{\partial F_k}{\partial x}(x_k(t), t) - w(t) \right] \dot{x}_k(t). \tag{4.2}$$

Formula (4.2) tells us to subtract the *industry* marginal productivity from the firm's marginal productivity. If there are no nonnegativity constraints, the envelope theorem, see equation (3.5), equates industry marginal productivity with optimal firm's marginal productivity and we are back in the ball game of (3.8).

The modification is quite intuitive. Imagine a single input-single output industry with two firms, $y_1 \leq x_1 \geq 0$ and $y_2 \leq 2x_2 \geq 0$. Then the industry production function is given by $y \leq 2x \geq 0$. Suppose $x_1(t) = x_2(t) = t$, $y_1 = t$ and $y_2 = 2t$. Both firms remain on their efficiency frontiers and, therefore, have zero efficiency change. Technical change is zero too, as the production functions do not change. Hence $\mathrm{PC}_1 = PC_2 = 0$. Now look at the industry. Technical change is zero. There is efficiency change though. The distance function, (3.2), reads $2x - y$. As a function of time it reads $2(t+t) - (t+2t) = t$. By the industry version of efficiency change expression (2.2) the latter becomes -1. Indeed, the growth of the inferior firm, 1, reduces efficiency. The allocation is wrong. All input should go to firm 2. The allocative efficiency changes, the second sum in (4.2), capture this. By equation (3.4) the shadow price is 2. The allocative efficiency change imputed to the first firm is $[1 - 2]1 = -1$. The allocative efficiency term efficiency term of the second firm is zero. If we would not have Kuhn–Tucker modified equation (3.8), but compared the actual marginal productivity to the optimal marginal productivity of firm 1, we would have missed the allocative efficiency term, simply because its marginal productivity is constant. The upshot is that firm 1's productivity is so low that it is irrelevant as a benchmark for efficiency change measurement.

An alternative procedure to incorporate nonnegativity constraints is to absorb them in the general production structure, $F(x(t), -y(t), t) \geq 0$. Then the just given generalization of (3.8) can be applied to net input structures. This approach, however, requires the use of subgradients instead of partial derivatives, and is not pursued here.

5. Concluding Remarks

Aggregate productivity is the sum of firm productivities *and* firm allocative efficiency changes. A firm's allocative efficiency change is measured by its excess marginal productivities (over and above the competitive economy wide ones), weighted by input changes.

The allocative efficiency correction term requires knowledge of the production function for each firm at each point in time, or, at the very least, the marginal products at both the observed inputs and at the optimally allocated inputs for each firm. Diewert (1992) largely dismisses the possibility of estimating these production functions. However, the logic of the aggregation of efficiency extends to the industries that make an economy (see Jorgenson et al., 2003).

Acknowledgment

I am grateful to three anonymous referees and editor Russell for suggestions that improved the paper.

References

Blackorby, C. and R. R. Russell. (1999). "Aggregation of Efficiency Indices." *Journal of Productivity Analysis* 12(1), 5–20.

Chambers, R., R. Färe and S. Grosskopf. (1996). "Productivity Growth in APEC Countries." *Pacific Economic Review* 1(3), 181–190.

Diewert, W. E. (1992). "The Measurement of Productivity." *Bulletin of Economic Research* 44(3), 163–198.

Färe, R. and S. Grosskopf. (2004). *New Directions: Efficiency and Productivity*. Boston: Kluwer Academic Publishers.

Färe, R. and D. Primont. (2003). "Luenberger Productivity Indicators: Aggregation Across Firms." *Journal of Productivity Analysis* 20(3), 425–435.

Johansen, L. (1972). *Production Functions*. Amsterdam: North-Holland.

Jorgenson, D., M. Ho and K. Stiroh. (2003). "Growth of US Industries and Investments in Information Technology and Higher Education." *Economic Systems Research* 15(3), 279–325.

Woertman, W. and Th. ten Raa. (2004). *Benefit and Expenditure Functions*. Draft, Tilburg University.

[18]

Don't Aggregate Efficiency But Disaggregate Inefficiency

Thijs ten Raa

Tilburg University, Box 90153,5000 LE Tilburg, the Netherlands tenRaa@UvT.nl

1 Introduction

Recently Bob Russell published an impossibility result with Chuck Blackorby. The gentlemen argue that it is impossible to aggregate efficiency indices. Since some of us make a descent living decomposing the efficiency of an economy into sectoral contributions the question is if we are crooks. This paper attempts to give an answer to this question.
Blackorby and Russell (1999) state:

> Perhaps more disturbing is the fact that the principal indexes proposed by Debreu (1951) and Farrell (1957), by Färe and Lovell (1978) and by Zieschang (1983) cannot satisfy these [aggregation] conditions for any technologies, even linear ones.

The subsequent relaxation of these aggregation conditions by Blackorby and Russell (1999) offers little comfort:

> In particular, the [relaxed] aggregation condition provides a rationalization of the Debreu/Farrell efficiency measure, albeit for a very restrictive (linear) class of technologies.

A first step in the process of recovery from bad news is to take stock of the issues. I shall clarify a number of things. First, what are efficiency measures? The Debreu/Farrell name, however much in the air as a reference for a general measure of efficiency, is misleading. The Debreu and Farrell measures would better be delineated vis-à-vis each other. Second, can we disaggregate these measures?

Predecessors disaggregating inefficiency, albeit implicitly, are Färe and Grosskopf (2004, pp. 110–14) who determine aggregate industry output (and the corresponding distance function) allowing for reallocations of inputs between firms and—the source they credit for this approach—Johansen (1972). This paper can be considered to generalize the approach and offer a dual analysis.

The upshot of this paper is a redirection of the measurement of efficiency: top-down instead of bottom-up. I hope the reader will feel better again.

2 Efficiency Measures: Debreu and Farrell or Diewert?

Consider an economy comprising l commodities, m consumers, with preference relationships $\succeq_i$ and observed consumption vectors $\mathbf{x}_i^0 \in \Re^l$ $(i = 1, \ldots, m)$, and n production units with sets of possible (net) input vectors $Y_j \subset \Re^l$ containing the observed input vector $\mathbf{y}_j^0$ $(j = 1, \ldots, n)$. A combination of consumption vectors and an input vector is *feasible* if the total sum does not exceed the vector of *utilizable physical resources*, $\mathbf{z}^0$, which is the datum of the economy. This constraint is binding for the observed inputs:

$$\sum \mathbf{x}_i^0 + \sum \mathbf{y}_j^0 = \mathbf{z}^0 \tag{1}$$

The *better set* of net consumption vectors is defined by

$$\mathbf{B} = \sum \mathbf{x}_i : \mathbf{x}_i \succeq_i \mathbf{x}_i^0, i = 1, \ldots, m + \sum Y_j \tag{2}$$

Debreu (1951) defines the coefficient of resource allocation by

$$\rho = Max\ \mathbf{p}(\mathbf{z}) \cdot \mathbf{z}/\mathbf{p}(\mathbf{z}) \cdot \mathbf{z}^0 \text{ subject to } \mathbf{z} \in \mathbf{B}^{min} \tag{3}$$

Coefficient ρ measures the distance from the set of minimally required physical resources, $\mathbf{z} \in \mathbf{B}^{min}$ to the utilizable physical resources, $\mathbf{z}^0$, in the metric of the supporting prices (which indicate welfare indeed). Debreu (1951, p. 284) proves that the distance or the Max in (3) is attained by

$$\mathbf{z} = \rho \mathbf{z}^0 \in \mathbf{B}^{min} \tag{4}$$

In modern terminology, this result means that ρ is the *input-distance function*, determined by the program

$$Min\ \rho \text{ subject to } \sum \mathbf{x}_i + \sum \mathbf{y}_j \leq \rho \mathbf{z}^0, \mathbf{x}_i \succeq_i \mathbf{x}_i^0, \mathbf{y}_j \in Y_j \tag{5}$$

Farrell (1957) decomposes efficiency in technical efficiency and allocative efficiency. He notes the similarity between his technical efficiency measure and the Debreu coefficient of resource utilization. Indeed, both concepts are defined through proportionate input contractions. Nonetheless, the analogy is sheer formality and confusing at a conceptual level. It suggests that Farrell takes the Debreu coefficient, augments it, and thus constructs a more encompassing overall measure. It is the other way round; the sway of the Debreu coefficient is far greater than that of Farrell's measure. Particularly Farrell's allocative efficiency measure is a partial (dis)equilibrium concept, conditioned on prices. It takes into account the cost reduction attainable by changing the mix of the inputs, given the prices of the latter. The Debreu coefficient, however, is a general (dis)equilibrium concept. It measures the technical and allocative inefficiency in the economy given only its fundamentals: resources, technology, and preferences. Prices are derived and enter the definition of the Debreu coefficient, see (3). Debreu *proves* that the coefficient can be freed from these prices, by formula (4) or nonlinear program (5). Prices remain implicit, however. They support the better set in the point of minimally required physical resources and will be revealed in this paper. The Debreu coefficient measures technical and allocative inefficiency, both in production and consumption, solving the formidable difficulty involved in assessing prices, referred to by Charnes, Cooper, and Rhodes (1978, p. 438). Farrell refrains from this, restricting himself to technical efficiency and price-conditioned allocative efficiency.

The formal analogy between the Debreu coefficient and the Farrell measure of technical efficiency prompted Färe and Lovell (1978) to coin the phrase "Debreu-Farrell measures of efficiency." This is confusing. Debreu's coefficient of resource allocation encompasses both Farrell's technical efficiency and his allocative efficiency measures, plus frees the latter from prices. On top of this, Debreu's coefficient also captures consumers' inefficiencies. The confusion persists. In a very recent review of Farrell's contribution Førsund and Sarafoglou (2002, footnote 4) state

> (Debreu) worked only from the resource cost side, defining his coefficient as the ratio between minimised resource costs of obtaining a given consumption bundle and actual costs, for given prices and a proportional contraction of resources.

Debreu (1951) calculates the resource costs not of a given consumption bundle, but of an (intelligently chosen) Pareto equivalent allocation. (And the prices are not given, but support the allocation.)

Yet, let me bridge the difference. Following Diewert (1983), I limit inefficiency to production by assuming Leontief preferences. Under this assumption Debreu's program (5) can be shown to reduce to

$$Min\ \rho \text{ subject to } \sum_i \mathbf{x}_i^0 + \sum_j \mathbf{y}_j \leq \rho \mathbf{z}^0, \mathbf{y}_j \in Y_j \tag{6}$$

The detail is in ten Raa (2003) who calls the consequent ρ the *Debreu-Diewert efficiency measure*.

3 An Example

Let us consider an economy producing a single consumption good. Denote the inputs by vector $\mathbf{I}$. The available stock of inputs is $\mathbf{I}^0$. The production possibilities are given by two production functions, one for each unit: F_1 and F_2. The observed inputs are $\mathbf{I}_1^0$ and $\mathbf{I}_2^0$. Efficiency program (6) reads

$$Min\ \rho \text{ subject to } \sum x_i^0 \leq F_1(\mathbf{I}_1) + F_2(\mathbf{I}_2) \text{ and } \mathbf{I}_1 + \mathbf{I}_2 \leq \rho \mathbf{I}^0 \tag{7}$$

The solution denotes the Debreu-Diewert efficiency of the economy. Denote the efficient inputs by $\mathbf{I}_1$ and $\mathbf{I}_2$ and contrast them with the observed inputs. The question is: How efficient are the units? It may very well be that both units produce the maximum output given their inputs, but that the distribution of inputs is inefficient. For example, if there is only one input and the units have the same, strictly concave production function, say F, then the efficient distribution of inputs is fifty/fifty. This example, however simple, conveys the message of Blackorby and Russell (1999). The efficiency of the units in the sense of maximizing output given the inputs does not imply that the constellation of the two units is efficient.

Is there no way to cope with this example? My idea is to look at profits, not at market prices, but at shadow prices. Choosing the consumption good as numeraire, the shadow prices of the inputs are their marginal products or the vector of partial derivatives $F'(\rho\mathbf{I}^0/2)$, evaluated at the optimum. These input prices will be intermediate, higher than the marginal product of a big unit, smaller than the marginal product of a small unit (assuming concavity). I shall consider the small unit relatively efficient. The big unit will pick up more inefficiency.

4 Back to the Model

Let the production possibility set be given by $Y_j = \{\mathbf{y}_j : F_j(\mathbf{y}_j) \geq 0\}$ where the differentiable functions F_j are concave. (In the previous example these functions map $(\mathbf{I}, -x)$ into $F_j(\mathbf{I}) - x$: the value of the production function of the previous section at input vector I minus output. Since the functions are concave the differentiability assumption can be dropped and the subsequent analysis would be in terms of subgradients.) Efficiency program (6) reads

$$Min\ \rho \text{ subject to } \sum_i \mathbf{x}_i^0 + \sum_j \mathbf{y}_j \leq \rho\mathbf{z}^0, F_j(\mathbf{y}_j) \geq 0 \tag{8}$$

Unlike the Blackorby and Russell (1999) condition, F_j need not be linear. Consequently, (8) is a nonlinear program. According to Wolfe (1961) the dual program is

$$Max_{\rho,\mathbf{y},\mathbf{p},\boldsymbol{\tau}}\ \rho - \mathbf{p}(\rho\mathbf{z}^0 - \sum \mathbf{y}_j - \sum \mathbf{x}_i^0) - \boldsymbol{\tau}\mathbf{F}(\mathbf{y}) \tag{9}$$
$$\text{subject to } \mathbf{p}\mathbf{z}^0 = 1, \mathbf{p} = \boldsymbol{\tau}\mathbf{F}'(\mathbf{y}), \text{ and } \mathbf{p}, \boldsymbol{\tau} \geq 0$$

and by his Theorem 2 (9) has the same solution value as (8). Here $\mathbf{F}$ is the vector with components F_j and $\mathbf{F}'$ is the matrix with the j-th row displaying the partial derivatives of F_j. Notice that the first two terms in (9) cancel by the first dual constraint.

The analysis becomes highly transparent if we assume constant returns to scale, or, in Blackorby and Russell (1999) jargon, linear homogeneity. In this case Blackorby and Russell (1999) argue that the inputs must be perfect substitutes and the outputs must be perfect substitutes. This prohibitive restriction rules out CES functions and even the case of fixed input coefficients, and reduces (9) to a linear program. Under general linear homogeneity, however, (9) remains a nonlinear program, but the third and fifth terms in (9) cancel by the second dual constraint and Euler's theorem. Hence only the fourth term remains and we obtain

$$Max_{\mathbf{y},\mathbf{p},\boldsymbol{\tau}}\ \mathbf{p}\sum \mathbf{x}_i^0 \text{ subject to } \mathbf{p}\mathbf{z}^0 = 1, \mathbf{p} = \boldsymbol{\tau}\mathbf{F}'(\mathbf{y}), \text{ and } \mathbf{p}, \boldsymbol{\tau} \geq 0 \tag{10}$$

And, by Wolfe's Theorem 2,

$$\rho = \mathbf{p}\sum \mathbf{x}_i^0 \tag{11}$$

Now value the observed inputs and resources, see equation (1), by the shadow prices. Substituting (10) and (11), and rearranging terms, I obtain

$$1 - \rho = \sum \mathbf{p}\mathbf{y}_j^0 \tag{12}$$

On the left hand side is inefficiency and on the right hand side are losses at shadow prices. (Remember $\mathbf{y}_j^0$ are net input vectors.) The shadow prices are given by the second dual constraint of (9) or (10), namely $\mathbf{p} = \boldsymbol{\tau}\mathbf{F}'(\mathbf{y})$. These are the marginal products of the efficient units. If a unit is inefficient, that is within its own frontier—$F_j(\mathbf{y}_j) > 0$—then $\tau_j = 0$ by the phenomenon of complementary slackness (which is equivalent to Wolfe's Theorem 2) and it plays no role in price formation.

5 Another Example

Consider an economy with one input (L) and one output (Y). The production possibilities for two units (1 and 2) are $Y \leq L$ and $Y \leq \beta L$, respectively. The observed allocation is $(Y_1^0, L_1^0) = (1/2, 1/2), (Y_2^0, L_2^0) = (1/2\ \beta, 1/2)$. Notice that both units are efficient in the sense of being on their frontiers. Blackorby and Russell (1999) argue that output (input) aggregation of efficiency indices is possible only if the efficiency indices are ratios of linear functions of input and output quantities and the aggregate index is a weighted average. Moreover, these functions must be common to all units. This implies the first of the following statements.

I. *The economy is efficient if and only if* $\beta = 1$.
II. If $\beta < 1$, the efficient allocation is $(Y_1, L_1) = (1/2 + 1/2\beta, 1/2 + 1/2\beta), (Y_2, L_2) = (0, 0)$. Hence efficiency $\rho = 1/2 + 1/2\ \beta$ and inefficiency $1 - \rho = 1/2 - 1/2\ \beta$.
III. If $\beta > 1$, the efficient allocation is $(Y_1, L_1) = (0, 0), (Y_2, L_2) = (1/2 + 1/2\ \beta, 1/2\beta^{-1} + 1/2)$. Hence efficiency $\rho = 1/2\ \beta^{-1}$ and inefficiency $1 - \rho = 1/2 - 1/2\beta^{-1}$.

To decompose inefficiency, let us first determine the shadow prices. The first dual constraint, see (9) or (10) normalizes the shadow price of the input to 1. The shadow price of the output is 1 in cases I and II and β^{-1} in case III.

I. Both units make zero losses at shadow prices, hence pick up zero inefficiency. This is in perfect agreement with Blackorby and Russell (1999).
II. At shadow prices the losses of the units are $1/2 - 1/2$ and $1/2 - 1/2\ \beta$, respectively. The inefficiency is imputed entirely to the second unit. Indeed, it should be out of business.
III. At shadow prices the losses of the units are $1/2 - 1/2\ \beta^{-1}$ and $1/2 - 1/2\ \beta\beta^{-1}$, respectively. The inefficiency is imputed entirely to the first unit. Indeed, it should be out of business.

The point of the example is that inefficiency has been decomposed in cases where efficiency cannot be aggregated according to Blackorby and Russell (1999). The result holds for nonlinear technologies, like CES functions, including the limiting case of a Leontief function.

6 Conclusion

To determine the efficiency of a constellation of production units we need the following data.

a. The inputs and outputs of each unit
b. The production possibilities of each unit

Notice that this is no more than what is required by Blackorby and Russell (1999).

I suggest we proceed as follows. The first step is to compute the efficiency of the system of the units. This is done by contracting the total input of the system subject to the condition that total output is preserved, allowing for reallocations of the inputs and outputs between the units. The percentage by which contraction is feasible is the inefficiency in the economy. The second step is to compute the shadow prices of the contraction program. They are the marginal products of the efficient units. The output shadow prices will be low, as they reflect best practice costs. The third step is to value the units (in terms of profits) at shadow prices. Under constant returns to scale the best practice units break even; their values are zero. The other units incur losses though. This paper has shown that the losses sum to the aggregate inefficiency. This completes the decomposition of inefficiency.

The inefficiency of a unit can have two sources. First, the unit may operate within its possibility frontier. Second, the unit may produce the wrong output vector, not the one implied by the optimal allocation of inputs between units. This allocative source of firm inefficiency should not be neglected. If one neglects it, one obtains impossibility results on the aggregation of efficiency indices. If one takes it into account, inefficiency can be disaggregated. The upshot is that efficiency scores may be aggregated when reallocations are allowed. This differs from the negative result obtained by Blackorby and Russell (1999). With Richard Nixon, let me conclude, "I am not a crook."

References

Blackorby, Charles and R. Robert Russell, "Aggregation of Efficiency Indexes", *Journal of Productivity Analysis* **12** (1999), 5–20.

Charnes, A., W.W. Cooper, and E. Rhodes, "Measuring the Efficiency of Decision Making Units", *European Journal of Operational Research* **2** (1978), 419–444.

Debreu, Gerard, "The Coefficient of Resource Utilization", *Econometrica* **19**(3) (1951), 273–292.

Diewert, W. Erwin, "The Measurement of Waste Within the Production Sector of an Open Economy", *Scandinavian Journal of Economics* **85**(2) (1983), 159–179.

Färe, Rolf, and Shawna Grosskopf, New Directions: Efficiency and Productivity, Kluwer, Boston, 2004.

Farrell, M.J., "The Measurement of Productive Efficiency", *Journal of the Royal Statistical Society Series A*, **120**(III) (1957), 253–281.

Førsund, Finn R., and Nikias Sarafoglou, "On the Origins of Data Envelopment Analysis", *Journal of Productivity Analysis* **17** (2002), 23–40.

Johansen, Leif, *Production Functions*, North-Holland, Amsterdam, 1972.

Jorgenson, Dale W., and Zvi Griliches, "The Explanation of Productivity Change", *Review of Economic Studies* **34**(3) (1967), 308–350.

ten Raa, Thijs, Debreu's Coefficient of Resource Utilization, the Solow Residual, and TFP: The Connection by Leontief Preferences, CentER DP 111, 2003.

Wolfe, Philip, "A Duality Theorem for Nonlinear Programming", *Quarterly of Applied Mathematics* **19**(3) (1961), 239–244.

Zieschang, K., "An Extended Farrell Technical Efficiency Measure", *Journal of Economic Theory* **33** (1983), 387–396.

[19]

J Prod Anal (2008) 30:191–199
DOI 10.1007/s11123-008-0112-8

Debreu's coefficient of resource utilization, the Solow residual, and TFP: the connection by Leontief preferences

Thijs ten Raa

Published online: 25 September 2008

Abstract Debreu's coefficient of resource utilization is freed from individual data requirements. The procedure is shown to be equivalent to the imposition of Leontief preferences. The rate of growth of the modified Debreu coefficient and the Solow residual are shown to add up to TFP growth. This decomposition is the neoclassical counterpart to the frontier analytic decomposition of productivity growth into technical change and efficiency change. The terms can now be broken down by sector as well as by factor input.

Keywords Efficiency · Productivity · Debreu's coefficient · Solow residual

JEL Classifications D24 · O47

1 Introduction

Total factor productivity (TFP) may grow by more efficient utilization of resources or by technical change. Debreu (1951) measured the utilization of resources and Solow (1957) measured technical change, but their models are remote. Solow's model is macro-economic and assumes perfect competition, while Debreu's model is micro-economic and assumes no technical change. In this paper, I show how the measures of Debreu and Solow can be commingled into TFP. I take Debreu's model as point of departure, because it is quite general and, therefore, accommodating. The drawback of Debreu's coefficient of resource utilization, however, is that it hinges on individual preferences data. I will free his coefficient from this prohibitive data requirement, by making Debreu's concept of a 'better' commodity set independent of the specifics of individual preferences. The procedure will be shown to be equivalent to the adoption of Leontief preferences, confirming Diewert's (1983) idea that such preferences remove misallocations between consumers as a source of inefficiency. The consequent coefficient of resource utilization yields a more conservative estimate of inefficiency than Debreu's coefficient resource of utilization. As a bonus, the procedure makes the measure of inefficiency a function of total consumption only, not the individual breakdown. This paves the way for macro-economic applications and Solow residual analysis. The Solow residual is generalized to Debreu's setting.

Neoclassical economics encounters some refreshing competition from frontier analysis. See Nishimizu and Page (1982), Färe et al. (1994), Färe and Grosskopf (1996), Kumar and Russell (2002) and the references given there. This literature provides a useful decomposition of productivity growth into technical change and efficiency change. I take the idea into the neoclassical general equilibrium realm. The connection is at a rather abstract level, for the mechanisms behind efficiency change are different in frontier analysis and neoclassical economics. Frontier analysis captures technological catch-up with the leader and the choice of inputs in terms of costs. Neoclassical analysis captures potential reallocations of resources between sectors. This type of efficiency change is harder to

This paper is an offspring of the workshop *Alternative measures of total factor productivity growth* held on 13 September 2002 at the Department of Econometrics and Operations Research of Tilburg University and co-sponsored by the Netherlands Organization for Scientific Research (Grant 460-02-031-A).

T. ten Raa (✉)
Tilburg University, Box 90153, 5000 LE Tilburg,
The Netherlands
e-mail: tenRaa@UvT.nl

detect. Frontier analytic inefficiency is exposed by the gap with the best practice, a conceptually straightforward concept. Neoclassical inefficiency, however, not only comprises gaps with production possibility frontiers, but also hidden misallocations. A nice exposition is Debreu (1951) and Diewert (2001) discusses the reduction to TFP. A contribution of my paper is that it shows how the tools of frontier analysis, particularly the input- and output-distance functions, can be applied to the measurement of allocative efficiency.

The pieces of the puzzle fit pleasingly well. More precisely, in this paper I show that TFP growth is the sum of technical change and efficiency change, where the former is the (generalized) Solow residual and the latter is the rate of growth of the modified coefficient of resource utilization.

2 The Debreu coefficient of resource utilization

Debreu (1951) measures the inefficiency of the allocation of resources in an economy by calculating how much less resources could attain the same level of satisfaction to the consumers. I will review his so-called coefficient of resource utilization.

The economy comprises m consumers with preference relationships $\succsim_i$ and observed consumption vectors $\mathbf{x}_i^0 \in \mathbb{R}^l$ ($i = 1, \ldots, m$), where l is the number of commodities. $Y \subset \mathbb{R}^l$ is the set of possible input vectors (*net* quantities of commodities consumed by the whole production sector during the period considered), including the observed one, $\mathbf{y}^0$. A combination of consumption vectors and an input vector is *feasible* if the total sum—the economy-wide *net* consumption—does not exceed the vector of *utilizable physical resources*, $\mathbf{z}^0 \in \mathbb{R}^l$.[1] Vector $\mathbf{z}^0$ is assumed to be at least equal to the sum of the observed consumption and input vectors, ensuring the feasibility of the latter.

The set of net consumption vectors that are at least as good as the observed ones is

$$\mathcal{B} = \left\{ \sum \mathbf{x}_i | \mathbf{x}_i \succsim_i \mathbf{x}_i^0, i = 1, \ldots, m \right\} + Y \tag{1}$$

The symbol $\mathcal{B}$ stands for 'better' set. The minimal resources required to attain the same levels of satisfaction that come with $\mathbf{x}_i^0$ belong to $\mathcal{B}^{\min}$, the South-western edge or subset of elements $\mathbf{z}$ that are minimal with respect to $\geqq$.[2] Assume that preferences are convex and continuous, and that production possibilities form a convex and closed set, then the separating hyperplane theorem yields a supporting price vector $\mathbf{p}(\mathbf{z}) > \mathbf{0}$ such that $\mathbf{z}' \in \mathcal{B}$ implies $\mathbf{p}(\mathbf{z}) \cdot \mathbf{z}' \geqq \mathbf{p}(\mathbf{z}) \cdot \mathbf{z}$.[3] The *Debreu coefficient of resource utilization* is defined by

$$\rho = \max_{\mathbf{z}} \{\mathbf{p}(\mathbf{z}) \cdot \mathbf{z} / \mathbf{p}(\mathbf{z}) \cdot \mathbf{z}^0 | \mathbf{z} \in \mathcal{B}^{\min}\} \tag{2}$$

Coefficient ρ measures the distance from the set of minimally required physical resources, $\mathbf{z} \in \mathcal{B}^{\min}$, to the utilizable physical resources, $\mathbf{z}^0$, in the metric of the supporting prices (which indicate welfare indeed). Debreu (1951, p. 284) shows that the distance or the max in (2) is attained by[4]

$$\mathbf{z} = \rho \mathbf{z}^0 \in \mathcal{B}^{\min} \tag{3}$$

In other words, the Debreu coefficient of resource utilization is the smallest fraction of the actually available resources that would permit the achievement of the levels of satisfaction that come with $\mathbf{x}_i^0$. Coefficient ρ is a number between zero and one, the latter indicating full efficiency. In modern terminology, this result means that ρ is the *input-distance function*, determined by the program

$$\rho = \min_r \left\{ r | \sum \mathbf{x}_i + \mathbf{y} \leqq r\mathbf{z}^0, \mathbf{x}_i \succsim_i \mathbf{x}_i^0, \mathbf{y} \in Y \right\} \tag{4}$$

There is also an output-distance function, but that one is opaque. The measurement of satisfaction is in terms of

[1] For example, if the last commodity, l, represents labor, and this is the only nonproduced commodity, then $\mathbf{z}^0 = Ne_l$, where N is the labor force and e_l the l-th unit vector.

[2] By convention, this vector inequality holds if it holds for all components.

[3] $\mathbf{p} > \mathbf{0}$ means that all components are positive. The prices are positive because of the min-superscript in $\mathbf{z} \in \mathcal{B}^{\min}$ and the fact that $\mathbf{z}$ is the *only* point in common to $\mathcal{B}$ and $\{\mathbf{z}' | \mathbf{z}' \leqq \mathbf{z}\}$; hence, $\mathbf{p}$ may be chosen such that $\mathbf{p} \cdot \mathbf{z}' < \mathbf{p} \cdot \mathbf{z}$ for $\mathbf{z}' \leqq \mathbf{z}$ (except $\mathbf{z}' = \mathbf{z}$). This argument requires no monotonicity and Debreu (1951) does not assume it indeed. An example is an exchange economy ($Y = \{0\}$) with one consumer and two commodities of which the quantities are nonnegative. Let $\mathbf{x} \succsim \mathbf{x}'$ if $(2 - x_1)^2 \leqq (2 - x_1')^2$. Let $\mathbf{x}^0 = \mathbf{z}^0 = (3\ 1)$. Then $\mathcal{B}^{\min} = \{\mathbf{x} | \mathbf{x} \succsim \mathbf{x}^0\}^{\min} = \{\mathbf{x} | 1 \leqq x_1 \leqq 3\}^{\min} = \{(1\ 0)\}$. In this point, any positive price vector renders $\mathcal{B} = \{\mathbf{x} | 1 \leqq x_1 \leqq 3\}$ more expensive.

[4] There are two, related caveats in Debreu's (1951) analysis: $\mathbf{z} = \rho \mathbf{z}^0 \in \mathcal{B}^{\min}$ need not exist and ρ may not be unique if the separating price vector is not unique. Consider again the exchange economy ($Y = \{0\}$) with one consumer and two commodities. Let $\mathbf{x} \succsim \mathbf{x}'$ if $\min(x_1, x_2) \geqq \min(x_1', x_2')$. Let $\mathbf{x}^0 = (1\ 1)$ and $\mathbf{z}^0 = (1\ 2)$. Then $\mathcal{B}^{\min} = \{\mathbf{x} | \mathbf{x} \succsim \mathbf{x}^0\}^{\min} = \{\mathbf{x} | \mathbf{x} \geqq (1\ 1)\}^{\min} = \{(1\ 1)\}$ contains no $\rho \mathbf{z}^0 = \rho(1\ 2)$. What is the coefficient of resource utilization? In this case, any $\mathbf{p} > \mathbf{0}$ separates $\mathcal{B} = \{\mathbf{x} | \mathbf{x} \geqq (1\ 1)\}$ and $\{\mathbf{z}' | \mathbf{z}' \leqq (1\ 1)\}$; hence (2) yields $\rho = \mathbf{p} \cdot (1\ 1) / \mathbf{p} \cdot (1\ 2) = (p_1 + p_2)/(p_1 + 2p_2)$, a number between 0.5 and 1. To resolve the multiplicity, we may address the efficiency problem in primal space. The preference relationship is represented by utility $\min(x_1, x_2)$. Subject to feasibility constraint $\mathbf{x} \leqq \mathbf{z}^0 = (1\ 2)$, the maximum utility is 1. This is attained by $\mathbf{x}^0 = (1\ 1)$. Hence the allocation is optimal. Following Debreu's (1951, p. 275) introduction, $\rho = 1$. This implies that $\mathbf{p} = (1\ 0)$. Indeed, this is the supporting price system of the second welfare theorem. However, it is not positive.

If the minimal $\rho \mathbf{z}^0$ belongs to $\mathcal{B}^{\min}$, then the prices in (2) are positive and the coefficient ρ generated by (4) solves (2), following Debreu (1951, p. 284). If the minimal $\rho \mathbf{z}^0$ does not belong to $\mathcal{B}^{\min}$, the prices in (2) are only nonnegative, but the coefficient ρ generated by (4) still solves (2).

utility, an ordinal concept that generally admits no aggregation over consumers.

3 The Farrell efficiency measure

Following ten Raa (2007), let me clear up some confusion on the relationship between Debreu and Farrell's efficiency measures. Farrell (1957) decomposes efficiency in technical efficiency and allocative efficiency. He notes the similarity between his technical efficiency and the Debreu coefficient of resource utilization. Indeed, both the Farrell technical efficiency measure and the Debreu coefficient of resource utilization are defined through proportionate input contractions. The analogy is sheer formality, but confusing at a conceptual level. It suggests that Farrell takes the Debreu coefficient, augments it, and thus constructs a more encompassing overall measure. It is the other way round; the sway of the Debreu coefficient is far greater than that of Farrell's measure. Particularly Farrell's allocative efficiency measure is a partial (dis)equilibrium concept, conditioned on prices. It takes into account the cost reduction attainable by changing the mix of the inputs, given the prices of the latter. The Debreu coefficient, however, is a general (dis)equilibrium concept. It measures the technical and allocative inefficiency in the economy given only its fundamentals: resources, technology, and preferences. Prices are derived and enter the definition of the Debreu coefficient, see (2). Debreu (1951) then *proves* that the coefficient can be freed from these prices, by Eq. 3 or nonlinear program (4). Prices remain implicit, however. They support the better set in the point of minimally required physical resources. The Debreu coefficient measures technical and allocative inefficiency, both in production and consumption, solving the formidable difficulty involved in assessing prices, referred to by Charnes et al. (1978, p. 438). Farrell refrains from this, restricting himself to technical efficiency and price-conditioned allocative efficiency.

The formal analogy between the Debreu coefficient and the Farrell measure of technical efficiency prompted Zieschang (1984) to coin the phrase "Debreu–Farrell measure of efficiency," a term picked up by Chakravarty (1992) and Grifell-Tatjé et al. (1998). This practice is confusing. Debreu's coefficient of resource allocation encompasses both Farrell's technical efficiency and his allocative efficiency measures, and frees the latter from prices. On top of this, Debreu's coefficient captures consumers' inefficiencies. The confusion persists. Färe et al. (2002) speak of the "Debreu–Farrell measure of technical efficiency." A recent review of Farrell's contribution states

> "(Debreu) worked only from the resource cost side, defining his coefficient as the ratio between minimized resource costs of obtaining a given consumption bundle and actual costs, for given prices and a proportional contraction of resources." Førsund and Sarafoglou (2002), footnote 4.

However, Debreu (1951) calculates the resource costs *not* of a given consumption bundle, but of an (intelligently chosen) Pareto equivalent allocation. (And the prices are not given, but support the allocation.) It is true, however, that the Debreu measure would become applicable if the aggregated consumption bundle can be considered given. The next section shows that this pragmatic approach is doable. The approach is exact if preferences are Leontief, as the subsequent section will prove.

4 Absent individual data: the Debreu–Diewert coefficient of resource utilization

Following Debreu (1951) a simple symbol $\mathcal{B}$ has been used to denote the 'better set.' Definition (1) reveals, however, that the set depends on the observed consumption vectors and on preferences. The informational requirements involved are prohibitive. To overcome this problem, I will define a version of the Debreu coefficient, namely the *Debreu Diewert coefficient of resource utilization*, ρ^*. Only in the next section it will transpire why I choose this name.

I want that the notion of 'better' set is independent of the specifics of preferences. For this purpose, all I assume is that preferences are weakly monotonic in the sense that they belong to

$$\mathcal{M} = \{ \succsim | (\mathbf{x}' \geqq \mathbf{x}) \text{ implies } (\mathbf{x}' \succsim \mathbf{x}) \} \tag{5}$$

I now define the tight better set as the intersection of all better sets over $\mathcal{M}$:

$$\mathcal{B}^* = \cap \left\{ \sum \mathbf{x}_i | \mathbf{x}_i \succsim \mathbf{x}_i^0, i = 1, \ldots, m \right\} + Y \tag{6}$$

The replacement of the better set, $\mathcal{B}$, by the tight better set, $\mathcal{B}^*$, implies that definition (2) produces the Debreu–Diewert coefficient ρ^* instead of the Debreu coefficient ρ. A comparison between these two coefficients is obtained by rewriting program (4):

$$\rho^* = \min_r \left\{ r | \sum \mathbf{x}_i + \mathbf{y} \leqq r\mathbf{z}^0, \mathbf{x}_i \succsim \mathbf{x}_i^0 \text{ for all } \succsim \in \mathcal{M}, \mathbf{y} \in Y \right\} \tag{7}$$

The constraint set of (7) is contained in the one of (4); hence the solution to program (4) must be sharper:

$$\rho \leqq \rho^* \tag{8}$$

In other words, use of the Debreu–Diewert coefficient will overestimate efficiency hence underestimate inefficiency. Debreu's (1951) measure of inefficiency reflects scope for

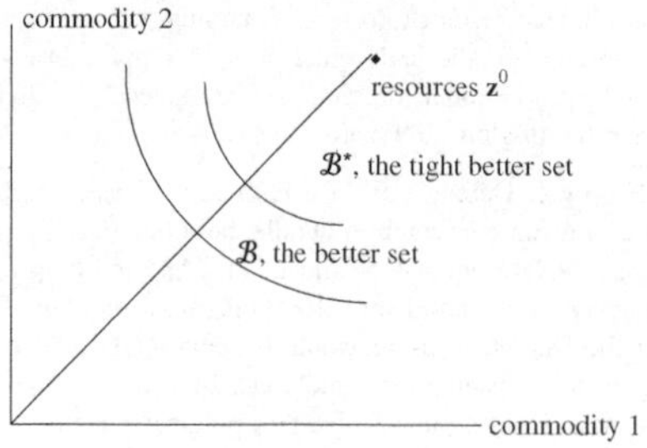

Fig. 1 Half the resources suffice to make consumers at least as well off. Two-thirds of the resources are needed to produce the total consumption vector. The Debreu coefficient of resource utilization is 1/2 and the Debreu–Diewert coefficient is 2/3

reallocation of resources between consumers with different tastes and, therefore, is quite high; the flipside of this observation is that the Debreu coefficient is relatively low. Figure 1 illustrates.

5 The Debreu–Diewert coefficient and Leontief preferences

I can be a bit more specific about the Debreu–Diewert coefficient of resource utilization. I will show that it is generated by Leontief preferences. As I noted in the introduction, Diewert (1983) first had the idea that such preferences remove misallocations between consumers as a source of inefficiency. This explains the name giving.

Leontief preferences $\succsim(\mathbf{a})$ with nonnegative bliss point $\mathbf{a} \in \mathbb{R}^l_+$ are defined for nonnegative consumption vectors by $\mathbf{x}' \succsim (\mathbf{a})\mathbf{x}$ if $\min x'_k/a_k \geqq \min x_k/a_k$ where the minimum is taken over commodities $k = 1,\ldots,l$. The minima exist if $\mathbf{a}$ is nonzero, which I assume.[5] The following lemma shows that the tight better set is obtained by imposing Leontief preferences on all individuals. Notice, however, that the preferences feature the observed individual consumption baskets as bliss points and, therefore, differ.

Lemma $\mathcal{B}^* = \{\sum \mathbf{x}_i | \mathbf{x}_i \succsim (\mathbf{x}_i^0)\mathbf{x}_i^0, i = 1,\ldots,m\} + Y = \{\mathbf{x} | \mathbf{x} \geqq \sum \mathbf{x}_i^0\} + Y.$

Proof Using the fact $\succsim(\mathbf{x}_i^0) \in \mathcal{M}$, I have that the first term of $\mathcal{B}^*$ in (6), $\cap\{\sum \mathbf{x}_i | \mathbf{x}_i \succsim_i \mathbf{x}_i^0, i = 1,\ldots,m\} \subset \{\sum \mathbf{x}_i | \mathbf{x}_i \succsim (\mathbf{x}_i^0)\mathbf{x}_i^0, i = 1,\ldots,m\} = \{\sum \mathbf{x}_i | \mathbf{x}_i \geqq \mathbf{x}_i^0\} = \{\mathbf{x} | \mathbf{x} \geqq \sum \mathbf{x}_i^0\} \subset \cap\{\sum \mathbf{x}_i | \mathbf{x}_i \succsim_i \mathbf{x}_i^0, i = 1,\ldots,m\}$, which is itself. The last inclusion is shown as follows. For $\mathbf{x} \geqq \sum \mathbf{x}_i^0$, allocate the surplus in any nonnegative way, for example by putting $\mathbf{x}_1 = \mathbf{x}_1^0 + \mathbf{x} - \sum \mathbf{x}_i^0, \mathbf{x}_2 = \mathbf{x}_2^0, \ldots, \mathbf{x}_m = \mathbf{x}_m^0$, then $\mathbf{x}_i \succsim_i \mathbf{x}_i^0$ for all $\succsim_i \in \mathcal{M}$. QED

The first equality in the Lemma implies that if the consumers have Leontief preferences, then the Debreu coefficient reduces to the Debreu–Diewert coefficient. The second equality in the Lemma, $\{\sum \mathbf{x}_i | \mathbf{x}_i \geqq \mathbf{x}_i^0\} = \{\mathbf{x} | \mathbf{x} \geqq \sum \mathbf{x}_i^0\}$, is a perfect aggregation result. Aggregated consumption is monotonic if and only if individual consumptions are. One might say that if preferences are Leontief with varying bliss points (according to the observed consumption baskets), there is a social welfare function. The better set, $\mathcal{B}$, is freed from preferences, $\succsim_i$, as well as from individual consumption baskets, $\mathbf{x}_i^0$. The tight better set, $\mathcal{B}^*$, depends only on the *total consumption vector*, $\sum \mathbf{x}_i^0$. This modification facilitates measurement of the coefficient of resource utilization. In fact, the tightening creates the option to determine the degree of efficiency in terms of outputs, resurrecting the output-distance function.

Corollary *Assume that the total consumption vector* $\sum \mathbf{x}_i^0$ *is nonnegative and nonzero. Assume that the production set* Y *features the impossibility to produce something from nothing and constant returns to scale. Then* $\gamma = 1/\rho^*$ *transforms the input-distance function program* (7) *into the* output-distance function *program*

$$\gamma = \max\left\{c | c \sum \mathbf{x}_i^0 + \mathbf{y} \leqq \mathbf{z}^0, \mathbf{y} \in Y\right\}$$

Proof By the Lemma, program (7) can be rewritten as

$$\rho^* = \min\left\{r | \sum \mathbf{x}_i + \mathbf{y} \leqq r\mathbf{z}^0, \mathbf{x}_i \succsim (\mathbf{x}_i^0)\mathbf{x}_i^0, i = 1,\ldots,m, \mathbf{y} \in Y\right\}$$

or

$$\rho^* = \min\left\{r | \mathbf{x} + \mathbf{y} \leqq r\mathbf{z}^0, \mathbf{x} \geqq \sum \mathbf{x}_i^0, \mathbf{y} \in Y\right\}$$

This can be simplified further to

$$\rho^* = \min\left\{r | \sum \mathbf{x}_i^0 + \mathbf{y} \leqq r\mathbf{z}^0, \mathbf{y} \in Y\right\}$$

The solution is positive. (Otherwise input vector $\mathbf{y} \leqq -\sum \mathbf{x}_i^0 \leqq 0$, but not equal to zero, would produce something from nothing.) The transformation is completed by multiplication by $c = 1/r$ and a change of variable ($c\mathbf{y}$ to $\mathbf{y}$), using constant returns to scale. QED

The output-distance function program informs us by which factor the total consumption vector can be expanded, given the resources.

6 Application to national accounts

The corollary shows that under constant returns to scale the inverse of the Debreu–Diewert coefficient of resource

[5] Situations like labor supply are covered by letting the commodity be leisure time. Division by zero is assumed to yield infinity.

utilization is the expansion factor of the economy, γ. ten Raa (2005) calculates γ for the Canadian economy, defines $1-1/\gamma$ as inefficiency, and decomposes the latter into productive inefficiency, allocative inefficiency, and trade inefficiency. It follows that ten Raa's (2005) measure of inefficiency is $1-\rho^*$. In view of inequality (8), this measure of inefficiency underestimates Debreu's (1951) degree of inefficiency, $1-\rho$. Debreu (1951) finds more scope for efficiency gains as marginal rates of substitution may be equalized across consumers. The Debreu–Diewert coefficient does not take into account this source of inefficiency.

ten Raa and Mohnen (2002) and ten Raa (2005) divide the commodities between produced goods and factor inputs, respectively. Use table **U** is a table depicting the use of goods by sectors and make table **V** is a table depicting the outputs of the sectors in terms of goods. $\mathbf{U}-\mathbf{V}^\top$ is the net input table; its dimension is that of goods by sectors.[6] **L** is the factor input table; its dimension is factor inputs by sectors. An element of $\mathbf{y} \in Y$ has components $(\mathbf{U}-\mathbf{V}^\top)\mathbf{s}$ and $\mathbf{Ls}$, and Y is defined by letting the allocation vector $\mathbf{s} \geqq 0$. Similarly, $\sum \mathbf{x}_i^0$ has components **f** and **0**, where **f** is the vector of final goods consumption, while $\mathbf{z}^0$ has components **0** and **N**, where **N** is the vector of factor endowments, and **z** has components **0** and **Ls**. The output-distance function program of the corollary becomes

$$\gamma = \max_{c,s}\{c \mid c\mathbf{f} + (\mathbf{U}-\mathbf{V}^\top)\mathbf{s} \leqq \mathbf{0}, \mathbf{Ls} \leqq \mathbf{N}, \mathbf{s} \geqq \mathbf{0}\} \tag{9}$$

The solution to this program yields the potential standard of living, relative to the observed one.[7] The shadow prices of the second constraint yield the factor productivities.

The standard interpretation of a sector is that of an industry, but conceptually it is possible to disaggregate it into firms, for example by using the reported data. Then program (9) will select for each industry best practice firms, which transform the industry inputs into potential industry output, in the sense of Johansen (1972).

[6] Superscript $^\top$ denotes transposition. The use and make tables are of opposite dimension in the System of National Accounts (ten Raa, 2005).

[7] Of course, any positive coefficient may be entered in the objective function and this is commendable, to scale the price level. As is, by the main theorem of linear programming, the factor input shadow prices fulfill $\mathbf{w}\cdot\mathbf{N}=\gamma$. Since γ is of the order one but **N** of the order millions, **w** will be tiny. A handy objective function is $\mathbf{e}\cdot\mathbf{f}c$, where **e** is the unit vector with all components one. The dual constraints then show that $\mathbf{p}\cdot\mathbf{f}=\mathbf{e}\cdot\mathbf{f}$ and $\mathbf{w}\cdot\mathbf{N}=\mathbf{p}\cdot\gamma\mathbf{f}$. In other words, the product prices are normalized at unity and the factor input prices fulfill the potential national income identity. The proof is as follows. Multiplication of the dual constraint associated with variable **s**, by **s**, yields $\mathbf{p}\cdot(\mathbf{U}-\mathbf{V}^\top)\mathbf{s}+\mathbf{w}\cdot\mathbf{Ls}=0$. Replace the two terms using the two respective constraints of program (14): $-\mathbf{p}\cdot\gamma\mathbf{f}+\mathbf{w}\cdot\mathbf{N}=0$, where (priced) inequalities are binding according to the phenomenon of complementary slackness. The product price normalization follows by the main theorem of linear programming or $\mathbf{w}\cdot\mathbf{N}=\mathbf{e}\cdot\mathbf{f}\gamma$.

7 Relationship with the Solow residual

This section is the centerpiece of the paper. The Debreu–Diewert coefficient of resources and a generalized Solow residual are tied up into TFP growth. What is productivity?

An economy transforms physical resources into final consumption by means of production. The ratio of consumption to the resources is called the *productivity* of the economy. A multi-input and output measure is the Malmquist index proposed by Caves, Christensen, and Diewert (1982). Productivity may grow because the production possibility set increases or because resources are better utilized. Productivity growth equals the sum of technical change and efficiency change. Technical change is the shift of the production possibility frontier and efficiency change is the increase in the coefficient of resource utilization. The two add to productivity growth according to Nishimizu and Page (1982), Färe et al. (1994), and ten Raa and Mohnen (2002). I will now uncover the relationship at the level of generality of the Debreu model.

The point of departure is the Debreu–Diewert coefficient of resource utilization (ρ^*), determined by program (7) or, using the Lemma,[8]

$$\rho^* = \min\left\{r \middle| \sum \mathbf{x}_i^0 + \mathbf{y} \leqq r\mathbf{z}^0, \mathbf{y} \in Y\right\} \tag{10}$$

Assuming free disposal, input may be added to $\mathbf{y} \in Y$ until the constraint is binding:

$$\sum \mathbf{x}_i^0 + \mathbf{y} = \rho^*\mathbf{z}^0 \tag{11}$$

This is the material balance.

Let **p** support the tight better set defined in (5), $\mathcal{B}^*$, in the sense introduced before (2).[9] According to the phenomenon of complementary slackness, non-linear program (10) yields[10]

$$\mathbf{p}\cdot\sum \mathbf{x}_i^0 = \rho^*\mathbf{p}\cdot\mathbf{z}^0 - \mathbf{p}\cdot\mathbf{y} \tag{12}$$

This is the identity between national product and national income; it holds even when there is no free disposal and, therefore, the material balance, (11), is not fulfilled. The national product is on the left hand side and on the right hand side is factor income plus profit. (Remember, **y** is net input, hence $-\mathbf{y}$ is net output.) All this is at the optimum allocation $(\sum \mathbf{x}_i^0, \mathbf{y}, \rho^*\mathbf{z}^0)$ and supporting (or competitive) prices **p**, not the actual allocation $(\sum \mathbf{x}_i^0, \mathbf{y}^0, \mathbf{z}^0)$ and prices.

The economy transforms resources $\mathbf{z}^0$ into consumption $\sum \mathbf{x}_i^0$. The ratio of the latter to the former constitutes the

[8] See the proof of the corollary.

[9] Footnote 4 shows that the supporting prices are not necessarily positive.

[10] The nonlinearity is due to production set Y.

level of TFP. Since the objects are vectors, they must weighed by prices, for which $\mathbf{p}$ is employed. The *level* of TFP is thus $\mathbf{p}\cdot\sum\mathbf{x}_i^0/\mathbf{p}\cdot\mathbf{z}^0$. If there are constant returns to scale, profit is zero, and, by Eq. 12:

$$\mathbf{p}\cdot\sum\mathbf{x}_i^0/\mathbf{p}\cdot\mathbf{z}^0=\rho^* \tag{13}$$

This equation shows that the level of TFP is equal to the Debreu–Diewert coefficient of resource utilization.

Another interesting connection is the following. Let all variables vary with time and let d denote a time derivative. *Total factor productivity growth* is the rate of growth of the level of TFP at *fixed* price weights:[11]

$$TFP=\mathbf{p}\cdot d\sum\mathbf{x}_i^0/\mathbf{p}\cdot\sum\mathbf{x}_i^0-\mathbf{p}\cdot d\mathbf{z}^0/\mathbf{p}\cdot\mathbf{z}^0 \tag{14}$$

The following proposition shows that TFP is the sum of the Solow residual, generalized to Debreu's framework, and the rate of growth of the Debreu–Diewert coefficient. The *generalized Solow residual* is defined by

$$SR=-\mathbf{p}\cdot d\mathbf{y}/\mathbf{p}\cdot\sum\mathbf{x}_i^0 \tag{15}$$

This expression features the change in optimal net output, $-\mathbf{y}$, and will be shown to be a generalized Solow residual indeed, evaluated at the frontier. The demonstration is in the next section, where the residual will be shown to measure the shift of the production possibility function.

Proposition *Under constant returns to scale, $TFP = SR + d\rho^*/\rho^*$.*

Proof Under constant returns to scale Eq. 13 holds. Substitution in Eq. 14 yields $TFP=[\mathbf{p}\cdot d\sum\mathbf{x}_i^0-\rho^*\mathbf{p}\cdot d\mathbf{z}^0]/\mathbf{p}\cdot\sum\mathbf{x}_i^0$. Substitution of the material balance, (11), and the product rule yield $TFP=[-\mathbf{p}\cdot d\mathbf{y}+\mathbf{p}\cdot\mathbf{z}^0d\rho^*]/\mathbf{p}\cdot\sum\mathbf{x}_i^0$. Substitution of Eqs. 13 and 15 yields the posted formula. QED

The first TFP term, SR, reflects *technical change*. The second TFP term, $d\rho^*/\rho^*$, is the rate of growth of the Debreu–Diewert coefficient of resource utilization and, therefore, represents *efficiency change*.

8 The Solow residual

Solow (1957) divides commodities between a single output and factor inputs. Denoting the latter by a vector $\mathbf{l}$, the producible output is $F(\mathbf{l},t)-s$, where $F(\cdot,t)$ is the production function at time t (presumed quasi-concave) and s is slack.[12] A net input vector $\mathbf{y}\in Y$ has components $-F(\mathbf{l},t)+s$ and $\mathbf{l}$, respectively. The production possibility set Y is obtained by letting $\mathbf{l}\geqq\mathbf{0}$ and $s\geqq0$. The vector of available resources, $\mathbf{z}^0$, has components 0 and $\mathbf{l}^0$, respectively. Let ρ^* be the Debreu–Diewert coefficient of resource utilization and $\mathbf{y}$ be the optimal net input vector, which solve efficiency program (10), then $\mathbf{y}$ has components $-F(\mathbf{l},t)$ and $\mathbf{l}=\rho^*\mathbf{l}^0$. The first or product component of the material balance, (11), reads

$$\left(\sum\mathbf{x}_i^0\right)_1-F(\mathbf{l},t)=\rho^*0=0 \tag{16}$$

The other or factor components read

$$0+\mathbf{l}=\rho^*\mathbf{l}^0 \tag{17}$$

An intuitive interpretation of the Debreu–Diewert coefficient of resource utilization, ρ^*, is in terms of actual output, $F(\mathbf{l}^0,t)-s^0$, where $F(\mathbf{l}^0,t)$ is potential output and s^0 is observed slack. Actual output could also be generated by optimal factor input $\mathbf{l}$ (with no slack). It follows that the actual/potential output ratio is $F(\mathbf{l},t)/F(\mathbf{l}^0,t)$. By Eq. 17, this is ρ^* if the production has constant returns to scale. *The Debreu–Diewert coefficient is the ratio of actual to potential output.*

As is well known, the solution $\mathbf{y}$ is supported by price vector $(1\,\mathbf{w})=(1\,\partial_1F(\mathbf{l},t))$ where ∂ denotes partial derivatives (with respect to $\mathbf{l}$ in this case) or marginal productivities.[13] I will now evaluate $SR=-\mathbf{p}\cdot d\mathbf{y}/\mathbf{p}\cdot\sum\mathbf{x}_i^0$ of definition (15) for this special setting. The numerator reduces to

$$-\mathbf{p}\cdot d\mathbf{y}=dF(\mathbf{l},t)-\mathbf{w}d\mathbf{l} \tag{18}$$

and the denominator is, in view of the first terms of (16) and (17),

$$\mathbf{p}\cdot\sum\mathbf{x}_i^0=\left(\sum\mathbf{x}_i^0\right)_1+0=F(\mathbf{l},t) \tag{19}$$

using (16). Hence the quotient is

$$\begin{aligned}SR&=-\mathbf{p}\cdot d\mathbf{y}/\mathbf{p}\cdot\sum\mathbf{x}_i^0\\&=dF(\mathbf{l},t)/F(\mathbf{l},t)-\sum_k[w_kl_k/F(\mathbf{l},t)]dl_k/l_k\end{aligned} \tag{20}$$

The expression on the right hand side is, indeed, the residual between the output growth rate and the input growth rates, where value shares weight the latter. The shares add up if the production function has constant returns to scale, by Euler's theorem. The input prices are competitive marginal productivities, which are high in the sense that they leave no room for profit. The use of lower, observed prices, will bias upwardly expression (20).

[11] Warning: I use TFP for TFP growth. No symbol is needed for the level of TFP.

[12] Slack scalar s should not be confused with allocation vector $\mathbf{s}$ of Sect. 5.

[13] If $F(\cdot,t)$ is not differentiable, a subgradient will do.

The main point of Solow (1957) was that the residual measures technical change, a result that is easily verified. By Eq. 18, $-\mathbf{p} \cdot d\mathbf{y} = dF(\mathbf{l}, t) - \partial_l F(\mathbf{l}, t) d\mathbf{l}$. But by total differentiation, $dF(\mathbf{l}, t) = \partial_l F(\mathbf{l}, t) d\mathbf{l} + \partial_t F(\mathbf{l}, t)$. Hence $SR = -\mathbf{p} \cdot d\mathbf{y} / \mathbf{p} \cdot \sum \mathbf{x}_i^0$ of definition (15) has a numerator $\partial_t F$ and we obtain, using Eq. 19,

$$SR = -\mathbf{p} \cdot d\mathbf{y} / \mathbf{p} \cdot \sum \mathbf{x}_i^0 = \partial_t F(\mathbf{l}, t) / F(\mathbf{l}, t) \quad (21)$$

The Solow residual measures the relative shift of the production function indeed.

Residual expression (20) can be generalized to multi-products. Then the output growth term is an output-value share weighted expression. Intermediate products can also be accommodated; this will be detailed in the next section. All are encompassed by definition (15): $SR = -\mathbf{p} \cdot d\mathbf{y} / \mathbf{p} \cdot \sum \mathbf{x}_i^0$, where $-\mathbf{y}$ is resource minimizing net output and $\sum \mathbf{x}_i^0$ is observed total consumption.

For constant returns to scale, the minimization of resources subject to total consumption—see program (10)—amounts to a maximization of consumption subject to available resources—program (9). As was shown there, this merely involves a change of variable from $\mathbf{y}$ to $c\mathbf{y}$ and a replacement of $\sum \mathbf{x}_i^0$ by $c \sum \mathbf{x}_i^0$. The expansion factors c in the numerator and in the denominator of the generalized Solow residual, $SR = -\mathbf{p} \cdot d\mathbf{y} / \mathbf{p} \cdot \sum \mathbf{x}_i^0$, cancel and its expression may therefore be reinterpreted in terms *maximal* consumption and sustaining optimal net output. The maximum consumption vector has the same proportions as the observed consumption vector. The prices in the generalized Solow residual are not affected at all, because of the constant returns to scale.

9 Productivity and efficiency decompositions

There are two further decompositions of TFP growth than in technical change and efficiency change. The first decomposition is in factor productivity growth rates; it sounds dull, but is not achieved in frontier analysis. The second decomposition is by input–output sector.

The decomposition by *factor* is standard neoclassical analysis, at least for the Solow residual. Assume constant returns to scale, then $\mathbf{p} \cdot \mathbf{y} = 0$ and the generalized Solow residual becomes

$$SR = -\mathbf{p} \cdot d\mathbf{y} / \mathbf{p} \cdot \sum \mathbf{x}_i^0 = d\mathbf{p} \cdot \mathbf{y} / \mathbf{p} \cdot \sum \mathbf{x}_i^0 \quad (22)$$

Remember, $\mathbf{y}$ is the vector of net inputs. $\mathbf{p}$ is the vector of shadow prices or marginal productivities. Equation 22 imputes the technical change term of TFP to the various inputs. It is very general. It reduces to the more familiar Jorgenson and Griliches (1967) form in the Solow world with a macro-economic production function, introduced in the previous section. There $\mathbf{y}$ has components $-F(\mathbf{l}, t)$ and $\mathbf{l}$, and $\mathbf{p} = (1\ \mathbf{w}) = (1\ \partial_l F(\mathbf{l}, t))$. Hence the numerator of the generalized Solow residual (22) reduces to $d\mathbf{p} \cdot \mathbf{y} = d\mathbf{w} \cdot \mathbf{l}$, while the denominator is $F(\mathbf{l}, t)$ by Eq. 19.

It follows that the Solow residual becomes

$$SR = -\mathbf{p} \cdot d\mathbf{y} / \mathbf{p} \cdot \sum \mathbf{x}_i^0 = \sum_k [w_k l_k / F(\mathbf{l}, t)] dw_k / w_k \quad (23)$$

The expression on the right hand side is the growth rate of the factor productivity, with components weighted by their value shares. The input prices are competitive marginal productivities, which are high in the sense that they leave no room for profit. The use of lower, observed prices, will bias downward expression (23), unlike expression (20), which was biased upward in this case. The (primal) expression (20) and the (dual) expression (23) thus provide inconsistent estimates when no competitive prices are used.

The inclusion of efficiency change amounts to proportional increases of the factor productivity growth rates. By Debreu's equation (3), the minimally required physical resources, $\mathbf{z}$, are proportional to the utilizable physical resources, $\mathbf{z}^0$.[14] In the world of Solow this proportionality is between minimal factor inputs $\mathbf{l}$ and observed factor inputs $\mathbf{l}^0$, see Eq. 16, or $\rho^* = l_k / l_k^0$, all k. Hence the efficiency change term of *TFP* reads, assuming constant returns to scale,

$$\begin{aligned} d\rho^* / \rho^* &= \sum_k [w_k l_k / F(\mathbf{l}, t)] d\rho^* / \rho^* \\ &= \sum_k [w_k l_k / F(\mathbf{l}, t)] (dl_k / l_k - dl_k^0 / l_k^0) \end{aligned} \quad (24)$$

Substituting expressions (23) and (24) into the Proposition (Sect. 7), all TFP-growth is now decomposed in terms of factor contributions:

$$TFP = \sum_k [w_k l_k / F(\mathbf{l}, t)] (dw_k / w_k + dl_k / l_k - dl_k^0 / l_k^0) \quad (25)$$

The leading term measures factor productivity growth and the remainder the factor utilization growth. For each factor, the value share of the factor weights the sum of the two growth measures.

The generalized Solow residual is decomposed by *sector* by adding the structure of Sect. 6. What follows is an activity variant of Hulten's (1978) analysis. In Sect. 6, the net input vector $\mathbf{y}$ sustaining maximal consumption has components $(\mathbf{U} - \mathbf{V}^\top)\mathbf{s}$ and $\mathbf{L}\mathbf{s}$, where $\mathbf{U}$ is a table depicting the use of goods by sectors, $\mathbf{V}$ a table depicting the outputs of the sectors in terms of goods, $\mathbf{L}$ the factor input table, and allocation vector $\mathbf{s} \geqq 0$. Similarly, $\sum \mathbf{x}_i^0$ has components $\mathbf{f}$ and $\mathbf{0}$, where $\mathbf{f}$ is the vector of final goods consumption. The maximal consumption is $\gamma\mathbf{f}$, which we

[14] See the disclaimer in footnote 4 though.

enter in the denominator, as discussed at the end of the last section. The respective prices are denoted $\mathbf{p}$ and $\mathbf{w}$, respectively; these are the shadow prices of program (9). The generalized Solow residual thus becomes

$$SR = -\{\mathbf{p} \cdot d[(\mathbf{U} - \mathbf{V}^\top)\mathbf{s}] + \mathbf{w} \cdot d(\mathbf{Ls})\}/\mathbf{p} \cdot (\gamma \mathbf{f}) \quad (26)$$

The shadow prices fulfill the dual constraint,

$$\mathbf{p}^\top(\mathbf{U} - \mathbf{V}^\top) + \mathbf{w} \cdot \mathbf{L} - \boldsymbol{\sigma}^\top = \mathbf{0} \quad (27)$$

where $\boldsymbol{\sigma}$ is the shadow price of $\mathbf{s} \geqq 0$. The product rule and substitution of Eq. 27 into expression (26) reduce the generalized Solow residual to

$$SR = -[\mathbf{p}^\top d(\mathbf{U} - \mathbf{V}^\top) \cdot \mathbf{s} + \mathbf{w}^\top d\mathbf{L} \cdot \mathbf{s} + \boldsymbol{\sigma}^\top d\mathbf{s}]/\mathbf{p} \cdot (\gamma \mathbf{f}) \quad (28)$$

By the phenomenon of complementary slackness,

$$\boldsymbol{\sigma} \cdot \mathbf{s} = 0 \quad (29)$$

expression (28) becomes

$$SR = (\mathbf{p}^\top d\mathbf{V}^\top - \mathbf{p}^\top d\mathbf{U} - \mathbf{w}^\top d\mathbf{L} + d\boldsymbol{\sigma})(diag\ \mathbf{Vp})^{-1} \times (diag\ \mathbf{Vp})\mathbf{s}/\mathbf{p} \cdot (\gamma \mathbf{f}) \quad (30)$$

Here $(\mathbf{p}^\top d\mathbf{V}^\top - \mathbf{p}^\top d\mathbf{U} - \mathbf{w}^\top d\mathbf{L} + d\boldsymbol{\sigma})(diag\ \mathbf{Vp})^{-1}$ is the row vector of sectoral Solow residuals, while $(diag\ \mathbf{Vp})\mathbf{s}/\mathbf{p} \cdot (\gamma \mathbf{f})$ is the vector of Domar weights, which add to the gross output/net output ratio of the economy, a number greater than one.[15]

To include sectoral efficiency changes, recall from Sect. 6 that the optimal (sustaining maximal consumption) and utilizable resources have only factor components, namely $\mathbf{Ls}$ and $\mathbf{N}$, respectively. Application of the phenomenon of complementary slackness and the main theorem of linear programming to (9) yields $\mathbf{w}^\top \mathbf{Ls} = \mathbf{w} \cdot \mathbf{N} = \gamma$. According to the Corollary, ρ^* is the inverse of this expression. It follows that the efficiency term of *TFP* becomes, substituting in the denominator $\mathbf{w}^\top \mathbf{Ls} = \mathbf{p}^\top(\mathbf{V}^\top - \mathbf{U})\mathbf{s} = \mathbf{p} \cdot (\gamma \mathbf{f})$ by Eqs. 27, 29, and material balance (9),[16]

$$\begin{aligned} d\rho^*/\rho^* &= -d(\mathbf{w}^\top \mathbf{Ls})/(\mathbf{w}^\top \mathbf{Ls}) \\ &= -\sum_j [d(\mathbf{w} \cdot \mathbf{l}_j s_j)/(\mathbf{p} \cdot \mathbf{v}_{j\cdot} s_j)] \cdot (\mathbf{p} \cdot \mathbf{v}_{j\cdot} s_j)/\mathbf{p} \cdot (\gamma \mathbf{f}) \end{aligned} \quad (31)$$

where the summation is over sectors. The efficiency growth is a Domar weighted average of optimal factor input reduction growth rates.

[15] This number is also called the Domar ratio. For any vector $\mathbf{x}$, *diag* $\mathbf{x}$ denotes the diagonal matrix with $\mathbf{x}$ on the diagonal.

[16] According to program (9), the material balance is an inequality. However, the premultiplication by the price vector eliminates the slack, by the phenomenon of complementary slackness. Alternatively, the material balance may be transformed to an equality in the same way that Eq. 11 was derived from program (10), assuming free disposal. Vectors $\mathbf{l}_j(\mathbf{v}_j)$ denotes the j-th column (row) of matrix $\mathbf{L}$ ($\mathbf{V}$).

A further specification is that of *input–output analysis*, where $\mathbf{U}$ and $\mathbf{V}$ are square matrices, $\mathbf{V}^\top\mathbf{s}$ is denoted $\mathbf{q}$, the vector of (optimal) gross outputs, and $\mathbf{A} = \mathbf{U}(\mathbf{V}^\top)^{-1}$ and $\mathbf{F} = \mathbf{L}(\mathbf{V}^\top)^{-1}$ are the matrices of (intermediate and factor) input coefficients. Expression (26) for the generalized Solow residual becomes

$$SR = -\{\mathbf{p} \cdot d[(\mathbf{A} - \mathbf{I})\mathbf{q}] + \mathbf{w} \cdot d(\mathbf{Fq})\}/\mathbf{p} \cdot (\gamma \mathbf{f}) \quad (32)$$

and price equation (27) reads

$$\mathbf{p}^\top(\mathbf{A} - \mathbf{I}) + \mathbf{w}^\top\mathbf{F} - (\mathbf{V}^{-1}\boldsymbol{\sigma})^\top = \mathbf{0} \quad (33)$$

Assume $\mathbf{s} > \mathbf{0}$.[17] As shadow prices are nonnegative, Eq. 29 sets the last term of Eq. 33 zero:

$$\mathbf{p}^\top(\mathbf{A} - \mathbf{I}) + \mathbf{w}^\top\mathbf{F} = \mathbf{0} \quad (34)$$

This permits the following rewrite of the generalized Solow residual, (32):

$$SR = -(\mathbf{p}^\top d\mathbf{A} + \mathbf{w}^\top d\mathbf{F})(diag\ \mathbf{p})^{-1}(diag\ \mathbf{p})\mathbf{q}/\mathbf{p} \cdot (\gamma \mathbf{f}) \quad (35)$$

This is essentially formula (12) of Wolff (1994).[18] The first half of this expression, $-(\mathbf{p}^\top d\mathbf{A} + \mathbf{w}^\top d\mathbf{F})(diag\ \mathbf{p})^{-1}$, is the row vector of sectoral Solow residuals and the remainder, $(diag\ \mathbf{p})\mathbf{q}/\mathbf{p} \cdot (\gamma \mathbf{f})$, is the vector of Domar weights, which add to the gross output/net output ratio of the economy, a number greater than one.[19] Expression (35) details the right hand side of Eq. 21: The generalized Solow residual measures the shift of the production function by means of reductions in intermediate and factor input coefficients.

The inclusion of sectoral efficiency changes is analogous to Eq. 31, obtained by substitution of $\mathbf{Ls} = \mathbf{Fq}$, Eq. 34, and material balance $(\mathbf{I} - \mathbf{A})\mathbf{q} = \gamma \mathbf{f}$:[20]

$$\begin{aligned} d\rho^*/\rho^* &= -d(\mathbf{w}^\top \mathbf{Fq})/(\mathbf{w}^\top \mathbf{Fq}) = -d[\mathbf{p}^\top(\mathbf{I} - \mathbf{A})\mathbf{q})]/\mathbf{p} \cdot (\gamma \mathbf{f}) \\ &= -\sum_k \{d[(p_k - \mathbf{p} \cdot \mathbf{a}_{\cdot k})q_k]/p_k q_k\} \cdot (p_k q_k)/\mathbf{p} \cdot (\gamma \mathbf{f}) \end{aligned} \quad (36)$$

where the summation is over commodities. The efficiency growth is a Domar weighted average of optimal factor input or value-added reduction growth rates.

[17] Well known sufficient conditions are $\mathbf{f} > \mathbf{0}$ and $\mathbf{A}$ has nonnegative Leontief inverse. For details see ten Raa (2005, Chapter 2).

[18] Wolff (1994) substitutes observed values for gross output $\mathbf{q}$ and final goods consumption $\gamma \mathbf{f}$, which are optimal. However, since gross output and final goods consumption are linked by the same Leontief inverse, $\mathbf{q}$ is obtained by inflating observed gross output by γ. As this factor cancels against the one in the denominator, the difference is immaterial.

[19] The input–output disaggregation, (35), is slightly different than the activity analytic one, (30), as sectors are now defined in terms of products, but the totals are the same. This wedge disappears when secondary products are absent (in the sense that output table $\mathbf{V}$ is diagonal).

[20] See footnote 16.

10 Conclusion

In this paper, I have interrelated the Debreu coefficient of resource utilization, the Solow residual, and TFP growth. Freed from individual data requirements, the Debreu coefficient's growth rate and the Solow residual sum to TFP growth. The procedure is equivalent to the imposition of Leontief preferences. The decomposition is the neo-classical counterpart to the decomposition of productivity growth into technical change and efficiency change made in frontier analysis and admits breakdowns by factor input as well as by sector.

Acknowledgments I gratefully acknowledge comments from Victoria Shestalova, Erwin Diewert, Rolf Färe, other participants of the Aggregation, Efficiency and Measurement Conference held on 23–25 May 2003 at the Department of Economics of University of California, Riverside, two anonymous referees and an anonymous associate editor.

References

Caves DW, Christensen LR, Erwin Diewert W (1982) The economic theory of index numbers and the measurement of input, output, and productivity. Econometrica 50(6):1393–1414. doi:10.2307/1913388

Chakravarty SR (1992) Efficiency and concentration. J Prod Anal 3:249–255. doi:10.1007/BF00158355

Charnes A, Cooper WW, Rhodes E (1978) Measuring the efficiency of decision making units. Eur J Operat Res 2:419–444. doi:10.1016/0377-2217(78)90138-8

Debreu G (1951) The coefficient of resource utilization. Econometrica 19(3):273–292. doi:10.2307/1906814

Diewert WE (1983) The measurement of waste within the production sector of an open economy. Scand J Econ 85(2):159–179. doi:10.2307/3439476

Diewert WE (2001) Which (old) ideas on productivity measurement are ready to use? In: Hulten CR, Dean ER, Harper MJ (eds) New developments in productivity analysis. University of Chicago Press, Chicago, pp 85–101

Färe R, Grosskopf S (1996) Productivity and intermediate products: a frontier approach. Econ Lett 50:65–70. doi:10.1016/0165-1765(95)00729-6

Färe R, Shawna G, Norris M, Zhang Z (1994) Productivity growth, technical progress, and efficiency change in industrialized countries. Am Econ Rev 84(1):66–83

Färe R, Grosskopf S, Zelenyuk V (2002) Finding common ground: efficiency indices. UPEG working paper 0305. Presented at the North American productivity workshop at Union College, Schenectady, NY

Farrell MJ (1957) The measurement of productive efficiency. J Roy Stat Soc Ser A (Gen) 120(III):253–281. doi:10.2307/2343100

Førsund FR, Sarafoglou N (2002). On the origins of data envelopment analysis. J Prod Anal 17:23–40. doi:10.1023/A:1013519902012

Grifell-Tatjé E, Lovell CAK, Pastor JT (1998) A quasi-malmquist productivity index. J Prod Anal 10(1):7–20. doi:10.1023/A:1018329930629

Hulten CR (1978) Growth accounting with intermediate inputs. Rev Econ Stud 45(3):511–518. doi:10.2307/2297252

Johansen L (1972) Production functions. North-Holland, Amsterdam

Jorgenson DW, Griliches Z (1967) The explanation of productivity change. Rev Econ Stud 34(3):308–350. doi:10.2307/2296675

Kumar S, Robert Russell R (2002) Technological change, technological catch-up, and capital deepening: relative contributions to growth and convergence. Am Econ Rev 92(3):527–548. doi:10.1257/00028280260136381

Nishimizu M, Page JM Jr (1982) Total factor productivity growth, technological progress and technical efficiency change: dimensions of productivity change in Yugoslavia. Econ J 92:920–936. doi:10.2307/2232675

ten Raa T (2005) The economics of input–output analysis. Cambridge University Press, Cambridge

ten Raa T (2007) Don't aggregate efficiency but disaggregate inefficiency. In: Färe R, Grosskopf S, Primont D (eds) Aggregation, efficiency, and measurement. Springer, Heidelberg, pp 145–51

ten Raa T, Mohnen P (2002) Neoclassical growth accounting and frontier analysis: a synthesis. J Prod Anal 18:11–128

Solow RM (1957) Technical change and the aggregate production function. Rev Econ Stat 39(3):312–320. doi:10.2307/1926047

Wolff EN (1994). Productivity measurement within an input–output framework. Region Sci Urban Econ 24(1):75–92. doi:10.1016/0166-0462(94)90020-5

Zieschang KD (1984) An extended farrell technical efficiency measure. J Econ Theory 33(2):387–396. doi:10.1016/0022-0531(84)90101-7

J Prod Anal (2011) 36:71–77
DOI 10.1007/s11123-010-0205-z

The Solow residual, Domar aggregation, and inefficiency: a synthesis of TFP measures

Thijs ten Raa · Victoria Shestalova

Published online: 29 December 2010

Abstract We consolidate and interrelate the four main approaches to the measurement and decomposition of total factor productivity growth, namely Solow's residual analysis, the index number approach, Data Envelopment Analysis, and Domar aggregation. Two new results link the general technology TFP growth measure to the industry Solow residuals and inefficiency.

Keywords TFP · Solow residual · Index numbers · Data envelopment analysis · Input–output analysis · Domar aggregation · Malmquist index

JEL Classification D24 · O47

1 Introduction

This paper presents a general framework that encompasses and interrelates the four main approaches to the measurement of total factor productivity (TFP)-growth: (1) Solow's aggregate production function model, (2) Index Numbers, (3) Data Envelopment Analysis (DEA), and (4) the Domar aggregation approach, which is associated with Input–Output (I–O) analysis. Our consolidating framework serves two purposes. It is a vehicle to review the different approaches to productivity measurement in the literature. Moreover, it is a breeding ground for new results. In particular, two propositions (3 and 4) link the general technology TFP growth measure to the industry Solow residuals and inefficiency.

A conceptual difference between these approaches is the treatment of prices. Traditional productivity indices use observed prices and rest on the assumption that the observed prices are competitive, so that factors are paid their marginal products. Under this assumption observed value shares are indeed the appropriate weights for the aggregation of the factor productivities into TFP. In the parametric literature adjustments are made for mark-ups and returns to scale (Diewert and Fox 2008). Frontier approaches, particularly DEA, make no behavioral assumption. Its TFP-growth measure, the so-called Malmquist index, is based on production statistics only and the value shares are generated by the shadow prices of the linear program that determines the production possibility frontier. The I–O analytical framework is on either side of the fence. As is well known, it accounts for intersectoral linkages and yields a TFP measure that is conceptually close to the macro-economic Solow residual; see, e.g., Wolff (1994). However, I–O can accommodate the shadow prices from a general equilibrium model, which moves its TFP-growth measure close to the DEA's (ten Raa 2008). Since shadow prices reflect marginal product values at the optimum, their use in computation does not conflict with the assumption of competitive pricing required by methods operating with observed prices. Hence, it is possible to reunite both these methodologies in one framework, capable of working with either of these prices.

Another difference lies in the assumption of optimizing behavior. The assumption provides economic justification to index numbers such as Törnqvist and Fisher's, but has the drawback that it bars inefficiencies. The TFP-growth measure arising in DEA makes no such assumption and has

T. ten Raa (✉)
Department of Econometrics and Operations Research, Tilburg University, P.O. Box 90153, 5000 LE Tilburg, The Netherlands
e-mail: tenRaa@UvT.nl

V. Shestalova
Netherlands Bureau for Economic Policy Analysis, P.O. Box 80510, 2508 GM The Hague, The Netherlands
e-mail: V.Shestalova@cpb.nl

the capacity to ascribe TFP growth to not only technical change but also efficiency change. In order to incorporate this attractive feature, we must relax the assumption of optimizing behavior.

The framework consists of (1) the technology, which in some cases is defined by means of a linear program; (2) data on inputs, net outputs, and either observed or shadow prices; and (3) rather general behavioral assumptions, such as the assumption on prices to reflect marginal products. The latter assumption is weaker that the assumption of profit maximizing behavior and allows for inefficiency. As a result, similarly to DEA, TFP growth includes both technical change and efficiency change. The former represents a shift of the production frontier and resembles the Solow residual as defined under the assumption of optimizing behavior, and the latter corresponds to a movement towards the frontier.

A novelty of this paper is the consolidation of all the four main alternative TFP-growth measures in a common theoretical framework. Although the economic literature contains excellent review articles on productivity indices, such as Diewert (1992) and Diewert and Nakamura (2003), to our knowledge this paper is the first to encompass all four main measures, including interrelating DEA efficiency measurement and Domar aggregation.

2 General framework

The measurement of TFP involves data, technological assumptions and possibly behavioral assumptions. We begin describing each of them in turn and define the concept of TFP growth that we use throughout this paper.

- **Data**. We assume that for each point of time t we observe of firms (industries or economies) the factor inputs x and the (net) outputs y, column vectors of different dimensions. We denote the prices of the outputs and the inputs by row vectors p and w, respectively. The prices can be either data or shadow prices of a maximization problem used to estimate technology.
- **Technology**. In each point of time the production possibility set is a subset in the commodity space of nonnegative factor inputs and unsigned net outputs, denoted by $P^t = \{(x,y) : \Phi(x,y,t) \leqslant 0\}$. The frontier is given by $\Phi(x,y,t) = 0$. We assume Φ to be continuous, piece-wise differentiable and convex in (x, y). A simple example, $\Phi(x,y,t) = y - tx$, illustrates why marginal products will be given by $-\partial\Phi/\partial x$ and the shift of the production function by $-\partial\Phi/\partial t$, both including a minus sign. We assume that the data are possible in the sense that all $(x(t), y(t))$ belong to P^t.
- **Behavioral assumptions**. If observed prices are used, they are assumed to reflect the marginal products on the production frontier. This assumption is weaker than those of cost minimization or profit maximization. In particular, productive and allocative inefficiencies are admitted. It should be mentioned that if price data are not used, shadow prices may fill the gap and will automatically reflect marginal products.
- **Definition of TFP**. TFP growth $\widehat{T}$ is defined as the (Solow) residual between the output and input growth rates, expressed by Divisia indices:

$$\widehat{T} = \sum \beta_j \widehat{y}_j - \sum \alpha_i \widehat{x}_i; \quad \alpha_i = w_i x_i / wx, \quad \beta_j = p_j y_j / py. \tag{1}$$

  Here the symbol $\widehat{\ }$ denotes the growth rate of a variable, for example, $\widehat{y}_j = \frac{dy_j}{dt} / y_j$. The weights in Eq. 1 may come from external value share data or from endogenous calculations. The distinction delineates the alternative approaches reviewed in this paper.

The first proposition shows that under rather general assumptions the Solow residual (1) can be decomposed into technical change and efficiency change. The first term measures the shift of the frontier by the partial derivative of the production frontier with respect to time. The second term measures the movement in the distance to the frontier. It is convenient to use input distance functions, as defined in DEA.[1] More precisely, for (non)frontier observations we have $\Phi(x,y,t)(<) = 0$ and we contract input x by a factor D so that y remains just producible from input Dx. By construction, for any producible (x, y) at time t there is $0 \leqslant D(x,y,t) \leqslant 1$ such that

$$\Phi[D(x,y,t)x, y, t] = 0. \tag{2}$$

Following Debreu (1951) distance function D is here defined by

$$D(x,y,t) = \min\{\theta : (\theta x, y) \in P^t\}. \tag{3}$$

Proposition 1 *Under constant returns to scale—meaning Φ is linearly homogeneous in (x, y)—and if prices reflect marginal products—meaning all $\frac{p_j}{w_i} = -\frac{\partial\Phi/\partial y_j}{\partial\Phi/\partial x_i}$—TFP growth decomposes into technical change and efficiency change:* $\widehat{T} = \frac{-\partial\Phi/\partial t}{\sum(\partial\Phi/\partial y_j)y_j} + \widehat{D}$.

Proof Differentiate Eq. 2 totally with respect to time:

$$\sum \frac{\partial\Phi}{\partial x_j}\left(D\frac{dx_j}{dt} + \frac{dD}{dt}x_j\right) + \sum \frac{\partial\Phi}{\partial y_j}\frac{dy_j}{dt} + \frac{\partial\Phi}{\partial t} = 0. \tag{4}$$

Rearrange the terms in Eq. 4:

[1] The results would carry through for an output orientation. Propositions 1, 3 and 4 will assume constant returns to scale, under which the two approaches are equivalent. Proposition 2 can be modified in the obvious way.

$$\sum \frac{\partial \Phi}{\partial y_j}\frac{dy_j}{dt} + \sum \frac{\partial \Phi}{\partial x_j}\frac{dx_j}{dt} D = -\frac{\partial \Phi}{\partial t} - \sum \frac{\partial \Phi}{\partial x_j} x_j \frac{dD}{dt}. \quad (5)$$

The derivatives of Φ in Eq. 5 are evaluated in the associated frontier point $(D(x, y, t)x, y, t)$. Here, by linear homogeneity, Euler's equation holds as follows: $\sum(\partial\Phi/\partial y_j)y_j = -\sum(\partial\Phi/\partial x_j)(Dx_j)$. Use either side of this equation to divide the terms in Eq. 5:

$$\frac{\sum(\partial\Phi/\partial y_j)dy_j/dt}{\sum(\partial\Phi/\partial y_j)y_j} - \frac{\sum(\partial\Phi/\partial x_j)dx_j/dt}{\sum(\partial\Phi/\partial x_j)x_j} = \frac{-\partial\Phi/\partial t}{\sum(\partial\Phi/\partial y_j)y_j} + \frac{1}{D}\frac{dD}{dt}. \quad (6)$$

By assumption vectors (p, w) and $(\partial\Phi/\partial y, -\partial\Phi/\partial x)$ are collinear, so that $\partial\Phi/\partial y$ and $-\partial\Phi/\partial x$ on the left hand side of Eq. 6 may be replaced by p and w, respectively. This turns the left hand side into $\widehat{T}$, defined by (1). □

The assumption of constant returns to scale can be dispensed. This would yield a third TFP component, namely a scale effect.

Following Färe and Grosskopf (2004), the leading, technical change term in Eq. 6 can also be expressed in the distance function and we shall do so for the two main representations of TFP growth, DEA and Domar aggregation. The next proposition shows the underpinning. It features free input disposability, which is defined by the condition that $(x, y) \in P^t, z \geqslant 0$ implies $(x + z, y) \in P^t$.

Proposition 2 *Under free input disposability,* $P^t = \{(x, y) : 1 - 1/D(x, y, t) \leqslant 0\}$.

Proof If $(x, y) \in P^t$, then, by definition of D, $0 \leqslant D(x, y, t) \leqslant 1$, and, therefore, $1 - 1/D(x, y, t) \leqslant 0$. Hence $(x, y) \in \{(x, y) : 1 - 1/D(x, y, t) \leqslant 0\}$. Conversely, if the latter holds, $0 \leqslant D(x, y, t) \leqslant 1$, and, therefore, $z = [1 - D(x, y, t)]\ x \geqslant 0$. By definition of D, $(D(x, y, t)x, y) \in P^t$. By free input disposability, $(D(x, y, t)x + z, y) = (x, y) \in P^t$. □

The upshot of this proposition is that we may reparametrize the production possibility set using $1 - 1/D$ instead of Φ. In particular, we will differentiate D instead of Φ when measuring technical change.

3 Approaches to the measurement of TFP growth

In this section we show how our framework encompasses the main measures of TFP growth and review the relevant literatures.

3.1 Solow residual

Solow (1957) analyzed a macro-economic model with one output and two inputs, capital and labor, interrelated by a production function, F. This situation can be derived from our framework by imposing a particular form on Φ, namely $\Phi(K, L, Y, t) = Y - F(K, L, t)$, and assuming no slack in production and proportionality between prices and marginal products. These assumptions were made by Solow (1957), imply production efficiency, $D = 1$ hence $\widehat{D} = 0$, and reduce Proposition 1 to $\widehat{T} = \frac{\partial F}{\partial t}/F$. This replicates Solow's result that TFP growth measures the shift of the aggregate production function under the assumptions.

3.2 Index numbers

Since our point of departure, definition (1), is the Divisia index, other conventional indices are encompassed. In discrete time, Christensen and Jorgenson (1970) approximate the Divisia index by the Törnqvist index,

$$\sum_j \sum_j \frac{1}{2}(\beta_j^t + \beta_j^{t+1})(\ln y_j^{t+1} - \ln y_j^t) - \sum_i \frac{1}{2}(\alpha_i^t + \alpha_i^{t+1}) \times (\ln x_i^{t+1} - \ln x_i^t), \quad (7)$$

and Diewert (1976) by the Fisher index,

$$\frac{1}{2}\left(\ln\frac{p^t y^{t+1}}{p^t y^t} + \ln\frac{p^{t+1}y^{t+1}}{p^{t+1}y^t}\right) - \frac{1}{2}\left(\ln\frac{w^t x^{t+1}}{w^t x^t} + \ln\frac{w^{t+1}x^{t+1}}{w^{t+1}x^t}\right). \quad (8)$$

These indices require observable price information. As in Sect. 3.1, we assume that there is no slack and that the prices reflect marginal products. This reduces TFP growth to technical change. Under the stronger assumption of price-taking profit maximization Diewert has shown that both indices are exact for certain functional forms. The Törnqvist index (7) is exact for the translog production function and, therefore, Diewert (1976) calls it the translog index. The Fisher index (8) is exact for a rather flexible functional form (a second order approximation to an arbitrary twice continuously differentiable aggregator function), a property Diewert (1976, p.117) calls 'superlative.'[2] Although the Törnqvist and Fisher productivity indices are exact for different production functions, most practical time-series applications yield similar numerical values; see Black et al. (2003). Diewert and Nakamura (2003) interrelate the physical and financial concepts of TFP growth for these indices, as well as for the Malmquist index, which we cover in Sect. 3.3.

[2] More specifically, Diewert (1992) proves that under certain parameter restrictions, the Fischer productivity index is exact for a time-dependent revenue function of the following form: $r^t(p, x) = \sigma_t(p^\top Apx^\top Cx + \alpha^t p \beta^t xp^\top B^t x)^{1/2}$, $A = A^\top$, $C = C^\top$, $t = 0,1$, where σ_t is a positive number, A, C, and B^t are parameter matrices, and α^t and β^t are parameter vectors.

3.3 Data envelopment analysis

In DEA technology Φ is constructed by the piece-wise linear envelopment of the available observations on inputs and outputs. Under constant returns to scale, the production possibility set represents a convex hull. There is no need to impose behavioral assumptions; DEA does not require them. The data requirement is reduced to outputs and inputs; DEA does not use the observed prices but shadow prices that reflect marginal values on the production frontier.

Because DEA subscribes to definition (3) of the distance function, Proposition 2 applies under free input disposability and we may use $\Phi = 1 - 1/D$. Consequently $\frac{\partial\Phi/\partial t}{\partial\Phi/\partial y_j} = \frac{\partial D/\partial t}{\partial D/\partial y_j}$ and, therefore, the technical change term in Proposition 1 becomes $\frac{-\partial D/\partial t}{\sum(\partial D/\partial y_j)y_j}$, the movement in the distance function D. Now by construction of the distance function, $\Phi(xD(x,y,t),y,t) = 0$, or, invoking constant returns to scale, $\Phi(x, y/D(x,y,t),t) = 0$. Differentiation with respect to y yields $\partial\Phi/\partial y \cdot [1/D - (y \cdot \partial D/\partial y)/D^2] = 0$. Hence, $(\partial D/\partial y_j)y_j = D$; and therefore the technical change is reduced to $\frac{\partial D(x,y,t)}{D\partial t}$.

Substituting the latter in Eq. 6 and using the differentiation rules yield:

$$\begin{aligned}\hat{T} &= \frac{dD(x,y,t)}{Ddt} - \frac{\partial D(x,y,t)}{D\partial t}\\ &= \frac{\partial \ln D(x,y,t)}{\partial x}\frac{dx}{dt} + \frac{\partial \ln D(x,y,t)}{\partial y}\frac{dy}{dt}\end{aligned} \tag{9}$$

In discrete time, the right hand side of this expression is approximated as $\ln D(x^{t+1},y^{t+1},\cdot) - \ln D(x^t,y^t,\cdot) = \ln\frac{D(x^{t+1},y^{t+1},\cdot)}{D(x^t,y^t,\cdot)}$. Evaluating this expression at t and $t+1$, taking the average of the two logarithms and exponentiating, one obtains the standard expression of Malmquist productivity index:

$$\left[\frac{D(x^{t+1},y^{t+1},t)}{D(x^t,y^t,t)}\frac{D(x^{t+1},y^{t+1},t+1)}{D(x^t,y^t,t+1)}\right]^{1/2}. \tag{10}$$

The decomposition of Malmquist index into technical change and efficiency change is well known; see Färe et al. (1989, 1996). If we assume inefficiency away, the efficiency change term drops out and the Malmquist index features only the technical change component. This component corresponds to technical change as defined by Solow under the assumptions of no slack and inputs paid by marginal products. The explicit price information in the expression of the Solow residual is replaced by the implicit shadow price information, derived from the shape of the frontier; see Coelli and Rao (2001).

Two important results from the DEA literature provide a link between the Malmquist index and two other TFP growth indices, namely, Törnqvist and Fisher indices. First, Caves et al. (1982) have shown that the Malmquist index becomes a Törnqvist productivity index (7) provided that the distance functions are of translog form with identical second order coefficients, and that the prices are those supporting cost minimization and profit maximization. Second, Färe and Grosskopf (1992) proved that under the assumption of profit maximizing behavior the Malmquist index is approximately equal to the Fisher productivity index (8). In both cases the assumption that prices support cost minimizing and profit maximizing behavior is crucial. Balk (1998) reviews comprehensively, including non-constant returns to scale.

3.4 Domar aggregation

In a multi-sectoral economy, aggregate TFP growth can be represented as a combination of industry productivity growths, the Domar (1961) aggregation. In this section we show how the Domar aggregation can be derived from our framework. For this purpose we use a functional form of Φ which reflects the I–O model of Leontief (1936) and assume no production slack and zero profits. No production slack is weaker than the assumption of optimizing behavior that underlies many TFP models. In addition to production slack there may be allocative inefficiencies, but these do not occur in Leontief's model.

I–O analysis is based on the gross outputs z_j (of industry j, $j = 1, \ldots, n$), interindustry transactions z_{kj} (the quantity of the intermediate input industry k supplies to industry j, at price p_k) and factor inputs x_{ij} (the quantity of factor input i utilized in the production of industry j, at price w_i). Letting e be the unit vector (all components equal to one), and introducing obvious vector and matrix notations, the utilized inputs are given by vector Xe and the net supply is given by $z - Ze$. The utilized inputs cannot exceed the available resources of the economy, given by vector x, and the net product supply must at least be the final demand vector, given by vector y. Hence the feasibility constraints are $Xe \leqslant x$ and $z - Ze \geqslant y$. In I–O analysis technology is represented by the input coefficients $a_{kj} = z_{kj}/z_j$ and $b_{ij} = x_{ij}/z_j$. With obvious matrix notation, (x, y) belongs to the I–O production possibility set if for some gross output vector $z \geq 0$ the feasibility constraints are fulfilled, $Bz \leqslant x$ and $z - Az \geqslant y$. The distance function of the I–O model is given by the following program:

$$D(x,y,t) = \min_{\theta,z}\theta \text{ subject to:}$$

$$[I - A(t)]z \geqslant y, B(t)z \leqslant \theta x, z \geqslant 0. \tag{11}$$

By Proposition 1, technical change is measured by $\frac{-\partial\Phi/\partial t}{\sum(\partial\Phi/\partial y_j)y_j}$. The following proposition provides the relation between this expression and the well known Domar aggregation (Wolff 1994), linking the general technology TFP growth measure to the industry Solow residuals under the assumption of technically efficient production.

Proposition 3 *In the I–O model technical change* $\frac{-\partial\Phi/\partial t}{\sum(\partial\Phi/\partial y_j)y_j}$ *is measured by the Domar weighted sum of industry Solow residuals,* $\widehat{T} = \sum \widehat{\tau}_j p_j z_j/py$, *where* $\widehat{\tau}_j = -\sum_k \frac{p_k z_{kj}}{p_j z_j}\widehat{a}_{kj} - \sum_i \frac{w_i x_{ij}}{p_j z_j}\widehat{b}_{ij}$, *and prices and production levels are the shadow prices and the optimal production levels of program* (11).

Proof Technology function Φ can be given by $\Phi(x,y,t) = \max\{B(t)[I-A(t)]^{-1}y - x\}$, where the maximum is taken with respect to factor input components. Here the distance function has been derived from the production possibility set. Because inputs are freely disposable in model (11), by Proposition 2 we may use $\Phi = 1 - 1/D$ and, as in Sect. 3.3, technical change is measured by $\frac{-\partial D/\partial t}{\sum(\partial D/\partial y_j)y_j}$. By program (11) the partials of the distance function with respect to output components are equal to the sensitivity of objective θ with respect to the first bound components, hence its Lagrange multipliers: $\partial D/\partial y_j = p_j$. The partials of the distance function with respect to time are determined by the sensitivity of the objective with respect to constraint coefficients. As shown in ten Raa (2005), Eq. 4.33, the derivative of $\max_q aq : C(t)q \leqslant b$ equals $-\lambda\frac{dC}{dt}q$, where λ is the row vector of Lagrange multipliers and q the optimum. Because in the present situation, $q = \begin{bmatrix}\theta \\ z\end{bmatrix}, a = (-1 \quad 0), \lambda = (p \quad w \quad \sigma)$ and $C(t) = \begin{bmatrix} 0 & A(t)-I \\ -x & B(t) \\ 0 & -I \end{bmatrix}$, the partial derivative of maximization objective $-\theta$ with respect to time equals $-(p \quad w \quad \sigma)\begin{bmatrix} 0 & dA/dt \\ 0 & dB/dt \\ 0 & 0\end{bmatrix}\begin{bmatrix}\theta \\ z\end{bmatrix} = -(pdA/dt + wdB/dt)z.$ It follows that $\frac{-\partial D/\partial t}{\sum(\partial D/\partial y_j)y_j} = \frac{-(pdA/dt + wdB/dt)z}{\sum p_j y_j}$. The numerator features $p\frac{dA}{dt}z = p_k\frac{da_{kj}}{dt}z_j = p_k(\frac{da_{kj}}{dt}/a_{kj})a_{kj}z_j = p_k\widehat{a}_{kj}z_{kj}$ and, similarly, $w\frac{dB}{dt}z = w_i\widehat{b}_{ij}z_{ij}$. Therefore we obtain the Domar aggregation expression for technical change in this model:

$$\frac{-\partial\Phi/\partial t}{\sum(\partial\Phi/\partial y_j)y_j} = \sum \widehat{\tau}_j p_j z_j/py, \qquad \widehat{\tau}_j = -\sum_k \frac{p_k z_{kj}}{p_j z_j}\widehat{a}_{kj} - \sum_i \frac{w_i x_{ij}}{p_j z_j}\widehat{b}_{ij}, \tag{12}$$

in which z_{ij} and x_{ij} correspond to the optimal production levels, and p_k and w_i are shadow prices. □

Since Proposition 3 has been proved for optimal production levels and shadow prices, it remains to show that under the additional assumptions of no slack and zero profits—stated at the beginning of this section—the use of this formula is also justified at observed prices and production levels.

The first assumption, no slack in production, means that the observed primary input x and net output y satisfy $\Phi(x,y,t) = \max\{B(t)[I-A(t)]^{-1}y - x\} = 0$, and therefore it is impossible to produce more y with less x. This follows that the primary input uses are at their frontier levels and sufficient to just produce net output y. Given a fixed proportion technology in production, the intermediate production must satisfy $z - Az = y$. Hence, we cannot increase y by their reallocation. Hence, the observed inputs and outputs can be used in Eq. 12 instead of those from the linear program. The assumption that there is no slack implies also that the efficiency change term, $\frac{1}{D}\frac{dD}{dt}$, equals to zero and the TFP growth is fully expressed by (12).

The other assumption, that industry profits are zero, reads:

$$p_j z_j = \sum_k p_k z_{kj} + \sum_i w_i x_{ij}, \text{ where } i,j,k = 1,\ldots n. \tag{13}$$

As long as Eq. 13 holds, the industry TFP growth in the Domar aggregation expression can be represented both in terms of output and input growth levels and in terms of the growth of technical coefficients: $\widehat{\tau}_j = -\sum_k \frac{p_k z_{kj}}{p_j z_j}\widehat{a}_{kj} - \sum_i \frac{w_i x_{ij}}{p_j z_j}\widehat{b}_{ij} = \widehat{z}_j - (\sum_k p_k z_{kj}\widehat{z}_{kj} + \sum_i w_i x_{ij}\widehat{x}_{ij})/(p_j z_j)$. Shadow prices satisfy the zero profit conditions by complementary slackness, but we need to impose the requirement of zero profits in order to justify the use of the observed prices instead of shadow prices.

4 Synthesis of domar aggregation and DEA

In this section we establish a relationship between DEA and Domar aggregation. The principal difference between the two lies in the data requirements and the behavioral assumptions. As we do not impose general restrictions on these factors, there is scope for synthesis. Our approach is to allow slack in the structural approach and to replace the observed prices by shadow prices. The obtained measure of TFP is based on the fundamentals of the economy, namely technology and preferences. The model draws from ten Raa and Mohnen (2001, 2002) and Shestalova (2001), but replaces their utility based output distance function by the input distance function used in this paper and, for simplicity, takes the one-country closed economy variant. Employing the distance function program (11) and combining Propositions 1 and 3, we obtain the next proposition, which allows technical inefficiency in the I–O model and shows how to measure it as well as technical progress.

Proposition 4 *Model* (11) *yields* $\widehat{T} = \sum \hat{\tau}_j p_j z_j / py + \widehat{D}$, *in which the first term is evaluated at shadow prices and optimal output levels.*

Proposition 4 intermingles the Domar approach with the DEA decomposition in technical and efficiency changes, where the technical change term is expressed in the Domar aggregation form (12) taken at shadow prices and optimal production levels from the linear program (11). While in DEA the potential for efficiency is determined by cross-sectional or intertemporal best practices, in this combined model the available production technology is represented by the observed technical coefficients and inefficiency stems from the suboptimal allocation of production within the system, or from underutilization of resources in industries.[3]

In the case of an open economy, international trade represents another source of TFP growth. An extension of the above model to the case of an open economy allows us to incorporate the effect of change in the terms-of-trade. This effect has been considered by ten Raa and Mohnen (2001, 2002) for the case of a small open economy, and by Shestalova (2001) for the case three large open economies. See also Diewert and Morrison (1986) on the effect of international trade on productivity.

5 Conclusion

The paper offers a common framework which links the main approaches to the measurement of TFP growth rates, namely, the original approach by Solow (1957), conventional TFP growth indices such as Fisher and Törnqvist indices, the structural Domar aggregation approach, and Data Envelopment Analysis. We have introduced a general framework that consolidates these approaches.

For all the main well known TFP growth indices, we review the main results established in the literature concerning the conditions under which these indices yield equivalent (or close) TFP growth measures. The condition of optimizing behavior appears to be crucial in this respect. This condition, which lends theoretical support to the conventional Divisia, Törnqvist or Fisher indices, while not required in the case of Malmquist indices, explains the main conceptual difference between the conventional index numbers and the DEA-based Malmquist indices. This allows the Malmquist indices to incorporate the effect of efficiency change which is neglected by the other indices.

Our framework augments the standard production function with an efficiency term (which is similar to the efficiency term that arises in DEA) and yields the TFP growth measure which is conceptually close to the Malmquist index. The measure encompasses both technical change and efficiency change. The framework interrelates the DEA approach with the other approaches. In particular, we show that in a multi-sectoral economy, the technical change component takes the Domar aggregation form known from the structural, I–O approach. Similarly to DEA, technical change is measured at shadow prices and production levels resulting from the linear program, and not at observable prices and production levels; and the efficiency is interpreted as the potential for boosting the production to reach the production possibility frontier. However, while in DEA the potential is determined by the observable best practice (possibly achieved by other market participants), in the augmented I–O model it comes from improving allocations of production factors within a multi sectoral economy.

Acknowledgments We are grateful to four anonymous referees and an Associate Editor for extremely careful comments. This paper is an offspring of the workshop *Alternative measures of total factor productivity growth* held on 13 September 2002 at the Department of Econometrics and Operations Research of Tilburg University and co-sponsored by the Netherlands Organization for Scientific Research (Grant 460-02-031-A).

References

Balk BM (1998) Industrial price, quantity and productivity indices, the micro-economic theory and an application. Kluwer Academic Publishers, Boston

Black M, Guy M, McLellan N (2003) Productivity in New Zealand 1988 to 2002, WP 03/06, New Zealand Treasury

Caves DW, Christensen LR, Diewert WE (1982) The economic theory of index numbers and the measurement of input, output and productivity. Econometrica 50(6):1393–1414

Christensen LR, Jorgenson RW (1970) U.S. real product and real factor input, 1929–1967. Rev Income Wealth 16:19–50

Coelli T, Prasada Rao DS (2001) Implicit value shares in Malmquist TFP index numbers, CEPA working paper no. 4/2001. University of New England, Armidale

Debreu G (1951) The coefficient of resource utilization. Econometrica 19(3):273–292

[3] Strictly speaking, DEA can incorporate other types of inefficiencies as well (for example, non-radial DEA models can account for the presence of a slack). However, we will not discuss those in this particular application, since the standard Malmquist indices based on DEA with constant returns to scale, which are typically used for the TFP measurement, do not consider them.

Diewert WE (1976) Exact and superlative index numbers. J Econom 4:115–146
Diewert WE (1992) Fisher ideal output, input and productivity indexes revisited. J Prod Anal 3:211–248
Diewert WE, Fox KJ (2008) On the estimation of returns to scale, technical progress and monopolistic markups. J Econom 145(1–2):174–193
Diewert WE, Morrison C (1986) Adjusting output and productivity indexes for changes in terms of trade. Econ J 96:659–679
Diewert WE, Nakamura A (2003) Index number concepts, measures and decompositions of productivity growth. J Prod Anal 19: 127–159
Domar ED (1961) On the measurement of technological change. Econ J LXXI:709–729
Färe R, Grosskopf S (1992) Malmquist indexes and fisher ideal indexes. Econ J 102(410):158–160
Färe R, Grosskopf S (1996) Intertemporal production frontiers: with dynamic DEA. Kluwer Academic Publishers, Boston
Färe R, Grosskopf S (2004) New directions: efficiency and productivity. Kluwer Academic Publishers, Boston
Färe R, Grosskopf S, Lindgren B, Roos P (1989) Productivity development in Swedish Hospitals: a Malmquist output index approach. Discussion paper No. 89-3. Southern Illinois University, Illinois
Leontief W (1936) Quantitative input and output relations in the economic system of the United States. Rev Econ Stat 18(3): 105–125
Shestalova V (2001) General equilibrium analysis of international TFP growth rates. Econ Syst Res 13(4):391–402
Solow RM (1957) Technical change and the aggregate production function. Rev Econ Stat 39(3):312–320
ten Raa T (2005) The economics of input–output analysis. Cambridge University Press, Cambridge
ten Raa T, Mohnen P (2002) Neoclassical growth accounting and frontier analysis: a synthesis. J Prod Anal 18(2):111–128
ten Raa T, Mohnen P (2001) The location of comparative advantages on the basis of fundamentals only. Econ Syst Res 13(1):93–108
ten Raa T (2008) Debreu's coefficient of resource utilization, the Solow residual, and TFP: the connection by Leontief preferences. J Prod Anal 30:191–199
Wolff EN (1994) Productivity measurement within an input–output framework. Reg Sci Urban Econ 24(1):75–92